This book is dedicated to my beautiful and endlessly patient wife, Tera. I was a zombie before I met you. Shuffling aimlessly through life and falling apart. You have breathed life into me and made me more alive than I have ever felt.

BLOOD SPLATTER

A GUIDE TO CINEMATIC ZOMBIE VIOLENCE, GORE AND SPECIAL EFFECTS

This book contains graphic text and images that some viewers may find offensive. Parental guidance is strongly recommended, but let's face it, the book is called Blood Splatter and has the words zombie, gore and violence in the subtitle. What did you expect, babies and puppies? If you are looking for puppies, one is killed on page 15 and a baby is killed on page 26. Just saying...

Front cover illustration

> Designed by Craig W. Chenery with assistance from Chris MacGibbon. Based on the cover of "Curse of the Cannibal Confederates". Image courtesy of Troma Entertainment.

> "Old Stock Film" by Flobele. Used with permission.

Back cover illustration

> Designed by Craig W. Chenery with assistance from Chris MacGibbon.

> "Old Stock Film" by Flobele. Used with permission.

ACKNOWLEDGEMENTS

I would like to extend a heartfelt thank you to everyone who has contributed to this book, offered support or provided inspiration and made it possible for it to become as in depth as it has.

Toby Sells

Boyd Banks
Steve Barton
Jon Bernthal
J.R. Bookwalter
Chris Bridges
Richard Burke
Everett Burrell
Greg Chown
Stuart Conran
Melissa Cowan
Gino Crognale
Andrew Currie
Chris Diani
Darcy Evellove
Tony Gardner
Colin Geddes
Kyle Glencross
Daniel Gommé
Emily Hagins
Robert Hall
Lloyd Kaufman
Roland Keates
Michael Kenworthy
Robert Kirkman
Matthew Kohnen
Robert Kurtzman
Joshua Long
Chris MacGibbon
Ed Martinez

Robert McCallum
Neil Morrill
Michael Mosher
Rusty Nails
Greg Nicotero
Jim Ojala
Christine Parker
Kieran Parker
Brian Paulin
Mike Peel
Joe Pilato
Nick Plantico
Marc Price
Chris Roe
George A. Romero
John Russo
Sean Sansom
Tom Savini
Todd Sheets
Warren Speed
Russ Streiner
William Stout
Daniel Symmes
Patricia Tallman
Wayne Toth
John Vulich
Cliff Wallace
Edgar Wright
Steven Yeun
Brian Yuzna

SPECIAL THANKS

Rhonda Aburomi
Hannah Bradshaw
Caley Brooks
Sam Brown
Duncan Brown
Scott Fensterer
Nicky Flint
Patrick Gardener
Charles F. Gray
Micah Henry
Chris Hudacek
Darren Jacques
Don Lamelin
Greg Longstreet
Tom Leingang

Angel Nickell
David Oakes
Mitch Palmer
Thorsten Pfeffer
Danny Renfroe
Luke Robinson
Mark Ross
David Sasich
Eli Sasich
Shane Shannon
Dane Paul Stewart
Josh Sweten
A.J. Taylor
Michele Toscan
Eduardo "Evil Ed" Verde

... and to every production company and studio for helping to bring these terrifying monsters to our living rooms and nightmares.

Mr. Bottom's family picture from "Fido" courtesy of Andrew Currie.

CONTENTS

CHAPTER ONE – Rise of the Dead..1
CHAPTER TWO – Viewing the Dead..4
CHAPTER THREE – Leading the Dead...201
CHAPTER FOUR – Raising the Dead..206
    Boyd Banks...207
    Steve Barton..210
    Chris Bridges..215
    Everett Burrell...219
    Stuart Conran...225
    Melissa Cowan...241
    Gino Crognalee...243
    Andrew Currie...247
    Tony Gardner..250
    Kyle Glencross...254
    Daniel Gommé...257
    Emily Hagins..261
    Lloyd Kaufman..265
    Michael Kenworthy......................................269
    Robert Kurtzman...273
    Joshua Long...278
    Ed Martinez...282
    Rob McCallum..285
    Neil Morrill..289
    Michael Mosher..292
    Greg Nicotero..296
    Jim Ojala...303
    Christine Parker..307
    Brian Paulin...311
    Mike Peel..314
    Nick Plantico..318
    Marc Price...321
    John Russo...326
    Sean Sansom...328
    Tom Savini...331
    Toby Sells..336
    Todd Sheets...342
    Warrren Speed...346
    John Vulich..349
    Cliff Wallace...353
CHAPTER FIVE – Journal of the Dead..358
    Index 370

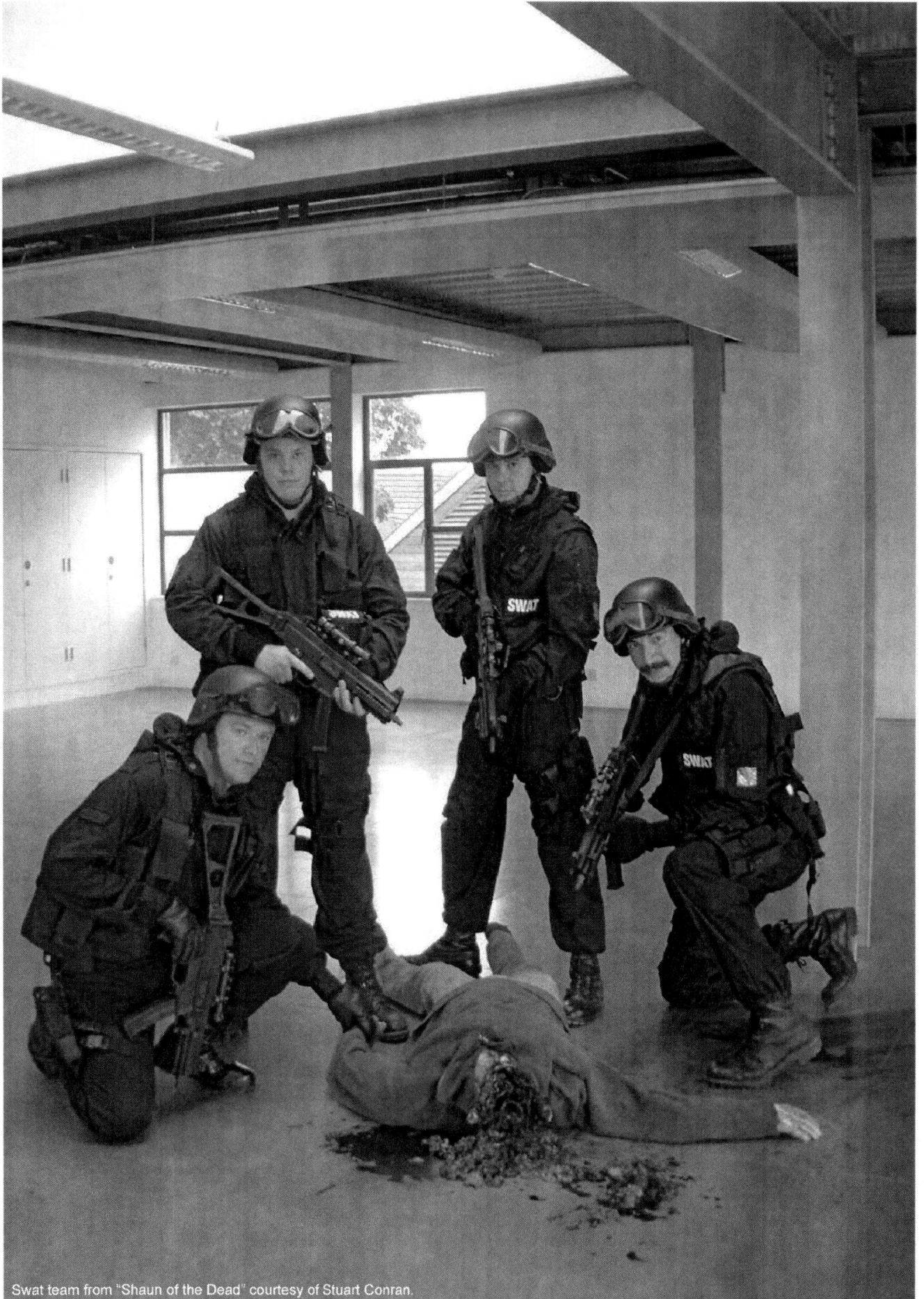

Swat team from "Shaun of the Dead" courtesy of Stuart Conran.

RISE OF THE DEAD

On October 18th, 1968 Variety Magazine published their review of George A. Romero's *Night of the Living Dead*. The conclusion was considerably less than favorable.

"[Night of the Living Dead] raises doubts about the moral health of filmgoers who cheerfully opt for this unrelieved orgy of sadism [and] on no level is the unrelieved grossness disguised by a feeble attempt at art or significance".

And so it began.

While the above summary is paraphrased, the intent of the review was clear. A new phase in horror had arrived and movie gore, especially that involving zombies, was never going to be the same. *Night of the Living Dead* was violent, intensely graphic, shocking and absolutely terrifying and had the complete opposite effect that Variety expected. Not only did the audience enjoy the so called "orgy of sadism", they clambered for more. While the stability of the moral health of filmgoers may have been in question, it was made quite apparent that there was a void in cinematic horror that this type of film filled. Contrary to Variety's opinions, the movie held considerable significance and ultimately become the measure that all zombie films would strive to become.

With Romero's bloodthirsty and savage zombies, the genre was forever changed. Zombies were no longer mindless minions, raised from their graves by voodoo or black magic, milling around in the background at the will of their masters. They now posed a significant threat to any human who was unfortunate enough to come in contact with them. Zombies had matured from Saturday matinee monsters and became terrifying creatures, relentless in their search for human flesh. George Romero established the rules for the zombie genre that almost every movie that followed would adhere to. Zombies crave human flesh and can only be stopped by destroying the brain. These rules have been ingrained into movie lore in much the same way as stakes kill vampires and silver bullets kill werewolves. In the years following *Night of the Living Dead*, filmmakers of all abilities from across the world stepped forward one by one to put their stamp on the genre. Zombie films have become synonymous with biting social commentaries and intense graphic violence.

Over the next forty years, as the genre continued to change and evolve, the special effects continued to improve. Effects studios and artists manipulated existing methods and created new ways of using makeup, latex and prosthetics to terrify and gross out audiences. With the advent of computer generated imagery in the 1990's, movies became even more graphic and realistic than ever. While the need for strong writing to produce legitimate scares was still required, the improvement of special effects allowed for the instant gratification that is so frequently craved by moviegoers.

For decades, movie and horror fans have enjoyed watching serial killers like Michael Myers and Jason Voorhees dismember. Demons like Pinhead and the Cenobites have tortured and maniacs like Freddy Krueger maimed. Their victims have suffered incredible and bloody demises as the effects envelope is constantly pushed. We are no stranger to blades, hooks, bullets, knives and a whole host of improvised weapons tearing into skin and ripping flesh. Gory on screen deaths and mutilations are now an expected element with any horror film and have shown critics such as Variety that gore is not only accepted, but relished. While many claim the core foundation of the zombie film is the underlying social commentary, there is no denying that the special effects and gore bring a very dedicated following of gorehounds. After all, not all zombie movies focus on social commentaries. Some concentrate on the cause of the outbreak, while others try to solve it. Many movies exist in the outbreak, while others try to simply survive it. However, the common factor amongst nearly all zombie films is the graphic nature in which they attack. Almost half a century later, *Night of the Living Dead* is still considered the grandfather of zombie blood splatter and has continued to influence film makers both amateur and professional from all over the globe.

With so much violence on screen, what makes the zombie film stand out among its peers? This appears to be a seemingly impossible feat as after all, the horror genre is no stranger to graphic violence and gore. Every year, movie after movie is released that delivers non-stop gore and blood. One possible reason is the blurring of fiction and reality. How are movies supposed to shock when daily life is constantly under an assault of graphic and bloody images? On almost any given day, you can pick up a newspaper, turn on the news or go online and you will be bombarded with stories and pictures of murder, serial killings, hate crimes and despair. Children are shot and drowned, animals are tortured and killed, the elderly are beaten and women are raped. During the hurricane Katrina tragedy in New Orleans, news channels had no hesitation in showing the bloated bodies of the dead floating down the streets of the French Quarter. In the aftermath of the September Eleventh attacks on the World Trade Center, viewers could see the planes slamming to the twin towers and people jumping from the burning buildings. The massive loss of life as the towers finally collapsed was shown live and unedited. Indeed the only thing the media apologized for was a New York firefighter shouting out "fuck" on live television. "I'm sorry you had to hear that", the newscaster mumbled as his cameraman continued to focus on the smoking towers. Two towers from which innocent men and women were jumping to their deaths. With this constant and unforgiving onslaught from the media, it becomes harder to shock and scare the audience with tales of murderers and serial killers. We are so used to seeing this on a daily basis that the impact is weakened considerably. The media and morality police are very quick to point the finger of blame at the entertainment industry for corrupting society and promoting violent content and desensitizing viewers. However, with the media in its perpetual state of exclusive up close and in your face delivery, it is hard to determine whether movies and video games have desensitized us to reality or if reality has desensitized us to movies and video games.

So what is left? What does the zombie movie offer that so many other films do not? How can the zombie film continue to shock audiences? The answer is simple. Zombie movies present the most rudimentary of animal instincts, the need to feed and stepping beyond that, the act of cannibalism. Even with the desensitizing of society, there are still a small handful of taboos that are still considered shocking and socially unacceptable, especially in western civilization. Murder, while a horrendous act, is so commonplace in the news, that most stories go unnoticed or with minimal impact and can no longer be considered a taboo. Watch the news on any given day and you will be hard pressed to find a news section that doesn't present a story where someone has been murdered. The zombie genre is one of the few that can touch on a social taboo without repulsing or offending the audience to the point of turning the film off and walking away. Of course the special effects can scare and shock, but not to the levels of depravity that is involved with crossing over the lines of other social taboos such as pedophilia, bestiality and incest. Zombies do not carry weapons. They do not shoot. They do not stab. They consume their victims and tear them apart limb from limb. There is something so savage and terrifying about being eaten alive. The new zombies of the post 1968 era no longer hide behind implied violence and poor makeup. Victims are pulled apart and consumed and nothing is left to the imagination. These terrifying visions have had audiences on the edges of their seats since the graveyard zombie attacked Barbara and Johnny all those years ago.

It is with the ability to touch on this taboo, that special effects artists have been able to create some of the most shocking scenes of gore and violence in the horror genre. While it is easy to credit the director with defining and shaping the zombie genre, there is no doubt that the zombie films of today would not be where they are if not for the special effects professionals. Special effects wizards such as Tom Savini and Greg Nicotero and effects crews all over the world have put some of the most violent and graphic scenes from horror cinema into zombie movies. Without them we would still be watching corpses with white face paint, black eye shadow and plastic teeth. Instead we see chunks of flesh and sinew torn from their victims limbs. Zombies are decapitated, hacked to pieces by helicopter blades and mutilated. Humans are ripped limb from limb and their intestines are ripped out of their stomach. Without the break through special effects, the zombie genre would likely have faded into the background as another worn out horror spin off. No longer relegated to being a background nuisance, zombies now stand out in films. Characters such as Dr. Tongue, Bub, Big Daddy and Tar Man have become ingrained in pop culture and are instantly recognizable to zombie fans world wide.

So where does Blood Splatter come in? There are already numerous books available on the market for zombie fans looking for information on zombie cinema. These books offer in depth reviews on plot and character development. However, while these books provide great detail on the structure of the film, few offer an analysis on the graphic content of the film. Zombie fans are interested in the story and quality of a zombie film, but as gorehounds, there is also a major interest in how intense and graphic a zombie film is. In other books, shot on video and lower budget films generally don't rate as well as high budget films, but so many of these films are crammed full of gore, violence and terrifying zombies. Instead of offering another analysis of zombie films, Blood Splatter provides detailed information about the gore factor. It presents how many zombies you can expect in a film, the quality of the makeup, how gory it is, the quality of the gore, how many people die and how many zombies die. Blood Splatter is an in depth look at the graphic nature of zombie cinema. Films have been reviewed based on a predetermined set of criteria to detail how gory the film is. Using this rating system removes any potential bias that is present in general films reviews.

Blood Splatter is different. It is a celebration of zombie movies and not a critique. All movies come to the table on an even playing ground. The goal of this book is not to determine the difference between a good or bad zombie film. Movies that rate low in this book do not necessarily constitute a bad movie experience, as much as high rated movies don't necessarily equal the best the genre has to offer. For example, the original *Dawn of the Dead* does not rate highly on zombie quality, as most zombies in the film are grey. Does it make the film any less of a classic? Of course not. Zombie fans know that it is a genre filled with films of all quality, but that is part of the charm. Even most low budget zombie film can have a fantastic amount of gore and with a good camera and a talented special effects artist, realistic gore and zombie effects are possible, as proven within these pages.

Blood Splatter also avoids detailing the definition of a zombie. In recent years, the genre has experienced a shift to include viral and plague movies such as *28 Days Later, Planet Terror* and *Quarantine*. The majority of zombie fans have embraced these as additions and thus they have been included. This recent shift can not be ignored, because it was a genre shift that turned zombies violent to begin with. The original Romero trilogy introduced us to cannibalistic zombies, *28 Days Later* and the remake of *Dawn of the Dead* introduced us to running and fast moving zombies. *Land of the Dead* and *Survival of the Dead* and elements of *Day of the Dead* saw zombies adapting to their environments and becoming intelligent. *Shaun of the Dead* and *Zombieland* made zombies funny, but retained the ability to scare. *The Walking Dead* showed that zombies used to be real people too. No doubt the genre will continue to change over the coming years and zombies will see a new evolution as director's bring original and genre expanding ideas to the table.

Finally, Blood Splatter is a thank you to every director, producer, writer, actor and special effects artist who has put time, money and love into a zombie film. It is this love of the genre that has kept it alive during periods when Hollywood interest dwindled. There are now hundreds of movies out there and that number is growing every year. Thank you for every bite, every groan and every rotting, shambling, bloody corpse that has ever made it onto film. Thank you for continuing to breath life into these horrific creatures. The genre would not be where it is without you.

For the fans, hopefully you are able to use this book to find a new favorite film. This research has uncovered dozens of films many of you may have never heard of and maybe you will find something obscure, something gory, something quirky or even just get reacquainted with an old friend. There are so many wonderful zombie movies out there to find, maybe you will be pointed in the direction of a few new ones.

2 VIEWING THE DEAD

Each movie has been graded on nine separate categories related to the special effects, violence and gore content of the film.

The first three statistics are timed entries.

- *First zombie appearance.* The time of the first obvious appearance of a zombie. A hand or a silhouette does not count as a zombie appearance, as many films use human characters to mislead the audience as a scare.

- *First human death.* The time of the first on screen human death. Implied or off screen deaths do not count.

- *First zombie death.* The time of the first on screen zombie death. Implied or off screen deaths do not count.

All times listed have been rounded to the nearest fifteen seconds as opposed to the exact second. This has been done for numerous reasons. Movies on PAL format play back 4% faster than those on NTSC and the events listed will occur at slightly different times. The goal of this book is to have worldwide appeal, so please accept that there may be some minor discrepancies depending on how the scene falls in a minute. For example, a zombie death scene occurring at 35:01 on a North American DVD could happen at 34:50 on a European DVD. All times listed are based on NTSC versions. Additionally, the films have been viewed on DVD, VHS and digital downloads and therefore minor time fluctuations can occur between different media types and release versions. Times may not match up exactly with the format viewed and are offered as approximate reference points.

The remaining six categories focus on the gore, violence and special effects and are graded from Very Low to Very High. These categories are amount of gore, gore quality, zombie quality, zombie count, zombie body count and human body count. Ratings are not dependent on those from other categories. A film with a zero gore count can still achieve a Very High rating in Zombie Counts and Zombie Deaths. As such, a film can score a Very High rating in gore but no zombies or humans die. Implied or off screen violence, is not counted in any category. For example, if a character is shot and killed on screen, but there is no squib effect, it will not count as an effects shot. The death will be counted towards the total, but the gunshot will not be listed.

While the goal of this book is to point zombie fans to gore and violence, it is not the intention to spoil the movies by specifically detailing which characters die. It is inevitable that this book will include new movies that the reader hasn't viewed before, therefore shot descriptions are vague when referencing characters. Only the characters gender is noted and names and roles are intentionally avoided. The reader can ascertain which gore effects are forthcoming but not who they happen to. The goal of this book is to entice and inform the reader, not spoil the film.

Amount of Gore

Very Low	No gore effects are present. (0)
Low	A few bites or gunshot wounds are shown. (1 – 5)
Average	A handful of graphic shots are shown. (6 – 10)
High	Multiple scenes of human on zombie violence. (11 – 24)
Very High	Constant graphic and excessive violence over multiple scenes. (25+)

Gore Quality

Very Low	Simulated zombie bites or heavy use of shadows to hide a graphic shot.
Low	Poor effects quality.
Average	Believable makeup for existing wounds, but may include blood/gore discoloration or visible latex lines.
High	More realistic effects showing exit wounds and aftermath.
Very High	Extremely graphic and realistic effects showing intense violence on humans and zombies.

Zombie Effects

Very Low	No makeup.
Low	Grey or green painted zombies and no decay.
Average	Passable skin color, but poor quality prosthetics.
High	Better quality prosthetics and makeup.
Very High	High quality CGI and/or prosthetic make up showing considerable damage and decay.

Zombie Count

Very Low	No zombies or an implied zombie presence. (0)
Low	A lone zombie is the antagonist. (1)
Average	A handful of individual zombies are present. (2 – 10)
High	A large group of zombies spread throughout the film. (11 – 29)
Very High	At numerous times through the movie, scenes are filled with the undead. (30+)

Zombie Body Count

Very Low	No zombies are killed on camera. (0)
Low	One zombie dies. (1)
Average	A handful of zombies die. (2 – 10)
High	A few skirmishes thin out the ranks. (11 – 19)
Very High	The undead suffer massive losses throughout the film. (20+)

Human Body Count

Very Low	No human characters are killed on camera. (0)
Low	One human dies. (1)
Average	A handful of humans die. (2 –5)
High	A few skirmishes thin out the ranks. (6 – 14).
Very High	Humans suffer massive losses throughout the film. (15+)

Effects Highlights

The gore effects from the film are highlighted. In the interests of preventing spoilers, character names or roles are not included.

28 DAYS LATER

Year: 2002   Length: 113 minutes
Director: Danny Boyle

STATISTICS

First Zombie: 5:00
First Human Death: 29:30
First Zombie Death: 17:00

Amount of Gore: Average
Gore Quality: Very High
Zombie Quality   High
Zombie Count: Very High
Zombie Deaths: High
Human Deaths: High

SUMMARY

Twenty eight days after a killer virus called "Rage" is accidentally unleashed from a British animal research facility and spread across the country, a small group of survivors are caught in a desperate fight to protect themselves from the infected. When they take shelter at a military facility, it becomes dangerously clear that the infected are not the only threat as the soldiers reveal their true intentions.

EFFECTS HIGHLIGHTS

4:45 – A woman vomits blood.

28:45 – A zombie is cut with a sword.

29:15 – Close up on a bite wound.

29:30 – A man's arm is cut off with a sword.

1:06:15 – An infected man is shot multiple times.

1:12:30 – A zombie throws up blood.

1:18:00 – A zombie steps on a land mine.

1:33:00 – A zombie is shot in the head.

1:37:45 – A soldier is stabbed with a bayonet.

1:41:45 – A man jams his thumbs in another man's eye sockets.

28 WEEKS LATER

Year: 2007   Length: 96 minutes
Director: Juan Carlos Fresnadillo

STATISTICS

First Zombie: 6:00
First Human Death: 7:45
First Zombie Death: 6:30

Amount of Gore: Very High
Gore Quality: Very High
Zombie Quality   High
Zombie Count: Very High
Zombie Deaths: Very High
Human Deaths: Very High

SUMMARY

Twenty eight weeks after the initial breakout of the "Rage" virus, the infected have died off and England is slowly being repopulated and cleansed. An American led NATO force enters London to assist with the reconstruction. The peace crumbles as an infected survivor is discovered and returned to the city. Before long, the disease breaks out again and rapidly spreads throughout the city. However, this time it is possible that one of the survivors could be carrying a cure.

EFFECTS HIGHLIGHTS

6:30 – A zombie is hit on the head with a crowbar.

27:30 – A woman rips the skin off of her face.

43:30 – A zombie pushes its thumbs into a woman's eyes.

46:00 – A zombie is shot in the head.

51:30 – A zombie is shot in the head.

51:45 – A zombie is shot in the head.

53:00 – A man is shot in the chest.

53:00 – A man is shot in the stomach.

53:30 – A man is shot in the back.

53:30 – A man is shot in the back.

53:30 – A man is shot in the back.

53:45 – A woman is shot in the back.

53:45 – A man is shot in the back.

53:45 – A man's lower arm is shot off.

53:45 – A man is shot in the head.

54:00 – A man is shot in the back.

54:15 – A zombie is shot in the face.

54:45 – A man is shot in the head.

1:12:45 – A helicopter pilot uses the helicopter blades to cut through a crowd of zombies.

1:12:45 – A zombie's head is cut in half.

1:12:45 – A helicopter pilot uses the helicopter blades to cut through a crowd of zombies.

1:12:45 – A zombie's head is cut in half.

1:13:00 – A helicopter pilot uses the helicopter blades to cut through a crowd of zombies.

1:13:00 – A zombie is decapitated.

1:13:00 – A zombie is decapitated.

1:13:00 – A helicopter pilot uses the helicopter blades to cut through a crowd of zombies.

1:13:00 – A zombie is cut in half.

1:13:00 – A zombie is cut in half.

1:13:00 – A helicopter pilot uses the helicopter blades to cut through a crowd of zombies.

1:13:00 – A zombie is decapitated.

1:13:00 – A zombie's arm is severed.

1:13:00 – A helicopter pilot uses the helicopter blades to cut through a crowd of zombies.

1:13:00 – A zombie is decapitated.

1:13:15 – A zombie is shot in the shoulder.

Location shots from "28 Weeks Later" courtesy of Roland Keates.

7

1:13:30 – A zombie has a massive hole in its side.

1:13:30 – The ground is littered with numerous severed body parts and moving torsos.

1:15:30 – A zombie vomits blood on a car window.

1:22:00 – A woman is repeatedly hit in the face with the butt of a rifle.

A GRAVE FOR THE CORPSES

Year: 2011   Length: 82 minutes
Director: S.N Sibley

STATISTICS

First Zombie: :15
First Human Death: :30
First Zombie Death: 7:00

Amount of Gore: High
Gore Quality: Low
Zombie Quality   Very Low
Zombie Count: Very High
Zombie Deaths: Very High
Human Deaths: High

SUMMARY

A police officer is bitten during a zombie attack and desperately tries to find a cure before he joins the ranks of the undead.

EFFECTS HIGHLIGHTS

:15 – A zombie rips out a boy's intestines.

7:00 – A zombie is shot in the head.

9:45 – A zombie eats a man's brains.

30:15 – A zombie rips out a man's intestines.

36:45 – A man is shot in the chest.

41:45 – A man drills into another man's neck.

53:30 – A zombie is stabbed with a chainsaw.

54:00 – A zombie is stabbed with a chainsaw.

54:15 – A zombie is stabbed with a chainsaw.

54:30 – A zombie is stabbed with a chainsaw.

57:45 – A zombie is stabbed with a chainsaw.

1:05:30 – A zombie is decapitated.

1:07:15 – A zombie bites a man's neck.

1:07:30 – A zombie rips out a man's tongue.

1:09:45 – A man rips off a zombie's penis.

1:10:45 – A man slices open a zombie's stomach.

1:11:30 – A zombie is shot in the hand.

1:11:45 – A zombie is shot in the head.

1:11:45 – A zombie is shot in the head.

1:11:45 – A zombie is shot in the head.

1:11:45 – A zombie is shot in the head.

1:11:45 – A zombie is shot in the head.

1:11:45 – A zombie is shot in the head.

1:12:00 – A zombie is shot in the chest.

A VIRGIN AMONG THE LIVING DEAD

Alternate Title: Christine, Princess of Eroticism
Year: 1973   Length: 78 minutes
Directors: Jesus Franco, Jean Rollin, Pierre Querut

STATISTICS

First Zombie: 1:15:45
First Human Death: 13:30
First Zombie Death: N/A

Amount of Gore: Very Low
Gore Quality: Low
Zombie Quality   Very Low
Zombie Count: Average
Zombie Deaths: Very Low
Human Deaths: Low

SUMMARY

A girl comes home to visit her estranged relatives in a remote castle for the reading of her father's will. She soon discovers that all of her relatives are all in fact dead and her decision to live with them turns into a nightmare.

EFFECTS HIGHLIGHTS

41:30 – Close up of a severed arm.

AAAH! ZOMBIES!!!

Alternate Title: Wasting Away
Year: 2007   Length: 91 minutes
Director: Matthew Kohnen

STATISTICS

First Zombie: 1:00
First Human Death: :45
First Zombie Death: 27:00

Amount of Gore: Average
Gore Quality: Low
Zombie Quality   Low
Zombie Count: Very High
Zombie Deaths: Average
Human Deaths: Very High

SUMMARY

After eating tainted food, a group of recently turned zombies struggle to come to grips with their new life as members of the undead. As they make their way through the days, they grasp the difficulties and challenges of their terrifying new life.

EFFECTS HIGHLIGHTS

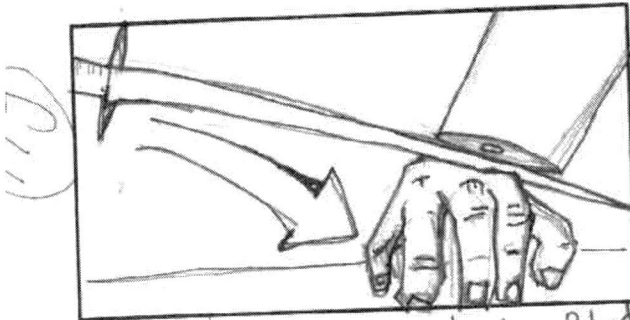

CU Hand chop not too Bloody

CU Nick RXNS Hold as MED CU thru dialogue push in for 32-33 Monologue

Bartender falls, sword in Head

2 shot Pool Players V steps behind grabs on turn. Dolly into Van. Pull back for drop & RXN. C thru shot.

low Profile, Tim Lands in Hold thru C's Grabble. Pull back thru walk

Rev. 2 shot OTS V Grabs

"Aaah! Zombies!!!" (Wasting Away) storyboards courtesy of Matthew Kohnen.

9

17C — Rev. Undercrank tim being beaten

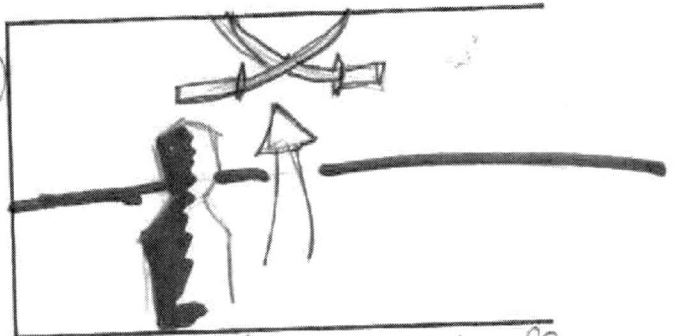

17D — Pool Player takes sword off wall, runs at us rushed Undercrank

17E — staggered 3 shot, lines Mike exits Rt. Nick DG? RxN C&V C exits CL after shot

17F — I crouching M enters CL line, h.t t out CR Pass OTS at Pool Players

17G — M falling on bar, enter CR fast Wally in w/ look RT. Hand on bar Pull back from RxN.; Bartender POPS UP camera left shot

17H — low Past Bar/hand Pool Player enters & chops Hold thru trying to pull out ?C Pull/thru Pushes Pool Player away C exits to Tim

13:30 – A woman crushes a cat.

15:00 – A man has a motorcycle handle bar sticking out of his chest.

19:14 – A man's hand is cut off with a machete.

28:30 – A man peels off part of his scalp.

29:30 – A man pulls the skin on his arm off.

38:45 – A man's finger is cut off in a door.

50:15 – A man's hand is pulled off.

1:00:15 – A zombie pulls a man's arm off.

1:01:13 – A severed head rolls down a bowling lane.

1:07:45 – A man holds a severed arm.

ADA: ZOMBILERIN DUGUNU

Year: 2010   Length: 73 minutes
Directors: Murat Emir Eren, Talip Ertürk

STATISTICS

First Zombie:	21:00
First Human Death:	23:00
First Zombie Death:	1:07:30
Amount of Gore:	Low
Gore Quality:	High
Zombie Quality:	Average
Zombie Count:	Very High
Zombie Deaths:	Average
Human Deaths:	High

SUMMARY

When a group of friends travel to a wedding, a horde of the undead crash the reception. Soon the celebration becomes a fight to survive as the wedding guests flee for their lives to escape the ravenous zombies.

EFFECTS HIGHLIGHTS

24:00 – A zombie eats a man's intestines.

24:30 – Close up of a half eaten dead body.

1:05:00 – A zombie has an open wound on its neck.

1:07:30 – A zombie is shot in the head.

AFTER SUNDOWN

Year: 2006   Length: 90 minutes
Director: Christopher Abram

STATISTICS

First Zombie:	20:31
First Human Death:	3:45
First Zombie Death:	50:00
Amount of Gore:	Average
Gore Quality:	High
Zombie Quality:	Average
Zombie Count:	Very High
Zombie Deaths:	Very High
Human Deaths:	Very High

SUMMARY

A century-old vampire rises from the dead to search for his offspring. With his legion of flesh-eating zombies, the vampire tears through a small Texas town leaving a trail of chaos and death in his wake.

EFFECTS HIGHLIGHTS

20:15 – A vampire spits blood into the mouth of a corpse.

44:15 – A man's heart is ripped from his chest.

48:00 – Close up of a bite mark.

48:45 – A zombie is missing the lower part of its arm.

50:00 – A zombie is stabbed in the head with a broom handle.

54:30 – A zombie eats a piece of flesh.

AGAINST THE DARK

Year: 2009   Length: 94 minutes
Director: Richard Crudo

STATISTICS

First Zombie:	:15
First Human Death:	31:30
First Zombie Death:	2:00
Amount of Gore:	High
Gore Quality:	Very High
Zombie Effects:	High
Zombie Count:	Very High
Zombie Deaths:	Very High
Human Deaths:	High

SUMMARY

When the population of Earth is infected with an unstoppable virus and transformed into flesh-eating monsters, a group of hunters chase the zombies to extinguish the menace. As the military prepares to bomb the area, hope of rescue is running out for six non-infected survivors who have taken refuge in an abandoned hospital teeming with the infected.

EFFECTS HIGHLIGHTS

:15 – A wroup of zombies tear at a pile of entrails.

1:00 – A group of zombies tear a body to pieces.

1:15 – Close up of a dead body.

6:00 – Zombies tear organs out of a women's stomach.

15:00 – Close up of a severed eyeball.

15:30 – A hallway is littered with fresh body parts.

16:00 – Dead bodies are suspended from the ceiling with their intestines spilling out.

19:45 – A zombie is decapitated.

28:30 – A severed arm lies in a trash can.

38:30 – Blood sprays out of a fallen zombies throat.

42:15 – A group of zombies eat a dead woman.

48:15 – A rotten corpse is propped up against a wall.

57:30 – A zombie bites off a man's arm.

59:15 – A man is shot in the chest.

1:07:30 – A zombie is stabbed in the back.

1:09:30 – A grenade vaporizes three zombies.

1:16:30 – A zombie's arm is cut off.

1:16:45 – A zombie is slashed across the neck.

1:21:45 – A zombie with a neck wound gushes blood.

ALIEN DEAD

Year: 1980   Length: 80 minutes
Director: Fred Olen Ray

STATISTICS

First Zombie:	12:00
First Human Death:	12:00
First Zombie Death:	1:04:30
Amount of Gore:	Low
Gore Quality:	Low
Zombie Effects:	Average
Zombie Count:	High
Zombie Deaths:	Low
Human Deaths:	High

SUMMARY

A meteorite plummets to Earth and collides with a houseboat, turning the passengers into flesh-eating zombies. At first, they feast on the alligators in the swamp, but once they run out, they turn on the local citizens.

EFFECTS HIGHLIGHTS

29:15 – A dog eats a dead man's torso.

29:45 – A woman is stabbed in the stomach with a pitchfork.

36:45 – A piece of flesh is found stuck on the propeller of a boat.

51:30 – A zombie eats a piece of flesh.

ALL SOULS DAY

Year: 2005   Length: 90 minutes
Director: Jeremy Kasten

STATISTICS

First Zombie:	17:15
First Human Death:	1:10:30
First Zombie Death:	55:45
Amount of Gore:	High
Gore Quality:	Very High
Zombie Effects:	Very High
Zombie Count:	Very High
Zombie Deaths:	Low
Human Deaths:	Average

SUMMARY

One hundred years ago, a Mexican soldier raided an ancient Aztec tomb and mercilessly murdered the towns inhabitants. Now, these tortured souls have returned from the dead to attack a group of travelers.

EFFECTS HIGHLIGHTS

49:30 – A man is shot in the stomach.

53:15 – A zombie spits out a piece of flesh.

55:30 – A zombie is stabbed in the chest with a pole.

55:45 – A zombie is shot in the head.

1:08:00 – A severed leg hits a car.

1:10:30 – A zombie spits out a piece of flesh.

1:17:30 – A man is shot in the back.

1:17:45 – A man is shot in the chest.

1:18:45 – A group of zombies eat various severed limbs.

1:22:15 – A group of zombies rip open a man's stomach.

1:26:30 – A man's arms are pulled off.

1:22:45 – A zombie is shot in the head.

AMERICAN ZOMBIE

Year: 2007   Length: 90 minutes
Director: Grace Lee

STATISTICS

First Zombie:	1:30
First Human Death:	N/A
First Zombie Death:	N/A
Amount of Gore:	Low
Gore Quality:	High
Zombie Effects:	Average
Zombie Count:	Very High
Zombie Deaths:	Very Low
Human Deaths:	Very Low

SUMMARY

Documentary filmmakers infiltrate a Los Angeles zombie community in an effort to document the undead subculture and monitor their daily lives. It doesn't take long to determine that the undead aren't much different from the rest of us - except for a few patches of maggot ridden, rotting flesh and the occasional taste for human flesh.

EFFECTS HIGHLIGHTS

5:15 – A man is shot in the stomach.

5:30 – A scalpel is drawn across a boy's forehead.

10:00 – A montage of zombies eating flesh.

33:15 – A bandage is removed from a zombie's abdomen to reveal a maggot infested wound.

34:30 – A zombie has a wound on its forehead.

35:00 – A zombie has a wound on its abdomen.

Working on the Deadites for "Army of Darkness" courtesy of Alterian Inc. and Tony Gardner.

13

ARMY OF DARKNESS

Year: 1992   Length: 81 minutes
Director: Sam Raimi

STATISTICS

First Zombie:	12:15
First Human Death:	10:15
First Zombie Death:	13:45

Amount of Gore:	Average
Gore Quality:	Average
Zombie Effects:	High
Zombie Count:	Very High
Zombie Deaths:	Very High
Human Deaths:	Very High

SUMMARY

A man is transported to 1300 A.D. England, where he must battle a massive army of the dead and retrieve the ancient book of the dead called the Necronomicon, so he can return home.

EFFECTS HIGHLIGHTS

10:15 – A man is shot in the back with a crossbow.

13:45 – A zombie is decapitated.

14:00 – A zombie's hand is cut off.

1:08:30 – A man is stabbed in the stomach.

1:08:45 – A man is stabbed in the stomach.

1:09:00 – A man is stabbed in the stomach.

1:12:45 – A zombie is stabbed in the stomach.

1:13:15 – A man is stabbed in the stomach.

1:15:15 – A zombie is stabbed in the chest.

THE ASTRO ZOMBIES

Year: 1968   Length: 91 minutes
Director: Ted V. Mikels

STATISTICS

First Zombie:	1:45
First Human Death:	5:00
First Zombie Death:	1:29:30

Amount of Gore:	Low
Gore Quality:	Very Low
Zombie Effects:	Very Low
Zombie Count:	Low
Zombie Deaths:	Low
Human Deaths:	Very High

SUMMARY

A mad scientist build a super human by murdering innocent victims and harvesting their parts. However, the creature goes on a murderous rampage.

EFFECTS HIGHLIGHTS

2:30 – A car is splattered with blood.

22:45 – A scientist drains blood out of a man.

33:45 – A woman is repeatedly stabbed in the chest.

43:15 – A man is shot in the chest.

1:28:45 – A man is decapitated with a sword.

1:28:45 – A man is stabbed in the head.

ATTACK GIRLS SWIM TEAM VS. THE UNDEAD

Alternate Title: Undead Pool
Year: 2007   Length: 78 minutes
Director: Kôji Kawano

STATISTICS

First Zombie:	16:30
First Human Death:	9:15
First Zombie Death:	24:15

Amount of Gore:	High
Gore Quality:	Very High
Zombie Effects:	Average
Zombie Count:	Average
Zombie Deaths:	Average
Human Deaths:	High

SUMMARY

When a deadly virus turns a Japanese high school full of students and teachers into flesh-eating zombies, it is up to the newest student to save the day. She soon discovers that the school swim team is immune to the disease and rallies her team mates to fight the undead horde.

EFFECTS HIGHLIGHTS

9:15 – A man is stabbed.

14:15 – A woman finds a dead body.

17:15 – A girl is covered in blood.

17:30 – A man cuts of a girls head with a metal ruler.

18:00 – An arm is cut off with a metal ruler.

18:15 – A leg is cut off.

18:15 – A head is cut off and a girl is covered in blood.

18:30 – A zombie eats an arm.

18:30 – An eyeball lies on the ground.

21:00 – A zombie spits out blood and flesh.

22:00 – A man is stabbed in the head with a pair of scissors.

42:30 – A girl is stabbed with a chainsaw.

1:12:15 – A naked woman is covered in blood.

AUTOMATON TRANSFUSION

Year: 2006   Length: 75 minutes

Director: Steven C. Miller

STATISTICS

First Zombie:	4:15
First Human Death:	4:30
First Zombie Death:	34:15

Amount of Gore:	High
Gore Quality:	Very High
Zombie Effects:	High
Zombie Count:	Very High
Zombie Deaths:	High
Human Deaths:	High

SUMMARY

When a U.S. Army experiment to turn corpses into a new form of military weapon goes awry, a group of teens find themselves fighting for their lives. As the undead destroy their home town, the teens take it upon themselves to end the rampage once and for all.

EFFECTS HIGHLIGHTS

4:15 – A zombie bites a chunk of flesh out of a man's neck.

4:30 – A man is snapped in half.

11:45 – A wound on a man's neck is gushing blood.

15:30 – A zombie tears the skin off of a man's cheek.

22:45 – Zombies pull a woman's body apart and rip out her organs.

23:00 – The remains of an eaten woman lay on the ground.

28:00 – A boy finds a severed head missing its skin.

33:00 – A zombie rips an organ out of a woman's stomach.

34:15 – A zombie is shot in the head.

35:00 – A group of zombies devour the remains of numerous victims.

35:30 – A woman's head is pulled off.

37:15 – A zombie rips off a woman's jaw.

38:00 – A man bludgeons a zombie with a hammer.

39:00 – A man is torn to pieces by a group of zombies.

39:00 – A zombie is shot in the face.

41:00 – A zombie stabbed in the eye with a shard of glass.

42:30 – Numerous body parts are scattered across the floor.

45:45 – A zombie is stabbed in the face with a chainsaw.

47:30 – A mans legs have been bitten off.

59:00 – A man is covered in blood.

1:00:00 – A woman is thrown over a balcony and hits her head on the swimming pool deck as she lands.

AUTUMN

Year: 2009   Length: 110 minutes
Director: Steven Rumbelow

STATISTICS

First Zombie:	16:15
First Human Death:	3:45
First Zombie Death:	N/A

Amount of Gore:	Low
Gore Quality:	High
Zombie Effects	Average
Zombie Count:	Very High
Zombie Deaths:	Very Low
Human Deaths:	Average

SUMMARY

A devastating virus sweeps the planet and kills millions. Before long, the dead are reanimating and they're hungry for flesh. The handful of remaining survivors have to deal with a rapidly changing world and the shocking realization that the dead are getting more intelligent with every passing day.

EFFECTS HIGHLIGHTS

2:30 – A girl is spitting up blood.

3:15 – Numerous other victims start coughing up blood.

10:36 – A group of zombies tear a dog to pieces.

28:39 – A man discovers rotting bodies lying in a bed

AWAKEN THE DEAD

Year: 2006   Length: 101 minutes
Director: Jeff Brookshire

STATISTICS

First Zombie:	11:00
First Human Death:	18:15
First Zombie Death:	6:00

Amount of Gore:	Low
Gore Quality:	Low
Zombie Effects:	Low
Zombie Count:	Very High
Zombie Deaths:	Very High
Human Deaths:	Average

SUMMARY

A murderer turned priest and a former prostitute find themselves trapped in a house while those outside succumb to a virus that's transforming the city's inhabitants into the living dead. Drawn to the house by a mysterious letter, the priest must now solve the missive's riddle if he and his companion are to survive.

EFFECTS HIGHLIGHTS

18:15 – Two zombies tear out and eat a man's

intestines.

24:45 – A zombie is stabbed in the eye with a kitchen knife.

38:30 – Blood drips out of a bullet wound on a zombie's forehead.

53:30 – A zombie pulls out another zombies eyeball with its teeth.

56:15 – A zombie's hand is put in a blender.

AXED

Year: 2011   Length: 30 minutes
Director: Joshua Long

STATISTICS

First Zombie: :45
First Human Death: 2:45
First Zombie Death: 1:15

Amount of Gore: Very High
Gore Quality: Very High
Zombie Effects: Very High
Zombie Count: Very High
Zombie Deaths: Very High
Human Deaths: Very High

SUMMARY

A desperate survivor of a zombie outbreak is forced to fight his way out of his neighborhood through a seemingly never ending army of the undead and a trigger happy militia. With both armies hell bent on destroying all signs of life in the shattered town, he finds himself in a fight for his life with danger at every turn.

EFFECTS HIGHLIGHTS

:45 – A man slips on a pile of intestines.

1:00 – A zombie's intestines are falling out of its stomach.

1:00 – A zombie eats its own intestines.

1:15 – A zombie is decapitated.

2:00 – A woman is injected into her neck.

2:15 – A woman coughs up blood.

2:45 – A woman is shot in the head.

3:15 – A zombie bites a woman's shoulder.

3:15 – A zombie eats a chunk of flesh.

3:30 – A zombie is shot in the head.

3:30 – A woman is shot in the head.

6:15 – A man is shot in the head.

8:30 – Three people are simultaneously shot in the head.

8:30 – A woman is shot in the head.

8:45 – A man and woman are shot in the head.

9:00 – A woman is shot in the head.

9:45 – A zombie bites of a man's finger.

9:45 – A zombie is shot in the head.

10:00 – A man bleeds from finger stumps.

10:00 – A zombie is shot in the chest.

10:00 – A zombie is shot in the eye.

10:00 – A zombie is shot in the chest.

10:15 – A man is shot in the head.

10:15 – A man is shot in the head.

10:30 – A zombie eats a severed limb.

10:45 – A zombie is shot in the chest.

13:15 – A group of zombies tear at a dead body.

13:30 – A dead woman's foot is sawed off.

14:00 – A zombie eats a dead woman's intestines.

14:00 – A zombie is hit by a car.

16:00 – A man steps in a pile of intestines.

18:00 – A man and a woman are shot in the chest.

18:00 – A woman is shot in the head.

18:15 – Two zombies tear out and eat a man's intestines.

19:00 – A zombie is shot in the chest.

19:30 – A man's hand is cut off with a machete.

19:30 – A man is shot in the head.

19:30 – A bloody stump squirts blood.

19:30 – A zombie bites an arm.

19:45 – A zombie eats a severed hand.

19:45 – A man is stabbed in the leg with shovel.

19:45 – A man is stabbed in the neck with a shovel.

19:45 – A zombie is shot in the head.

19:45 – A zombie is shot in the head.

19:45 – A zombie is shot in the head.

20:15 – A man's stomach is sliced open with a knife.

20:15 – A group of zombies tear open a man's stomach.

20:15 – A group of zombies eat a man's intestines.

20:30 – A man shoots himself in the head.

20:30 – A zombie eats a piece of flesh.

20:30 – A zombie vomits blood on a woman.

20:45 – A zombie stabs a woman in the chest.

20:45 – A zombie eats a piece of flesh.

21:00 – A zombie eats a piece of flesh.

21:15 – A zombie is stabbed in the chest.

21:15 – A zombie bites a man's neck.

21:30 – A zombie is cut on the arm with a machete.

21:30 – A zombie bites a man's nose.

22:15 – A man cuts a zombie's head open with an axe.

22:30 – Close up of a smashed zombie skull.

23:00 – A zombie eats a dead zombies brain.

23:15 – A zombie is shot in the head.

23:15 – A zombie is shot in the head.

23:30 – A zombie rips open a man's throat.

23:45 – A group of zombies tear open a man's stomach.

24:00 – A zombie is shot in the head.

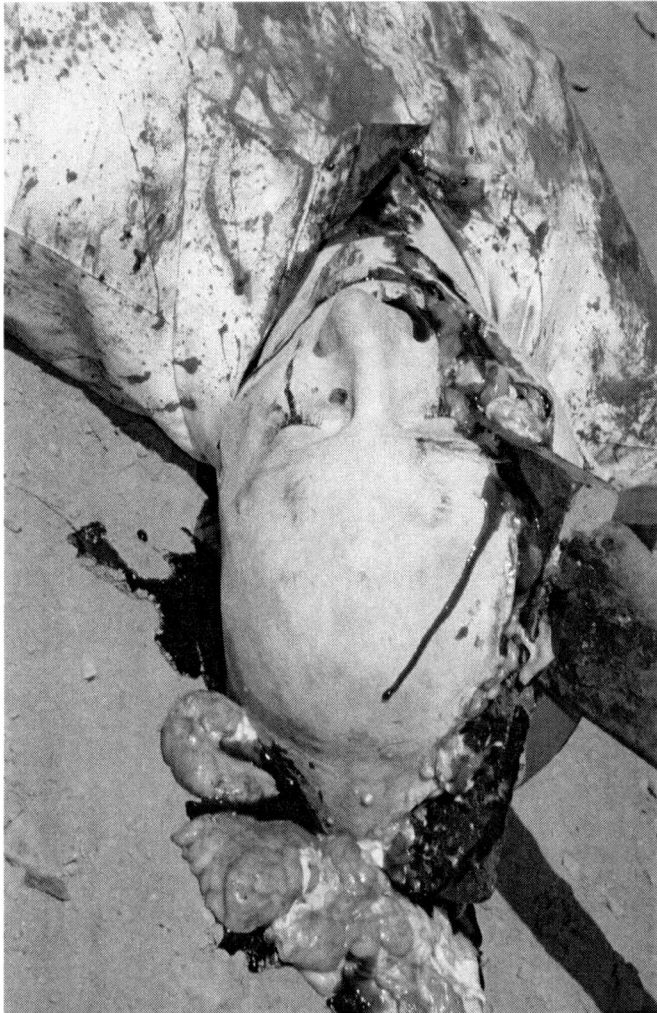

Behind the scenes of "Axed" courtesy of Joshua Long

25:00 – A zombie is shot in the head.

25:00 – A zombie is shot in the head.

25:00 – A zombie is shot in the head.

26:45 – A zombie is shot in the head.

27:00 – A zombie is shot in the head.

BATTLE GIRL

Alternate Title: The Living Dead In Tokyo Bay
Year: 1991   Length: 73 minutes
Director: Kazuo 'Gaira' Komizu

STATISTICS

First Zombie:	8:30
First Human Death:	8:00
First Zombie Death:	18:15

Amount of Gore:	Average
Gore Quality:	Very Low
Zombie Effects:	Very Low
Zombie Count:	Average
Zombie Deaths:	Very Low
Human Deaths:	Low

SUMMARY

After a meteor crashes into Tokyo Bay, an strange virus causes the dead to come back to life and feast on the living. It's up to one woman army Keiko, to restore order and save her home from the dead.

EFFECTS HIGHLIGHTS

25:15 – A zombie is stabbed in the arm.

25:30 – A woman beheads a zombie with a garrote wire.

26:45 – A zombie is sliced with an invisible laser.

33:15 – A zombie is shot in the head.

48:30 – A zombie bites a man's neck.

55:45 – A man's arm is ripped off.

56:00 – An arrow pierces a zombie's head.

BATTLEFIELD BASEBALL

Year: 2003   Length: 87 minutes
Director: Yûdai Yamaguchi

STATISTICS

First Zombie:	11:00
First Human Death:	18:15
First Zombie Death:	6:00

Amount of Gore:	Low
Gore Quality:	Low
Zombie Effects:	Very Low
Zombie Count:	Very High
Zombie Deaths:	Very High
Human Deaths:	High

SUMMARY

The students of Seido High School are worried when their team is set to face the zombie baseball team of Gedo High. However, Seido's newest student, Jubei may just be their secret weapon.

EFFECTS HIGHLIGHTS

1:00 – A man catches a baseball and explodes.

1:45 – A baseball field is littered with body parts.

38:15 – A baseball field is covered in body parts.

43:45 – A man is impaled with multiple baseball bats.

1:17:15 – A zombie is shot in the head.

BEAST WITHIN

Alternate Title: Virus Undead
Year: 2008   Length: 95 minutes
Director: Wolf Wolff, Ohmuthi

STATISTICS

First Zombie:	50:45
First Human Death:	2:00
First Zombie Death:	50:45

Amount of Gore:	Average
Gore Quality:	High
Zombie Effects:	High
Zombie Count:	Average
Zombie Deaths:	Average
Human Deaths:	High

SUMMARY

When a new strain of avian flu turns its victims into zombies, a group of survivors holed up in a mansion must fight off an onslaught from flesh-eating monsters as well as the infected birds.

EFFECTS HIGHLIGHTS

7:45 – A bird flies into a car's windshield.

20:15 – A dead animal is skinned.

47:30 – A man bites another man's arm.

48:15 – Close up of a bite mark.

50:45 – A zombie is shot in the mouth.

1:02:45 – A zombie is shot multiple times in the chest.

1:20:15 – A woman drops a sickle off of a roof and it stabs a zombie in the head.

1:23:15 – A zombie is shot in the head.

BENEATH STILL WATERS

Year: 2005   Length: 92 minutes
Director: Brian Yuzna

STATISTICS

First Zombie:	9:00
First Human Death:	8:30
First Zombie Death:	1:32:00

Amount of Gore: Average
Gore Quality: Very High
Zombie Effects: Very High
Zombie Count: High
Zombie Deaths: Low
Human Deaths: High

SUMMARY

After an evil force consumes a small town and its residents, authorities build a dam and flood the town, submerging it forever. Forty years later, when the history of the area has been forgotten, the creature returns. Only now, it is thirsty to wreak havoc on the inhabitants of a neighboring town.

EFFECTS HIGHLIGHTS

8:30 – A boy's head is ripped in half.

10:45 – The skin melts off of a man's face.

23:00 – A severed arm is floating in a lake.

49:00 – A man pulls a severed head from the water.

50:00 – Severed limbs float to the surface of a lake.

51:00 – Close up of a waterlogged severed head.

1:10:45 – A zombie bites off a woman's neck.

1:14:00 – A zombie rips a man's head in half.

1:15:00 – Close up of a dead body.

1:24:15 – A zombie cuts its limbs off with a saw.

BENEATH THE SURFACE

Year: 2007   Length: 90 minutes
Director: Blake Reigle

STATISTICS

First Zombie: 27:45
First Human Death: 25:15
First Zombie Death: N/A

Amount of Gore: Low
Gore Quality: High
Zombie Effects: Very Low
Zombie Count: Very Low
Zombie Deaths: Low
Human Deaths: Very Low

SUMMARY

A high school outcast brings the love of his life back from the dead to expose the truth behind her apparent suicide.

EFFECTS HIGHLIGHTS

1:21:30 – A man is stabbed in the neck with a razor blade.

1:23:00 – A machete is drawn across a man's stomach.

THE BEYOND

Alternate Title: Seven Doors of Death
Year: 1981   Length: 87 minutes
Director: Lucio Fulci

STATISTICS

First Zombie: 56:30
First Human Death: 6:30
First Zombie Death: 1:12:30

Amount of Gore: High
Gore Quality: High
Zombie Effects: High
Zombie Count: High
Zombie Deaths: Average
Human Deaths: High

SUMMARY

A young woman inherits an old hotel in Louisiana, but the run down building hides a dark secret. Beneath the hotel lies of one of the entrances to Hell. Soon, evil forces start rising up and violently attacking the occupants one by one.

EFFECTS HIGHLIGHTS

3:45 – A man is slashed on the cheek

4:30 – The man is whipped with chains.

5:00 – Nails are hammered through a man's wrists.

17:30 – A finger hooks a man's eye out of its socket.

21:00 – Blood pours out of a dead man's mouth.

22:00 – A surgeon stitches up a wound.

28:15 – Acid is poured on a woman's face.

50:00 – A tarantula bites a man below the eye.

50:15 – A second spider tears the skin off the man's nose.

50:30 – Another spider pulls out the man's eyeball.

57:30 – A woman is impaled on a nail and it punctures through her eye socket, pushing her eyeball out.

1:04:00 – A dog bites a chunk of flesh out of a woman's neck.

1:04:00 – A dog bites a woman's ear off.

1:12:15 – A zombie is shot in the arm.

1:15:15 – A man is stabbed in the face with shards of glass.

1:18:30 – A zombie is shot in the chest.

1:18:45 – A zombie is shot in the head.

BEYOND RE-ANIMATOR

Year: 2003   Length: 95 minutes
Director: Brian Yuzna

STATISTICS

First Zombie: 4:45
First Human Death: 5:15
First Zombie Death: 6:00

Amount of Gore:	High
Gore Quality:	High
Zombie Effects:	High
Zombie Count:	Average
Zombie Deaths:	Average
Human Deaths:	High

SUMMARY

Dr. Herbert West has spent fourteen years in prison for accidentally killing a girl during one of his experiments. While incarcerated he has continued to perfect his reanimation methods on rats. When the new prison doctor asks West to help him with a project he's working on, the reanimation begins again and before long, the prison is full of the living dead.

EFFECTS HIGHLIGHTS

1:45 – A boy plays with an eyeball.

4:45 – A zombie is missing its jaw.

5:45 – A man shoots a zombie through the eye.

24:15 – A zombie bites a man's arm.

26:00 – Close up of a bite mark.

47:15 – A zombie bites off a man's ear.

1:11:45 – A woman is hacked into pieces.

1:12:15 – A severed arm lies on the floor.

1:18:00 – A zombie is shot multiple times in the back.

1:20:00 – A zombie bites off a man's penis.

1:20:30 – A zombie hangs from the ceiling with its legs and lower torso missing.

1:22:45 – A rat gnaws a severed penis.

1:24:0 – A man's eye swells up just before his stomach explodes.

1:24:30 – A zombie is missing most of its flesh.

1:27:15 – A zombie is beaten with a walking stick.

BIG TITS ZOMBIE

Alternate Title: The Big Tits Dragon:
Year: 2010   Length: 73 minutes
Director: Takao Nakano

STATISTICS

First Zombie:	1:15
First Human Death:	33:15
First Zombie Death:	1:45

Amount of Gore:	High
Gore Quality:	Average
Zombie Effects:	Average
Zombie Count:	Very High
Zombie Deaths:	Average
Human Deaths:	High

SUMMARY

An ancient Book of the Dead is discovered in the catacombs that run beneath a strip club. When one of the desperate strippers raises an army of the undead, the rest of the dancers must group together to stop the zombies.

EFFECTS HIGHLIGHTS

1:45 – A zombie is cut in half with a chainsaw.

2:00 – A zombie is stabbed in the head with a sword.

2:45 – A zombie is stabbed in the neck with a chainsaw.

3:30 – A zombie is decapitated with a chainsaw.

32:15 – A woman's finger is bitten off by a zombie.

32:45 – Zombies tear open a woman's torso.

35:00 – A zombie bites a woman's leg.

36:00 – A fountain of blood splashes on a wall.

37:45 – Close up of a pulsing bite wound.

41:15 – A woman finds a severed hand on the floor.

47:15 – Two zombies are decapitated with a chainsaw.

47:15 – A group of zombies eat a woman's innards.

48:00 – A zombie's arm is cut off with a sword and is then decapitated.

48:00 – A zombie is cut in half with a chainsaw.

57:00 – Close up of a bite mark.

1:01:00 – A zombie is cut in half with a chainsaw.

1:01:15 – A zombie is stabbed through the head.

1:02:15 – A zombie is decapitated with a chainsaw.

1:02:45 – A topless woman is covered in blood.

BIO COPS

Year: 2000   Length: 89 minutes
Director: Wai-Man Cheng

STATISTICS

First Zombie:	3:15
First Human Death:	3:45
First Zombie Death:	4:30

Amount of Gore:	Average
Gore Quality:	Average
Zombie Effects:	Average
Zombie Count:	Very High
Zombie Deaths:	Average
Human Deaths:	High

SUMMARY

A top secret experiment to make a vaccine that makes people intolerable to pain, goes awry and turns the patients into zombies.

EFFECTS HIGHLIGHTS

5:00 – Close up of a bite mark.

39:45 – A man's arms is ripped off.

43:00 – A zombie has a chunk of flesh in its mouth

43:15 – A zombie bites a man's arm.

50:00 – A zombie's arm is severed.

56:30 – Blood flows under a door.

58:00 – A zombie rips the heart out of another zombie's chest.

BIO ZOMBIE

Year: 1998   Length: 94 minutes
Director: Wilson Yip

STATISTICS

First Zombie:	11:45
First Human Death:	12:45
First Zombie Death:	13:00
Amount of Gore:	High
Gore Quality:	Low
Zombie Effects:	Average
Zombie Count:	Very High
Zombie Deaths:	Average
Human Deaths:	High

SUMMARY

Two lazy mall clerks unwittingly raise an army of zombies when they crash into a biochemical company employee with their car, causing him to spill cans of tainted soda.

EFFECTS HIGHLIGHTS

12:45 – Body parts are thrown out of a crate.

28:30 – A man is pulled under a car by a zombie.

52:15 – A man is bitten on the neck.

52:35 – A streak of blood covers a wall.

53:00 – A zombie is shot in the head.

1:02:00 – A zombie's head is pulled off.

1:04:30 – A zombie eats a chunk of meat.

1:06:45 – A zombie is in the head.

1:16:15 – A power drill is placed in a zombie's mouth.

1:18:00 – A man's arm is pulled off.

1:26:00 – Zombies eat various body parts.

1:35:00 – A zombie's head is ripped off.

BIOPHAGE

Year: 2010   Length: 72 minutes
Director: Mark Rapp

STATISTICS

First Zombie:	3:15
First Human Death:	50:15
First Zombie Death:	38:15
Amount of Gore:	Low
Gore Quality:	Average
Zombie Effects:	Average
Zombie Count:	Very High
Zombie Deaths:	Average
Human Deaths:	Average

SUMMARY

An epidemic turns most of the human race into zombie-like Biophages. Two survivors travel to a research hospital after their mission to find signs of human life fails.

EFFECTS HIGHLIGHTS

41:45 – A zombie eats flesh off of a severed deer leg.

42:30 – A zombie is shot in the head.

1:03:20 – A severed head lies on the floor.

BLACK MAGIC 2

Alternate Title: Bewitch Tame Head
Year: 1976   Length: 89 minutes
Director: Meng Hua Ho

STATISTICS

First Zombie:	1:05:45
First Human Death:	1:30
First Zombie Death:	1:23:30
Amount of Gore:	High
Gore Quality:	High
Zombie Effects:	Average
Zombie Count:	High
Zombie Deaths:	High
Human Deaths:	Average

SUMMARY

When an evil wizard wreaks havoc by raising a small army of zombies, a pair of scientists attempt to thwart him by uncovering the mysterious source of his dark powers.

EFFECTS HIGHLIGHTS

3:30 – A dead alligator is sliced open.

10:30 – A man removes a nail from a woman's head.

11:30 – Close up of an infected wound.

12:30 – Worms crawl under a man's skin.

35:30 – A man hammers a large nail into a woman's head.

42:00 – A man's hair and finger nails start to fall out.

42:45 – A man's face melts.

45:15 – Close up of a rotting a corpse.

45:45 – The abdomen of a corpse is cut open with a scalpel.

1:02:00 – A wound on a woman's chest swells up and bursts.

1:06:45 – A man cuts open a zombie's back, releasing pus and worms.

1:07:30 – A man stabs himself in the cheek with a nail.

1:07:45 – A man impales his hands on two large nails.

1:09:50 – A man holds two eyeballs in his hands.

1:23:15 – A man pulls a nail out of a zombie's head causing it to melt.

1:27:15 – Blood pours from a wound on a zombie's head.

1:31:00 – A zombie melts.

BLOOD CREEK

Year: 2009   Length: 90 minutes
Director: Joel Schumacher

STATISTICS

First Zombie:	42:00
First Human Death:	11:15
First Zombie Death:	51:00

Amount of Gore:	High
Gore Quality:	Very High
Zombie Effects:	High
Zombie Count:	Average
Zombie Deaths:	Low
Human Deaths:	Average

SUMMARY

A man and his brother go on a mission of revenge and become trapped in the middle of a harrowing occult experiment dating back to the days of the Third Reich.

EFFECTS HIGHLIGHTS

10:30 – Close up of a man's back wound.

24:00 – A man stabs a dog repeatedly in the chest.

26:45 – A man is shot in the arm.

27:00 – A man is shot in the stomach.

32:45 – A man treats a bloody wound.

44:30 – A horse bites a man on the shoulder.

44:45 – A horse has a large cut on its neck.

44:45 – A horse is shot.

45:00 – A horse is hit with multiple gun shots.

51:00 – A zombie is stabbed under the chin.

51:15 – A zombie's head is smashed with a club.

51:30 – A zombie's head is split in two.

1:00:15 – A zombie punches a man in the stomach, ripping a hole in him.

1:05:45 – A zombie hammers a spike into its forehead.

1:08:00 – A zombie is strangled with a strip of barbed wire and the head is severed.

BLOOD MOON RISING

Year: 2009   Length: 80 minutes
Director: Brian Skiba

STATISTICS

First Zombie:	1:30

First Human Death:	8:45
First Zombie Death:	4:15

Amount of Gore:	Average
Gore Quality:	High
Zombie Effects:	Average
Zombie Count:	Very High
Zombie Deaths:	Very High
Human Deaths:	Average

SUMMARY

When the devil's daughter raises an army of zombies and vampires from hell, the fate of the world rests in the hands of her hippie great-great-granddaughter and comic book geek friend.

EFFECTS HIGHLIGHTS

3:30 – A woman is bitten on the neck and blood pours down her arms.

4:15 – A zombie is shot in the head with a shotgun, destroying its head.

4:30 – A zombie is shot in the head, cracking the top part of its skull.

8:30 – A man is bitten, sending blood spraying across a table.

15:15 – A woman stabs a body as blood covers a wall.

23:45 – A woman shoots a zombie in the head.

35:00 – A zombie is shot in the neck.

39:30 – A zombie is shot in the head.

BLOOD OF THE BEAST

Year: 2003   Length: 74 minutes
Director: Georg Koszulinski

STATISTICS

First Zombie:	17:30
First Human Death:	11:00
First Zombie Death:	N/A

Amount of Gore:	Very Low
Gore Quality:	Very Low
Zombie Effects:	Very Low
Zombie Count:	High
Zombie Deaths:	Very Low
Human Deaths:	Low

SUMMARY

After the third world war claimed the lives of billions, over ninety-eight percent of the surviving males are rendered infertile. To ensure the survival of the human race, human clones are created. However, the experiment to reproduce life goes horribly wrong when the clone population mutates into an army of relentless zombies with a thirst for blood.

EFFECTS HIGHLIGHTS

10:30 – A wound on a man's neck pumps blood.

BLOODLUST ZOMBIES

Year: 2011   Length: 80 minutes
Director: Dan Lantz

STATISTICS

First Zombie:	20:15
First Human Death:	20:15
First Zombie Death:	30:00
Amount of Gore:	High
Gore Quality:	Very High
Zombie Effects:	High
Zombie Count:	High
Zombie Deaths:	Average
Human Deaths:	Low

SUMMARY

A lab accident at a top secret military weapons manufacturer exposes staff to a chemical that causes victims to become blood-lusting killers. The building goes into a security lock down and the remaining uninfected staff find themselves trapped inside and in a fight for their lives against the zombies.

EFFECTS HIGHLIGHTS

27:00 – A zombie bites a man's neck.

27:00 – Blood squirts out of a wound on a man's neck.

29:15 – A man has a bite mark on his neck.

30:00 – A zombie is shot in the head.

31:30 – A zombie bites a woman's neck.

31:45 – A zombie is stabbed in the chest with a test tube.

32:15 – A woman bleeds from a neck wound.

40:45 – A zombie is shot in the head.

41:00 – A zombie is shot in the chest.

57:15 – A zombie spits out a piece of flesh.

57:30 – A zombie is shot in the chest.

59:15 – A zombie's hand is cut off in a door.

1:00:15 – A zombie is shot in the chest.

1:03:00 – A zombie is shot in the head.

1:03:15 – A zombie is shot in the chest.

1:03:45 – A zombie is shot in the chest.

1:04:45 – A woman is covered in blood.

1:13:30 – A zombie is decapitated.

BLOODPIGS

Year: 2010   Length: 85 minutes
Director: Brian Paulin

STATISTICS

First Zombie:	5:30
First Human Death:	2:30
First Zombie Death:	10:15

Amount of Gore:	Very High
Gore Quality:	High
Zombie Effects:	High
Zombie Count:	Very High
Zombie Deaths:	High
Human Deaths:	High

SUMMARY

When food supplies dry up after a worldwide zombie outbreak, the survivors turn to eating each other. When humans begin to run low, they start to eat the flesh of the undead.

EFFECTS HIGHLIGHTS

4:00 – A man slices a woman's skin.

5:15 – A woman's skin is ripped off her face.

10:00 – A zombie bites a chunk of flesh out of a girls neck.

10:15 – A zombie is stabbed in the chest with a sword.

10:15 – A man pulls a sword up through a zombie's skull and rips its head off.

12:00 – A field is full of bloody carcasses.

16:15 – A man cuts a section of skin off of a dead zombie's stomach.

22:30 – A zombie rips organs out of another zombie's stomach.

45:15 – A zombie is decapitated with a sword.

49:15 – A man is stabbed in the neck.

50:00 – A head is cleaved in half with an axe.

55:00 – Blood squirts out of a wound on a man's neck.

55:00 – A man cuts off a zombie's arm with a sword.

56:00 – A man rips off a woman's butt cheeks.

56:00 – A man tears the skin off of a woman's back.

56:45 – A man rips open a woman's chest.

57:00 – A man stabs a zombie in the head.

57:30 – A pregnant woman's stomach explodes.

58:00 – A man slices a piece of skin off of a man's face.

58:15 – A man is stabbed in the neck.

58:15 – A man stomps on a skull, crushing it.

1:00:15 – The back of a zombie's head explodes.

1:00:30 – Close up of a few dead bodies.

1:01:15 – A car spins its wheels on a zombie's head.

1:02:15 – A man's head is shoved in to an engine.

1:03:30 – A man cuts off a zombie's head with a sword.

1:11:15 – A zombie's tongue is ripped out of its mouth.

1:11:30 – A zombie is eating flesh.

1:12:15 – A zombie is stabbed in the chest with a sword.

1:13:10 – A zombie's arm is cut off.

1:14:00 – Blood spurts out of a wound.

1:16:00 – A man shoots himself in the head.

1:17:15 – The heads of two zombie's are ripped off.

"Bloodpigs" courtesy of Brian Paulin.

1:17:45 – A man bleeds from a wound on his neck.
1:18:00 – A man's head is pulled off.
1:18:45 – Pieces of skin are pulled off dead bodies.

BLOODSUCKERS FROM OUTER SPACE

Year: 1984   Length: 79 minutes
Director: Glen Coburn

STATISTICS

First Zombie:	5:15
First Human Death:	5:15
First Zombie Death:	N/A
Amount of Gore:	Low
Gore Quality:	Low
Zombie Effects:	Low
Zombie Count:	Very High
Zombie Deaths:	Very Low
Human Deaths:	Average

SUMMARY

When an alien intelligence invades a small Texas town, it turns the locals into flesh-eating zombies. Two survivors must elude both the undead and the military to solve the mystery and prevent the epidemic from spreading.

EFFECTS HIGHLIGHTS

4:30 – A man coughs up blood.
44:45 – A man cuts off a zombie's arm with a machete.
50:15 – A man uses a chainsaw to cut off a zombie's head.
1:03:00 – Blood soaks a shower curtain

BONE SICKNESS

Year: 2004   Length: 98 minutes
Director: Brian Paulin

STATISTICS

First Zombie:	18:30
First Human Death:	3:00
First Zombie Death:	56:00
Amount of Gore:	Very High
Gore Quality:	High
Zombie Effects:	High
Zombie Count:	Very High
Zombie Deaths:	High
Human Deaths:	Very High

SUMMARY

A woman caring for her terminally ill husband turns to alternative remedies to fight his degenerative bone disease. However she unknowingly creates a walking corpse, hungry for human flesh.

EFFECTS HIGHLIGHTS

3:15 – An axe is pulled out of a dead man's head.
13:45 – A man is stabbed in the cheek with a sharpened stick.
13:45 – A man has his throat slit.
15:00 – A doctor cuts open a body during a post mortem surgery.
21:00 – Maggots crawl out of a decomposed arm.
30:30 – A toilet bowl is full of worms.
31:30 - A man vomits blood and worms.
31:45 – The man subsequently eats the bloodied pile of worms.
38:00 – Close up of a dead and bloodied body.
46:45 – A zombie rips open a woman's stomach and pulls out her intestines.
54:00 – A man's hand is cut off with an axe.
55:15 – A man is shot in the head.
56:00 – A zombie is stabbed in the neck with a circular saw.
56:00 – A zombie's body is cut into pieces with a saw.
1:00:00 – A man smashes the barrel of a gun into a zombie's face.
1:00:15 – A zombie removes the gun from its face.

1:00:30 – A garage door is slammed down on a zombie's head, crushing it.

1:02:00 – A zombie bites a chunk out of a woman's neck.

1:02:15 – A zombie pulls out a woman's intestines.

1:07:15 – A zombie eats from a dead body.

1:07:30 – A zombie bites a chunk out of a man's neck.

1:08:00 – A head is cracked open and brains spill out.

1:08:30 – A zombie rips open a man's stomach.

1:10:10 – A woman's legs are torn off by a zombie

1:10:30 – A zombie is shot in the head.

1:10:45 – A man's head is torn in half.

1:11:30 – Zombies pull off a man's head.

1:11:30 – A man is bitten on the neck.

1:11:45 – Half of a zombie's skull is blown off.

1:12:00 – A man's torso is ripped open.

1:12:15 – Zombies pull the skin off a man's face.

1:12:15 – A man's jaw is impaled on his rifle.

1:12:15 – A zombie rips off a man's jaw.

1:12:30 – A zombie is shot in the eye.

1:13:15 – A woman is impaled on a shard of glass.

1:13:45 – Numerous body parts are scattered on the floor.

1:14:00 – A group of zombies eat from multiple dead bodies.

1:14:30 – A zombie drinks blood squirting out a severed head.

1:15:15 – A zombie eats the brains out of a dead man's skull.

1:15:45 – A zombie is shot in the head with an assault rifle.

1:15:45 – zombie is shot in the head with an assault rifle.

1:16:00 – A falling piece of wood cleaves a zombie skull in two.

1:16:30 – Close up of a severed head squirting out blood.

1:18:30 – Close up of a rotten head.

1:19:30 – A zombie spits out worms.

1:19:45 – A zombie pulls chunks of skin off of its face.

1:20:00 – The zombie cracks its face open, revealing a skull full of worms.

1:24:30 – A cut on a man's neck gushes blood.

1:24:30 – A zombie bites a chunk of flesh out of a man.

1:24:45 – A zombie pries open a man's chest with two sticks.

1:25:15 – A man's skull is bashed in with a rock.

1:25:45 – A zombie stabs a man's skull with a stick and pries the top of his head off.

1:26:40 – A man is repeatedly stabbed in the back with a bone.

1:29:00 – A zombie rips the skin off of a man's face.

1:29:30 – A zombie cuts into a man's head with an axe.

Brian Paulin and Rich George on the set of "Bone Sickness" courtesy of Brian Paulin.

1:29:45 – A zombie pries a man's head in half.

1:30:15 – A zombie rips the skin off of a body.

1:33:30 – A zombie rips a man's spine out of his torso.

1:33:45 – A zombie rips a man's intestines out of his anus.

1:34:00 – A zombie eats a dead man's intestine.

1:34:30 – A man blows himself and a zombie up with a hand grenade.

1:34:30 – Zombies chew on various body parts.

1:35:00 – A group of zombies rip a baby out of a pregnant woman's stomach.

THE BONEYARD

Year: 1991   Length: 98 minutes
Director: James Cummins

STATISTICS

First Zombie:	16:00
First Human Death:	1:14:15
First Zombie Death:	1:02:30
Amount of Gore:	Low
Gore Quality:	Average
Zombie Effects:	Average
Zombie Count:	Average
Zombie Deaths:	Average
Human Deaths:	Average

SUMMARY

A psychic medium gets involved in a child-murder case that leads her and her detective partner to a mortuary, where the real trouble begins. The creepy parlor owner claims that the three mummified corpses in question are not children but ancient demons with an a appetite that can only be sated by human flesh.

EFFECTS HIGHLIGHTS

48:00 – A zombie is eating a dead body.

1:01:30 – A zombie pulls a chunk of slime from its head and shoves it in a woman's mouth.

1:20:15 – A zombie is stabbed with the blade of a fork lift truck.

BONG OF THE DEAD

Year: 2011   Length: 91 minutes
Director: Thomas Newman

STATISTICS

First Zombie:	8:00
First Human Death:	N/A
First Zombie Death:	26:00
Amount of Gore:	Very High
Gore Quality:	Very High

Zombie Effects:	Very High
Zombie Count:	Very High
Zombie Deaths:	Very High
Human Deaths:	Very Low

SUMMARY

After the world is taken over by ravenous flesh-eating zombies, two pot smoking best friends figure out a way to benefit from the apocalypse. They turn zombies into a special fertilizer that is used specifically for growing marijuana.

EFFECTS HIGHLIGHTS

6:00 – An abscess on a man's head bursts.

7:15 – A man stabs himself in the cheek with a fork.

9:15 – Two zombies eat each other's intestines.

25:15 – A man jams his thumbs into a zombie's eye sockets.

50:15 – A group of zombie's eat a dead body.

51:45 – A zombie eats a severed leg.

52:00 – A zombie is shot in the head.

1:02:45 – A zombie is shot in the head.

1:15:15 – A zombie is cut up with a weed wacker.

1:19:30 – A zombie is cut up with a lawn mower.

1:19:45 – Close up of severed body parts.

1:20:00 – A zombie is cut up with a lawn mower.

1:20:00 – Close up of severed body parts.

1:20:00 – A zombie is cut up with a lawn mower.

1:21:00 – A zombie's foot is shot off..

1:21:00 – A zombie is shot in the head

1:21:00 – A zombie is shot in the head.

1:21:15 – A zombie is shot in the head.

1:21:45 – A zombie is shot in the head.

1:22:15 – A zombie gives birth to a baby.

1:22:15 – A zombie eats a new born baby.

1:22:15 – A zombie is shot in the chest.

1:22:15 – A zombie is shot in the chest.

1:22:30 – A zombie is stabbed in the chest.

1:22:45 – A zombie is shot in the head.

1:22:45 – A zombie is stabbed in the chest.

1:25:00 – A zombie's throat is slit.

THE BOOK OF ZOMBIE

Year: 2010   Length: 61 minutes
Directors: Paul Cranefield, Scott Kragelund, Erik Van Sant

STATISTICS

First Zombie:	9:45
First Human Death:	12:45
First Zombie Death:	27:30'
Amount of Gore:	High

Gore Quality: High
Zombie Effects: High
Zombie Count: Very High
Zombie Deaths: Average
Human Deaths: High

SUMMARY

A small Utah town gets a visit from the undead when all of the townspeople of Mormon faith suddenly turn into flesh-eating zombies. A group of 'non-believers' who remain unaffected by the mysterious epidemic must fight to survive the night and resort to original ways to dispose of the dead.

EFFECTS HIGHLIGHTS

9:45 – A cat is ripped in half.

12:30 – A zombie eats a man's severed arm.

27:00 – A zombie is shot in the forehead.

27:30 – A zombie is stabbed in the head with a machete

28:30 – A zombie's face melts.

33:30 – A zombie is shot in the head with an arrow.

41:00 – A zombie bites a man's arm.

41:15 – A zombie is shot in the head.

47:45 – A zombie bites a woman's neck.

48:00 – A zombie has a chunk of flesh in its mouth.

49:00 – A zombie is stabbed in the eyes with a broken pool cue.

49:15 – A man throws a hammer at a zombie's head.

49:30 – A woman decapitates a zombie with a machete.

50:00 – A woman crushes a zombie's skull.

50:15 – A man jams his thumbs in a zombie's eye sockets, gouging out its eyes.

50:30 – A woman cuts off a zombie's hand with a machete.

50:45 – A zombie's head is cut in half.

51:20 – A zombie is cut in half with an axe.

52:20 – A zombie is disemboweled with a machete.

53:15 – A can of soda melts a zombie's face.

BOY EATS GIRL

Year: 2005   Length: 80 minutes
Director: Stephen Bradley

STATISTICS

First Zombie: 35:30
First Human Death: 57:30
First Zombie Death: 35:30

Amount of Gore: High
Gore Quality: Very High
Zombie Effects: High
Zombie Count: Very High
Zombie Deaths: High

Human Deaths: High

SUMMARY

When a heart broken teenager commits suicide, ho mother brings him back to life with an ancient ritual. However, there is one major change, he is now a flesh-craving zombie who struggles to control his emotions and thirst for flesh.

EFFECTS HIGHLIGHTS

55:30 – A zombie has a golf club handle jammed in its mouth, knocking its teeth out.

56:00 – A zombie is stabbed in the hand with a pair of scissors.

59:30 – A zombie is stabbed in the eye with a high heeled shoe.

1:03:00 – A zombie is stabbed in the eye with a garden stake light.

1:04:15 – A tree trimmer shreds a zombie.

1:04:30 – The front wheel of a tractor lift crushes a zombie's head.

1:04:30 – A zombie is decapitated.

1:04:45 – Close up of a severed arm.

1:04:45 – A tree trimmer shreds a zombie.

1:04:30 – Close up of a headless body.

1:04:30 – A pair of severed legs fall over, spilling intestines on the ground.

1:04:45 – A torso is missing its legs.

1:05:00 – A zombie is stabbed in the head.

1:04:30 – Close up of a headless body.

1:04:45 – A tree trimmer shreds a zombie.

1:05:00 – Close up of various body parts.

1:07:15 – The tractor continues to hack zombies.

1:08:30 – A zombie's head is pulled off.

BRAIN DEAD

Year: 2007   Length: 95 minutes
Director: Kevin Tenney

STATISTICS

First Zombie: 31:30
First Human Death: 4:30
First Zombie Death: 1:24:15

Amount of Gore: High
Gore Quality: Very High
Zombie Effects: High
Zombie Count: Average
Zombie Deaths: Average
Human Deaths: Low

SUMMARY

When a small crater crash-lands and releases a slimy

parasitic agent that transforms the residents into brain-eating zombies, a nearby sleepy fishing port town is consumed with terror. Cornered in an abandoned fishing lodge, six strangers are forced to band together to stave off the flesh-eating creatures.

EFFECTS HIGHLIGHTS

4:15 – Close up of a wound on a man's forehead.

4:45 – A zombie jams its thumbs in a man's eyes and pulls his head apart.

17:30 – A man is shot in the head.

23:00 – A zombie is shot repeatedly in the chest.

23:15 – A zombie vomits a black fluid onto a cops face.

37:15 – A fishing hook pierces a woman's thumb.

39:00 – A woman trips over the body of the man whose head was ripped in half.

43:30 – A woman is shot in the leg.

44:30 – A zombie punches a woman in the head and its fist pierces the back of her skull, her brain in its hand.

44:30 – A woman's body stumbles around with a massive hole in her head.

57:00 – A zombie is shot in the arm, severing it at the shoulder.

59:45 – A man shoots a zombie with a shotgun, severing the torso from its legs.

1:00:15 – A zombie is shot in the head and covers a man's face in slime.

1:00:30 – Close up of a dead zombie.

1:07:15 – A woman opens a cabinet door and finds severed heads inside.

1:15:30 – Close up of a dead zombie.

1:16:15 – A zombie is hit on the shoulder with a machete, slicing its arm off.

1:16:30 – A zombie is decapitated.

1:18:30 – A zombie rips a woman's head off and pulls her brains out.

1:20:45 – A man finds a severed head on a couch.

1:21:15 – A man shoots himself in the head, covering the wall behind him with blood.

1:24:15 – A zombie is decapitated.

1:25:00 – A decapitated zombie head explodes.

BRAINDEAD

Alternate Title: Dead Alive
Year: 1992   Length: 104 minutes
Director: Peter Jackson

STATISTICS

First Zombie:	31:30
First Human Death:	4:30
First Zombie Death:	1:24:15

Amount of Gore:	Very High
Gore Quality:	Very High
Zombie Effects:	Very High
Zombie Count:	Very High
Zombie Deaths:	Very High
Human Deaths:	High

SUMMARY

When a young man's mother is bitten by a Sumatran rat-monkey, she gets sick and dies. Before long, she comes back to life as a zombie, killing and eating anyone who dares comes to the house. Her son, tries to entertain guests, while keeping his hungry mother fed and satisfied.

EFFECTS HIGHLIGHTS

4:00 – A man's hand is cut off.

4:15 – A man's arm is cut off.

16:30 – A monkey's arm is ripped off.

18:00 – A woman is bitten on the arm.

23:45 – Close up of an infected wound.

24:45 – A piece of skin falls off of a woman's face.

27:15 – A woman's ear falls off.

29:30 – A bed is soaked with blood from a dead dog.

31:30 – A zombie jams its fingers into a woman's face and snaps her head backwards.

32:45 – A zombie's head is snapped backwards

37:00 – A zombie is stabbed in the eye with a hypodermic needle.

37:15 – A zombie is stabbed in the nose with a hypodermic needle.

41:30 – A zombie's head explodes.

47:15 – The skin is ripped off of a man's chest.

48:45 – A zombie's arm is ripped off.

48:45 – The zombie's other arm is pulled off.

49:00 – A zombie's legs are broken off.

49:00 – A zombie is decapitated.

49:30 – A man is impaled on a statue.

50:15 – Food falls out of a slit in a zombie's throat.

50:30 – A zombie stabs itself through the back of its head with a fork.

50:30 – A zombie's head is titled back and food put in its neck.

53:45 – A zombie bites off the lip of another zombie.

1:06:15 – A zombie is stabbed in the head with a rake.

1:10:45 – A zombie rips open a mans chest and pulls out his rib cage.

1:11:00 – The skin is pulled off of a man's head

1:11:00 – A zombie bites a chunk of flesh out of a woman's neck.

1:11:15 – A zombie punches a woman in the stomach and pulls out an organ.

1:11:45 – A woman stabs a zombie in the arm with a

pair of scissors and cuts through the wrist.

1:12:45 – The skin is stripped from a man's legs

1:13:00 – A zombie punches a woman in the back of her head and its fist exits through her mouth.

1:13:30 – A zombie eats an arm.

1:13:45 – A man crosses a bloody floor, stepping on miscellaneous body parts.

1:15:00 – A man pulls out a zombie's tooth with a pair of pliers.

1:15:15 – The man pulls out a second tooth.

1:16:00 – A zombie is impaled on a broken door.

1:16:15 – A zombie's head is cut in half with a pair of shears.

1:16:30 – A zombie's intestines fall out.

1:18:30 – A baby zombie vomits green blood.

1:19:30 – A zombie's hand is cut off.

1:21:45 – Two zombie's are stabbed in the head.

1:22:30 – Close up of a large pile of bodies and limbs on the floor.

1:22:45 – A zombie is impaled with a broom handle.

1:23:15 – A blood pours out of a zombie's neck.

1:24:15 – A zombie falls over a railing and explodes when it hits the floor.

1:24:45 – A man is ripped in half.

1:25:45 – A man cuts through a crowd of zombies using a lawn mower. Multiple shots of severed limbs and blood spray.

1:26:15 – The man takes a second pass with the lawn mower.

1:26:30 – A severed head is put in a blender.

1:27:00 – Close up of a head beneath the lawn mower.

1:27:15 – A woman drops body parts in a blender.

1:28:15 – A woman rips a man's head off of his body and smashes it on a table.

1:29:15 – A torso is mangled in a lawn mower.

1:30:00 – A woman's head is ripped in half.

1:34:30 – A giant mutant is cut open from the inside.

BRIDE OF RE-ANIMATOR

Year: 1990   Length: 96 minutes
Director: Brian Yuzna

STATISTICS

First Zombie:	2:30
First Human Death:	1:45
First Zombie Death:	2:30
Amount of Gore:	High
Gore Quality:	High
Zombie Effects:	High
Zombie Count:	Average
Zombie Deaths:	Average
Human Deaths:	Average

SUMMARY

On the set of "Braindead" courtesy of Stuart Conran.

29

This page and opposite, setting up effects on the set of "Braindead" courtesy of Stuart Conran.

31

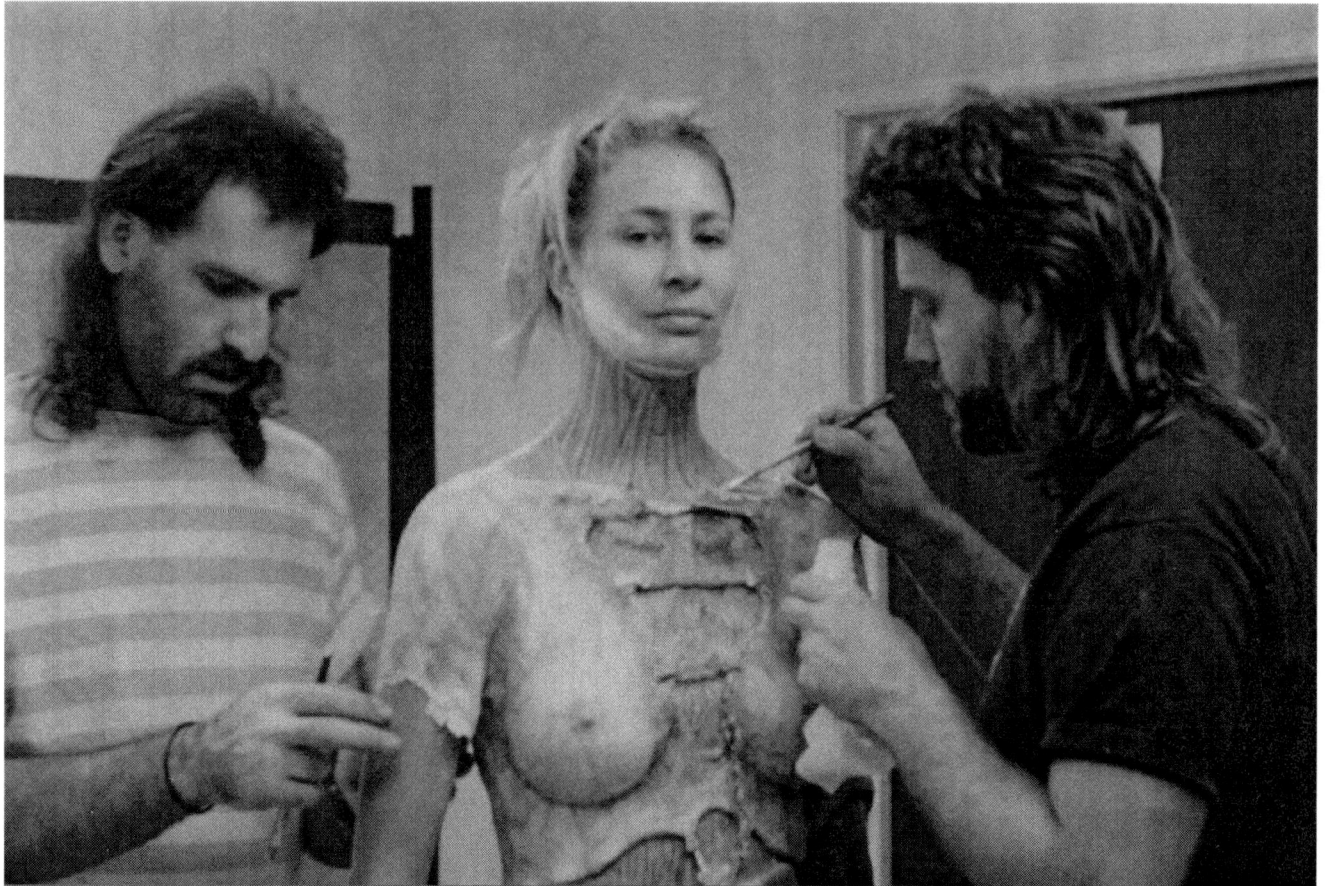

Robert Kurtzman and Howard Berger of KNB EFX make up Kathleen Kinmont for "Bride of Re-animator" courtesy of Robert Kurtzman.

Doctor's Herbert West and Dan Cain's experiments with the dead lead them to discover the secret to creating human life and they proceed to create a perfect woman from dead tissue and body parts.

EFFECTS HIGHLIGHTS

1:45 – Two doctors work on an injured man, pulling shrapnel from his body.

10:30 – A man unwraps a severed head.

40:00 – A cut up body is spread out on a table.

40:45 – Blood squirts out of an artery.

51:45 – A man's arm is cut off with a machete.

53:15 – A zombie rips a dog's leg off.

58:45 – A man draws a scalpel across a woman's chest.

59:00 – Two doctors crack open a woman's chest.

1:27:00 – A zombie rips its heart out of its chest.

1:28:00 – A man pulls a zombie's hand off.

1:28:00 – A zombie's arm falls off.

BUBBA'S CHILI PARLOR

Year: 2008   Length: 84 minutes
Director: Joey Evans

STATISTICS

First Zombie:	2:30
First Human Death:	10:45
First Zombie Death:	14:00
Amount of Gore:	Average
Gore Quality:	Average
Zombie Effects:	Average
Zombie Count:	Very High
Zombie Deaths:	Very High
Human Deaths:	Low

SUMMARY

Bubba's Chili Parlor becomes ground zero for a worldwide zombie epidemic after Bubba unwittingly serves chili infected with a mutated strain of Mad Cow Disease.

EFFECTS HIGHLIGHTS

8:15 – A zombie chews on a severed leg

10:45 – A zombie bites a chunk of flesh out of a woman's neck

14:00 – A zombie is shot in the head.

36:00 – A zombie's arm is shot off with an assault rifle

36:15 – The zombie's other arm is shot off.

36:30 – A gunman shoots off a zombie's right leg.

42:15 – A zombie is shot in the head.

42:30 – A zombie is shot in the head, leaving brain splatter on the car behind it.

42:30 – A zombie is shot in the head.

42:45 – A zombie is eating intestines.

42:45 – A fourth zombie is shot in the head.

42:45 – A fifth zombie is shot in the head.

43:00 – A final zombie is shot on the head.

43:30 – A severed zombie head rolls across the floor.

1:03:00 – Blood oozes out of a wound in a man's head.

BURIAL GROUND

Alternate Title: The Nights of Terror
Year: 1981   Length: 85 minutes
Director: Andrea Bianchi

STATISTICS

First Zombie:	3:45
First Human Death:	25:15
First Zombie Death:	32:00
Amount of Gore:	Very High
Gore Quality:	Very High
Zombie Effects:	Very High
Zombie Count:	Very High
Zombie Deaths:	High
Human Deaths:	High

SUMMARY

A professor opens a mysterious underground crypt, only to unleash dozens of hungry zombies in search of prey.

EFFECTS HIGHLIGHTS

4:15 – A zombie bites a man's neck.

24:15 – A group of zombies are shot in the chest.

25:15 – A man's intestines are ripped out.

32:00 – A zombie's skull is bashed in with a rock.

32:15 – A second zombie has its skull bashed it.

39:30 – A woman's hand is stabbed with a spike.

40:15 – A woman is decapitated with a scythe.

41:15 – A man finds a headless torso.

42:30 – A large spike is ripped out of a hand.

42:45 – A group of zombie's eat the entrails of a dead woman.

44:15 – A zombie is shot in the head.

44:30 – A zombie is shot in the head.

44:45 – A zombie is shot in the head.

44:45 – A zombie is shot in the head.

45:00 – A zombie is shot in the head.

47:15 – A woman's face is scratched by a piece of glass.

52:30 – A zombie is stabbed with a spear multiple times.

53:15 – A zombie's arms is cut off with a sword

53:30 – A man cuts into a zombie's head.

54:15 – A woman cuts off a zombie's hand.

54:45 – A man bashes in a zombie's skull.

55:15 – A woman decapitates a zombie.

1:00:30 – A zombie is eating the flesh off of a boy's severed arm.

1:07:30 – A zombie bites a man's neck.

1:07:45 – A zombie eats a man's intestines.

1:14:45 – A zombie bites a chunk of flesh out of a man's neck.

1:15:15 – A group of zombies tear out a man's intestines.

1:21:30 – A zombie bites off a woman's nipple.

BUTT CRACK

Year: 1998   Length: 68 minutes
Director: Jim Lasen

STATISTICS

First Zombie:	36:00
First Human Death:	24:00
First Zombie Death:	56:45

Amount of Gore:	Low
Gore Quality:	Average
Zombie Effects:	Average
Zombie Count:	Average
Zombie Deaths:	Average
Human Deaths:	Average

SUMMARY

When a couch potato is killed by his roommate, his vindictive sister raises him from the dead so he can avenge his murder.

EFFECTS HIGHLIGHTS

56:00 – A zombie bites a man's neck.

56:30 – A zombie rips a man's arm off.

58:15 – A zombie rips a man's throat out.

58:30 – A zombie is shot in the chest.

CANNIBAL APOCALYPSE

Year: 1980   Length: 96 minutes
Director: Antonio Margheriti

STATISTICS

First Zombie:	55:00
First Human Death:	5:30
First Zombie Death:	55:15

Amount of Gore:	High
Gore Quality:	High
Zombie Effects:	Average
Zombie Count:	Average
Zombie Deaths:	Low
Human Deaths:	Very High

SUMMARY

Two Vietnam veterans return from the war changed men. Not only are they carrying the scars of war, they bring back a highly contagious virus that turns people into blood thirsty cannibals when bitten.

EFFECTS HIGHLIGHTS

5:30 – A man is shot in the chest.

6:15 – A man bites a woman's wrist.

7:30 – Two men eat pieces of flesh.

21:45 – A man bites a woman's neck.

21:45 – A man's nose is broken.

29:45 – Close up of a bloody wound on a man's head.

55:00 – A zombie eats a piece of flesh.

55:15 – A zombie is shot in the head.

58:30 – A zombie bites off a man's tongue.

1:05:30 – A zombie cuts a dead man's leg with a saw.

1:09:15 – A man's eye is pushed into the socket.

1:09:30 – A zombie bites a man's neck.

1:09:45 – A man's head is smashed against a window.

CEMETERY MAN

Alternate Title: Dellamorte Dellamore
Year: 1994   Length: 105 minutes
Director: Michele Soavi

STATISTICS

First Zombie:	1:15
First Human Death:	24:00
First Zombie Death:	1:15

Amount of Gore:	High
Gore Quality:	Very High
Zombie Effects:	Very High
Zombie Count:	High
Zombie Deaths:	High
Human Deaths:	High

SUMMARY

A cemetery watchman keeps guard over an overactive cemetery where the dead don't seem to want to stay dead for very long. As the corpses rise, the watchman quickly sends them back to their graves.

EFFECTS HIGHLIGHTS

1:15 – A zombie is shot in the head.

5:00 – A zombie is stabbed in the head with a shovel.

22:30 – A woman is bitten on the arm.

22:45 – A zombie is stabbed in the head with a cross.

28:00 – A zombie is shot in the head.

34:45 – After falling off a motorcycle, a woman's head is run over by a bus.

38:45 – A zombie is shot in the head.

38:45 – A zombie is shot in the head.

38:45 – A zombie is shot in the head.

38:45 – A zombie is shot in the head.

39:45 – A zombie is smashed in the face with a vase.

45:45 – A woman and a zombie are shot in the head.

48:45 – A man pulls off a zombie's head.

55:15 – A zombie bites a man's shoulder.

1:02:00 – A man is shot in the face.

1:08:00 – A severed zombie head bites a chunk of flesh out of a man's neck.

1:30:00 – A woman is shot in the eye.

1:30:30 – A man is shot in the head.

1:31:15 – A woman is shot in the head.

CHILDREN OF THE LIVING DEAD

Year: 2001   Length: 90 minutes
Director: Tor Ramsey

STATISTICS

First Zombie:	2:00
First Human Death:	24:15
First Zombie Death:	2:15

Amount of Gore:	High
Gore Quality: :	Average
Zombie Effects:	Average
Zombie Count:	Very High
Zombie Deaths:	Very High
Human Deaths:	Average

SUMMARY

A businessman relocates the bodies of the local cemetery into a mass grave so he can build a car dealership. However, a long dead serial murderer rises from his grave and sets out to create his own army of the undead.

EFFECTS HIGHLIGHTS

2:15 – A zombie is shot in the head.

4:15 – Two zombies are shot in the head

11:45 – A zombie is shot in the chest.

11:45 – Blood sprays out of the back of a zombie's head.

52:30 – A severed ear falls to the ground.

1:14:15 – A zombie is shot in the head

1:15:30 – A zombie is shot through the chest.

1:19:00 – A zombie is shot in the head.

1:19:00 – A zombie is shot in the head.

1:19:15 – Two zombie's are shot on the head.

1:19:30 – A zombie is shot in the head.

CHILDREN SHOULDN'T PLAY WITH DEAD THINGS

Year: 1973   Length: 87 minutes
Director: Bob Clark

STATISTICS

First Zombie:	1:04:00
First Human Death:	1:07:00
First Zombie Death:	N/A

Amount of Gore:	Very Low
Gore Quality:	Low
Zombie Effects:	High
Zombie Count:	Very High
Zombie Deaths:	Very Low
Human Deaths:	Average

SUMMARY

A group of actors and their director travel to a island rich in tales of evil curses and demons. They exhume a recently deceased body and attempt to raise the dead.

EFFECTS HIGHLIGHTS

1:17:15 – A zombie is eating a dead man's torso.

CHOKING HAZARD

Year: 2004   Length: 81 minutes
Director: Marek Dobes

STATISTICS

First Zombie:	:15
First Human Death:	27:30
First Zombie Death:	17:00

Amount of Gore:	Low
Gore Quality:	High
Zombie Effects:	High
Zombie Count:	High
Zombie Deaths:	Very Low
Human Deaths:	Low

SUMMARY

A group of students on a self-help retreat ponder the meaning of life, but when zombie woodsmen emerge, the group finds itself locked in mortal battle.

EFFECTS HIGHLIGHTS

1:00 – A zombie is shot in the mouth.

26:15 – A zombie bites a man's fingers.

C.H.U.D II BUD THE C.H.U.D

Year: 1989   Length: 84 minutes
Director: David Irving

STATISTICS

First Zombie:	6:00
First Human Death:	30:30

First Zombie Death: 1:06:30

Amount of Gore:	Average
Gore Quality:	Average
Zombie Effects:	Average
Zombie Count:	High
Zombie Deaths:	Average
Human Deaths:	Average

SUMMARY

When a covert military experiment to create a race of super-soldiers goes wrong, a legion of blood-thirsty zombies are unleashed upon a quiet suburban neighborhood.

EFFECTS HIGHLIGHTS

45:45 – A zombie's head is knocked off.

1:05:45 – A zombie's head is impaled on a Bunsen burner.

1:06:30 – A zombie explodes.

1:15:00 – A zombie rips its heart out of its chest.

1:16:00 – A frozen zombie falls to the ground and shatters.

1:16:30 – A group of frozen zombies explode.

CITY OF THE LIVING DEAD

Year: 1980   Length: 92 minutes
Director: Lucio Fulci

STATISTICS

First Zombie:	4:00
First Human Death:	3:15
First Zombie Death:	1:20:15

Amount of Gore:	High
Gore Quality:	Very High
Zombie Effects:	Very High
Zombie Count:	High
Zombie Deaths:	Average
Human Deaths:	Average

SUMMARY

A priest hangs himself in a church's cemetery causing the gates of Hell to open and the dead begin to rise. A New York City reporter and a young psychic, find themselves in a race against time to close the gates.

EFFECTS HIGHLIGHTS

3:15 – A man hangs himself.

10:15 – Close up of a rotten dead body.

30:30 – A woman's eyes bleed.

31:00 – A woman spits up her intestines.

31:30 – The back of a man's head is ripped off.

56:15 – A power drill pierces a man's cheek.

1:00:45 – A woman vomits after being covered in maggots.

1:06:15 – A zombie rips off the back of a woman's head.

1:19:00 – A zombie rips off the back of a man's head.

1:24:30 – A woman's eyes bleed.

1:24:45 – A zombie is stabbed in the torso with a cross.

COLIN

Year: 2008   Length: 97 minutes
Director: Marc Price

STATISTICS

First Zombie:	5:03
First Human Death:	16:00
First Zombie Death:	6:45

Amount of Gore:	Very High
Gore Quality:	High
Zombie Effects:	Very High
Zombie Count:	Very High
Zombie Deaths:	High
Human Deaths:	High

SUMMARY

When a man is bitten by a zombie, he is slowly transformed into one of the living dead and struggles to survive in a world where zombies and humans don't mix.

EFFECTS HIGHLIGHTS

4:15 – Close up of a bite wound.

6:30 – A zombie is repeatedly stabbed in the head.

14:00 – A zombie slices itself on a metal bracket.

16:00 – A man's legs are broken as he is pulled into an open window.

18:30 – A man clubs a zombie in the head.

19:30 – A zombie bites off a man's lip.

21:00 – A zombie bites off a man's ear.

23:00 – A zombie rips out a man's intestines.

26:45 – A zombie bites a woman's wrist.

32:00 – A dead body has a massive wound on its neck.

34:15 – A woman stabs a zombie in the forehead with a power drill.

34:30 – A group of zombies rip out a man's intestines.

34:30 – A zombie is stabbed with an umbrella.

35:00 – Zombies pull out a woman's intestines.

35:45 – A zombie pulls out a woman's spine.

36:15 – A zombie bites a man's arm.

36:30 – A zombie bites a man's neck.

36:45 – Two zombies snap off a man's foot.

39:30 – Zombies eat the remains of their victims.

40:15 – A woman's head is smacked against a wall.

1:10:00 – A zombie is shot in the head.

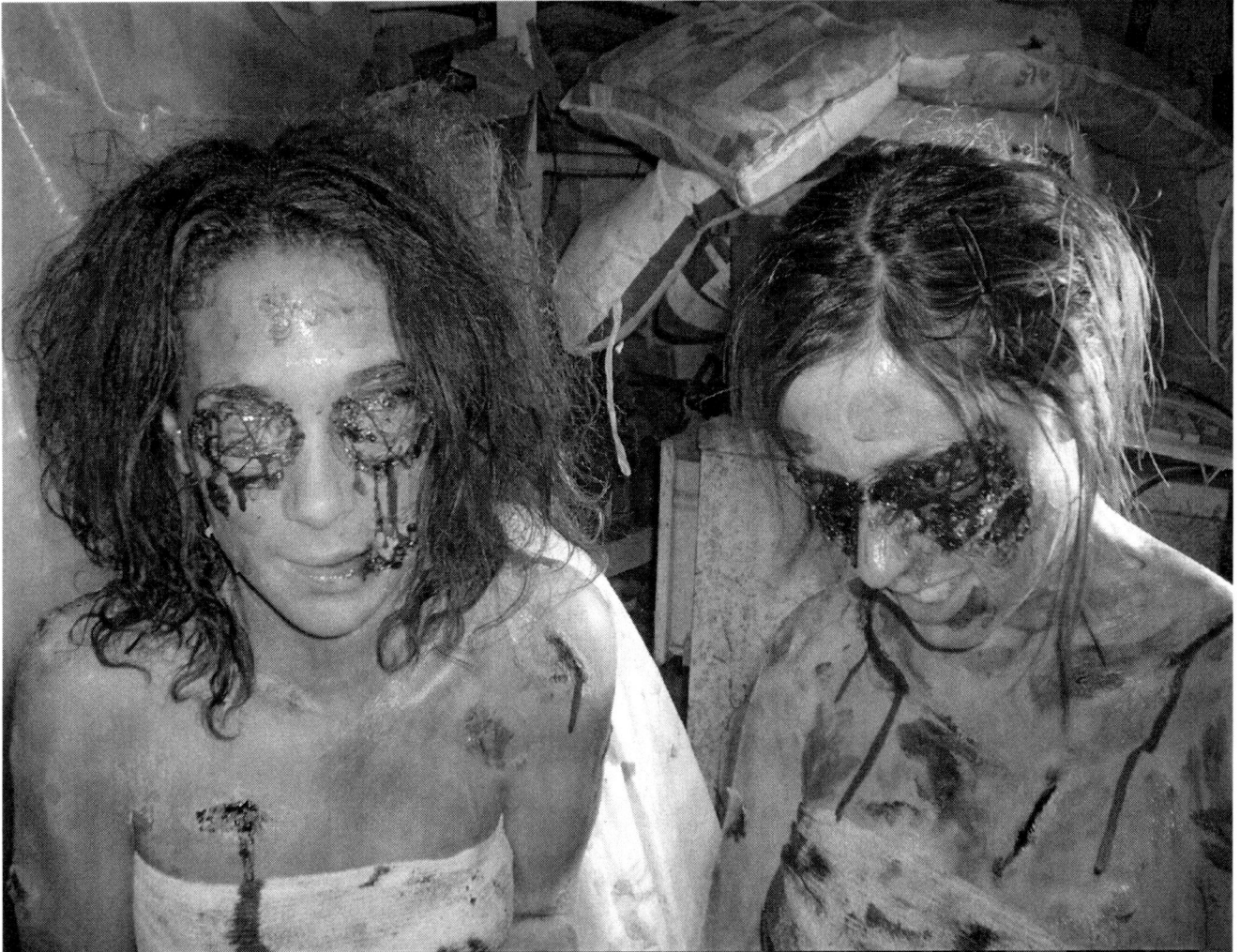

Michelle Webb makes up zombies for "Colin" courtesy of Nowhere Fast Film Productions and Marc Price.

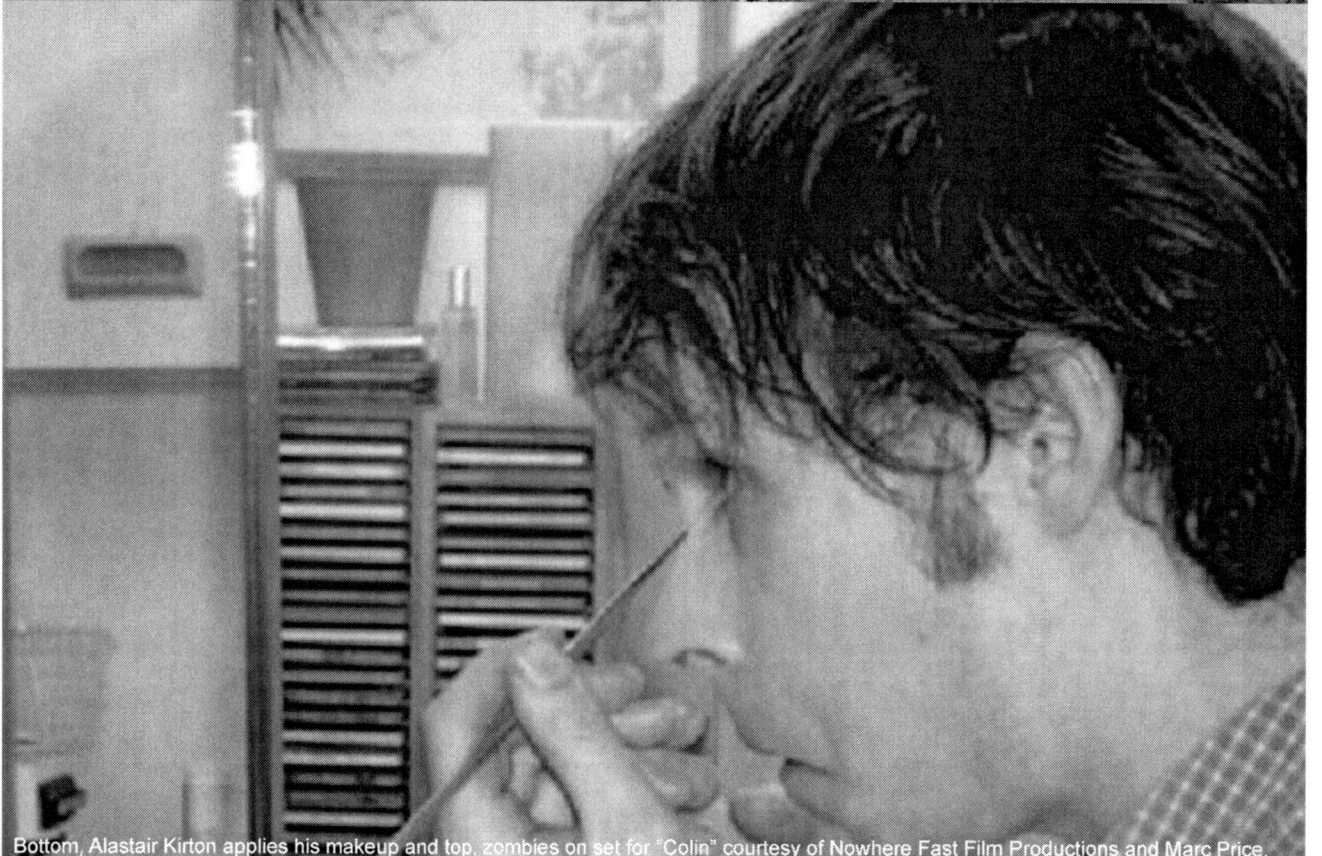

Bottom, Alastair Kirton applies his makeup and top, zombies on set for "Colin" courtesy of Nowhere Fast Film Productions and Marc Price.

1:10:30 – A pipe bomb blows up a group of zombies.

1:10:45 – A zombie is eating intestines.

1:11:30 – A man uses a catapult to shoot a razor blade at a zombie's head.

1:12:30 – A woman falls on a pipe bomb and explodes.

1:12:45 – A zombie has skin falling off of its face.

1:13:45 – A zombie rips the skin off of a man's face.

1:14:00 – A zombie is stabbed in the eye.

1:24:45 – A woman is bitten on the cheek.

1:25:00 – A zombie's head is smashed in with a barbell.

CORPSES

Year: 2004　　　Length: 90 minutes
Director: Rolfe Kanefsky

STATISTICS

First Zombie:	2:15
First Human Death:	4:30
First Zombie Death:	49:45
Amount of Gore:	Average
Gore Quality:	High
Zombie Effects:	Average
Zombie Count:	High
Zombie Deaths:	Average
Human Deaths:	High

SUMMARY

An undertaker discovers a way to bring the dead back to life when he happens upon a serum that allows him to revive corpses for an hour at a time. However, if the zombies don't receive their medicine after an hour, they will die. After he receives an eviction letter from the bank, he sends his zombies off on a crime spree to steal money and pay the bank.

EFFECTS HIGHLIGHTS

4:30 – A man's intestines are pulled apart by a group of zombies.

34:15 – A pair of zombies hold the limbs of a recently killed victim.

35:30 – A zombie shoves its hand into a woman's chest.

35:45 – A man falls to the floor clutching his bleeding throat.

36:30 – A man's head is impaled on a pole.

37:00 – A zombie's severed arm lies on the floor.

1:02:30 – A man catches a severed zombie head and the headless body falls on him.

1:10:45 – Two severed zombie heads roll out of an open door.

1:17:00 – A man's arms are pulled off by a group of zombies.

1:20:15 – A woman's chest explodes.

COWBOYS AND ZOMBIES

Alternate Title: The Dead and the Damned
Year: 2011　　　Length: 82 minutes
Director: Rene Perez

STATISTICS

First Zombie:	30:45
First Human Death:	1:30
First Zombie Death:	39:15
Amount of Gore:	Very High
Gore Quality:	High
Zombie Effects:	High
Zombie Count:	Very High
Zombie Deaths:	Very High
Human Deaths:	Average

SUMMARY

In 1849, a group of gold miners from Jamestown, California discover a meteorite that has crashed. While trying to move the rock, they unknowingly release alien spoors that turn the town's population into flesh-eating zombies.

EFFECTS HIGHLIGHTS

1:30 – A man is shot in the neck.

1:30 – A man is shot in the chest.

2:00 – A man is shot in the foot.

31:15 – A zombie eats a severed arm.

32:30 – A zombie pulls off a woman's lower leg.

39:15 – A zombie is shot in the head.

1:05:45 – A zombie is hit in the head with a machete.

1:07:30 – A zombie pulls an axe out of its neck.

1:07:45 – A zombie bites a hole in a man's chest.

1:08:00 – A zombie is shot in the head.

1:09:30 – A zombie is eating a man's intestines.

1:10:15 – A zombie is shot in the head.

1:10:15 – A zombie is shot in the head.

1:10:30 – A zombie is shot in the chest.

1:10:30 – A zombie is shot in the head.

1:11:00 – A zombie is shot in the head.

1:11:30 – A zombie is shot in the head.

1:11:30 – A zombie is shot in the head.

1:11:30 – A zombie is shot in the head.

1:12:00 – A zombie is shot in the head.

1:12:30 – A zombie is shot in the chest.

1:12:45 – A zombie is shot in the head.

1:12:45 – A zombie is shot in the chest.

1:13:00 – A zombie is shot in the head.

1:13:00 – A zombie is shot in the head.

1:14:45 – A zombie is shot in the head.

1:17:30 – A zombie is shot in the head.

This page and opposite, miscellaneous zombies on the set of "Cowboys and Zombies" courtesy of Ed Martinez.

On the set of "Creatures From The Pink Lagoon" courtesy of Chris Diani.

42

CREATURES FROM THE PINK LAGOON

Year: 2006   Length: 71 minutes
Director: Chris Diani

STATISTICS

First Zombie: 37:45
First Human Death: 48:30
First Zombie Death: 42:45

Amount of Gore: High
Gore Quality: Average
Zombie Effects: Average
Zombie Count: High
Zombie Deaths: Average
Human Deaths: Average

SUMMARY

Five friends gather at a beach house for a birthday celebration only to have their party crashed by a horde of gay men who have been turned into zombies thanks to some toxin-infected mosquitoes.

EFFECTS HIGHLIGHTS

33:00 – A man grabs a severed arm

40:45 – A zombie's penis falls off.

40:45 – A zombie bites a man's arm.

41:00 – A zombie throws up blood.

42:45 – A zombie throws up blood

47:45 – A zombie bites a man's arm.

48:00 – A zombie bites the man's hand off.

48:45 – A zombie throws up.

49:45 – A zombie's rip open a man's stomach.

52:30 – A zombie throws up.

54:30 – Two zombies throw up.

CURSE OF THE CANNIBAL CONFEDERATES

Alternate Title: Curse of the Screaming Dead
Year: 1982   Length: 91 minutes
Director: Tony Malanowski

STATISTICS

First Zombie: :30
First Human Death: 1:07:00
First Zombie Death: 49:00

Amount of Gore: High
Gore Quality: Average
Zombie Effects: High
Zombie Count: Very High
Zombie Deaths: High
Human Deaths: Average

SUMMARY

A group of hunters stop at a church graveyard in the woods. Unbeknownst to them, the site is the location where a group of Confederate soldiers were captured and tortured to death by the Union Army. Soon the soldiers have risen from their graves to torment the hunters.

EFFECTS HIGHLIGHTS

50:15 – A zombie shot in the head and explodes

50:30 – A zombie's head explodes.

1:04:45 – A zombie's head explodes.

1:05:15 – A zombie's head explodes.

1:05:15 – A zombie's head explodes.

1:05:30 – A zombie's head explodes.

1:07:00 – Zombies tear out a man's intestines.

1:08:00 – A zombie eats a man's organ.

1:08:15 – Multiple scenes of zombies eating a man's organs and ripping more from his body.

1:11:30 – A group of zombies tear at another corpse.

1:16:00 – A zombie is shot in the head and explodes.

1:19:00 – A zombie is shot in the head and explodes.

1:25:45 – A man is strangled to death.

DANCE OF THE DEAD

Year: 2008   Length: 87 minutes
Director: Gregg Bishop

STATISTICS

First Zombie: 20:15
First Human Death: 20:30
First Zombie Death: 30:30

Amount of Gore: High
Gore Quality: Very High
Zombie Effects: Very High
Zombie Count: Very High
Zombie Deaths: High
Human Deaths: Average

SUMMARY

When the dead arise on prom night, the only people who can save the school are the losers who couldn't even get a prom date in the first place.

EFFECTS HIGHLIGHTS

2:00 – A man cuts off a hand with a pair of shears.

21:45 – A zombie carries a severed head.

30:30 – A zombie is shot in the head.

30:30 – A zombie is shot in the head.

31:00 – A man rips off a zombie's arm.

31:15 – A zombie is stabbed with a baseball bat.

31:30 – A man rips off a zombie's arm.

31:30 – A man stabs a zombie in the mouth with a severed arm.

43

This page and opposite "Curse of the Cannibal Confederates" courtesy of Tony Malanowski.

44

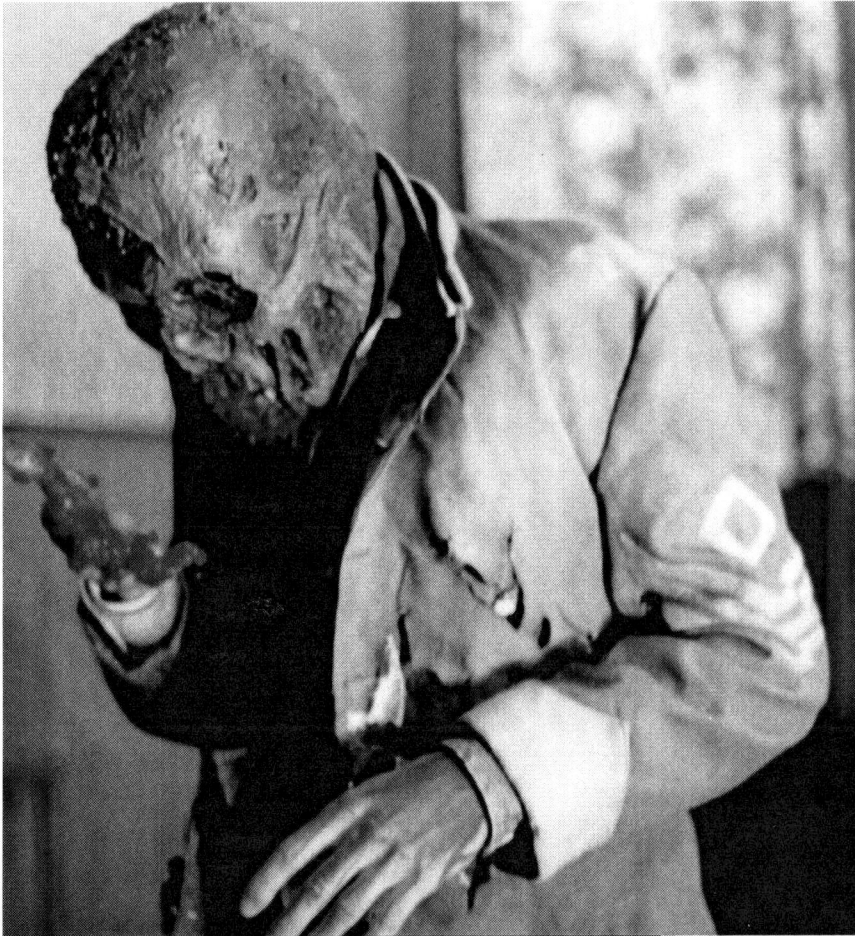

31:45 – A man stabs a zombie with a baseball bat and rips its torso in half.

31:45 – A man pulls off a zombie's head.

34:15 – A zombie is stabbed in the eye with a high heeled shoe.

58:30 – A man rips a zombie's head and spine out of its body.

1:07:00 – A zombie is shot in the head.

1:07:00 – A zombie is shot in the head.

1:07:00 – A zombie is shot in the head.

1:07:15 – A zombie is decapitated.

1:11:00 – A zombie bites off a man's tongue.

1:12:15 – A woman smashes a severed head.

1:14:00 – Two zombies eat each other.

1:15:15 – A man is torn to pieces by a group of zombies.

1:15:45 – A man cuts a zombie's head in two with an axe.

DAWN OF THE DEAD

Year: 1978   Length: 127 minutes
Director: George A. Romero

STATISTICS

First Zombie:	9:30
First Human Death:	6:45
First Zombie Death:	10:15
Amount of Gore:	Very High
Gore Quality:	High
Zombie Effects:	Average
Zombie Count:	Very High
Zombie Deaths:	Very High
Human Deaths:	Very High

SUMMARY

Following the events of *Night of the Living Dead,* four survivors take refuge in an abandoned shopping mall in Pennsylvania. Before long, they have acclimated to life without the living dead but the peace is soon shattered when a biker gang lays siege to the mall in an attempt to take it over.

EFFECTS HIGHLIGHTS

6:45 – A man is shot in the head with a rifle.

7:00 – A man is shot in the chest with a shotgun.

7:15 – Another man is shot in the chest with a shotgun.

8:15 – A man is shot in the head with a shotgun.

8:45 – A man is shot in the back.

9:15 – A severed arm is laying on the floor.

9:30 – A zombie is missing its right foot.

1:15 – A zombie is missing part of its scalp.

10:15 – A zombie is shot in the chest and head.

10:15 – A zombie is shot in the head.

10:45 – A zombie bites a chunk of flesh out of a woman's shoulder.

10:45 – A zombie bites a chunk of flesh out of a woman's arm.

14:45 – A group of zombies are eating various body parts.

15:15 – A zombie is shot in the head.

20:15 – A zombie is shot in the head.

23:15 – A zombie is hit on the head with a hammer.

24:00 – A helicopter blade slices off the top of a zombie's head.

24:45 – A zombie is shot in the arm.

25:00 – A zombie is shot in the head.

25:15 – A zombie is shot in the chest.

42:15 – A zombie is shot in the head.

44:30 – A zombie is stabbed in the ear with a screwdriver.

1:03:15 – A zombie is shot in the chest.

1:03:45 – A zombie is shot in the back of the head.

1:04:00 – A zombie is shot in the forehead.

1:05:00 – A truck runs over a zombie.

1:06:30 – A zombie is shot in the forehead.

1:08:15 – A man is bitten on the wrist.

1:08:15 – A man is bitten on the calf.

1:12:15 – A zombie is shot in the forehead.

1:12:15 – A second zombie is shot in the forehead.

1:12:30 – A third zombie is shot in the forehead.

1:15:00 – A zombie is shot in the head.

1:15:00 – A zombie digs is fingers into a man's leg wound.

1:15:00 – A zombie is shot in the head.

1:15:45 – A zombie is shot in the eye.

1:17:45 – A zombie is shot in the head.

1:44:15 – Numerous zombies are shot in the chest with a machine gun.

1:49:00 – A zombie is stabbed in the head with a machete.

1:49:15 – Multiple zombies are shot in the head and chest.

1:49:15 – A zombie is decapitated.

1:49:15 – More zombies are shot.

1:52:45 – A man is shot in the arm.

1:53:00 – A zombie is stabbed in the neck.

1:55:00 – A group of zombies tear off a man's arm.

1:55:00 – A zombie bites a man's neck.

1:55:15 – A man's torso is ripped open.

1:55:30 – A group of zombies eat entrails.

1:55:45 – A man's leg is bitten.

1:56:15 – A zombie is shot in the head.

1:57:45 – Zombies fight over severed body parts.

2:01:15 – A zombie is shot in the head.

2:03:30 – A zombie is shot in the head.

DAWN OF THE DEAD (DIRECTORS CUT)

Year: 1978   Length: 139 minutes
Director: George A. Romero

STATISTICS

First Zombie:	9:45
First Human Death:	7:30
First Zombie Death:	10:30
Amount of Gore:	Very High
Gore Quality:	High
Zombie Effects:	Average
Zombie Count:	Very High
Zombie Deaths:	Very High
Human Deaths:	Very High

SUMMARY

The Director's edit of the original film which adds twelve minutes of new footage.

EFFECTS HIGHLIGHTS

7:30 – A man is shot in the head with a rifle.

7:45 – A man is shot in the chest with a shotgun.

8:00 – A man is shot in the chest with a shotgun.

8:45 – A man is shot in the head with a shotgun.

9:15 – A man is shot in the back.

9:45 – A severed arm is lying on the floor.

9:45 – A zombie is missing its right foot.

10:30 – A zombie is missing part of its scalp.

10:30 – A zombie is shot in the chest and head.

10:30 – A zombie is shot in the head.

11:00 – A zombie bites a chunk of flesh out of a woman's shoulder.

11:00 – A zombie bites a chunk of flesh out of the woman's arm.

14:15 – A group of zombies are eating various body parts.

14:45 – A zombie is shot in the head.

22:15 – A zombie is shot in the head.

25:45 – A zombie is hit on the head with a hammer.

26:45 – A helicopter blade slices off the top of a zombie's head.

27:45 – A zombie is shot in the arm.

28:00 – A zombie is shot in the head.

28:30 – A zombie is shot in the chest.

40:30 – A zombie is shot in the head.

45:45 – A zombie is shot in the head.

47:30 – A zombie is shot in the head.

48:15 – A zombie is stabbed in the ear with a screwdriver.

1:08:15 – A zombie is shot in the chest.

1:09:15 – A zombie is shot in the back of the head.

1:09:45 – A zombie is shot in the forehead.

1:10:45 – A truck runs over a zombie.

1:12:00 – A zombie rips its arm off.

1:12:15 – A zombie is shot in the forehead.

1:12:15 – A second zombie is shot in the forehead.

1:14:15 – A man is bitten on the wrist.

1:14:30 – A man is bitten on the calf.

1:14:45 – A zombie is shot in the head.

1:19:15 – A zombie is shot in the forehead.

1:19:15 – A second zombie is shot in the forehead.

1:19:15 – A third zombie is shot in the forehead.

1:21:30 – Two zombies are shot in the chest.

1:22:15 – A zombie is shot in the head.

1:22:30 – A zombie digs its fingers into a man's leg wound.

1:22:30 – A zombie is shot in the head.

1:23:15 – A zombie is shot in the eye.

1:25:30 – A zombie is shot in the head.

1:52:15 – Numerous zombies are shot in the chest with a machine gun.

1:58:45 – A zombie is stabbed in the head with a machete.

1:59:00 – Multiple zombies are shot in the head and chest.

1:59:15 – A zombie is decapitated.

1:59:15 – A zombie is shot in the head.

1:59:15 – A zombie is hit with a mace.

1:59:15 – A man cuts off a zombie's head with a machete.

2:00:00 – More zombies are shot.

2:02:45 – A zombie's hand is cut off.

2:03:15 – A man is shot in the arm.

2:03:45 – A zombie is stabbed in the neck.

2:06:15 – A group of zombies tear off a man's arm.

2:06:15 – A zombie bites a man's neck.

2:06:30 – A zombie chews on a severed arm.

2:06:30 – A man's torso is ripped open.

2:06:45 – A group of zombies eat entrails.

2:07:15 – A man's leg is bitten.

2:08:00 – A zombie is shot in the head.

2:09:30 – Zombies eat various severed body parts.

2:09:45 – Zombies fight over severed body parts.

2:13:15 – A zombie is shot in the head.

2:15:30 – A zombie is shot in the head.

Airport building and Monroeville Mall escalator from "Dawn of the Dead" courtesy of Roland Keates.

DAWN OF THE DEAD (EUROPEAN EDIT)

Year: 1978   Length: 96 minutes
Director: George A. Romero

STATISTICS

First Zombie: 10:45
First Human Death: 8:00
First Zombie Death: 11:30

Amount of Gore: Very High
Gore Quality: High
Zombie Effects: Average
Zombie Count: Very High
Zombie Deaths: Very High
Human Deaths: Very High

SUMMARY

The European edit of the original film which adds twelve minutes of new footage.

EFFECTS HIGHLIGHTS

8:00 – A man is shot in the head.

8:15 – A man is shot in the chest.

8:30– Another man is shot in the chest.

8:30 – A man is shot in the back.

8:45 – A man is shot in the chest.

9:45 – A man is shot in the head.

10:15 – A man is shot in the back.

10:45 – A severed arm is lying on the floor.

10:45 – A zombie is missing its right foot.

11:15 – A zombie is missing part of its scalp.

11:30 – A zombie is shot in the chest and head.

11:45 – A zombie is shot in the head.

12:00 – A zombie bites a chunk of flesh out of a woman's shoulder.

12:00 – A zombie bites a chunk of flesh out of a woman's arm.

12:15 – A zombie is shot in the chest.

16:45 – A group of zombies are eating various body parts.

17:00 – A zombie is shot in the head.

17:15 – A zombie eats a severed arm.

17:15 – A zombie tears at a piece of flesh.

17:45 – A zombie eats a severed arm.

22:15 – A zombie is shot in the head.

24:45 – A zombie is hit on the head with a hammer.

25:45 – A zombie is shot in the back.

35:15 – A zombie is shot in the head.

35:30 – A zombie is shot in the chest.

35:30 – A zombie is shot in the head.

36:30 – A zombie is shot in the head.

41:00 – A zombie is shot in the head.

43:00 – A zombie is stabbed in the ear with a screwdriver .

59:00 – A zombie is shot in the chest.

59:30 – A zombie is shot in the back of the head.

1:00:00 – A zombie is shot in the forehead.

1:01:15 – A truck runs over a zombie

1:02:45 – A zombie rips its arm off.

1:03:00 – A zombie is shot in the head.

1:03:15 – A zombie is shot in the head.

1:03:30 – A zombie is shot in the chest.

1:04:30 – A zombie is shot in the head.

1:04:45 – A man is bitten on the wrist.

1:05:00 – A man is bitten on the calf.

1:05:15 – A zombie is shot in the head.

1:08:45 – A zombie is shot in the head.

1:09:00 – A zombie is shot in the head.

1:09:00 – A zombie is shot in the head.

1:09:00 – A zombie is shot in the head.

1:10:30 – A zombie is shot in the chest.

1:11:00 – A zombie is shot in the head.

1:11:15 – A zombie digs its fingers into a man's leg wound.

1:11:15 – A zombie is shot in the head.

1:12:00 – A zombie is shot in the eye.

1:13:15 – A zombie is shot in the chest.

1:14:00 – A zombie is shot in the head.

1:37:30 – A zombie is shot in the head.

1:37:45 – A zombie is shot in the head.

1:43:45 – A zombie is stabbed in the head with a machete.

1:43:45 – Multiple zombies are shot in the chest.

1:43:45 – A zombie is decapitated.

1:43:45 – A zombie is shot in the chest and head.

1:44:00 – A zombie is hit with a mace.

1:44:00 – A man cuts off a zombie's head with a machete.

1:44:30 – A zombie is shot in the chest.

DAWN OF THE DEAD

Year: 2004   Length: 96 minutes
Director: Zack Snyder

STATISTICS

First Zombie: 5:00
First Human Death: 29:30
First Zombie Death: 17:00

Amount of Gore: Very High
Gore Quality: Very High
Zombie Effects: Very High

Zombie Count: Very High
Zombie Deaths: Very High
Human Deaths: Average

SUMMARY

A group of survivors hide in a mall in a desperate attempt to hide from the undead. When the numbers of the surrounding dead start to grow, the refugees formulate a plan to escape from the mall and head to a deserted island.

EFFECTS HIGHLIGHTS

5:15 – A zombie is missing its lips.

5:30 – A man is bitten on the neck.

6:00 – A jet of blood squirts out of a man's neck.

8:00 – A man is ran over by an ambulance.

15:30 – A zombie is missing half of its right arm.

15:45 – A zombie is shot in the chest.

21:30 – A zombie eats from a dead body.

22:00 – A man cuts his arm on a piece of metal.

22:15 – A zombie is stabbed in the head with a wooden handle.

22:30 – A zombie is shot in the shoulder.

26:30 – Close up of a scratch mark.

27:45 – A wound on a man's arm is stitched up.

29:30 – A zombie is shot in the head.

30:00 – A zombie is shot in the head.

41:00 – A zombie is hit by a truck.

41:00 – A zombie is hit by a truck.

41:00 – A zombie is hit by a truck.

41:00 – A zombie is hit by a truck.

41:00 – A zombie is hit by a truck.

41:45 – A zombie is shot in the chest.

41:45 – A zombie is shot in the chest.

41:45 – A zombie is shot in the head.

42:00 – A zombie is shot in the head.

42:00 – A zombie is shot in the head.

42:15 – A zombie is shot in the head.

48:45 – A zombie is stabbed in the eye with a poker.

56:30 – A zombie is shot in the head.

57:00 – A zombie is shot in the head.

1:04:15 – A zombie is missing both of its lower legs.

1:05:00 – A zombie is shot in the head.

1:05:15 – A zombie is shot in the head.

1:05:30 – A zombie is shot in the head.

1:09:45 – A zombie is shot in the head.

1:10:00 – A woman is shot in the stomach.

1:10:00 – A man is shot in the chest.

1:10:00 – A woman is shot in the stomach.

1:10:00 – A man is shot in the stomach.

1:10:00 – A woman is shot in the chest.

1:10:15 – A woman is shot in the chest.

1:24:30 – A zombie is shot in the head.

1:24:30 – A zombie is shot in the head.

1:24:30 – A zombie is shot in the head.

1:24:45 – A zombie is shot in the head.

1:25:00 – A zombie is shot in the head.

1:26:15 – A zombie is shot in the head.

1:28:00 – A zombie is shot in the head.

1:29:00 – A zombie is shot in the chest.

1:29:00 – A zombie is shot in the chest.

1:29:00 – A zombie is shot in the chest.

1:29:00 – A zombie is shot in the chest.

1:31:15 – A zombie's leg is cut with a chainsaw.

1:31:45 – A zombie is shot in the head.

1:33:00 – A woman shoulder is cut with a chainsaw.

1:34:45 – A zombie is shot in the head.

1:34:45 – A zombie is shot in the head.

1:35:15 – A zombie is shot in the chest.

1:37:15 – A zombie is shot in the head.

1:37:30 – A zombie is shot in the chest.

1:38:30 – Close up of a bite mark.

1:41:30 – A severed zombie head is in an ice chest.

DAWN OF THE LIVING DEAD

Alternate Title: Evil Grave: Curse of the Maya
Year: 2004   Length: 80 minutes
Director: David Heavener

STATISTICS

First Zombie: 23:15
First Human Death: 38:15
First Zombie Death: N/A

Amount of Gore: High
Gore Quality: High
Zombie Effects: Average
Zombie Count: Average
Zombie Deaths: Very Low
Human Deaths: High

SUMMARY

When a couple move into a new home in the desert, they find that it rests upon the burial ground of a murdered family. Soon the dead family rises to seek justice.

EFFECTS HIGHLIGHTS

38:15 – A zombie rips a man's heart out of his chest.

39:30 – A zombie bites a chunk of flesh out of a woman's neck.

40:30 – A zombie rips out a man's intestines.

41:30 – A zombie bites a man's neck.

48:00 – A man is shot in the chest.

48:15 – A woman is shot in the back.

On the set of Crossroads Mall for "Dawn of the Dead" courtesy of A.J. Taylor.

On the set of Crossroads Mall for "Dawn of the Dead" courtesy of A.J. Taylor.

On the set of "Dawn of the Dead" courtesy of A.J. Taylor

53

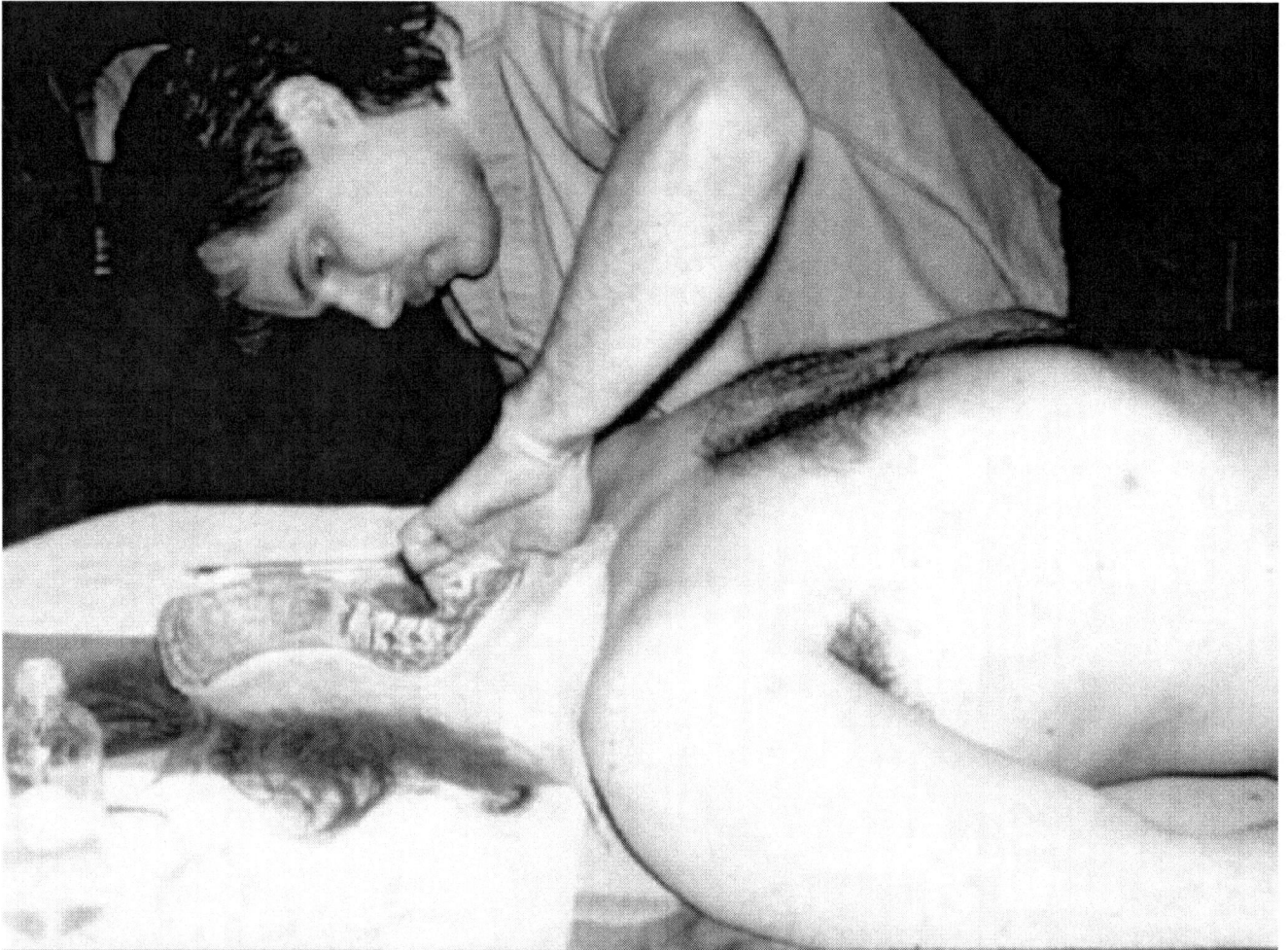

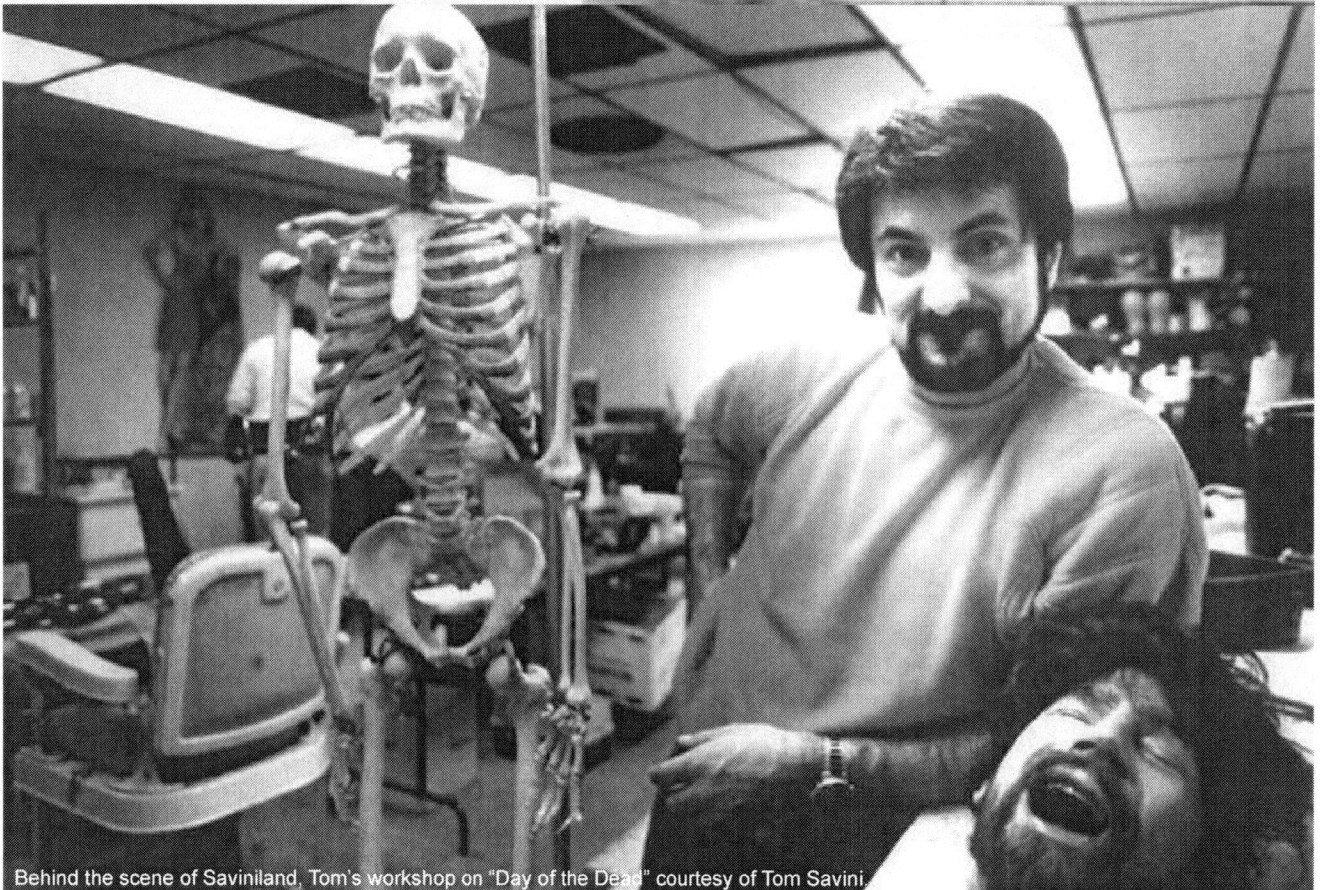

Behind the scene of Saviniland, Tom's workshop on "Day of the Dead" courtesy of Tom Savini.

53:15 – A zombie bites off a man's ear.

53:45 – A man's stomach is ripped open.

53:45 – Zombies pull off a man's head.

54:00 – Zombies feast on a decimated body.

54:45 – A zombie is stabbed in the arm.

54:45 – A zombie's arm is cut off.

DAY OF THE DEAD

Year: 1985   Length: 102 minutes
Director: George A. Romero

STATISTICS

First Zombie:	4:45
First Human Death:	58:30
First Zombie Death:	26:45
Amount of Gore:	Very High
Gore Quality:	Very High
Zombie Effects:	Very High
Zombie Count:	Very High
Zombie Deaths:	High
Human Deaths:	High

SUMMARY

In a world over run by the undead, a group of scientists and soldiers have taken shelter in an underground bunker. The scientists are desperately seeking a way to control the zombies, while the military wants to kill as many zombies as possible. Before long, fighting erupts between the two groups. Their differences are put on hold when the dead infiltrate the base.

EFFECTS HIGHLIGHTS

4:45 – A zombie is missing its lower jaw.

23:00 – A zombie on an operating table is missing the skin on its chest.

26:30 – A zombie sits up on an operating table and its stomach and intestines fall out of its open chest.

26:45 – A zombie is stabbed in the head with a drill.

58:30 – A zombie rips out a man's throat.

58:45 – A zombie bites a man on the wrist.

58:45 – A zombie is shot in the head.

59:22 – A man is shot in the head.

1:00:00 – A man's arm is cut off with a machete.

1:08:00 – A man finds a severed head.

1:11:00 – A zombie eats a piece of flesh.

1:12:15 – A man is shot in the chest.

1:14:45 – A man is shot in the head.

1:19:15 – A zombie is stabbed in the mouth with a shovel.

1:19:30 – A zombie is bludgeoned with a piece of wood.

1:22:30 – A zombie is shot in the head.

1:23:30 – A zombie bites a man's throat.

1:23:45 – A zombie bites a chunk of flesh out of a

man's chest.

1:27:00 – A man's head is pulled off of his body.

1:27:30 – A zombie is shot in the chest.

1:28:00 – A zombie rips off a man's eyelid.

1:28:00 – A zombie bites off a man's fingers.

1:28:15 – A zombie is shot in the head.

1:30:00 – A zombie is shot in the head.

1:30:15 – Two more zombies are shot in the head.

1:30:30 – A man shoots himself in the head.

1:30:45 – A zombie is shot in the head.

1:31:30 – A zombie is shot in the head.

1:31:45 – A zombie is shot in the head.

1:34:45 – A man is ripped in half by a group of zombies.

1:35:15 – Multiple shots of zombies eating various body parts.

1:35:30 – Multiple shots of zombies eating various body parts.

1:35:45 – Multiple shots of zombies eating various body parts.

DAY OF THE DEAD

Year: 2008   Length: 96 minutes
Director: Steve Miner

STATISTICS

First Zombie:	10:00
First Human Death:	10:30
First Zombie Death:	40:30
Amount of Gore:	Very High
Gore Quality:	Very High
Zombie Effects:	High
Zombie Count:	Very High
Zombie Deaths:	Very High
Human Deaths:	High

SUMMARY

When a small Colorado town is overrun by the flesh hungry dead, a small group of survivors try to escape the overrun city in a last ditch attempt to stay alive. Meanwhile, military and scientific experts clash as they try to arrive at a solution.

EFFECTS HIGHLIGHTS

10:30 – A piece of skin is thrown on the floor.

17:30 – A man finds two dead bodies.

24:00 – A zombie bites a large piece of flesh off of a woman's face.

28:00 – A zombie eats a severed arm.

28:15 – A zombie bites a woman's torso

29:15 – A zombie eats a dead body.

36:00 – A zombie is missing the lower parts of its legs.

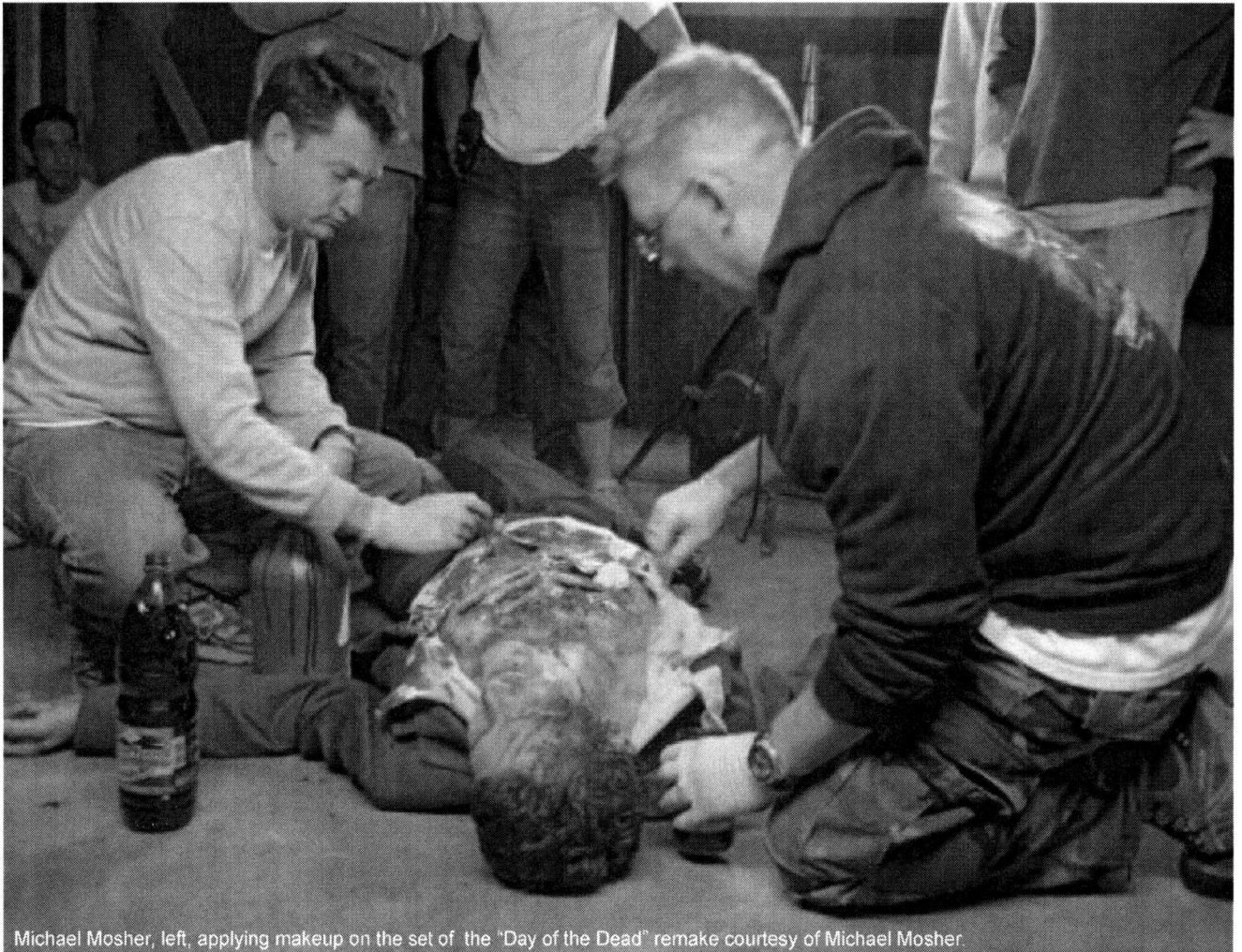

Michael Mosher, left, applying makeup on the set of the "Day of the Dead" remake courtesy of Michael Mosher.

37:15 – A zombie pulls out its eye and eats it.

44:00 – A zombie is shot in the head.

44:15 – A zombie is stabbed in the neck.

44:15 – A woman kicks off a zombie's head.

44:30 – A zombie is smashed in the head.

44:30 – A zombie is decapitated.

44:45 – A zombie is stabbed in the head.

45:30 – A zombie is clubbed in the head.

45:30 – A zombie is decapitated

45:30 – A zombie is decapitated.

46:45 – A group of zombies are set on fire.

47:00 – A zombie is stabbed in the head with a crutch.

49:30 – A zombie falls off a ladder.

52:45 – A zombie is stabbed in the head.

55:30 – A group of zombies are run over.

56:00 – A zombie is hit by a truck.

57:13 – A woman finds a half-eaten body.

1:00:15 – Four zombies are shot in the head.

1:13:00 – A zombie is decapitated.

1:14:00 – A bloodied body falls to the ground.

1:19:00 – A zombie's head is pulled off.

DAY OF THE DEAD 2: CONTAGIUM

Year: 2005   Length: 103 minutes
Directors: Ana Clavell, Glenn Dudelson

STATISTICS

First Zombie:	3:00
First Human Death:	2:15
First Zombie Death:	3:30
Amount of Gore:	Very High
Gore Quality:	Very High
Zombie Effects:	Very High
Zombie Count:	Very High
Zombie Deaths:	Very High
Human Deaths:	Very High

SUMMARY

In the late 1960's, an unexplained viral outbreak ravaged a Pennsylvania military hospital. The contaminated victims were quarantined and burned alive to contain the virus. Years later, the site is reopened as a treatment center for mental health patients and the virus spreads once again.

EFFECTS HIGHLIGHTS

2:15 – A man is shot in the head.

2:15 – Two more people are shot in the head.

2:15 – A man is shot in the head.

3:15 – A man's throat is ripped out.

3:45 – A zombie is shot in the head.

3:45 – A zombie is shot in the head.

4:00 – A zombie is shot in the head.

4:30 – A zombie is shot in the head.

5:15 – A man is shot in the head.

7:45 – A zombie bites a man's wrist

8:00 – A zombie is shot in the neck.

8:00 – A zombie is shot in the head.

8:30 – A zombie is shot in the head.

8:45 – A zombie is shot in the head.

9:00 – A man is shot in the head.

9:15 – A zombie is shot in the face.

9:15 – A zombie is shot in the head.

9:45 – A zombie is shot in the head.

43:00 – A man is bitten on the wrist.

44:45 – A man picks at wounds on his arm.

59:00 – Close up of a wound on a man's arm.

1:05:45 – A man pulls off his fingernail.

1:07:45 – Close up of a bloody body.

1:09:30 – A zombie eats a man's hand.

1:10:15 – A man is shot in the chest.

1:12:00 – A man's head is pulled off.

1:16:30 – A man picks up a severed hand.

1:16:45 – A zombie is eating a dead body.

1:20:30 – A zombie bites a man's wrist.

1:22:15 – A zombie bites a man's skull.

1:23:45 – A zombie is eating a dead body.

1:24:00 – A group of zombies are eating a dead body.

1:28:15 – A room full of zombies are eating various body parts.

1:28:45 – A zombie eats the fingers off of a severed arm.

1:32:15 – A zombie's arms are pulled off.

1:32:15 – A zombie's head is pulled off.

1:32:30 – A group of zombies tear open a zombie's stomach.

1:33:15 – A zombie eats a piece of flesh.

1:34:45 – A zombie punches through a man's chest.

1:39:00 – A zombie spits out a mouthful of blood.

DAY X

Year: 2005   Length: 81 minutes
Director: Jason Hack

STATISTICS

First Zombie:	2:45
First Human Death:	7:15
First Zombie Death:	3:30
Amount of Gore:	Average
Gore Quality:	High
Zombie Effects:	High
Zombie Count:	Very High
Zombie Deaths:	Average
Human Deaths:	High

SUMMARY

A mysterious epidemic sweeps through the population and turns its victims into zombies. A handful of uninfected citizens escape the outbreak by hiding in a deserted steel mill.

EFFECTS HIGHLIGHTS

3:30 – A zombie is shot in the head.

7:15 – A man vomits.

23:45 – A group of zombies eat a dead body.

27:45 – A man's torso is pulled to pieces.

27:45 – A man's head is ripped off.

39:15 – A zombie is shot in the head.

1:04:00 – A woman's torso is ripped open.

1:09:00 – A woman is torn to pieces.

DAYS OF DARKNESS

Year: 2005   Length: 81 minutes
Director: Jake Kennedy

STATISTICS

First Zombie:	3:30
First Human Death:	44:45
First Zombie Death:	5:00
Amount of Gore:	Very High
Gore Quality:	Very High
Zombie Effects:	High
Zombie Count:	Very High
Zombie Deaths:	High
Human Deaths:	High

SUMMARY

After a comet hits the Earth, a cloud of toxic dust fills the sky, turning thousands of humans into zombies. A group of survivors fight to stay ahead of the growing undead horde.

EFFECTS HIGHLIGHTS

4:00 – A man is bitten on the wrist.

5:00 – A man cleaves a zombie's head with a machete.

6:30 – A zombie is stabbed repeatedly in the chest with a knife.

8:00 – A group of zombies eat various body parts.

26:45 – A group of zombies eat various body parts.

33:00 – A man uses a knife to poke at an open wound on a zombie's abdomen.

36:15 – Two severed fingers fall to the floor.

38:45 – A zombie is shot in the chest.

43:45 – A zombie is smashed in the head.

43:45 – A zombie's arm is cut off with a machete.

44:00 – A man cuts off a zombie's hand.

44:00 – A man stabs a zombie with a machete.

44:15 – A zombie is stabbed with a pole.

44:45 – A zombie bites a chunk out of a man's neck.

50:15 – A man cuts into a zombie's torso.

51:00 – A man removes the top of a dead zombie's skull, exposing the brain.

54:45 – A creature bites a man's neck.

1:05:45 – A woman is stabbed in the head.

1:09:30 – A group of zombies bite a woman's neck.

1:09:45 – A zombie eats a woman's intestines.

1:21:45 – The back of a man's head explodes.

THE DEAD

Year: 2010   Length: 105 minutes
Directors: Howard J. Ford, Jonathan Ford

STATISTICS

First Zombie:	1:00
First Human Death:	3:30
First Zombie Death:	2:00

Amount of Gore:	Very High
Gore Quality:	Very High
Zombie Effects:	High
Zombie Count:	Very High
Zombie Deaths:	Very High
Human Deaths:	High

SUMMARY

When the last evacuation flight out of war-torn Africa crashes not long after take off, an American soldier emerges as the sole survivor in a country where the dead are returning to life and attacking the living.

EFFECTS HIGHLIGHTS

1:15 – A broken bone is sticking out of a zombie's leg.

2:00 – A zombie is shot in the head.

3:00 – A man bleeds from a neck wound.

4:30 – A zombie bites a mans arm.

4:45 – A zombie is shot in the head.

5:45 – A zombie is shot in the head.

5:45 – A zombie eats a piece of flesh.

5:45 – A zombie is shot in the shoulder.

6:00 – A zombie is shot in the head.

6:30 – A zombie is shot in the shoulder.

7:00 – A zombie eats a piece of flesh.

7:00 – A zombie is shot in the head.

7:00 – A zombie eats a piece of flesh.

7:00 – A zombie is shot in the head

7:30 – A zombie eats a piece of flesh.

11:45 – A zombie is shot in the face.

12:45 – A zombie bites a man's arm.

13:00 – A zombie bites a man's neck.

13:30 – A zombie is shot in the head.

13:30 – A zombie is shot in the head.

13:45 – A zombie is shot in the head.

15:00 – Close up of bloodied body parts.

17:45 – A zombie is shot in the head.

25:00 – A zombie is shot in the head.

27:30 – A truck runs over a zombie's head.

30:30 – A zombie is shot in the back.

30:45 – A zombie is shot in the head.

31:00 – A zombie is shot in the head.

49:00 – A man crushes a zombie's skull.

54:15 – A zombie is stabbed in the head.

1:17:15 – A zombie bits a man's leg.

DEAD AIR

Year: 2008   Length: 97 minutes
Director: Corbin Bernsen

STATISTICS

First Zombie:	25:15
First Human Death:	2:00
First Zombie Death:	27:00

Amount of Gore:	Average
Gore Quality:	High
Zombie Effects:	High
Zombie Count:	Very High
Zombie Deaths:	Average
Human Deaths:	Average

SUMMARY

A bioterrorist attack infects Americans with a disease that turns them into zombies fill with a murderous rage. A local radio jockey is locked down in his studio and talks to listeners struggling to stay alive amid the mayhem.

EFFECTS HIGHLIGHTS

2:00 – A man is shot in the head.

27:30 – A man is scratched on his neck.

30:15 – A zombie has a flap of skin falling off of its face.

51:30 – A zombie is stabbed in the chest with a broom handle.

1:15:30 – A zombie is stabbed in the back with a pair of scissors.

1:16:45 – A zombie is shot in the head.

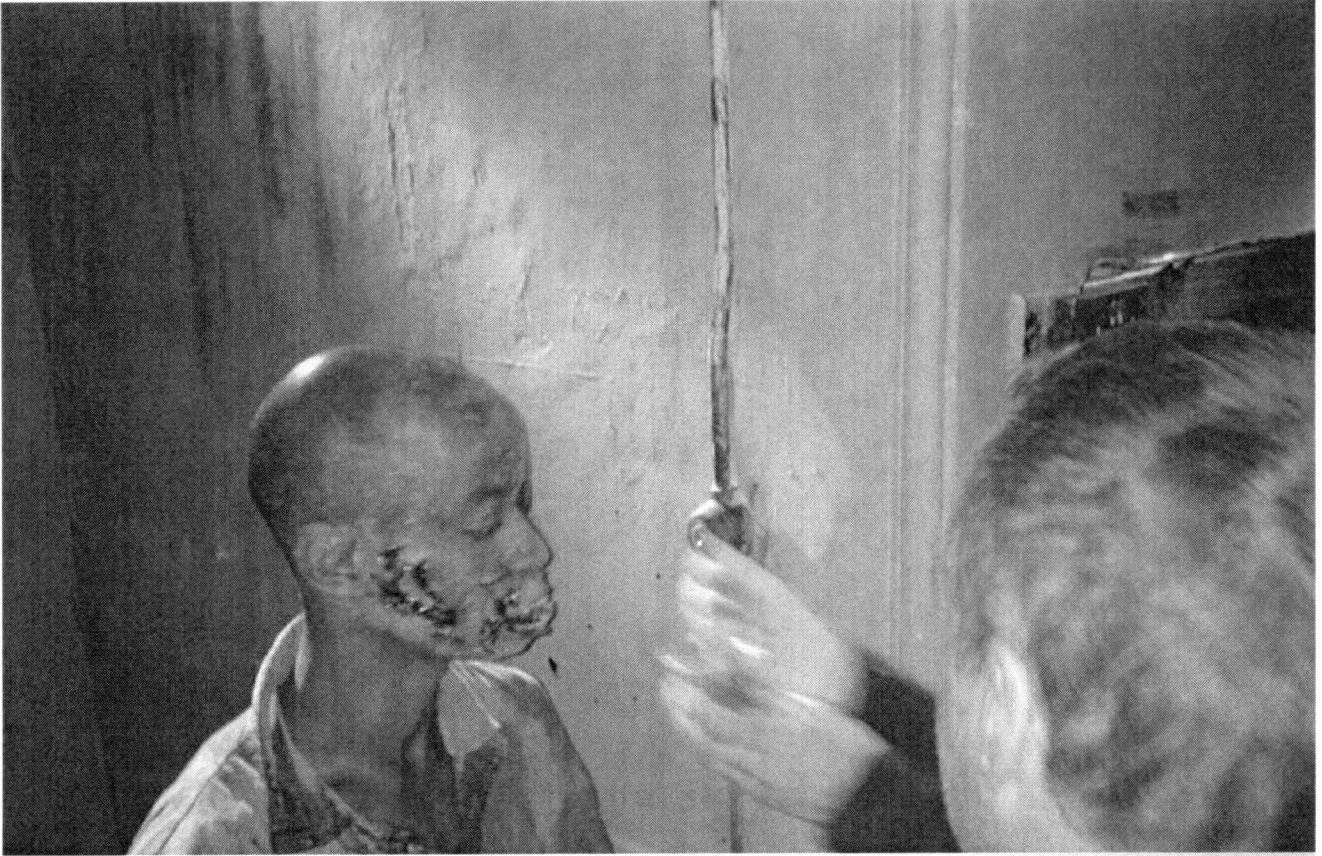

On location with "The Dead" courtesy of Howard and Jon Ford.

59

1:17:00 – A zombie pulls a bullet out of the back of its head.

1:18:00 – A zombie bites a man's neck.

DEAD AND BREAKFAST

Year: 2004   Length: 88 minutes
Director: Matthew Leutwyler

STATISTICS

First Zombie:	42:15
First Human Death:	34:45
First Zombie Death:	45:30
Amount of Gore:	Very High
Gore Quality:	Very High
Zombie Effects:	High
Zombie Count:	High
Zombie Deaths:	High
Human Deaths:	High

SUMMARY

Six friends spend the night at a bed and breakfast, they become the prime suspects when the owner and chef are killed. The situation soon changes when the towns people become possessed by an evil spirit and turn into zombies and lay siege on the hotel.

EFFECTS HIGHLIGHTS

16:45 – A dead body has a knife in its throat.

34:30 – A man is stabbed in the chest.

34:45 – A man is stabbed in the head with a hammer.

38:32 – Blood splatter sprays a wall.

42:45 – A man is shot in the chest.

44:45 – A zombie is stabbed in the eye with a drumstick.

45:30 – A zombie is stabbed in the forehead with a cymbal.

45:45 – A zombie is stabbed in the head with a set of antlers.

46:00 – A man is hacked in the neck with an axe.

46:00 – A man is decapitated with an axe.

48:15 – A zombie uses a decapitated head as a hand puppet.

56:45 – A zombie is shot in the neck and decapitated.

57:00 – A severed head is kicked at a wall.

59:30 – A zombie is shot in the head, shearing off everything over the jaw.

1:00:30 – A zombie's arm is shot off.

1:05:30 – A zombie is shot in the face.

1:06:45 – A zombie is stabbed in the head with a hammer.

1:07:15 – A zombie is shot in the chest.

1:11:00 – A zombie is cut on the neck with a chainsaw.

Eric Palidino in "Dead and Breakfast" courtesy of Michael Mosher.

1:11:15 – The zombie struggles with the chainsaw, squirting blood everywhere, until it collapses.

1:13:00 – A man is stabbed in the chest.

1:13:00 – A zombie is stabbed in the neck with a shovel.

1:14:00 – A woman uses a power drill to pierce a zombie's head.

1:15:00 – A man cuts a bone out of a severed leg.

1:16:15 – A zombie is stabbed in the back of the head.

1:16:30 – A zombie has garden shears sticking out of its stomach.

1:16:30 – A zombie is shot in the face, blowing a hole through its head.

1:17:30 – A zombie is shot in the head.

1:20:00 – A zombie is shot with an arrow.

1:20:15 – A woman cuts through a group of zombies with a chainsaw.

1:21:00 – A zombie is stabbed with a bone.

DEAD AND BURIED

Year: 1981   Length: 94 minutes
Director: Gary Sherman

STATISTICS

First Zombie:	12:30
First Human Death:	9:00

First Zombie Death: N/A

Amount of Gore:	Average
Gore Quality:	Average
Zombie Effects:	Low
Zombie Count:	High
Zombie Deaths:	Very Low
Human Deaths:	Average

SUMMARY

A small coastal town harbors a dark secret where, after a series of violent murders committed by mobs of townspeople against tourists, the dead bodies start to come back to life.

EFFECTS HIGHLIGHTS

9:00 – A man is tied to a pole and set on fire.

12:30 – Close up of a badly burned body.

30:00 – A nurse stabs a patient in the eye with a hypodermic needle.

43:15 – During a struggle in a car, a woman's hair is ripped off of her scalp.

44:30 – A severed arm is stuck in the grill of a car.

58:45 – A man inserts eyes into a dead woman.

1:05:15 – Chemicals are inserted in a man's nose causing massive lesions and bleeding.

1:13:30 – Close up of a human heart.

1:15:00 – A man's hands are cracking.

1:20:30 – A man's throat is slit.

1:27:30 – A man sticks two large tubes into his torso.

1:30:45 – The skin on a man's fingers has split open.

DEAD AND DEADER

Year: 2006   Length: 89 minutes
Director: Patrick Dinhut

STATISTICS

First Zombie:	3:15
First Human Death:	3:45
First Zombie Death:	3:30

Amount of Gore:	Very High
Gore Quality:	Very High
Zombie Effects:	High
Zombie Count:	Very High
Zombie Deaths:	High
Human Deaths:	High

SUMMARY

A Special Forces soldier stationed in Cambodia is bitten by a radioactive scorpion. Back on US soil, he soon turns into a half-zombie while the rest of his squad has completely turned into zombies. He must kill his squad mates to prevent the infection from spreading.

EFFECTS HIGHLIGHTS

3:30 – A zombie is shot in the head.

3:45 – A zombie is shot in the head.

11:30 – A zombie cuts open its arm with a scalpel and pulls out a scorpion.

17:45 – A zombie is stabbed in the chest.

19:00 – A zombie bites a chunk of flesh out of a woman's arm.

19:45 – A zombie bites off a man's finger.

20:30 – A man cuts a zombie's neck with an electric knife.

20:30 – A zombie's head is put into a ceiling fan.

21:00 – A zombie's hand is put into a meat grinder.

21:15 – A zombie is decapitated.

35:45 – A zombie bites a man's throat.

37:15 – A zombie eats a severed leg.

37:15 – A zombie eats a severed arm.

37:15 – A zombie rips flesh out of a man's neck.

38:30 – A zombie is stabbed with a set of antlers.

38:45 – A zombie is decapitated with an axe.

58:00 – A zombie is shot in the head.

58:15 – A zombie is stabbed with a cattle prod.

1:07:00 – Two zombies are shot in the head.

1:10:45 – A zombie's stomach is cut open with a saw.

1:12:00 – A man's arms are ripped off.

1:12:15 – A zombie is shot in the head.

1:12:30 – A zombie is shot in the head

1:12:30 – A woman is shot in the head.

1:15:30 – A group of zombies are eating various body parts.

DEAD AND ROTTING

Year: 2002   Length: 72 minutes
Director: David P. Barton

STATISTICS

First Zombie:	30:30
First Human Death:	N/A
First Zombie Death:	N/A

Amount of Gore:	Low
Gore Quality:	High
Zombie Effects:	High
Zombie Count:	Average
Zombie Deaths:	Very Low
Human Deaths:	Very Low

SUMMARY

Three friends unknowingly release the wrath of an aged witch, when they become accomplices to the murder of her son. Transformed into a beautiful young woman, the witch seduces the three friends and then uses the men's own undead spawn to destroy them.

EFFECTS HIGHLIGHTS

15:45 – A bloody torso is in a closet.

29:00 – Gore falls from between a woman's legs.

40:30 – A man is missing the top of his head.

43:15 – A man knocks off a zombie's jaw.

1:08:15 – A rotten head is covered in maggots.

DEAD CLOWNS

Year: 2003   Length: 95 minutes
Director: Steve Sessions

STATISTICS

First Zombie:	22:15
First Human Death:	55:30
First Zombie Death:	1:24:15

Amount of Gore:	Low
Gore Quality:	High
Zombie Effects:	High
Zombie Count:	High
Zombie Deaths:	Low
Human Deaths:	Average

SUMMARY

A violent hurricane awakens an army of zombie clowns who were left to die after a circus train accident and are bent on revenge.

EFFECTS HIGHLIGHTS

27:15 – A zombie has part of its head missing.

49:15 – Zombies eat the remains of a dead body.

54:00 – A woman's throat has been slit.

55:30 – A woman is stabbed in the eye with a meat thermometer.

55:45 – A zombie eats an eyeball.

1:03:30 – A zombie smashes a man's head in.

1:06:15 – Zombies eat a dead body.

1:15:00 – A zombie cuts a man's wrist with a knife.

1:15:30 – A zombie eats a severed hand.

1:19:45 – A zombie eats an organ.

1:20:00 – A group of zombies eat a dead body.

1:23:15 – A man finds a dead body.

1:24:15 – A zombie is shot in the head.

1:31:15 – A bloody severed arm is on the floor.

DEAD COUNTRY

Year: 2008   Length: 75 minutes
Director: Andrew Merkelbach

STATISTICS

First Zombie:	1:30
First Human Death:	5:00
First Zombie Death:	13:30

Amount of Gore:	Low
Gore Quality:	Low
Zombie Effects:	Low
Zombie Count:	High
Zombie Deaths:	High
Human Deaths:	Very Low

SUMMARY

A space ship explodes in the sky above a small rural town showering the population with a deadly alien virus, spreading a zombie plague upon the town folk. The alien responsible for the plague, joins forces with the locals to battle the zombies and prevent the outbreak from spreading.

EFFECTS HIGHLIGHTS

8:30 – A man finds a severed arm.

13:30 – A zombie is decapitated.

24:00 – Two zombies are shot in the head.

29:15 – A zombie is eating intestines.

DEAD CREATURES

Year: 2000   Length: 90 minutes
Director: Andrew Parkinson

STATISTICS

First Zombie:	1:00
First Human Death:	21:30
First Zombie Death:	N/A

Amount of Gore:	Low
Gore Quality:	Low
Zombie Effects:	Low
Zombie Count:	High
Zombie Deaths:	High
Human Deaths:	Very Low

SUMMARY

A group of young women are cursed with the need to feed on human flesh. They are forced to abandon their lives to prowl the streets searching for victims.

EFFECTS HIGHLIGHTS

19:00 – A zombie eats a piece of meat.

21:30 – A man is impaled through the head.

30:00 – Two women cut up a dead body.

33:15 – A woman picks at a bloody chunk of dead meat.

34:45 – A man saws off a dead body' head.

38:30 – A man urinates blood.

45:15 – A group of woman cut flesh off of a dead body.

1:11:15 – A man is impaled through the head.

1:25:00 – A man bleeds through a gaping wound in his neck.

THE DEAD HATE THE LIVING

Year: 2000   Length: 90 minutes
Director: David Parker

STATISTICS

First Zombie: 1:15
First Human Death: 5:00
First Zombie Death: 1:03:30

Amount of Gore: Average
Gore Quality: Very High
Zombie Effects: High
Zombie Count: High
Zombie Deaths: Average
Human Deaths: Average

SUMMARY

While shooting a horror movie in an abandoned hospital, a group of friends discover a corpse and decide to use it in their film. They unknowingly unleash an army of zombies who prey on the crew.

EFFECTS HIGHLIGHTS

5:00 – A zombie draws a scalpel across a woman's throat.

17:45 – A zombie is missing part of its scalp.

49:30 – A man pulls a headless torso out of a window.

1:03:30 – A woman punches a zombie in the face, collapsing the skull.

1:05:15 – A zombie punches a man through the chest and rips out his intestines.

1:10:00 – A man stabs a zombie with a chainsaw

1:10:15 – A man stabs a zombie in the head with a machete.

1:22:15 – A zombie claws a chunk of skin off of a man's neck.

1:22:15 – A man jams his fingers in a zombie's eyes.

DEAD HEAT

Year: 1988   Length: 84 minutes
Director: Mark Goldblatt

STATISTICS

First Zombie: 18:00
First Human Death: 4:45
First Zombie Death: 34:30

Amount of Gore: High
Gore Quality: High
Zombie Effects: High
Zombie Count: Average
Zombie Deaths: Average
Human Deaths: Very High

SUMMARY

Two police officers visit a pharmaceutical company they suspect of some underhanded business. Inside, they uncover a room that can raise people from the dead, making them virtually indestructible. When one of the cops dies, he is reanimated and they set out to bring his murderer to justice.

EFFECTS HIGHLIGHTS

20:45 – A man is shot in the chest.

27:45 – A zombie has an open wound on his wrist.

32:30 – A zombie is shot in the chest.

34:30 – A zombie is electrocuted.

34:45 – A zombie is stabbed with an umbrella pole.

38:45 – A zombie sees a rotten skeleton in the mirror.

42:30 – A man is shot in the stomach.

45:45 – A woman stitches up a wound in a zombie's hand.

59:30 – A woman starts to melt.

1:08:45 – A zombie picks chunks of flesh off its face.

1:13:15 – A man is shot in the chest.

1:14:00 – A man is shot in the chest.

1:14:30 – A zombie is shot multiple times in the chest.

1:15:00 – A woman is shot in the chest.

1:15:00 – A man is shot in the chest.

1:17:30 – A zombie is shot in the chest.

DEAD HEIST

Year: 2007   Length: 75 minutes
Director: Bo Webb

STATISTICS

First Zombie: 1:30
First Human Death: 37:00
First Zombie Death: 56:00

Amount of Gore: High
Gore Quality: Very High
Zombie Effects: High
Zombie Count: Very High
Zombie Deaths: Very High
Human Deaths: Average

SUMMARY

After committing a bank robbery, four thieves are forced to seek shelter inside when the small town they are in experiences an attack by the living dead.

EFFECTS HIGHLIGHTS

37:00 – A man is shot in the chest.

37:30 – A man is shot in the chest.

45:15 – A zombie is shot in the chest.

45:15 – A zombie bites a man's neck.

47:45 – A zombie bites a man's wrist.

47:45 – A zombie bites a man's neck.

1:00:00 – A group of zombies eat a man.

1:02:15 – A zombie is shot in the head.

1:05:30 – A zombie is shot repeatedly in the chest.

1:10:30 – A zombie is stabbed in the back.

1:11:00 – A zombie is stabbed in the chest.

1:12:00 – A man stabs himself in the chest.

DEAD HUNTER

Year: 2003   Length: 75 minutes
Director: Julián Lara

STATISTICS

First Zombie:	5:45
First Human Death:	5:45
First Zombie Death:	12:15
Amount of Gore:	High
Gore Quality:	High
Zombie Effects:	High
Zombie Count:	Very High
Zombie Deaths:	Very High
Human Deaths:	High

SUMMARY

During the excavation of an old subway tunnel, the workers who had died in the collapse twenty years earlier emerge as flesh-eating zombies and go on a bloodthirsty rampage. It is up to an elite team of zombie killers called "Deadhunters" to combat the outbreak before it spreads.

EFFECTS HIGHLIGHTS

5:30 – A man has a wound on his chest.

12:15 – A zombie is shot repeatedly in the head.

12:30 – A man vomits.

36:30 – A zombie eat a woman's brain.

38:45 – A zombie rips out a man's intestines.

39:30 – A group of zombies tear a man's torso apart.

58:00 – Blood sprays out of a dead zombie's head.

58:30 – A zombie eats a man's intestines.

59:30 – A zombie carries a severed head.

1:10:45 – A man bites off a zombie's eyeball.

DEAD LIFE

Year: 2005   Length: 92 minutes
Director: William Victor Schotten

STATISTICS

First Zombie:	24:45
First Human Death:	36:15
First Zombie Death:	36:15
Amount of Gore:	High

Gore Quality:	High
Zombie Effects:	Average
Zombie Count:	Very High
Zombie Deaths:	Average
Human Deaths:	High

SUMMARY

A deadly virus runs rampant through Midwest America killing the living and reviving the dead. A group of friends struggle to survive, as one by one they are killed by the undead.

EFFECTS HIGHLIGHTS

3:00 – A man pulls his intestines out.

16:00 – A man vomits blood.

28:45 – A zombie eats a man's stomach.

29:30 – A zombie bites off a man's penis.

30:45 – A zombie has a bloody wound on its back.

35:45 – A zombie bites into a man's stomach

36:00 – A zombie bites a chunk of flesh out of a man's neck.

41:00 – A zombie rips off a woman's scalp.

47:15 – Close up of a woman's bloody scalp.

56:00 – A zombie bites a chunk of flesh off of a woman's face.

59:30 – A zombie has part of its breast missing.

58:00 – A zombie bites a chunk of flesh off of its arm.

1:07:15 – A zombie bites a man's arm.

1:14:15 – A zombie bites a chunk of flesh off of a man's neck.

DEAD MEAT

Year: 2004   Length: 80 minutes
Director: Conor McMahon

STATISTICS

First Zombie:	1:45
First Human Death:	2:15
First Zombie Death:	55:30
Amount of Gore:	High
Gore Quality:	High
Zombie Effects:	Average
Zombie Count:	Very High
Zombie Deaths:	High
Human Deaths:	Average

SUMMARY

A mutated strain of mad cow disease infects the Irish countryside turning people into flesh-eating zombies. A pair of survivors must band together to combat the outbreak.

EFFECTS HIGHLIGHTS

4:15 – Flies and maggots crawl over a dead animal

lying in the road.

9:00 – A zombie bites a man's neck.

9:45 – A quick succession of rapid shots as a man bludgeons a zombie's head with a steering wheel lock.

16:30 – A vacuum cleaner sucks a zombie's eye out of its socket.

27:15 – A zombie is stabbed through the chest with the handle of a shovel.

29:00 – A shovel is embedded in a zombie's head.

29:45 – A woman uses a high heeled shoe to stab a zombie in the face.

29:45 – A zombie is decapitated by a shovel.

35:00 – A woman stabs a zombie in the eye with a branch.

44:00 – While driving, a man hits a zombie with a bat, knocking its jaw off.

1:06:15 – The top of a zombie's head is cut off with a shovel.

1:07:15 – After being almost decapitated, a zombie's head falls off of its neck, squirting blood.

1:08:00 – A zombie is stabbed in the mouth repeatedly with a shovel until the top of its head is cleaved off.

1:09:45 – A man's arm is cut off.

DEAD MEN WALKING

Year: 2005   Length: 85 minutes
Director: Peter Mervis

STATISTICS

First Zombie:	:00
First Human Death:	22:15
First Zombie Death:	:15
Amount of Gore:	High
Gore Quality:	Very High
Zombie Effects:	High
Zombie Count:	Very High
Zombie Deaths:	Average
Human Deaths:	High

SUMMARY

A plague infects a maximum-security prison, turning everyone inside into zombies. A group of armed guards band together with the rest of the survivors to exterminate the undead

EFFECTS HIGHLIGHTS

:15 – A zombie is shot, covering a wall with blood.

20:30 – A prison guard shoots a zombie under the chin, destroying its jaw.

31:15 – A zombie bites a large chunk of flesh out of a man's arm.

31:30 – A zombie bites a man's torso.

33:00 – A zombie is shot in the head.

50:30 – A man shoots himself in the head.

51:45 – Numerous body parts are scattered across the floor.

53:45 – A zombie bites a woman's cheek.

54:45 – A group of zombies tear open a man's torso.

55:15 – A second man is torn to pieces by zombies.

1:02:00 – A child's intestines are pulled out.

1:03:15 – A man's torso is ripped apart.

DEAD MOON RISING

Year: 2007   Length: 93 minutes
Director: Mark E. Poole

STATISTICS

First Zombie:	12:00
First Human Death:	17:00
First Zombie Death:	23:00
Amount of Gore:	Very High
Gore Quality:	Very High
Zombie Effects:	High
Zombie Count:	Very High
Zombie Deaths:	High
Human Deaths:	High

SUMMARY

A disease transforms most of earths population into flesh-eating zombies. The employees of Cheapskate Car Rentals are taken by surprise when they fail to recognize the threat until it falls on their doorstep.

EFFECTS HIGHLIGHTS

12:30 – A zombie spits up blood.

17:00 – A group of zombies rip open a girls stomach.

20:30 – A man is covered in blood.

28:00 – A man hits a zombie in the head with a bat.

28:15 – Two people beat a zombie with bats.

29:00 – A zombie spits up blood.

38:30 – A group of zombies rip the entrails out of a woman's stomach.

38:30 – A zombie eats a severed arm.

39:45 – A woman has open wounds on her back.

39:45 – A woman bites off a man's tongue.

43:45 – A group of zombies rip open a woman's stomach.

44:00 – A woman's stomach is ripped open.

45:45 – A woman beheads a zombie.

50:00 – A man is torn to pieces by a group of zombies.

56:45 – A man is torn to pieces by a group of zombies.

1:04:30 – A woman cuts a zombie with a chainsaw.

1:04:45 – A woman is covered in blood.

1:08:00 – A zombie bites a chunk of flesh out of a

man's neck.

1:09:45 – A man shoots himself in the head.

1:15:00 – A large crowd of zombies are shot at with a machine gun.

1:15:15 – A zombie is shot multiple times in the chest.

1:24:00 – A man is ripped apart by a group of zombies.

THE DEAD NEXT DOOR

Year: 1989   Length: 78 minutes
Director: J.R. Bookwalter

STATISTICS

First Zombie: 1:30
First Human Death: 32:45
First Zombie Death: 9:15

Amount of Gore: High
Gore Quality: High
Zombie Effects: High
Zombie Count: Very High
Zombie Deaths: Average
Human Deaths: High

SUMMARY

A viral epidemic turns humans into the living dead and it is up to a government-run zombie squad to try to find a cure and keep the survivors from succumbing to the disease. Things become much more complicated when one of their own gets bitten and joins the ranks of the undead.

EFFECTS HIGHLIGHTS

1:30 – A zombie bites a chunk of flesh out of a man's neck.

3:30 – A zombie is eating intestines.

8:15 – A zombie bleeds from a bullet wound in its forehead.

8:45 – A zombie is decapitated.

9:15 – A headless zombie squirts blood from its neck.

10:30 – A man's fingers are bitten off.

17:30 – A zombie bites a man's throat.

17:45 – A zombie's head is split in two.

21:45 – A severed tongue is moving.

22:15 – A zombie bites a chunk of flesh out of a man's wrist.

32:30 – A man is cut on the shoulder with a machete.

34:45 – A zombie eats a piece of flesh.

40:30 – A group of zombies tear a dead body apart.

43:30 – A car runs over a zombie's head.

51:30 – A man is shot in the chest.

56:30 – A zombie's skin melts.

56:45 – A man is shot in the shoulder.

1:01:15 – A group of zombies tear a man's stomach

open.

1:07:00 – A man is bitten on the neck.

1:07:30 – A zombie is stabbed in the head.

1:08:00 – Zombies pull the skin off of a man's face.

1:08:30 – A group of zombies rip open a man's stomach.

1:10:15 – A zombie eats a piece of flesh.

THE DEAD OUTSIDE

Year: 2008   Length: 84 minutes
Director: Kerry Anne Mullaney

STATISTICS

First Zombie: 1:45
First Human Death: N/A
First Zombie Death: 53:15

Amount of Gore: Low
Gore Quality: Average
Zombie Effects: Average
Zombie Count: High
Zombie Deaths: Average
Human Deaths: Very Low

SUMMARY

After a neurological pandemic has consumed the population, two survivors come together on an isolated farm. When a mysterious stranger arrives, they are confronted with a new enemy even deadlier than the one outside the fence.

EFFECTS HIGHLIGHTS

53:15 – A zombie is shot in the head.

1:13:45 – A zombie is shot in the shoulder.

THE DEAD PIT

Year: 1989   Length: 95 minutes
Director: Brett Leonard

STATISTICS

First Zombie: 27:15
First Human Death: 2:15
First Zombie Death: 10:45

Amount of Gore: High
Gore Quality: Very High
Zombie Effects: High
Zombie Count: Very High
Zombie Deaths: Average
Human Deaths: Average

SUMMARY

A mad doctor is shot dead and entombed in the basement of an abandoned mental hospital. Twenty years later, an earthquake cracks the seal to the Dead Pit, freeing the undead doctor to continue his experiments.

EFFECTS HIGHLIGHTS

2:15 – A man is stabbed in the eye with a needle.

6:45 – A man is missing the top part of his scalp.

7:00 – Close up of a pile of dead bodies.

8:15 – A man is shot in the forehead.

27:15 – A woman is stabbed in the eye.

40:15 – A man has been stabbed in the eye.

41:00 – A dead woman has a large hole in her forehead.

42:15 – A zombie holds a severed head.

1:00:30 – A dead woman has a large hole in her forehead.

1:08:30 – A group of zombies rip off the top of a man's head and pull out his brain.

1:12:00 – A zombie has part of its scalp missing.

1:14:00 – A zombie is holding a brain.

1:21:15 – A group of zombies are holding brains.

1:22:15 – A zombie's face melts.

1:27:15 – A zombie puts a needle in a man's exposed brain.

1:29:15 – A zombie's face melts.

1:34:00 – A zombie holds a brain.

DEAD SNOW

Year: 2009   Length: 91 minutes
Director: Tommy Wirkola

STATISTICS

First Zombie:	1:45
First Human Death:	2:15
First Zombie Death:	55:30

Amount of Gore:	Very High
Gore Quality:	Very High
Zombie Effects:	High
Zombie Count:	Very High
Zombie Deaths:	High
Human Deaths:	High

SUMMARY

A ski vacation turns terrifying for a group of medical students, as they find themselves confronted by an army of Nazi zombies.

EFFECTS HIGHLIGHTS

26:45 – A man's throat is slit.

31:00 – A man finds a dead body with its intestines spilling out onto its lap.

42:15 – A zombie's hand is cut off.

45:21 – A zombie reaches into a man's eye socket and cracks his skull in two.

51:00 – A severed head sits among a collection of helmets.

55:30 – A bayonet impales a zombie's eye.

55:30 – A zombie is kicked into a tree branch and tears open its stomach, spilling its intestines.

56:15 – A man falls off a cliff and grabs a zombie's intestines, using them as a rope.

57:00 – A woman stomps on a zombie's head, crushing its skull.

1:05:15 – A man stitches up a wound in his neck.

1:08:45 – A zombie's arm is cut off with a chainsaw.

1:08:45 – A zombie is stabbed in the chest.

1:09:00 – A zombie is cut in two.

1:10:15 – A zombie is crushed under a snow mobile.

1:12:00 – Five zombies tear a man apart.

1:15:45 – A man cuts his right arm off with a chainsaw and cauterizes it.

DEAD SUMMER

Year: 2005   Length: 70 minutes
Director: Eddie Benevich

STATISTICS

First Zombie:	1:45
First Human Death:	2:15
First Zombie Death:	55:30

Amount of Gore:	Low
Gore Quality:	Low
Zombie Effects:	Average
Zombie Count:	High
Zombie Deaths:	Average
Human Deaths:	Average

SUMMARY

After a plague turns many residents of a small town into zombies, the living and the undead avoid each other until some teens discover a chemical that turns the slow moving zombies into hostile flesh eaters.

EFFECTS HIGHLIGHTS

10:15 – A zombie bites a chunk of flesh from a man's neck.

30:15 – A zombie is beaten with a tire iron.

58:00 – Close up of a bloody dead body.

THE DEAD UNDEAD

Year: 2010   Length: 89 minutes
Directors: Matthew R. Anderson, Edward Conna

STATISTICS

First Zombie:	7:30
First Human Death:	40:30
First Zombie Death:	12:45

This page and opposite, concept sketches of the demise Dr. Ramzi from "The Dead Pit" courtesy of Ed Martinez.

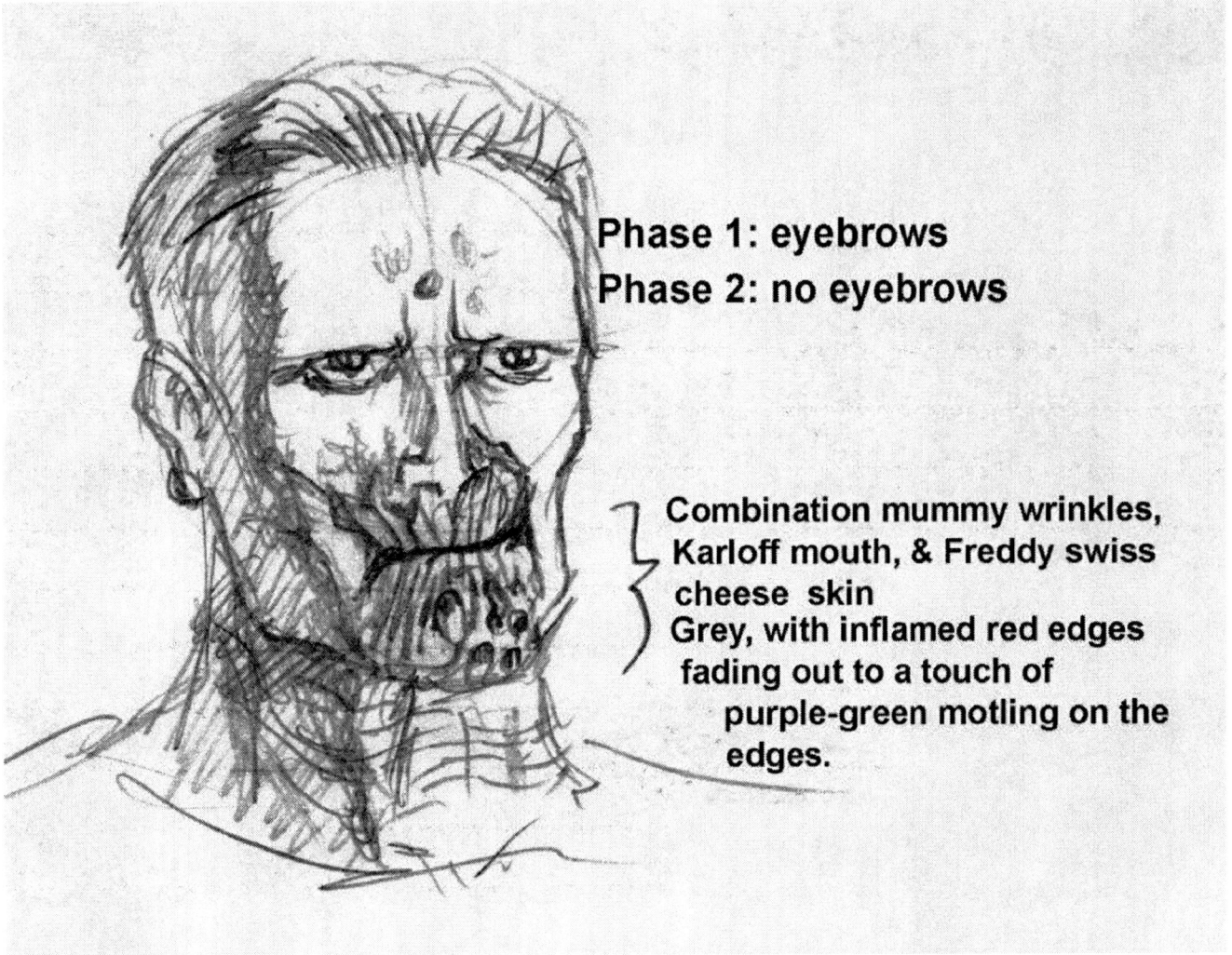

Phase 1: eyebrows

Phase 2: no eyebrows

Combination mummy wrinkles, Karloff mouth, & Freddy swiss cheese skin

Grey, with inflamed red edges fading out to a touch of purple-green motling on the edges.

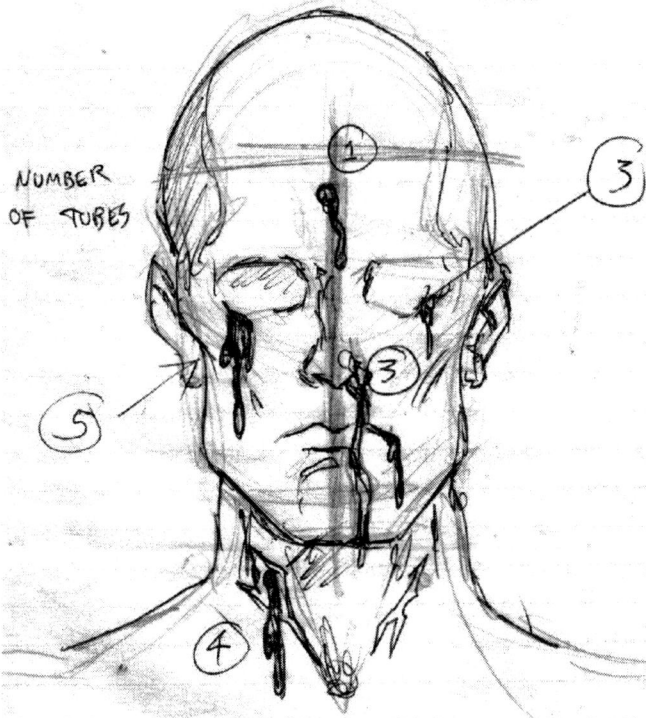

MAJOR BOSCO EXITS

NUMBER OF TUBES

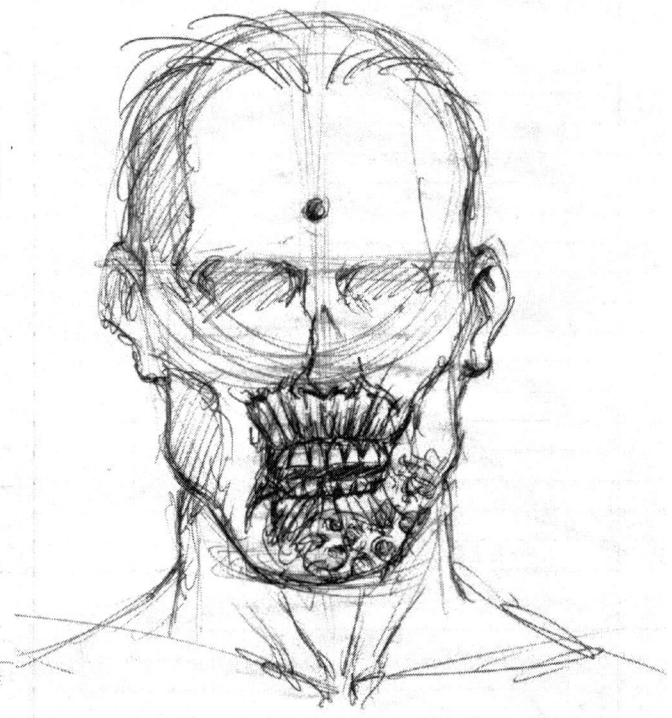

STAGE I

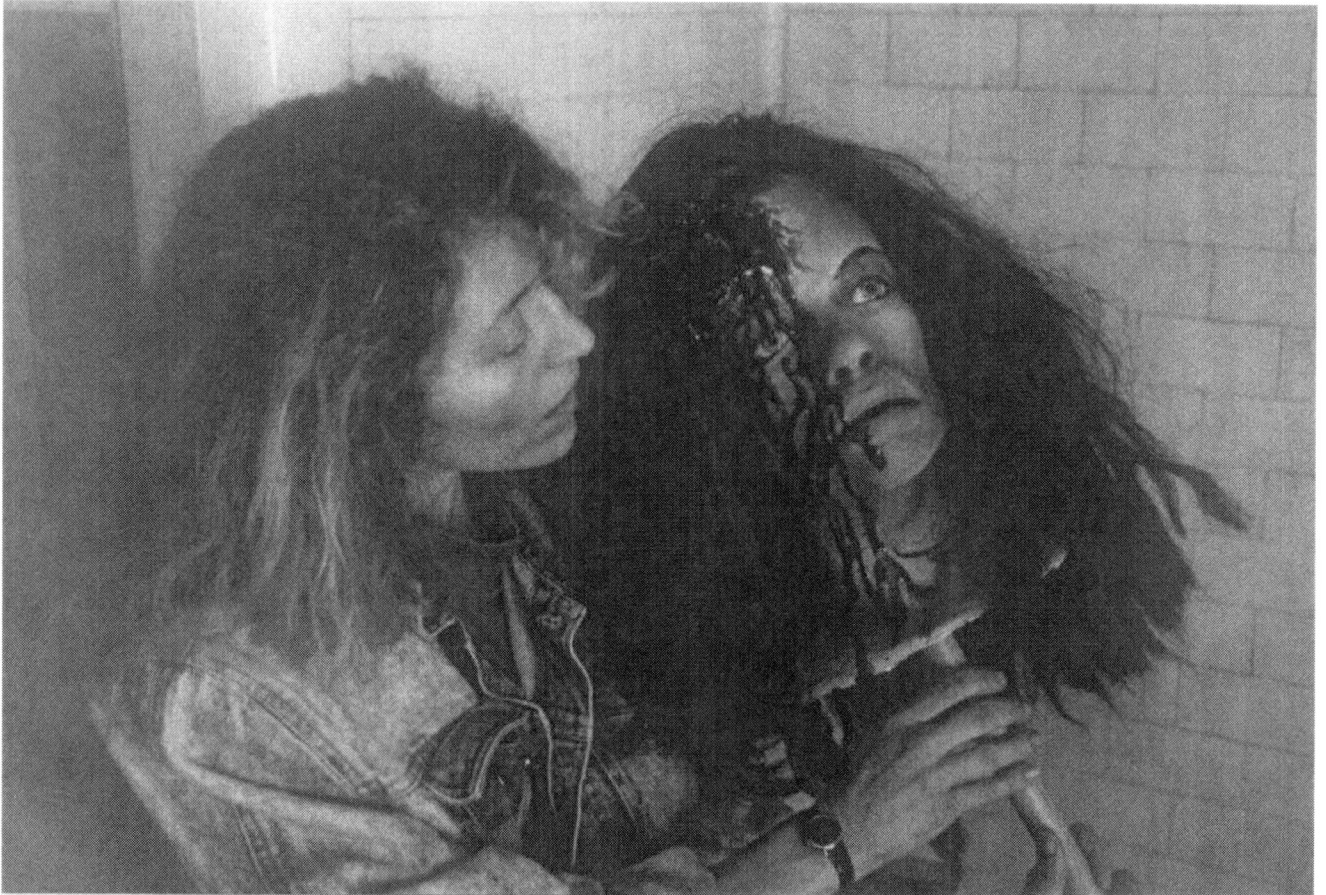

This page and opposite, behind the scenes of "The Dead Pit" courtesy of Ed Martinez.

70

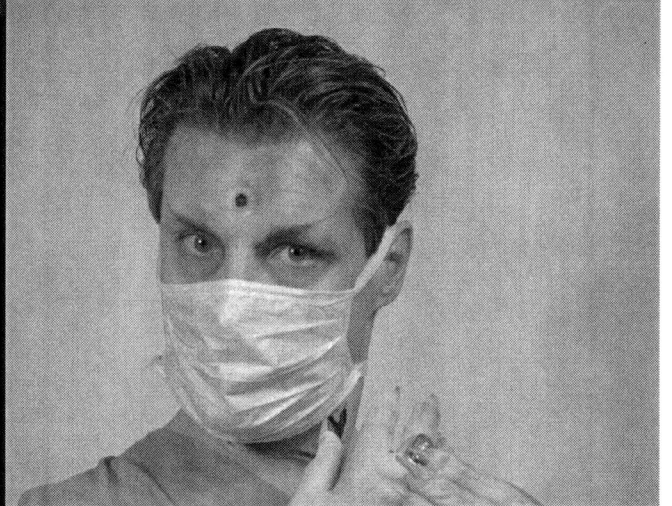

This page and opposite behind the scenes "The Dead Pit" courtesy of Ed Martinez.

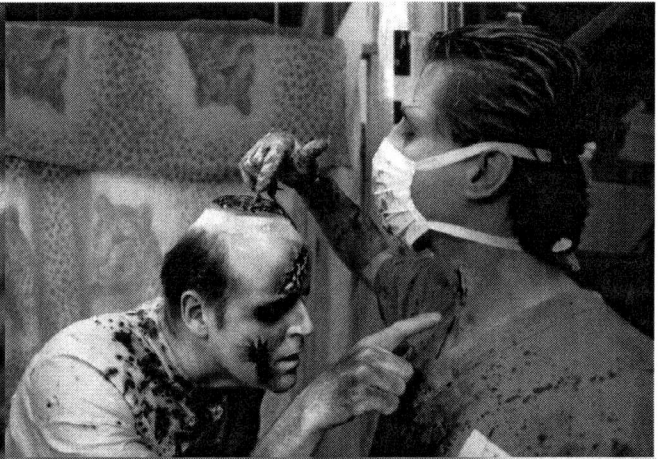
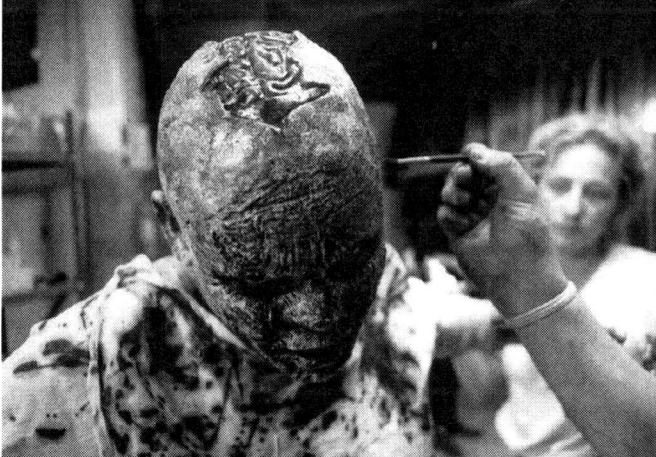

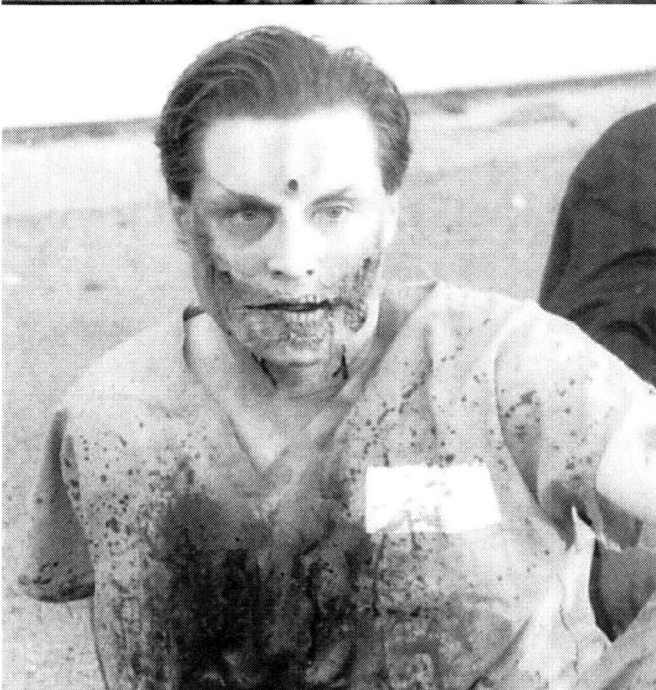

73

Amount of Gore:	Very High
Gore Quality:	Very High
Zombie Effects:	High
Zombie Count:	Very High
Zombie Deaths:	Very High
Human Deaths:	Very High

SUMMARY

Vampires battle zombies while trying to hide their own identity and prevent the infection from spreading across the globe.

EFFECTS HIGHLIGHTS

13:15 – A zombie is shot in the head.

14:45 – A man's throat is cut by a zombie.

15:00 – A zombie is shot in the chest.

32:00 – The top of a zombie's head is shot off.

32:00 – A zombie is shot in the head.

32:15 – A zombie is shot in the chest.

32:30 – A zombie's lower leg is shot off.

32:45 – A zombie is shot in the chest.

32:45 – A zombie is shot in the head.

35:30 – A zombie is shot in the chest.

35:30 – A zombie is shot in the chest.

36:00 – A zombie is shot in the chest.

40:45 – A man is stabbed in the stomach with a sword.

42:00 – A man is stabbed in the chest with a sword.

55:15 – A man is shot in the chest.

56:45 – A man is shot in the chest.

1:07:15 – A woman is shot in the forehead.

1:08:00 – A man is shot in the chest.

1:10:30 – Two zombies are shot in the chest.

1:11:00 – A zombie is shot in the chest.

1:20:45 – A zombie is stabbed in the chest.

1:21:15 – A zombie is stabbed in the chest.

1:21:45 – A zombie is shot multiple times in the chest.

DEADGIRL

Year: 2008   Length: 101 minutes
Directors: Marcel Sarmiento, Gadi Harel

STATISTICS

First Zombie:	14:00
First Human Death:	1:10:30
First Zombie Death:	N/A

Amount of Gore:	High
Gore Quality:	Very High
Zombie Effects:	High
Zombie Count:	Average
Zombie Death:	Very Low
Human Deaths:	Average

SUMMARY

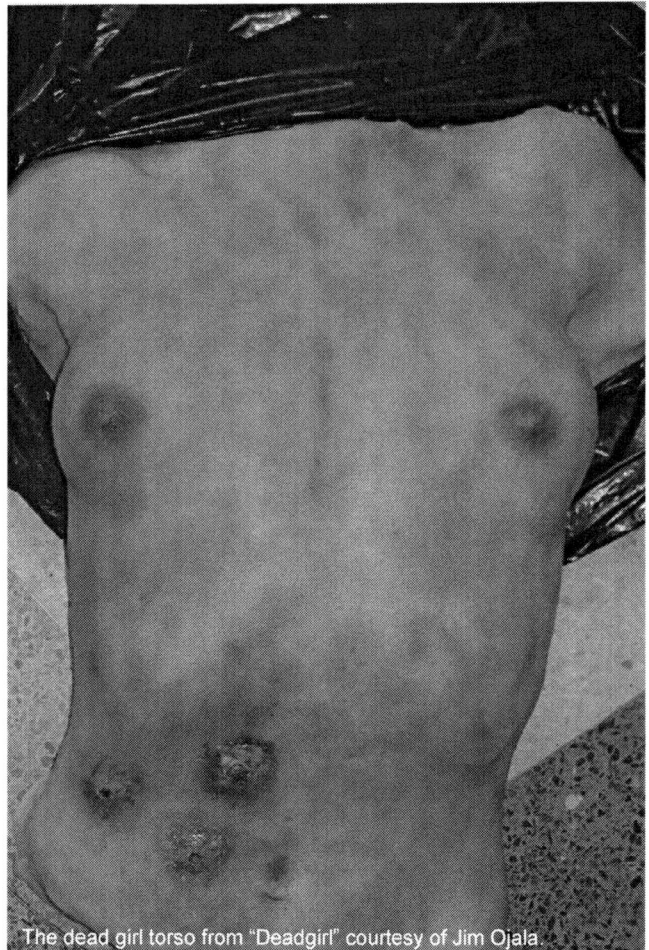

The dead girl torso from "Deadgirl" courtesy of Jim Ojala.

Two friends break into a deserted mental hospital and find the naked body of a woman on a gurney covered in plastic. All is not as it seems, as the door to the boiler room had been rusted shut for years. Things turn sour when one of the friends suggests they take sexual advantage of her. It doesn't take long for her lust for flesh to be revealed.

EFFECTS HIGHLIGHTS

49:00 – An infected wound leaks pus.

49:15 – A man inserts a finger into a gunshot wound on a zombie's torso.

1:00:45 – A zombie bites a man's penis.

1:08:30 – A zombie bites a chunk of flesh out of a dog.

1:10:30 – A man bleeds from his rectum.

1:10:30 – A man's intestines trail out of his rectum.

1:12:30 – A zombie bites a man's stomach.

1:16:45 – A woman is hit with a tire iron.

1:23:45 – A man clutches the stump of his arm.

1:29:15 – A woman has a bloody wound on her back.

1:29:30 – A man is missing the top part of his lip.

DEADLANDS: THE RISING

Year: 2006   Length: 72 minutes

Director: Gary Ugarek

STATISTICS

First Zombie: 21:15
First Human Death: 26:30
First Zombie Death: 26:00

Amount of Gore: Average
Gore Quality: High
Zombie Effects: Average
Zombie Count: Very High
Zombie Death: Low
Human Death: Low

SUMMARY

A biochemical weapon explosion causes the dead to come back to life. It is up to five survivors to make a stand against an ever growing army of zombies.

EFFECTS HIGHLIGHTS

26:30 – A group of zombies pull out a man's intestines.

29:30 – A zombie rips out a woman's throat.

31:30 – A woman finds a pile of intestines on the floor.

48:45 – A zombie digs its finger into a man's flesh.

48:45 – A zombie bites a chunk of flesh out of a man's neck.

49:00 – A group of zombies rip open a man's torso.

DEADLANDS 2: TRAPPED

Year: 2008   Length: 82 minutes
Director: Gary Ugarek

STATISTICS

First Zombie: 7:30
First Human Death: 40:30
First Zombie Death: 12:45

Amount of Gore: Low
Gore Quality: High
Zombie Effects: High
Zombie Count: Very High
Zombie Death: Very Low
Human Death: Low

SUMMARY

Six strangers are trapped inside a movie theater after the government tests nerve gas on the residents of a small town and brings an army of the dead back to life.

EFFECTS HIGHLIGHTS

22:30 – A man's torso is ripped open by a group of zombies.

38:00 – A zombie pulls the skin off of a man's face.

41:00 – A zombie tears into flesh.

41:00 – A zombie bites skin off of a man's face.

1:18:15 – A man has a bloody wound on his face.

DEATH METAL ZOMBIES

Year: 1995   Length: 90 minutes
Director: Todd Jason Cook

STATISTICS

First Zombie: 1:45
First Human Death: 2:15
First Zombie Death: 55:30

Amount of Gore: High
Gore Quality: Average
Zombie Effects: Average
Zombie Count: Very High
Zombie Deaths: Average
Human Deaths: Average

SUMMARY

When a music fan wins an album by the band "Living Corpse", he discovers that it has a hidden song on it called "Zombiefied", which turns its listeners into zombies.

EFFECTS HIGHLIGHTS

1:30 – A man's chest is crushed.

21:45 – A man is stabbed in the shoulder.

22:00 – A woman is bitten on the wrist.

34:45 – A man is impaled on a metal pole.

38:15 – A man sits on a knife.

39:00 – A zombie punches through a man's chest.

41:15 – A woman is stabbed in the chest.

42:15 – A zombie eats a dead woman's intestines.

45:45 – A woman finds a bloody skeleton.

58:30 – A woman is stabbed in the mouth.

1:06:45 – A zombie holds the blood stump after its hand is severed.

1:07:30 – A zombie is stabbed in the stomach.

1:07:30 – A zombie is stabbed in the stomach.

1:13:45 – A zombie's face melts.

DEATH VALLEY: THE REVENGE OF BLOODY BILL

Year: 2004   Length: 82 minutes
Director: Byron Werner

STATISTICS

First Zombie: 7:15
First Human Death: 8:30
First Zombie Death: 7:15

Amount of Gore: High
Gore Quality: Very High
Zombie Effects: High
Zombie Count: Very High

Zombie Deaths: High
Human Deaths: Average

SUMMARY

A group of college students stumble upon a small abandoned town called Sunset Valley, where they must fight a group of zombies led by a Confederate soldier seeking revenge for his grisly execution.

EFFECTS HIGHLIGHTS

7:15 – A zombie is shot in the head.

8:30 – A zombie rips out a man's throat.

23:30 – A zombie bites a man's arm.

27:30 – A zombie eats a piece of flesh.

28:00 – A zombie bites a woman's cheek.

33:15 – A woman is covered in blood.

37:15 – A zombie is shot in the head.

41:00 – A man's head is crushed.

43:15 – Close up of a bloody bite mark.

52:45 – A zombie rips out a man's organs.

53:15 – A zombie is shot in the head.

58:00 – A zombie bites off a man's fingers.

1:04:45 – A woman is stabbed in the stomach.

1:13:45 – A zombie is decapitated.

DEMON SLAUGHTER

Year: 2006   Length: 62 minutes
Director: Ryan Cavalline

STATISTICS

First Zombie: 2:15
First Human Death: 5:00
First Zombie Death: 39:30

Amount of Gore: High
Gore Quality: Average
Zombie Effects: Average
Zombie Count: Average
Zombie Deaths: Average
Human Deaths: Average

SUMMARY

A mobster flees into the woods to begin a new life as an normal citizen, but his plans are foiled when he realizes that he's being hunted by the walking dead.

EFFECTS HIGHLIGHTS

6:00 – A man is shot in the forehead.

7:15 – Close up of a bullet wound in a man's forehead.

35:00 – A severed head rolls across the floor.

44:00 – A zombie is missing an arm.

44:00 – An eyeball hangs out of an eye socket.

45:30 – A zombie has a gaping wound in its chest.

46:00 – Blood squirts out of a stump.

47:15 – Close up of a crushed head.

47:30 – A group of zombies eat a dead body.

49:00 – A zombie is cut with an axe.

DEVIL'S PLAYGROUND

Year: 2010   Length: 92 minutes
Director: Mark McQueen

STATISTICS

First Zombie: 15:30
First Human Death: 8:15
First Zombie Death: 16:30

Amount of Gore: High
Gore Quality: Very High
Zombie Effects: High
Zombie Count: Very High
Zombie Deaths: High
Human Deaths: High

SUMMARY

After 30,000 people test a new performance enhancing drug, an unexpected side effect turns all but one into blood thirsty zombies. A hardened mercenary sets out to find the lone unaffected woman and bring her back to safety.

EFFECTS HIGHLIGHTS

16:00 – A man is shot in the head.

16:15 – A zombie bites a man's neck.

16:30 – A zombie is shot repeatedly in the head.

17:00 – Close up of a bite wound on a hand.

19:30 – Various body parts are on the floor.

22:15 – A man is stabbed in the chest

23:00 – A man is shot in the head.

25:00 – A zombie bites a man's neck.

25:30 – A zombie bites a chunk of flesh off of a woman's neck.

38:30 – A zombie is impaled through the eye on a metal shard.

43:30 – A zombie bites a man's fingers

43:30 – A zombie is stabbed in the eye with a crowbar.

44:15 – A woman clutches a bloody wound on her neck.

45:15 – Close up of a bite wound on a man's wrist

45:45 – A man's fingers are cut off.

1:02:00 – A zombie hit in the head with a hammer.

1:18:30 – A woman has a piece of rebar impaled in her neck.

1:22:00 – A woman is shot in the leg.

1:23:30 – Close up of a bite wound on a man's face.

1:26:15 – A zombie is hit in the head with a pipe.

1:26:15 – A zombie is hit in the head with a hammer.

DIARY OF THE DEAD

Year: 20067   Length: 95 minutes
Director: George A. Romero

STATISTICS

First Zombie:	2:15
First Human Death:	2:45
First Zombie Death:	3:00
Amount of Gore:	Very High
Gore Quality:	Very High
Zombie Effects:	Very High
Zombie Count:	Very High
Zombie Deaths:	High
Human Deaths:	High

SUMMARY

A group of college filmmakers are shooting a low budget horror film in the woods when news of the dead rising breaks. They document the terrifying unfolding events as they desperately try to safely make it to a friend's mansion.

EFFECTS HIGHLIGHTS

2:30 – A zombie is shot repeatedly in the chest.

2:45 – A zombie is shot in the head.

2:45 – A woman is bitten in the face by a zombie.

20:30 – A woman has a gunshot wound on her cheek.

23:30 – A zombie is shot in the chest.

23:30 – A zombie is shot in the head.

24:00 – A zombie is shocked in the head by a defibrillator.

24:15 – A zombie is shot in the head.

27:30 – A zombie rolls off of a hospital bed and its intestines fall out onto the floor.

30:00 – A man is bitten on the arm.

30:00 – A zombie is stabbed in the chest with an IV pole.

30:30 – A zombie is stabbed in the head with an IV pole.

30:15 – A zombie is shot in the head.

34:00 – A zombie hangs from noose beneath a bridge.

35:45 – A group of zombies are blown up with dynamite.

36:30 – A zombie's nose is pulled off.

36:45 – A zombie bites off a man's ear.

38:15 – A zombie is shot in the head.

38:15 – A zombie is stabbed in the back with a scythe.

38:30 – A zombie is shot in the head.

39:00 – A man stabs himself in the face with a scythe, killing a zombie standing behind him.

50:45 – A glass container of hydrochloric acid is smashed on a zombie's head.

59:15 – A zombie is shot in the head with an arrow.

59:30 – A zombie is eating a severed hand.

1:05:45 – A zombie bites a man's neck.

1:06:00 – A zombie is shot in the head.

1:06:00 – A zombie is shot in the head.

1:06:30 – A man is shot in the chest.

1:22:15 – A zombie's head is cut in two.

1:23:00 – A man is shot in the head.

1:26:30 – A zombie is shot in the head.

DIE AND LET LIVE

Year: 2006   Length: 74 minutes
Director: Justin Channell

STATISTICS

First Zombie:	:45
First Human Death:	35:30
First Zombie Death:	1:30
Amount of Gore:	High
Gore Quality:	High
Zombie Effects:	High
Zombie Count:	Very High
Zombie Deaths:	Low
Human Deaths:	High

SUMMARY

A party is interrupted by the escaped flesh-hungry test subjects of a secret experimental virus that revives the dead.

EFFECTS HIGHLIGHTS

1:30 – A zombie is shot in the head.

3:45 – A zombie bites a chunk of flesh out of a woman's neck.

9:30 – A zombie bites a woman's neck.

29:30 – A zombie bites a chunk of flesh out of a woman's neck.

29:30 – A zombie bites a woman's arm.

30:15 – A zombie bites a man's arm.

35:15 – A zombie bites a chunk of flesh out of a man's neck.

35:15 – A zombie bites a man's leg.

35:30 – A zombie bites a man's neck.

40:30 – A zombie bites a chunk of flesh out of a man's arm.

47:45 – Two zombies rip open a man's stomach.

49:45 – A severed arm is thrown to the floor.

1:04:30 – A zombie bites a piece of flesh off of a woman's face.

1:05:00 – A zombie bites a chunk of flesh out of a woman's arm.

1:05:15 – Blood pours out of a wound on a woman's

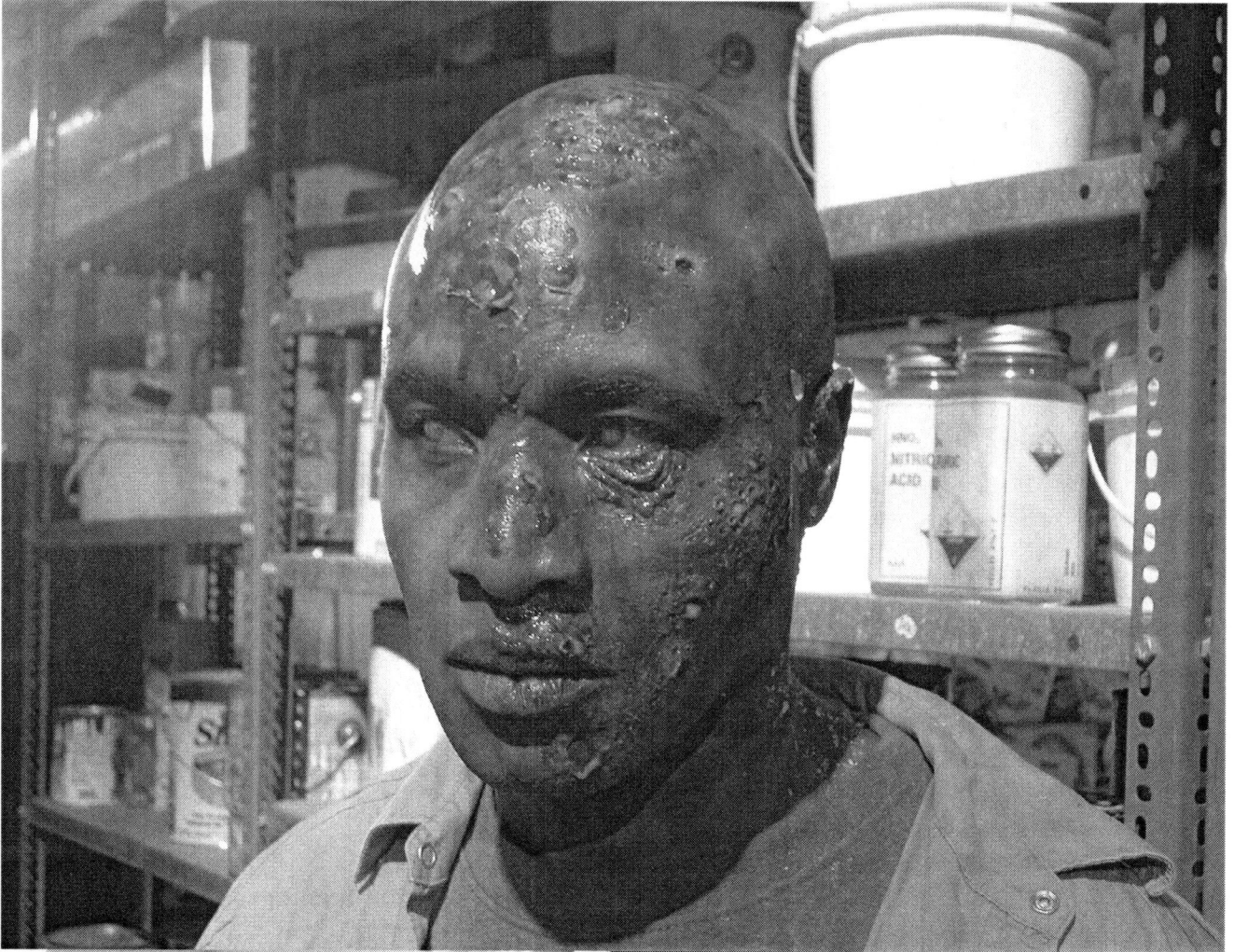

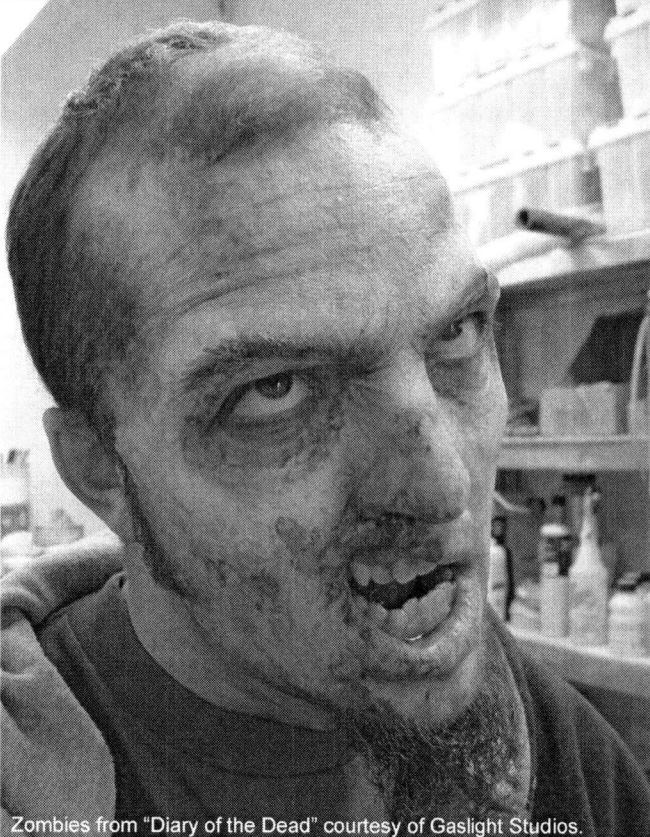

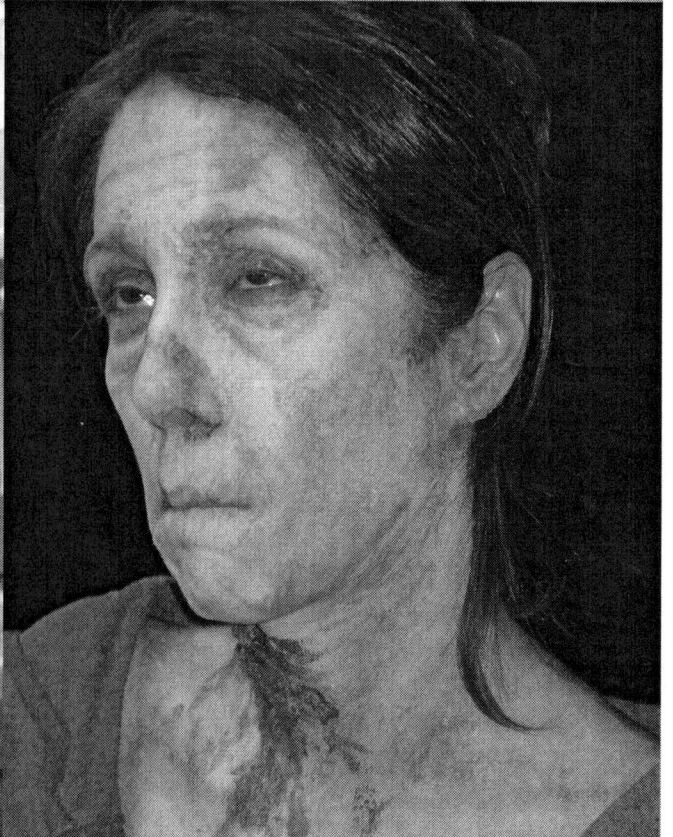

Zombies from "Diary of the Dead" courtesy of Gaslight Studios.

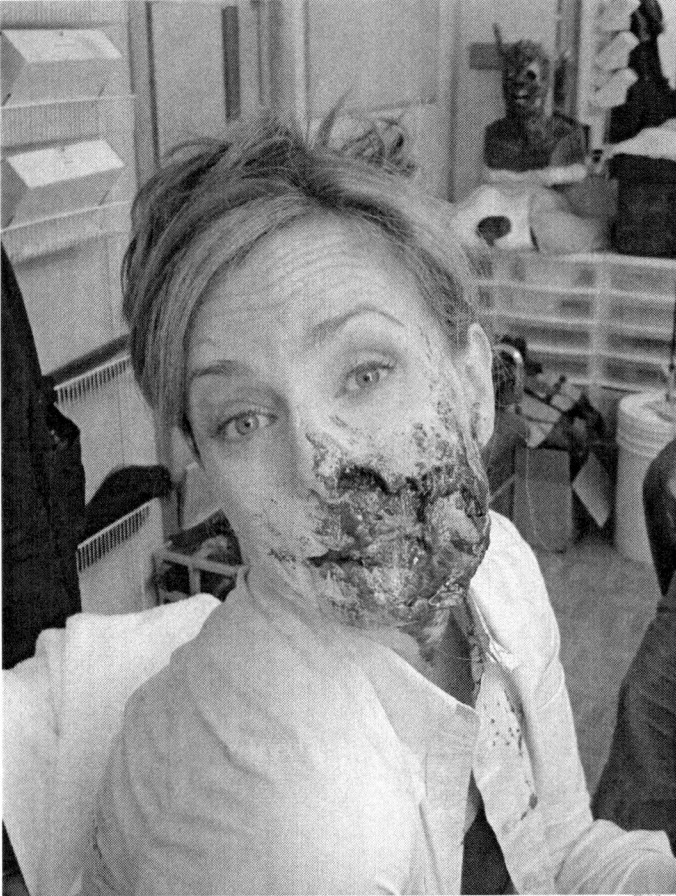

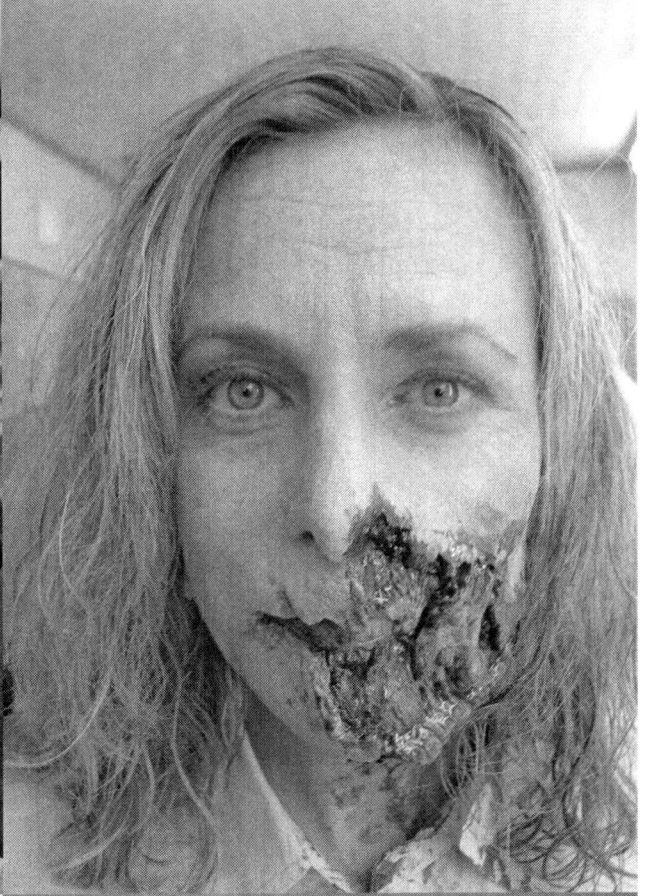

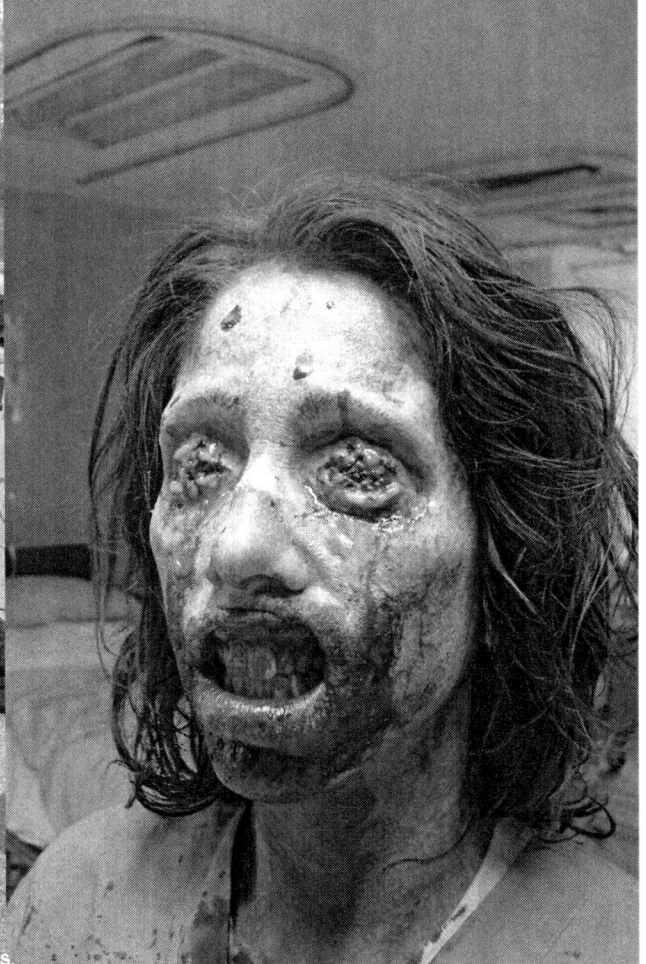

Zombies and victim from "Diary of the Dead" courtesy of Gaslight Studios.

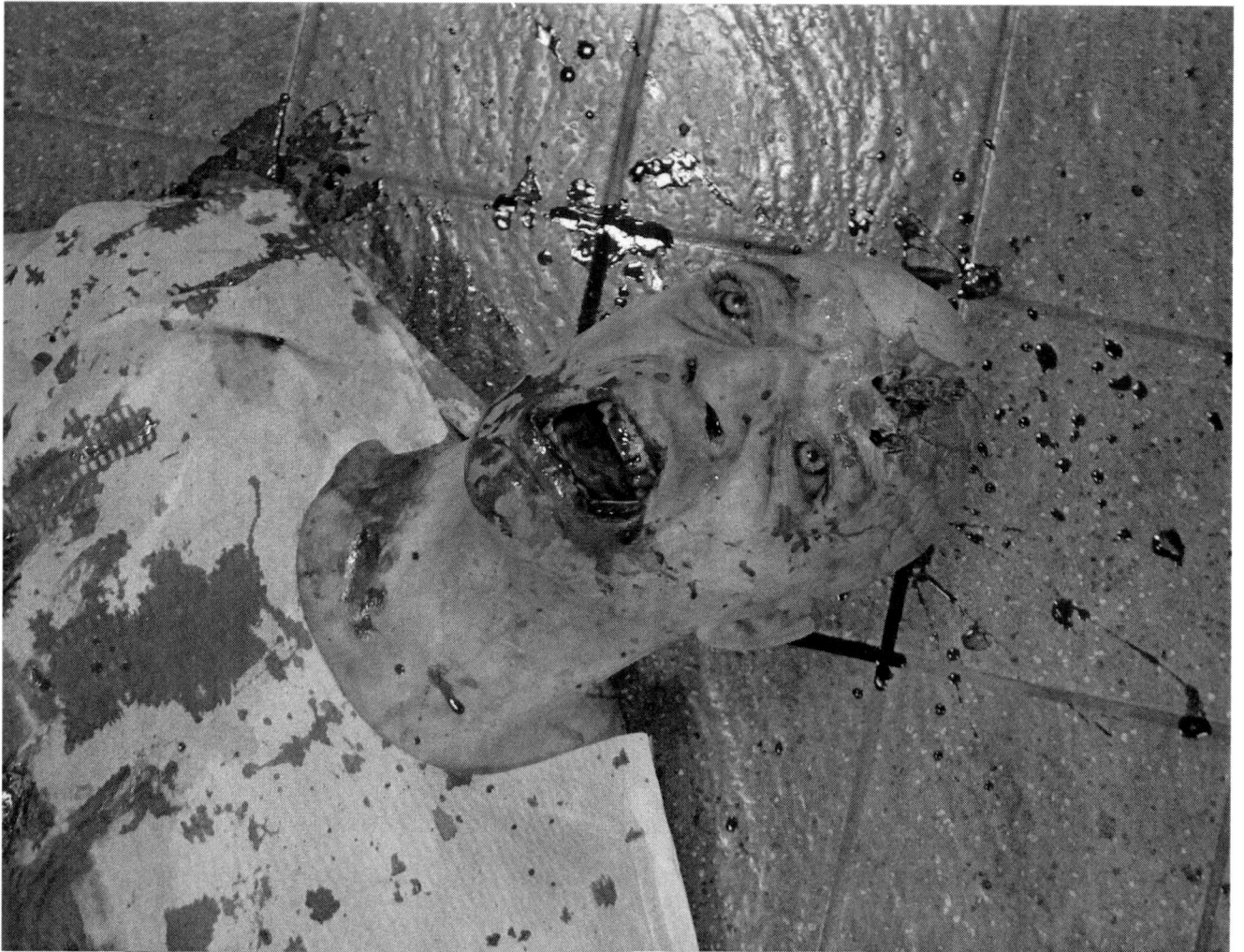

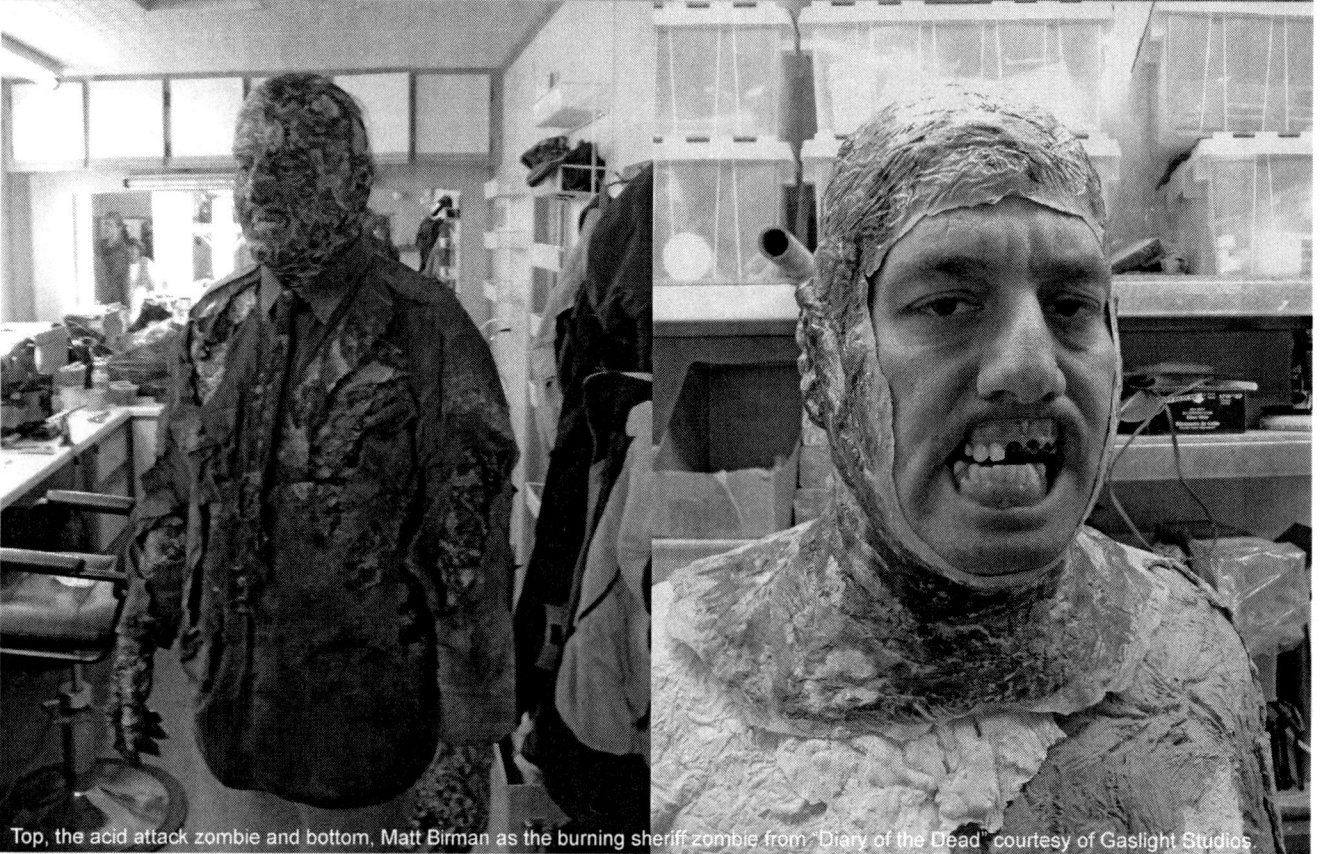

Top, the acid attack zombie and bottom, Matt Birman as the burning sheriff zombie from "Diary of the Dead" courtesy of Gaslight Studios.

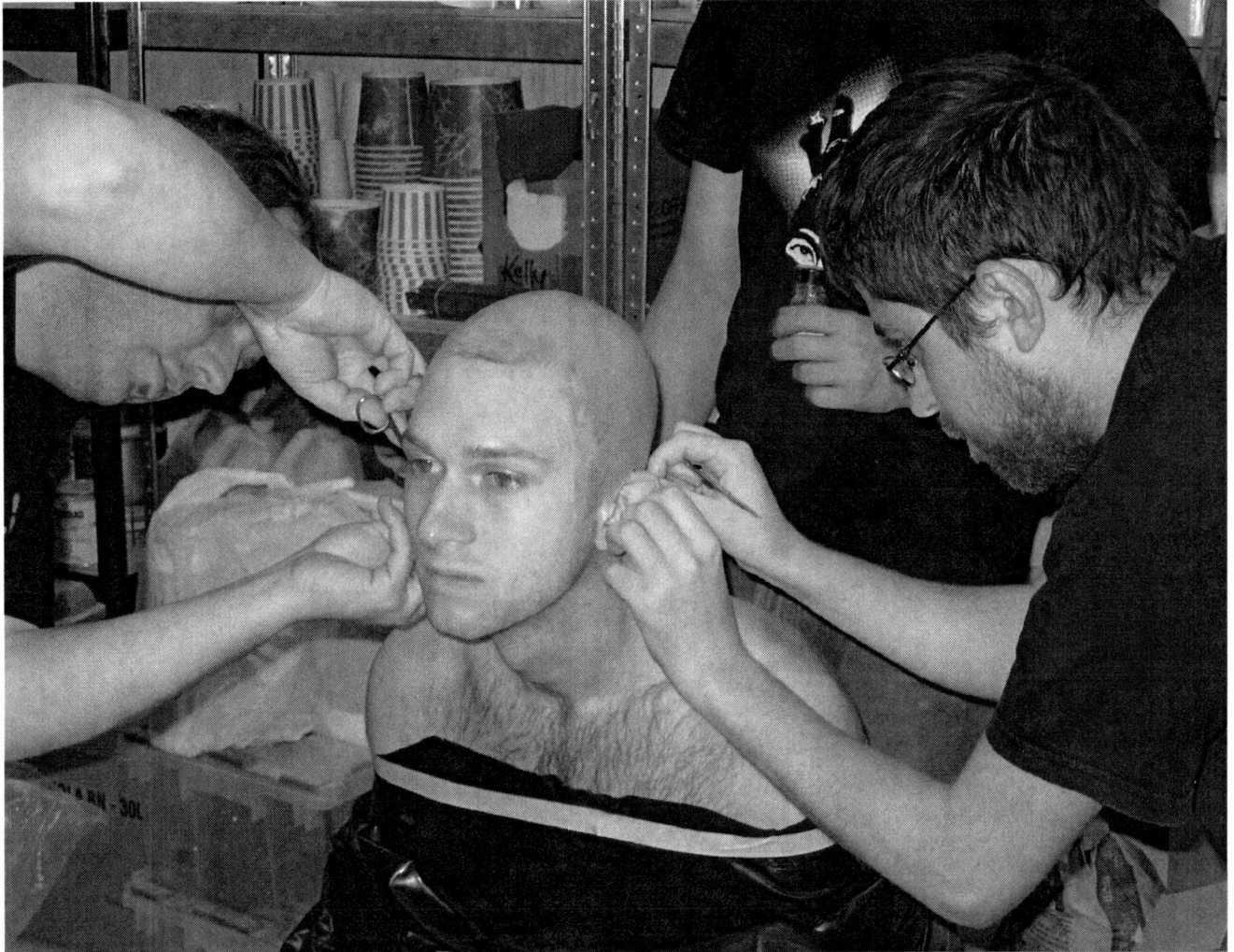

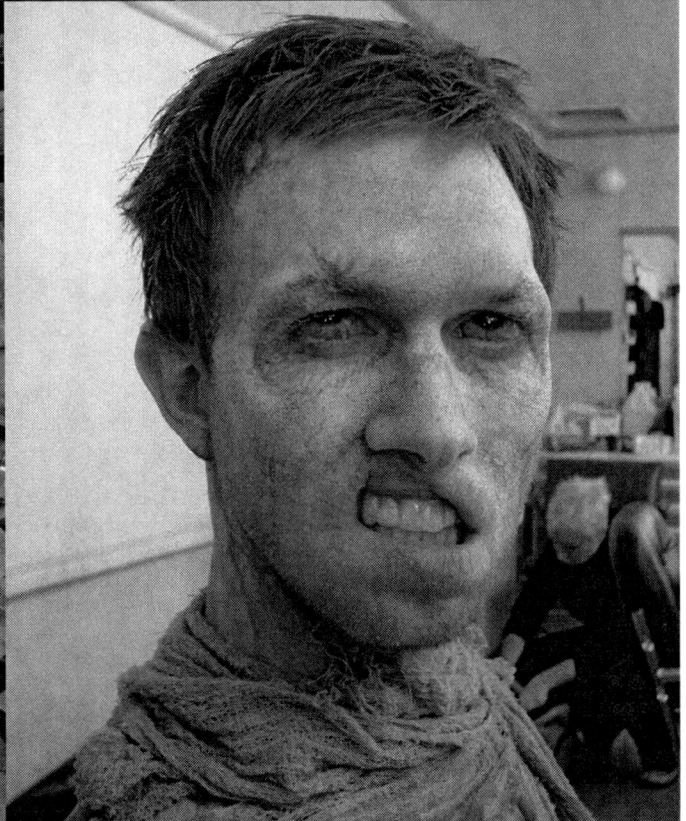

Top, Kyle Glencross and Neil Morrill make up Philip Riccio. Bottom, Riccio in makeup for "Diary of the Dead" courtesy of Gaslight Studios.

neck.

1:05:30 – Two zombies bite a chunk of flesh out of a man's neck.

1:07:15 – A zombie bites a chunk of flesh out of a man's arm.

DIE YOU ZOMBIE BASTARDS!

Year: 2005   Length: 97 minutes
Director: Caleb Emerson

STATISTICS

First Zombie:	18:00
First Human Death:	4:30
First Zombie Death:	44:15
Amount of Gore:	High
Gore Quality:	High
Zombie Effects:	Average
Zombie Count:	High
Zombie Deaths:	Average
Human Deaths:	Average

SUMMARY

After his wife is kidnapped, a good-hearted serial killer sets out to reclaim the woman he loves.

EFFECTS HIGHLIGHTS

4:30 – A man is decapitated with a scythe.

4:45 – Two men are decapitated with a scythe.

10:15 – A woman opens a box filled with body parts.

10:30 – A man and woman eat a piece of flesh.

11:30 – A man pulls a blanket of human flesh out of a bag.

13:15 – A man holds a severed arm.

21:45 – A man and woman eat a severed head.

24:15 – A man rips of a zombie's genitals.

54:15 – A man punches a hole in a zombie's back and pulls out its organs.

1:05:30 – A man bites off a zombie's fingers.

1:05:30 – A zombie's head explodes.

1:29:00 – A man is missing his legs.

1:29:45 – A zombie's face melts.

1:34:00 – A man eats from a severed head.

DIE ZOMBIELAGER

Year: 2005   Length: 85 minutes
Director: Jonas Wolcher

STATISTICS

First Zombie:	2:45
First Human Death:	1:30

First Zombie Death:	3:45
Amount of Gore:	Very High
Gore Quality:	High
Zombie Effects:	High
Zombie Count:	Very High
Zombie Deaths:	Very High
Human Deaths:	Average

SUMMARY

Sweden has been overrun by an army of the living dead. The police are powerless and a team of zombie hunters are called in to solve the problem and help clean up the city.

EFFECTS HIGHLIGHTS

1:30 – Blood sprays across a shower wall.

3:45 – A zombie is shot in the shoulder.

4:15 – A zombie is shot in the head.

18:45 – A man's torso is cut with a blade.

19:45 – Skin is sliced off of a man's face.

21:45 – A zombie eats a dead woman's arm.

29:15 – A zombie eats a dead woman's arm.

29:30 – A zombie eats a piece of flesh.

29:45 – A zombie eats a piece of flesh.

33:15 – A zombie is shot in the chest.

38:15 – A zombie is shot in the chest.

41:45 – A zombie bites a chunk of flesh off of a woman's neck.

43:15 – A zombie is stabbed in the head with a pen.

48:45 – A zombie is shot in the torso.

49:15 – A zombie is shot in the chest.

50:45 – A zombie is shot in the head.

58:15 – A zombie picks at a bloody wound on its stomach.

1:00:45 – A zombie is shot in the leg.

1:01:45 – A zombie is shot in the back.

1:01:45 – A second zombie is shot in the back.

1:02:15 – A zombie is shot in the chest.

1:03:15 – A zombie is shot in the arm.

1:04:00 – A zombie is shot in the stomach.

1:04:30 – A zombie is shot in the stomach.

1:05:00 – A zombie is shot in the chest.

1:05:45 – A zombie eats its own entrails.

1:06:30 – A zombie eats a dead zombie's entrails.

DIENER

Year: 2010   Length: 76 minutes
Director: Patrick Horvath

STATISTICS

First Zombie:	23:00
First Human Death:	6:15
First Zombie Death:	53:15

Amount of Gore: Average
Gore Quality: High
Zombie Effects: High
Zombie Count: Average
Zombie Death: Low
Human Deaths: Average

SUMMARY

After a roaming serial killer kills a waitress and a cook at a deserted diner, they refuse to stay dead and reanimate to torment the serial killer and hapless customers who visit the diner.

EFFECTS HIGHLIGHTS

6:00 – A man is stabbed in the back with a knife.

24:45 – A zombie bites a man on the neck.

38:15 – A man hammers a nail into a zombie's head.

45:00 – A man's fingers are cut with a knife.

53:15 – A zombie is decapitated.

1:07:00 – A zombie is shot in the chest.

1:07:45 – A zombie's throat is cut with a machete.

1:09:00 – A woman is shot in the shoulder.

1:09:45 – A zombie bites a man's neck.

1:11:30 – A man is torn apart by a group of zombies.

DOGHOUSE

Year: 2009   Length: 89 minutes
Director: Jake West

STATISTICS

First Zombie: 22:00
First Human Death: 25:00
First Zombie Death: 35:45

Amount of Gore: High
Gore Quality: Very High
Zombie Effects: Very High
Zombie Count: Very High
Zombie Deaths: Average
Human Deaths: Average

SUMMARY

Trying to cheer up a recently dumped colleague, a group of men travel to a remote English village. When they get there, they find that the only inhabitants are a bunch of female, men-hating zombies. The retreat soon becomes a fight for their lives as they try to escape the village.

EFFECTS HIGHLIGHTS

20:00 – Close up of a severed hand.

22:00 – Body parts are scattered across a backyard.

22:00 – A zombie is eating a piece of flesh.

23:30 – A man is stabbed through the hand with a knife.

25:00 – The bloodied body of a man is pinned to a fence.

26:30 – A zombie cuts a man's head in half with an axe.

33:30 – A man's leg is cut with an axe.

35:30 – A zombie is hit in the mouth with a golf ball.

35:45 – A zombie is decapitated with a sword.

38:30 – A zombie is shot in the head.

42:15 – A zombie cuts off a man's finger.

45:30 – A zombie eats a severed head.

47:00 – A zombie is cutting up body parts.

53:30 – A man stabs a zombie in the head.

1:02:30 – A man is stabbed in the chest with a sword.

1:03:45 – A zombie is stabbed with a sword.

1:05:45 – A zombie's eyeballs are hanging out of its sockets.

1:11:45 – A man is repeatedly stabbed in the chest with a pair of scissors.

1:12:15 – A man is stabbed with a bottle.

1:15:30 – A zombie is hit by a bus.

DOOMED

Year: 2007   Length: 96 minutes
Director: Michael Su

STATISTICS

First Zombie: 14:30
First Human Death: 8:30
First Zombie Death: 15:15

Amount of Gore: High
Gore Quality: High
Zombie Effects: High
Zombie Count: Very High
Zombie Deaths: Average
Human Deaths: Average

SUMMARY

On a new television reality show, a group of dangerous convicted felons are placed on a remote island to compete for a $50 million jackpot and their freedom. However, they soon find out they are not alone on the island and find themselves in a struggle to survive against the island undead inhabitants.

EFFECTS HIGHLIGHTS

8:00 – A man is cut on the back with a knife.

8:15 – A man is stabbed in the chest.

34:45 – A zombie is stabbed in the neck.

39:45 – A zombie is stabbed in the side of its chest.

40:00 – A zombie is shot in the head.

42:30 – A zombie is shot in the head.

43:00 – A zombie is shot in the head.

45:45 – A zombie is shot in the head with an arrow.

1:00:30 – A zombie is stabbed in the back with a sword.

1:04:00 – A woman cuts a zombie on the chest with a sword.

1:04:30 – A zombie is stabbed with a sword.

1:04:30 – A man cuts a zombie's throat.

1:09:00 – A zombie is stabbed in the chest.

DORM OF THE DEAD

Year: 2006   Length: 75 minutes
Director: Donald Farmer

STATISTICS

First Zombie:	2:15
First Human Death:	5:00
First Zombie Death:	39:30
Amount of Gore:	Average
Gore Quality:	Low
Zombie Effects:	Low
Zombie Count:	High
Zombie Deaths:	Average
Human Deaths:	Average

SUMMARY

During a zombie attack, two stuck up college girls try to ensure a mutual enemy is converted to the ranks of the undead.

EFFECTS HIGHLIGHTS

4:15 – A zombie bites a chunk of flesh out of a man's shoulder.

16:30 – A group of zombies are eating a dead body.

20:30 – A zombie eats a piece of flesh.

39:30 – A zombie is shot in the head.

40:00 – A zombie rips off a man's arm.

45:15 – A zombie eats a piece of flesh.

59:15 – A zombie eats a piece of meat.

1:04:30 – A zombie is shot in the head.

EATERS: RISE OF THE DEAD

Year: 2011   Length: 94 minutes
Directors: Luca Boni, Marco Ristori

STATISTICS

First Zombie:	4:30
First Human Death:	1:18:30
First Zombie Death:	16:45
Amount of Gore:	Very High
Gore Quality:	Very High
Zombie Effects:	Very High
Zombie Count:	Very High
Zombie Deaths:	High
Human Deaths:	Average

SUMMARY

The entire planet has been devastated by the Great Epidemic. A deadly plague has left no corner untouched and has set loose a horde of the undead. Three men try to find an answer to what has happened to the human race.

EFFECTS HIGHLIGHTS

4:30 – A man operates on a zombie's face.

15:30 – A zombie is shot in the chest.

16:45 – A zombie is shot in the face.

21:30 – A zombie eats its own intestines.

22:30 – A zombie is shot in the head.

25:15 – A zombie is shot in the head.

28:30 – Close up of a severed head.

30:15 – A man cuts up a dead body.

33:15 – A zombie is decapitated.

36:15 – A zombie is cut in half by a truck.

36:30 – A zombie is shot in the head.

43:15 – A zombie is shot in the leg.

43:15 – A zombie is shot in the head.

43:15 – Close up of a dead zombie.

43:30 – A zombie bites a man's neck.

43:45 – A zombie claws at a bloody wound on its neck.

48:15 – A couple mop up a pile of blood and guts.

49:15 – A man vomits.

51:30 – A man injects himself in the arm.

54:00 – A zombie is shot in the head.

55:15 – Close up of a bloodied dead body.

59:15 – A zombie is stabbed in the head with a machete.

59:15 – A man pulls a machete out of a zombie's head.

1:06:15 – A zombie is shot in the head.

1:06:45 – A zombie is shot in the head.

1:07:00 – A zombie is shot in the throat.

1:07:00 – A zombie is shot in the head with an arrow.

1:07:15 – A zombie is hit in the head with an axe.

1:08:00 – A zombie is shot in the head.

1:09:00 – A zombie is shot in the head.

1:11:45 – Close up of a bloodied dead body.

1:15:00 – A man draws a scalpel across his arm.

1:18:30 – A man's head is bashed in with a statue.

1:19:00 – A zombie is shot in the head.

1:19:00 – A zombie is shot in the chest.

1:19:00 – A zombie is shot in the head.

1:19:15 – A zombie is shot in the head.

1:20:15 – A zombie is shot in the head.

1:20:30 – A zombie is shot in the leg.

1:24:30 – A man picks up a severed hand.

1:25:00 – A man injects a syringe into a zombie's stomach.

1:25:45 – A man is shot in the head.

EDGES OF DARKNESS

Year: 2009   Length: 87 minutes
Directors: Blaine Cade, Jason Horton

STATISTICS

First Zombie:	1:00
First Human Death:	1:45
First Zombie Death:	1:09:45

Amount of Gore:	High
Gore Quality:	Very High
Zombie Effects:	High
Zombie Count:	Very High
Zombie Deaths:	Average
Human Deaths:	High

SUMMARY

Three stories follow survivors as they adjust to life among the living dead. A girl captured by vampires discovers a way to fight back, a writer uses a disturbing energy source to power his computer and a mercenary protects a boy who harbors a whole new kind of evil.

EFFECTS HIGHLIGHTS

1:30 – A zombie eats a piece of meat.

1:45 – A group of zombies tear flesh off of a man.

2:45 – Zombies tear a body apart.

3:15 – Zombies pull the organs out of a dead bodies.

3:30 – A zombie chews on a severed arm.

4:30 – A zombie chews on a piece of flesh.

57:15 – A woman bites another woman's arm.

1:09:45 – A zombie is shot in the head.

1:10:15 – A zombie is stabbed in the head with an axe.

1:16:30 – A zombie is hit in the head with a bowling ball.

1:18:45 – A woman is stabbed in the stomach.

1:19:30 – A woman is hit in the head repeatedly with a lamp.

ELECTRIC ZOMBIES

Year: 2006   Length: 90 minutes
Director: John Specht

STATISTICS

First Zombie:	N/A
First Human Death:	30:30
First Zombie Death:	N/A

Amount of Gore:	Low
Gore Quality:	Average
Zombie Effects:	Very Low
Zombie Count:	Very Low
Zombie Death:	Very Low
Human Deaths:	High

SUMMARY

A government plot to thwart the country's enemies using top secret transmission technology goes awry when cell phone signals turn users into zombies.

EFFECTS HIGHLIGHTS

10:45 – A man is repeatedly stabbed with a screwdriver.

30:45 – Close up of a bullet wound on a man's forehead.

54:30 – Close up of wounds on a man's arm and face.

55:15 – A man's penis falls off.

EROTIC NIGHTS OF THE LIVING DEAD

Alternate Title: Sexy Nights of the Living Dead Year: 1980   Length: 104 minutes
Director: Joe D'Amato

STATISTICS

First Zombie:	12:00
First Human Death:	12:45
First Zombie Death:	1:25:15

Amount of Gore:	High
Gore Quality:	High
Zombie Effects:	High
Zombie Count:	Very High
Zombie Deaths:	Average
Human Deaths:	Average

SUMMARY

A callous American hotel developer purchases a cursed island where the businessman wants to build a resort. However, when he arrives, the living dead start to rise from their graves.

EFFECTS HIGHLIGHTS

12:45 – A zombie bites a chunk of flesh out of a man's neck.

29:00 – A dead body is crawling with maggots.

29:45 – A zombie bites a man's neck

1:24:30 – A man jams his fingers into a zombie's eyes.

1:24:45 – A zombie stabbed in the chest.

1:25:15 – A zombie is decapitated.

1:26:45 – A woman bites off a man's penis.

1:28:00 – A group of zombies eat a dead body.

1:34:00 – A zombie is shot in the head.

1:36:45 – A zombie is shot in the head.

1:37:00 – A zombie is shot in the head.

1:37:15 – A zombie is shot in the face.

EVIL

Alternate Title: To Kako
Year: 2005   Length: 83 minutes
Director: Yorgos Noussias

STATISTICS

First Zombie:	9:15
First Human Death:	11:45
First Zombie Death:	23:45

Amount of Gore:	Very High
Gore Quality:	Very High
Zombie Effects:	High
Zombie Count:	Very High
Zombie Deaths:	High
Human Deaths:	Average

SUMMARY

A cab driver and a teenager lead a group of survivors against a horde of the living dead that have taken over Athens.

EFFECTS HIGHLIGHTS

11:45 – A zombie bites a woman's neck.

16:00 – A zombie pulls off a man's arm.

16:15 – A group of zombies tear open a man's stomach.

17:00 – Intestines fall out of a zombie's stomach.

23:45 – A man rips off a zombie's arm.

36:00 – A zombie is shot in the head.

42:15 – A dead woman is hanging on a butcher's hook.

42:45 – A zombie is stabbed in the chest.

43:15 – A zombie is decapitated.

43:30 – A zombie is stabbed in the stomach.

44:00 – A zombie is decapitated.

44:00 – A zombie is stabbed in the stomach.

44:15 – A zombie is stabbed in the foot.

44:15 – A zombie is stabbed in the eye.

44:30 – A zombie is stabbed in the head with an axe handle.

45:00 – A man punches his fist through a zombie's chest.

45:15 – A zombie is decapitated.

45:30 – A zombie's head is crushed.

45:45 – A zombie is stabbed in the back.

46:15 – A zombie is stabbed in the throat.

46:30 – A man jams his thumbs into a zombie's eyes.

46:45 – A zombie is shot in the head.

47:00 – A legless zombie crawls across the floor.

47:00 – A zombie's head is cut in half.

56:00 – A zombie is hit by a car.

56:45 – A dead body has most of its face missing.

57:45 – A zombie is shot in the chest.

1:02:15 – A zombie is stabbed in the eye with a shoe.

1:09:15 – A woman is shot in the head.

1:10:15 – A zombie is shot in the mouth.

1:11:15 – A zombie is stabbed in the back.

1:12:00 – A woman rips out a zombie's intestines.

1:12:45 – A zombie is decapitated.

EVIL 2: IN THE TIME OF HEROES

Alternate Title: To Kako 2
Year: 2009   Length: 88 minutes
Director: Yorgos Noussias

STATISTICS

First Zombie:	3:00
First Human Death:	4:45
First Zombie Death:	3:30

Amount of Gore:	Very High
Gore Quality:	High
Zombie Effects:	High
Zombie Count:	Very High
Zombie Deaths:	Very High
Human Deaths:	High

SUMMARY

Alternating between ancient and modern-day Greece, a young warrior and his taxi driver friend attempt to control and use their newly acquired special powers to defeat hordes of flesh-eating zombies.

EFFECTS HIGHLIGHTS

3:00 – A man's throat is slit.

3:30 – A zombie is decapitated.

3:30 – A man is stabbed in the chest.

4:00 – A zombie is stabbed in the chest.

8:30 – A zombie is hit by a car.

13:15 – A man is shot in the head.

24:45 – A zombie is shot in the head.

25:45 – A woman is shot in the head.

28:45 – A man is decapitated.

37:15 – A zombie is decapitated.

40:15 – A zombie is shot in the head.

40:30 – A zombie bites a man on the neck.

40:45 – A man stomps on a zombie's head.

41:00 – A zombie is sliced across the stomach.

41:00 – A zombie is stabbed in the head.

41:15 – A zombie is stabbed in the head.

41:30 – A zombie is shot in the head.

41:30 – A zombie is shot in the head.

41:30 – A zombie bites a man on the neck.

41:30 – A zombie is decapitated.

49:45 – A zombie bites a man on the arm.

51:30 – A zombie is decapitated.

53:30 – A woman is shot in the head.

59:00 – A man is shot in the neck.

59:00 – A man's arm is broken.

1:13:15 – A zombie is stabbed in the chest.

1:13:30 – A man punches his fist through a zombie's head.

1:13:30 – A man stomps on a zombie's head.

1:14:00 – A zombie is decapitated.

1:14:00 – A zombie is decapitated.

1:14:15 – A zombie's head is cut in two.

1:15:00 – A zombie is disemboweled with a sword.

1:15:00 – A zombie bites a woman's arm.

1:15:15 – A zombie bites a man's shoulder.

1:15:30 – A boomerang decapitates multiple zombies.

1:18:00 – A man rips out a zombie's intestines.

1:18:15 – A zombie is decapitated.

THE EVIL DEAD

Year: 1981   Length: 85 minutes
Director: Sam Raimi

STATISTICS

First Zombie:	36:30
First Human Death:	36:15
First Zombie Death:	1:19:30
Amount of Gore:	High
Gore Quality:	High
Zombie Effects:	Average
Zombie Count:	Average
Zombie Deaths:	Average
Human Deaths:	Low

SUMMARY

A group of friends travel to a remote cabin in the woods, where they unknowingly release evil demons.

EFFECTS HIGHLIGHTS

36:45 – A zombie stabs a woman in the ankle with a pencil.

43:30 – A zombie scratches a man's face.

45:00 – A man cuts a zombie's hand off.

45:30 – A zombie bites its hand off.

47:30 – A man cuts a zombie's hand off with an axe.

47:30 – A man cuts a zombie's leg off with an axe.

58:45 – A man is stabbed in the arm.

59:45 – A zombie is impaled on a knife.

1:06:15 – A zombie is decapitated.

1:08:15 – A zombie is shot in the chest.

1:16:15 – A zombie is shot in the face.

1:16:45 – A man jams his thumbs into a zombie's eye sockets.

1:20:45 – An arm bursts through a zombie's chest.

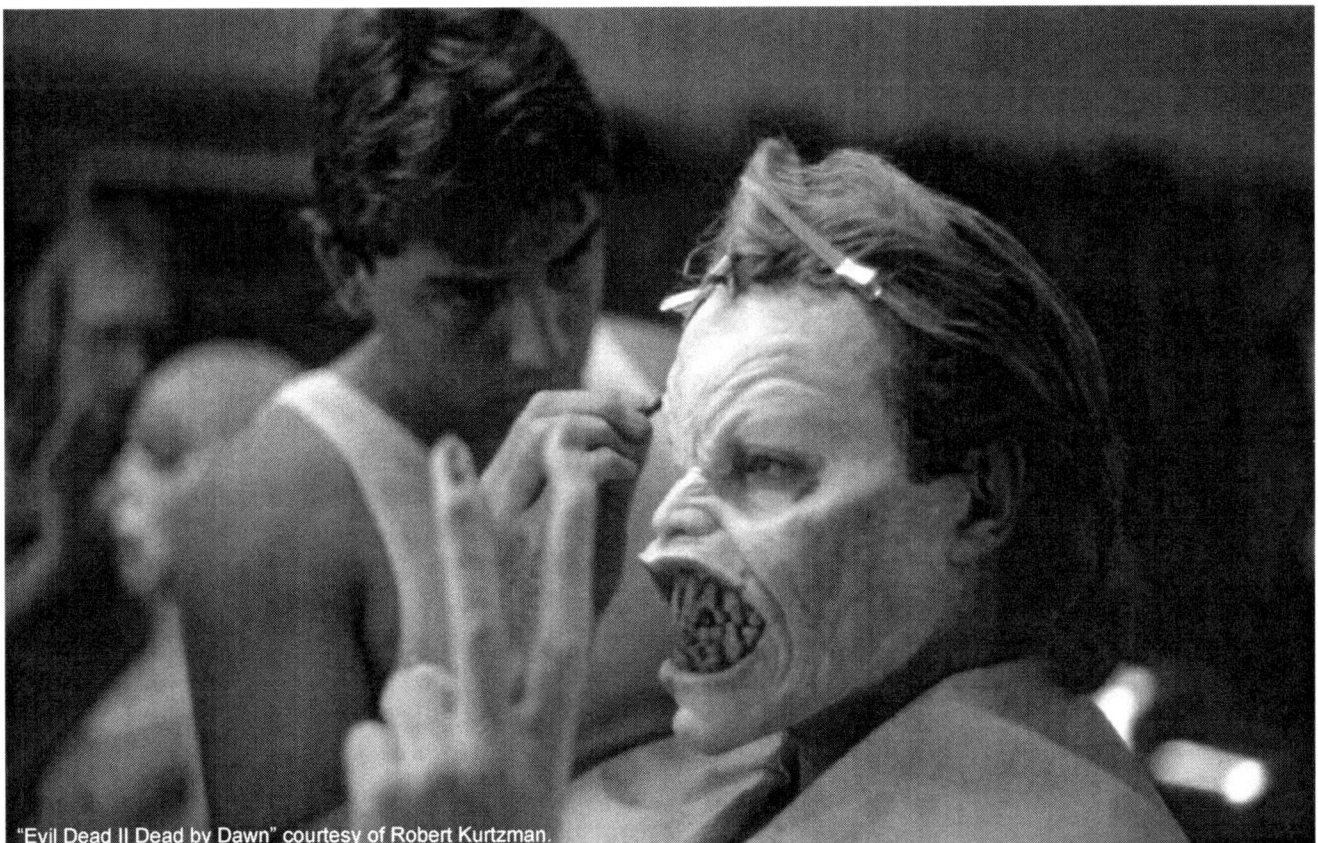

"Evil Dead II Dead by Dawn" courtesy of Robert Kurtzman.

1:20:45 – An arm bursts through a zombie's back.

EVIL DEAD II: DEAD BY DAWN

Year: 1987   Length: 84 minutes
Director: Sam Raimi

STATISTICS

First Zombie: 6:00
First Human Death: N/A
First Zombie Death: 45:30

Amount of Gore: Average
Gore Quality: High
Zombie Effects: Average
Zombie Count: Average
Zombie Deaths: Low
Human Deaths: Very Low

SUMMARY

The lone survivor of the previous demon attacks hides out in a cabin with a group of strangers while more demons continue their attack.

EFFECTS HIGHLIGHTS

6:15 – A zombie is decapitated.

18:45 – A zombie's head falls off.

21:00 – A zombie cuts itself with a chainsaw.

30:00 – A man stabs himself in the hand.

31:30 – Close up of a severed hand.

41:45 – A woman swallows an eyeball.

51:45 – A woman holds a severed hand.

1:00:30 – A man is stabbed in the stomach.

1:13:15 – A zombie's arm is cut off with a chainsaw.

1:13:30 – A zombie is shot in the head.

EXHUMED

Year: 2003   Length: 87 minutes
Director: Brian Clement

STATISTICS

First Zombie: :45
First Human Death: 19:00
First Zombie Death: 9:30

Amount of Gore: High
Gore Quality: High
Zombie Effects: High
Zombie Count: Average
Zombie Deaths: Average
Human Deaths: Average

SUMMARY

Three stories spanning centuries of individuals given the power to raise the dead, The first is set in feudal Japan where two men fight the living dead. The second is in 1940's USA where a detective is probing a rash of grave robbing's and finally, a post-apocalyptic future finds vampires and werewolves facing off.

EFFECTS HIGHLIGHTS

9:30 – A man is bitten on the leg.

9:30 – A zombie is stabbed in the head with a sword.

13:45 – Close up of a bite wound on a man's leg.

17:00 – A zombie's hand is cut off.

17:30 – A man cuts a zombie's throat.

19:00 – A man is cut in half with a sword.

51:30 – A zombie is shot in the chest.

57:00 – A zombie's head is smashed against the floor.

58:30 – A zombie is cut with a chainsaw.

58:45 – A zombie is cut with a chainsaw.

1:02:45 – A man's head is smashed against the wall.

1:03:30 – A man is shot in the head.

1:03:45 – A man's face is ripped off.

FEEDING THE MASSES

Year: 2004   Length: 74 minutes
Director: Richard Griffin

STATISTICS

First Zombie: 4:30
First Human Death: 11:15
First Zombie Death: 5:00

Amount of Gore: Low
Gore Quality: High
Zombie Effects: High
Zombie Count: Very High
Zombie Deaths: Average
Human Deaths: High

SUMMARY

A small group of news reporters and their military escort set out to expose the truth about a zombie outbreak that the government is trying to silence.

EFFECTS HIGHLIGHTS

11:15 – A woman has a bloody wound on her neck.

32:45 – A zombie bites a dead body's neck.

46:15 – A zombie bites a chunk of flesh out of a woman's neck.

FIDO

Year: 2006   Length: 91 minutes
Director: Andrew Currie

STATISTICS

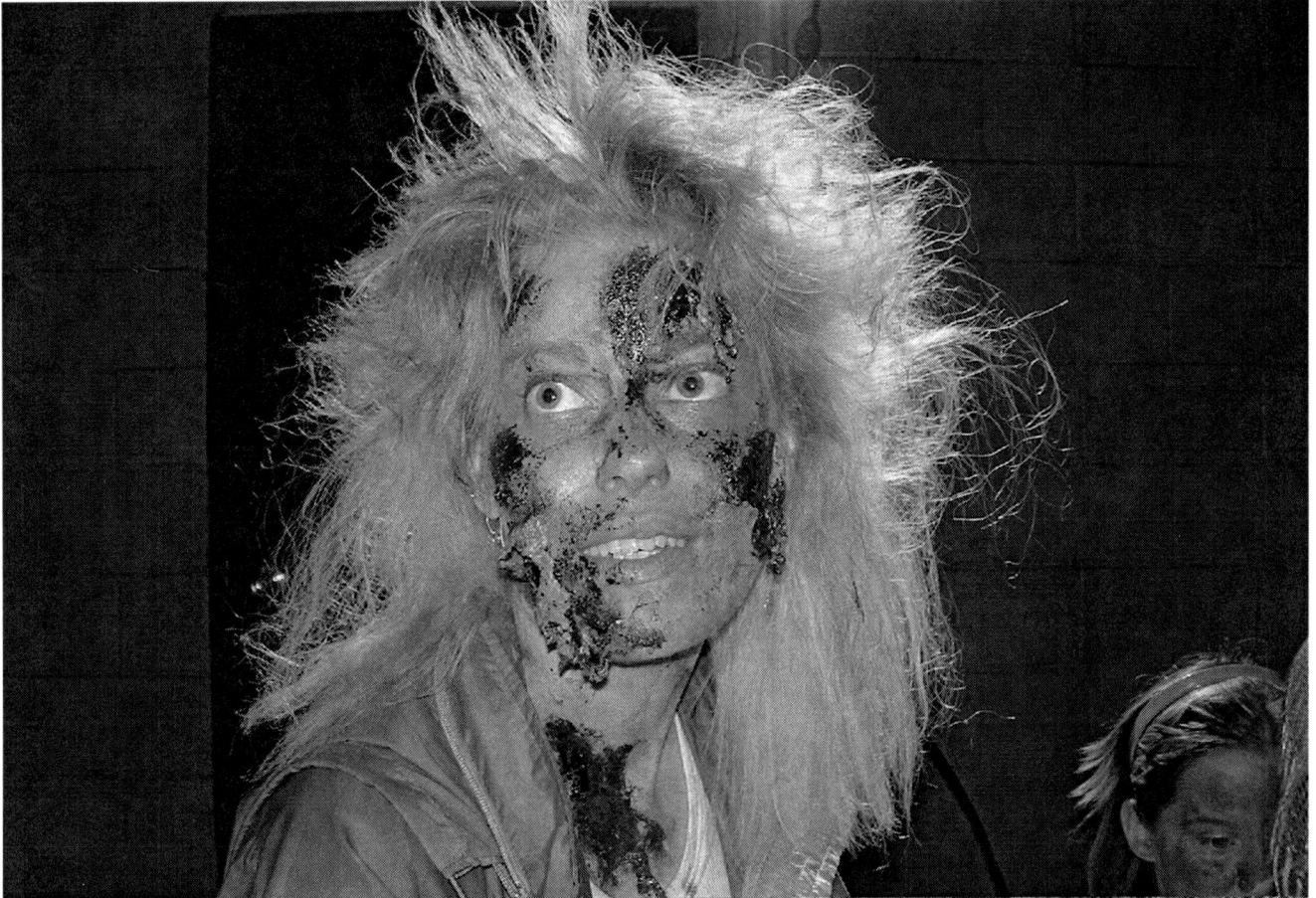

A zombie and victim from "Feeding the Masses" courtesy of Don Lamelin.

Funeral zombie extras on the set of 'Fido' courtesy of Charles F. Gray.

A ZomCon van and zombie extras on the set of "Fido" courtesy of Charles F. Gray.

Zombie extras on the set of "Fido" courtesy of Charles F. Gray.

92

DOMESTIC SECURITY

Z9 31

A5 ZOMCON D7

THE SAFEST PLACE IS HERE

C7 50

A5 WILLARD D7

Embossed characters

C7 50

Z9 31

Number Sequences are start guides - if more are needed
than specified continue with higher numbers

ZomCon license plate designs from "Fido" courtesy of Andrew Currie.

93

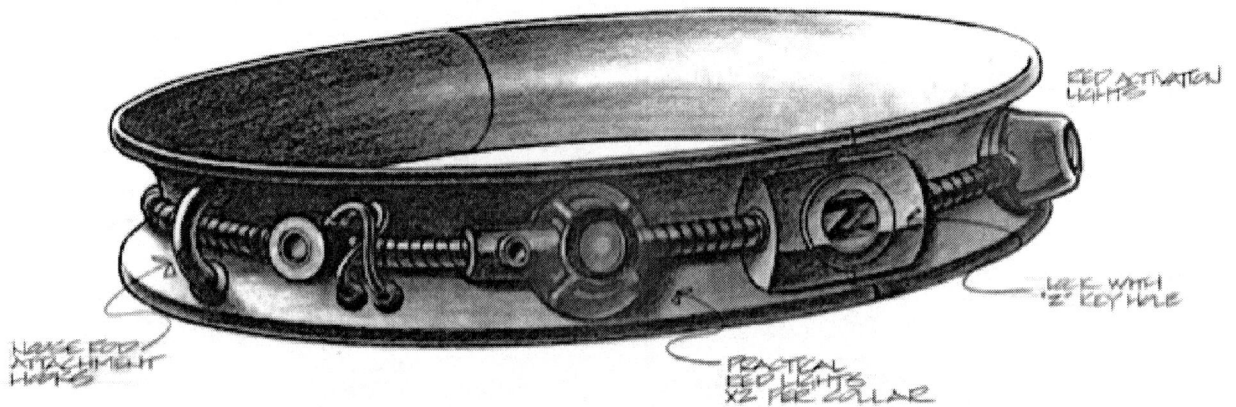

ZomCon propaganda and production sketch from "Fido" courtesy of Andrew Currie.

First Zombie:	5:00
First Human Death:	29:30
First Zombie Death:	17:00
Amount of Gore:	Very High
Gore Quality:	Very High
Zombie Effects:	High
Zombie Count:	Very High
Zombie Deaths:	High
Human Deaths:	High

SUMMARY

A young boy's best friend in the whole world is a six foot tall and rotting zombie named Fido. When Timmy is captured and held captive by two bullies, it is up to Fido to rescue him.

EFFECTS HIGHLIGHTS

:30 – A zombie eats a chunk of flesh.

1:00 – A man sticks a metal probe into a zombie's forehead.

23:15 – A zombie is eating a severed limb.

23:15 – Close up of a dead body with a severed arm.

31:45 – A zombie bites off a man's ear.

32:45 – A severed arm lies on the ground.

33:15 – A zombie's head is cut off.

51:00 – A zombie is shot in the chest.

53:30 – A zombie is shot in the head.

56:00 – A zombie is run over.

1:17:30 – A zombie is shot in the head.

1:22:30 – A man is shot in the chest.

1:22:45 – A man is bitten on the neck.

1:23:00 – Three zombies are shot in the head in quick succession.

1:23:15 – A zombie pulls out a man's intestines.

1:23:30 – A zombie is shot in the head.

1:24:15 – A zombie is shot in the head.

FISTFUL OF BRAINS

Year: 2008   Length: 90 minutes
Director: Christine Parker

STATISTICS

First Zombie:	26:15
First Human Death:	29:45
First Zombie Death:	1:18:30
Amount of Gore:	Very High
Gore Quality:	High
Zombie Effects:	High
Zombie Count:	Very High
Zombie Deaths:	Average
Human Deaths:	Average

SUMMARY

In the late 1800s, the small town of Shadowhawk is targeted by a mysterious man selling the townsfolk a potion claiming to offer immortality. Instead the potion turns them into zombies, forced to join his ever growing army of the undead.

EFFECTS HIGHLIGHTS

26:30 – A man picks up a severed hand.

40:00 – A zombie pulls a man's heart out of his chest.

40:00 – A zombie rips out a man's intestines.

42:30 – Blood seeps out of a wound on a zombie's arm.

43:30 – A zombie pulls a chunk of flesh off of a man's chest.

44:00 – A zombie bites a piece of flesh off of a woman's chest.

45:00 – The flesh on a zombie's leg is missing.

48:15 – A zombie bites a piece of flesh out of a man's neck.

48:30 – A zombie eats a chunk of flesh.

48:30 – A zombie pulls off a man's head.

51:30 – A zombie pulls flesh off of a woman's chest.

52:00 – A zombie has a severed breast in its mouth.

1:07:00 – A group of zombies are eating various body parts.

1:10:00 – A man is shot in the chest.

1:15:30 – A group of zombies tear open a man's torso.

1:18:30 – A zombie's head is pulled off.

1:19:30 – A zombie eats a brain scattered across the floor.

1:19:30 – A group of zombies are eating body parts.

1:20:00 – A zombie is shot in the head.

1:23:15 – A zombie is decapitated.

FLESH FREAKS

Year: 2000   Length: 79 minutes
Director: Conall Pendergast

STATISTICS

First Zombie:	16:45
First Human Death:	2:15
First Zombie Death:	44:45
Amount of Gore:	High
Gore Quality:	Very High
Zombie Effects:	High
Zombie Count:	High
Zombie Deaths:	High
Human Deaths:	Average

SUMMARY

Deep within the jungles of Central America scientists experiment with a parasite that feasts on corpses and then reanimates them as flesh-eating zombies.

EFFECTS HIGHLIGHTS

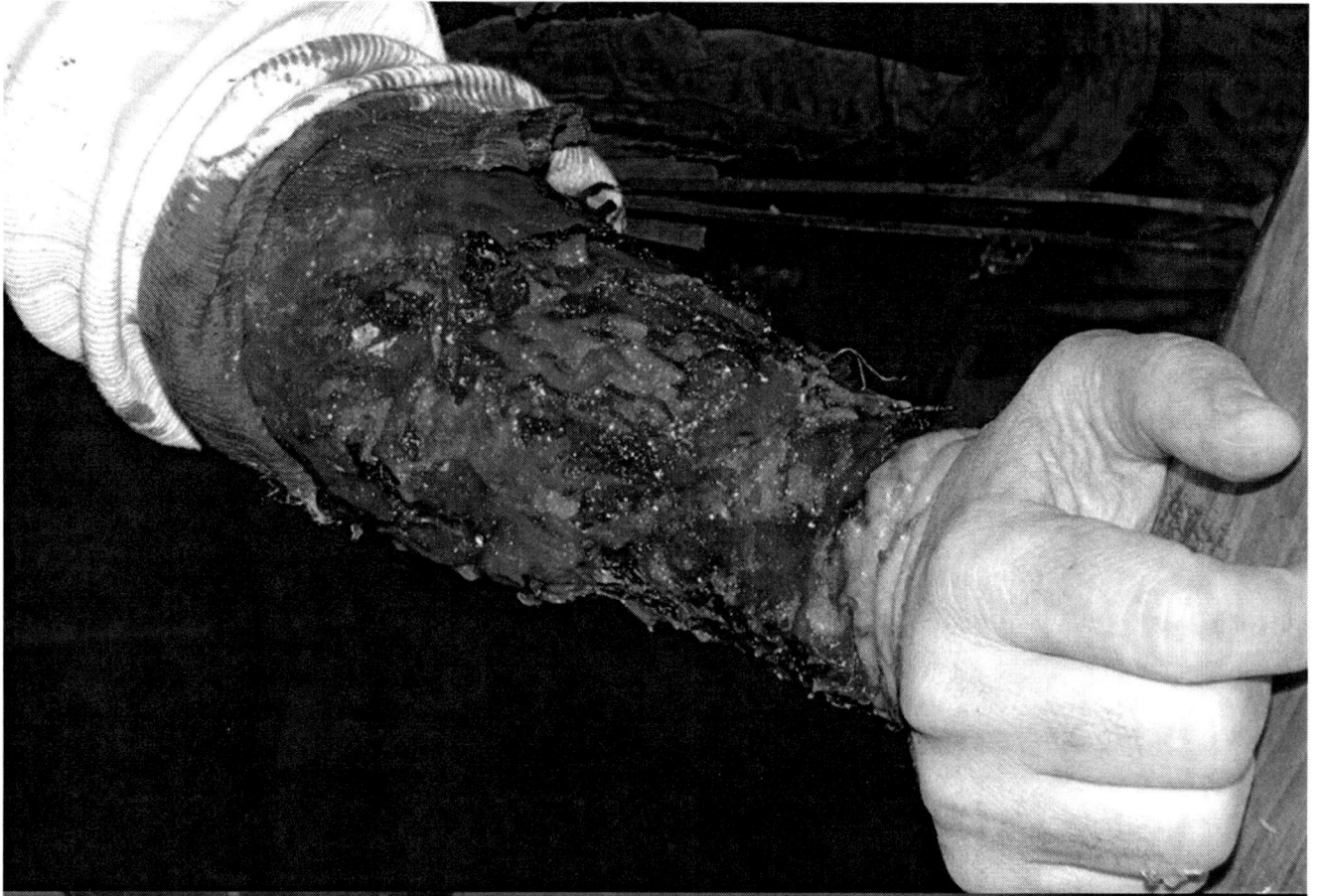

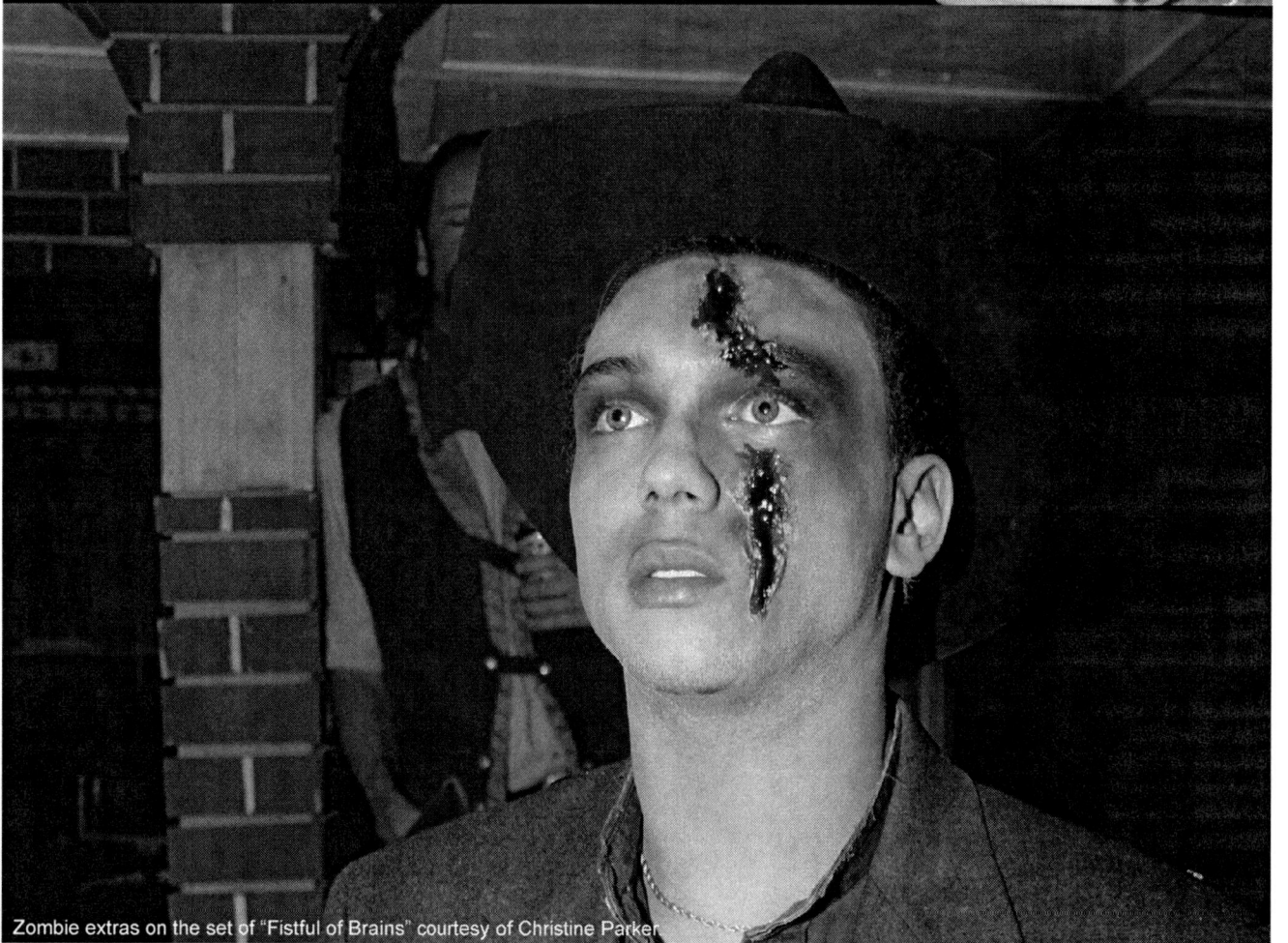

Zombie extras on the set of "Fistful of Brains" courtesy of Christine Parker.

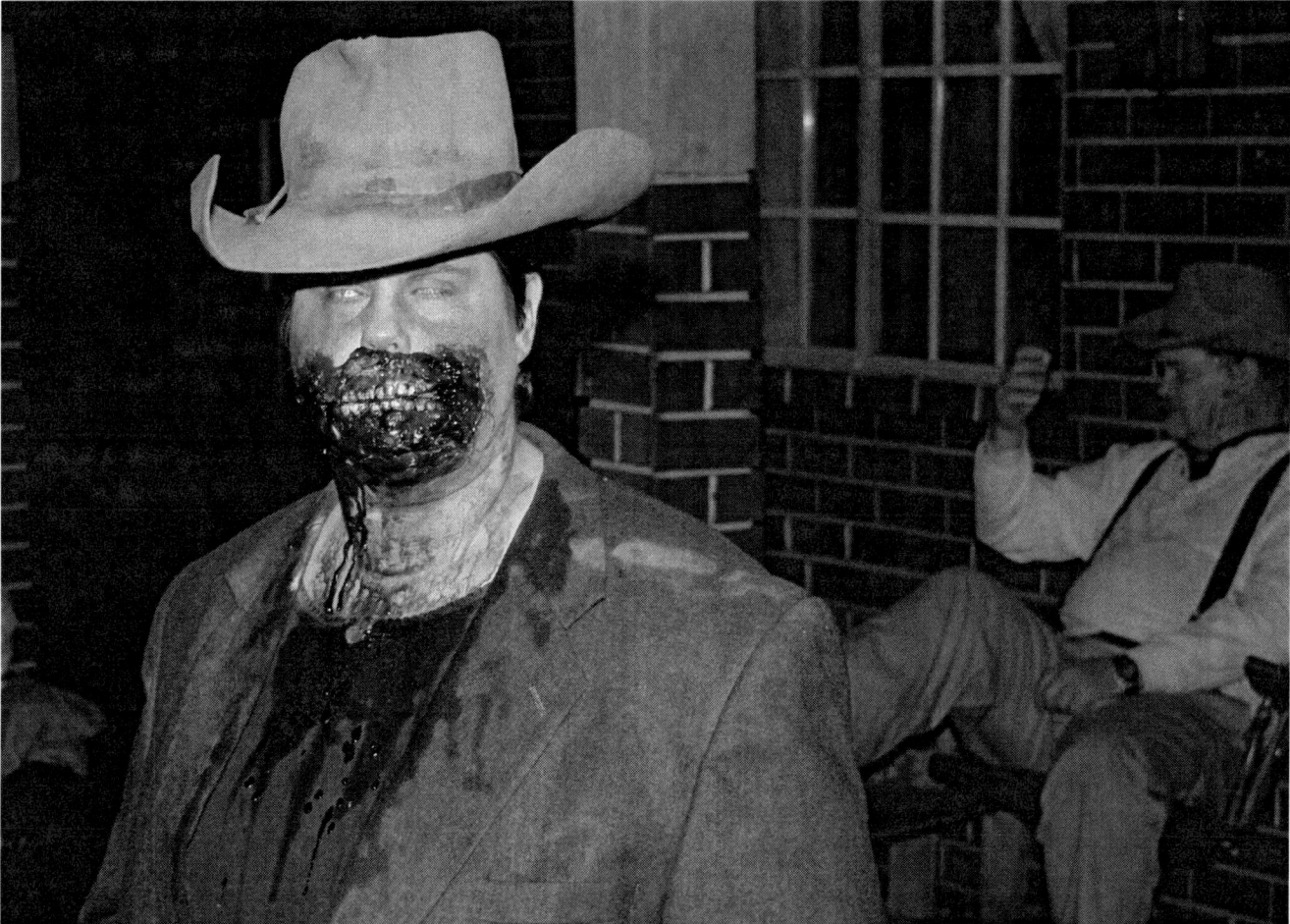

2:45 – Close up of a pile of body parts.

17:00 – A zombie slices a man's hand with a scalpel.

44:00 – A zombie slices a woman's hand with a scalpel.

44:30 – A zombie is hit with the blades of an oscillating fan, spraying blood everywhere.

49:45 – A woman finds a bloody dead body.

50:45 – A woman stabs a zombie in the eye with a stick.

1:01:00 – A man is stabbed in the hand with a nail.

1:02:15 – A man is stabbed in the head with a nail.

1:04:30 – A zombie is stabbed in the head with a broom handle.

1:05:15 – A zombie rips a man's heart out of his chest.

1:06:30 – A zombie is stabbed in the head with a nail.

1:07:15 – A zombie is stabbed in the head with a nail.

1:09:45 – A zombie is stabbed in the head with a crowbar.

1:11:00 – A zombie is stabbed in the head with a pair of scissors.

1:11:15 – A zombie is stabbed in the head with a piece of metal.

1:13:30 – A man is stabbed in the head with a pair of scissors.

1:14:45 – A zombie is stabbed with a pair of scissors.

FLESHEATER

Year: 1988   Length: 88 minutes
Director: S. William Hinzman

STATISTICS

First Zombie:	9:00
First Human Death:	9:00
First Zombie Death:	33:45

Amount of Gore:	High
Gore Quality:	High
Zombie Effects:	High
Zombie Count:	High
Zombie Deaths:	Very High
Human Deaths:	High

SUMMARY

A group of college students on a Halloween hayride stumble across a group of flesh-eating zombies. They are soon fighting for their lives as they try to escape and warn the authorities.

EFFECTS HIGHLIGHTS

9:00 – A man bleeds from a neck wound.

15:00 – A zombie is stabbed in the arm with a pitch fork.

15:15 – A man is stabbed in the chest with a pitch fork.

15:45 – A zombie pulls a woman's organs out of her stomach.

22:00 – A zombie bites a chunk of flesh out of a woman's neck.

33:45 – A zombie is shot in the head.

34:15 – A man's head is cut with an axe.

45:45 – A zombie is shot in the shoulder.

46:00 – A zombie is shot in the head.

46:00 – A zombie is shot in the head.

46:45 – A zombie is shot in the head.

48:15 – Entrails spill out of a dead body.

1:02:15 – A zombie bites a chunk of flesh out of a man's neck.

1:03:30 – A woman is stabbed in the leg with a hook.

1:04:45 – A zombie punches its hand through a woman's chest.

1:10:45 – A zombie is shot in the head.

1:11:15 – A zombie is shot in the head.

1:11:30 – A zombie is shot in the head.

1:14:00 – A zombie eats from a dead body.

1:14:15 – A zombie is shot in the head.

1:14:45 – A zombie is shot in the chest.

1:18:45 – A woman is shot in the head.

1:18:45 – A man is shot in the head.

FLIGHT OF THE LIVING DEAD

Year: 2007   Length: 89 minutes
Director: Scott Thomas

STATISTICS

First Zombie:	19:15
First Human Death:	19:00
First Zombie Death:	48:45

Amount of Gore:	High
Gore Quality:	Very High
Zombie Effects:	Very High
Zombie Count:	Very High
Zombie Deaths:	Very High
Human Death:	High

SUMMARY

A transatlantic flight from Los Angeles to Paris is carrying the dead body of an infected scientist. After the plane hits major turbulence, the body is set free from its coffin and the flesh-eating monster sets off on rampage. Before long, the entire flight is filled with the living dead.

EFFECTS HIGHLIGHTS

13:30 – A broken bone sticks out of a man's leg.

19:00 – A woman is shot in the chest.

48:30 – A woman is shot in the side of her torso.

51:30 – A zombie bites a woman's neck.

55:00 – Close up of a bite wound on a woman's arm.

1:04:00 – A woman's legs are chewed off.

1:05:45 – A zombie chews on a severed arm.

1:08:45 – A zombie is shot in the head.

1:08:45 – A zombie is shot in the head.

1:09:30 – A zombie bites a chunk of flesh out of a woman's neck.

1:11:45 – A zombie is shot in the head.

1:13:45 – A zombie is shot in the head.

1:20:15 – A zombie is shot in the head.

1:20:15 – A zombie is decapitated.

1:21:45 – A zombie's skin has been burned off.

1:22:00 – A zombie is stabbed in the head with an umbrella.

1:24:00 – A zombie is sucked into a plane's engines

1:24:30 – A zombie is shot in the head.

1:28:30 – A zombie is shot in the chest.

1:28:30 – A zombie is shot in the head.

1:30:15 – A zombie is missing its legs.

FOREST OF THE DEAD

Year: 2007   Length: 79 minutes
Director: Brian Singleton

STATISTICS

First Zombie: 54:30
First Human Death: 36:00
First Zombie Death: 58:00

Amount of Gore: High
Gore Quality: High
Zombie Effects: Average
Zombie Count: Average
Zombie Deaths: Average
Human Deaths: Average

SUMMARY

A group of friends go on a camping trip and split into two groups. One group is turned into flesh-eating monsters and the other takes cover in the darkness and plans their escape.

EFFECTS HIGHLIGHTS

36:00 – A man's head is ripped off.

49:30 – A woman falls and cuts her arm.

55:00 – Two zombies pull a man in half.

55:15 – A zombie pulls intestines out of a torso.

57:45 – A zombie is eating a piece of flesh.

58:00 – A zombie is stabbed in the mouth with a stick.

58:00 – A zombie is eating a piece of flesh.

59:15 – A man is bitten on the neck.

59:15 – A zombie is stabbed in the eye with a stick.

59:30 – A zombie's head is crushed with a rock.

59:45 – A zombie pulls the skin off of a man's face.

1:01:45 – A zombie rips the skin off of a man's chest.

1:02:15 – A zombie is eating a piece of flesh.

1:02:30 – A zombie's face is cut with a machete.

1:02:45 – A woman cuts a zombie's arms off.

1:02:45 – A woman cuts off a zombie's head.

1:03:00 – A woman decapitates a zombie

1:06:45 – A zombie eats a dead body.

1:07:00 – A zombie is stabbed in the neck with a pitchfork.

THE FOREVER DEAD

Year: 2007   Length: 102 minutes
Director: Christine Parker

STATISTICS

First Zombie: 17:15
First Human Death: 20:00
First Zombie Death: 51:30

Amount of Gore: Very High
Gore Quality: High
Zombie Effects: Average
Zombie Count: Very High
Zombie Deaths: Average
Human Deaths: Average

SUMMARY

A diseased laboratory rabbit escapes and turns the residents of a local community into zombies. A group of survivors struggle to stat alive and deal with their own inner demons. Some of which are more frightening than the zombies they are trying to avoid.

EFFECTS HIGHLIGHTS

8:30 – A rabbit bites a man's face.

11:30 – A rabbit bites a man's ankle.

17:15 – A zombie bites a man's neck.

19:45 – A woman stabs a zombie in the eye.

20:00 – A zombie pulls off a woman's scalp.

22:15 – A zombie is shot in the head.

28:00 – A zombie bites a woman's lip off.

28:30 – A zombie eats a piece of flesh.

29:30 – A zombie spits blood in a woman's face.

35:00 – A man accidentally stabs himself in the stomach with a branch.

39:45 – A group of zombies eat a dead body.

42:30 – A zombie bites a man's neck.

43:15 – A zombie bites a chunk of flesh out of a man's neck.

45:30 – A man's torso is ripped apart by a group of zombies.

51:00 – A man jams his thumbs into a zombie's eyes.

51:30 – A man stabs a zombie in the head with a shovel.

56:00 – A zombie eats a piece of flesh.

1:17:45 – A man peels off a zombie's scalp.

1:18:00 – A man pulls out a zombie's brain.

1:30:45 – A zombie eats a severed arm.

1:34:15 – A group of zombies rip open a man's chest.

1:34:30 – A zombie bites off a man's tongue.

1:35:30 – Zombies tear a dead body apart.

1:37:30 – A rabbit is crushed with a rock.

GANGS OF THE DEAD

Year: 2007   Length: 88 minutes
Director: Duane Stinnett

STATISTICS

First Zombie:	13:15
First Human Death:	2:45
First Zombie Death:	20:15

Amount of Gore:	Average
Gore Quality:	Very High
Zombie Effects:	High
Zombie Count:	Very High
Zombie Deaths:	High
Human Deaths:	High

SUMMARY

When two rival Los Angeles gangs meet at an abandoned downtown warehouse, they find the place crawling with zombies. Along with an undercover cop, the gangs must put aside their differences and work together if they hope to survive the brutal onslaught and blood lust of the evil undead.

EFFECTS HIGHLIGHTS

22:15 – A woman's arm is bitten off.

22:30 – A zombie bites a chunk of skin.

44:30 – A man is shot in the head.

1:07:30 – A man is electrocuted.

1:08:45 – A zombie is shot in the head.

1:13:15 – A man's head is ripped in half by a group of zombies.

GARDEN OF THE DEAD

Year: 1974   Length: 85 minutes
Director: John Hayes

STATISTICS

First Zombie:	27:45
First Human Death:	23:15
First Zombie Death:	43:45

Amount of Gore:	Average
Gore Quality:	Average
Zombie Effects:	Average
Zombie Count:	Average
Zombie Deaths:	Average
Human Deaths:	High

SUMMARY

A group of inmates on a chain gang start sniffing formaldehyde to get high. After a failed prison break, they are shot down and buried. Before long, the dead convicts rise from their graves and lay siege on the prison.

EFFECTS HIGHLIGHTS

23:15 – A man is shot in the back.

GHOST GALLEON

Year: 1974   Length: 85 minutes
Director: Amando de Ossorio

STATISTICS

First Zombie:	34:45
First Human Death:	1:00:45
First Zombie Death:	N/A

Amount of Gore:	Low
Gore Quality:	High
Zombie Effects:	High
Zombie Count:	Average
Zombie Death:	Very Low
Human Deaths:	Average

SUMMARY

A group of young attractive models are adrift at sea when their boat suddenly loses radio contact. They soon discover a ghost ship floating nearby and go on board to investigate. Later, a crew of rescuers lead a mission to retrieve the missing girls, only to discover the ghost ship is inhabited by the undead Templar Knights.

EFFECTS HIGHLIGHTS

57:45 – A zombie scratches a woman's neck.

1:00:45 – A zombie cuts a woman's neck with a sword.

1:01:15 – A zombie eats a severed hand.

GHOST LAKE

Year: 2004   Length: 112 minutes
Director: Jay Woelfel

STATISTICS

First Zombie:	41:45
First Human Death:	2:30
First Zombie Death:	1:44:30

Amount of Gore:	Very Low
Gore Quality:	Very Low
Zombie Effects:	High

Zombie Count: High
Zombie Deaths: High
Human Deaths: High

SUMMARY

After the death of her parents, a young woman visits her family's lake side summer house. In the depths of grief, her fragile state of mind is rocked by visions in which the dead are rising from the waters and feeding on the living.

EFFECTS HIGHLIGHTS

N/A

GHOUL SCHOOL

Year: 1990   Length: 90 minutes
Director: Timothy O'Rawe

STATISTICS

First Zombie: 24:15
First Human Death: 16:45
First Zombie Death: 1:02:30

Amount of Gore: High
Gore Quality: Average
Zombie Effects: Low
Zombie Count: High
Zombie Deaths: Average
Human Deaths: Average

SUMMARY

While looking for buried treasure, two social rejects accidentally release a deadly chemical into the schools water system, turning all who drink it into the undead.

EFFECTS HIGHLIGHTS

16:45 – A man is shot in the chest.

24:45 – A woman's arm is pulled off.

24:45 – A woman's leg is pulled off.

24:45 – A woman's arm is pulled off.

24:45 – A woman's leg is pulled off.

25:15 – A woman's torso is ripped open.

35:15 – A zombie is eating a severed leg.

48:15 – A man's throat is slit.

48:30 – A zombie rips out a man's intestines.

52:30 – A dead woman is missing her scalp.

56:15 – An eye is impaled.

1:02:30 – A zombie is hit in the head with a tire iron.

1:03:30 – A zombie bites a woman's neck.

1:04:15 – A zombie is stabbed in the mouth with a drum stick.

1:04:30 – A zombie eats a man's intestines.

1:04:30 – A zombie is shot in the hand.

THE GHOULS

Year: 2003   Length: 81 minutes
Director: Chad Ferrin

STATISTICS

First Zombie: 20:15
First Human Death: 20:15
First Zombie Death: 50:15

Amount of Gore: Very High
Gore Quality: Very High
Zombie Effects: High
Zombie Count: High
Zombie Deaths: Average
Human Deaths: Low

SUMMARY

A sleazy video journalist who specializes in cruel and graphic videos finds himself in a fight for his life when he discovers zombies living beneath the streets of Los Angeles.

EFFECTS HIGHLIGHTS

1:00 – A man's throat is slit.

2:45 – Blood seeps out of an open wound.

3:30 – A woman is repeatedly stabbed in the chest.

14:45 – A man's throat is slit.

15:00 – A man's stomach is slit open.

16:00 – A man is shot repeatedly in the chest.

22:15 – A zombie spits blood on a man's chest.

32:30 – A zombie holds a piece of flesh.

33:15 – A zombie pulls out a man's tongue.

35:15 – A zombie bites a woman's neck.

35:30 – A zombie bites a woman's arm.

37:00 – A zombie eats from a dead body.

37:30 – A zombie eats a piece of meat.

38:00 – A zombie eats from a dead body.

39:15 – A zombie eats from a dead body.

40:15 – A zombie intestines are falling out of its stomach.

41:30 – A man stitches up a wound on a zombie.

44:15 – A zombie bites a woman's shoulder.

44:15 – A zombie bites a chunk of flesh out of a woman's shoulder.

46:45 – A man is hit in the head with a piece of wood.

47:00 – A group of zombies eat a dead body.

47:30 – A zombie rips an organ out of a man's stomach.

48:30 – A man finds a legless body.

49:30 – A zombie claws at an open wound on a man's arm.

50:15 – A zombie is shot in the chest.

53:00 – A woman spits up blood.

53:15 – A woman vomits in a man's face.

58:45 – A man finds a skinned body.

1:00:30 – A zombie eats a dead woman.

1:01:15 – A zombie pulls an organ out of a dead body.

1:02:45 – A zombie eats its own arm.

1:03:30 – A zombie slits another zombie's throat.

1:03:45 – A hook is pulled out of a man's back.

1:05:30 – A zombie bleeds from a wound in its neck.

1:09:00 – A zombie is shot through the hand .

GIRL'S ZOMBIE

Year: 2011   Length: 86 minutes
Director: Masahiro Aso

STATISTICS

First Zombie:	10:00
First Human Death:	46:30
First Zombie Death:	23:00
Amount of Gore:	Low
Gore Quality:	High
Zombie Effects:	Average
Zombie Count:	Very High
Zombie Deaths:	Very High
Human Deaths:	Average

SUMMARY

A group of Yakuza gangsters make a living from stealing. When one of them is killed, the survivors are captured and forced to take their assailants is where the money is hidden. Unbeknownst to all, it is in a forest full of zombies.

EFFECTS HIGHLIGHTS

1:05:00 – A zombie is shot in the head.

THE GRAPES OF DEATH

Year: 1978   Length: 90 minutes
Director: Jean Rollin

STATISTICS

First Zombie:	10:00
First Human Death:	46:30
First Zombie Death:	23:00
Amount of Gore:	High
Gore Quality:	High
Zombie Effects:	High
Zombie Count:	Very High
Zombie Deaths:	Average
Human Deaths:	Average

SUMMARY

A young woman discovers that the pesticide being sprayed on the local vineyards is turning people who drink the wine into killer zombies.

EFFECTS HIGHLIGHTS

10:45 – A man has a wound on his face.

20:45 – A dead woman has had her throat slit.

22:30 – A zombie has a wound on her chest.

23:00 – A zombie is stabbed with a pitchfork.

27:15 – A zombie has a bloody wound on it forehead.

36:15 – An eyeball falls out of a dead man's eye socket.

45:45 – A woman has been nailed to a door.

46:30 – A zombie cuts a woman's head off with an axe.

1:21:45 – A man is shot in the chest.

1:23:30 – A man is shot in the back.

GRAVE MISTAKE

Year: 2008   Length: 94 minutes
Director: Shawn Darling

STATISTICS

First Zombie:	4:30
First Human Death:	28:45
First Zombie Death:	24:30
Amount of Gore:	High
Gore Quality:	High
Zombie Effects:	Very High
Zombie Count:	Very High
Zombie Deaths:	High
Human Deaths:	Average

SUMMARY

An abusive stepfather manages to infect his family's entire hometown with a deadly virus that turns its inhabitants into flesh-eating zombies. As the dead return to life, his stepson desperately searches for his mother and tries to escape to a safe zone set up by the National Guard.

EFFECTS HIGHLIGHTS

26:00 – A woman puts her foot through a zombie's stomach.

28:30 – A zombie bites a woman's neck.

36:15 – A zombie pulls a man's head off.

36:15 – A group of zombies pull a man's body apart.

40:15 – A zombie is hit in the face with a pole.

43:30 – A zombie is shot in the head.

48:45 – A zombie is stabbed in the eye with a crowbar.

49:00 – A zombie's head explodes.

1:01:00 – A zombie is shot in the head.

1:02:45 – A zombie's head is cut in half with a sword.

1:02:45 – A zombie is stabbed with a hedge trimmer.

1:07:30 – A zombie bites off a woman's fingers.

1:08:00 – A zombie bites off a man's foot.

1:10:15 – A zombie rips open a man's back.

1:13:15 – A woman's hand is cut off in a door.

1:17:45 – A zombie rips a man's head off.

1:20:30 – A zombie is smashed in the head with a computer monitor.

1:23:30 – A zombie pulls off a woman's jaw.

1:24:00 – A zombie is shot in the head.

1:30:00 – A zombie is shot in the head.

GRAVEYARD ALIVE

Year: 2003   Length: 80 minutes
Director: Elza Kephart

STATISTICS

First Zombie:	4:45
First Human Death:	34:45
First Zombie Death:	16:00
Amount of Gore:	Average
Gore Quality:	Average
Zombie Effects:	Low
Zombie Count:	Average
Zombie Death:	Low
Human Death:	Low

SUMMARY

When a shy nurse treats a handsome woodsman, he bites her on the hand and infects her with a virus that turns her into a ravishing zombie sex kitten. While trying to adjust to her new cravings for flesh, she uses her new found sexuality to go head to head with her arch rival and win back her old love.

EFFECTS HIGHLIGHTS

35:15 – A zombie stabs a man with a scalpel.

35:30 – A zombie eats a piece of flesh.

39:30 – A zombie eats a piece of flesh

50:00 – A zombie is eating a severed leg.

50:45 – A zombie peels skin off of its face.

58:15 – A woman picks up a severed hand.

1:06:45 – A zombie bites a man's torso.

1:13:15 – A zombie stabs a woman in the stomach.

1:15:30 – A zombie is eating a man's intestines.

GRAVEYARD DISTURBANCE

Year: 1987   Length: 96 minutes
Director: Lamberto Bava

STATISTICS

First Zombie:	50:15
First Human Death:	N/A
First Zombie Death:	1:33:45
Amount of Gore:	Low
Gore Quality:	High

Zombie Effects:	High
Zombie Count:	High
Zombie Death:	Low
Human Death:	Very Low

SUMMARY

A group of teenagers accept a bet and spend a night in the catacombs beneath a nearby church. It doesn't take long for the group to find out that something evils lies in the darkness as a group of zombies emerge to hunt them down.

EFFECTS HIGHLIGHTS

1:30:45 – A zombie pulls its face off.

GUT PILE

Year: 1997   Length: 75 minutes
Director: Jerry O'Sullivan

STATISTICS

First Zombie:	43:15
First Human Death:	30:45
First Zombie Death:	N/A
Amount of Gore:	Average
Gore Quality:	High
Zombie Effects:	High
Zombie Count:	Low
Zombie Deaths:	N/A
Human Death:	Very Low

SUMMARY

When a hunter accidentally shoots a fellow sportsman, he buries the body deep in the woods. A year later, the corpse digs itself out of its grave and searches for the hunter, thirsty for revenge.

EFFECTS HIGHLIGHTS

4:45 – A dead body bleeds from a head wound.

30:45 – A man's arms and legs are cut off with an axe.

32:30 – An eyeball hangs out of a severed head.

40:15 – A man pulls a stick out of his leg.

42:30 – A dead body has a massive wound on its chest.

44:00 – A man steps in a pile of intestines.

HARD ROCK ZOMBIES

Year: 1984   Length: 90 minutes
Director: Krishna Shah

STATISTICS

First Zombie:	44:45
First Human Death:	2:30
First Zombie Death:	1:32:30
Amount of Gore:	High
Gore Quality:	High

Zombie Effects: Low
Zombie Count: High
Zombie Deaths: High
Human Deaths: High

SUMMARY

During a layover in a small rural town, the members of a rock band are killed by a family of rednecks. Determined to not let death get in the way, they rise from their graves to put on the show of their lives.

EFFECTS HIGHLIGHTS

3:00 – A woman cuts off a man's hand.

36:15 – A man's organs fall out of his stomach.

39:45 – A man's hand is pinned to a tree.

40:30 – A man is attacked with a weed wacker.

48:45 – A man is stabbed in the throat.

55:30 – A zombie pulls a man's head off.

1:07:15 – A woman finds a severed head.

1:09:15 – A zombie is eating its hand.

1:11:00 – A zombie is eating its legs.

1:12:30 – A girl is playing with a severed head.

1:12:45 – A zombie is eating its intestines.

1:21:30 – A sidewalk is littered with severed heads.

1:33:15 – A zombie eats the skin off of its face.

HELL OF THE LIVING DEAD

Alternate Title: Night of the Zombies
Year: 1980   Length: 101 minutes
Director: Bruno Mattei

STATISTICS

First Zombie:	8:00
First Human Death:	5:45
First Zombie Death:	31:30

Amount of Gore:	Very High
Gore Quality:	High
Zombie Effects:	High
Zombie Count:	Very High
Zombie Deaths:	High
Human Deaths:	High

SUMMARY

A chemical leak at a remote research lab in Papua New Guinea transforms the employees into zombies. A commando team heads into the jungle to investigate. The squad meets a tough female reporter and her cameraman boyfriend chasing the story, but soon they're all fighting for their lives as the contagion spreads.

EFFECTS HIGHLIGHTS

8:00 – A zombie bites a chunk of flesh out of a man's neck.

8:45 – Two zombies eat from a dead body.

17:00 – A man is shot in the chest.

17:45 – A man is shot in the head.

18:00 – Four men are shot in the chest.

21:15 – Close up of an infected wound.

29:30 – A zombie child is eating a man's intestines.

30:45 – A zombie is shot repeatedly in the chest.

31:00 – A zombie is shot repeatedly in the chest.

32:30 – A bloody dead body hangs from the ceiling

33:15 – A zombie is shot in the head.

39:45 – A group of men rip open an animal.

50:00 – A zombie bites a chunk of flesh out of a man's neck.

50:15 – A zombie bites a chunk of flesh out of a man's neck.

50:15 – A zombie is shot in the head.

50:30 – A zombie bites off a man's fingers.

50:45 – A zombie bites a chunk of flesh out of a man's leg.

50:45 – A zombie is shot in the head.

50:45 – A zombie eats a piece of flesh.

50:45 – A zombie bites off a man's fingers.

51:00 – A zombie eats a piece of flesh.

51:00 – A group of zombies eat various body parts.

1:01:30 – A zombie is shot in the chest.

1:02:00 – A zombie is shot in the head.

1:03:15 – A zombie is shot in the head.

1:14:00 – A zombie is shot in the chest.

1:04:15 – A zombie is shot in the head.

1:28:30 – A zombie bites a man's neck.

1:28:30 – A zombie bites a man's leg.

1:29:00 – A zombie is shot in the chest.

1:30:00 – A zombie is hit in the head with a rifle butt.

1:36:15 – A zombie pulls out a woman's tongue.

1:36:15 – A woman's eyeballs are pushed out of her head.

1:39:00 – A group of zombies bite a woman.

HELL'S GROUND

Year: 2007   Length: 77 minutes
Director: Omar Khan

STATISTICS

First Zombie:	27:45
First Human Death:	2:45
First Zombie Death:	N/A

Amount of Gore:	Average
Gore Quality:	Very High
Zombie Effects:	High
Zombie Count:	Average
Zombie Death:	Very Low

Human Deaths: Average

SUMMARY

A group of friends traveling to a concert are forced to take a detour. Before long, they have become lost in the woods and encounter a family of flesh-eating zombies.

EFFECTS HIGHLIGHTS

2:45 – A man is stabbed in the chest with a hook.

25:45 – Close up of a bloody wound on a man's leg.

29:30 – A group of zombies tear apart a dead body.

39:15 – A man holds a severed head.

47:30 – A man is stabbed in the chest.

52:00 – A man cuts off man's leg.

1:02:30 – A man removes a mace from a man's head.

1:12:45 – A woman stabs a man in the chest.

HIDE AND CREEP

Year: 2004   Length: 85 minutes
Director: Chuck Hartsell, Chance Shirley

STATISTICS

First Zombie: 8:45
First Human Death: 37:00
First Zombie Death: 37:15

Amount of Gore: High
Gore Quality: High
Zombie Effects: Average
Zombie Count: Very High
Zombie Deaths: High
Human Death: Low

SUMMARY

The residents of a small southern town find themselves fighting for their lives against a bloodthirsty horde of the undead and a strange flying saucer.

EFFECTS HIGHLIGHTS

15:00 – A zombie eats a piece of flesh.

31:00 – A zombie is shot in the chest.

31:15 – A zombie is shot in the chest.

33:00 – A zombie is stabbed in the eye with a dart.

37:00 – A zombie bites the back of a man's head.

52:00 – A man eats a piece of flesh.

1:07:30 – A zombie is shot in the head.

1:07:30 – A zombie is shot in the head.

1:07:30 – A zombie is shot in the head.

1:07:30 – A zombie is shot in the head.

1:10:45 – Two zombies are hit by a car.

1:14:15 – A zombie is shot in the head.

1:16:30 – A zombie is cut in the head with a machete.

HIGH SCHOOL GIRL ZOMBIE

Year: 2010   Length: 86 minutes
Director: Masashi Minami

STATISTICS

First Zombie: 1:45
First Human Death: 1:30
First Zombie Death: 13:30

Amount of Gore: High
Gore Quality: High
Zombie Effects: Average
Zombie Count: Very High
Zombie Deaths: High
Human Deaths: Average

SUMMARY

When a woman receives a phone call telling her that an assassin is trying to kill her, she heads out to track down the villain. On her travels she encounters a swarm of zombies.

EFFECTS HIGHLIGHTS

13:30 – A zombie is shot in the head.

14:15 – A zombie is decapitated.

18:00 – A group of zombies eat a dead body.

43:00 – Close up of a bloody dead body.

48:00 – A zombie is decapitated.

55:15 – A zombie is decapitated.

58:45 – A group of zombies eat a dead body.

1:00:30 – A zombie rips out its intestines.

1:00:30 – A zombie rips out its intestines.

1:02:00 – A zombie is stabbed in the chest.

1:03:45 – A zombie is shot in the head.

1:12:45 – A zombie is decapitated.

HOOD OF THE LIVING DEAD

Year: 2005   Length: 86 minutes
Director: Eduardo Quiroz, Jose Quiro

STATISTICS

First Zombie: 31:15
First Human Death: 31:15
First Zombie Death: 40:30

Amount of Gore: Low
Gore Quality: Average
Zombie Effects: Average
Zombie Count: High
Zombie Deaths: Average
Human Deaths: Average

SUMMARY

After the murder of his younger brother, a promising scientists does the unthinkable to bring his sibling back to life. Using a recently discovered serum that regenerates dying cells, he resurrects his brother. However, the creature who has returned is not the boy he remembered.

EFFECTS HIGHLIGHTS

52:00 – A zombie eats a dead dog.
1:06:15 – A zombie bites a man on the arm.

THE HORDE

Year: 2009   Length: 86 minutes
Directors: Yannick Dahan, Benjamin Rocher

STATISTICS

First Zombie:	19:30
First Human Death:	11:30
First Zombie Death:	20:45

Amount of Gore:	Very High
Gore Quality:	Very High
Zombie Effects:	Very High
Zombie Count:	Very High
Zombie Deaths:	Very High
Human Deaths:	High

SUMMARY

A siege on a high rise apartment complex goes wrong and a group of police officers find themselves teaming up with the gangsters they were trying to arrest to defend against an army of the dead.

EFFECTS HIGHLIGHTS

11:00 – A man is shot in the shoulder.
11:30 – A man is shot in the chest.
14:30 – A man is shot in the chest.
16:45 – A man is shot in the leg.
19:30 – A zombie bites a man's neck.
19:45 – A zombie is shot in the arm.
19:45 – A zombie is shot in the arm.
19:45 – A man is shot in the chest.
19:45 – A zombie is shot in the chest.
20:00 – A man is shot in the chest.
20:00 – A zombie is shot in the chest.
20:00 – A zombie is shot in the chest.
20:00 – A zombie is shot in the chest.
20:00 – A zombie is shot in the arm.
20:00 – A zombie is shot in the shoulder.
20:00 – A man is shot in the chest.
20:00 – A zombie is shot in the chest.
20:00 – A zombie is shot in the chest.
20:00 – A zombie is shot in the arm.
20:00 – A zombie is shot in the chest.
20:00 – A zombie is shot in the chest.

20:00 – A zombie is shot in the shoulder.
20:00 – A man is shot in the chest.
20:00 – A zombie is shot in the shoulder.
20:00 – A zombie is shot in the chest.
20:00 – A man is shot in the chest.
20:15 – A zombie is shot in the arm.
20:15 – A man is shot in the chest.
20:15 – A zombie is shot in the chest.
20:15 – A zombie is shot in the chest.
20:15 – A zombie is shot in the chest.
20:15 – A zombie is shot in the chest.
20:30 – A zombie bites a man's chest.
20:45 – A zombie is shot in the head.
58:00 – A zombie holds a severed head.
1:01:30 – A man is shot in the head.
1:11:15 – A zombie is eating a man's intestines.
1:11:45 – A zombie is shot in the shoulder.
1:12:15 – A zombie's head is smashed repeatedly into a cement pillar.
1:15:45 – A zombie is shot in the head.
1:15:45 – A zombie is shot in the head.
1:15:45 – A zombie is shot in the head.
1:17:45 – A zombie is stabbed in the shoulder.
1:17:45 – A zombie is decapitated.
1:18:00 – A zombie is stabbed in the head.
1:19:30 – A zombie is shot in the face.
1:19:45 – A zombie is shot in the neck.
1:20:15 – A zombie is shot in the chest.
1:20:30 – A zombie is shot in the face.
1:21:30 – A zombie is shot in the chest.
1:21:45 – A zombie is shot in the chest.

HORRORS OF WAR

Year: 2006   Length: 99 minutes
Directors: Peter John Ross, John Whitney

STATISTICS

First Zombie:	3:00
First Human Death:	2:00
First Zombie Death:	53:30

Amount of Gore:	Average
Gore Quality:	Average
Zombie Effects:	High
Zombie Count:	Average
Zombie Deaths:	Average
Human Deaths:	Very High

SUMMARY

With Allied forces closing in, Hitler unleashes a secret weapon on his enemies. A new breed of platoon that consists of the living dead. U.S. soldiers go behind enemy lines to find and destroy Hitler's horde of zombie soldiers.

EFFECTS HIGHLIGHTS

8:20 – A man is shot in the leg.

58:30 – A zombie breaks a man's arm in half.

1:13:30 – A zombie is shot in the head.

1:20:00 – A bloody dead body falls to the floor.

1:21:00 – A zombie is shot in the chest.

1:23:00 – A man is impaled on a pole.

1:23:45 – A zombie has a gaping hole in its stomach.

1:25:30 – A man is shot in the head.

HOT WAX ZOMBIES ON WHEELS

Year: 2000   Length: 90 minutes
Director: Michael Roush

STATISTICS

First Zombie:	10:15
First Human Death:	N/A
First Zombie Death:	N/A
Amount of Gore:	Very Low
Gore Quality:	Very Low
Zombie Effects:	Very Low
Zombie Count:	Average
Zombie Deaths:	Very Low
Human Deaths:	Very Low

SUMMARY

A band of hairless zombies on motorcycles terrorize a sleepy fishing village, intent on ridding the world's human population of body hair. It is up to a group of locals join together and battle the zombies.

EFFECTS HIGHLIGHTS

N/A

HOUSE BY THE CEMETERY

Year: 1981   Length: 87 minutes
Director: Lucio Fulci

STATISTICS

First Zombie:	12:45
First Human Death:	2:15
First Zombie Death:	N/A
Amount of Gore:	Average
Gore Quality:	Average
Zombie Effects:	Average
Zombie Count:	Low
Zombie Deaths:	Very Low
Human Deaths:	Average

SUMMARY

A family moves into a house where the previous owner had conducted horrific experiments. They soon find the house has become a portal for evil.

EFFECTS HIGHLIGHTS

2:15 – A woman is stabbed in the head.

42:45 – A woman is stabbed in the chest.

53:45 – Miscellaneous body parts are scattered across a room.

59:30 – A woman's throat is slit.

1:00:45 – A severed head rolls down a flight of stairs.

1:12:00 – An arm is cut off with an axe.

1:15:15 – A man stabs a zombie in the chest.

1:16:00 – A zombie rips out a man's throat.

HOUSE OF THE DEAD

Year: 2003   Length: 90 minutes
Director: Uwe Boll

STATISTICS

First Zombie:	15:30
First Human Death:	33:00
First Zombie Death:	33:15
Amount of Gore:	Very High
Gore Quality:	Very High
Zombie Effects:	Very High
Zombie Count:	Very High
Zombie Deaths:	Very High
Human Deaths:	Average

SUMMARY

A group of partying teenagers arrive on an remote island ready to join a rave, only to discover the island has been over run by zombies. Narrowly escaping with their lives, they take refuge in a house where things get even more dangerous.

EFFECTS HIGHLIGHTS

15:30 – A zombie has its hand through a man's chest.

33:00 – A zombie is shot in the chest.

33:15 – A zombie is shot in the head.

34:45 – A zombie is shot in the chest.

35:15 – A zombie is shot in the head.

37:15 – A zombie is shot in the head.

39:15 – A zombie is shot in the head.

40:00 – A zombie is shot in the stomach.

40:00 – A zombie is shot in the chest.

40:15 – A zombie is shot in the chest.

40:30 – A zombie is shot in the head.

40:45 – A zombie is shot in the head.

41:15 – A zombie is shot in the head.

51:15 – A zombie is shot in the head.

51:15 – A zombie is shot in the head.

51:45 – A zombie is shot in the chest.

51:45 – A zombie is shot in the head.

51:45 – A zombie is shot in the head.

51:45 – A zombie is shot in the head.

52:00 – A zombie is shot in the chest.

52:00 – A zombie is shot in the chest.

52:15 – A zombie is shot in the head.

52:45 – A zombie is shot in the head.

53:00 – A zombie is shot in the chest.

53:00 – A zombie is shot in the chest.

54:15 – A zombie is shot in the head.

54:30 – A zombie is shot in the chest.

54:30 – A zombie is shot in the stomach.

54:30 – A zombie is shot in the stomach.

54:30 – A zombie is shot in the chest.

54:30 – A zombie is shot in the chest.

54:45 – A zombie is shot in the head.

55:00 – Three zombies are shot through the chest with the same bullet.

55:15 – A zombie is hit in the chest with an axe.

55:15 – A zombie is shot in the chest.

55:30 – A zombie is shot in the chest.

55:30 – A zombie is shot in the chest.

55:30 – A zombie is shot in the chest.

55:45 – A zombie is shot in the chest.

55:45 – A zombie is shot in the chest.

56:15 – A zombie is shot in the chest.

56:30 – A zombie is shot in the chest.

57:00 – A zombie is shot in the chest.

57:00 – A severed head rolls across the ground.

58:30 – A zombie is shot in the head.

58:30 – A zombie is shot in the chest.

58:45 – A zombie is shot in the head.

59:30 – A woman's legs are cut off with an axe.

1:00:15 – A zombie's arm is cut off.

1:01:00 – A zombie is shot in the head.

1:16:30 – A zombie is stabbed in the chest.

1:19:30 – A zombie is stabbed in the chest.

1:22:00 – A woman is stabbed in the chest.

1:22:00 – A zombie is decapitated.

1:22:45 – A zombie's head is crushed.

HOUSE OF THE DEAD 2

Year: 2005   Length: 95 minutes
Director: Michael Hurst

STATISTICS

First Zombie:	5:15
First Human Death:	3:45
First Zombie Death:	12:45
Amount of Gore:	High

A pair of zombies on the set of "House of the Dead" courtesy of Brightlight Pictures.

Gore Quality:	Very High
Zombie Effects:	Very High
Zombie Count:	Very High
Zombie Deaths:	Very High
Human Deaths:	High

SUMMARY

A deadly virus breaks out at a university turning everyone on campus into zombies. Twenty nine days later, a team of scientists and soldiers are sent in to deal with the problem and locate patient zero in hopes of finding a cure.

EFFECTS HIGHLIGHTS

10:15 – Close up of a bloody wound on a man's hand.

12:45 – A zombie is shot in the head.

25:15 – A zombie is shot in the chest.

28:30 – A man's arm is cut off with a machete.

36:00 – A zombie is shot in the head.

50:15 – Close up of a bloody neck wound.

50:15 – A zombie is shot in the head.

52:15 – A man spits up blood.

52:15 – A zombie eats a man's heart.

1:05:15 – A zombie is shot in the head.

1:06:00 – A group of zombies eat a dead body.

1:08:00 – A zombie is shot in the chest.

1:08:15 – A zombie is shot in the chest.

1:08:15 – A zombie is shot in the chest.

1:08:15 – A zombie is shot in the stomach.

1:08:15 – A zombie is shot in the stomach.

1:08:30 – A zombie is shot in the chest.

1:11:00 – A zombie is shot in the head.

1:12:45 – A zombie is shot in the head.

1:14:00 – A zombie's stomach is cut open.

1:14:15 – A man covers himself with blood and gore.

1:18:00 – A zombie is shot in the chest.

1:18:00 – A zombie is shot in the chest.

1:20:15 – A zombie is shot in the head.

HUNTING CREATURES

Year: 2004   Length: 73 minutes
Director: Oliver Kellisch, Andreas Pape

STATISTICS

First Zombie:	8:30
First Human Death:	8:15
First Zombie Death:	9:15

Amount of Gore:	Very High
Gore Quality:	High
Zombie Effects:	High
Zombie Count:	Very High
Zombie Deaths:	Very High
Human Deaths:	High

SUMMARY

After a top secret experiment in an abandoned factory goes wrong, the resulting contamination turns a group of nearby party goers into flesh-eating zombies.

EFFECTS HIGHLIGHTS

8:15 – A man's face is burned.

8:45 – A man has a gushing wound on his wrist.

9:45 – A zombie is shot in the chest.

18:00 – A man is shot in the chest.

24:00 – A dead body is missing skin.

31:00 – A zombie is shot in the chest.

33:30 – A man bleeds from an ankle bite.

37:30 – A zombie is stabbed in the chest.

37:45 – A zombie is stabbed in the mouth.

39:30 – A zombie is shot in the head.

40:30 – A zombie eats from a dead man's torso.

40:45 – A zombie is shot in the chest.

42:30 – A zombie's arm is cut off.

42:45 – A zombie is stabbed in the chest.

43:00 – A zombie is eating a severed hand.

46:30 – A zombie is eating a severed limb.

48:15 – A group of zombies are shot in the chest.

48:15 – A zombie's intestines fall out.

48:30 – A zombie is stabbed in the chest.

48:45 – A zombie rips out a man's spinal cord.

48:45 – A man cuts into a zombie's torso.

49:00 – A zombie is decapitated.

49:00 – A zombie is stabbed in the chest.

49:00 – A man rips open a zombie's stomach.

49:15 – A man cuts open a zombie's torso.

49:30 – A zombie's head is pulled off.

53:00 – A zombie is shot in the chest.

56:00 – A zombie's leg is broken.

56:15 – A zombie is shot in the chest.

56:30 – A man is shot in the head.

57:45 – A man cuts off a zombie's leg.

58:00 – A group of zombies eat various severed limbs.

58:30 – A zombie rips off a man's face.

1:00:00 – A man rips out a zombie's organs.

1:00:15 – A zombie is stabbed in the chest.

1:00:15 – A zombie is shot in the head.

1:00:15 – Two zombies are shot in the head.

1:00:30 – A zombie is shot in the head.

1:00:45 – A zombie bites a man's leg.

1:00:45 – A zombie is shot in the neck.

1:01:30 – A man shoots himself in the head.

1:02:00 – A man is disemboweled with a sword.

1:02:45 – Two zombies rip out a man's intestines.

1:05:45 – A man shoots himself in the head.

1:07:15 – Various body parts are buried in piles of rubble.

I AM OMEGA

Year: 2007   Length: 90 minutes
Director: Griff Furst

STATISTICS

First Zombie: 1:45
First Human Death: 2:00
First Zombie Death: 4:00

Amount of Gore: High
Gore Quality: High
Zombie Effects: Very High
Zombie Count: Very High
Zombie Deaths: High
Human Death: Low

SUMMARY

A lethal plague has killed or mutated every human on Earth except one. As the planet's last survivor he finds himself in a war with the deadly zombies that have taken over the planet.

EFFECTS HIGHLIGHTS

21:00 – A zombie is slashed across the stomach.

33:00 – A zombie is shot in the chest.

44:00 – A zombie's head is smashed against a van.

45:00 – A zombie's head explodes.

45:00 – A zombie is cut on the stomach.

45:15 – A zombie is stabbed in the head.

52:30 – A zombie is shot in the head.

52:30 – A zombie is shot in the head.

1:09:30 – A man is shot in the chest.

I SELL THE DEAD

Year: 2008   Length: 85 minutes
Director: Glenn McQuaid

STATISTICS

First Zombie: 28:15
First Human Death: 3:30
First Zombie Death: 30:45

Amount of Gore: Average
Gore Quality: High
Zombie Effects: High
Zombie Count: Average
Zombie Deaths: Low
Human Deaths: Average

SUMMARY

An 19th century grave robber facing execution by the guillotine confesses his sins to a priest, revealing a shocking life that has been filled with supernatural adventures.

EFFECTS HIGHLIGHTS

3:30 – Close up of a severed head.

57:00 – A boy holds a bloodied rabbit.

1:02:15 – A man's throat is slit.

1:06:30 – Close up of a bite mark.

1:06:30 – A woman is stabbed in the head.

1:10:15 – A zombie eats a piece of flesh.

1:14:45 – Close up of a headless zombie.

1:14:45 – A man is sliced across the forehead.

1:15:00 – A zombie holds a severed head.

INSANE IN THE BRAIN

Year: 2007   Length: 90 minutes
Director: Chad Hendricks

STATISTICS

First Zombie: 1:00
First Human Death: 9:30
First Zombie Death: 55:15

Amount of Gore: Low
Gore Quality: Average
Zombie Effects: Average
Zombie Count: Average
Zombie Death: Low
Human Death: Low

SUMMARY

Pheromones seeping from a nearby brothel cause the dead to start rising. Two local police officers are sent out on a mission to stem the increasing ranks of the dead.

EFFECTS HIGHLIGHTS

9:30 – A woman's head explodes after giving a zombie oral sex.

24:45 – A zombie pulls a man's penis off.

JOHNNY SUNSHINE

Year: 2008   Length: 79 minutes
Director: Matt Yeager

STATISTICS

First Zombie: 3:30
First Human Death: 7:15
First Zombie Death: 21:00

Amount of Gore: High
Gore Quality: High
Zombie Effects: High
Zombie Count: High
Zombie Deaths: Average

Human Deaths: Average

SUMMARY

Johnny Sunshine is a beautiful and cold-blooded assassin whose zombie-killing skills are shown on the world's most popular reality television show. When she discovers that her producer has arranged to have her killed, she takes revenge into her own hands.

EFFECTS HIGHLIGHTS

6:15 – A woman stabs a man in the stomach.

13:30 – A woman pulls out a man's tongue.

20:00 – A zombie is eating from a dead body.

20:45 – A zombie is stabbed in the neck.

38:45 – A woman puts staples in another woman's breasts.

49:15 – A woman drill into a zombie's leg.

1:01:15 – A zombie is stabbed in the neck.

1:01:30 – A zombie is stabbed in the chest.

1:02:00 – A zombie is stabbed in the head.

1:04:00 – A man's face is smashed against a counter.

1:15:45 – A man is stabbed in the ear with a hypodermic needle.

JUNK

Year: 2000   Length: 83 minutes
Director: Atsushi Muroga

STATISTICS

First Zombie:	1:30
First Human Death:	1:45
First Zombie Death:	35:30

Amount of Gore:	Very High
Gore Quality:	High
Zombie Effects:	High
Zombie Count:	Very High
Zombie Deaths:	Very High
Human Deaths:	Average

SUMMARY

Four bottom of the rung thieves meet their Yakuza connection at an abandoned lab to off load stolen jewelry from a recent heist. They soon find themselves trapped when the meeting place is overrun by the living dead.

EFFECTS HIGHLIGHTS

1:45 – A zombie bites a chunk of flesh out of a man's neck.

10:30 – A man is stabbed in the foot with a pair of scissors.

33:00 – A man is stabbed in the throat.

34:45 – A zombie eats a man's intestines.

35:00 – A zombie eats a piece of flesh.

35:15 – A zombie is shot in the stomach.

35:15 – A zombie's intestines fall out.

35:30 – A zombie is shot in the head.

35:30 – A zombie is shot in the head.

35:30 – A zombie is shot in the head.

38:15 – A man is shot in the chest.

39:00 – A zombie bites a man's neck.

40:30 – A zombie is shot in the chest.

40:45 – A zombie is shot in the head.

45:30 – A woman is shot in the arm.

47:00 – A zombie is shot in the chest.

50:30 – A zombie eats a piece of flesh.

50:45 – A zombie eats intestines.

52:15 – A zombie eats a piece of its own flesh.

52:30 – A zombie is shot in the chest.

52:30 – A zombie is shot in the shoulder.

52:30 – A zombie is shot in the stomach.

52:45 – A zombie is shot in the stomach.

52:45 – A zombie is shot in the head.

54:00 – A zombie is shot in the head.

54:15 – A zombie is stabbed in the head.

54:15 – A zombie is shot in the head.

56:45 – A woman has a bloody wound on her leg.

1:06:00 – A zombie eats a piece of flesh.

1:07:45 – A group of zombies eat pieces of flesh.

1:09:15 – A severed head is thrown down a flight of stairs.

1:09:45 – A zombie pulls off a dead man's hand.

1:10:00 – A zombie is shot in the head.

1:11:15 – A zombie is stabbed in the stomach with a pole.

1:11:30 – Close up of a bloody wound filled with maggots.

1:12:15 – A zombie is cut in half with a shovel.

1:12:45 – A woman reaches into the torso of a dead zombie.

1:13:00 – A zombie is shot in the head.

LAND OF THE DEAD

Year: 2005   Length: 93 minutes
Director: George A. Romero

STATISTICS

First Zombie:	2:30
First Human Death:	23:00
First Zombie Death:	4:30

Amount of Gore:	Very High
Gore Quality:	Very High
Zombie Effects:	Very High
Zombie Count:	Very High
Zombie Deaths:	Very High

Human Deaths: Very High

SUMMARY

The world has been overrun by the living dead and the last humans have moved into a walled city to protect themselves from the threat outside. When one of the citizens steals an armored vehicle for ransom, the safety of the city is put in jeopardy.

EFFECTS HIGHLIGHTS

4:30 – A zombie is shot in the eye with a crossbow.

9:00 – A zombie's head is impaled with a flag pole.

9:15 – A zombie is decapitated by machine gun fire.

9:45 – A zombie's head is crushed by another zombie.

13:15 – A zombie is shot through the chin with a crossbow.

14:00 – A zombie bites a chunk of flesh out of a man's wrist.

14:30 – A zombie is shot in the head.

14:45 – A man shoots himself in the head.

24:48 – A man uses a statue to bludgeon a zombie.

29:37 – A man is shot in the head

38:45 – Numerous zombies are shot in the head.

40:00 – A zombie rips a man's eye lid.

40:00 – A group of zombies eat various body parts.

50:45 – Close up of a half-eaten leg.

51:00 – A zombie is eating meat off of a leg bone.

51:30 – A group of zombies are eating body parts.

51:45 – A zombie reaches into a dead body's mouth and rips out its tongue.

52:45 – A zombie with its head hanging from its spinal column bites a man on the arm.

59:00 – After a zombie takes a bite out of a man's neck, more zombies pull him apart.

1:06:00 – A man's head is pulled off of his shoulders.

1:06:30 – A zombie cuts a man's hand off with a meat cleaver.

1:06:30 – A man falls on a grenade.

1:08:13 – A woman is bitten on the cheek and a large chunk of flesh is pulled off.

1:11:15 – A zombie slices a man's face.

1:13:45 – A zombie rips a man's throat out with its teeth while another is scooping a brain out of a skull.

1:14:00 – A man's skin is pulled off of his face.

1:14:00 – A man is torn in half.

1:15:45 – Two zombies pull an arm apart.

1:17:45 – A man's neck is bitten, spraying blood across a window.

1:18:00 – A woman's belly button piercing is ripped out.

1:19:45 – A zombie runs its finger down the side of a

vehicle, causing its finger nails to fall off.

1:20:15 – A lowering bridge decapitates a zombie.

1:21:15 – A vehicle crushes numerous zombies under its wheels.

1:28:30 – A huge group of zombies are eating the remains of multiple dead humans.

LET SLEEPING CORPSES LIE

Alternate Title: The Living Dead at Manchester Morgue
Year: 1974   Length: 92 minutes
Director: Jorge Grau

STATISTICS

First Zombie:	14:45
First Human Death:	6:15
First Zombie Death:	26:00
Amount of Gore:	Average
Gore Quality:	High
Zombie Effects:	High
Zombie Count:	Average
Zombie Deaths:	Average
Human Deaths:	High

SUMMARY

A new crop pesticide used by local farmer's in England's Lake District has devastating effects when it brings the dead back to life.

EFFECTS HIGHLIGHTS

1:02:00 – Close up of a leg wound.

1:02:15 – Zombies pull out a mans intestines.

1:02:30 – Zombies gorge on a victim.

1:10:15 – A severed hand is grasping a car door handle.

1:18:45 – A zombie eats a piece of flesh.

1:22:30 – A zombie tears off a woman's breast.

1:22:30 – Two zombies pull out a woman's intestines.

1:24:15 – A man slices off a zombie's pectoral muscle.

1:24:15 – A man is cut in the head with an axe.

1:26:00 – Close up of a dead body.

LINNEA QUIGLEY'S HORROR WORKOUT

Year: 1990   Length: 60 minutes
Director: Kenneth J. Hall

STATISTICS

First Zombie:	7:30
First Human Death:	9:45
First Zombie Death:	N/A
Amount of Gore:	Low

112

"Land of the Dead" test audience screening storyboards for missing scenes courtesy of Greg Chown.

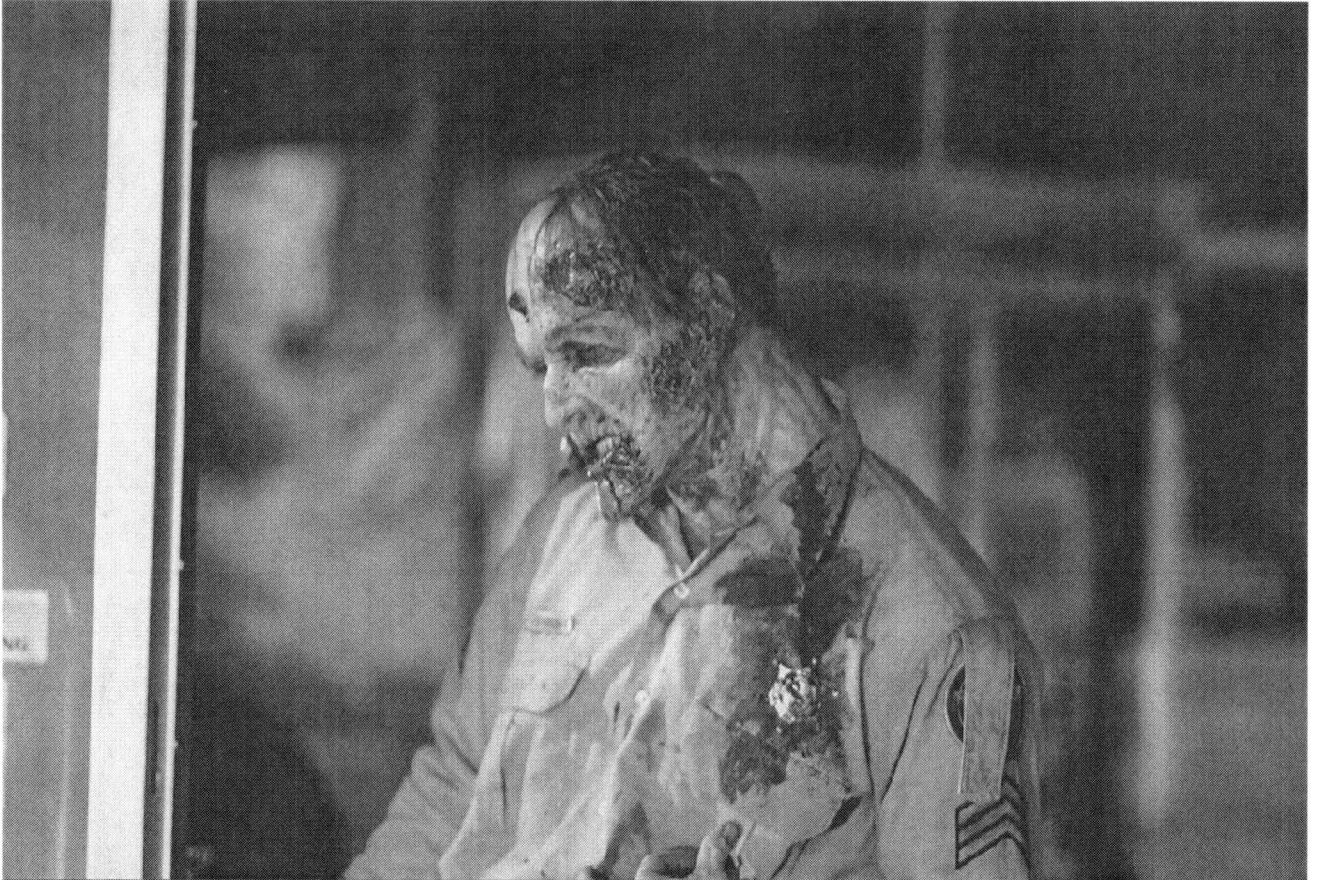
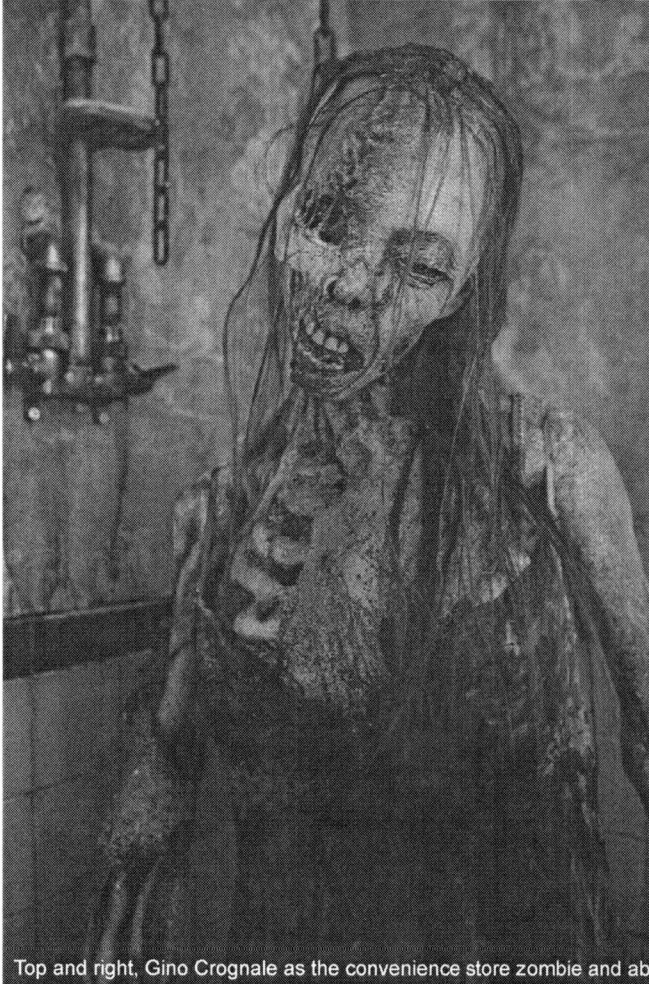

Top and right, Gino Crognale as the convenience store zombie and above, a zombie from "Land of the Dead" courtesy of Gino Crognale.

114

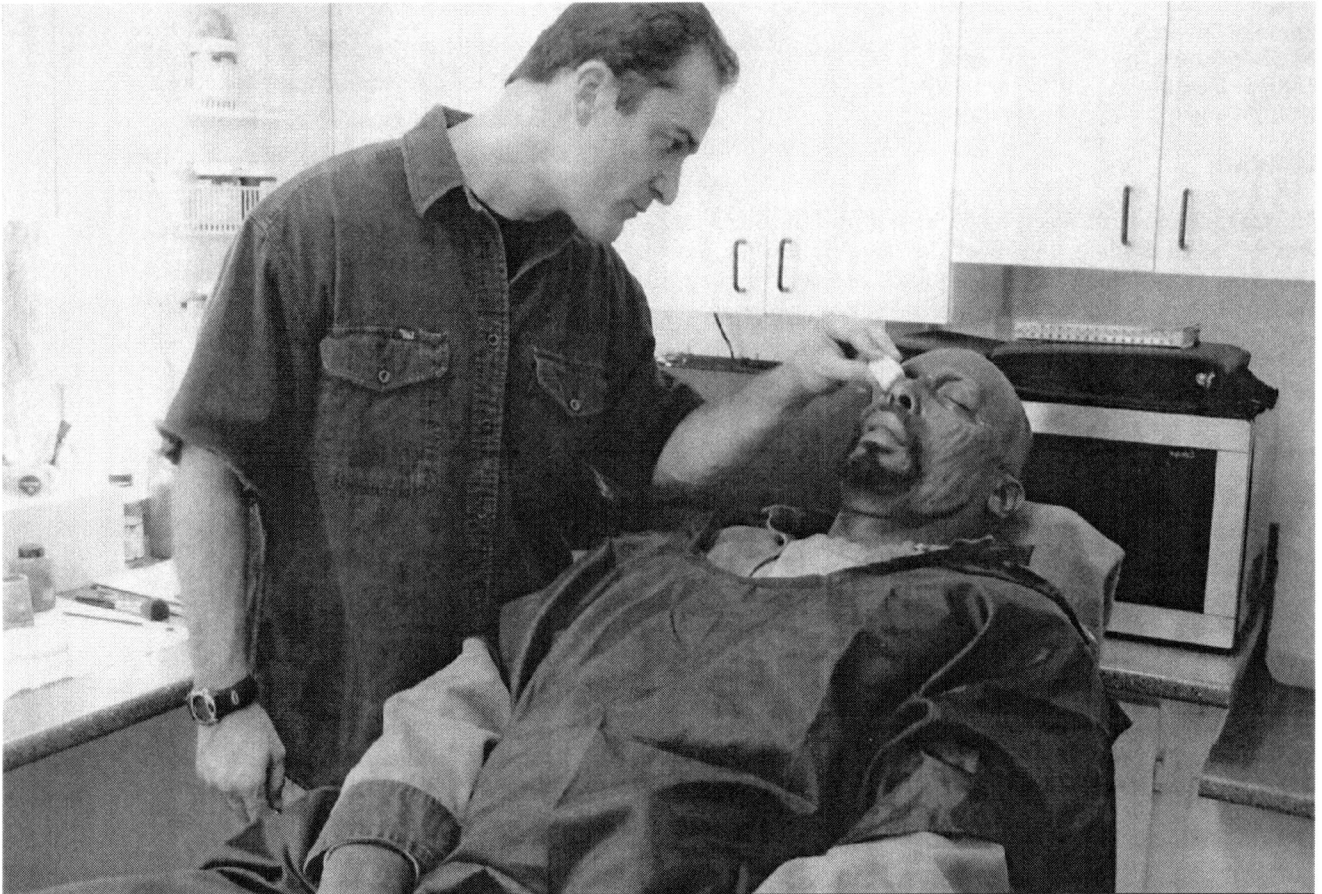

Top, Gino Crognale applies makeup to Eugene Clarke   Above, Gino and Greg Nicotero on "Land of the Dead" courtesy of Gino Crognale.

Gore Quality: Average
Zombie Effects: High
Zombie Count: Average
Zombie Deaths: Very Low
Human Deaths: Average

SUMMARY

Linnea Quigley is followed home by a group of zombies where she leads them in a pool side aerobic routine as she tries to get them back in shape. Later she invites some girlfriends over for a slumber party and some more exercise.

EFFECTS HIGHLIGHTS

23:45 – A woman pulls off a zombie's arm.

51:45 – A woman is decapitated.

52:45 – A woman is stabbed in the stomach with a power drill.

54:15 – A woman is holding a severed hand.

LIVING A ZOMBIE DREAM

Year: 1996   Length: 90 minutes
Director: Todd Reynolds

STATISTICS

First Zombie: 21:00
First Human Death: 14:45
First Zombie Death: N/A

Amount of Gore: Very High
Gore Quality: High
Zombie Effects: High
Zombie Count: Average
Zombie Death: Very Low
Human Deaths: Average

SUMMARY

When a young man discovers that his girlfriend has been dating his brother behind his back, he leaves his sibling stranded in bad area of town. A deranged serial killer finds the lost brother and kills him. The young man sets out to take revenge on the murderer, but the killer won't stay dead.

EFFECTS HIGHLIGHTS

1:00 – A man's throat is slit.

2:45 – Blood seeps out of an open wound.

14:45 – A man's throat is slit.

15:00 – A man's stomach is slit open.

16:00 – A man is shot repeatedly in the chest.

22:15 – A zombie spits blood on a man's chest.

32:30 – A zombie holds a piece of flesh.

33:15 – A zombie pulls out a man's tongue.

35:15 – A zombie bites a woman's neck.

35:30 – A zombie bites a woman's arm.

37:00 – A zombie eats from a dead body.

37:30 – A zombie eats a piece of meat.

38:00 – Zombies eat from a dead body.

39:15 – Zombies eat from a dead body.

40:15 – A zombie intestines falling out of its stomach.

41:30 – A man stitches up a wound on a zombie.

44:15 – A zombie bites a woman's shoulder.

44:15 – A zombie bites a woman's shoulder.

46:45 – A man is hit in the head with a piece of wood.

47:30 – A zombie rips an organ out of a man's stomach.

49:30 – A zombie claws at a wound on a man's arm.

53:00 – A woman spits up blood.

53:15 – A woman vomits in a man's face.

1:00:30 – A zombie eats a dead woman.

1:01:15 – A zombie pulls an organ out of a dead body.

1:02:45 – A zombie eats its own arm.

1:03:30 – A zombie slits another zombie's throat.

THE LIVING DEAD GIRL

Year: 1982   Length: 86 minutes
Director: Jean Rollin

STATISTICS

First Zombie: 7:30
First Human Death: 8:15
First Zombie Death: N/A

Amount of Gore: Average
Gore Quality: Average
Zombie Effects: Low
Zombie Count: Low
Zombie Death: Very Low
Human Deaths: High

SUMMARY

When her grave is disturbed by both an earthquake and a toxic waste spill, a deceased girl rises from the dead and sets out to find her sister. Her sister decides to help satisfy her undead sibling's bloodlust by luring innocent victims into their lair.

EFFECTS HIGHLIGHTS

7:30 – A zombie sticks its fingers into a man's eyes.

9:15 – A zombie cuts a man's throat.

28:15 – A man bleeds from a neck wound.

28:45 – A zombie cuts a woman's throat.

56:00 – A zombie cuts a woman's stomach.

1:15:15 – A woman draws a sword across another woman's stomach.

1:17:30 – A woman is set on fire.

1:17:45 – A woman hits a man with an axe.

1:21:45 – A zombie bites a woman's neck.

1:23:30 – A zombie bites a woman's arm.

LIVELIHOOD

Year: 2005   Length: 105 minutes
Director: Ryan Graham

STATISTICS

First Zombie:	22:15
First Human Death:	4:00
First Zombie Death:	1:36:30

Amount of Gore:	Average
Gore Quality:	Low
Zombie Effects:	Low
Zombie Count:	High
Zombie Deaths:	Low
Human Deaths:	Average

SUMMARY

A partying 80's rocker, a corporate office worker and a bitchy mother-in-law all perish under strange circumstances. A short time later, the dead start to rise and the three victims find that picking up where they left off isn't as easy as they had hoped.

EFFECTS HIGHLIGHTS

14:45 – A man is decapitated.

27:15 – A zombie's hand falls off.

56:15 – A zombie holds its intestines.

1:01:00 – A zombie is decapitated.

1:02:00 – A woman reattaches a zombie's head.

1:24:15 – A zombie's arm falls off.

1:35:30 – A zombie is impaled through the stomach.

1:36:30 – A zombie is cut in the head with a machete.

THE MAD

Year: 2007   Length: 83 minutes
Director: John Kalangis

STATISTICS

First Zombie:	24:45
First Human Death:	25:00
First Zombie Death:	33:00

Amount of Gore:	Average
Gore Quality:	Very High
Zombie Effects:	High
Zombie Count:	High
Zombie Deaths:	Average
Human Deaths:	Average

SUMMARY

While on a cross country trip, a doctor and his daughter pull in to a small town pit stop. Unknown to them, the organic meat served at the diner contains a mutated virus that turns people into the undead.

EFFECTS HIGHLIGHTS

25:00 – A woman is stabbed in the head.

25:00 – A man bleeds from a wound in his throat.

25:00 – A zombie is eating a chunk of flesh.

27:15 – A zombie bites a man's foot.

44:30 – A severed head is thrown through a door.

53:30 – A zombie is shot with a harpoon gun.

MAKE OUT WITH VIOLENCE

Year: 2008   Length: 105 minutes
Director: Deagol Brothers

STATISTICS

First Zombie:	3:30
First Human Death:	2:15
First Zombie Death:	N/A

Amount of Gore:	Average
Gore Quality:	High
Zombie Effects:	High
Zombie Count:	Low
Zombie Death:	Very Low
Human Death:	Low

SUMMARY

After the disappearance of teenage classmate, the lives of two brothers take a turn for the worse when they accidentally discover her body. To their surprise, the girl has returned to life as one of the living dead. The brothers hide the girl in their family's abandoned summer house while they search for a way to bring her back to life.

EFFECTS HIGHLIGHTS

49:45 – A zombie eats a mouse.

1:37:30 – A bed is covered with the remains of a dead dog.

MALLORCA ZOMBIE

Year: 2011   Length: 93 minutes
Directors: Marc Albertí, Jaume Alçina, Juanjo Durán, Juan Fernandez, Juan Ortega, Frederic Tort, Alex Vargas

STATISTICS

First Zombie:	:30
First Human Death:	17:00
First Zombie Death:	1:13:30

Amount of Gore:	High
Gore Quality:	High
Zombie Effects:	High
Zombie Count:	Very High
Zombie Deaths:	Low
Human Deaths:	Average

SUMMARY

Seven stories of how survivors try to live through and cope with the zombie apocalypse.

EFFECTS HIGHLIGHTS

17:00 – A man is stabbed in the eye with a carrot.

34:00 – A man is hit in the head with a baseball bat.

39:45 – A zombie pulls a chunk of flesh off of its face.

40:15 – A zombie is eating a severed limb.

44:15 – A zombie eats a chunk of flesh.

50:30 – Two zombies eat a piece of flesh.

50:45 – Zombies eat flesh.

1:08:30 – A zombie is eating a woman's face.

1:12:15 – A zombie bites a chunk of skin out of a woman's neck.

1:13:00 – A group of zombies tear a man apart.

1:13:30 – A man stabs a zombie in the head with a key chain.

1:22:15 – A zombie is shot in the head.

MANSION OF THE LIVING DEAD

Year: 1982   Length: 89 minutes
Director: Jesus Franco

STATISTICS

First Zombie: :15
First Human Death: 48:00
First Zombie Death: 1:28:00

Amount of Gore: Very Low
Gore Quality: Very Low
Zombie Effects: Average
Zombie Count: Average
Zombie Deaths: Average
Human Deaths: Average

SUMMARY

A 17th-century monastery unleashes a horde of zombies upon a group of young women who are vacationing at an island resort.

EFFECTS HIGHLIGHTS

N/A

MEAT MARKET

Year: 2000   Length: 90 minutes
Director: Brian Clement

STATISTICS

First Zombie: :00
First Human Death: 11:00
First Zombie Death: 3:30

Amount of Gore: High
Gore Quality: Average
Zombie Effects: Average
Zombie Count: Very High
Zombie Deaths: Very High
Human Deaths: High

SUMMARY

Two former employees of a medical research company attempt to leak details of questionable practices that return the dead to life.

EFFECTS HIGHLIGHTS

5:15 – A zombie eats a piece of flesh.

16:45 – A zombie eats a piece of flesh.

17:30 – A zombie eats a piece of flesh.

20:30 – A zombie eats a piece of flesh.

28:00 – A zombie bites a man's neck.

33:45 – A zombie is shot in the head.

34:00 – A zombie is shot in the chest.

36:15 – A car crushes a zombie's head.

49:15 – A zombie is shot in the chest.

50:45 – A zombie's head is cut with a circular saw.

1:07:30 – A man crushes a zombie's skull with his elbow.

1:13:30 – A surgeon cuts open a dead body.

1:22:15 – A zombie is stabbed in the head.

1:26:45 – A zombie is shot in the head.

1:27:45 – A zombie pulls a man's head off.

1:28:00 – A zombie is shot in the head.

MEAT MARKET 2

Year: 2001   Length: 80 minutes
Director: Brian Clement

STATISTICS

First Zombie: :15
First Human Death: 18:45
First Zombie Death: 5:45

Amount of Gore: Very High
Gore Quality: High
Zombie Effects: High
Zombie Count: Very High
Zombie Deaths: High
Human Deaths: High

SUMMARY

When a group of survivors take refuge in what they believe is a safe zone, they soon find themselves under attack. It soon becomes clear that the biggest threat isn't necessarily the zombies.

EFFECTS HIGHLIGHTS

5:45 – A zombie is shot in the head with a crossbow.

7:15 – A zombie is shot in the head with a crossbow.

9:30 – A zombie is shot in the head.

31:15 – A man cuts a zombie's head in half .

40:45 – A woman pulls out a zombie's intestines.

40:45 – A man pulls off a zombie's hand.

41:15 – A zombie eats a piece of flesh.

46:45 – A woman bites off a man's fingers.

50:00 – Maggots crawl through a bloody wound on a man's arm.

51:45 – A group of people eat various body parts.

54:30 – A man's face is missing its skin.

54:45 – A zombie's head is crushed in a door.

57:00 – A man shoots himself in the head.

1:01:15 – A zombie is shot in the chest.

1:01:45 – A severed hand falls the floor.

1:03:00 – A zombie rips open a man's stomach.

1:03:00 – A zombie eats a severed hand.

1:03:00 – A group of zombies eat a man's intestines.

1:03:30 – A zombie is shot in the chest.

1:04:00 – A zombie ea a man's face.

1:04:30 – A group of zombies eat various body parts.

1:05:30 – A zombie is shot in the head.

1:05:30 – A group of zombies eat various body parts.

1:07:15 – A zombie is eating a man's intestines.

1:07:30 – A man eats his own intestines.

1:08:30 – A group of zombies eat various body parts.

1:09:15 – A man shoots himself in the head.

1:10:00 – A zombie is shot in the head.

1:10:15 – A group of zombies eat various body parts.

1:10:15 – A zombie is shot in the head.

MORTUARY

Year: 2005   Length: 93 minutes
Director: Tobe Hooper

STATISTICS

First Zombie:	37:45
First Human Death:	1:19:15
First Zombie Death:	1:14:00

Amount of Gore:	Low
Gore Quality:	High
Zombie Effects:	High
Zombie Count:	High
Zombie Deaths:	Average
Human Death:	Very Low

SUMMARY

A recently widowed woman retreats to California with her two children to try to start a new life. To make ends meet, she runs a local mortuary and finds out that the resident corpses won't stay dead. Soon she is facing an army of the walking dead.

EFFECTS HIGHLIGHTS

55:15 – A woman stitches up a dead body's arm.

1:08:15 – A woman's hand is sliced open.

1:19:15 – A zombie punches through a man's chest.

MOTORCROSS ZOMBIES FROM HELL

Year: 2007   Length: 78 minutes
Director: Gary Robert

STATISTICS

First Zombie:	54:45
First Human Death:	1:06:15
First Zombie Death:	55:30

Amount of Gore:	Average
Gore Quality:	High
Zombie Effects:	Average
Zombie Count:	High
Zombie Deaths:	Average
Human Death:	Low

SUMMARY

A motocross racer prepares to race against the undefeated Team Skullz. However, he has no idea that his opponents are really zombies and the race for victory becomes a fight for survival.

EFFECTS HIGHLIGHTS

38:45 – A severed head is thrown to the floor.

42:45 – Body parts are scattered on the ground.

1:06:00 – A man is shot in the chest.

1:06:15 – Zombies rip open a man's torso.

1:06:30 – A zombie is shot in the head.

1:09:45 – A zombie is shot in the chest.

MUD ZOMBIES

Year: 2008   Length: 105 minutes
Director: Rodrigo Aragão

STATISTICS

First Zombie:	23:00
First Human Death:	29:15
First Zombie Death:	26:30

Amount of Gore:	Very High
Gore Quality:	Very High
Zombie Effects:	Very High
Zombie Count:	Very High
Zombie Deaths:	Very High
Human Deaths:	Average

SUMMARY

A small fishing town in Brazil finds its way of life threatened when zombies start to emerge from the contaminated swamp to terrorize the community. As the town's residents are killed one by one, a survivor fights for his life.

EFFECTS HIGHLIGHTS

17:15 – A man has multiple lacerations on his face.

23:30 – A zombie is stabbed in the eye with a fork.

24:45 – A zombie is shot in the chest.

26:15 – A zombie is shot in the eye.

28:30 – A zombie bites a man on the shoulder.

31:15 – A zombie bites off a man's fingers.

31:30 – A zombie is shot in the head.

34:00 – A zombie is shot in the head.

41:15 – A man cuts off a zombie's hand with an axe.

45:45 – A zombie is hit in the head with an axe.

45:45 – A zombie is decapitated.

1:08:00 – A zombie eats from a dead body.

1:22:15 – A man stabs a zombie in the neck.

1:22:15 – A man cuts a zombie's head in half with an axe.

1:22:45 – Brains spill out of a zombie's open skull.

1:23:15 – A woman pulls of a zombie's jaw.

1:24 :00 – A man cuts a zombie's head in half.

1:27:00 – A tentacle crawls out of a woman's mouth.

1:27:45 – A man cuts a zombie's head with an axe.

1:37:15 – A zombie's eyes swell up.

1:40:00 – A zombie is decapitated.

1:40:15 – A man cuts off the top of a zombie's head.

1:40:30 – A zombie's hand is cut off.

1:40:30 – A zombie's head is cut in half.

1:40:30 – A zombie is decapitated.

MULVA ZOMBIE ASS KICKER

Year: 2001   Length: 50 minutes
Director: Chris Seaver

STATISTICS

First Zombie:	2:00
First Human Death:	15:45
First Zombie Death:	N/A
Amount of Gore:	Average
Gore Quality:	Average
Zombie Effects:	Average
Zombie Count:	Very High
Zombie Death:	Very Low
Human Deaths:	Average

SUMMARY

On Halloween night, a chocolate addict and her misfit group of friends go on a bloody zombie hunting rampage to fight for their Halloween candy.

EFFECTS HIGHLIGHTS

15:45 – A zombie punches a man in the face and pulls his brain out.

16:30 – A group of zombies rip out a man's intestines.

36:45 – A zombie bleeds from a neck wound.

38:15 – A zombie pulls off a man's arm.

38:45 – A man stabs himself with a sword.

42:00 – A man jams his thumbs into a zombie's eyes.

48:00 – A zombie's heart is ripped out.

48:45 – A man pulls out a zombie's tongue.

52:45 – A zombie bleeds from its arm stumps.

MUTANT VAMPIRE ZOMBIES FROM THE HOOD

Year: 2008   Length: 81 minutes
Director: Thunder Levin

STATISTICS

First Zombie:	13:30
First Human Death:	13:30
First Zombie Death:	14:30
Amount of Gore:	High
Gore Quality:	Very High
Zombie Effects:	High
Zombie Count:	Very High
Zombie Deaths:	Very High
Human Deaths:	High

SUMMARY

After the citizens of Los Angeles have been turned into flesh-eating zombies, a handful of cops and gang members are forced to create an unlikely alliance to fend off the relentless horde of the living dead. Breaking free of the city, they make their way to a compound up the coast where a scientist may hold the key to survival.

EFFECTS HIGHLIGHTS

13:15 – A man has a bloody wound on his neck.

17:45 – A zombie pulls off a woman's arm.

19:45 – A zombie is shot in the head.

20:00 – A zombie is shot in the head.

22:00 – A zombie eats a man's intestines.

23:15 – A zombie is shot in the head.

27:15 – A zombie's intestines are falling out of its stomach.

28:15 – A zombie is shot in the head.

35:00 – A zombie is shot in the head.

37:15 – A zombie is shot in the head.

38:15 – A zombie eats a severed arm.

40:30 – A zombie is shot in the head.

42:30 – Close up of a bloody bite mark on a man's neck.

47:15 – A zombie eats a piece of flesh.

47:15 – A zombie eats a severed penis.

47:30 – A zombie is shot in the head.

47:30 – Two zombies are shot in the head.

47:30 – Another zombie is shot in the head.

50:15 – A woman pulls an organ out of a dead zombie.

51:45 – A group of zombies eat various body parts.

54:45 – A zombie eats a severed foot.

56:30 – A zombie receives oral sex from a severed head.

1:15:45 – A zombie is shot in the head.

1:19:00 – A zombie is shot in the head.

MY DEAD GIRLFRIEND

Year: 2006   Length: 73 minutes
Director: Brett Kelly

STATISTICS

First Zombie:	23:45
First Human Death:	18:15
First Zombie Death:	N/A
Amount of Gore:	Low
Gore Quality:	Average
Zombie Effects:	Low
Zombie Count:	Average
Zombie Deaths:	Very Low
Human Deaths:	Low

SUMMARY

After a young man accidentally backs over his girlfriend with his car and killing her, he uses an ancient book of magic to revive her. Unfortunately, she comes back to life as a flesh-eating zombie. Now, he must keep his friends and family from uncovering the truth.

EFFECTS HIGHLIGHTS

43:00 – A zombie bites a man's neck.

58:30 – A zombie is eating a piece of flesh.

1:00:15 – A zombie bites a man's arm.

1:03:15 – Two zombies eat a piece of flesh.

THE NECRO FILES

Year: 1997   Length: 72 minutes
Director: Matt Jaissle

STATISTICS

First Zombie:	15:30
First Human Death:	5:30
First Zombie Death:	1:01:45

Amount of Gore:	High
Gore Quality:	Average
Zombie Effects:	High
Zombie Count:	Low
Zombie Deaths:	Low
Human Deaths:	High

SUMMARY

A dead cannibal rapist returns to life as a flesh-eating zombie sex maniac. Two police officers, a satanic cult and a demon fetus each try to stop the violent creature before he can kill again.

EFFECTS HIGHLIGHTS

7:00 – A man rips out a woman's intestines.

8:00 – A man cuts off a woman's nipple and eats it.

12:00 – A man is shot in the chest.

12:00 – A man is shot in the head.

15:45 – A zombie rips off a man's penis.

15:45 – A zombie stabs a man in the neck with a severed penis.

16:00 – A zombie rips out a man's intestines.

24:45 – A zombie rips open a man's stomach.

25:45 – A zombie rips open a woman's back.

31:00 – Two men find a decimated body.

34:30 – A man finds a dead woman.

35:00 – A zombie shoots a man in the head.

50:15 – A woman is stabbed in the chest.

1:01:15 – A zombie is stabbed in the head.

1:01:30 – A zombie's hand is cut off with an axe.

1:01:30 – A zombie's foot is cut off with an axe.

1:01:45 – A zombie's penis is cut off with an axe.

THE NEIGHBOR ZOMBIE

Year: 2010   Length: 89 minutes
Directors: Young-Geun Hong, Young-doo Oh, Hoon Ryoo

STATISTICS

First Zombie:	13:30
First Human Death:	39:45
First Zombie Death:	28:00
Amount of Gore:	Average
Gore Quality:	Very High
Zombie Effects:	High
Zombie Count:	High
Zombie Deaths:	Average
Human Deaths:	Average

SUMMARY

An AIDS vaccine has unintended consequences when millions of innocent people are transformed into zombies. Families are torn apart as loved ones succumb to the disease.   Four different stories highlight the struggles families suffer when faced with having to kill a loved one who has become a zombie.

EFFECTS HIGHLIGHTS

10:45 – A man's foot is cut in half.

12:00 – A man eats a severed foot.

17:15 – A zombie's eye falls out.

26:45 – A woman cuts off one of her fingers.

30:00 – A woman stitches up a wound on a zombie's face.

39:45 – A woman is shot in the head.

NIGHTMARE CITY

Year: 1990   Length: 92 minutes
Director: Umberto Lenzi

STATISTICS

First Zombie:	8:45
First Human Death:	9:00
First Zombie Death:	1:10:45

Amount of Gore:	Very High
Gore Quality:	Average
Zombie Effects:	Average
Zombie Count:	Very High
Zombie Deaths:	High
Human Deaths:	Very High

SUMMARY

An airplane exposed to deadly radiation lands at an airport and is surrounded by the military. When the cargo hold is opened, blood thirsty zombies swarm out on to the runway. Armed with weapons and teeth they go on a terrifying rampage across the city.

EFFECTS HIGHLIGHTS

8:45 – A man is stabbed in the chest.

9:15 – A man's throat is slit.

9:30 – A zombie is shot in the chest.

10:00 – A zombie's arm is shot off.

20:45 – A man is stabbed in the neck.

21:15 – A woman is stabbed in the chest.

21:30 – A woman is hit in the head with an axe.

22:00 – A woman is stabbed in the chest.

22:15 – A zombie slices off a woman's breast with a knife.

39:30 – A man's throat is slit.

46:15 – A zombie is stabbed in the shoulder.

46:30 – A man is stabbed in the stomach.

47:30 – A woman is stabbed in the chest.

50:30 – A woman is stabbed in the chest.

57:15 – A man is shot in the stomach with a harpoon gun.

57:30 – A woman is stabbed in the chest.

1:02:45 – A woman is stabbed in the chest.

1:03:00 – A woman is stabbed in the eye.

1:03:15 – A woman is stabbed in the chest.

1:09:00 – A zombie is cut in the shoulder with an axe.

1:17:00 – A zombie's head is hit with a candlestick.

1:22:00 – A zombie is shot in the head.

1:24:00 – A zombie is shot in the chest.

1:24:15 – A zombie is shot in the head.

1:24:45 – A zombie is shot in the head.

1:35:30 – A zombie is shot in the head.

1:27:00 – A zombie is shot in the head.

NIGHT LIFE

Alternate Title: Grave Misdemeanours
Year: 1989   Length: 89 minutes
Director: David Acomba

STATISTICS

First Zombie:	57:30
First Human Death:	1:06:45
First Zombie Death:	1:15:00

Amount of Gore:	Average
Gore Quality:	High
Zombie Effects:	High
Zombie Count:	Average
Zombie Deaths:	Average
Human Deaths:	Average

SUMMARY

A high school student spends his evening working at his uncle's mortuary. One night he finds himself facing a group of zombies as the bullies that tormented him return from the dead after a fatal car accident.

EFFECTS HIGHLIGHTS

4:30 – A boy holds a severed arm.

38:45 – A man stabs a dead body in the back with a small drainage pipe.

1:05:45 – A zombie is drilled in the eye.

1:09:15 – A man punches his hand through a zombie's chest.

1:09:30 – A zombie is shot in the chest.

1:15:00 – A zombie's head is split open with an axe.

1:15:00 – A zombie is impaled on a metal pole.

1:20:30 – A zombie falls into a wood chipper.

1:20:45 – A zombie is shot in the head.

NIGHT OF THE BUMS

Year: 1998   Length: 71 minutes
Director: Charles E. Cullen

STATISTICS

First Zombie: 17:30
First Human Death: 24:15
First Zombie Death: 57:15

Amount of Gore: Very High
Gore Quality: Average
Zombie Effects: Very Low
Zombie Count: High
Zombie Deaths: High
Human Deaths: Average

SUMMARY

Three witches create a deadly concoction disguised as wine, that transforms the homeless into flesh-eating ghouls.

EFFECTS HIGHLIGHTS

23:00 – A woman is torn in half.

24:00 – A woman is stabbed in the neck.

24:15 – A zombie pulls off a woman's head.

25:00 – A zombie carries a severed head.

29:15 – A man's brains are spilling out on a sidewalk.

31:45 – A zombie bites a woman's neck.

33:30 – A zombie pulls off a woman's leg.

34:00 – A zombie is shot in the chest.

34:00 – A zombie is shot in the head.

34:00 – A zombie is shot in the shoulder.

35:00 – A zombie pulls a man's hand off.

35:30 – A man bleeds from the stump of his arm.

41:00 – A group of zombies tear open a woman's stomach.

41:15 – A zombie eats a woman's intestines.

41:15 – A zombie eats a severed hand.

43:45 – A zombie bites a baby's back.

44:00 – A zombie holds a pair of severed baby legs.

44:15 – A legless baby crawls across the ground.

45:00 – Blood squirts out of a headless torso.

46:15 – A man's finger is cut off.

57:15 – A zombie is shot in the chest.

59:00 – A zombie is shot in the chest.

59:15 – A zombie is shot in the head and chest.

59:30 – A zombie is shot in the head.

59:30 – A zombie is shot in the head.

1:00:30 – A zombie is shot in the stomach.

1:00:30 – A zombie is shot in the chest.

1:02:00 – A zombie is shot in the head.

1:02:15 – A zombie is shot in the head.

1:02:15 – A zombie is shot in the throat.

1:03:45 – A zombie is shot in the head.

1:04:00 – A zombie's throat is slashed.

NIGHT OF THE COMET

Year: 1984   Length: 95 minutes
Director: Thom Eberhardt

STATISTICS

First Zombie: 14:45
First Human Death: 15:00
First Zombie Death: 1:27:15

Amount of Gore: Low
Gore Quality: High
Zombie Effects: High
Zombie Count: Average
Zombie Deaths: Low
Human Deaths: High

SUMMARY

The Earth is struck by a comet and those who have survived fight for their lives against the evils that have taken over.

EFFECTS HIGHLIGHTS

38:00 – A woman rips the skin off of a zombie's hand.

1:01:00 – A man is shot in the chest.

NIGHT OF THE CREEPS

Year: 1986   Length: 90 minutes
Director: Fred Dekker

STATISTICS

First Zombie: 24:00
First Human Death: 58:00
First Zombie Death: 1:01:30

Amount of Gore: High
Gore Quality: High
Zombie Effects: High
Zombie Count: High
Zombie Deaths: Average
Human Deaths: Low

SUMMARY

Two college fraternity brothers thaw out a frozen corpse they found in their school clinic, releasing hidden space slugs that slither out and escape. Anyone infected by the slugs is promptly turned into a flesh-eating zombie. Before long, the campus is overrun by the living dead.

EFFECTS HIGHLIGHTS

35:45 – A dead body's head is split in half.

45:00 – A cat is missing its eyes.

50:15 – A dead body is missing its brain.

58:00 – A woman's head is cut in half with an axe.

1:01:30 – A zombie is shot in the head.

1:14:15 – A zombie is shot in the head.

1:15:00 – A zombie has no skin on its face.

1:15:45 – A zombie is shot in the head.

1:16:15 – A zombie is shot in the head.

1:16:30 – A zombie is shot in the head.

1:17:30 – A zombie is shot in the face.

1:18:00 – A zombie is stabbed in the face with a hammer.

1:18:15 – A zombie's head explodes.

NIGHT OF THE LIVING DEAD

Year: 1968   Length: 96 minutes
Director: George A. Romero

STATISTICS

First Zombie:	6:15
First Human Death:	7:00
First Zombie Death:	16:45
Amount of Gore:	High
Gore Quality:	High
Zombie Effects:	Low
Zombie Count:	Very High
Zombie Deaths:	Average
Human Deaths:	Average

SUMMARY

The dead have started rising from their graves and a group of survivors trapped in a house, must fight off the living dead and each other.

EFFECTS HIGHLIGHTS

12:15 – Close up of a bloody dead body.

43:30 – A zombie is shot in the chest.

43:45 – A zombie is shot in the chest.

1:07:45 – A zombie is shot in the chest.

1:10:15 – A zombie is shot in the chest.

1:13:00 – A zombie eats a piece of flesh.

1:13:00 – Two zombies fight over a pile of intestines.

1:13:00 – More zombies eat flesh.

1:13:15 – A zombie eats a piece of flesh.

1:13:15 – A zombie eats a piece of flesh.

1:13:15 – A zombie eats a severed hand.

1:13:15 – A zombie eats a piece of flesh.

1:22:30 – A zombie eats a piece of flesh.

NIGHT OF THE LIVING DEAD

Year: 1990   Length: 92 minutes
Director: Tom Savini

STATISTICS

First Zombie:	5:00
First Human Death:	6:00
First Zombie Death:	15:30
Amount of Gore:	High
Gore Quality:	Very High
Zombie Effects:	Very High
Zombie Count:	Very High
Zombie Deaths:	High
Human Deaths:	Average

SUMMARY

A group of survivors take refuge inside a farmhouse as a the dead come back to life to lay siege in this updated retelling of the 1968 classic directed by special effects master, Tom Savini.

EFFECTS HIGHLIGHTS

5:15 – A zombie is stabbed with a wreath stand.

5:30 – A man is stabbed in the hand with a wreath stand.

6:00 – A man hits his head against a gravestone.

6:15 – A zombie is stabbed with a wreath stand.

12:15 – A severed hand falls from a balcony.

15:30 – A zombie is stabbed in the head with a crowbar.

28:15 – Close up of a bloody dead body.

51:30 – A zombie is shot in the stomach.

51:30 – A zombie is shot in the chest.

51:30 – A zombie is shot in the chest.

51:45 – A zombie is shot in the head.

57:15 – A zombie is shot in the head.

57:45 – A zombie is shot in the head.

1:05:15 – A zombie is shot in the chest.

1:09:00 – A man is shot in the stomach.

1:09:15 – A zombie is shot in the head.

1:11:45 – A group of zombies eat a dead body.

1:12:15 – A zombie is shot in the head.

1:13:15 – A zombie is shot in the head.

1:13:30 – A zombie picks up a severed hand.

1:13:45 – A zombie eats a piece of flesh.

1:14:00 – A zombie eats a mouse.

1:22:00 – A zombie is shot in the head.

1:22:15 – A man is shot in the head.

NIGHT OF THE LIVING DEAD 30TH ANNIVERSARY

Year: 1998   Length: 93 minutes
Directors: George A. Romero, John Russo

STATISTICS

First Zombie:	7:00
First Human Death:	12:00
First Zombie Death:	21:45

Amount of Gore:	High
Gore Quality:	High
Zombie Effects:	Low
Zombie Count:	Very High
Zombie Deaths:	Very High
Human Deaths:	Average

SUMMARY

Producer and writer John Russo takes over the directing and adds brand new scenes and characters to the original film.

EFFECTS HIGHLIGHTS

17:15 – Close up of a bloody dead body.

34:30 – A zombie is missing half of an arm.

35:00 – Brains fall out of an open skull.

44:00 – A zombie is shot in the chest.

44:15 – A zombie is shot in the chest.

1:01:15 – A zombie is shot in the chest.

1:06:15 – A zombie eats a piece of flesh.

1:06:15 – A group of zombies eat flesh.

1:06:15 – A group of zombies fight over a pile of intestines.

1:06:30 – A zombie eats intestines.

1:06:45 – A pair of zombies eat flesh.

1:06:45 – A zombie eats a piece of flesh.

1:07:00 – A zombie eats a piece of flesh.

1:07:00 – A zombie eats a severed arm.

1:07:00 – A zombie eats a piece of flesh.

1:09:30 – A zombie eats a piece of flesh.

1:16:00 – A zombie eats a piece of flesh.

NIGHT OF THE LIVING DEAD 3D

Year: 2006   Length: 80 minutes
Director: Jeff Broadstreet

STATISTICS

First Zombie:	6:00
First Human Death:	36:00
First Zombie Death:	29:15

Amount of Gore:	Average
Gore Quality:	Very High
Zombie Effects:	Very High
Zombie Count:	Very High
Zombie Deaths:	Average
Human Deaths:	Average

SUMMARY

The horror classic gets a modern day retelling in 3D.

EFFECTS HIGHLIGHTS

29:00 – A zombie is stabbed in the chest.

42:00 – A zombie is shot in the chest.

42:15 – A zombie is shot in the head.

58:45 – A zombie is stabbed in the mouth with a shovel.

1:12:00 – A group of zombies tear out a man's intestines.

1:13:00 – A group of zombies eat entrails.

1:14:15 – A man has a crowbar sticking out of his chest.

1:15:30 – A zombie is shot in the head.

NIGHT OF THE LIVING DORKS

Year: 2004   Length: 89 minutes
Director: Mathias Dinter

STATISTICS

First Zombie:	6:00
First Human Death:	36:00
First Zombie Death:	29:15

Amount of Gore:	Low
Gore Quality:	Average
Zombie Effects:	Average
Zombie Count:	Average
Zombie Deaths:	N/A
Human Deaths:	N/A

SUMMARY

Three uncool high school friends decide to try a old voodoo ritual then die in a car accident. They soon find themselves alive and well, but as members of the living dead. However, while they were not exactly cool as the living, being a zombie has its advantages.

EFFECTS HIGHLIGHTS

40:45 – A zombie eats a severed foot.

41:00 – A zombie pulls another zombie's ear off.

1:13:30 – A man pulls off a zombie's hand.

NIGHT OF THE SEAGULLS

Alternate Title: Night of the Death Cult
Year: 1975   Length: 89 minutes
Director: Amando de Ossorio

STATISTICS

First Zombie:	25:15
First Human Death:	4:45
First Zombie Death:	1:14:15

Amount of Gore:	Low
Gore Quality:	High
Zombie Effects:	High
Zombie Count:	High

Top and right, on the set of "Night of the Living Dead 3D". Above, Sid Haig in between takes courtesy of Daniel Symmes.

Zombie Deaths: Average
Human Deaths: Average

SUMMARY

The fourth entry in the Blind Dead saga. A young doctor and his wife take up residency in a seaside village and fight off an attack by the undead Templar Knights, who have risen from watery graves to collect human sacrifices.

EFFECTS HIGHLIGHTS

8:00 – A woman is stabbed in the chest.

8:00 – A man cuts out a woman's heart.

1:26:00 – A zombie bleeds from its eye sockets.

NINJA'S VS. ZOMBIES

Year: 2008   Length: 99 minutes
Director: Justin Timpane

STATISTICS

First Zombie: 2:15
First Human Death: 4:45
First Zombie Death: 47:15

Amount of Gore: High
Gore Quality: High
Zombie Effects: Average
Zombie Count: Very High
Zombie Deaths: Average
Human Deaths: Average

SUMMARY

Three ninja's find themselves in a battle to the death to save mankind from an army of the dead.

EFFECTS HIGHLIGHTS

5:30 – A woman stabs a zombie in the neck.

17:45 – A zombie is eating a severed arm.

24:00 – A severed arm is tossed in the air.

24:15 – A zombie eats from a dead body.

47:00 – A zombie is stabbed in the chest.

47:00 – A zombie is stabbed under the chin.

47:15 – A zombie is stabbed in the chest.

47:15 – A zombie is cut in half.

47:30 – A zombie is impaled on a pole.

47:30 – A zombie is decapitated.

51:00 – A zombie is decapitated.

51:15 – A zombie is decapitated.

51:30 – A man is stabbed in the chest.

52:45 – A man holds a severed head

1:02:15 – A zombie is decapitated.

1:02:15 – A zombie is shot in the head.

1:02:30 – A zombie is shot in the chest.

1:02:30 – A zombie is decapitated.

1:04:15 – A zombie bites a man's neck.

NUDIST COLONY OF THE DEAD

Year: 1991   Length: 90 minutes
Director: Mark Pirro

STATISTICS

First Zombie: 23:00
First Human Death: 1:10:15
First Zombie Death: N/A

Amount of Gore: High
Gore Quality: Average
Zombie Effects: Low
Zombie Count: Average
Zombie Deaths: Very Low
Human Deaths: Average

SUMMARY

A judge orders the Sunny Buttocks Nudist Camp to be closed down in an attempt to stop the nudist community. The camp members enter into a suicide pact, vowing to return for vengeance. Five years later, a group of campers on the old camp site start disappearing as the dead nudists return to life.

EFFECTS HIGHLIGHTS

26:15 – Close up of a severed head.

31:30 – A zombie's ear falls off.

46:30 – A woman finds two severed heads floating in a pool.

47:30 – A woman finds a spine and severed limbs in a tent.

52:00 – Close up of a bloody wound.

52:00 – Various dead bodies and limbs are scattered in a field.

52:30 – A woman holds a severed head.

1:03:45 – A man's hand is cut off.

1:03:45 – A man's arm is cut off.

1:04:15 – A man finds a severed head in a bag.

1:04:30 – A man is cut in half.

OASIS OF THE ZOMBIES

Year: 1983   Length: 82 minutes
Director: Jesus Franco

STATISTICS

First Zombie: 34:45
First Human Death: 9:15
First Zombie Death: 1:17:00

Amount of Gore: Average

Gore Quality:	Average
Zombie Effects:	High
Zombie Count:	High
Zombie Deaths:	Average
Human Deaths:	Very High

SUMMARY

During World War II, the Nazis buried over $6 million in gold in the Sahara Desert. Fifty years later, a man stumbles on the secret in his late father's diaries and sets out to find it, unaware of the zombies that guard the hidden treasure.

EFFECTS HIGHLIGHTS

9:00 – A man is stabbed in the hand with a pen.

37:00 – A zombie bites a woman's breast.

38:00 – A zombie pulls out a woman's intestines.

OC BABES AND THE SLASHER OF ZOMBIE TOWN

Year: 2008   Length: 72 minutes
Director: Creep Creepersin

STATISTICS

First Zombie:	35:45
First Human Death:	32:15
First Zombie Death:	N/A

Amount of Gore:	Low
Gore Quality:	Average
Zombie Effects:	Low
Zombie Count:	Average
Zombie Deaths:	Very Low
Human Deaths:	Average

SUMMARY

A group of Orange County locals find themselves trapped in a bar, surrounded by zombies on the outside and a serial killer within.

EFFECTS HIGHLIGHTS

51:30 – A man is stabbed in the neck.

ONE DARK NIGHT

Year: 1983   Length: 89 minutes
Director: Tom McLoughlin

STATISTICS

First Zombie:	1:12:00
First Human Death:	1:18:00
First Zombie Death:	1:24:00

Amount of Gore:	Low
Gore Quality:	Average

Zombie Effects:	High
Zombie Count:	Average
Zombie Deaths:	Average
Human Deaths:	Average

SUMMARY

As part of an initiation into a club, a young girl is forced to spend the night in a mausoleum. However, the dare becomes terrifying when forces from beyond the grave start to revive the dead.

EFFECTS HIGHLIGHTS

1:17:15 – A woman tears the skin off of a zombie's face.

1:17:45 – A woman put her foot into a zombie's stomach.

1:21:30 – A man knocks off a zombie's jaw.

1:24:00 – A zombie's head swells up.

1:24:00 – A zombie's face melts.

ONECHANBARA

Year: 2008   Length: 86 minutes
Director: Yôhei Fukuda

STATISTICS

First Zombie:	1:00
First Human Death:	4:30
First Zombie Death:	1:30

Amount of Gore:	Very High
Gore Quality:	High
Zombie Effects:	High
Zombie Count:	Very High
Zombie Deaths:	Very High
Human Deaths:	High

SUMMARY

In the not-too-distant future, the world has been ravaged by a zombie outbreak. Aya, clad in only a bikini and a cowboy hat fights of swarms of hungry zombies in the search for her father's killer.

EFFECTS HIGHLIGHTS

1:30 – A zombie is shot in the head.

5:30 – Three zombies evaporate in a cloud of blood.

5:45 – A woman cuts through a group of zombies with a sword.

5:45 – A zombie is decapitated.

5:45 – A zombie's arm is cut off.

6:00 – A woman kicks a zombie in the head, crushing it.

6:00 – A zombie is cut in half.

7:00 – A large group of zombies evaporate in a cloud of blood.

7:15 – A severed zombie head is balanced on the tip of

a sword.

9:00 – A zombie's arm is cut off.

9:15 – A zombie is shot in the head.

9:30 – A zombie is shot in the head.

13:45 – A man picks up a severed head.

17:45 – A man's throat is slit.

28:15 – A woman pulls off a man's arm.

30:45 – Two zombies are shot in the head.

34:00 – A zombie eats from a dead body.

50:30 – A zombie is decapitated.

58:30 – A large group of zombies are attacked with a sword.

58:45 – A zombie is decapitated.

58:45 – Various limbs are cut off of zombies.

1:01:00 – A zombie is shot in the head.

1:02:00 – A zombie sticks its fingers into a man's eyes.

1:02:15 – Multiple zombies are killed with a sword.

1:03:15 – A man stabs a zombie in the back.

1:05:45 – A woman is shot in the head.

1:15:00 – A woman is stabbed in the chest.

OUTPOST

Year: 2007   Length: 90 minutes
Director: Steve Barker

STATISTICS

First Zombie:	55:15
First Human Death:	55:30
First Zombie Death:	1:20:45
Amount of Gore:	High
Gore Quality:	Very High
Zombie Effects:	High
Zombie Count:	High
Zombie Deaths:	Average
Human Deaths:	Average

SUMMARY

A team of mercenaries embark on a mission to escort a civilian to a deserted military post in Eastern Europe. The squad soon find themselves trapped in an underground bunker with a bloodthirsty survivor of violent and deadly Nazi experiments

EFFECTS HIGHLIGHTS

54:45 – A bullet is hammered into a man's kneecap.

55:00 – A man is stabbed in the eye with a bullet casing.

55:15 – A man is stabbed in the stomach.

58:15 – A man is stabbed in the mouth.

1:03:15 – A man is stabbed in the stomach with a pick axe.

1:03:45 – A man's head is crushed against a wall.

1:07:45 – A zombie is shot in the head.

1:16:30 – A zombie is shot in the chest.

1:18:00 – A zombie is stabbed in the stomach.

1:22:30 – A zombie's intestines fall out of its stomach.

1:31:45 – A zombie bites a chunk of flesh out of a woman's neck.

1:31:45 – A zombie is shot in the head.

OZONE

Year: 1993   Length: 78 minutes
Director: J.R. Bookwalter

STATISTICS

First Zombie:	11:15
First Human Death:	4:30
First Zombie Death:	57:00
Amount of Gore:	High
Gore Quality:	High
Zombie Effects:	Average
Zombie Count:	High
Zombie Deaths:	Average
Human Deaths:	High

SUMMARY

Two police officers are on the hunt for the kingpin responsible for creating an addictive drug called Ozone, an addictive drug which side effects include turning those who use it into the undead.

EFFECTS HIGHLIGHTS

4:15 – A vein on a man's arm swells and bursts.

4:15 – Veins burst on a man's neck.

4:30 – A man's head explodes.

7:45 – A man is shot in the chest.

11:45 – A man is shot in the chest.

12:00 – A man's hand is cut off with a piece of glass.

17:45 – A man's skin melts off of his face.

23:45 – A man picks up a severed finger.

30:30 – A car runs over a man's head.

36:30 – A man is cut on the shoulder.

36:45 – A man is cut on the leg.

37:45 – A man is cut on the chest.

38:30 – Blisters swell up on a man's arm.

42:00 – A man's face swells up.

42:15 – A woman's face swells up.

56:15 – A man is shot in the chest.

57:00 – A zombie is shot in the head.

1:07:15 – A zombie is shot in the chest.

1:12:00 – A zombie slices its stomach open with a knife.

PARIS BY NIGHT OF THE LIVING DEAD

Year: 2009   Length: 12 minutes
Director: Grégory Morin

STATISTICS

First Zombie: 1:30
First Human Death: 1:30
First Zombie Death: 2:45

Amount of Gore: Very High
Gore Quality: Very High
Zombie Effects: High
Zombie Count: Very High
Zombie Deaths: Very High
Human Deaths: Low

SUMMARY

A pair of lovers fight their way out of a zombie infested Paris.

EFFECTS HIGHLIGHTS

1:30 – A group of zombies rip out a man's intestines.

2:45 – A zombie is shot in the head.

2:45 – A zombie is shot in the chest.

2:45 – A zombie is shot in the head.

3:00 – A zombie is shot in the chest.

3:00 – Two zombies are shot in the chest.

3:15 – A zombie is shot in the chest.

3:15 – A zombie is shot in the head.

3:15 – A zombie's head explodes.

3:30 – A zombie is shot in the chest.

3:30 – Two zombies are shot in the chest.

3:45 – A zombie is shot in the chest.

3:45 – A zombie is shot in the face.

3:45 – A zombie is stabbed in the eye with a gun barrel.

4:00 – A zombie is cut in half.

4:00 – A zombie's head is cut in half.

4:00 – A zombie is shot in the head.

4:15 – A zombie shot in the head.

4:30 – A zombie is decapitated.

4:30 – A zombie is cut in the stomach with a chainsaw.

4:30 – A second zombie is cut in the stomach with a chainsaw.

4:30 – A third zombie is cut in the stomach with a chainsaw.

5:15 – A zombie bites a man's leg.

6:00 – A zombie is hit with a missile.

7:30 – A zombie bites a woman's wrist.

12:00 – A zombie eats a piece of flesh.

PATHOGEN

Year: 2006   Length: 67 minutes
Director: Emily Hagins

STATISTICS

First Zombie: 34:15
First Human Death: 1:03:5
First Zombie Death: 43:45
Amount of Gore: Average
Gore Quality: High
Zombie Effects: Average
Zombie Count: Very High
Zombie Deaths: Low
Human Deaths: Low

SUMMARY

A zombie epidemic breaks out when bacteria found in the local water turns those who drink it into the undead. A group of middle school students try to save their friends, their town and themselves in spite of the overwhelming odds against them.

EFFECTS HIGHLIGHTS

43:00 – A zombie is stabbed in the eye.

59:00 – A zombie is eating a dead body.

1:03:15 – A boy is decapitated.

PLAGA ZOMBIE

Year: 1997   Length: 69 minutes
Directors: Pablo Parés, Hernán Sáez

STATISTICS

First Zombie: 2:30
First Human Death: 10:45
First Zombie Death: 20:45

Amount of Gore: High
Gore Quality: Average
Zombie Effects: Average
Zombie Count: Very High
Zombie Deaths: High
Human Deaths: Average

SUMMARY

Two men take to the streets to fight for their lives with any weapon they can find against a zombie outbreak sweeping the country.

EFFECTS HIGHLIGHTS

7:45 – A section of a man's stomach is cut open.

12:15 – A man has open sores on his back.

13:15 – A man's stomach swells up and explodes.

19:00 – A zombie is stabbed in the eye with a pen.

31:15 – A zombie cuts off a man's hand.

41:15 – Close up of a severed hand.

43:00 – A man crushes a zombie's head.

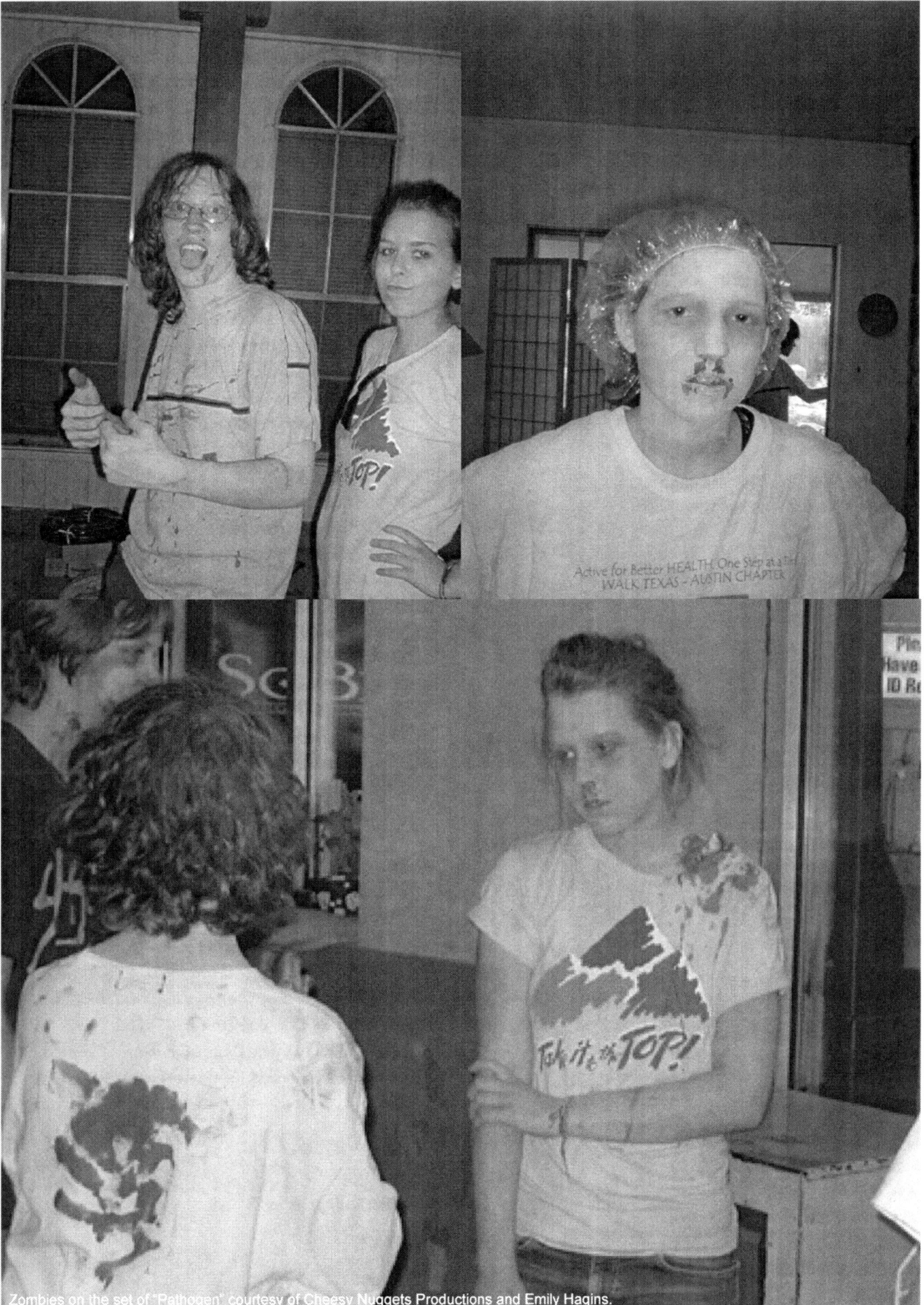

Zombies on the set of "Pathogen" courtesy of Cheesy Nuggets Productions and Emily Hagins.

49:45 – A zombie rubs a brain in a man's face.

52:45 – A zombie is stabbed in the neck with a stick.

54:00 – A zombie's throat is slit.

55:15 – A man punches through a zombie's chest.

56:00 – A zombie is stabbed repeatedly with a pen.

57:15 – A zombie's tongue is cut off with sheers.

57:15 – A zombie is stabbed in the ear with a pencil.

57:30 – A man pulls off a zombie's leg.

57:30 – A man pulls out a zombie's intestines.

58:00 – A man cuts a zombie's leg with a machete.

58:00 – A man knocks off a zombie's head.

58:15 – A zombie's torso is ripped open.

58:30 – A zombie is stabbed with a pole.

1:04:00 – A zombie is shot in the head.

PLAGA ZOMBIE 2: ZONA MUTANTE

Year: 2001   Length: 101 minutes
Directors: Pablo Parés, Hernán Sáez

STATISTICS

First Zombie:	9:30
First Human Death:	26:45
First Zombie Death:	12:45

Amount of Gore:	Very High
Gore Quality:	High
Zombie Effects:	Average
Zombie Count:	Very High
Zombie Deaths:	High
Human Deaths:	High

SUMMARY

A group of aliens unleash a deadly virus that turns humans into the living dead. Three men trapped inside a quarantined town must use their wits, bravery and brains to fight their way to freedom through the zombies standing in their way.

EFFECTS HIGHLIGHTS

10:00 – A zombie is holding a severed head.

12:00 – A man pulls a zombie's arm off.

12:18 – A man jams his fist into a zombie's neck and pulls out its spine.

12:30 – A man breaks a zombie's leg in half.

12:45 – A man bites a tendon off a severed arm.

12:45 – A man rips a zombie in half.

13:00 – A zombie is stabbed in the mouth with a severed arm.

13:00 – A zombie bites the skin on a man's back.

18:05 – A zombie holds a severed leg.

20:00 – A zombie's intestines are falling out of its stomach.

20:15 – A zombie sprays a man with stomach bile.

20:30 – A man rips out a zombie's intestines.

21:00 – A man pokes a bloody wound with a stick.

21:15 – A hand is sticking out of a dead zombie's mouth.

26:45 – A severed hand is thrown to the floor.

28:15 – A zombie's head is split in half.

28:30 – A zombie is decapitated.

30:15 – A zombie is stabbed in the head with a wooden pole.

31:00 – A zombie is stabbed in the eyes with a wooden poles.

39:15 – Two zombies are decapitated.

58:45 – A body has been torn to pieces.

1:10:30 – A zombie eats a pile of intestines.

1:16:45 – A zombie is decapitated.

1:17:00 – A man punches his fist through a zombie's skull.

1:17:30 – A zombie's throat is slit.

1:20:30 – A man steps on a zombie's neck.

1:20:30 – A zombie is stabbed in the stomach.

1:20:45 – A zombie is stabbed in the stomach.

1:20:45 – A zombie's face is pulled off.

1:21:13 – A zombie is decapitated.

1:21:15 – A zombie is stabbed in the stomach.

1:21:15 – A zombie is stabbed in the stomach.

1:21:30 – A zombie is stabbed in the head.

1:21:30 – A zombie's scalp is ripped open.

1:24:00 – A man cuts a zombie's eye out with a knife.

1:24:15 – A zombie's arm is cut open.

1:24:15 – A zombie is cut in half.

1:27:00 – A zombie's head is pulled off.

1:27:15 – The top of zombie's skull is cut off with a sword.

1:27:45 – A man's head is smashed against a wall.

1:32:15 – Fluid leaks from a zombie's mouth.

1:32:15 – Fluid leaks from a zombie's back.

1:32:15 – Fluid leaks from a zombie's hand.

1:32:15 – The skin on a zombie's back splits open.

1:32:15 – The skin on a zombie's leg splits open.

1:32:30 – A zombie leaks fluid from various contusions.

1:32:45 – A zombie pulls its skin off.

THE PLAGUE

Year: 2006   Length: 86 minutes
Director: Hal Masonberg

STATISTICS

First Zombie:	25:00
First Human Death:	49:45

First Zombie Death: 28:00

Amount of Gore: High
Gore Quality: Very High
Zombie Effects: High
Zombie Count: Low
Zombie Deaths: Average
Human Deaths: Low

SUMMARY

A mysterious illness infects every child on the planet ,leaving them in a coma. A decade later, they awaken as blood thirsty zombies and begin to attack the adults.

EFFECTS HIGHLIGHTS

26:00 – Close up of a head wound.

28:00 – A zombie spits up blood.

29:00 – A woman's jaw is broken.

40:45 – A zombie is shot in the chest.

43:00 – A man has a broken leg.

44:00 – A man is injected with a syringe.

1:02:15 – A zombie is shot in the back.

1:05:45 – A zombie is shot in the shoulder.

1:06:15 – A zombie bleeds from a bullet wound.

1:14:30 – A man is shot in the back.

1:14:30 – A zombie is shot in the head.

PLAGUERS

Year: 2008   Length: 86 minutes
Director: Brad Sykes

STATISTICS

First Zombie: :30
First Human Death: 29:00
First Zombie Death: 42:00

Amount of Gore: High
Gore Quality: Very High
Zombie Effects: Very High
Zombie Count: High
Zombie Deaths: Average
Human Deaths: High

SUMMARY

A group of space pirates hijack a fuel-transport vessel that is heading for Earth. During the boarding an alien virus known as "Thanatos" is accidentally released. The highly contagious disease mutates its victims into bloodthirsty and nearly indestructible zombies. The pirates and crew are forced to band together to destroy the virus and infected crew before the ship reaches Earth and destroys the entire planet.

EFFECTS HIGHLIGHTS

29:00 – A man is stabbed in the neck.

30:45 – A zombie is stabbed in the head.

34:15 – A zombie is shot in the chest.

39:00 – A man is bitten on the neck.

39:15 – A zombie is shot in the chest.

42:00 – A zombie is shot in the head.

42:15 – A zombie's head is cut in half.

1:08:15 – A zombie rips open a man's stomach.

1:08:15 – A zombie rips the skin off of a man's chest.

1:09:00 – A zombie is stabbed in the neck.

1:09:15 – A zombie's throat is slit.

1:11:30 – A zombie is stabbed in the neck.

1:11:45 – A woman's lips are bitten off.

1:15:00 – A zombie rips off a man's arm.

1:15:30 – A woman is stabbed in the stomach.

PLANET TERROR

Year: 2007   Length: 107 minutes
Director: Robert Rodriguez

STATISTICS

First Zombie: 27:45
First Human Death: 11:00
First Zombie Death: 44:30

Amount of Gore: Very High
Gore Quality: Very High
Zombie Effects: Very High
Zombie Count: Very High
Zombie Deaths: Very High
Human Deaths: Very High

SUMMARY

An experimental biochemical weapon is released into the air and turns thousands of people into zombie-like creatures. It is up to a rag-tag group of survivors to try to stop the infection and find those who are behind its release.

EFFECTS HIGHLIGHTS

8:30 – A woman has a piece of metal stuck in her leg.

10:45 – A man's testicle is thrown on the ground.

11:45 – A man is shot in the chest.

11:45 – A man is shot in the chest.

11:45 – A man is shot in the chest.

11:45 – A man is shot in the chest.

11:45 – A jar of testicles is dropped on the ground.

12:15 – The skin on a man's face starts to blister.

12:30 – The skin on three men's faces melts.

17:15 – A woman pulls a piece of metal out of her leg.

22:15 – Close up of a bite wound.

23:15 – A man's tongue is blistered and infected.

23:45 – A blister squirts blood in a man's face.

24:15 – Close up of an infected bite wound.

25:30 – A man is stabbed in the arm with a syringe.

25:45 – A man is stabbed in the arm with a syringe.
25:45 – A man is stabbed in the arm with a syringe.
28:00 – A group of zombies tear a woman apart.
30:00 – A zombie holds a severed leg.
30:00 – A woman is missing her lower leg.
38:15 – The back of a woman's head is missing.
40:15 – A woman is stabbed in the wrist with a syringe.
42:30 – A man is missing the top part of his finger.
44:15 – A man is bitten on the arm.
44:15 – A man is missing the lower half of his left arm.
44:30 – A zombie bites a man's chest.
44:30 – A zombie is shot in the back.
44:30 – A zombie is shot in the back.
44:30 – A zombie is shot in the stomach.
44:30 – A zombie bites the skin off of a man's face.
44:45 – A zombie is shot in the chest twice.
45:00 – A zombie is shot in the face.
45:00 – A zombie is shot in the face.
45:15 – A zombie is stabbed in the chest with a pistol.
45:30 – A zombie is shot in the chest.
45:30 – A zombie is shot in the back.
45:45 – A zombie is shot in the head.
47:15 – A man has an open wound on his chest.
47:45 – A zombie wipes blood on a man's face.
49:30 – A woman breaks her hand.
51:15 – A pair of zombies tear open a man's stomach.
51:30 – A zombie's throat is slit.
52:00 – A zombie is stabbed in the back.
53:30 – A zombie is stabbed in the chest.
1:00:15 – A young boy has a bullet wound in his head.
1:08:15 – A group of zombies tear a man to pieces.
1:08:15 – A zombie is shot in the head.
1:08:15 – A zombie is shot in the head.
1:08:15 – A zombie is shot in the head.
1:08:30 – A zombie is shot in the chest.
1:08:30 – A zombie is shot in the chest.
1:08:30 – A zombie is shot in the chest.
1:08:30 – A zombie is shot in the chest.
1:08:30 – A zombie is shot in the back.
1:08:30 – A zombie is shot in the back.
1:09:30 – A zombie is shot in the chest.
1:09:30 – A zombie is shot in the chest.
1:09:30 – A zombie is shot in the chest.
1:09:45 – A zombie is shot in the back.
1:09:45 – A zombie is shot in the head.
1:10:15 – A zombie is shot in the back.
1:12:15 – A zombie is run over by a truck.
1:12:15 – A zombie is run over by a truck.
1:12:15 – A zombie is run over by a truck.
1:12:30 – A dog is run over by a truck.

1:12:30 – A zombie is run over by a truck.
1:12:30 – A zombie is run over by a truck.
1:13:15 – A group of zombies are shot in the chest.
1:17:45 – The skin on a man's face starts to blister.
1:19:00 – A man is shot in the chest.
1:22:15 – The skin on a man's face starts to blister.
1:25:00 – A man is stabbed in the eye with a wooden leg.
1:25:15 – The skin on a man's face starts to blister.
1:25:45 – A man's penis melts and falls off.
1:26:00 – A man is stabbed in the leg with a syringe.
1:26:15 – A man is stabbed in the eye with a syringe.
1:26:30 – The skin on a man's face starts to melt.
1:26:30 – A man is shot in the chest.
1:27:15 – A man vomits.
1:29:00 – A zombie is shot in the chest.
1:29:00 – A zombie is shot in the chest.
1:29:00 – A zombie is shot in the chest.
1:30:15 – A man is shot in the head.
1:32:45 – A zombie is shot in the chest.
1:32:45 – A zombie is shot in the chest.
1:32:45 – A zombie is shot in the chest.
1:32:45 – A zombie is shot in the chest.
1:32:45 – A zombie is shot in the chest.
1:32:45 – A zombie is shot in the chest.
1:33:15 – A zombie is shot in the chest.
1:33:15 – A zombie is shot in the chest.
1:33:15 – A zombie is shot in the chest.
1:33:15 – A zombie is shot in the chest.
1:33:30 – A zombie is shot in the chest.
1:33:45 – A zombie is shot in the back.
1:33:45 – A man is shot in the stomach.
1:34:00 – A zombie is shot in the chest.
1:34:00 – A man is shot in the chest.
1:34:00 – A zombie is shot in the chest.
1:34:15 – A zombie is shot in the chest.
1:34:15 – A zombie is shot in the neck.
1:35:00– A zombie is shot in the chest.
1:36:00 – A helicopter cuts through a crowd of zombies.
1:38:45 – A zombie is shot in the head.

PLATOON OF THE DEAD

Year: 2009   Length: 82 minutes
Director: John Bowker

STATISTICS

First Zombie:	5:15
First Human Death:	4:30
First Zombie Death:	15:30
Amount of Gore:	High

Gore Quality: Average
Zombie Effects: Average
Zombie Count: High
Zombie Deaths: High
Human Deaths: Average

SUMMARY

Three soldiers take refuge in an abandoned house. While they attempt to plan their next move, they are attacked by platoon of zombies.

EFFECTS HIGHLIGHTS

2:15 – A man has been impaled on a branch.

6:45 – A man finds a pile of intestines.

31:15 – A zombie's arm is shot off at the elbow.

49:45 – A group of zombies rip out a woman's intestines.

1:09:45 – A woman pulls out a man's eyeball.

PONTYPOOL

Year: 2008   Length: 97 minutes
Director: Bruce McDonald

STATISTICS

First Zombie: 1:04:15
First Human Death: N/A
First Zombie Death: N/A

Amount of Gore: Low
Gore Quality: Very High
Zombie Effects: Very High
Zombie Count: High
Zombie Death: Very Low
Human Deaths: Very Low

SUMMARY

A radio shock-jock struggles to keep his show on the air and report to his audience as a mass of infected people lay siege to the radio station.

EFFECTS HIGHLIGHTS

1:07:30 – A zombie vomits blood.

PORNO HOLOCAUST

Year: 1981   Length:Very Low13 minutes
Director: Joe D'Amato

STATISTICS

First Zombie: 1:11:00
First Human Death: 1:11:15
First Zombie Death: 1:42:45

Amount of Gore: Low
Gore Quality: Average
Zombie Effects: Average
Zombie Count: Low

Zombie Death: Low
Human Deaths: Average

SUMMARY

A group of castaways wash ashore on a deserted island. However, they are unaware that a sex-crazed zombie is also stalking the island. After he rapes several of the women, the survivors must find a way to either escape the island or kill the bloodthirsty and perverted creature.

EFFECTS HIGHLIGHTS

1:14:15 – A man is hit in the face with a rock.

1:14:30 – A man is hit in the face with a piece of wood.

1:34:25 – A man has a bloody wound on his chest.

1:40:15 – A dead woman is bleeding from the vagina.

POULTRYGEIST

Year: 2006   Length: 103 minutes
Director: Lloyd Kaufman

STATISTICS

First Zombie: 2:15
First Human Death: 4:15
First Zombie Death: 1:13:00

Amount of Gore: Very High
Gore Quality: High
Zombie Effects: Average
Zombie Count: Very High
Zombie Deaths: Very High
Human Deaths: High

SUMMARY

When a fast food restaurant is built on the site of an ancient Indian burial ground, the food becomes possessed and those who eat it turn into zombies.

EFFECTS HIGHLIGHTS

4:00 – A man spits up blood.

4:15 – A hand pulls a pair of boxes out of a man's anus.

23:00 – Blood sprays out of a man's anus.

23:15 – A zombie bursts out of a man's stomach.

38:15 – A man falls in a meat grinder.

50:15 – A dead chicken bites a man's penis.

51:30 – A man is stabbed in the anus with a broom.

1:03:45 – A man bites the head off a zombie chicken.

1:08:15 – A zombie bites off a man's head.

1:08:45 – A zombie cuts a man's arm off.

1:09:00 – A zombie pulls off a man's leg.

1:09:15 – A group of zombies rip open a man's stomach.

1:09:30 – A group of zombies rip open a man's stomach.

The zombie chicken from "Poultrygeist" courtesy of Jim Ojala.

1:09:45 – A zombie rips off a woman's face.

1:10:00 – A zombie slices off a man's face.

1:10:15 – A zombie rips a man's head off.

1:10:30 – A zombie rips off a man's testicles.

1:10:45 – A zombie rips a man's eye out.

1:11:00 – A zombie rips out a woman's breast implants.

1:11:30 – A pair of zombies pull off a man's legs.

1:12:30 – A zombie rips out a man's spine.

1:13:00 – A man is shot in the chest.

1:13:00 – A zombie is shot in the chest.

1:13:15 – A man is shot in the back.

1:14:30 – A zombie bites off a man's nose.

1:15:00 – A zombie is shot in the chest.

1:18:45 – A man holds a severed head.

1:25:45 – A man's head is crushed.

1:32:45 – A zombie's head explodes.

PREMUTOS: LORD OF THE LIVING DEAD

Year: 1997   Length: 106 minutes
Director: Olaf Ittenbach

STATISTICS

First Zombie:	1:15
First Human Death:	9:15
First Zombie Death:	11:45
Amount of Gore:	Very High
Gore Quality:	Very High
Zombie Effects:	Very High
Zombie Count:	Very High
Zombie Deaths:	Very High
Human Deaths:	Very High

SUMMARY

Centuries ago, a brutal fallen angel called Premutos ruled the earth. When an ancient book of evil is accidentally uncovered, Premutos returns to terrorize the innocent, leading an army of the dead.

EFFECTS HIGHLIGHTS

1:00 – A man is missing half of his right arm.

1:00 – Close up of a severed head.

1:15 – Close up of a severed head.

1:15 – A man is stabbed in the back.

1:15 – A man is stabbed in the stomach.

1:30 – Close up of numerous dead bodies.

1:45 – Flesh and organs merge into a skeleton.

2:00 – A group of zombies tear a man apart.

2:00 – Flesh and organs merge into a skeleton.

2:30 – A man is stabbed in the back.

4:45 – Close up of a bloody skeleton.

5:45 – A zombie is shot in the head.

5:45 – A zombie bites off a man's hand.

6:00 – A zombie bites a man's face.

9:15 – A man is stabbed in the face with a shovel.

11:15 – A zombie vomits blood.

11:45 – A zombie rips the flesh off of its face.

11:45 – A zombie's head explodes.

11:45 – A severed hand falls to the floor.

12:00 – Close up of a bloody body.

12:15 – A man is stabbed in the eye with a pick axe.

12:15 – A man is shot in the head.

13:00 – A man's penis is bitten off.

13:15 – A man shoots himself in the head.

13:15 – A zombie is shot in the head.

13:30 – A man is shot in the stomach.

18:45 – A woman holds a severed head.

29:15 – A man throws a severed head.

30:00 – A man is hit in the face with an axe.

30:15 – A man's hand is cut off.

30:15 – A man is hit in the head with an axe.

33:45 – A man's arm is shot off.

33:45 – A man is shot in the chest.

34:00 – A man is shot in the chest.

34:45 – A zombie is stabbed in the chest.

35:00 – A zombie is stabbed in the chest.

35:00 – A zombie is stabbed in the head.

35:00 – A zombie is stabbed in the chest.

35:30 – A man carries a severed head.

51:15 – A man is stabbed in the cheek.

51:15 – A man is stabbed in the chest.

51:30 – A severed head falls to the ground.

56:15 – A woman holds a severed head.

1:01:00 – A pole pierces a man's stomach.

1:01:00 – A cork screw pierces a man's stomach.

1:01:15 – A man is cut with barbed wire.

1:01:15 – A pole pierces a man's head.

1:01:15 – A man pulls a pole out of his mouth.

1:01:45 – A man pulls a piece of metal out of his leg.

1:01:45 – A man pulls a piece of metal out of his stomach.

1:10:00 – A zombie bites a man's arm.

1:10:15 – A zombie rips open a man's stomach.

1:10:30 – A zombie bites a man's face.

1:10:45 – A zombie's throat is slit.

1:13:30 – A zombie is stabbed in the chest with a pole.

1:13:45 – A zombie is stabbed in the stomach with a scythe.

1:13:45 – A zombie is stabbed in the face with a scythe.

1:14:30 – A woman is stabbed with a pole.

1:14:30 – A zombie rips a woman's head off.

1:16:00 – Close up of a bloodied dead body.

1:16:30 – A man is stabbed in the face.

1:23:15 – A zombie is shot in the chest.

1:23:15 – A zombie is shot in the arm.

1:23:30 – A zombie is shot in the head.

1:23:30 – A zombie is cut with a sword.

1:23:45 – A zombie is stabbed in the chest.

1:24:00 – A zombie is shot in the chest.

1:24:00 – A zombie is shot in the chest.

1:24:00 – A zombie is shot in the chest.

1:24:15 – A zombie is shot in the chest.

1:24:15 – A zombie is shot in the head.

1:24:30 – A zombie is cut in half.

1:25:45 – A zombie is shot in the head.

1:26:00 – A zombie is decapitated.

1:26:15 – A zombie is shot in the head.

1:26:15 – A zombie is shot in the head.

1:26:15 – A zombie is shot in the head.

1:26:15 – A zombie is shot in the head.

1:26:45 – A zombie rips off a woman's leg.

1:27:00 – A group of zombies rip off a woman's head.

1:27:45 – A zombie is shot in the chest.

1:27:45 – A zombie is shot in the chest.

1:27:45 – A zombie is shot in the head.

1:27:45 – A zombie is shot in the head.

1:27:45 – A zombie is shot in the head.

1:27:45 – A zombie is shot in the chest.

1:28:00 – A zombie is shot in the head.

1:28:00 – A zombie is shot in the head.

1:28:15 – A zombie is shot in the chest.

1:28:15 – A zombie is shot in the chest.

1:28:15 – A zombie's throat is slit.

1:28:15 – A zombie is shot in the chest.

1:28:30 – A zombie is shot in the chest.

1:28:45 – A zombie is shot in the back.

1:28:45 – A zombie is shot in the head.

1:28:45 – A zombie's head is smashed.

1:29:00 – A zombie's chest explodes.

1:29:15 – A zombie is shot in the chest.

1:29:15 – A zombie is shot in the chest.

1:29:30 – A zombie is shot in the chest.

1:29:30 – A zombie is shot in the chest.

1:29:30 – A zombie is shot in the chest.

1:30:00 – A zombie is stabbed with a chainsaw.

1:30:00 – A zombie's arm is pulled off.

1:30:15 – A zombie is shot in the head.

1:30:30 – A zombie is stabbed with a chainsaw.

1:30:30 – A zombie is stabbed in the stomach.

1:30:30 – A zombie is shot in the chest.

1:30:30 – A zombie is shot in the head.

1:31:00 – A zombie is shot in the head.

1:31:15 – A zombie's arm is cut off.

1:31:15 – A zombie is stabbed with a chainsaw.

1:31:15 – A zombie is decapitated with a chainsaw.

1:31:30 – A zombie is shot in the chest.

1:31:30 – A zombie is shot in the chest.

1:32:00 – A group of zombies rip open a man's torso.

1:32:00 – A group of zombies eat a man's intestines.

1:32:45 – A zombie is shot in the chest.

1:32:45 – A zombie is shot in the chest.

1:33:00 – A zombie is hit in the head with a pick axe.

1:33:15 – A zombie is shot in the chest.

1:33:30 – A zombie is shot in the chest.

1:33:30 – A zombie's hand is shot off.

1:33:30 – A zombie is shot in the chest.

1:34:00 – A zombie is hit in the head with an axe.

1:34:30 – A zombie's hand is cut off with an axe.

1:34:30 – A zombie's leg is cut off with an axe.

1:34:30 – A zombie's foot is cut off with an axe.

1:34:45 – A zombie pulls an axe out of its head.

1:34:45 – Close up of a mangled zombie.

1:34:45 – A zombie is shot in the head.

1:35:00 – A zombie is shot in the chest.

1:35:00 – A zombie is shot in the chest.

1:35:00 – A zombie is shot in the chest.

1:35:00 – A zombie is shot in the chest.

1:35:15 – A zombie bites a man's neck.

1:35:15 – A group of zombies tear open a man's torso.

1:36:30 – A zombie is shot by a tank.

1:37:30 – A zombie is shot in the head.

1:37:30 – A zombie is shot in the chest.

1:37:30 – A zombie is shot in the chest.

1:37:30 – A zombie is shot in the chest.

1:37:30 – A zombie is shot in the chest.

1:37:45 – A zombie is shot in the chest.

1:37:45 – A zombie is shot in the head.

1:37:45 – A zombie is shot in the chest.

1:37:45 – A zombie is shot in the stomach.

1:37:45 – A zombie is shot in the chest.

1:37:45 – A zombie is shot in the stomach.

1:37:45 – A zombie is shot in the chest.

PSYCHOMANIA

Year: 1973   Length: 85 minutes
Director: Don Sharp

STATISTICS

First Zombie:	38:45
First Human Death:	47:45
First Zombie Death:	N/A
Amount of Gore:	Very Low
Gore Quality:	Very Low
Zombie Effects:	Very Low
Zombie Count:	Average
Zombie Deaths:	Very Low
Human Deaths:	High

SUMMARY

A British motorcycle gang called The Living Dead wreaks havoc in their small English town. When the leader of the gang is killed in a motorcycle accident, he returns from the dead through a seance. He encourages the rest of the gang to die to ensure they can continue to terrorize the locals past death.

EFFECTS HIGHLIGHTS

N/A

QUARANTINE

Year: 2008   Length: 89 minutes
Director: John Erick Dowdle

STATISTICS

First Zombie:	19:45
First Human Death:	24:45
First Zombie Death:	25:30
Amount of Gore:	High
Gore Quality:	Very High
Zombie Effects:	High
Zombie Count:	High
Zombie Deaths:	Average
Human Deaths:	Average

SUMMARY

A television reporter and her cameraman are trapped inside a building that has been quarantined by the CDC. They soon discover that there has been a mysterious viral outbreak that turns humans into bloodthirsty zombies.

EFFECTS HIGHLIGHTS

19:30 – A zombie bites a man's neck.

22:30 – A man falls to his death.

25:30 – A zombie is shot in the chest.

30:15 – A man steps on a rat.

37:15 – Close up of a broken leg.

46:30 – A zombie is hit with a video camera.

1:07:00 – A man is shot in the head.

QUARANTINE 2: TERMINAL

Year: 2011   Length: 86 minutes
Director: John Pogue

STATISTICS

First Zombie:	16:00
First Human Death:	53:15
First Zombie Death:	38:30
Amount of Gore:	High
Gore Quality:	Very High
Zombie Effects:	High
Zombie Count:	Very High
Zombie Deaths:	Average
Human Deaths:	Average

SUMMARY

A virus that a turns its victims into zombies infects the passengers of a plane. When the aircraft lands, the authorities seal off the jet to let the virus run its course, killing everyone onboard. Realizing that they've been left to die, the passengers plan their escape.

EFFECTS HIGHLIGHTS

21:00 – A woman bleeds from a bite mark on her face.

38:30 – A zombie is shot in the head.

40:30 – A woman spits up blood.

52:30 – A zombie bites a chunk of flesh out of a man's neck.

53:15 – A man is shot in the chest.

53:15 – A man is shot in the chest.

1:01:00 – A zombie falls off of a balcony.

1:03:00 – A zombie is shot in the chest.

1:03:00 – A zombie is shot in the stomach.

1:04:30 – A man is shot in the chest.

1:07:00 – A man injects himself in the eye.

1:15:00 – A zombie is shot in the chest.

1:15:45 – A zombie is hit in the face with a pole.

THE QUICK AND THE UNDEAD

Year: 2006   Length: 78 minutes
Director: Gerald Nott

STATISTICS

First Zombie:	:15
First Human Death:	32:00
First Zombie Death:	:45
Amount of Gore:	High
Gore Quality:	Very High
Zombie Effects:	High
Zombie Count:	Very High
Zombie Deaths:	High
Human Deaths:	Average

SUMMARY

After a viral outbreak decimates the earth's population, hordes of the undead roam the land. A bounty hunter and his untrustworthy sidekick hunt down the creatures in an apocalyptic world, while the rest of humanity struggles to survive.

EFFECTS HIGHLIGHTS

3:00 – A man injects himself in the arm.

6:45 – A man throws body parts on to the ground.

8:15 – A group of zombies eat various severed body parts.

9:15 – A zombie is shot in the head.

9:15 – A zombie is shot in the head.

10:00 – A zombie is shot in the head.

10:00 – A zombie is shot in the head.

10:15 – A zombie is shot in the head.

12:15 – A zombie is shot in the head.

13:30 – A man is shot in the chest

19:15 – A zombie eats a severed arm.

25:15 – Close up of a bite mark.

31:45 – A group of zombies tear open a man's stomach.

41:15 – A man is shot in the head.

44:30 – A zombie's hand is smashed with a shovel.

44:45 – A zombie is stabbed in the head with a power drill.

48:00 – A zombie's torso is cut open.

48:15 – A man pulls out a zombie's entrails.

1:01:30 – A zombie crushes a man's head.

1:04:15 – A group of zombies rip open a man's torso.

1:06:30 – A man is shot in the shoulder.

1:06:30 – A zombie is shot in the head.

THE RAGE

Year: 2007   Length: 99 minutes
Director: Robert Kurtzman

STATISTICS

First Zombie:	5:15
First Human Death:	3:00
First Zombie Death:	11:00
Amount of Gore:	Very High
Gore Quality:	Very High
Zombie Effects:	Very High
Zombie Count:	High
Zombie Deaths:	High
Human Deaths:	High

SUMMARY

An insane scientist experiments with a rage-inducing virus by testing it on unsuspecting victims. He unleashes a blood thirsty horde of mutant zombies who

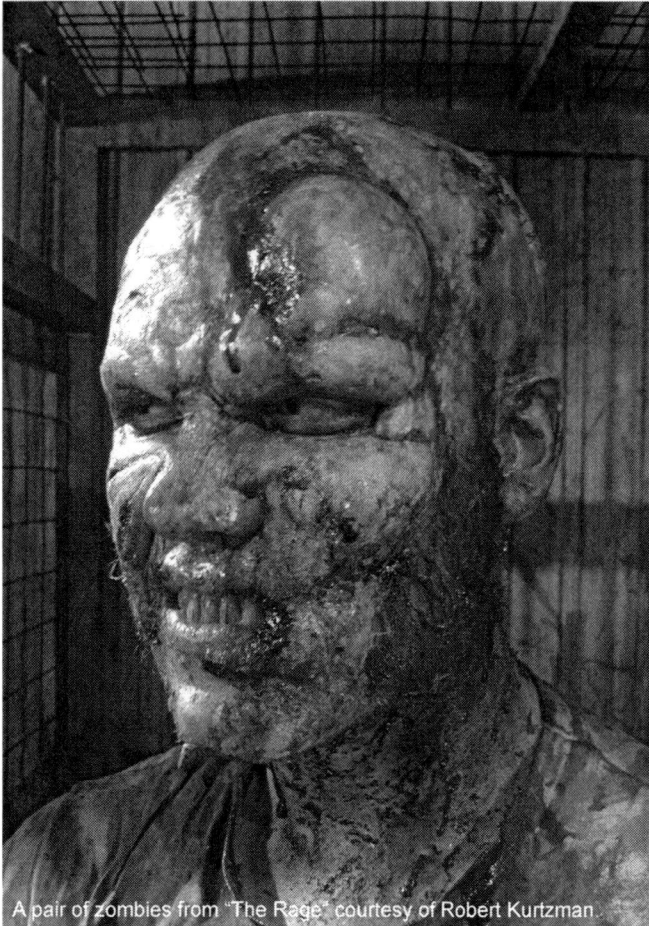

A pair of zombies from "The Rage" courtesy of Robert Kurtzman

soon break free.

EFFECTS HIGHLIGHTS

3:00 – A woman has a massive wound in the side of her head and part of her brain is exposed.

5:15 – A pair of caged zombies are tearing flesh off of bones.

8:00 – Using a scalpel, a surgeon cuts into a man's head.

8:45 – Part of the man's skull is lifted off.

10:15 – A zombie bites a man on the arm.

11:00 – A zombie is shot in the head.

11:15 – A zombie is stabbed in the chest with a meat hook.

11:30 – A zombie scratches a man's face.

11:45 – A zombie is cut in the chest with an axe.

12:00 – A zombie cuts a dead body with an axe.

12:15 – A man stabs a zombie in the chest with a saw.

12:15 – A man is stabbed repeatedly in the chest with a saw.

18:00 – A man is stabbed in the head with a saw.

18:30 – A zombie rips a woman's eyes out.

21:45 – Birds peck at a dead zombie.

27:00 – A man finds a pile of intestines on the floor.

27:15 – A man finds a bloody and half eaten body.

27:15 – A bird vomits on a man.

28:30 – A zombie is eating a dead body.

32:30 – A zombie is eating a dead body.

33:30 – An RV runs over a zombie.

35:45 – Vultures peck at a dead zombie.

37:45 – A severed head is thrown through a window.

38:15 – A bird is stabbed in the head.

39:30 – A bird vomits in a man's face.

39:45 – Birds peck at a man's face.

40:00 – A severed head falls to the ground.

40:15 – A woman is covered in body parts.

46:30 – Close up of a pile of body parts.

47:00 – A bird is hit with a baseball bat.

50:15 – A woman falls in the remains of a half-eaten animal.

52:15 – A bird's head is cut off.

53:30 – A woman hits a zombie in the head with an axe.

53:30 – A zombie is stabbed in the chest with a pole.

54:00 – A zombie's head explodes.

1:00:00 – A zombie drills into a woman's head.

1:08:30 – A man pulls an arm off a dead body.

1:09:45 – A zombie is shot in the chest.

1:10:00 – A zombie is shot in the head.

1:10:15 – A zombie is shot in the head.

1:14:00 – A room is filled with bloody body parts.

1:15:15 – A zombie is stabbed in the head with a screwdriver.

1:15:30 – A zombie is hit in the head with a hammer.

1:15:45 – A zombie is hung on a butcher's hook.

1:16:30 – A zombie is stabbed through the chest with a saw.

1:16:45 – A zombie is stabbed in the anus with a pole.

1:17:30 – A zombie is cut to pieces with a cleaver.

1:20:30 – A man cuts off a zombie's head.

1:20:45 – A woman cuts a severed head in half.

RAIDERS OF THE LIVING DEAD

Year: 1986   Length: 86 minutes
Directors: Brett Piper, Samuel M. Sherman

STATISTICS

First Zombie:	23:30
First Human Death:	27:30
First Zombie Death:	26:30

Amount of Gore:	High
Gore Quality:	Average
Zombie Effects:	Average
Zombie Count:	High
Zombie Deaths:	Very High
Human Deaths:	Low

SUMMARY

A reporter is trying to find the scoop on whether zombies really exist. He follows his leads to an abandoned island prison, where he discovers a mad scientist who is reanimating the dead.

EFFECTS HIGHLIGHTS

13:45 – A man is electrocuted.

24:30 – A zombie impales its arm on a branch.

38:45 – A zombie is shot in the arm.

39:00 – A zombie is shot in the head.

1:18:45 – A zombie is hit in the chest with an arrow.

1:22:15 – A man is impaled through the chest.

RE-ANIMATOR

Year: 1985   Length: 86 minutes
Director: Stuart Gordon

STATISTICS

First Zombie:	38:30
First Human Death:	1:30
First Zombie Death:	40:45

Amount of Gore:	High

Gore Quality:	Very High
Zombie Effects:	High
Zombie Count:	Average
Zombie Deaths:	Low
Human Deaths:	Average

SUMMARY

An egotistical but brilliant medical student develops a serum that can repair dead tissue and reanimate the dead. However, when he reanimates his first corpse, he doesn't factor in certain complications.

EFFECTS HIGHLIGHTS

1:30 – A man's eyes swell up and burst.

14:45 – A man peels off a dead man's scalp.

15:15 – A man pulls off the top of a dead man's skull.

39:45 – A zombie bites off a man's fingers.

40:30 – A zombie is stabbed through the chest with a bone saw.

55:00 – A man is decapitated with a shovel.

1:08:00 – A man's head is smashed against a wall.

1:16:00 – A zombie crushes a severed head.

1:16:45 – A tentacle bursts out of a zombie's chest.

1:19:00 – A zombie's arm is cut off with an axe.

REC

Year: 2007   Length: 78 minutes
Directors: Jaume Balagueró, Paco Plaza

STATISTICS

First Zombie:	12:45
First Human Death:	21:15
First Zombie Death:	N/A

Amount of Gore:	Low
Gore Quality:	High
Zombie Effects:	High
Zombie Count:	Average
Zombie Deaths:	Average
Human Deaths:	Very Low

SUMMARY

A television reporter and her cameraman are trapped inside a building that has been quarantined. They soon discover that there has been an outbreak of a mysterious virus that turns humans into bloodthirsty zombies.

EFFECTS HIGHLIGHTS

14:15 – A zombie bites a man's neck.

29:45 – A man is injected in the cheek.

REC 2

Year: 2009   Length: 84 minutes
Directors: Jaume Balagueró, Paco Plaza

First Zombie: 13:30
First Human Death: 54:45
First Zombie Death: 23:45

Amount of Gore: Average
Gore Quality: Very High
Zombie Effects: High
Zombie Count: Very High
Zombie Deaths: Average
Human Deaths: Low

SUMMARY

A medical officer and a SWAT team return to the scene of the original outbreak to try to contain the disease and prevent it from spreading.

EFFECTS HIGHLIGHTS

23:45 – A zombie is shot in the head.

28:30 – A zombie is shot in the chest.

30:00 – A zombie is shot in the chest.

31:45 – A zombie is shot in the chest.

36:15 – A zombie spits up blood.

50:30 – A man is shot in the neck.

54:45 – A man is shot in the head.

54:45 – A zombie is shot in the head.

1:11:00 – A zombie is shot in the head.

1:16:00 – A zombie vomits into a woman's mouth.

REDNECK ZOMBIES

Year: 1989   Length: 84 minutes
Director: Pericles Lewnes

STATISTICS

First Zombie: :00
First Human Death: 40:30
First Zombie Death: 1:24:30

Amount of Gore: Very High
Gore Quality: Average
Zombie Effects: Average
Zombie Count: Very High
Zombie Deaths: Average
Human Deaths: Average

SUMMARY

A group of Rednecks find a missing barrel of radioactive waste and decide to use it in part of their moonshine distillery, turning all who drink it into zombies.

EFFECTS HIGHLIGHTS

:30 – A zombie bleeds from a wound on its neck.

8:45 – Close up of a body missing its torso.

8:45 – A group of zombies tear open a torso.

9:00 – A zombie eats a piece of flesh.

34:15 – A man cuts himself with a razor.

40:15 – The skin melts off of two men's faces.

44:15 – A zombie pulls off a woman's scalp.

45:00 – A zombie eats a piece of flesh.

47:15 – A zombie bites a woman's neck.

47:30 – A zombie pulls flesh off of a woman's neck.

48:15 – Close up of a body missing its top half.

52:45 – Close up of a body missing its top half.

1:07:45 – A man cuts open a dead bodies stomach.

1:10:45 – A man holds a pair of severed hands.

1:15:15 – A zombie eats a piece of flesh.

1:15:45 – A zombie eats a piece of flesh.

1:15:45 – A zombie eats a piece of flesh.

1:16:30 – A zombie is shot in the stomach.

1:16:30 – A zombie gouges out a man's eyes.

1:16:45 – A man's head is crushed.

1:17:00 – A zombie eats an eyeball.

1:20:30 – A group of zombies tear open a man's stomach.

1:20:45 – A man is ripped in half.

1:21:00 – A zombie eats a piece of flesh.

1:21:00 – A zombie eats a piece of flesh.

1:21:00 – A zombie eats a piece of flesh.

1:21:45 – A man vomits.

1:22:15 – A zombie bites a man's arm.

1:22:15 – A zombie bites a man's neck.

1:23:45 – A zombie eats a piece of flesh.

1:24:30 – A zombie is hit in the head with a hammer.

1:25:15 – A zombie is decapitated.

1:26:00 – A zombie is stabbed in the head with a spoon.

1:27:45 – A zombie is shot in the head.

1:28:30 – A zombie eats a piece of flesh.

1:28:30 – A zombie eats a piece of flesh.

1:28:30 – A zombie eats a piece of flesh.

1:28:45 – A zombie eats a piece of flesh.

1:29:30 – A zombie eats a piece of flesh.

1:31:00 – A zombie is stabbed in the mouth.

RESIDENT EVIL

Year: 2002   Length: 101 minutes
Director: Paul W.S. Anderson

STATISTICS

First Zombie: 27:00
First Human Death: 6:45
First Zombie Death: 40:00

Amount of Gore: High
Gore Quality: Very High
Zombie Effects: Very High

Zombie Count: Very High
Zombie Deaths: High
Human Deaths: High

SUMMARY

When a highly contagious disease called the T-Virus leaks from a top-secret underground facility, it turns all of the resident scientists into blood thirsty zombies. With only three hours on the clock, an elite military task force is sent in to contain the outbreak before it spreads to the outside world.

EFFECTS HIGHLIGHTS

32:45 – A man has four of his fingers cut off by a laser beam.

32:45 – A woman is decapitated by a laser beam.

33:30 – A cross hatched laser beam slices a man into cubes.

39:45 – A zombie is shot in the leg.

41:30 – A zombie is missing half of its face.

42:30 – A zombie is shot in the chest.

42:45 – A zombie is shot in the chest.

50:00 – A zombie dog is shot in the head.

1:25:15 – A mutant zombie is shot in the head.

1:25:30 – A mutant zombie is shot in the head.

1:26:00 – A mutant zombie is stabbed in the tongue.

1:26:30 – A zombie is shot in the chest.

RESIDENT EVIL: AFTERLIFE

Year: 2010   Length: 96 minutes
Director: Paul W.S. Anderson

STATISTICS

First Zombie: 3:30
First Human Death: 8:15
First Zombie Death: 5:00

Amount of Gore: Very High
Gore Quality: Very High
Zombie Effects: Very High
Zombie Count: Very High
Zombie Deaths: Very High
Human Deaths: Very High

SUMMARY

Alice fights zombies and mutants as she heads to a rumored sanctuary in Los Angeles, which may just be nothing more than a deadly trap set by the ruthless Umbrella Corporation to capture her.

EFFECTS HIGHLIGHTS

3:30 – A zombie bites a man's neck.

7:15 – A man spits up blood.

8:15 – Three men are stabbed with shurikens.

8:15 – Two men are sliced with a sword.

8:15 – A man is decapitated.

8:15 – Two men are decapitated.

8:15 – Two men are stabbed in the stomach.

9:00 – A man is stabbed in the head.

9:45 – A woman is shot in the chest.

10:30 – A man is shot in the head.

12:00 – A man is shot in the chest.

12:15 – A woman is shot in the head.

12:00 – A man is shot in the chest.

12:45 – A woman is shot in the chest.

49:30 – A zombie is shot in the face.

49:30 – A zombie is shot in the chest.

54:45 – A zombie is shot in the head.

57:30 – A zombie is stabbed in the head.

57:30 – A zombie is shot in the chest.

1:01:15 – A zombie is shot in the chest.

1:01:15 – A zombie is shot in the chest.

1:01:15 – A zombie is shot in the chest.

1:01:15 – A zombie is shot in the chest.

1:01:15 – A zombie is shot in the chest.

1:01:15 – A zombie is shot in the chest.

1:01:30 – A zombie is shot in the chest.

1:01:30 – A zombie is shot in the chest.

1:01:30 – A zombie is shot in the chest.

1:01:30 – A zombie is shot in the chest.

1:01:30 – A zombie is shot in the chest.

1:01:30 – A zombie is shot in the chest.

1:01:45 – A zombie is shot in the leg.

1:01:45 – A zombie is shot in the chest.

1:01:45 – A zombie is shot in the chest.

1:01:45 – A zombie is shot in the chest.

1:02:00 – A zombie is shot in the chest.

1:03:15 – A zombie is shot in the head.

1:03:15 – A zombie is shot in the head.

1:03:30 – A zombie is shot in the head.

1:03:30 – A zombie is shot in the chest.

1:03:30 – A zombie is shot in the chest.

1:03:30 – A zombie is shot in the head.

1:03:45 – A zombie is shot in the head.

1:04:00 – A zombie is shot in the chest.

1:04:00 – A zombie is shot in the chest.

1:04:00 – A zombie is shot in the chest.

1:05:30 – A zombie is shot in the neck.

1:07:45 – A zombie is shot in the head.

1:22:30 – A man is stabbed in the leg.

1:23:15 – A zombie dog is shot in the chest.

1:23:45 – A zombie dog is stabbed with a piece of glass.

1:23:45 – A woman is stabbed in the arm.

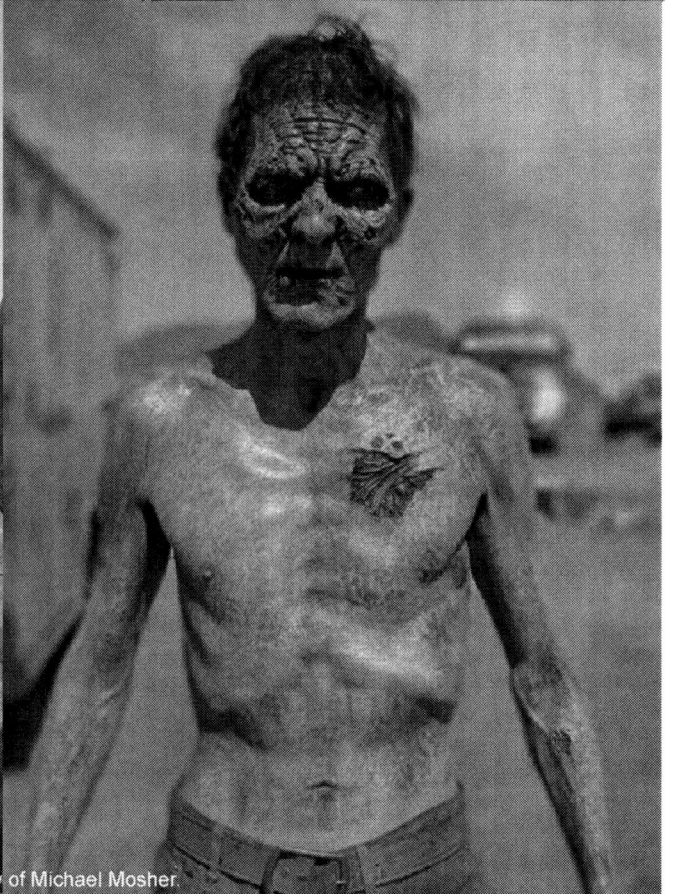

Michael Mosher with zombies from "Resident Evil: Extinction" courtesy of Michael Mosher

144

1:24:00 – A zombie is stabbed in the head.

1:24:15 – A zombie is shot in the head.

RESIDENT EVIL: APOCALYPSE

Year: 2004   Length: 94 minutes
Director: Alexander Witt

STATISTICS

First Zombie:	6:45
First Human Death:	11:45
First Zombie Death:	6:45
Amount of Gore:	High
Gore Quality:	Very High
Zombie Effects:	Very High
Zombie Count:	Very High
Zombie Deaths:	High
Human Deaths:	Very High

SUMMARY

The T-Virus has escaped from the research lab and has wiped out most of the population of Raccoon City. A group of soldiers are sent in to the ravaged city to locate a scientists daughter and they soon discover a new threat is walking among the dead that is even deadlier than the relentless horde of zombies.

EFFECTS HIGHLIGHTS

11:45 – Close up of a bite mark.

22:15 – Close up of a severed arm.

28:00 – A mutant is shot in the head.

28:45 – A zombie is shot in the chest.

29:00 – A zombie is stabbed in the head.

36:30 – A zombie is shot in the chest.

45:15 – A zombie is shot in the leg.

53:45 – A zombie dog is shot in the chest.

53:45 – A zombie is shot in the head.

53:45 – A zombie is shot in the head.

1:12:00 – A man is shot in the chest.

1:12:15 – A zombie is shot in the back.

1:12:45 – A man is shot in the chest.

1:13:00 – A man is shot in the chest.

1:13:00 – A zombie is shot in the chest.

1:14:00 – A man is shot in the chest.

1:14:00 – A man is shot in the neck.

1:14:00 – A man is shot in the chest.

1:24:15 – A man bleeds from his eyes.

RESIDENT EVIL: EXTINCTION

Year: 2007   Length: 95 minutes
Director: Russell Mulcahy

STATISTICS

First Zombie:	6:30
First Human Death:	5:00
First Zombie Death:	18:30
Amount of Gore:	Very High
Gore Quality:	Very High
Zombie Effects:	Very High
Zombie Count:	Very High
Zombie Deaths:	Very High
Human Deaths:	Very High

SUMMARY

Desperately short of food and fuel, the survivors of the Raccoon City catastrophe travel across the Nevada desert, hoping to make it to Alaska. Their quest seems hopeless until Alice joins the caravan and aids in their fight against the evil Umbrella Corp.

EFFECTS HIGHLIGHTS

4:45 – A woman is shot in the stomach.

10:45 – A man is kicked under the chin.

11:45 – A zombie dog is impaled on a spike.

18:30 – A zombie is shot in the head with an arrow.

24:45 – A zombie is shot in the leg.

25:00 – A zombie is shot in the back.

26:15 – Close up of a bite mark.

26:15 – A zombie is injected.

39:15 – A woman is attacked by a flock of birds.

40:30 – A man is attacked by a flock of birds.

50:45 – Close up of a bite mark.

59:00 – A zombie is shot in the chest.

59:00 – A zombie is shot in the chest.

59:00 – A zombie is shot in the chest.

59:00 – A zombie is shot in the chest.

59:00 – A zombie is shot in the head.

59:15 – A zombie is shot in the shoulder.

59:15 – A zombie is shot in the head.

59:15 – A zombie is shot in the chest.

59:30 – A zombie is shot in the head.

59:30 – A zombie is shot in the neck.

59:30 – A zombie is shot in the head.

59:30 – A zombie is shot in the head.

59:45 – A zombie is shot in the chest.

59:45 – A zombie is shot in the head.

1:00:00 – A zombie's throat is slit.

1:00:00 – A zombie's throat is slit.

1:00:00 – A zombie is shot in the chest.

1:00:00 – A zombie is shot in the chest.

1:00:15 – A zombie is shot in the head.

1:00:15 – A zombie is shot in the chest.

1:00:30 – A zombie's throat is slit.
1:00:30 – A zombie is shot in the head.
1:00:45 – A zombie is shot in the head.
1:00:45 – A zombie is shot in the head.
1:01:15 – A zombie's throat is slit.
1:01:15 – A zombie is stabbed in the head.
1:01:15 – A zombie's throat is slit.
1:01:30 – A zombie is stabbed in the stomach.
1:01:45 – A zombie is stabbed in the stomach.
1:01:45 – A zombie is stabbed in the stomach.
1:01:45 – A zombie is stabbed in the head.
1:01:45 – A zombie eats a woman's stomach.
1:03:00 – A zombie is shot in the head.
1:03:15 – A zombie is shot in the head.
1:03:30 – A zombie is shot in the back.
1:03:30 – A zombie is shot in the back.
1:03:30 – A zombie is shot in the back.
1:03:45 – A zombie is shot in the head.
1:03:45 – A zombie is shot in the head.
1:04:45 – A zombie is shot in the head.
1:05:00 – Close up of a bite mark.
1:06:30 – A man is shot in the chest.
1:06:30 – A man is shot in the head.
1:06:45 – A zombie is shot in the head.
1:08:15 – A zombie is shot in the chest.
1:08:45 – A man is stabbed in the head.
1:12:00 – A zombie is hit by a truck.
1:12:00 – A zombie is hit by a truck.
1:14:45 – Close up of a pile of dead bodies.
1:21:15 – A zombie is stabbed in the shoulder.
1:23:00 – A zombie is sliced with a sword.
1:25:45 – A zombie is sliced by a laser.

RETARDEAD

Year: 2008   Length: 102 minutes
Directors: Rick Popko, Dan West

STATISTICS

First Zombie: 48:45
First Human Death: 55:00
First Zombie Death: 1:03:45

Amount of Gore: Very High
Gore Quality: High
Zombie Effects: Average
Zombie Count: Very High
Zombie Deaths: Very High
Human Deaths: High

SUMMARY

A mad scientist turns students into super intelligent, but cannibalistic zombies. An FBI agent on the case, works to convince the scientist's assistant to reveal how to stop the doctor's evil plans.

EFFECTS HIGHLIGHTS

21:45 – A man pulls a string of blood and sinew out of his nose.
25:45 – A man is injected in the brain.
49:00 – A group of zombies tear open a man's stomach.
55:00 – A zombie rips a man's head off.
55:15 – A zombie eats flesh of off a dead man's spine.
55:45 – A zombie bites a baby's neck.
56:00 – A zombie bites a man's neck.
56:45 – A zombie eats a piece of flesh.
57:45 – A pair of zombies eat from a dead body.
57:45 – A zombie eats a piece of flesh.
58:00 – A zombie pulls flesh out of an eye socket.
58:15 – A zombie bites a man's neck.
58:30 – A zombie rips out a woman's intestines.
58:45 – A zombie eats a piece of flesh.
58:45 – A zombie eats a severed foot.
58:45 – A zombie eats a piece of flesh.
59:00 – A zombie eats from a dead body.
59:00 – A zombie eats intestines.
59:15 – A dog eats a dead body.
1:03:45 – A zombie is shot in the head.
1:04:15 – A zombie is shot in the head.
1:04:15 – A zombie is shot in the head.
1:04:15 – A zombie is shot in the head.
1:04:15 – A zombie is shot in the head.
1:04:45 – A zombie is shot in the head.
1:08:30 – A man is missing the top part of his skull.
1:17:30 – A zombie is shot in the head.
1:17:30 – A group of zombies tear open a man's stomach.
1:19:45 – Three men are covered in blood.
1:20:15 – A man rips open a dead bodies stomach and pulls out its organ's.
1:21:00 – A man vomits in a bucket.
1:21:00 – A man continues to pull organ's out of a body.
1:21:00 – A man vomits.
1:21:15 – A man continues to pull organ's out of a body.
1:21:15 – A man vomits on another man.
1:26:00 – A group of zombies tear open a man's stomach.
1:26:15 – A group of zombies eat flesh and intestines.
1:26:15 – A group of zombies pulls the skin off of a man's head.
1:31:15 – A zombie is shot in the head.
1:31:30 – A zombie is shot in the chest.

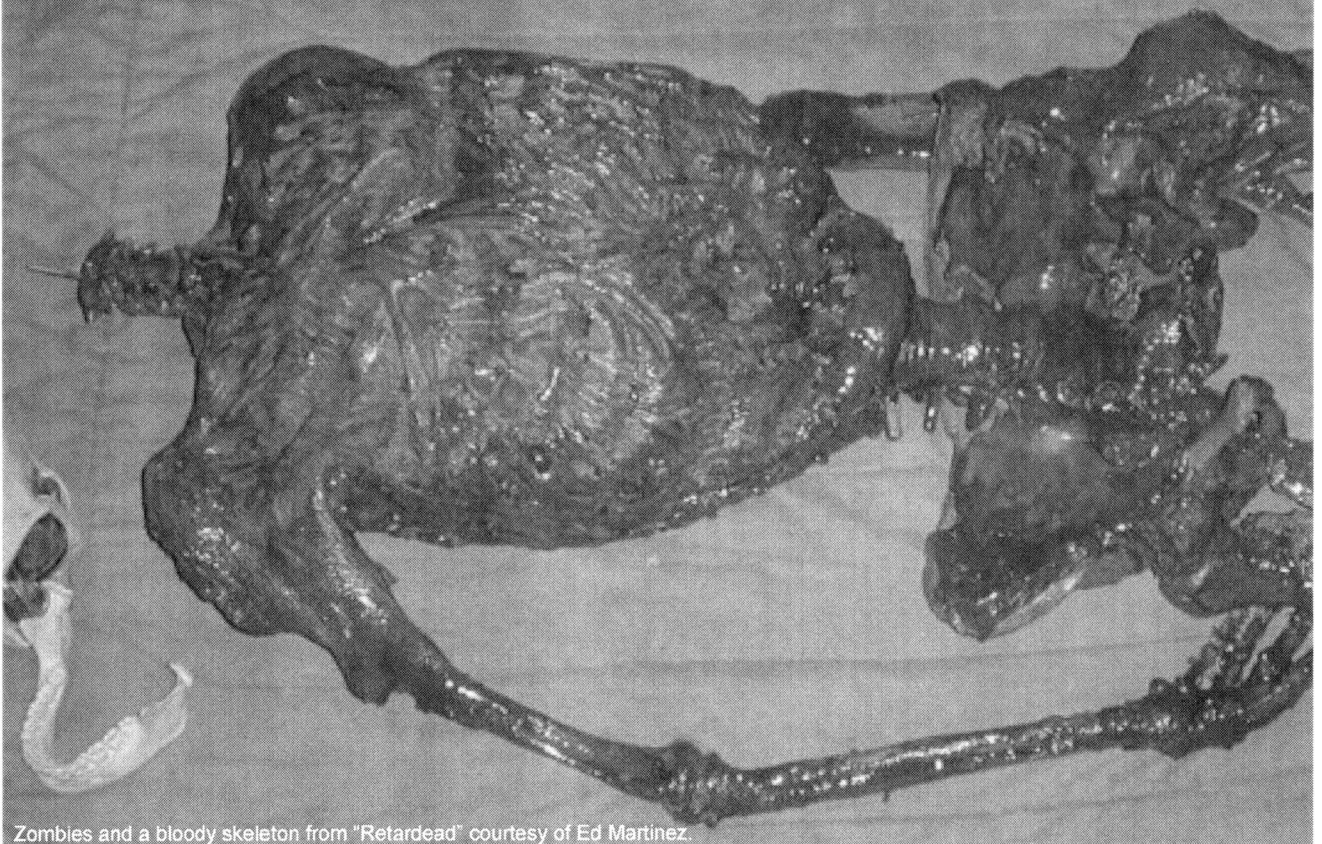

Zombies and a bloody skeleton from "Retardead" courtesy of Ed Martinez.

147

1:31:30 – A zombie is shot in the chest.

1:31:30 – A zombie is shot in the chest.

1:31:30 – A zombie is shot in the chest.

1:31:30 – A zombie is shot in the head.

1:31:30 – A zombie is shot in the chest.

1:31:45 – A zombie is shot in the chest.

1:31:45 – A zombie is stabbed with a chainsaw.

1:32:15 – A zombie's face melts.

1:32:30 – A zombie's face melts.

1:32:30 – A zombie bites a chunk of flesh out of a man's arm.

1:32:45 – A zombie pulls off a man's arm.

1:33:00 – A zombie eats a severed arm.

1:33:15 – A zombie is hit in the head with a machete.

1:33:15 – A zombie is stabbed in the head.

RETURN IN RED

Year: 2005   Length: 102 minutes
Director: Tyler Tharpe

STATISTICS

First Zombie:	1:24:45
First Human Death:	1:30:45
First Zombie Death:	N/A
Amount of Gore:	Low
Gore Quality:	High
Zombie Effects:	Average
Zombie Count:	Average
Zombie Deaths:	Low
Human Deaths:	Very Low

SUMMARY

The residents of a small town are turned into blood thirsty zombies after a science experiment testing the effect of electromagnetic frequencies on the human brain goes wrong.

EFFECTS HIGHLIGHTS

1:24:00 – Close up of a severed arm.

1:29:30 – A zombie stabs itself in the mouth with a screwdriver.

1:30:30 – A zombie is stabbed in the stomach.

1:31:00 – A zombie is stabbed with a fork lift.

1:31:30 – A zombie is stabbed in the head with a fork lift.

RETURN OF THE BLIND DEAD

Year: 1973   Length: 91 minutes
Director: Amando de Ossorio

STATISTICS

First Zombie:	17:30
First Human Death:	2:45
First Zombie Death:	44:30
Amount of Gore:	High
Gore Quality:	High
Zombie Effects:	High
Zombie Count:	Very High
Zombie Deaths:	Very High
Human Deaths:	Very High

SUMMARY

500 years ago, the Templar Knights were blinded and executed for committing human sacrifices. Now, the knights have returned from the grave as the Blind Dead to terrorize a rural Portuguese village during it's centennial celebration.

EFFECTS HIGHLIGHTS

1:45 – A man's faced is burned by a torch.

1:45 – Close up of a burned eye.

12:30 – A man slices a piece of skin off of a woman's breast.

13:00 – A man pulls out a woman's heart.

14:30 – A woman is stabbed in the chest.

45:45 – A man is cut on the face with a sword.

45:45 – A man is cut on the forehead with a sword.

46:00 – A man is cut on the face with a sword.

46:00 – A man is stabbed in the head.

1:07:15 – A man's hand is cut off with a sword.

1:07:30 – A man is stabbed in the stomach.

1:13:00 – A man is stabbed in the stomach.

1:18:16 – A woman is stabbed in the stomach.

1:20:00 – A man is decapitated.

1:20:15 – Close up of a headless body.

THE RETURN OF THE LIVING DEAD

Year: 1985   Length: 91 minutes
Director: Dan O'Bannon

STATISTICS

First Zombie:	8:15
First Human Death:	46:15
First Zombie Death:	N/A
Amount of Gore:	High
Gore Quality:	High
Zombie Effects:	High
Zombie Count:	Very High
Zombie Deaths:	Very Low
Human Deaths:	Average

SUMMARY

Tony Gardner holding a zombie torso and below, props from "The Return of the Living Dead" courtesy of Alterian Inc. and Tony Gardner.

149

When a strange military chemical leaks into rain clouds, the dead in a local graveyard rise up from the ground and terrorize the locals trapped in a medical supply center.

EFFECTS HIGHLIGHTS

9:00 – A zombies skin melts off.

17:15 – Half of a stuffed dog starts moving.

23:15 – A man hits a zombie in the head with a pickaxe.

23:45 – A man saws off a zombie's head.

32:15 – Close up of a severed arm.

46:15 – A zombie bites a man's head.

55:00 – A zombie is eating a man's brain.

57:30 – A zombie is eating a man's brain.

1:01:45 – A zombie bites a man's head.

1:01:45 – A zombie is cut in half.

1:09:00 – A dead man's brains spill out.

1:20:00 – A zombie's head is knocked off.

RETURN OF THE LIVING DEAD PART II

Year: 1988   Length: 89 minutes
Director: Ken Wiederhorn

STATISTICS

First Zombie: 7:30
First Human Death: 34:45
First Zombie Death: 1:04:00

Amount of Gore: High
Gore Quality: Very High
Zombie Effects: Very High
Zombie Count: Very High
Zombie Deaths: Very High
Human Deaths: Average

SUMMARY

A group of curious children discover a military canister containing the remains of the Tar Man zombie. The children accidentally open the canister releasing both the zombie inside and the chemical used to raise the dead.

EFFECTS HIGHLIGHTS

15:30 – A man cuts the head off of a dead body.

15:45 – A man cuts a finger off of a dead body.

27:00 – A woman punches her fist through a zombie's face.

28:00 – A man hits a zombie on the head with a crowbar.

34:45 – A zombie bites a man's head.

36:30 – A man holds a severed head.

37:15 – A man stabs a severed head with a screwdriver.

41:30 – A zombie is stabbed in the stomach with a poker.

46:15 – A zombie's hand is cut off.

57:30 – A zombie is cut in half with a shotgun.

57:45 – A pair of legs walk around.

58:30 – A man rips off a zombie's arm.

1:01:45 – A zombie bites a man's head.

1:05:30 – A woman pulls off a zombie's jaw.

1:12:45 – A zombie eats a brain.

1:20:45 – A zombie is stabbed in the mouth with a screwdriver.

1:22:15 – A zombie's eyes burst.

RETURN OF THE LIVING DEAD 3

Year: 1993   Length: 90 minutes
Director: Brian Yuzna

STATISTICS

First Zombie: 9:15
First Human Death: 13:30
First Zombie Death: N/A

Amount of Gore: Very High
Gore Quality: Very High
Zombie Effects: Very High
Zombie Count: High
Zombie Deaths: Very Low
Human Deaths: High

SUMMARY

After his girlfriend dies in a motorcycle accident, her boyfriend uses Trioxin to reanimate her. However, the creature that returns to life is not the same woman he once loved.

EFFECTS HIGHLIGHTS

12:15 – A zombie bites off a man's fingers.

12:30 – A zombie stabs a man with a scalpel.

13:00 – A zombie is shot in the back.

24:15 – A woman drills into a severed arm.

30:30 – The skin on a zombie's head peels off.

31:00 – A zombie eats a piece of flesh.

36:30 – A zombie bites a man's wrist.

38:15 – A zombie stabs itself in the hand with a pin.

38:45 – A man is shot in the head.

39:15 – A zombie eats a man's brain.

40:45 – A cop is stabbed in the eye with a crowbar.

41:15 – A zombie is shot in the chest.

43:30 – A zombie pierces its skin with a spring.

1:00:00 – A zombie pulls a piece of metal out of its heel.

Top, the cast of "Return of the Living Dead Part II". Bottom, Michael Kenworthy and Marsha Dietlein courtesy of Michael Kenworthy.

151

1:00:15 – A zombie stabs its hand with a piece of metal.

1:02:15 – A zombie cuts its leg.

1:02:15 – A zombie pierces its thumb with a piece of metal.

1:02:30 – A zombie pulls a chain through holes in its neck.

1:07:15 – A man is shot in the leg.

1:07:45 – A man's head is pulled from his body and his spine is exposed.

1:08:45 – A zombie bites a man's lip and pulls the skin from his face.

1:09:30 – A zombie bites a woman's neck.

1:11:30 – A zombie is decapitated.

1:14:15 – A zombie is eating a man's brains.

1:23:00 – A zombie's arm is shot off.

1:28:15 – Close up of a bite mark.

RETURN OF THE LIVING DEAD: NECROPOLIS

Year: 2005   Length: 88 minutes
Director: Ellory Elkayem

STATISTICS

First Zombie:	7:45
First Human Death:	8:00
First Zombie Death:	8:15
Amount of Gore:	Very High
Gore Quality:	Very High
Zombie Effects:	Very High
Zombie Count:	Very High
Zombie Deaths:	Very High
Human Deaths:	High

SUMMARY

A group of high school student discover that the uncle of one of their group is conducting experiments that raise the dead. However, the nephew discovers that two of his uncle's test subjects are his parents and he tries to set them free.

EFFECTS HIGHLIGHTS

8:00 – A zombie bites a man's head.

8:15 – A zombie is shot in the head.

16:45 – Close up of a severed arm.

24:00 – A zombie eats a brain.

28:15 – A man is bitten on the neck.

37:45 – A zombie is shot in the stomach.

37:45 – A zombie is shot in the stomach.

37:45 – A zombie is shot in the head.

38:30 – A zombie is shot in the head.

53:00 – A zombie is shot in the stomach.

53:00 – A zombie is shot in the chest.

53:00 – A man's head is ripped off.

53:15 – A group of zombies tear open a man's torso.

53:15 – A zombie bites a man's head.

53:30 – A zombie bites a man's neck.

53:30 – A zombie is shot in the head.

56:45 – Close up of a bite mark.

57:15 – A zombie is shot in the stomach.

57:15 – A zombie is shot in the stomach.

57:15 – A zombie is shot in the stomach.

57:30 – A zombie is shot in the head.

58:45 – A zombie is shot in the stomach.

59:30 – A zombie is shot in the stomach.

59:30 – Two zombies are shot in the chest.

59:30 – A zombie is shot in the chest.

59:30 – Two zombies are shot in the chest.

59:30 – A zombie is shot in the chest.

59:45 – A zombie is shot in the chest.

59:45 – Two zombies are shot in the chest.

1:01:15 – A zombie bites a man's head.

1:02:00 – A zombie is shot in the chest.

1:02:00 – A zombie is shot in the chest.

1:03:15 – A zombie is shot in the stomach.

1:03:15 – A zombie is shot in the head.

1:03:15 – A zombie is shot in the stomach.

1:03:15 – A zombie is shot in the chest.

1:03:15 – A zombie is shot in the chest.

1:03:15 – A zombie is shot in the chest.

1:03:15 – A zombie is shot in the head.

1:03:15 – A zombie is shot in the chest.

1:03:30 – A zombie is shot in the head.

1:04:45 – A car runs over a zombie's head.

1:11:15 – A zombie is shot in the chest.

1:11:15 – A zombie is shot in the chest.

1:11:30 – A zombie bites a boy's head.

1:13:15 – A zombie is disintegrated by a hand grenade.

1:13:30 – Close up of a severed arm and entrails.

1:16:15 – A zombie is disintegrated by a hand grenade.

1:16:45 – A zombie is shot in the chest

1:17:00 – A zombie is shot in the chest

1:17:00 – A zombie is shot in the chest

1:17:15 – A zombie is shot in the stomach.

1:17:15 – A zombie is shot in the chest.

1:17:15 – A zombie is shot in the chest.

1:17:15 – Two zombies are shot in the chest.

1:17:30 – A zombie is shot in the chest.

1:17:30 – A zombie is shot in the chest.

1:17:30 – A zombie is shot in the stomach.

1:17:30 – A zombie is shot in the chest.

1:18:00 – A vehicle runs over a zombie's head.

Zombies from "Return of the Living Dead 3" courtesy of Wayne Toth.

1:18:45 – An armored vehicle destroys a zombie.

RETURN OF THE LIVING DEAD: RAVE TO THE GRAVE

Year: 2005   Length: 86 minutes
Director: Ellory Elkayem

STATISTICS

First Zombie: 5:15
First Human Death: 5:15
First Zombie Death: 5:30

Amount of Gore: Very High
Gore Quality: Very High
Zombie Effects: Very High
Zombie Count: Very High
Zombie Deaths: Very High
Human Deaths: Very High

SUMMARY

A group of college students uncover a drum filled with the reanimation chemical, Trioxyn-5. After one of the group uses it to get high, they assume it is safe to start selling it as a recreational party drug. They distribute the drug at a Halloween rave, transforming hundreds of users into flesh-eating zombies.

EFFECTS HIGHLIGHTS

5:15 – A zombie bites a man's skull.

5:30 – A zombie is shot in the chest.

5:30 – A zombie is shot in the head.

5:45 – A zombie is stabbed in the head.

6:00 – A man bleeds from his eyes.

6:00 – A man is bitten on the neck.

6:15 – A zombie is shot in the chest.

6:15 – A zombie is shot in the head.

31:45 – A woman is scratched on her shoulder.

33:15 – A zombie bites a man's skull.

33:30 – A zombie is stabbed in the eyes with a pair of drumsticks.

33:30 – A zombie is decapitated.

36:30 – Close up of a severed zombie head.

49:15 – Close up of an infected bite wound.

52:15 – A zombie bites a man's neck.

56:30 – A zombie bites a man's skull.

56:45 – A zombie eats a piece of flesh.

59:45 – A zombie bites a woman's buttocks.

1:00:00 – A zombie is shot in the head.

1:00:00 – A zombie is shot in the head.

1:00:15 – A zombie is shot in the chest.

1:00:15 – A zombie is shot in the chest.

1:00:15 – A woman is shot in the back.

1:01:00 – A zombie is stabbed in the ears with a pair of pencils.

1:01:00 – A zombie is hit on the head with an axe.

1:01:30 – A zombie is shot in the chest.

1:12:00 – A zombie is stabbed in the head.

1:12:30 – A zombie eats a severed arm.

1:13:00 – A zombie bites a woman's head.

1:16:15 – A zombie is shot in the head.

1:16:30 – A zombie is shot in the head.

1:18:00 – A zombie bites a man's head.

1:19:00 – A zombie is shot in the chest.

1:19:15 – A zombie bites a man's head.

1:19:45 – A zombie is shot in the head.

1:19:45 – A zombie bites a man's face.

1:21:00 – A zombie is shot in the head.

1:21:00 – A zombie is shot in the head.

1:22:15 – A zombie is shot in the head.

1:22:45 – A zombie bites a man's head.

1:23:00 – A zombie bites a man's face.

1:23:00 – A zombie is shot in the chest.

1:23:00 – A zombie is shot in the head.

1:23:00 – A zombie is shot in the head.

1:23:15 – A zombie bites a man's head.

1:24:00 – A zombie is shot in the head with an arrow.

REVENGE OF THE LIVING DEAD GIRLS

Year: 1987   Length: 73 minutes
Director: Peter B. Harsone

STATISTICS

First Zombie: 24:00
First Human Death: 6:45
First Zombie Death: N/A

Amount of Gore: Low
Gore Quality: High
Zombie Effects: Average
Zombie Count: Average
Zombie Deaths: Very Low
Human Deaths: High

SUMMARY

When toxic waste contaminates the milk supply in a small town, three teenage girls who drink it are killed. When the chemical waste accidentally spills on their graves, the girls' corpses rise from the dead to take revenge on the culprits.

EFFECTS HIGHLIGHTS

27:45 – A zombie stabs a woman in the eye with a high heeled shoe.

42:15 – A zombie bites off a man's penis.

42:30 – Zombies have pulled out a man's entrails.

1:03:45 – A zombie slides a sword into a woman's vagina.

1:05:45 – A woman's stomach is torn open.

THE REVOLTING DEAD

Year: 2003   Length: 87 minutes
Director: Michael Su

STATISTICS

First Zombie:	25:30
First Human Death:	30:45
First Zombie Death:	N/A
Amount of Gore:	Low
Gore Quality:	High
Zombie Effects:	High
Zombie Count:	Average
Zombie Deaths:	Very Low
Human Deaths:	Average

SUMMARY

The evil owners of a mortuary have been grave robbing, but when they disturb the grave of a druid priest, his sister raises the dead to exact revenge against the mortuary.

EFFECTS HIGHLIGHTS

30:15 – A man breaks a finger off of a dead body's hand.

1:02:00 – A zombie's eyeball is visible through cuts in its eyelids.

1:21:00 – A group of zombies tear open a woman's stomach.

1:21:15 – A zombie pulls off a man's head.

1:21:15 – A group of zombies tear at a dead body.

THE RISING DEAD

Year: 2007   Length: 112 minutes
Director: Brent Cousins

STATISTICS

First Zombie:	11:15
First Human Death:	1:35:00
First Zombie Death:	12:15
Amount of Gore:	High
Gore Quality:	High
Zombie Effects:	High
Zombie Count:	Very High
Zombie Deaths:	Very High
Human Deaths:	Low

SUMMARY

The use of biological weapons instigates World War IV, causing the dead to rise from their graves and terrorize humanity.

EFFECTS HIGHLIGHTS

5:00 – A woman has been cut in half.

12:15 – A zombie is shot in the head.

14:15 – A zombie is shot in the head.

14:45 – A zombie is stabbed with an axe.

15:00 – A zombie is killed with an axe.

26:45 – A zombie is shot in the neck.

26:45 – A zombie is shot in the chest.

26:45 – A zombie is shot in the neck.

26:45 – A zombie is shot in the neck.

33:30 – A zombie is shot in the head.

37:45 – A zombie is shot in the head.

37:45 – A zombie is shot in the head.

39:00 – A zombie bites a woman's neck.

40:00 – A severed arm crawls across the floor.

42:15 – A man stomps on a zombie's head.

43:30 – A woman is attacked by a severed arm.

59:30 – A zombie's head is cut off with a saw.

1:02:30 – A zombie is stabbed in the chest.

1:02:45 – A zombie is decapitated.

1:03:00 – A zombie is stabbed in the head.

1:03:15 – A zombie is cut in half.

1:03:30 – Two zombies are decapitated.

1:23:15 – A zombie is stabbed in the head.

1:24:30 – A woman cuts off a man's hand.

THE ROOST

Year: 2005   Length: 81 minutes
Director: Ti West

STATISTICS

First Zombie:	43:00
First Human Death:	59:30
First Zombie Death:	1:12:30
Amount of Gore:	Low
Gore Quality:	High
Zombie Effects:	High
Zombie Count:	Average
Zombie Deaths:	Low
Human Deaths:	Low

SUMMARY

A group of friends suffer a near fatal car accident, while traveling to a Halloween night wedding. Leaving the scene of the accident, they set off to seek help. Instead they find themselves faced with hungry zombies and a horde of killer vampire bats.

EFFECTS HIGHLIGHTS

24:00 – Close up of an animal carcass.

58:15 – A zombie spits up blood.

59:30 – Close up of a bloody neck wound.

1:12:30 – A zombie has a pole sticking through its chest.

ROUTE 666

Year: 2001   Length: 90 minutes
Director: William Wesley

STATISTICS

First Zombie:	7:00
First Human Death:	8:30
First Zombie Death:	1:17:30

Amount of Gore:	Average
Gore Quality:	High
Zombie Effects:	High
Zombie Count:	Average
Zombie Deaths:	Average
Human Deaths:	High

SUMMARY

After disappearing from the government's witness protection program, a mob informer is hiding out in the Arizona desert. As a pair of federal agents try to find the man, they make their way along the dangerous and zombie infested stretch of highway known as Route 666.

EFFECTS HIGHLIGHTS

35:45 – A man is stabbed in the side of his stomach.

38:00 – A man is stabbed with a jackhammer.

51:15 – A man's hand is crushed in a car door.

1:11:00 – A man is stabbed with a jackhammer.

1:12:15 – A man is shot in the chest.

1:17:30 – A zombie is stabbed with a jackhammer.

1:18:00 – A zombie is shot in the chest.

1:20:45 – A man is shot in the chest.

SABBATH

Year: 2005   Length: 80 minutes
Director: William Victor Schotten

STATISTICS

First Zombie:	10:15
First Human Death:	1:00:00
First Zombie Death:	41:45

Amount of Gore:	High
Gore Quality:	High
Zombie Effects:	Average
Zombie Count:	Very High
Zombie Deaths:	High
Human Deaths:	Low

SUMMARY

Four strangers must team up to fight for survival when the dead start coming back to life. However, it isn't just zombies the survivors face, as the undead are joined by demons and the grim reaper himself.

EFFECTS HIGHLIGHTS

9:30 – A woman's face melts.

11:00 – Blood and gore is splashed over a tree.

11:15 – Close up of a pile of body parts.

37:00 – A zombie bites a man's neck.

48:30 – A zombie is hit in the head with a baseball.

48:30 – A zombie is hit in the head with a baseball.

49:00 – A zombie bites a man's leg.

49:15 – A zombie is hit in the head with a baseball.

1:00:45 – Close up of a pile of body parts.

1:00:45 – A man spits up blood.

1:01:15 – A zombie eats intestines.

1:07:15 – A zombie carries a legless torso.

SARS WARS

Year: 2004   Length: 95 minutes
Director: Taweewat Wantha

STATISTICS

First Zombie:	5:15
First Human Death:	6:15
First Zombie Death:	22:15

Amount of Gore:	High
Gore Quality:	Average
Zombie Effects: Average	
Zombie Count:	Very High
Zombie Deaths:	High
Human Deaths:	Average

SUMMARY

After a deadly SARS outbreak sweeps the globe and turns its victims into flesh-eating zombies, Thailand stands alone as the only nation to escape the pandemic. However, the virus finds its way into a Bangkok apartment complex and it's up to an unlikely hero to make his way into the building and clear out the threat.

EFFECTS HIGHLIGHTS

11:00 – A man has an infected wound on his neck

18:15 – A zombie is stabbed in the neck with an electric iron.

20:00 – A zombie is shot in the back.

20:30 – A zombie is shot in the head with a shotgun.

29:45 – A man is shot in the back of the head.

37:00 – A zombie is stabbed in the head with a sword.

40:00 – Body parts are scattered on the floor.

42:00 – A zombie's head explodes.

45:15 – A zombie bites a woman's neck.

46:45 – Numerous zombie limbs are cut off with a sword.

47:00 – A zombie is cut in two.

53:30 – A zombie is decapitated with an axe.

54:00 – A zombie baby bursts out of a zombie's stomach.

1:00:00 – A group of zombies explode.

1:24:15 – A headless torso is sitting behind a desk.

THE SERPENT AND THE RAINBOW

Year: 1988   Length: 98 minutes
Director: Wes Craven

STATISTICS

First Zombie: 39:30
First Human Death: 1:15:30
First Zombie Death: N/A

Amount of Gore: Low
Gore Quality: Average
Zombie Effects: High
Zombie Count: Low
Zombie Deaths: Very Low
Human Deaths: Average

SUMMARY

An American anthropologist travels to Haiti to research rumors about a drug used by local black magic practitioners that can turn people into zombies.

EFFECTS HIGHLIGHTS

4:15 – A man sticks a needle into another man's face.

1:02:45 – A woman is decapitated.

SEVERED: FOREST OF THE DEAD

Year: 2006   Length: 95 minutes
Director: Carl Bessai

STATISTICS

First Zombie: 8:30
First Human Death: 27:45
First Zombie Death: 19:30

Amount of Gore: High
Gore Quality: Very High
Zombie Effects: Very High
Zombie Count: High
Zombie Deaths: High
Human Deaths: Average

SUMMARY

When a forestry company genetically engineers trees,

a group of lumberjacks and environmental activists become ravenous flesh-eating zombies after being exposed to the tainted sap.

EFFECTS HIGHLIGHTS

7:15 – A man is hit in the shoulder with a chainsaw.

18:45 – A zombie is eating a dead body.

23:15 – A zombie is eating a dead body.

42:45 – Close up of a severed arm.

42:45 – Close up of a severed leg.

43:15 – Close up of an open wound on a man's leg.

49:30 – Close up of a severed head.

50:45 – Close up of a dead zombie.

59:45 – A group of zombies eat a dead body.

1:09:00 – A zombie is shot in the chest.

1:09:15 – A zombie is shot in the head.

1:09:15 – A zombie is shot in the chest.

1:10:45 – A man is stabbed in the hand.

1:18:45 – A zombie is shot in the leg.

1:19:15 – A zombie is shot in the chest.

1:19:15 – A zombie is shot in the chest.

1:21:00 – A man is shot in the chest.

1:24:45 – A severed head is mounted on a pole.

1:26:15 – A zombie eats from a dead body.

SHADOW: DEAD RIOT

Year: 2006   Length: 81 minutes
Director: Derek Wan

STATISTICS

First Zombie: 36:45
First Human Death: 4:45
First Zombie Death: 38:00

Amount of Gore: Very High
Gore Quality: Very High
Zombie Effects: Very High
Zombie Count: Very High
Zombie Deaths: Average
Human Deaths: Very High

SUMMARY

An imprisoned serial killer is put to death for murdering pregnant women. Twenty years later the prison has been turned into a women's penitentiary and the body of the serial killer has risen from the grave to take out his revenge.

EFFECTS HIGHLIGHTS

:30 – A man carves into his skin.

1:45 – A man is bitten on the neck.

4:45 – A man is stabbed in the face.

4:45 – A man is shot in the back.

5:00 – A man is shot in the chest.

5:00 – A man is shot in the chest.

5:00 – A man is shot in the head.

5:00 – A man is shot in the head.

5:00 – A man is shot in the head.

5:00 – A man is shot in the chest.

5:00 – A man is shot in the chest.

33:15 – A man explodes.

38:00 – A zombie jams a night stick through a man's head.

52:30 – A woman is bitten on the neck.

54:15 – A zombie's eye is pulled out.

58:30 – A man is stabbed in the eye with a syringe.

1:02:30 – A zombie is shot in the head.

1:06:00 – A door cuts off a zombie's arm.

1:07:30 – A zombie pulls out a woman's stomach.

1:07:45 – A zombie is stabbed in the eye.

1:10:45 – A zombie bites off a woman's tongue.

1:11:00 – A zombie is impaled on a pole.

1:12:00 – A zombie's head is pulled off.

1:12:15 – A zombie is missing its legs.

1:13:15 – A woman is stabbed in the head.

1:21:45 – A zombie explodes.

SHADOWS OF THE DEAD

Year: 2004   Length: 92 minutes
Director: Carl Lindbergh

STATISTICS

First Zombie:	8:30
First Human Death:	1:08:00
First Zombie Death:	N/A
Amount of Gore:	Low
Gore Quality:	Average
Zombie Effects:	Low
Zombie Count:	Average
Zombie Deaths:	Very Low
Human Deaths:	Average

SUMMARY

A man and his girlfriend take a weekend getaway and stumble upon a dead body that infects them with a deadly virus that turns them into zombies. They take shelter in an abandoned shack and struggle with their rising hunger for human flesh.

EFFECTS HIGHLIGHTS

1:06:45 – A woman bleeds from a neck wound.

SHATTER DEAD

Year: 1994   Length: 84 minutes
Director: Scooter McCrae

STATISTICS

First Zombie:	4:15
First Human Death:	N/A
First Zombie Death:	42:45
Amount of Gore:	High
Gore Quality:	High
Zombie Effects:	Low
Zombie Count:	High
Zombie Deaths:	Average
Human Deaths:	Very Low

SUMMARY

After the Angel of Death impregnates a mortal woman, the flow of life is disrupted causing the dead come back to life. However, these zombies only want to coexist with the living.   The living want their world back and a bloody war breaks out between the living and the dead.

EFFECTS HIGHLIGHTS

4:45 – A zombie picks at a bloody arm wound.

9:00 – A zombie carries a severed head.

42:45 – A zombie is shot in the head.

42:45 – A zombie is shot in the head.

42:45 – A zombie is shot in the head.

44:15 – Close up of a zombie's bloodied face.

44:45 – A zombie is shot in the head.

45:30 – A zombie is shot in the stomach.

48:15 – A zombie holds a bloodied baby.

50:30 – A man is shot in the hand.

51:30 – A zombie's head is smashed with the butt of a rifle.

59:30 – Close up a zombie's slit wrists.

1:11:45 – A zombie is shot in the head.

1:12:15 – Close up of a bloodiy zombie.

SHAUN OF THE DEAD

Year: 2004   Length: 94 minutes
Director: Edgar Wright

STATISTICS

First Zombie:	12:30
First Human Death:	22:00
First Zombie Death:	32:15
Amount of Gore:	Very High
Gore Quality:	Very High
Zombie Effects:	Very High
Zombie Count:	Very High
Zombie Deaths:	High
Human Deaths:	High

SUMMARY

When a slacker's girlfriend dumps him the night the dead return to life, he sets out with his best friend to rescue his mum, win back his girlfriend and take

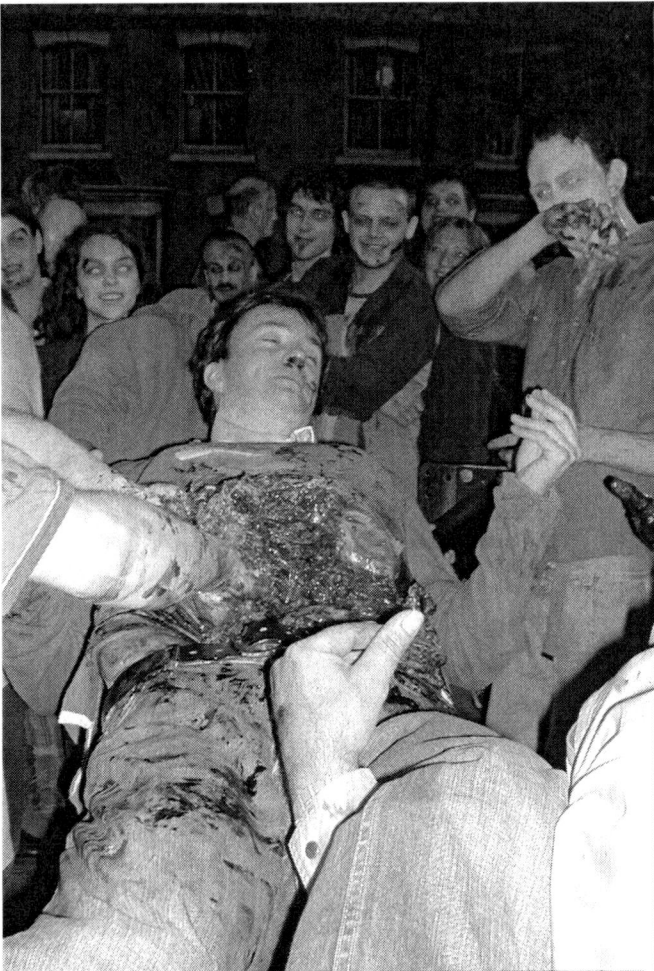

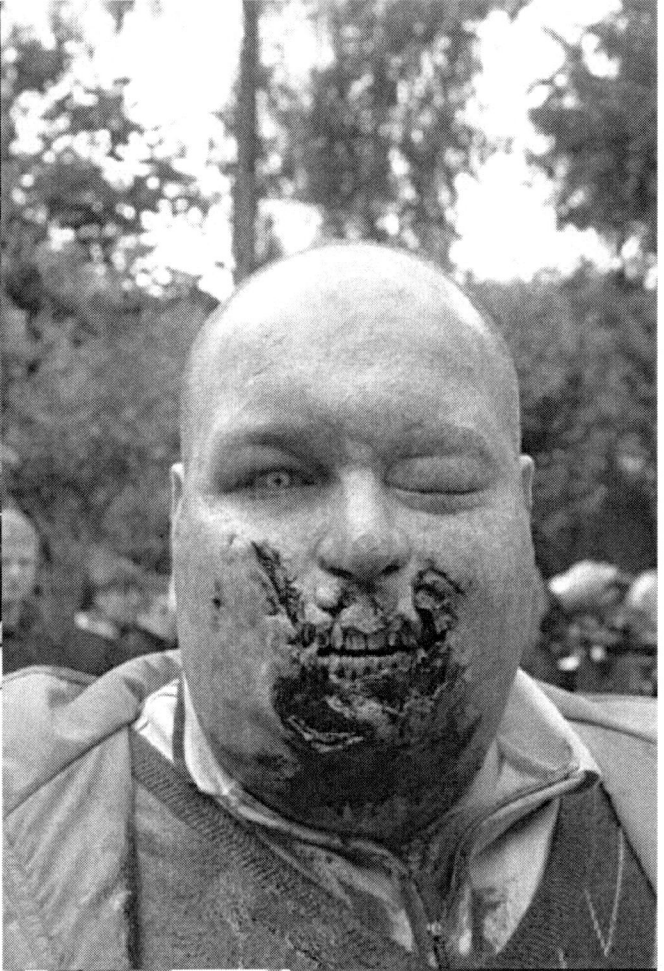

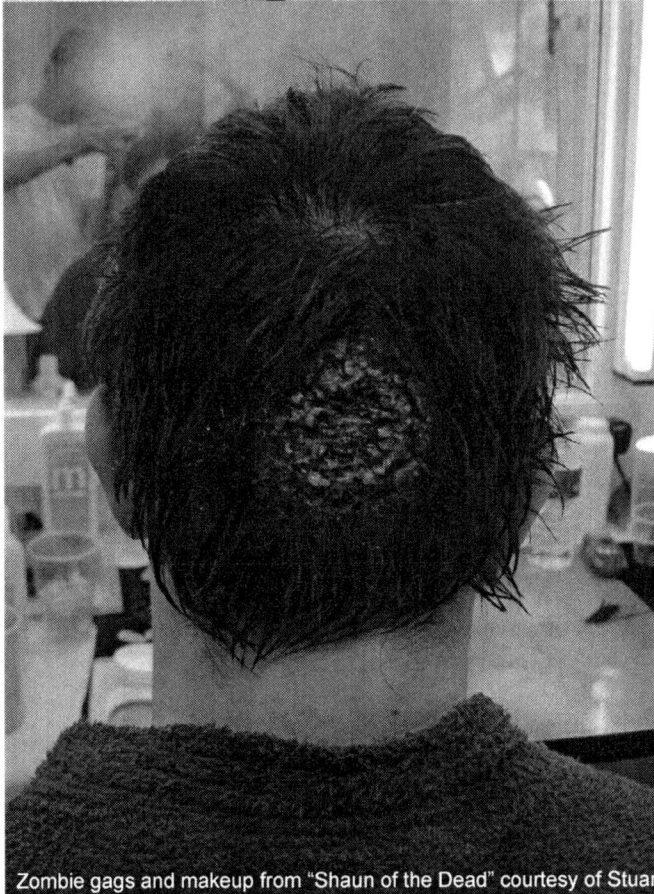

Zombie gags and makeup from "Shaun of the Dead" courtesy of Stuart Conran.

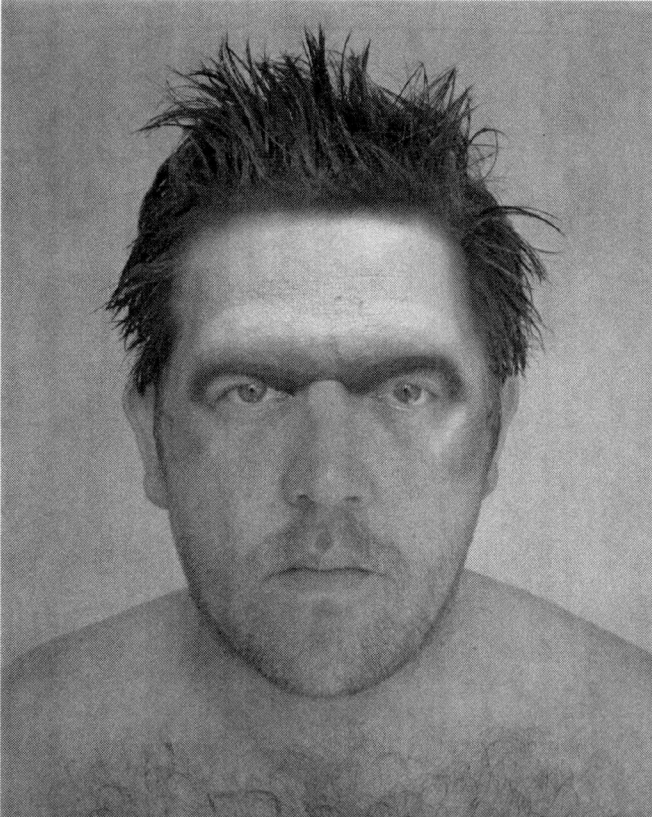

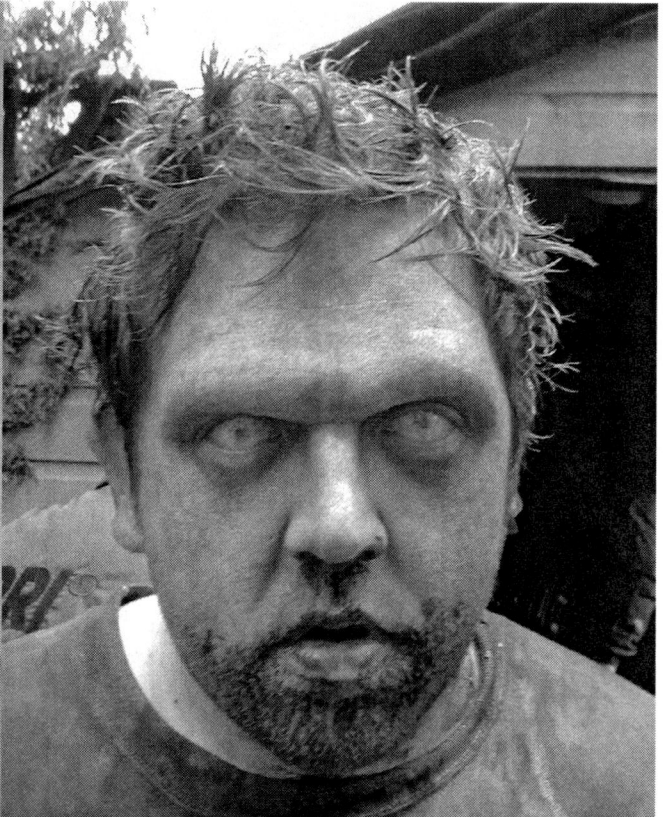

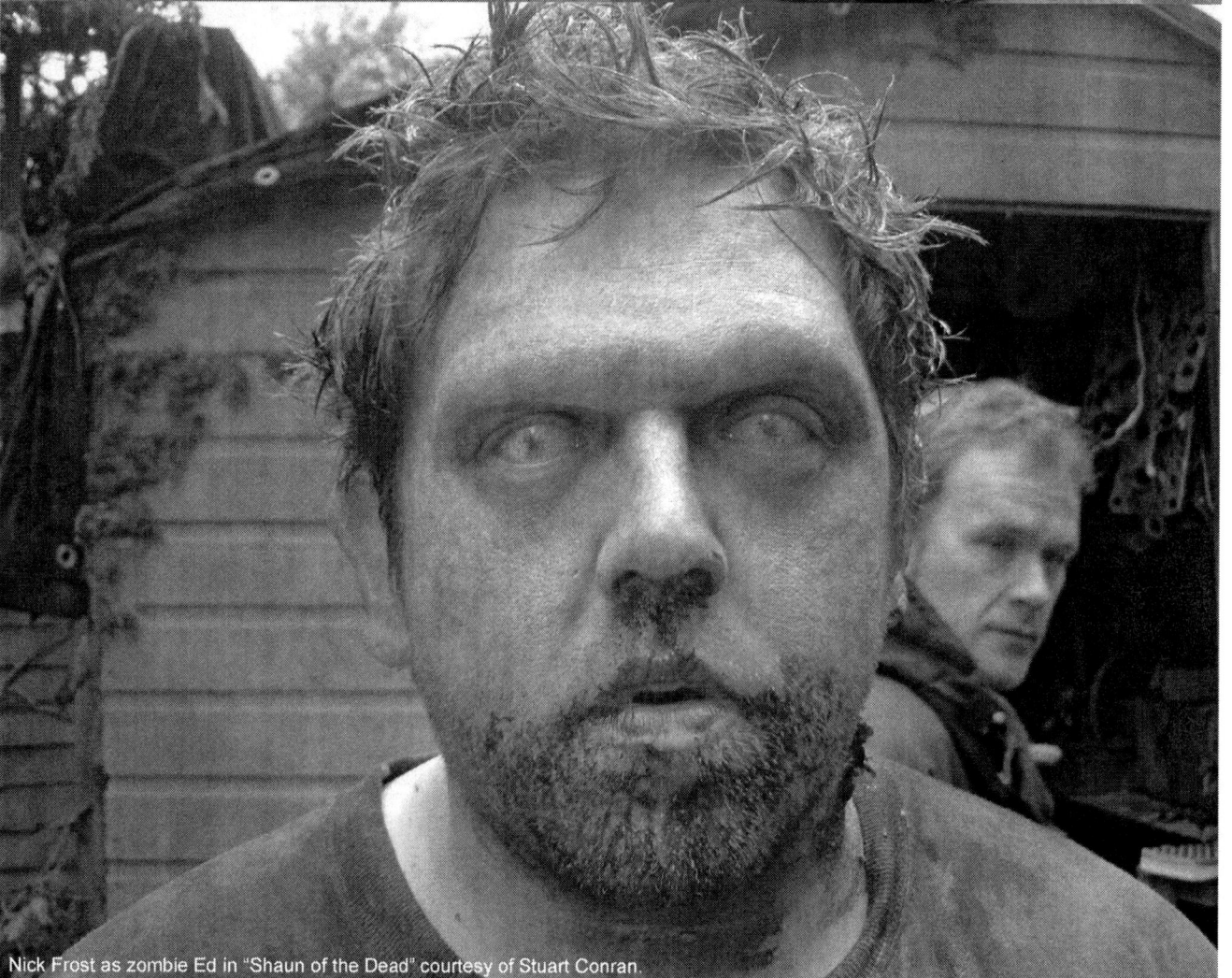

Nick Frost as zombie Ed in "Shaun of the Dead" courtesy of Stuart Conran.

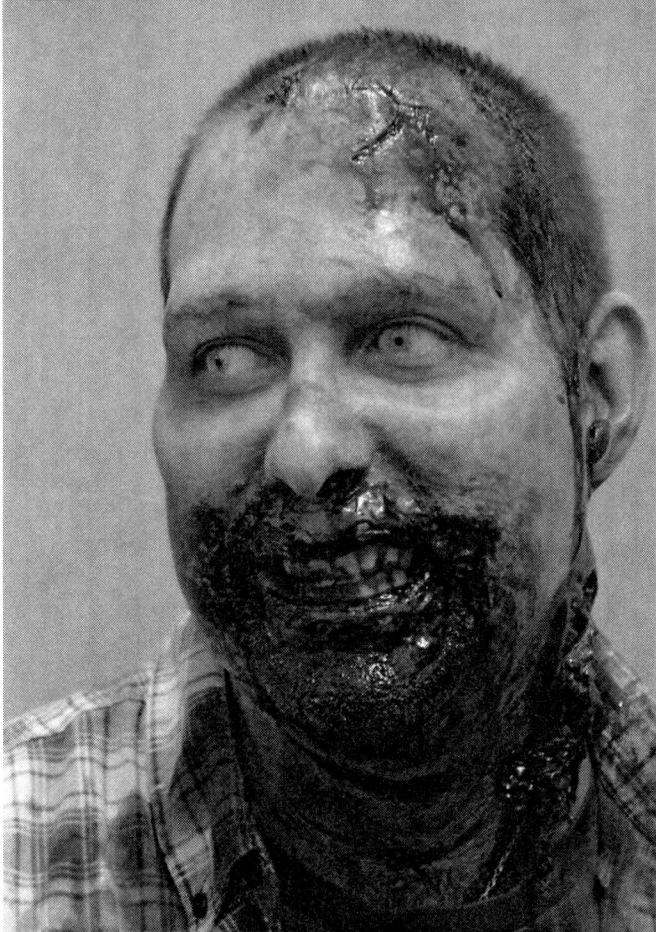

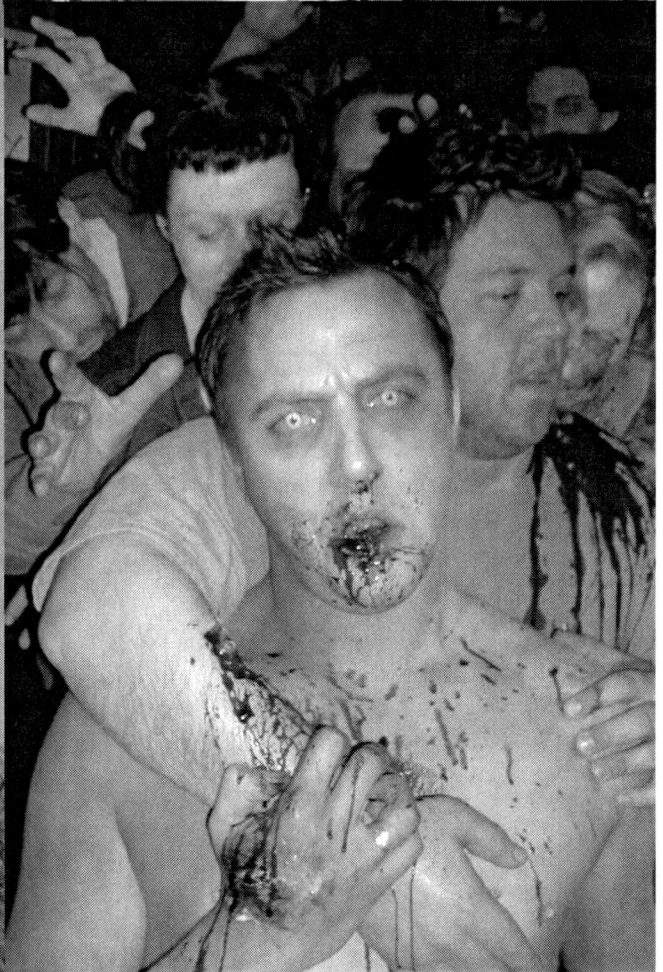

Top and center Bill Nighy and zombies from "Shaun of the Dead" courtesy of Stuart Conran. Bottom, Whites Lines courtesy of Luke Robinson.

161

shelter at the local pub.

EFFECTS HIGHLIGHTS

22:00 – A zombie bites a man's head off.
30:15 – A zombie is impaled on a pole.
32:00 – A zombie has an arm missing.
32:15 – A glass ashtray is smashed over a zombie's head.
33:45 – A zombie is stabbed in the face with a vinyl record.
46:45 – A zombie bites a man's neck.
55:15 – A group of zombies are eating a corpse.
1:00:45 – A zombie is stabbed with a steel pole.
1:13:15 – A man is hit in the head with a dart.
1:15:30 – Close up of a bite mark.
1:16:00 – A zombie is shot in the chest.
1:16:15 – A zombie is shot in the shoulder.
1:16:15 – A zombie is shot in the neck.
1:16:30 – A zombie is shot in the head.
1:22:30 – A group of zombies tear open a man's stomach.
1:22:45 – A man's arms and legs are pulled off.
1:23:15 – A zombie is shot in the shoulder.
1:23:15 – A zombie is shot in the head.
1:23:15 – A zombie is shot in the shoulder.
1:23:45 – A zombie bites a man's arm.
1:24:00 – A zombie bites a man's neck.
1:24:00 – A zombie is shot in the head.
1:25:15 – A zombie is shot in the head.
1:25:15 – A zombie is shot in the head.
1:30:15 – A truck crushes a zombie's head.
1:30:30 – A truck hits a zombie.
1:30:30 – A zombie is shot in the chest.
1:30:30 – A zombie is shot in the chest.
1:30:30 – A zombie is shot in the chest.
1:30:30 – A zombie is shot in the chest.
1:30:45 – A zombie is shot in the head.

SHOCK WAVES

Year: 1977   Length: 85 minutes
Director: Ken Wiederhorn

STATISTICS

First Zombie:	28:30
First Human Death:	44:30
First Zombie Death:	N/A
Amount of Gore:	Very Low
Gore Quality:	Very Low
Zombie Effects:	High
Zombie Count:	Average
Zombie Deaths:	Very Low
Human Deaths:	High

SUMMARY

Off the coast of Florida, an indestructible army of undead Nazi's created during World War II have come back from the dead to kill all who get in their path.

EFFECTS HIGHLIGHTS

N/A

SICK AND THE DEAD

Year: 2009   Length: 90 minutes
Directors: Jordy Dickens, Brockton McKinney

STATISTICS

First Zombie:	1:00
First Human Death:	24:45
First Zombie Death:	10:45
Amount of Gore:	Very High
Gore Quality:	High
Zombie Effects:	Average
Zombie Count:	Very High
Zombie Deaths:	Very High
Human Deaths:	Average

SUMMARY

Three struggling survivors fight to maintain their way of life after a zombie plague sweeps across the globe. A year after the outbreak, the three men experience personality changes as they try to survive the outbreak.

EFFECTS HIGHLIGHTS

1:15 – A zombie is hit with a car.
2:30 – A zombie eats the flesh off of a severed skull.
10:45 – A zombie bleeds from a head wound.
10:45 – A zombie is stabbed in the forehead.
11:30 – A man bludgeons a zombie's skull.
11:45 – A zombie's skull is crushed.
12:15 – A zombie is decapitated.
17:00 – Close up of an arm wound.
17:15 – A zombie spits out a piece of flesh.
17:45 – Close up of a headless torso.
19:45 – A zombie bleeds from a head wound.
20:45 – A zombie is eating a piece of flesh.
21:00 – A zombie bleeds from a head wound.
37:15 – A man is stabbed in the head.
38:45 – A man pulls out a man's intestines.
41:45 – Close up of a pair of slit wrists.
44:15 – A zombie has been impaled on wooden spikes.
50:45 – A zombie is shot in the crotch with an arrow.
51:00 – A zombie is shot in the head with an arrow.
53:00 – A zombie is stabbed in the head.
53:15 – A zombie's arm is pulled off.

55:45 – A zombie is shot in the head.

55:45 – A man is stabbed in the back.

1:03:30 – A zombie is stabbed in the head with a pipe.

1:03:30 – A zombie is decapitated.

1:04:45 – A zombie's head is crushed.

1:11:15 – A man is shot in the chest.

1:16:00 – A zombie bites a man's fingers.

1:16:15 – A zombie eats a severed finger.

1:16:15 – A zombie eats a piece of flesh.

SIEGE OF THE DEAD

Year: 2010   Length: 59 minutes
Director: Marvin Kren

STATISTICS

First Zombie:	00:30
First Human Death:	41:45
First Zombie Death:	5:45
Amount of Gore:	Low
Gore Quality:	High
Zombie Effects:	High
Zombie Count:	Very High
Zombie Deaths:	Very High
Human Deaths:	Average

SUMMARY

A virus spreads across Berlin, turning people into zombies. A man and a teenager barricade themselves in an apartment when raging hordes of zombies swarm the building.

EFFECTS HIGHLIGHTS

6:30 – A woman is bitten on the neck.

52:30 – Close up of a bite on a man's arm.

SKIN CRAWL

Year: 2007   Length: 85 minutes
Director: Justin Wingenfeld

STATISTICS

First Zombie:	1:02:15
First Human Death:	1:02:45
First Zombie Death:	N/A
Amount of Gore:	Low
Gore Quality:	Average
Zombie Effects:	Low
Zombie Count:	Low
Zombie Deaths:	Very Low
Human Deaths:	Average

SUMMARY

When a woman is murdered by her husband, a witches curse brings her back from the dead to get revenge on her husband and his mistress.

EFFECTS HIGHLIGHTS

43:30 – A woman is stabbed in the stomach.

1:07:15 – A zombie rips out a man's intestines.

1:10:15 – A woman vomits blood and maggots.

SPECIAL DEAD

Year: 2006   Length: 90 minutes
Directors: Thomas L. Phillips, Sean Simmons

STATISTICS

First Zombie:	3:00
First Human Death:	17:15
First Zombie Death:	12:45
Amount of Gore:	High
Gore Quality:	High
Zombie Effects:	High
Zombie Count:	High
Zombie Deaths:	Average
Human Deaths:	Average

SUMMARY

When a zombie outbreak sweeps through a ranch for the mentally handicapped, a group of campers and their counselors try to survive the onslaught.

EFFECTS HIGHLIGHTS

6:45 – A zombie bites a man's leg.

17:15 – A man's head is hit repeatedly against a tree.

27:45 – A zombie is stabbed in the chest.

38:00 – A zombie is decapitated.

40:15 – A zombie bites a woman's neck.

40:15 – A zombie is shot in the head.

49:15 – A zombie is eating a dead chicken.

51:30 – A zombie's arm is smashed with various tools.

1:05:30 – Close up of a pair of severed zombie feet.

1:05:45 – A zombie's intestines fall out.

1:06:15 – A zombie is shot with an arrow.

1:06:30 – A zombie is stabbed in the chest.

1:08:00 – A zombie's head is pulled off.

1:10:30 – The skin on a zombie's face is pulled off.

1:15:00 – A zombie is shot in the head.

STACY

Year: 2001   Length: 80 minutes
Director: Naoyuki Tomomatsu

STATISTICS

First Zombie:	1:45
First Human Death:	48:45
First Zombie Death:	7:45

Amount of Gore:	High
Gore Quality:	Very High
Zombie Effects:	High
Zombie Count:	Very High
Zombie Deaths:	High
Human Deaths:	High

SUMMARY

Teenage girls across the world suddenly start dying and later reemerge as zombies. The government hires a vigilante groups to hunt down the dead girls and end the zombie threat.

EFFECTS HIGHLIGHTS

1:45 – A zombie bites a severed limb.

4:15 – Close up on a pile of intestines.

6:45 – A zombie's arm is ripped off.

7:15 – A zombie is missing an eye.

7:30 – A zombie's leg snaps in half.

7:45 – A zombie is shot in the face.

39:00 – A man slices a zombie's throat.

39:15 – A man pulls off a zombie's head.

42:30 – A legless zombie crawls across the floor.

42:45 – A zombie is shot in the head.

43:30 – A zombie's head is cut up with a chainsaw.

48:45 – A group of zombies rip open a man's chest.

51:15 – A zombie is shot in the eye.

53:15 – A zombie is decapitated.

1:05:15 – A zombie pulls off a man's hand.

1:05:15 – A zombie pulls off a man's arm.

1:05:30 – A zombie bites a man's neck.

1:05:45 – A zombie pulls off a man's head.

1:06:00 – A group of zombies devour a dead body.

STIFF ODDS

Year: 2004   Length: 84 minutes
Director: Caleb Allen

STATISTICS

First Zombie:	12:15
First Human Death:	48:15
First Zombie Death:	N/A

Amount of Gore:	High
Gore Quality:	Average
Zombie Effects:	Low
Zombie Count:	Average
Zombie Deaths:	Very Low
Human Deaths:	Average

SUMMARY

The grim reaper works a second job as a bookmaker for the dead, who place bets on who on earth will be the next to die. When he has difficulty paying off a debt, he is forced to hire a group of zombies to help him fix a few wagers in his favor.

EFFECTS HIGHLIGHTS

15:30 – A man's head is twisted 180 degrees.

21:45 – A woman's face is smashed into a road.

1:00:30 – A woman is shot in the head.

1:01:00 – Close up of gore splattered across a windshield.

1:01:30 – A zombie picks up a severed arm.

1:04:30 – A woman rips off a man's nipples.

1:06:15 – A woman is missing an arm.

1:11:00 – A zombie's head is smashed against a car.

1:11:15 – A zombie is missing its head.

1:11:30 – A zombie's torso is ripped open.

1:15:00 – A zombie's intestines are ripped out.

1:15:00 – A zombie's head is crushed.

THE STINK OF FLESH

Year: 2005   Length: 85 minutes
Director: Scott Phillips

STATISTICS

First Zombie:	1:30
First Human Death:	6:30
First Zombie Death:	3:15

Amount of Gore:	Very High
Gore Quality:	High
Zombie Effects:	Average
Zombie Count:	Very High
Zombie Deaths:	High
Human Deaths:	Average

SUMMARY

A man has survived the zombie holocaust by using his wits, but when he meets two fellow survivors, he is drawn into a world of bizarre sexual experimentation.

EFFECTS HIGHLIGHTS

3:15 – A spike is hammered into a zombie's head.

6:15 – A zombie eats a piece of flesh.

6:15 – A zombie eats a piece of flesh.

7:15 – A zombie eats a piece of flesh.

16:00 – A zombie bites a man's neck.

16:15 – A zombie bites a woman's stomach.

16:15 – A zombie bites a man's neck.

20:30 – A zombie is shot in the head.

33:45 – A zombie is shot in the head.

38:00 – A strip of material is peeled off of a bloody wound.

41:30 – A zombie bites a chunk of flesh out of a man's face.

41:30 – A zombie bites a piece of intestine.

42:00 – A zombie eats a piece of flesh.

42:15 – A zombie bites a man's chest.

42:15 – A zombie bites a man's chest.

42:45 – Close up of a bloody dead zombie.

1:03:30 – A zombie's face is smashed into a rock.

1:11:15 – A zombie bites a man's neck.

1:12:30 – A man is stabbed in the neck with a pair of scissors.

1:14:00 – A zombie bites a chunk of flesh out of a man's neck.

1:14:45 – A zombie is stabbed in the head.

STORM OF THE DEAD

Year: 2005   Length: 88 minutes
Director: Bob Cook

STATISTICS

First Zombie: 44:45
First Human Death: 10:00
First Zombie Death: N/A

Amount of Gore: Low
Gore Quality: Average
Zombie Effects: Low
Zombie Count: Low
Zombie Deaths: Very Low
Human Deaths: Average

SUMMARY

After a massive hurricane hits Florida, the President calls up the Army and authorizes the troops to shoot any looters. But when they accidentally kill the grandson of a powerful voodoo queen, they find themselves in a fight for their lives as the dead return to life to take revenge on the soldiers.

EFFECTS HIGHLIGHTS

44:15 – Close up of a severed hand.

1:19:15 – A zombie eats a piece of flesh.

1:19:45 – Close up of a severed hand.

STRIPPERLAND

Year: 2011   Length: 103 minutes
Director: Sean Skelding

STATISTICS

First Zombie: :30
First Human Death: 41:45
First Zombie Death: 5:45

Amount of Gore: Very High
Gore Quality: High
Zombie Effects: High
Zombie Count: Very High
Zombie Deaths: Very High
Human Deaths: Average

SUMMARY

A devastating virus breaks out across the country causing the majority of the female population to turn into lethal flesh-eating zombie strippers. A small band of survivors embark on a dangerous cross country mission to get to a save haven in Portland, Oregon.

EFFECTS HIGHLIGHTS

:30 – A zombie is hit in the face with a baseball bat.

2:15 – A zombie bites off a man's penis.

2:30 – A zombie bites off a man's cheek.

2:45 – A zombie eats a man's intestines.

2:45 – A man's eyes are pulled out and eaten.

4:15 – A zombie eats a piece of flesh.

4:30 – A group of zombies eat a man's intestines.

4:30 – A group of zombies eat a man's intestines.

5:00 – A zombie pulls out a woman's intestines.

5:15 – A zombie holds a pair of severed arms.

5:45 – A zombie is shot in the chest.

5:45 – A zombie is shot in the chest.

6:00 – A zombie is shot in the chest.

6:00 – A zombie is shot in the head.

10:15 – A man is punched in the head, splitting it in half.

11:30 – A zombie eats a severed arm.

11:45 – A zombie eats a piece of flesh.

18:30 – A zombie is shot in the stomach.

23:00 – A zombie is shot in the chest.

41:45 – A man's intestines are pulled out.

43:00 – A zombie's arm is cut off.

43:00 – A zombie is decapitated.

43:00 – A zombie is stabbed in the stomach.

43:11 – A zombie's head is cut with a sword.

43:15 – A zombie's arm is cut off.

43:30 – A zombie is stabbed in the neck.

44:00 – A car runs over a zombie's head.

45:00 – A zombie eats a piece of flesh.

49:45 – A zombie is cut with a chainsaw.

50:00 – An arm and foot are cut off with a chainsaw.

50:00 – A zombie is cut in the head with a chainsaw.

50:00 – An arm and leg are cut off with a chainsaw.

50:00 – A zombie stabbed in the chest with a chainsaw.

50:15 – A hand is cut off with a chainsaw.

50:15 – An arm and leg are cut off with a chainsaw.

50:15 – A zombie is cut in the neck with a chainsaw.

50:30 – An arm is cut off with a chainsaw.

50:30 – A zombie is stabbed in the mouth with a chainsaw.

50:45 – An arm and hand are cut off.

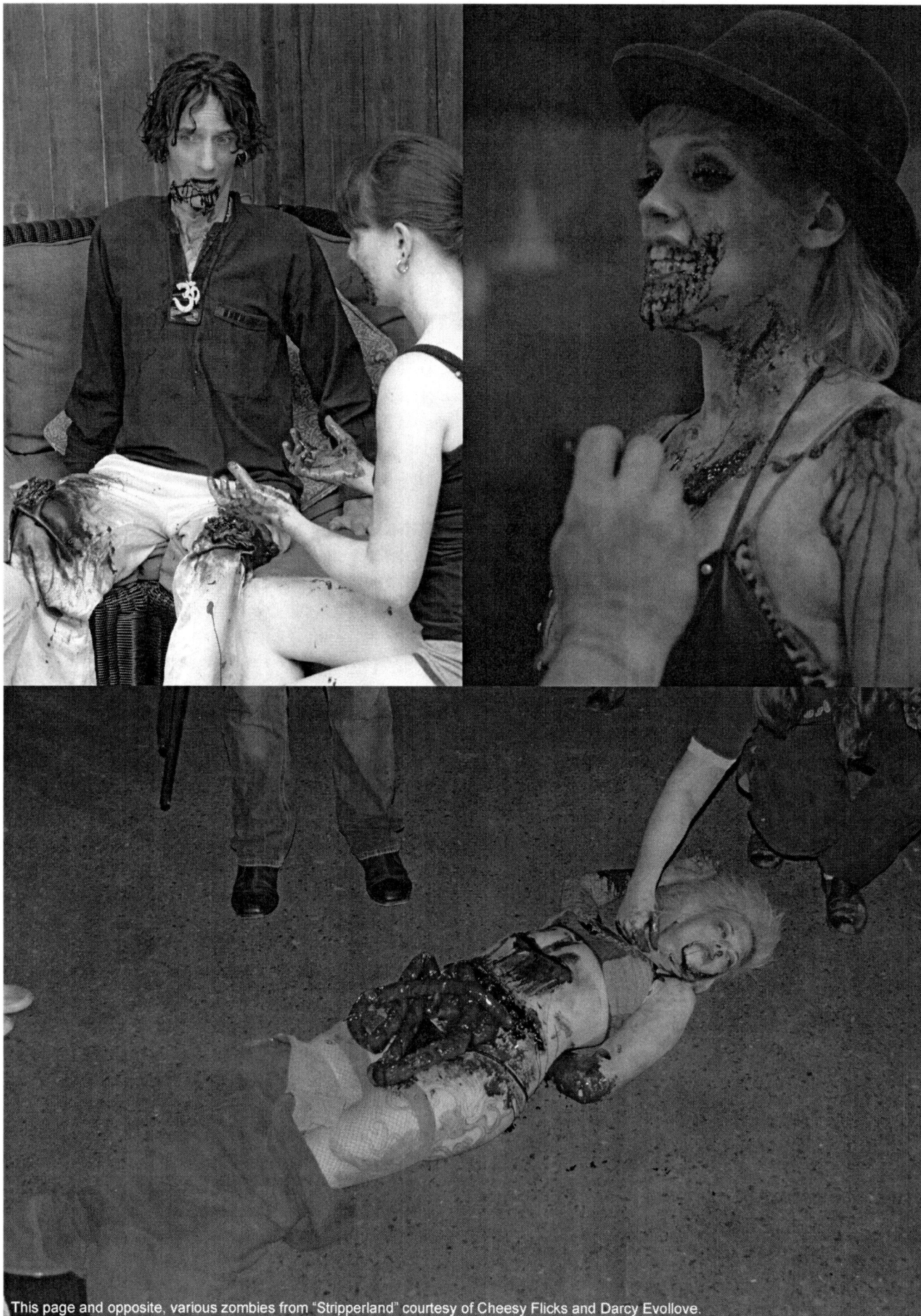

This page and opposite, various zombies from "Stripperland" courtesy of Cheesy Flicks and Darcy Evollove.

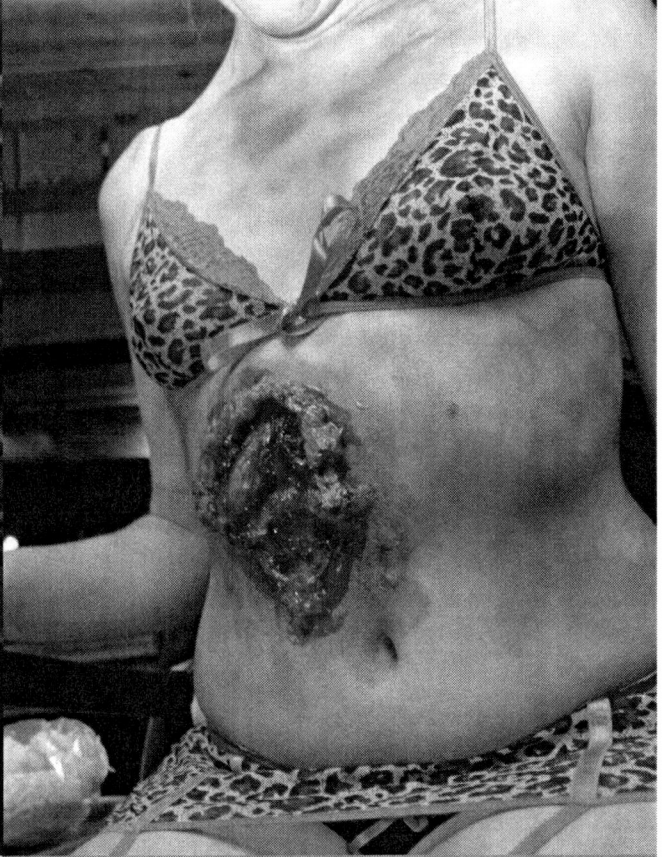

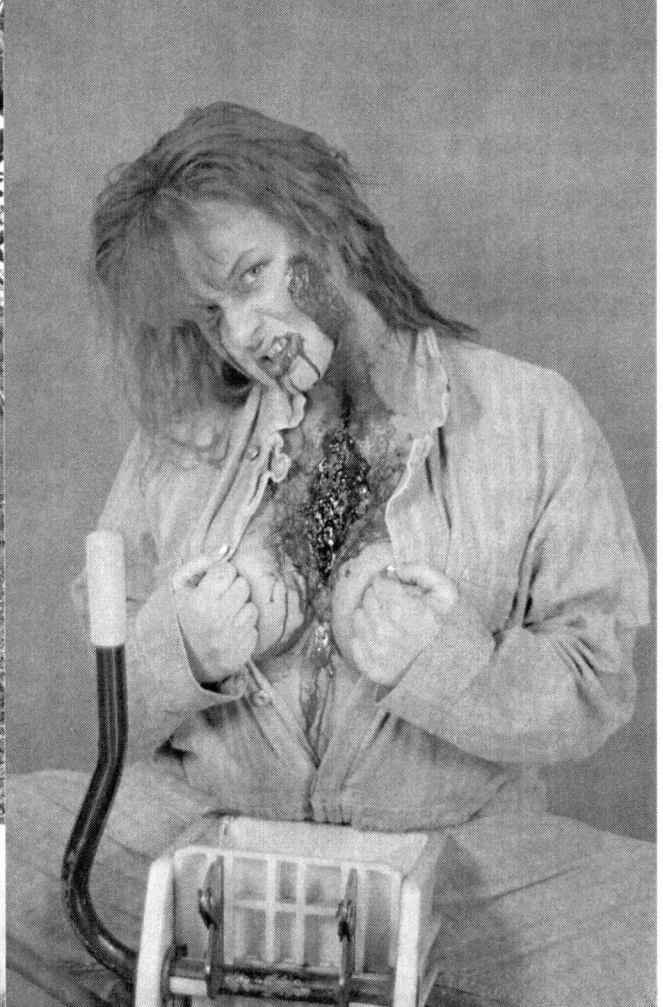

1:03:45 – A zombie bites a man's neck.

1:04:15 – Two zombies pull off a man's legs.

1:04:30 – A man's intestines are pulled out.

1:13:00 – A man is shot in the back.

1:13:15 – A man bleeds from a wound in his stomach.

1:16:15 – A zombie is eating a severed arm.

1:29:45 – A zombie is stabbed in the throat.

1:29:45 – A zombie is stabbed in the head.

1:30:00 – A zombie is stabbed in the chest.

1:30:15 – A zombie is shot in the chest.

1:31:30 – A zombie is shot in the chest.

1:31:30 – A zombie is stabbed in the head.

1:31:30 – A zombie is shot in the chest.

1:31:45 – A zombie is stabbed in the head.

1:32:00 – A zombie is stabbed in the head.

1:32:00 – A zombie is shot in the chest.

1:32:00 – A zombie is shot in the chest.

1:32:00 – A zombie is stabbed in the head.

1:35:00 – Multiple zombies are shot in the chest.

1:35:15 – A zombie is stabbed in the chest with a vinyl record.

1:35:15 – A zombie is hit in the head with a golf ball.

1:35:15 – A zombie is hit in the head with a golf ball.

SURVIVAL OF THE DEAD

Year: 2010   Length: 86 minutes
Director: George A. Romero

STATISTICS

First Zombie: 1:00
First Human Death: 2:15
First Zombie Death: 1:45

Amount of Gore: Very High
Gore Quality: Very High
Zombie Effects: Very High
Zombie Count: Very High
Zombie Deaths: Very High
Human Deaths: Very High

SUMMARY

A small group of rogue National Guards take shelter on an island populated by two feuding families with differing views on how to treat those who have turned into zombies.

EFFECTS HIGHLIGHTS

1:45 – A zombie is shot in the head.

2:00 – A zombie bites a man's face.

2:15 – A man is shot in the head.

2:15 – A zombie is shot in the head.

4:00 – A zombie is shot in the head.

6:45 – A woman is shot in the chest.

15:15 – A man is shot in the shoulder.

16:00 – Severed zombie's heads are impaled on branches.

16:00 – A zombie is shot in the head.

16:15 – A zombie is shot in the head.

16:15 – A zombie is shot in the head.

16:15 – A zombie is shot in the head.

16:15 – A zombie is shot in the head.

16:30 – A zombie is shot in the head.

17:15 – A man is shot in the stomach.

17:45 – A man is shot in the head.

23:45 – A zombie is shot in the head.

25:45 – A zombie steps on a land mine.

27:15 – A zombie is shot in the head.

27:45 – A man bites a zombie's finger off.

28:00 – A zombie is shot in the head.

29:15 – A man places a fire extinguisher in a zombie's mouth and its head explodes.

29:15 – A zombie is shot in the head.

29:45 – A zombie is shot in the head.

30:45 – A zombie is shot in the head.

30:45 – A zombie is shot in the head.

31:15 – A zombie is shot in the head.

31:15 – A zombie is shot in the head.

31:15 – A zombie is shot in the head.

31:30 – A zombie bites a man's neck.

31:30 – A zombie is shot in the head.

34:15 – A zombie is stabbed in the head.

35:45 – Close up of a dead woman with a gunshot wound in her head.

38:45 – A zombie's head catches fire.

42:30 – A man is shot in the head.

45:15 – A zombie is shot in the head.

46:30 – A zombie is shot in the head.

46:45 – A zombie is stabbed in the foot with a rake.

47:00 – A zombie is shot in the head.

47:00 – Close up of a severed foot.

47:00 – A zombie is shot in the head.

47:45 – A zombie is shot in the head.

54:15 – A man is shot in the head.

1:11:00 – A man is shot in the leg.

1:11:30 – A zombie bites a woman's hand.

1:12:45 – A man is shot in the chest.

1:12:45 – A man is shot in the stomach.

1:13:30 – A zombie is shot in the head.

1:13:30 – A group of zombies tear a man apart.

1:13:30 – A zombie is shot in the head.

1:13:30 – A zombie is shot in the head.

1:13:30 – A zombie is shot in the head.

1:13:30 – A zombie is shot in the head.

1:13:45 – A zombie bites a man on the neck.

1:13:45 – A zombie is shot in the head.

1:13:45 – A group of zombies tear a man apart.

1:14:00 – A zombie is shot in the head.

1:14:00 – A zombie rips off a man's scalp.

1:14:15 – A zombie is shot in the head.

1:14:30 – A zombie is shot in the chest.

1:14:30 – A zombie is shot in the head.

1:14:30 – A zombie is stabbed in the eye with a shotgun barrel.

1:14:30 – A zombie is shot in the head.

1:14:45 – A zombie is shot in the head.

1:14:45 – A zombie is stabbed in the head with an axe.

1:14:45 – A zombie is stabbed in the crotch with a fire poker.

1:15:00 – A zombie bites a man's arm.

1:15:30 – A zombie is shot in the head.

1:15:45 – A zombie is shot in the chest.

1:15:45 – A zombie is shot in the head.

1:17:15 – A man is shot in the chest.

1:17:15 – A man is shot in the chest.

1:17:45 – A zombie bites a horse.

1:18:45 – A woman is shot in the head.

1:20:30 – A group of zombies eat a horse.

MICHAEL JACKSON'S THRILLER

Year: 1983   Length: 13 minutes
Director: John Landis

STATISTICS

First Zombie:	6:45
First Human Death:	N/A
First Zombie Death:	N/A

Amount of Gore:	Very Low
Gore Quality:	Very Low
Zombie Effects:	High
Zombie Count:	High
Zombie Deaths:	Very Low
Human Deaths:	Very Low

SUMMARY

Michael Jackson's seminal music video that introduced the long form music video to the undead. A night at the movies turns into a nightmare when Michael and his date are attacked by a hoard of the living dead on their way home.

EFFECTS HIGHLIGHTS

7:45 – A zombie has a gaping wound in its stomach.

7:45 – A zombie's arm falls off.

TOKYO ZOMBIE

Year: 2005   Length: 103 minutes
Director: Sakichi Sato

STATISTICS

First Zombie:	7:15
First Human Death:	59:30
First Zombie Death:	7:30

Amount of Gore:	Average
Gore Quality:	Average
Zombie Effects:	Low
Zombie Count:	Very High
Zombie Deaths:	Average
Human Deaths:	High

SUMMARY

Two factory workers must use their jujitsu skills and join forces with other survivors to fight off a horde of zombies that attack Tokyo.

EFFECTS HIGHLIGHTS

7:30 – A zombie is decapitated.

13:15 – A zombie bites a chunk of flesh out of a woman's neck.

25:00 – A man pulls off a zombie's head.

25:15 – A zombie is decapitated.

57:15 – A zombie bites a chunk of flesh out of a man's leg.

59:15 – A zombie punches a hole in a man's chest.

59:30 – A zombie pulls out a man's intestines.

1:11:30 – A zombie is shot in the head.

1:28:00 – A zombie's head swells up.

TOMBS OF THE BLIND DEAD

Year: 1971   Length: 86 minutes
Director: Amando de Ossorio

STATISTICS

First Zombie:	20:15
First Human Death:	37:15
First Zombie Death:	1:06:30

Amount of Gore:	High
Gore Quality:	High
Zombie Effects:	High
Zombie Count:	Average
Zombie Deaths:	Low
Human Deaths:	Average

SUMMARY

A group of people stumble on an abandoned monastery that is home to the deadly Templar Knights. These evil and dead creatures are a group of 13th century knights

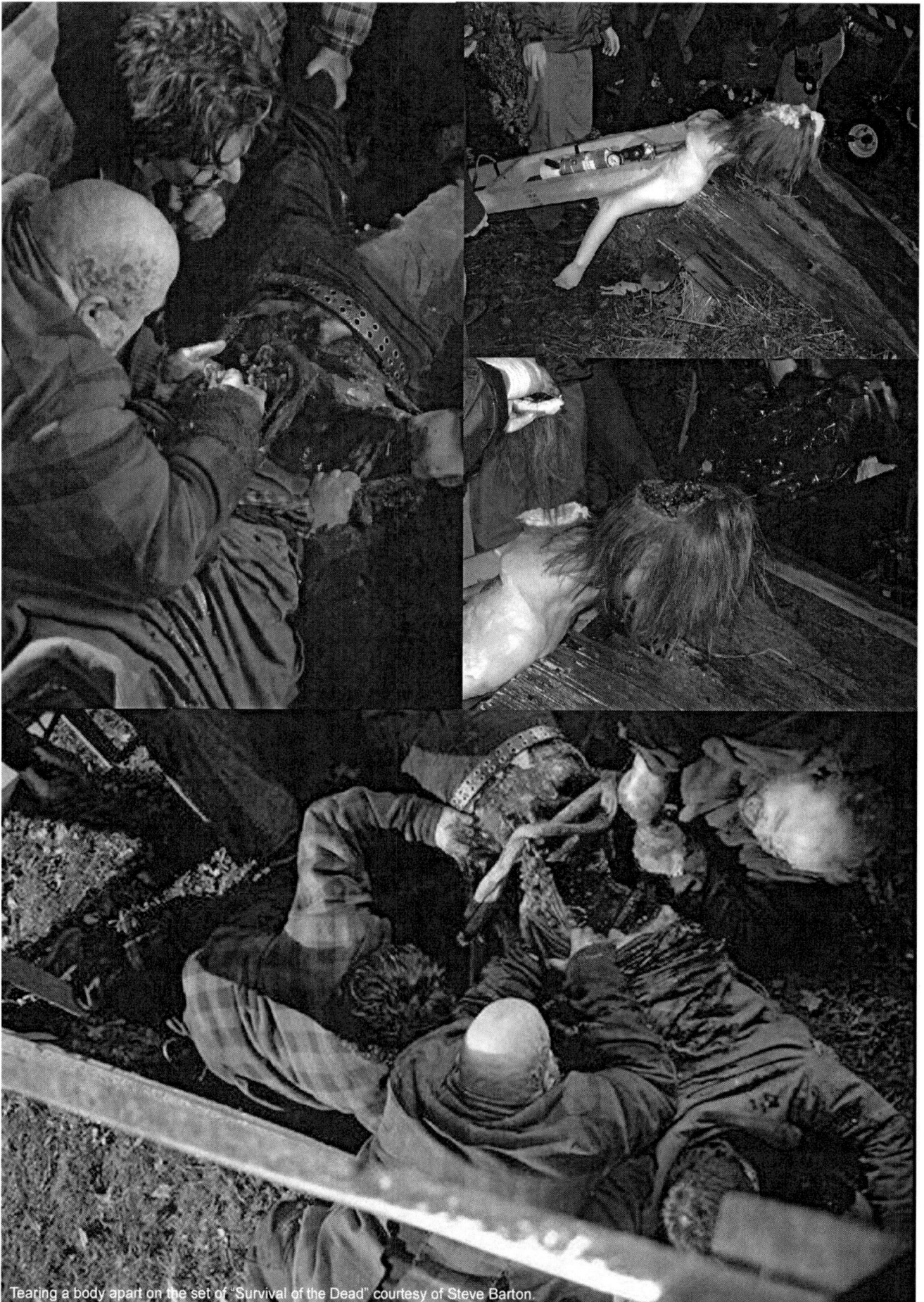

Tearing a body apart on the set of "Survival of the Dead" courtesy of Steve Barton.

? OF THE DEAD

SCENE	SLATE	TAKE	ROLL
87	4	1	A49

DIR: GEORGE A. ROMERO
ADAM SWICA, csc

DAY	SND
EXT	13

Behind the scenes on "Survival of the Dead" courtesy of Steve Barton.

who sought eternal life by drinking human blood and were executed for their sins.

EFFECTS HIGHLIGHTS

37:15 – Close up of a dead body.

44:00 – Close up of a dead body.

44:30 – Close up of a dead body.

52:00 – A zombie bites a man's neck.

57:00 – A woman is sliced on the chest.

57:00 – A woman is sliced on the chest.

57:00 – A woman is sliced on the chest.

57:00 – A woman is sliced on the stomach.

57:00 – A woman is sliced on the stomach.

1:25:00 – A man's hand is cut off.

1:25:15 – Close up of a bloodied stump.

1:33:15 – A child is covered in blood.

UNDEAD

Year: 2003   Length: 104 minutes
Directors: Michael Spierig, Peter Spierig

STATISTICS

First Zombie: 7:15
First Human Death: 7:00
First Zombie Death: 12:15

Amount of Gore: Very High
Gore Quality: High
Zombie Effects: High
Zombie Count: Very High
Zombie Deaths: Very High
Human Deaths: Average

SUMMARY

After a meteor shower, a deadly disease starts to spread across the countryside, turning those infected into blood thirsty zombies. A group of survivors meet at an old farmhouse and must learn to work together to overcome the threat.

EFFECTS HIGHLIGHTS

7:45 – A man has a hole in his chest.

7:45 – A man's head is destroyed.

11:00 – Close up of a bite wound on a man's leg.

12:15 – A zombie holds a bloodied skull.

12:15 – A zombie is cut in half.

12:45 – A zombie is shot in the chest.

13:15 – A shotgun blast cuts a zombie in half.

18:45 – A zombie punches through a woman's head.

19:00 – A zombie eats a brain.

27:45 – A zombie is missing half of its head.

33:45 – A man shoots a fish.

33:45 – A man shoots a fish.

37:45 – A zombie's arm is pulled off.

38:00 – A man shoots a severed arm.

39:00 – A zombie is shot in the chest.

39:00 – A zombie is shot in the head.

39:15 – A zombie is shot in the chest.

39:30 – Two zombies are stabbed in the head.

40:00 – A zombie's stomach falls onto the floor.

40:15 – A zombie is cut in half.

40:45 – A zombie is shot in the chest.

41:45 – A zombie is shot in the head.

44:45 – A zombie is shot in the head.

46:30 – A zombie is hit by a truck.

1:06:00 – A severed zombie arm holds a man's shoulder.

1:06:30 – A zombie is shot in the head.

1:06:30 – A zombie is shot in the neck.

1:07:15 – A zombie's head explodes.

1:07:45 – A zombie is stabbed in the head with a shovel.

1:08:00 – A zombie's face is ripped off.

1:09:00 – A zombie is shot in the head with a circular saw blade.

1:09:15 – A zombie is decapitated.

1:09:15 – A zombie is cut in half.

1:09:15 – A zombie is decapitated.

1:09:15 – A zombie is decapitated.

1:09:30 – A zombie is decapitated.

1:14:45 – A zombie is shredded by an airplane's propeller.

1:32:30 – A necklace charm is embedded in a man's chest.

UNDEAD OR ALIVE

Year: 2007   Length: 91 minutes
Director: Glasgow Phillips

STATISTICS

First Zombie: 2:15
First Human Death: 58:15
First Zombie Death: 44:15

Amount of Gore: Very High
Gore Quality: High
Zombie Effects: Very High
Zombie Count: Very High
Zombie Deaths: Average
Human Deaths: Low

SUMMARY

A rogue soldier teams up with hapless cowboy to rob a corrupt sheriff and leave town with the help of an Apache warrior princess. The robbery turns out to be the easy part, as the dead start coming back to life.

EFFECTS HIGHLIGHTS

2:30 – A zombie bites the head off of a chicken.

3:15 – A zombie is stabbed in the hand.

3:30 – A woman is bitten on the head.

31:30 – A zombie bites off a man's fingers.

31:30 – A zombie bites a man's neck.

31:45 – A zombie bites off a man's toe.

33:15 – A zombie bites a woman's back.

40:45 – A zombie is hit in the leg with an arrow.

40:45 – A zombie is hit in the chest with an arrow.

40:45 – A zombie is hit in the arm with an arrow.

41:00 – A zombie is shot in the chest.

43:30 – A zombie is stabbed in the mouth.

44:15 – A zombie's head is cut off with a shovel.

55:30 – A zombie bites off a man's lip.

58:15 – A zombie eats a man's brains with a spoon.

58:30 – A zombie holds a severed head.

58:45 – A zombie is shot in the chest.

58:45 – A zombie is shot in the chest.

59:15 – A zombie is shot in the head.

59:15 – A zombie is shot in the head.

1:00:00 – A zombie is shot in the knee.

1:00:00 – A zombie is shot in the knee.

1:00:15 – A zombie is eating a dead horse.

1:01:30 – A zombie's arm is cut off.

1:10:45 – A zombie's throat is slit.

1:10:45 – A zombie is decapitated.

1:13:15 – A zombie is stabbed in the chest.

1:18:15 – A zombie bites a man's face.

1:20:30 – A zombie's head is cut in half.

1:20:30 – A zombie is decapitated.

URBAN EVIL

Year: 2005   Length: 86 minutes
Directors: Art Carnage, Ted Nicolaou, James Black

STATISTICS

First Zombie: 25:45
First Human Death: 36:00
First Zombie Death: N/A

Amount of Gore: Average
Gore Quality: High
Zombie Effects: Very Low
Zombie Count: Average
Zombie Deaths: Very Low
Human Deaths: Average

SUMMARY

A collection of three separate urban horror stories that start with "Demonic Tunes" and follows an infamous record producer who wants to turn a hip-hop group into an army of zombies. In "The Killing Kind", a teenager puts his grandmother's spirit into a doll to take out revenge after she's attacked and "Hidden Evil" tells the story of a specter who's freed from the cellar of an old high school.

EFFECTS HIGHLIGHTS

27:00 – A man is electrocuted.

36:30 – A man is stabbed in the chest with a needle.

52:45 – A woman is stabbed in the shoulder.

1:08:30 – A man is hit by a van.

1:09:45 – A man is impaled on a metal pole.

1:14:30 – A man's head is cut in half with a piece of glass.

1:20:45 – A man's heart is ripped out.

VAMPIRES VS. ZOMBIES

Year: 2004   Length: 75 minutes
Director: Vince D'Amato

STATISTICS

First Zombie: 1:45
First Human Death: 1:11:15
First Zombie Death: 2:00

Amount of Gore: High
Gore Quality: High
Zombie Effects: Average
Zombie Count: Average
Zombie Deaths: Average
Human Deaths: Low

SUMMARY

A group of vampires face off against an army of the undead in a battle to decide the fate of humankind.

EFFECTS HIGHLIGHTS

2:00 – A zombie is hit by a car and decapitated.

15:45 – A man is bitten on the neck.

17:30 – A zombie bleeds from multiple wounds on its face.

27:15 – A vampire is staked in the chest.

27:30 – A vampire is decapitated.

31:00 – A man picks up a severed head.

50:00 – A zombie is stabbed in the chest.

58:30 – A woman punches a zombie through its head.

1:03:15 – A vampire is stabbed in the chest.

1:03:30 – A zombie bites a man's neck.

1:11:15 – A zombie eats an organ.

1:11:15 – A woman's intestines have been ripped out.

VENGEANCE OF THE

ZOMBIES

Year: 1973   Length: 90 minutes
Director: León Klimovsky

STATISTICS

First Zombie:	17:30
First Human Death:	18:00
First Zombie Death:	1:24:00

Amount of Gore:	Average
Gore Quality:	Average
Zombie Effects:	Low
Zombie Count:	Average
Zombie Deaths:	Average
Human Deaths:	High

SUMMARY

A mysterious Indian mystic uses voodoo to resurrect zombies from the grave to do his evil bidding.

EFFECTS HIGHLIGHTS

18:00 – A man is hit in the face with an axe.

37:00 – A man is stabbed in the back.

38:30 – A dead man's throat is slit.

43:15 – A man is stabbed in the neck.

56:00 – A man slices his own throat.

1:00:15 – A woman's severed head falls off her shoulders.

1:24:30 – A woman is shot in the chest.

VERSUS

Year: 2000   Length: 119 minutes
Director: Ryûhei Kitamura

STATISTICS

First Zombie:	1:15
First Human Death:	4:30
First Zombie Death:	1:15

Amount of Gore:	Very High
Gore Quality:	High
Zombie Effects:	Average
Zombie Count:	Very High
Zombie Deaths:	Very High
Human Deaths:	High

SUMMARY

A criminal on the run heads into the Forest of Resurrection to meet with a group of gangsters. When one of the gang is killed, it becomes apparent that the forest holds strange powers over the dead.

EFFECTS HIGHLIGHTS

1:15 – A zombie is cut in half.

13:00 – A man is shot in the chest.

15:45 – A zombie is shot in the head.

15:45 – A zombie is shot in the back.

16:00 – A zombie is shot in the chest.

16:00 – A zombie is shot in the chest.

16:00 – A zombie is shot in the chest.

16:15 – A zombie is shot in the chest.

16:00 – A zombie is shot in the chest.

16:00 – A zombie is shot in the chest.

17:15 – A zombie is repeatedly shot in the back.

32:00 – A zombie is shot in the chest.

32:45 – A zombie's arm falls off.

34:00 – A zombie's intestines fall out.

35:00 – A zombie is shot in the head.

35:15 – A zombie is decapitated.

35:45 – Two zombies are shot in the head.

36:45 – A zombie is shot in the head.

36:45 – A zombie is shot in the head.

37:00 – A zombie is shot in the head.

38:15 – A zombie is stabbed in the head.

47:30 – Two zombies are shot in the head.

48:30 – A zombie is shot in the head.

55:45 – A zombie punches through a man's chest.

56:00 – A man is shot in the head.

56:15 – A zombie eats a man's heart.

1:05:15 – A zombie punches through another zombie's skull.

1:10:15 – A car cuts a zombie in half.

1:37:00 – A man cuts a zombie is cut into pieces.

1:37:30 – A woman is shot in the stomach.

1:39:00 – A man stomps on a zombie's head.

1:46:00 – A man catches a severed hand.

1:52:45 – A man is stabbed in the chest.

1:59:00 – A man is decapitated.

THE VIDEO DEAD

Year: 1987   Length: 90 minutes
Director: Robert Scott

STATISTICS

First Zombie:	5:00
First Human Death:	8:45
First Zombie Death:	N/A

Amount of Gore:	High
Gore Quality:	Average
Zombie Effects:	High
Zombie Count:	Average
Zombie Deaths:	Very Low
Human Deaths:	High

SUMMARY

When a pair of teenagers discover an abandoned

Zombies on the set of "The Video Dead" courtesy of Dale Hall Jr.

175

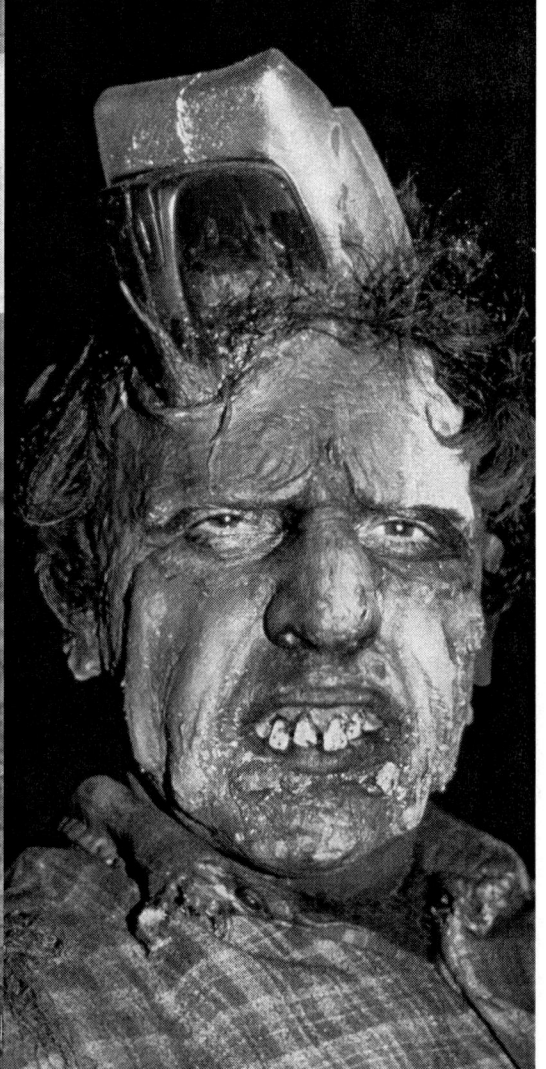

Zombies on the set of "The Video Dead" courtesy of Dale Hall Jr.

television in their new home, they open a doorway that allows the dead to crawl through.

EFFECTS HIGHLIGHTS

31:15 – A man cuts off a zombie's hand with an axe.

32:00 – A severed hand starts moving.

38:45 – A zombie is stabbed in the head with an iron.

58:15 – A zombie is hit in the chest with an arrow.

58:30 – A zombie is hit in the chest with an arrow.

58:30 – A zombie is hit in the chest with an arrow.

1:00:30 – A zombie is cut in half with a chainsaw.

1:06:30 – A zombie is hit in the stomach with an arrow.

1:06:45 – A zombie is hit in the back with an arrow.

1:07:00 – A zombie is hit in the back with an arrow.

1:07:00 – A zombie is hit in the back with an arrow.

1:07:00 – A zombie is hit in the back with an arrow.

1:07:30 – A zombie is hit in the stomach with an arrow.

1:09:45 – A man is stabbed in the chest with an arrow.

1:11:45 – A zombie is decapitated.

1:11:45 – A man is stabbed in the chest with a chainsaw.

1:21:45 – A zombie's face starts cracking and leaking fluid.

1:22:00 – A zombie's head falls off.

1:22:30 – A zombie eats a severed zombie head.

WILD ZERO

Year: 1999   Length: 97 minutes
Director: Tetsuro Takeuchi

STATISTICS

First Zombie:	23:15
First Human Death:	10:45
First Zombie Death:	41:45

Amount of Gore:	Very High
Gore Quality:	High
Zombie Effects:	Average
Zombie Count:	Very High
Zombie Deaths:	Very High
Human Deaths:	Average

SUMMARY

When zombies take over the world, only legendary Japanese garage rock band Guitar Wolf stands in their way.

EFFECTS HIGHLIGHTS

10:45 – A man is shot in the head.

10:45 – A man is missing two fingers.

11:15 – A man draws a knife across the back of his hand.

11:30 – A man draws a knife across the back of a man's hand.

11:45 – Close up of a severed finger.

28:15 – A zombie is shot in the chest.

29:15 – A group of zombies tear a dead body apart.

34:15 – A group of zombies are eating intestines.

34:45 – A zombie bites a chunk of flesh out of a man's arm.

35:00 – A zombie is shot in the chest.

41:45 – A zombie is shot in the head.

43:45 – A zombie is shot in the head.

44:00 – A zombie is shot in the head.

1:01:15 – A zombie is shot in the head.

1:01:15 – A zombie is shot in the chest.

1:01:45 – A zombie is shot in the head.

1:04:00 – A zombie is hit in the head with an axe.

1:08:00 – A zombie bites a chunk of flesh out of a man's shoulder.

1:08:00 – A zombie is shot in the stomach.

1:08:15 – A zombie is shot in the head.

1:10:30 – Close up of a headless zombie torso.

1:17:15 – A zombie is shot in the stomach.

1:17:15 – A zombie is shot in the head.

1:17:30 – A zombie is shot in the stomach.

1:17:30 – A zombie is shot in the stomach.

1:19:30 – A zombie is shot in the head.

1:19:30 – A zombie is shot in the head.

1:22:30 – A zombie is shot in the stomach.

WISEGUYS VS. ZOMBIES

Year: 2003   Length: 110 minutes
Director: Adam Minarovich

STATISTICS

First Zombie:	48:45
First Human Death:	26:00
First Zombie Death:	1:12:45

Amount of Gore:	Very High
Gore Quality:	Low
Zombie Effects:	Low
Zombie Count:	High
Zombie Deaths:	High
Human Deaths:	Average

SUMMARY

Two hitmen are given the task of transporting three bodies and a new street drug to Florida. On their travels they encounter hillbilly zombies that have been created by the very drug they are trying to deliver.

EFFECTS HIGHLIGHTS

4:00 – A man bleeds from a head wound.

26:00 – A man is shot in the chest.

26:00 – A man is shot in the head.

49:00 – A zombie bites a man's neck.

49:45 – A man spits up blood.

51:00 – A zombie bites a chunk of flesh out of a man's neck.

1:12:45 – A zombie is shot in the head.

1:15:30 – A zombie's head explodes.

1:17:00 – A zombie's head is cut off with a chainsaw.

1:17:30 – A man rips out a zombie's intestines.

1:17:45 – A zombie bites a chunk of flesh out of a man's neck.

1:21:45 – a zombie's stomach is cut open with a chainsaw.

ZOMBIE

Year: 1979   Length: 91 minutes
Director: Lucio Fulci

STATISTICS

First Zombie: :15
First Human Death: 7:15
First Zombie Death: 7:45

Amount of Gore: Very High
Gore Quality: Very High
Zombie Effects: High
Zombie Count: Very High
Zombie Deaths: Very High
Human Deaths: Average

SUMMARY

A woman travels to a remote Caribbean island to try and locate her missing father, but a voodoo curse has covered the island and has brought the dead back to life.

EFFECTS HIGHLIGHTS

:15 – A zombie is shot in the head.

6:45 – Close up of a severed hand.

7:00 – The skin on a zombie's arm is ripped off.

7:15 – A zombie bites a man's neck.

7:45 – A zombie is shot in the chest.

30:00 – A man injects himself with a syringe.

36:30 – A zombie pulls a chunk of flesh off of a shark.

37:15 – A shark bites off a zombie's arm.

44:30 – A zombie's fingers are cut off in a door.

46:00 – A woman's eye is pierced by a splinter of wood.

55:15 – A zombie is shot in the head.

1:01:30 – A group of zombies eat a dead body.

1:03:15 – A zombie is shot in the head.

1:10:30 – A zombie bites a chunk of flesh out of a woman's neck.

1:11:00 – A zombie is shot in the back.

1:11:00 – A zombie is shot in the back.

1:11:15 – A zombie's head is crushed with a gravestone.

1:15:30 – Close up of a foot wound.

1:18:30 – A zombie's head is smashed open.

1:19:00 – A zombie bites a chunk of flesh out of a man's face.

1:19:30 – A zombie is eating a piece of flesh.

1:19:30 – A zombie is shot in the chest.

1:19:45 – A zombie is shot in the head.

1:20:30 – A zombie bites a chunk of flesh out of a man's arm.

1:21:30 – A zombie is shot in the head.

1:21:45 – A zombie is shot in the chest.

1:21:45 – A zombie is shot in the chest.

1:23:00 – A zombie is shot in the back.

1:23:15 – A zombie is shot in the head.

1:23:30 – A zombie is shot in the head.

1:23:45 – A zombie is shot in the chest.

1:24:00 – A zombie's burning arm falls off.

1:24:15 – A zombie is shot in the head.

1:25:30 – A zombie is hit in the head.

1:25:30 – A zombie is hit in the head.

ZOMBIE 3

Year: 1988   Length: 96 minutes
Directors: Lucio Fulci, Bruno Mattei

STATISTICS

First Zombie: 23:00
First Human Death: 3:15
First Zombie Death: 24:00

Amount of Gore: High
Gore Quality: High
Zombie Effects: High
Zombie Count: Very High
Zombie Deaths: Very High
Human Deaths: High

SUMMARY

A group of soldiers find themselves under attack after a rogue team of scientists raise the dead. The soldiers meet up with a group of tourists and take refuge in an abandoned hotel.

EFFECTS HIGHLIGHTS

9:15 – A man has infected wounds on his face and hands.

9:30 – A man cuts his hand off with a machete.

10:30 – A woman's head is smashed against a mirror.

12:00 – A woman has been pinned to a door.

20:00 – A man has an infected wound on his face.

30:15 – A wound on a man's face starts bleeding.

40:45 – A zombie is shot in the back.

43:00 – A zombie bites a chunk of flesh out of a man's neck.

52:30 – A group of zombies eat a man's intestines.

52:45 – A zombie is shot in the back.

53:15 – A zombie is shot in the head.

53:45 – A zombie is shot in the chest.

53:45 – A zombie is stabbed in the neck.

54:00 – A zombie is shot in the back.

56:15 – A zombie is shot in the chest.

1:04:15 – A man is shot in the chest.

1:13:00 – A zombie pulls the skin off of a woman's face.

1:13:15 – A hand bursts out of a pregnant woman's stomach.

1:14:45 – A zombie is stabbed with a pick axe.

1:14:45 – A man is shot in the chest.

1:14:45 – A man is shot in the chest.

1:14:45 – A man is shot in the chest.

1:21:15 – A man is shot in the chest.

ZOMBIE 4: AFTER DEATH

Year: 1988   Length: 84 minutes
Director: Claudio Fragasso

STATISTICS

First Zombie:	10:15
First Human Death:	10:15
First Zombie Death:	51:15
Amount of Gore:	High
Gore Quality:	Average
Zombie Effects:	High
Zombie Count:	Very High
Zombie Deaths:	Very High
Human Deaths:	High

SUMMARY

Years after a voodoo priest has turned the residents of a remote island into the living dead, a group of soldiers arrive and find themselves being hunted by the ravenous horde.

EFFECTS HIGHLIGHTS

10:45 – A zombie pulls out a man's eye.

10:45 – A zombie rips the skin off of a man's face.

16:30 – A man is bitten on the neck.

49:45 – A zombie stabbed in the shoulder with a pair of scissors.

53:45 – A zombie is shot in the head.

56:00 – A zombie is shot in the head.

56:15 – A zombie is shot in the head.

1:03:45 – A man is shot in the leg.

1:08:15 – A man is shot in the shoulder.

1:08:15 – A man is shot in the knee cap.

1:10:00 – A man is shot in the chest.

1:14:45 – A zombie is shot in the head.

1:21:15 – A zombie punches through a man's chest.

1:21:30 – A woman's face starts to rot.

1:21:45 – A woman pulls her eye out.

ZOMBIE 5: KILLING BIRDS

Year: 1987   Length: 90 minutes
Directors: Claudio Lattanzi, Joe D'Amato

STATISTICS

First Zombie:	45:45
First Human Death:	4:00
First Zombie Death:	N/A
Amount of Gore:	High
Gore Quality:	Average
Zombie Effects:	Average
Zombie Count:	Average
Zombie Deaths:	Very Low
Human Deaths:	High

SUMMARY

Twenty years ago, a cuckolded husband was pecked to death by pet birds that belonged to his wife, whom he murdered. A group of student ornithologists head for the Louisiana bayou to study birds and they take refuge in the deserted house.

EFFECTS HIGHLIGHTS

3:45 – A man's throat is slit.

6:15 – A woman's throat is slit.

6:45 – A man is stabbed in the head.

7:15 – A woman's throat is slit.

8:15 – A bird claws out a man's eye.

8:15 – A bird claws out a man's eye.

46:00 – A woman has been nailed to a wall.

56:45 – A woman's head is smashed into a wall.

1:10:30 – A woman's head is ripped off.

1:16:45 – A necklace cuts into a man's neck.

1:17:15 – A man's fingers are cut off.

ZOMBIE 90: EXTREME PESTILENCE

Year: 1991   Length: 75 minutes
Director: Andreas Schnaas

STATISTICS

First Zombie:	5:00
First Human Death:	11:00
First Zombie Death:	5:15

Amount of Gore: Very High
Gore Quality: Average
Zombie Effects: Average
Zombie Count: Very High
Zombie Deaths: Average
Human Deaths: High

SUMMARY

Two doctors join forces to try and stop a mysterious outbreak of the living dead that has swept through the countryside.

EFFECTS HIGHLIGHTS

2:45 – A surgeon removes a man's organs.

5:00 – A zombie pulls out its intestines.

5:15 – A zombie is shot in the head.

10:30 – A man's torso is cut with a chainsaw.

11:00 – A zombie pulls out a man's intestines.

14:00 – A zombie slices off a woman's breast with a knife.

14:15 – A zombie pulls out a woman's organs.

15:30 – A zombie bites off a woman's finger.

15:45 – A woman's torso is cut open with a knife.

18:45 – A zombie is shot in the head.

22:00 – Two zombies rip open a man's torso and pull out his intestines.

30:15 – A zombie's arm is cut off with a machete.

30:45 – A zombie is shot in the chest.

31:00 – A zombie is shot in the chest.

31:00 – A zombie's intestines fall onto a man's face.

31:15 – A man jams his thumbs into a zombie's eye socket.

32:00 – A zombie is stabbed in the head.

34:45 – A large maggot exits a gunshot wound.

34:45 – A large maggot crawls into a man's eye.

44:45 – A zombie's hands are cut off.

45:00 – A zombie's head is cut in half.

48:30 – A man's intestines are pulled out.

48:30 – A man is cut in the head with a machete.

48:45 – A man is stabbed in the stomach.

49:00 – A group of zombies rip open a man's torso.

49:45 – A man is stabbed in the stomach.

50:15 – A man is decapitated.

52:00 – A group of zombies tear apart a dead body.

54:45 – A zombie is shot in the head.

55:30 – A zombie is cut with a chainsaw.

56:15 – A zombie's fingers are cut off with a chainsaw.

57:00 – A zombie's head is cut in half with a chainsaw.

1:03:30 – A zombie is decapitated.

1:04:00 – A zombie is decapitated.

1:04:15 – A zombie's hand is cut off.

1:04:45 – A zombie is decapitated.

1:05:15 – A zombie's head is crushed.

1:09:00 – A zombie pulls out a man's intestines.

ZOMBIE APOCALYPSE NOW

Year: 2010   Length: 68 minutes
Director: Germán Magariños

STATISTICS

First Zombie: 3:45
First Human Death: 5:15
First Zombie Death: 6:30

Amount of Gore: Very High
Gore Quality: Average
Zombie Effects: Low
Zombie Count: Very High
Zombie Deaths: Average
Human Deaths: High

SUMMARY

In a city overrun with zombies, a sexual deviant is recognized as the most important hunter of the undead. Hired by the Catholic Church to kill zombies, he uses his earnings to fulfill his perverted desires.

EFFECTS HIGHLIGHTS

4:00 – A man is hit in the back with an axe.

4:15 – A man's hand is cut off with a shovel.

4:45 – A zombie rips out a man's intestines.

5:30 – A zombie pulls the skin off of a man's face.

6:15 – A zombie is stabbed in the chest.

6:30 – A zombie is shot in the chest.

14:15 – A zombie bites a man's neck.

15:15 – A zombie is shot in the head.

15:30 – A zombie is shot in the head.

21:30 – A man is cut on the shoulder with a saw.

24:00 – A man is stabbed with a knife.

24:15 – A man's intestines are pulled out.

26:15 – A group of zombies pull out a man's intestines.

36:45 – A woman's forehead is cut with a knife.

40:30 – A zombie pulls out a woman's intestines.

48:30 – A man draws a knife across a dead man's stomach.

49:30 – A man hammers a stake into a dead man's neck.

51:45 – Two zombies pull out a man's intestines.

57:00 – A zombie bites off a man's penis.

57:45 – A zombie rips open a man's stomach.

1:01:30 – A man is cut open with a knife.

1:02:15 – Two men eat a man's intestines.

1:03:15 – A zombie bites a man's shoulder.

1:03:30 – A group of zombies eat a man's intestines.

1:04:15 – A zombie is stabbed in the chest.

1:05:00 – A zombie is stabbed in the stomach.

ZOMBIE BLOODBATH

Year: 1993   Length: 70 minutes
Director: Todd Sheets

STATISTICS

First Zombie: 1:30
First Human Death: 2:00
First Zombie Death: 23:30

Amount of Gore: High
Gore Quality: Average
Zombie Effects: Average
Zombie Count: Very High
Zombie Deaths: High
Human Deaths: Very High

SUMMARY

A meltdown at a nuclear power plant turns the community into a group of flesh-eating zombies.

EFFECTS HIGHLIGHTS

1:45 – A man's skin melts.

2:00 – A group of zombies tear open a man's torso.
2:00 – A man's skin melts.
2:00 – A group of zombies tear open a man's torso.
2:30 – A woman vomits blood.
3:00 – A woman's skin melts.
3:00 – A man's skin melts.
20:30 – A group of zombies tear open a man's stomach.
23:30 – A zombie is shot in the head.
27:00 – A zombie pulls out a woman's eyes.
27:30 – A group of zombies tear open a woman's stomach.
33:15 – A group of zombies tear out a man's intestines.
34:45 – A man spits out his intestines.
55:00 – A group of zombies tear out a man's intestines.
56:45 – A group of zombies tear out a man's intestines.
1:01:15 – A group of zombies tear out a man's intestines.
1:02:15 – A group of zombies tear out a man's intestines.
1:02:15 – A group of zombies tear out a woman's intestines.

"Zombie Bloodbath" courtesy of Todd Sheets.

181

ZOMBIE BLOODBATH 2: RAGE OF THE UNDEAD

Year: 1995   Length: 98 minutes
Director: Todd Sheets

STATISTICS

First Zombie: 32:00
First Human Death: 28:30
First Zombie Death: 40:45

Amount of Gore: Very High
Gore Quality: Average
Zombie Effects: Average
Zombie Count: Very High
Zombie Deaths: Average
Human Deaths: High

SUMMARY

A demonic scarecrow resurrects the dead as zombies who feast on the living. A group of survivors do their best to stay alive and out last this terrifying nightmare.

EFFECTS HIGHLIGHTS

4:45 – A man cuts off a woman's fingers.

5:45 – A group of people claw at a man's face.

6:15 – A man plays with gore.

7:45 – A man's hands are nailed to a piece of wood.

8:15 – A group of people tear open a man's stomach.

28:30 – A woman is shot in the vagina.

36:49 – A group of zombies tear a man's eyes out.

40:30 – A zombie is stabbed in the mouth with a crowbar.

43:45 – A man puts his hand in a bloody wound.

46:15 – A man is forced to eat gore.

54:45 – A woman steps on broken glass.

56:30 – A man is stabbed under the chin.

57:30 – A group of zombies tear open a man's back.

58:30 – A group of zombies tear at a dead body.

59:00 – A man is stabbed in the stomach.

59:30 – A man is stabbed in the stomach.

1:04:00 – A man is pulled in half by a group of zombies.

1:04:15 – A group of zombies eat a man's intestines.

1:04:45 – A group of zombies eat a man's intestines.

1:05:45 – Close up of a bleeding wound.

1:06:45 – A woman's head is pulled off.

1:07:15 – A zombie eats a woman's arm.

1:18:30 – A woman's torso is ripped open.

1:18:45 – A group of zombies pull two dead women apart.

1:19:00 – A zombie's face melts.

1:19:15 – A zombie's face melts.

1:19:45 – A group of zombies pull out a woman's intestines.

1:20:00 – A zombie's face melts.

1:20:30 – A group of zombies eats a woman's intestines.

1:20:45 – A zombie's face melts.

1:21:00 – A zombie's head explodes.

1:26:15 – A group of zombies rip out a man's intestines.

ZOMBIE BLOODBATH 3: ZOMBIE ARMAGEDDON

Year: 2000   Length: 90 minutes
Director: Todd Sheets

STATISTICS

First Zombie: 0:00
First Human Death: 1:45
First Zombie Death: 36:15

Amount of Gore: Average
Gore Quality: Average
Zombie Effects: Average
Zombie Count: Very High
Zombie Deaths: Low
Human Deaths: High

SUMMARY

A Group of teenagers find themselves trapped in a high school as an army of the undead fight to get inside.

EFFECTS HIGHLIGHTS

:15 – Two zombies eat a severed arm.

1:45 – A zombie rips out a man's intestines.

36:00 – A man cuts off a zombie's head.

36:15 – A man decapitates a zombie.

42:30 – A group of zombies rip out a man's intestines.

45:45 – Two zombies rip out a man's intestines.

1:06:30 – A man jams his thumbs into a zombie's eye.

1:12:30 – A woman's intestines have been ripped out.

ZOMBIE CAMP OUT

Year: 2002   Length: 91 minutes
Director: Joshua D. Smith

STATISTICS

First Zombie: 2:00
First Human Death: 51:30
First Zombie Death: 53:00

Amount of Gore: Very High
Gore Quality: High
Zombie Effects: Average
Zombie Count: Very High

Zombie Deaths: High
Human Deaths: High

SUMMARY

A radioactive meteorite crashes into a cemetery near where a group of friends are on a weekend camping trip. Soon, the dead are returning to life and the campers must try and make it out alive.

EFFECTS HIGHLIGHTS

2:15 – A zombie pulls a man's arm off.
36:30 – A zombie is shot in the chest.
36:30 – A zombie is shot in the stomach.
36:30 – A zombie is shot in the chest.
36:45 – A group of zombies tear the skin off of a man's face.
43:30 – A zombie bites a man's neck.
50:45 – A zombie bites a woman on the neck.
50:45 – A woman bleeds from an open wound.
51:15 – A group of zombies pull a woman's arms off.
51:30 – A woman trips and smashes her head against a rock.
51:45 – A zombie eats a severed arm.
52:45 – A zombie is shot in the stomach.
53:00 – A zombie is shot in the chest.
53:00 – A zombie is shot in the stomach.
53:00 – A zombie is shot in the chest.
53:15 – A zombie is shot in the stomach.
53:15 – A zombie is shot in the chest.
53:15 – A zombie is shot in the stomach.
53:15 – A zombie is shot in the head.
53:30 – A zombie is shot in the stomach.
54:00 – A zombie is shot in the chest.
54:00 – A zombie is shot in the chest.
56:15 – A group of zombies eat a dead dog.
56:45 – A zombie is hit in the head with a baseball bat.
57:15 – A man's eyeball is hanging out of its socket.
1:13:15 – A woman's arm is ripped off.
1:18:15 – A group of zombies tear the skin off of a man's face.
1:20:45 – A piece of a zombie's face falls off.
1:21:00 – Blood pours out of a zombie's eye.

ZOMBIE DEATH HOUSE

Year: 1987   Length: 90 minutes
Director: John Saxon

STATISTICS

First Zombie: 41:45
First Human Death: 6:45
First Zombie Death: 1:03:15

Amount of Gore: High
Gore Quality: High
Zombie Effects: Average
Zombie Count: High
Zombie Deaths: Low
Human Deaths: High

SUMMARY

A renegade federal agent uses a new drug to create an army of unbeatable warriors.

EFFECTS HIGHLIGHTS

6:45 – A man is shot in the chest.
10:15 – A man is shot in the chest.
10:15 – A man is shot in the chest.
10:15 – A man is shot in the chest.
10:15 – A man is shot in the chest.
43:15 – A zombie rips off a man's hand.
44:45 – A man is stabbed in the chest.
48:30 – A man's throat is slit.
54:15 – A zombie pulls a man's head off.
54:30 – A zombie is shot in the chest.
1:03:15 – A zombie is shot in the chest.
1:21:30 – A zombie's arm is cut off.
1:31:30 – A zombie is shot in the chest.

ZOMBIE DIARIES

Year: 2006   Length: 85 minutes
Directors: Michael Bartlett, Kevin Gates

STATISTICS

First Zombie: 1:30
First Human Death: 49:45
First Zombie Death: 27:00

Amount of Gore: Average
Gore Quality: Very High
Zombie Effects: High
Zombie Count: Very High
Zombie Deaths: Average
Human Deaths: Average

SUMMARY

A mysterious plague has ravaged the planet and reanimates the dead, transforming them into flesh-eating zombies. Video cameras from a documentary film crew, a couple fleeing London and a group of survivors taking refuge in a barn capture the zombie attack in real time.

EFFECTS HIGHLIGHTS

20:15 – A dead man's intestines are spilled on the floor.
27:00 – A zombie is shot in the head.
33:45 – A zombie is shot in the head.
34:30 – A zombie is shot in the head.

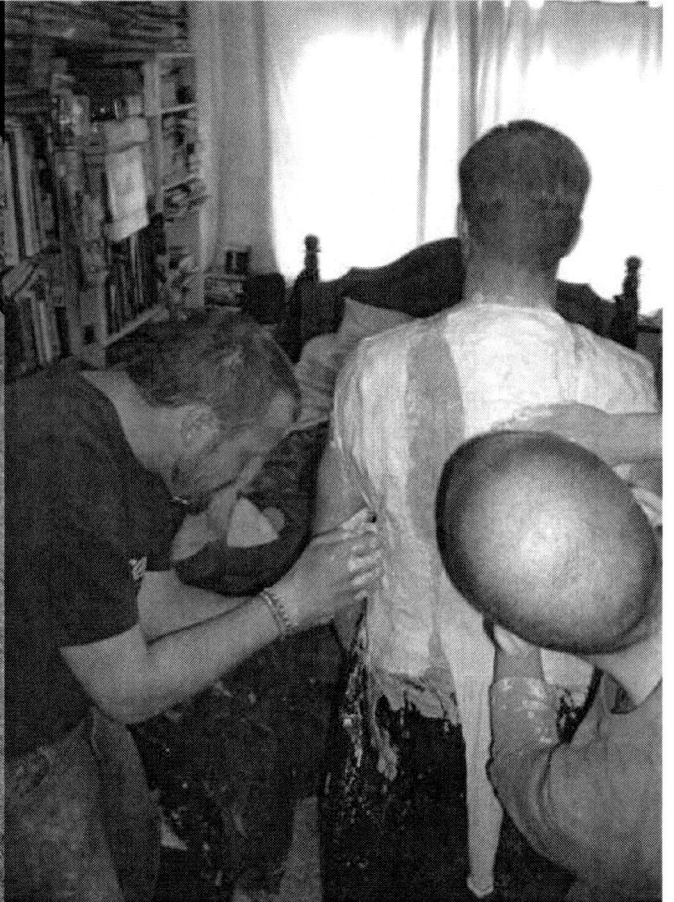

Zombies on set and in production for "Zombie Diaries" courtesy of Mike Peel.

47:45 – A zombie is eating a woman's intestines.

53:00 – A man's hand is missing a finger.

1:00:30 – A zombie is shot in the head.

1:03:00 – A child is shot in the head.

1:13:15 – A man's fingers are cut off with garden shears.

ZOMBIE DIARIES 2: WORLD OF THE DEAD

Year: 2011   Length: 88 minutes
Directors: Michael Bartlett, Kevin Gates

STATISTICS

First Zombie:	5:45
First Human Death:	46:15
First Zombie Death:	12:45

Amount of Gore:	High
Gore Quality:	Very High
Zombie Effects:	High
Zombie Count:	Very High
Zombie Deaths:	Very High
Human Deaths:	High

SUMMARY

Three months after a virus wipes out 99.9% of the world's population, a surviving band of soldiers and civilians have taken refuge in a military barracks. When the base is overrun, the survivors try to make their way to the coast.

EFFECTS HIGHLIGHTS

10:00 – A woman vomits blood.

13:15 – A zombie eats a man's intestines.

13:30 – A zombie bites a man's neck.

15:45 – A group of zombies eat a dead body.

34:30 – A zombie is shot in the head.

38:00 – A zombie is shot in the head.

38:15 – A zombie is shot in the head.

38:15 – A zombie is shot in the head.

39:00 – A zombie is shot in the head.

47:45 – A group of zombies rip open a man's stomach.

1:03:00 – A woman is stabbed in the chest.

1:04:15 – A man is shot in the head.

ZOMBIE DRIFTWOOD

Year: 2010   Length: 75 minutes
Director: Bob Carruthers

STATISTICS

First Zombie:	16:30
First Human Death:	N/A

First Zombie Death:	27:45

Amount of Gore:	High
Gore Quality:	High
Zombie Effects:	High
Zombie Count:	Very High
Zombie Deaths:	Average
Human Deaths:	Very Low

SUMMARY

Tourists on a cruise ship are turned into zombies and two heavy metal fans must battle against zombie Armageddon, armed with only a baseball bat, booze and a set of bagpipes.

EFFECTS HIGHLIGHTS

21:15 – A pair of severed hands are holding onto a wall.

21:45 – A zombie's intestines are exposed.

27:45 – A zombie's head is crushed with a guitar.

27:45 – A man knocks a zombie's head off.

31:30 – A pile of intestines is on the floor.

31:30 – A severed hands moves.

32:15 – A zombie's penis is pulled off.

35:15 – Multiple zombie arms are cut off.

35:15 – A zombie is decapitated.

36:00 – A zombie picks up a severed arm.

43:30 – A zombie is stabbed in the neck with a pool cue.

43:30 – A zombie is hit in the head with an eight ball.

50:30 – A severed zombie arm falls to the floor.

52:45 – A zombie is decapitated.

56:45 – Close up of a severed zombie arm.

1:01:30 – A zombie pulls its ear off.

1:01:30 – A zombie bleeds from its ears.

1:10:45 – A zombie eats a severed hand.

ZOMBIE FARM

Year: 2009   Length: 90 minutes
Director: Ricardo Islas

STATISTICS

First Zombie:	35:30
First Human Death:	53:00
First Zombie Death:	1:16:00

Amount of Gore:	Average
Gore Quality:	High
Zombie Effects:	High
Zombie Count:	Very High
Zombie Deaths:	Low
Human Deaths:	Average

SUMMARY

A voodoo priestess gives an abused wife a potion that turns her husband into a zombie.

36:15 – A zombie is shot in the head.

46:30 – A zombie is impaled on a fishing pole.

1:09:00 – A group of zombies eat intestines.

1:16:00 – A zombie's brains are eaten.

1:16:45 – A zombie is stabbed with a pair of scissors.

1:19:30 – A zombie is stabbed in the mouth.

ZOMBIE HOLOCAUST

Year: 1980   Length: 84 minutes
Director: Marino Girolami

STATISTICS

First Zombie:	49:15
First Human Death:	15:15
First Zombie Death:	N/A
Amount of Gore:	Very High
Gore Quality:	High
Zombie Effects:	High
Zombie Count:	Average
Zombie Deaths:	Very Low
Human Deaths:	High

SUMMARY

When body parts go missing from a hospital, experts recognize the signature of Moluccas island tribe that worships the cannibal god, Kito. An expedition is arranged to travel to Moluccas to track down the last faithful to Kito. When they arrive on the island, they find themselves on the run not only from cannibals, but blood thirsty zombies that are being raised from the dead by a local witch doctor.

EFFECTS HIGHLIGHTS

3:30 – The hand of a dead body is cut off.

5:15 – Close up of a bloodied stump.

5:30 – A man cuts into a dead body's stomach.

6:00 – A man pulls out a pile of organs.

14:15 – A man cuts into a dead body's stomach.

14:15 – A man removes an organ from a dead body.

15:15 – A man jumps from a window.

17:30 – Intestines have fallen out of a dead body.

17:45 – Intestines have fallen out of a dead body.

30:00 – A woman finds a severed head infested with maggots.

36:30 – Close up of a disemboweled dead body.

40:30 – A man is impaled on a bamboo trap.

40:45 – A man's throat is slit.

41:00 – A man's intestines are pulled out.

41:00 – A group of cannibals eat a man's intestines.

41:15 – A man is shot in the back.

44:45 – A man is cut in the head with a machete.

45:00 – A man has been impaled on a bamboo pole.

48:00 – A man is shot in the chest.

48:15 – A man is stabbed in the chest.

48:15 – A man's intestines are pulled out.

48:30 – A group of men eat a man's intestines.

49:00 – A man's eye is pulled out and eaten.

49:00 – A man's eye is pulled out.

50:45 – Close up of a bloodied dead body.

ZOMBIE HONEYMOON

Year: 2005   Length: 83 minutes
Director: David Gebroe

STATISTICS

First Zombie:	11:00
First Human Death:	13:15
First Zombie Death:	12:15
Amount of Gore:	High
Gore Quality:	Very High
Zombie Effects:	Very High
Zombie Count:	Low
Zombie Deaths:	Low
Human Deaths:	High

SUMMARY

The honeymoon is over for a pair of newlyweds when a zombie stumbles out of the ocean and infects the groom. Slowly he turns into a flesh-eating zombie as his bride struggles to control his appetite while accepting his changes.

EFFECTS HIGHLIGHTS

12:00 – A zombie vomits on a man's face.

29:45 – A man's intestines have been pulled out.

45:15 – A zombie bites a woman's arm.

45:30 – A zombie bites a woman's neck.

48:00 – A zombie bites a man's neck.

1:01:45 – A zombie bites a man's chest.

1:08:30 – A zombie bites a man's face.

1:08:30 – A zombie bites a man's arm.

1:08:45 – A zombie is shot in the chest.

1:09:00 – A zombie bites a woman's neck.

1:13:15 – Close up of a severed head.

1:15:30 – A zombie vomits blood.

ZOMBIE HUNTER RIKA

Year: 2008   Length: 86 minutes
Director: Ken'ichi Fujiwara

STATISTICS

First Zombie:	1:30

First Human Death:	48:00		First Zombie:	16:30
First Zombie Death:	4:30		First Human Death:	17:30
			First Zombie Death:	N/A

Amount of Gore:	Very High
Gore Quality:	Very High
Zombie Effects:	High
Zombie Count:	Very High
Zombie Deaths:	Very High
Human Deaths:	Average

Amount of Gore:	Average
Gore Quality:	Average
Zombie Effects:	Low
Zombie Count:	Low
Zombie Deaths:	Very Low
Human Deaths:	Very High

SUMMARY

After a woman is bitten by a zombie, her father surgically removes her arm and replaces it with an arm of a famous zombie hunter.

EFFECTS HIGHLIGHTS

1:30 – A zombie eats a severed arm.

2:00 – A zombie spits out a piece of flesh.

2:45 – A man spits up blood.

4:30 – A man's arm is cut off.

10:00 – A zombie eats a severed arm.

11:45 – A car runs over a zombie's head.

13:15 – A zombie eats a man's intestines.

13:30 – A zombie eats a severed arm.

14:30 – Two zombies eat another zombie's intestines.

15:45 – A zombie is hit in the head with a wrench.

23:15 – A zombie bites a woman's neck.

25:30 – A zombie's arm is cut off.

25:45 – A zombie spits up blood.

26:45 – A zombie is stabbed in the head with a sword.

27:45 – A man cuts off a girls arm.

31:30 – A group of zombies eat various body parts.

44:30 – A zombie's eye falls out,

47:15 – A zombie bites off a woman's tongue.

47:45 – A zombie tears a chunk of flesh out of a woman's shoulder.

1:02:15 – A zombie is cut in half.

1:03:45 – A zombie rips open a man's neck.

1:04:30 – A zombie decapitated.

1:04:45 – A zombie is shot in the head.

1:04:45 – Two more zombies are shot in the head.

1:05:15 – A zombie's brain falls on the ground.

1:10:30 – A zombie pulls out a man's intestines.

1:17:15 – A zombie bites a man's neck.

1:19:15 – A zombie is stabbed in the head.

ZOMBIE ISLAND MASSACRE

Year: 1984   Length: 95 minutes
Director: John N. Carter

STATISTICS

SUMMARY

A group of tourists visit an island in the Caribbean and witness a local voodoo ritual. Before long, they are in a fight for their lives as they find themselves under attack by the living dead.

EFFECTS HIGHLIGHTS

17:30 – A man is hit on the head.

42:00 – A woman is impaled on a wooden spike.

52:15 – A man is decapitated.

1:05:30 – A head is impaled on a pole.

1:10:45 – A man is stabbed with a spear.

1:11:00 – A woman is grazed by a spear.

1:11:00 – A man is shot in the stomach.

1:15:45 – A man is shot in the stomach.

1:18:00 – A man is shot in the chest.

1:18:15 – A woman is hit in the head with a machete.

ZOMBIE LAKE

Year: 1981   Length: 90 minutes
Director: Jean Rollin

STATISTICS

First Zombie:	3:45
First Human Death:	11:00
First Zombie Death:	1:24:15

Amount of Gore:	Low
Gore Quality:	Average
Zombie Effects:	Low
Zombie Count:	Average
Zombie Deaths:	Average
Human Deaths:	Very High

SUMMARY

In a small French village, German soldiers who were killed and thrown into the lake by the resistance during World War II, come back from the dead.

EFFECTS HIGHLIGHTS

11:00 – A zombie bites a woman's neck.

34:15 – A man is shot in the eye.

1:19:00 – A zombie bites a woman's neck.

ZOMBIE NIGHT

Year: 2003   Length: 93 minutes
Director: David J. Francis

STATISTICS

First Zombie: 1:00
First Human Death: 20:45
First Zombie Death: 16:15

Amount of Gore: High
Gore Quality: High
Zombie Effects: High
Zombie Count: Very High
Zombie Deaths: High
Human Deaths: High

SUMMARY

Nuclear fallout causes a plague of the living dead to rise up across the globe. A group of survivor's try to stay one step ahead of the undead.

EFFECTS HIGHLIGHTS

1:15 – A zombie bites a man's neck.

1:45 – A zombie eats a man's intestines.

12:00 – Close up of a pile of dead bodies.

15:15 – Close up of a pile of dead bodies.

16:00 – A zombie has a bloody wound on its neck.

16:15 – A zombie is shot in the head.

17:00 – A zombie is shot in the head.

27:15 – A zombie's leg is shot off.

27:30 – A zombie eats a severed leg.

30:30 – A zombie bites a man's wrist.

37:30 – A zombie spits out a piece of flesh.

40:00 – A zombie bites a man's leg.

40:15 – A zombie is shot in the head.

56:45 – Close up of a bloody dead body.

1:03:30 – A woman's throat is slit.

1:10:45 – A zombie is shot in the head.

1:14:00 – A zombie eats a piece of flesh.

1:14:00 – A zombie is shot in the chest.

1:14:00 – A zombie is shot in the chest.

1:14:00 – A zombie is shot in the chest.

1:14:15 – A zombie eats a woman's intestines.

1:25:00 – A zombie eats a dead body.

ZOMBIE PENETRATOR

Year: 2007   Length: 65 minutes
Directors: P. Saelor, Pakito Bien Tonibadoiro

STATISTICS

First Zombie: 2:00
First Human Death: 27:45

First Zombie Death: 39:15

Amount of Gore: Low
Gore Quality: High
Zombie Effects: Average
Zombie Count: High
Zombie Deaths: Average
Human Deaths: Average

SUMMARY

An alien invasion turns locals into zombies causing the handful of survivors to fight for their lives against an army of the undead.

EFFECTS HIGHLIGHTS

37:45 – A group of zombies eat various body parts.

54:15 – A zombie holds a severed leg.

56:45 – A man rips off a zombie's leg.

ZOMBIE RAMPAGE

Year: 1989   Length: 89 minutes
Director: Todd Sheets

STATISTICS

First Zombie: 24:00
First Human Death: 14:00
First Zombie Death: 39:30

Amount of Gore: High
Gore Quality: High
Zombie Effects: High
Zombie Count: Very High
Zombie Deaths: Low
Human Deaths: High

SUMMARY

A gang plots to revive its fallen members, but a rival gang, believing they will control the zombies if they raise them first, perform the ritual instead. The zombies fall under no ones control and attack both of the gangs.

EFFECTS HIGHLIGHTS

13:00 – A man stabs a woman in the chest.

13:45 – A woman is stabbed in the face.

30:30 – A zombie rips out a woman's tongue.

30:30 – A group of zombies rip open a woman's stomach.

31:30 – A group of zombies eat a baby.

39:30 – A zombie bites a man's arm.

39:30 – A zombie is shot in the head.

44:45 – A zombie rips out a man's intestines.

45:00 – A zombie pulls off a man's arm.

45:45 – Zombies eat various body parts.

47:00 – Zombies pull the skin off of a man's face.

50:30 – A woman is stabbed in the back.

54:15 – A group of zombies rip out a woman's intestines.

59:45 – A man shoots himself in the head.

1:07:00 – A zombie rips open a dead body.

1:11:15 – A zombie eats a severed leg.

ZOMBIE SELF DEFENSE FORCE

Year: 2006   Length: 75 minutes
Director: Naoyuki Tomomatsu

STATISTICS

First Zombie: 7:15
First Human Death: 3:30
First Zombie Death: 8:30

Amount of Gore: Very High
Gore Quality: High
Zombie Effects: High
Zombie Count: Very High
Zombie Deaths: Very High
Human Deaths: High

SUMMARY

When a UFO crashes and releases strange radiation, confusion turns to terror as the dead rise and attack the living in a cannibalistic frenzy. Soon, a group of soldiers and a handful of civilians are holed up in a secluded hotel, surrounded by the zombie horde.

EFFECTS HIGHLIGHTS

8:00 – A zombie bites a chunk of flesh out of a man's neck.

8:15 – A man spits up blood.

8:15 – A zombie's arm is snapped off.

8:15 – A zombie is stabbed in the mouth with a stick.

9:15 – A zombie bites off a man's fingers.

11:00 – A man spits up blood.

12:30 – A zombie bites a man's neck.

20:00 – A zombie is shot in the head.

29:30 – A pregnant zombie's stomach explodes.

31:00 – A zombie pulls a man's eyes out of his sockets.

33:45 – A baby zombie bites a man's arm.

35:00 – A zombie is shot in the head.

52:15 – A zombie is stabbed in the stomach.

52:45 – A zombie bites a man on the shoulder.

52:45 – A man is shot in the head.

53:00 – A zombie is stabbed in the chest with a sword.

55:15 – A zombie bites a woman on the arm.

55:15 – A zombie is stabbed in the stomach.

57:45 – Two zombies bite a woman's legs.

59:45 – A group of zombies tear a man's stomach open.

1:01:00 – A woman is decapitated.

1:01:30 – Two zombies are eating pieces of flesh.

1:08:15 – A zombie rips off a woman's arm.

1:09:30 – A zombie is cut in half with a sword.

1:12:00 – A zombie holds a severed head.

ZOMBIE STRIPPERS

Year: 2008   Length: 94 minutes
Director: Jay Lee

STATISTICS

First Zombie: 7:00
First Human Death: 12:30
First Zombie Death: 6:00

Amount of Gore: Very High
Gore Quality: Very High
Zombie Effects: Very High
Zombie Count: Very High
Zombie Deaths: Very High
Human Deaths: High

SUMMARY

A top secret government re-animation virus gets released into wild and infects the dancers at a Nebraska strip club. As the virus spreads, the zombie strippers turn their club into an erotic sensation that is to die for.

EFFECTS HIGHLIGHTS

6:00 – A zombie is shot in the head.

7:15 – A zombie is shot in the head.

10:15 – Close up of a bite mark

11:15 – A zombie is shot in the head.

27:45 – A zombie bites a woman's neck.

28:00 – A woman bleeds from an open neck wound.

36:00 – A zombie bites off a man's penis.

36:30 – A zombie eats a severed arm.

37:45 – Close up of a severed head.

46:00 – A zombie rips a man's head in half.

46:00 – A zombie bites off a man's tongue.

47:00 – A zombie is missing its jaw.

53:45 – A zombie eats a piece of flesh.

53:45 – A zombie eats a piece of flesh.

1:01:30 – A zombie bites a woman's arm.

1:01:30 – A zombie bites a woman's neck.

1:05:30 – A zombie is scratched on the chest.

1:05:45 – A zombie rips off a man's arm.

1:05:45 – A man is thrown against a wall.

1:07:00 – A man pulls off a zombie's scalp.

1:07:45 – A man is hit in the head with a pool ball.

1:12:00 – A zombie is shot in the chest.

1:12:00 – A zombie is shot in the chest.

1:12:00 – A zombie is shot in the chest.

1:12:15 – A zombie is shot in the chest.

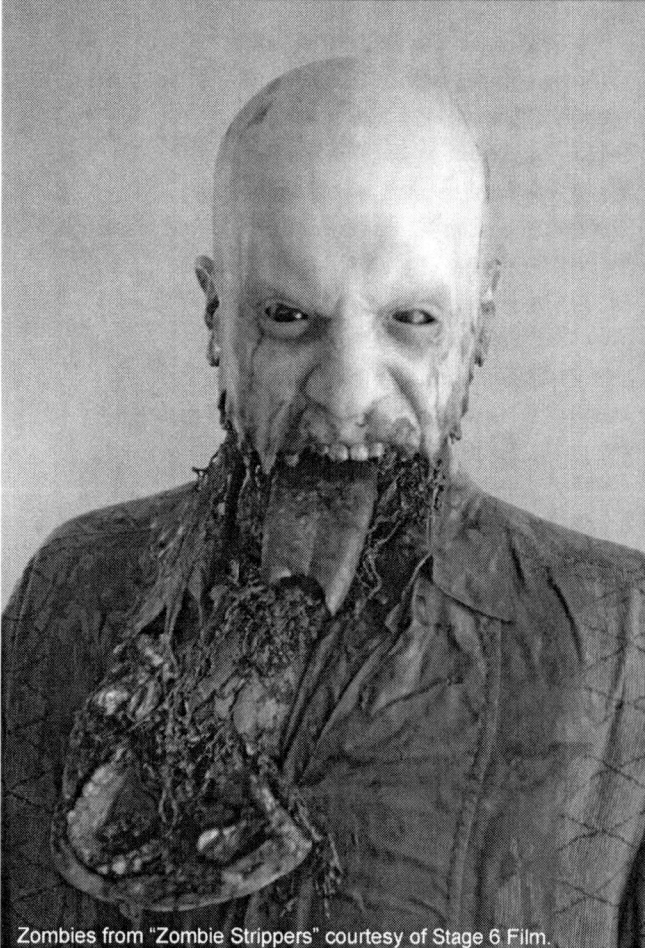

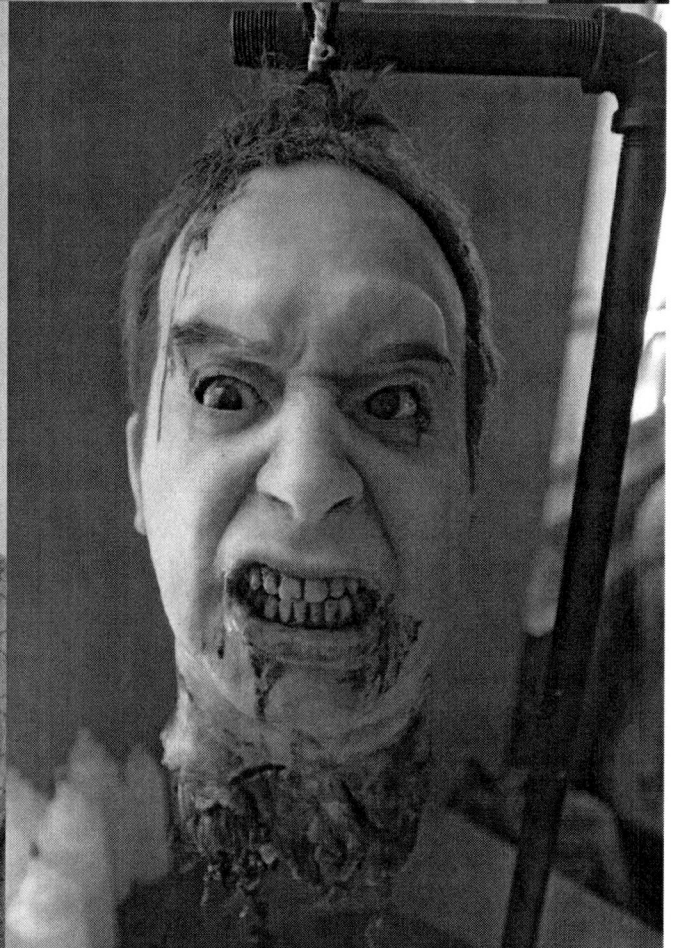

Zombies from "Zombie Strippers" courtesy of Stage 6 Film.

1:12:15 – A zombie is shot in the chest.

1:12:15 – A zombie is shot in the chest.

1:12:15 – A zombie is holding a heart.

1:16:00 – A group of zombies tear a man apart.

1:16:45 – A zombie bites a woman's neck.

1:17:00 – A man punches a hole in a zombie's stomach.

1:17:15 – A zombie rips off a man's scalp.

1:17:45 – A zombie is shot in the head.

1:17:45 – A zombie is stabbed in the head.

1:17:45 – A zombie is stabbed in the head.

1:17:45 – A zombie is stabbed in the head.

1:17:45 – A wall is splattered with blood.

1:19:00 – The skin is pulled off of a zombie's arm.

1:19:30 – The skin is pulled off of a zombie's legs.

1:19:45 – A zombie is shot in the head.

1:19:45 – A zombie is stabbed in the head.

1:19:45 – A zombie's head is cut in half.

1:20:15 – A zombie is missing an arm.

1:20:45 – A zombie is shot in the head.

1:21:00 – A zombie is shot repeatedly.

1:21:15 – A zombie is shot in the head.

1:23:45 – A zombie is stabbed in the throat.

1:23:45 – Two zombie heads are crushed.

1:28:45 – A zombie is shot in the head.

1:29:00 – A zombie is shot in the head.

1:29:15 – A zombie is shot in the head.

ZOMBIE UNDEAD

Year: 2010   Length: 79 minutes
Director: Rhys Davies

STATISTICS

First Zombie: 7:15
First Human Death: 13:30
First Zombie Death: 7:15

Amount of Gore: High
Gore Quality: Very High
Zombie Effects: High
Zombie Count: Very High
Zombie Deaths: Low
Human Deaths: Average

SUMMARY

When a zombie outbreak occurs, a woman and her dying father are directed to an evacuation facility on the outskirts of town.

EFFECTS HIGHLIGHTS

7:15 – A zombie is hit on the head with a sword.

13:30 – A group of zombies tear out a woman's intestines.

16:30 – A zombie eat a man's intestines.

29:45 – A woman stabs a zombie in the head.

37:30 – A zombie bites a chunk of flesh out of a man's neck.

37:45 – A man stabs a zombie in the head.

49:00 – A dead body's intestines are exposed.

51:15 – A woman vomits.

56:15 – A zombie is hit in the chest with a sledgehammer.

1:03:00 – A man is shot in the head.

1:04:45 – A woman jams her thumbs into a zombie's eyes.

1:11:30 – A zombie is shot in the chest.

ZOMBIE WARS

Year: 2008   Length: 80 minutes
Director: David A. Prior

STATISTICS

First Zombie: 2:45
First Human Death: 14:30
First Zombie Death: 2:45

Amount of Gore::   Very High
Gore Quality: :   Very High
Zombie Effects::   High
Zombie Count::   Very High
Zombie Deaths::   Very High
Human Deaths: Average

SUMMARY

Decades after a zombie epidemic has devastated the globe, a small group of freedom fighters have discovered that the undead are increasing in intelligence and have started breeding humans for food.

EFFECTS HIGHLIGHTS

2:45 – A zombie is shot in the head.

3:00 – A zombie is decapitated.

3:00 – A severed zombie head is shot in the forehead.

3:15 – A zombie is shot in the head.

3:15 – A zombie is shot in the head.

3:30 – A zombie is shot in the head.

4:45 – A man rips off a zombie's arm.

5:00 – A zombie is shot in the head.

14:00 – A zombie is shot in the head.

14:00 – A zombie is shot in the head.

14:15 – A zombie is decapitated.

14:15 – A zombie bites a chunk of flesh out of a man's neck.

14:15 – A zombie is shot in the head.

14:30 – A man is shot in the head.

14:45 – A zombie is shot in the head.

Behind the scenes of "Zombie Women of Satan" courtesy of Growling Clown Entertainment and Warren Speed.

14:45 – A zombie is shot in the head.

14:45 – A zombie is shot in the head.

14:45 – A zombie is shot in the head.

15:00 – A group of zombies rip open a man's torso.

15:00 – A zombie is shot in the head.

15:00 – A zombie is shot in the head.

15:45 – A zombie is shot in the head.

16:30 – A zombie is shot in the head.

16:30 – A zombie is shot in the head.

20:30 – A group of zombies rip open a man's torso.

30:15 – A group of zombies rip open a torso.

34:30 – A zombie's head is impaled on a nail.

38:45 – A zombie is shot in the head.

38:45 – A zombie is shot in the head.

39:00 – A zombie is shot in the head.

39:00 – A zombie is decapitated.

56:15 – A zombie is shot in the head.

57:00 – A zombie is shot in the head.

57:15 – A zombie's arm is cut off with a garden hoe.

57:30 – A zombie is shot in the head.

57:45 – A zombie is shot in the head.

58:00 – A zombie is shot in the head.

58:15 – A zombie is shot in the head.

58:30 – A zombie is shot in the head.

58:30 – A zombie is shot in the head.

58:30 – A zombie is shot in the head.

58:45 – A zombie is shot in the head.

58:45 – A zombie is shot in the head.

59:00 – A zombie is shot in the head.

59:15 – A zombie is shot in the head.

59:15 – A zombie is shot in the head.

59:30 – A zombie is shot in the head.

59:30 – A man kicks off a zombie's head.

1:01:00 – A zombie is stabbed in the head.

1:02:00 – A zombie is shot in the head.

1:02:00 – A zombie is shot in the head.

1:02:45 – A zombie is shot in the head.

1:05:45 – A zombie is shot in the head.

1:05:45 – A zombie is shot in the head.

1:09:15 – A zombie is shot in the head.

1:09:15 – A zombie bites a man's neck.

ZOMBIE WOMEN OF SATAN

Year: 2009   Length: 85 minutes
Directors: Steve O'Brien, Warren Speed

STATISTICS

First Zombie:	7:30
First Human Death:	46:30
First Zombie Death:	7:45

Amount of Gore:	High
Gore Quality:	Very High
Zombie Effects:	High
Zombie Count:	Very High
Zombie Deaths:	Very High
Human Deaths:	Very High

SUMMARY

A group of misfits find themselves at a farm that is home to a combined cult for women and zombie research laboratory. After the zombie virus is mistakenly added to a bowl of punch, the women are turned into zombies and sent on a bloody rampage.

EFFECTS HIGHLIGHTS

3:30 – A woman is injected in the stomach.

7:45 – A zombie is stabbed in the head.

25:15 – A man draws a scalpel across a zombie's stomach.

30:15 – A zombie bites a woman's neck.

34:30 – A woman vomits.

34:30 – A zombie is hit in the head with a pipe.

38:45 – A zombie is beaten with a golf club.

45:30 – A man is bitten on the neck.

51:30 – A zombie is hit in the head with a golf club.

52:45 – A zombie is stabbed in the head.

56:00 – A zombie is hit in the head with a golf club.

1:00:30 – A zombie is stabbed in the head with a branch.

1:06:15 – A woman is stabbed in the head with a screwdriver.

1:09:30 – Close up of a bite wound on a woman's face.

1:10:00 – A man is decapitated with a chainsaw.

1:10:00 – A zombie's head is cut in half with a chainsaw.

1:10:15 – Close up of a severed head.

1:16:30 – Blood sprays across a wall.

1:16:45 – A zombie is stabbed in the eye with a high heeled shoe.

1:18:30 – A man is shot in the neck.

1:19:00 – A man is stabbed in the eye.

1:19:00 – A woman is shot in the head.

1:19:15 – A man pulls his eye out.

ZOMBIEGEDDON

Year: 2003   Length: 81 minutes
Director: Chris Watson

STATISTICS

First Zombie:	7:45
First Human Death:	12:00
First Zombie Death:	8:00

Amount of Gore:	High
Gore Quality:	High
Zombie Effects:	Average
Zombie Count:	High
Zombie Deaths:	Average
Human Deaths:	Average

SUMMARY

Satan has created a new and horrible species of zombie that craves human flesh. The only ones who can save humanity are two shady cops.

EFFECTS HIGHLIGHTS

7:45 – A zombie is cut on the chest.

7:45 – A zombie is stabbed in the chest with the tip of an axe.

8:00 – A man stomps on a zombie's head.

11:30 – A man is shot in the chest.

16:15 – A zombie rips out a man's heart.

16:30 – A man's organs fall on the floor.

25:00 – A man is shot in the stomach.

32:15 – A man is shot in the chest.

36:45 – A zombie bites a chunk of flesh out of a woman's back.

37:45 – Close up on a bloodied brain.

38:00 – A zombie is shot in the head.

38:00 – Close up on a dead zombie.

40:30 – A zombie vomits on a man.

44:00 – A zombie is stabbed in the head.

45:45 – A zombie's arm is broken.

48:30 – A zombie's stomach is ripped open.

56:00 – A zombie is stabbed in the chest with the tip of an axe.

56:00 – A man stomps on a zombie's head.

1:01:30 – A zombie eats a piece of flesh.

1:06:00 – A zombie's heart is ripped out.

1:09:00 – A man is shot in the chest.

ZOMBIELAND

Year: 2009   Length: 88 minutes
Director: Ruben Fleischer

STATISTICS

First Zombie:	:45
First Human Death:	3:00
First Zombie Death:	7:00

Amount of Gore:	Very High
Gore Quality:	Very High
Zombie Effects:	Very High
Zombie Count:	Very High
Zombie Deaths:	Very High
Human Deaths:	Average

SUMMARY

A traveling college student meets up with a group of roamers while trying to find his way home to his family.

EFFECTS HIGHLIGHTS

1:00 – A zombie bites a man's leg.

1:30 – A man is bitten on the neck.

1:45 – A zombie is shot in the chest.

2:00 – A zombie bites a woman's ankle.

3:00 – A woman slides across a road.

3:15 – A zombie spits up blood.

6:45 – A zombie is shot in the chest.

17:00 – A zombie's ankle is broken.

20:15 – A zombie eats a dead man's intestines.

22:45 – A zombie is smashed in the head with a banjo.

22:45 – A zombie is smashed in the head with a bat.

23:00 – A zombie is smashed in the head with a bat.

23:00 – A zombie is smashed in the head with a bat.

29:30 – Close up on a pair of severed arms.

41:45 – A zombie is shot in the head.

42:00 – A zombie is crushed by a piano.

53:45 – A man is shot in the chest.

1:06:45 – A zombie is shot in the chest.

1:07:00 – A zombie is shot in the chest.

1:09:15 – A zombie is shot in the chest.

1:09:30 – A zombie is shot in the chest.

1:09:30 – A zombie is shot in the chest.

1:09:30 – A zombie is shot in the chest.

1:09:30 – A zombie is shot in the chest.

1:10:30 – A zombie is shot in the head.

1:11:30 – A truck runs over a zombie.

1:13:15 – A zombie is shot in the chest.

1:13:15 – A zombie is shot in the chest.

1:13:30 – A zombie is shot in the chest.

1:13:15 – A zombie is shot in the head.

1:13:15 – A zombie is shot in the chest.

1:13:15 – A zombie is shot in the head.

1:13:15 – A zombie is shot in the head.

1:13:45 – A zombie is shot in the head.

1:13:45 – A zombie is shot in the chest.

1:14:00 – A zombie is shot in the head.

1:14:15 – A zombie falls off of a tower.

1:14:30 – A zombie is shot in the head.

1:14:45 – A zombie is shot in the chest.

1:15:45 – A zombie is shot in the chest.

1:16:15 – A zombie is shot in the head.

1:18:15 – A zombie's head is smashed with a mallet.

1:18:45 – A zombie falls off of a tower.

ZOMBIES ANONYMOUS

Year: 2006   Length: 118 minutes
Director: Marc Fratto

STATISTICS

First Zombie:	7:30
First Human Death:	29:15
First Zombie Death:	1:06:15
Amount of Gore:	Very High
Gore Quality:	Very High
Zombie Effects:	High
Zombie Count:	High
Zombie Deaths:	Average
Human Deaths:	High

SUMMARY

In a world where zombies coexist with ordinary people, the undead are considered second-class citizens. A a woman is shot by her boyfriend and must learn to adjust to her new zombie lifestyle.

EFFECTS HIGHLIGHTS

3:15 – A woman is shot in the chest.

3:15 – A woman is shot in the head.

17:45 – A zombie eats raw meat.

25:30 – Close up on a dead mouse.

25:45 – A zombie eats a dead mouse.

28:15 – A zombie has a bloody wound on its face.

29:15 – A zombie is shot in the head.

33:30 – A zombie eats a piece of flesh.

39:00 – A zombie bites a woman's neck.

42:00 – A man is shot in the chest.

42:00 – A zombie is stabbed in the head.

42:15 – A zombie is shot in the head.

46:15 – A zombie eats a piece of flesh.

57:15 – A zombie is shot in the head.

57:30 – A zombie is shot in the head.

57:45 – A zombie is shot in the head.

58:15 – A man holds a severed head.

58:30 – A zombie is shot in the back.

1:03:30 – A zombie is shot in the head.

1:03:45 – A zombie is shot in the head.

1:03:45 – A zombie is shot in the head.

1:04:30 – A man is shot in the head.

1:04:45 – A woman is stabbed in the chest.

1:05:15 – A zombie is shot in the head.

1:05:45 – A zombie breaks off a man's jaw.

1:05:45 – A zombie eats a piece of flesh.

1:06:15 – A zombie pulls a man's head off.

1:06:15 – A group of zombies rip open a woman's

Tony Gardner applies makeup to a zombie on "Zombieland" courtesy of Alterian Inc. and Tony Gardner.

Top, preparing a zombie, bottom, Woody Harrelson, Emma Stone and Bill Murray in "Zombieland" courtesy of Alterian Inc. and Tony Gardner.

196

Zombies on the set of "Zombieland" courtesy of Alterian Inc. and Tony Gardner.

stomach.

1:13:00 – A zombie eats a severed arm.

1:14:15 – A zombie bites a man's leg.

1:14:45 – A zombie bites a man's leg.

1:15:00 – A zombie is stabbed in the head.

1:15:00 – A zombie pulls out a zombie's eye.

1:16:30 – A zombie bites a man's hand.

1:17:45 – A zombie bites a man's neck.

1:18:15 – A zombie is shot in the head.

1:18:15 – A zombie is shot in the head.

1:18:30 – A zombie is shot in the head.

1:18:30 – A zombie bites a woman's hand.

1:19:30 – A woman is shot in the back.

1:19:15 – A group of zombies tear open a woman's stomach.

1:25:45 – A zombie cuts off a man's testicles.

1:26:15 – A zombie bites a man's neck.

1:26:45 – A zombie shoots a man in the leg.

ZOMBIES GONE WILD

Year: 2007   Length: 102 minutes
Director: Gary Robert

STATISTICS

First Zombie:	1:06:45
First Human Death:	1:25:15
First Zombie Death:	1:19:00
Amount of Gore:	Low
Gore Quality:	Average
Zombie Effects:	Average
Zombie Count:	High
Zombie Deaths:	Average
Human Deaths:	Low

SUMMARY

Three men take a spring break trip and get more than they bargained for when they meet a group of female zombies who prey on vacationers.

EFFECTS HIGHLIGHTS

3:30 – The hand of a dead body is cut off.

1:24:30 – A zombie rips out a man's intestines.

1:25:15 – Close up on a dead body.

1:36:45 – A group of zombies tear open a man's stomach.

ZOMBIES OF MASS DESTRUCTION

Year: 2009   Length: 89 minutes
Director: Kevin Hamedani

STATISTICS

First Zombie:	1:00
First Human Death:	32:45
First Zombie Death:	42:45
Amount of Gore:	Very High
Gore Quality:	Very High
Zombie Effects:	High
Zombie Count:	Very High
Zombie Deaths:	High
Human Deaths:	Average

SUMMARY

When zombies assault a small town, a ragtag group of locals join forces to repel the deadly onslaught.

EFFECTS HIGHLIGHTS

1:15 – A man accidentally impales a zombie with his walking stick.

27:45 – A zombie bites a man's neck.

28:00 – A zombie peels the skin off of a man's face.

31:15 – A zombie impales itself on a poker.

32:45 – A girl is hit by a car, severing her arm.

33:15 – A zombie's eye falls out.

34:30 – A headless torso bleeds from a chest wound.

34:45 – A zombie eats a piece of flesh.

34:45 – A zombie eats a piece of flesh.

34:45 – A zombie eats a piece of flesh.

35:30 – A zombie bites a woman's wrist.

35:45 – A man cuts a zombie's arm with an axe.

35:45 – A zombie's arm is cut off with an axe.

42:45 – A zombie is shot in the head.

43:00 – Close up on a severed arm.

45:00 – A zombie is shot in the head.

45:15 – A zombie is cut on the neck with a weed wacker.

45:30 – A zombie is shot in the head.

45:45 – A zombie is cut on the stomach with a weed wacker.

48:15 – A zombie's arm is cut off.

48:15 – A zombie's throat is slit.

48:15 – A zombie is stabbed in the mouth.

48:15 – A zombie's stomach is slit open.

48:45 – A zombie is shot in the chest.

49:15 – A man pulls a zombie's head off.

53:30 – A zombie eats a piece of flesh.

59:00 – A woman's foot is nailed to the floor.

59:45 – A man is stabbed in the head with a hammer.

1:00:30 – A nail is pulled out of a woman's foot.

1:01:00 – A zombie eats a man's intestines.

1:07:00 – Close up on a headless torso.

1:09:15 – A zombie is stabbed through the mouth.

1:14:15 – A woman is missing her lower lip.

1:16:30 – A zombie is shot in the head.

1:16:45 – A zombie is shot in the head.

1:19:00 – A zombie rips a man's arm off.

1:19:15 – A zombie eats a man's torso.

1:19:45 – A zombie is shot in the head.

1:20:30 – A zombie is shot in the stomach.

1:20:45 – A zombie is shot in the head.

ZOMBIES OF SUGAR HILL

Year: 1974   Length: 91 minutes
Director: Paul Maslansky

STATISTICS

First Zombie:	23:15
First Human Death:	7:00
First Zombie Death:	N/A
Amount of Gore:	Low
Gore Quality:	Low
Zombie Effects:	Low
Zombie Count:	Average
Zombie Deaths:	Very Low
Human Deaths:	Average

SUMMARY

When her boyfriend is brutally murdered by gangsters, a woman calls upon the help of Baron Zamedi, Lord of the Dead, to get revenge on the murderers.

EFFECTS HIGHLIGHTS

:30 – A man pours blood out of a headless chicken.

29:30 – Close up on a severed head.

54:15 – A man bleeds from a head wound.

ZOMBIES THE BEGINNING

Year: 2007   Length: 91 minutes
Director: Bruno Mattei

STATISTICS

First Zombie:	2:45
First Human Death:	1:08:30
First Zombie Death:	18:15
Amount of Gore:	Very High
Gore Quality:	High
Zombie Effects:	High
Zombie Count:	Very High
Zombie Deaths:	Very High
Human Deaths:	Low

SUMMARY

A zombie outbreak spreads through a colony of humans and they lose contact with the outside world. A woman who has dealt with the dead before, is forced to go back with a squad of soldiers to wipe out the menace once and for all.

EFFECTS HIGHLIGHTS

5:00 – A zombie bites a woman's neck.

18:15 – A zombie is shot in the head.

30:15 – Close up on a bloody dead body.

43:30 – A zombie baby bursts out a woman's stomach.

46:45 – A zombie rips a piece of flesh off of a man.

48:45 – A zombie is shot in the chest.

48:45 – A zombie is shot in the head.

50:15 – A zombie's arm is cut off in a door.

51:15 – A van crushes a zombie.

56:45 – A woman is cut in half.

1:05:00 – A zombie is shot in the chest.

1:05:00 – A zombie is shot in the chest.

1:05:15 – A zombie is shot in the chest.

1:05:15 – A zombie is shot in the chest.

1:05:15 – A zombie is shot in the head.

1:05:15 – A zombie is shot in the head.

1:05:15 – A zombie is shot in the head.

1:05:30 – A zombie is shot in the head.

1:05:30 – A zombie is shot in the chest.

1:05:30 – A zombie is shot in the stomach.

1:05:45 – A zombie is shot in the stomach.

1:05:45 – A zombie is shot in the stomach.

1:05:45 – A zombie is shot in the head.

1:06:15 – A zombie bites a man's neck.

1:08:00 – A group of zombies tear a man apart.

1:10:45 – A zombie is shot in the stomach.

1:12:00 – Two men explode.

1:12:00 – A zombie is shot in the chest.

1:12:15 – A zombie bites a man's arm.

1:12:15 – A zombie is shot in the head.

1:26:00 – A zombie is shot in the head.

1:26:00 – A zombie is shot in the head.

1:26:15 – A zombie is shot in the head.

ZOMBIES, ZOMBIES, ZOMBIES

Year: 2008   Length: 82 minutes
Director: Jason Murphy

STATISTICS

First Zombie:	:30
First Human Death:	2:00
First Zombie Death:	2:00
Amount of Gore:	Very High
Gore Quality:	High
Zombie Effects:	Average

Zombie Count:	Very High
Zombie Deaths:	Very High
Human Deaths:	High

SUMMARY

A experimental drug produces an army of zombies and it is up to a small group of strippers to fight back.

EFFECTS HIGHLIGHTS

2:00 – A zombie is stabbed in the head with a pair of ice skates.

2:15 – A zombie is hit in the head with a machete.

31:45 – A woman spits up blood.

32:00 – A zombie bites a woman's neck.

32:00 – A zombie bites off a woman's arm.

32:15 – A zombie eats a severed arm.

32:30 – A severed arm falls to the floor.

37:30 – A wall is splattered with blood.

45:15 – A zombie is shot in the head.

45:15 – A zombie is shot in the stomach.

46:15 – A group of zombies tear open a man's stomach.

57:00 – A zombie is shot in the shoulder.

57:15 – A zombie is shot in the shoulder.

57:15 – A zombie is shot in the shoulder.

57:45 – A zombie is stabbed in the head.

1:01:30 – A woman is shot in the chest.

1:05:15 – Close up on a bite mark.

1:06:00 – A man is bitten on the neck.

1:06:00 – A zombie is shot in the head.

1:07:00 – A zombie is hit in the head with a weed wacker.

1:07:15 – A zombie's throat is cut with a chainsaw.

1:07:15 – A zombie's face is cut off.

1:07:30 – A zombie is hit in the head with a hammer.

1:07:30 – A zombie is cut on the neck with a chainsaw.

1:07:45 – A zombie is decapitated.

1:08:15 – A zombie is stabbed in the head with a bat.

1:08:30 – A zombie is stabbed in the head with a chainsaw.

1:08:30 – A zombie is missing half of an arm.

1:08:45 – a zombie's arm is shot off.

1:08:45 – a zombie's head is shot off.

1:09:15 – A zombie is stabbed in the head with a shoe.

1:10:45 – A zombie bites a man's face.

1:11:00 – A zombie explodes.

1:12:15 – A zombie bites a man's arm.

1:13:30 – Two zombies explode.

1:14:00 – A severed head falls to the floor.

1:14:45 – A zombie is shot in the face.

1:15:45 – A zombie is stabbed in the head with a pole.

1:17:30 – Zombies tear open a man's stomach.

1:17:30 – A zombie explodes.

1:17:30 – A zombie explodes.

1:17:30 – A zombie explodes.

1:17:30 – Two zombies explode.z

1:17:45 – A zombie explodes.

1:17:45 – A zombie explodes.

1:17:45 – A zombie explodes.

1:18:00 – A zombie explodes.

1:18:00 – A zombie explodes.

1:18:00 – A zombie explodes.

ZOMBIEZ

Year: 2005   Length: 83 minutes
Director: John Bacchus

STATISTICS

First Zombie:	1:45
First Human Death:	2:30
First Zombie Death:	12:00

Amount of Gore:	High
Gore Quality:	Average
Zombie Effects:	Low
Zombie Count:	High
Zombie Deaths:	High
Human Deaths:	Average

SUMMARY

A young woman finds herself besieged by a group of zombies and she is forced to fight off the seemingly endless horde in order to save her husband.

EFFECTS HIGHLIGHTS

2:30 – A man's intestines are ripped out.

2:45 – A man eats intestines.

10:15 – A zombie is pulling out a man's intestines.

12:30 – A zombie eats a piece of flesh.

23:15 – Close up on a piece of flesh.

23:45 – An axe is drawn across a woman's wrist.

25:45 – An axe is drawn across a woman's throat.

25:45 – Close up on a piece of flesh.

26:00 – Close up on a piece of flesh.

37:30 – A group of zombies tear open a man's stomach.

38:00 – A group of zombies eat intestines and organs.

43:00 – A man's stomach falls out.

56:45 – A man's intestines fall out.

59:30 – A zombie cuts off a woman's finger.

1:00:30 – A piece of intestine hangs from a hook.

1:03:30 – Close up on a piece of flesh.

1:17:45 – A knife is stuck in a zombie's neck.

3 RANKING THE DEAD

The reviews in chapter three graded the films on a predetermined set of criteria. The following lists are based on the results from these reviews. All movies that received the highest ratings are listed below.

- Most Gore - Movies that contain over twenty shots of gore.
- Best Gore - Movies that contain realistic and highly graphic content.
- Best Zombie Effects - Movies that contain realistic looking zombies
- Most Zombies - Movies that contain over thirty zombies.
- Most Zombie Deaths - Movies that contain over twenty zombie deaths.
- Most Human Deaths - Movies that contain over fifteen human deaths.

MOST GORE

28 Weeks Later
Axed
Bloodpigs
Bone Sickness
Bong Of The Dead
Braindead
Burial Ground
Colin
Cowboys And Zombies
Dawn Of The Dead
Dawn Of The Dead (Directors Cut)
Dawn Of The Dead (European Edit)
Dawn Of The Dead
Day Of The Dead
Day Of The Dead
Day Of The Dead 2: Contagium
Days Of Darkness
The Dead
Dead And Breakfast
Dead And Deader
Dead Moon Rising
Dead Snow
The Dead Undead
Diary Of The Dead
Die Zombielager
Eaters: Rise Of The Dead
Evil
Evil 2: In The Time Of Heroes
Fido

Fistful Of Brains
The Forever Dead
The Ghouls
Hell Of The Living Dead
House Of The Dead
Hunting Creatures
Junk
Land Of The Dead
Living A Zombie Dream
Meat Market 2
Mud Zombies
Nightmare City
Night Of The Bums
Onechanbara
Paris By Night Of The Living Dead
Plaga Zombie 2: Zona Mutante
Planet Terror
Poultrygeist
Premutos: Lord Of The Living Dead
The Rage
Redneck Zombies
Resident Evil: Extinction
Resident Evil: Afterlife
Retardead
Return Of The Living Dead 3
Return Of The Living Dead: Necropolis
Return Of The Living Dead: Rave To The Grave
Shadow: Dead Riot
Shaun Of The Dead

Sick And The Dead
The Stink Of Flesh
Stripperland
Survival Of The Dead
Undead
Undead Or Alive
Versus
Wild Zero
Wiseguys Vs. Zombies
Zombie
Zombie 90: Extreme Pestilence
Zombie Apocalypse Now

Zombie Bloodbath 2: Rage Of The Undead
Zombie Camp Out
Zombie Holocaust
Zombie Hunter Rika
Zombie Self Defense Force
Zombie Strippers
Zombie Wars
Zombieland
Zombies Anonymous
Zombies Of Mass Destruction
Zombies The Beginning
Zombies, Zombies, Zombies

BEST GORE

28 Days Later
28 Weeks Later
Against The Dark
All Souls Day
Attack Girls Swim Team Vs. The Undead
Automaton Transfusion
Axed
Beneath Still Waters
Blood Creek
Bloodlust Zombies
Bong Of The Dead
Boy Eats Girl
Brain Dead
Braindead
Burial Ground
Cemetery Man
City Of The Living Dead
Dance Of The Dead
Dawn Of The Dead
Day Of The Dead
Day Of The Dead
Day Of The Dead 2: Contagium
Days Of Darkness
The Dead
Dead And Breakfast
Dead And Deader
The Dead Hate The Living
Dead Heist
Dead Moon Rising
The Dead Pit
Dead Snow
The Dead Undead
Deadgirl
Death Valley: The Revenge Of Bloody
Devil's Playground
Diary Of The Dead
Doghouse
Eaters: Rise Of The Dead
Edges Of Darkness
Evil
Fido
Flesh Freaks
Flight Of The Living Dead

Gangs Of The Dead
The Ghouls
Hell's Ground
The Horde
House Of The Dead
House Of The Dead 2
Land Of The Dead
The Mad
Mud Zombies
Mutant Vampire Zombies From The Hood
The Neighbor Zombie
Night Of The Living Dead
Night Of The Living Dead 3D
Outpost
Paris By Night Of The Living Dead
The Plague
Planet Terror
Pontypool
Premutos: Lord Of The Living Dead
Quarantine
Quarantine 2
The Quick And The Undead
The Rage
Re-animator
Rec 2
Resident Evil
Resident Evil: Apocalypse
Resident Evil: Extinction
Resident Evil: Afterlife
Return Of The Living Dead Part II
Return Of The Living Dead 3
Return Of The Living Dead: Necropolis
Return Of The Living Dead: Rave To The Grave
Sars Wars
Shadow: Dead Riot
Shaun Of The Dead
Stacy
Survival Of The Dead
Zombie
Zombie Diaries
Zombie Diaries 2: World Of The Dead
Zombie Honeymoon
Zombie Hunter Rika

Zombie Strippers
Zombie Undead
Zombie Wars
Zombie Women Of Satan

Zombieland
Zombies Anonymous
Zombies Of Mass Destruction

BEST ZOMBIES

All Souls Day
Axed
Beneath Still Waters
Bong Of The Dead
Braindead
Burial Ground
Cemetery Man
City Of The Living Dead
Colin
Dance Of The Dead
Dawn Of The Dead
Day Of The Dead
Day Of The Dead 2: Contagium
Diary Of The Dead
Doghouse
Eaters: Rise Of The Dead
Flight Of The Living Dead
Grave Mistake
The Horde
House Of The Dead
House Of The Dead 2
I Am Omega
Land Of The Dead

Mud Zombies
Night Of The Living Dead
Night Of The Living Dead 3D
Pontypool
Premutos: Lord Of The Living Dead
The Rage
Resident Evil
Resident Evil: Apocalypse
Resident Evil: Extinction
Resident Evil: Afterlife
Return Of The Living Dead Part II
Return Of The Living Dead 3
Return Of The Living Dead: Necropolis
Return Of The Living Dead: Rave To The Grave
Sars Wars
Shadow: Dead Riot
Shaun Of The Dead
Survival Of The Dead
Undead Or Alive
Zombie Honeymoon
Zombie Strippers
Zombieland

MOST ZOMBIES

28 Days Later
28 Weeks Later
A Grave For The Corpses
Aaah! Zombies!!
Ada: Zombilerin Dugunu
After Sundown
Against The Dark
American Zombie
All Souls Day
Army Of Darkness
Automaton Transfusion
Autumn
Awaken The Dead
Axed
Battlefield Baseball
Big Tits Zombie
Bio Cops
Bio Zombie
Biophage
Blood Moon Rising
Bloodpigs
Bloodsuckers From Outer Space
Bone Sickness
Bong Of The Dead
The Book Of Zombie

Boy Eats Girl
Braindead
Bubba's Chili Parlor
Burial Ground
Children Of The Living Dead
Children Shouldn't Play With Dead
  Things
Colin
Cowboys And Zombies
Curse Of The Cannibal Confederates
Dance Of The Dead
Dawn Of The Dead
Dawn Of The Dead (Directors Cut)
Dawn Of The Dead (European Edit)
Dawn Of The Dead
Day Of The Dead
Day Of The Dead
Day Of The Dead 2: Contagium
Day X
Days Of Darkness
The Dead
Dead Air
Dead And Deader
Dead Heist
Dead Hunter

Dead Life
Dead Meat
Dead Men Walking
Dead Moon Rising
The Dead Next Door
The Dead Pit
Dead Snow
The Dead Undead
Deadlands: The Rising
Deadlands 2: Trapped
Death Metal Zombies
Death Valley: The Revenge Of Bloody
Devil's Playground
Diary Of The Dead
Die And Let Live
Die Zombielager
Doghouse
Doomed
Eaters: Rise Of The Dead
Edges Of Darkness
Erotic Nights Of The Living Dead
Evil
Evil 2: In The Time Of Heroes
Feeding The Masses
Fido
Fistful Of Brains
Flight Of The Living Dead
The Forever Dead
Gangs Of The Dead
Girl's Zombie
The Grapes Of Death
Grave Mistake
Hell Of The Living Dead
Hide And Creep
High School Girl Zombie
The Horde
House Of The Dead
House Of The Dead 2
Hunting Creatures
I Am Omega
Junk
Land Of The Dead
Mallorca Zombie
Meat Market
Meat Market 2
Mud Zombies
Mutant Vampire Zombies From The Hood
Nightmare City
Night Of The Living Dead
Night Of The Living Dead 30th Anniversary
Night Of The Living Dead
Night Of The Living Dead 3d
Ninja's Vs. Zombies
Onechanbara
Paris By Night Of The Living Dead
Pathogen
Plaga Zombie
Plaga Zombie 2: Zona Mutante

Planet Terror
Poultrygeist
Premutos: Lord Of The Living Dead
Quarantine 2
The Quick And The Undead
Rec 2
Redneck Zombies
Resident Evil
Resident Evil: Apocalypse
Resident Evil: Extinction
Resident Evil: Afterlife
Retardead
Return Of The Blind Dead
The Return Of The Living Dead
Return Of The Living Dead Part II
Return Of The Living Dead: Necropolis
Return Of The Living Dead: Rave To The Grave
The Rising Dead
Sabbath
Sars Wars
Shadow: Dead Riot
Shaun Of The Dead
Sick And The Dead
Siege Of The Dead
Stacy
The Stink Of Flesh
Stripperland
Survival Of The Dead
Tokyo Zombie
Undead
Undead Or Alive
Versus
Wild Zero
Zombie
Zombie 3
Zombie 4: After Death
Zombie 90: Extreme Pestilence
Zombie Apocalypse Now
Zombie Bloodbath
Zombie Bloodbath 2: Rage Of The Undead
Zombie Bloodbath 3: Zombie Armageddon
Zombie Camp Out
Zombie Diaries
Zombie Diaries 2: World Of The Dead
Zombie Driftwood
Zombie Farm
Zombie Night
Zombie Rampage
Zombie Self Defense Force
Zombie Strippers
Zombie Undead
Zombie Wars
Zombie Women Of Satan
Zombieland
Zombies Of Mass Destruction
Zombies The Beginning
Zombies, Zombies, Zombies

MOST ZOMBIE DEATHS

28 Weeks Later
A Grave for the Corpses
After Sundown
Against The Dark
Army Of Darkness
Awaken The Dead
Axed
Battlefield Baseball
Blood Moon Rising
Bong Of The Dead
Braindead
Bubba's Chili Parlor
Children Of The Living Dead
Cowboys And Zombies
Dawn Of The Dead
Dawn Of The Dead (Directors Cut)
Dawn Of The Dead (European Edit)
Dawn Of The Dead
Day Of The Dead
Day of The Dead 2: Contagium
The Dead
Dead Heist
Dead Hunter
The Dead Undead
Die Zombielager
Evil 2: In The Time Of Heroes
Flesheater
Flight Of The Living Dead
Girl's Zombie
The Horde
House Of The Dead
House Of The Dead 2
Hunting Creatures
Junk
Land Of The Dead
Meat Market
Mud Zombies

Mutant Vampire Zombies From The Hood
Night Of The Living Dead 30th Anniversary
Onechanbara
Paris By Night Of The Living Dead
Planet Terror
Poultrygeist
Premutos: Lord Of The Living Dead
Raiders Of The Living Dead
Resident Evil
Resident Evil: Extinction
Resident Evil: Afterlife
Retardead
Return Of The Blind Dead
Return Of The Living Dead Part II
Return Of The Living Dead: Necropolis
Return Of The Living Dead: Rave To The Grave
The Rising Dead
Sick And The Dead
Siege Of The Dead
Stripperland
Survival Of The Dead
Undead
Versus
Wild Zero
Zombie
Zombie 3
Zombie 4: After Death
Zombie Diaries 2: World Of The Dead
Zombie Hunter Rika
Zombie Self Defense Force
Zombie Strippers
Zombie Wars
Zombie Women Of Satan
Zombieland
Zombies The Beginning
Zombies, Zombies, Zombies

MOST HUMAN DEATHS

28 Weeks Later
After Sundown
Army Of Darkness
The Astro Zombies
Bone Sickness
Cannibal Apocalypse
Dawn Of The Dead
Dawn Of The Dead (Directors Cut)
Dawn Of The Dead (European Edit)
Day Of The Dead 2: Contagium
Dead Heat
The Dead Undead
Horrors Of War
Land Of The Dead
Nightmare City
Oasis Of The Zombies

Planet Terror
Premutos: Lord Of The Living Dead
Resident Evil: Apocalypse
Resident Evil: Extinction
Return Of The Blind Dead
Return Of The Living Dead: Rave To The Grave
Shadow: Dead Riot
Survival Of The Dead
Zombie Bloodbath
Zombie Island Massacre
Zombie Lake
Zombie Women Of Satan

4 RAISING THE DEAD

The following interviews were conducted over a fourteen month period in 2010 and 2011. Each interviewee graciously gave considerable time out of their busy schedules to discuss their careers and in many cases going back twenty, thirty or even forty years to recollect their journey's in the zombie genre. To provide insight on the genre as a whole, these interviews represent movies from all corners of the world of zombie cinema. Many of the professionals listed here have been interviewed for the first time and all provide an interesting insight into the creation of a genre we all hold to such high esteem.

INTERVIEW LIST

Actors

Boyd Banks...207
Steve Barton...210
Melissa Cowan..241
Michael Kenworthy.....................................269

Directors

Andrew Currie 247
Emily Hagins 261
Lloyd Kaufman 265
Joshua Long...278
Christine Parker......................................307
Brian Paulin...311
Marc Price...321
Todd Sheets 342
Warrren Speed 346

SFX Artists

Chris Bridges..215
Everett Burrell.......................................219
Stuart Conran 225
Gino Crognalee 243

Tony Gardner...250
Kyle Glencross 254
Robert Kurtzman 273
Ed Martinez..282
Michael Mosher 292
Neil Morrill...289
Greg Nicotero..296
Jim Ojala 303
Mike Peel...314
Sean Sansom 328
Tom Savini..331
Toby Sells...336
John Vulich 349
Cliff Wallace 353

Storyboard Artist

Rob McCallum 285

Production

Daniel Gommé 257
Nick Plantico...318
John Russo 326

BOYD BANKS

- Stripperland (2011) Maestro
- Pontypool (2008) Jay/Osama
- Diary of the Dead (2007) White Man
- Land of the Dead 2005) Butcher
- Dawn of the Dead (2004) Tucker

Blood Splatter: You have starred in some high profile zombie films, namely Zack Synder's re-envisioning of *Dawn of the Dead, Land of the Dead, Diary of the Dead* and some more obscure zombie features such as *Pontypool* and *Stripperland.* How did you get into the zombie genre?

Boyd Banks: The genre actually ended up on my front doorstep. I live in Toronto and the city offers fantastic tax credits to filmmakers and this attracts certain genres at certain times. It goes in cycles with what is popular here. For a while we were inundated with costume dramas and then it shifted to horror. The horror genre has been really good to both Toronto and myself. For many years it became the zombie capital of the world, as production companies jumped to take advantage of the tax credits and shoot films out here. The *Dawn of the Dead* remake was being shot here and I decided to audition for the role of Tucker. The rest, as they say, is history.

BS: Are you a fan of zombie films?

BB: Absolutely, I love zombie movies. I think they are awesome. I am a huge fan and have been one for a long time and god knows I've been in enough of them in recent years.

BS: So what do you look for in a zombie film either as an actor or as a fan?

BB: I have two criteria for a good zombie film whether I'm acting in it or watching it as a fan. A zombie movie has to have a social commentary of some type. I love the commentaries they have on us as a society. It's like holding up a mirror and showing our deepest and darkest secrets. It also has to be very gory with a lot of people and zombies dying in it. Let's face it, bloodshed is very much expected in any zombie film. If a zombie movie has both of those, then I am happy.

BS: So which is your favorite zombie film that you worked on?

BB: That's a really hard question and to be honest, I can't answer that. It's like picking your favorite child. I have really enjoyed every film I have been fortunate enough to work on. Each one holds good memories.

BS: What about your favorite one that you haven't worked on?

BB: Oh, it definitely has to be the originals. It has to be the original Romero trilogy. Of course I know there were zombie films before then, but this really was the beginning for the modern zombie for me. They changed everything and made the movies what they are today.

BS: What are your thoughts on the recent influx of amateur zombie films?

BB: Zombie movies today are like the garage bands in the 1960's and 1970's. Back then, everyone in the suburbs had a garage band. With camera's now being a lot more affordable and much better quality than they used to be, we're seeing loads of amateur filmmakers jumping into the genre and I think that is a great thing. I find the people who make zombie movies are so level headed, it's hilarious. They are the calmest, nicest people and yet they come up the most evil and sickening ways to die. It's such a contrast.

BS: Was it a genre you specifically went after?

BB: I was in the right place at the right time to be perfectly honest. When George Romero moved to Toronto, he basically brought the genre with him. Even though George wasn't involved with the *Dawn of the Dead* remake, zombies were here to stay.

BS: How did you get the role of Tucker in *Dawn of the Dead*?

BB: I wasn't offered the gig. I worked hard and auditioned just like I do for every role. I work for scale and I keep my mouth shut. These are the two things I have going for me. *(laughs)*

BS: Were you aware of the controversy surrounding the remake?

BB: Actually, I was yes. I had worked with George previously on *Bruiser* before *Dawn of the Dead* and my agent personally advised me to take it off of my resume before auditioning for *Land of the Dead*, but George knew anyway. He was really cool about it and is always giving me work. George Romero has been really good to me. Hell, the undead have been really good to me. I have a lot to be thankful for.

BS: Did you experience any animosity on the set of *Land of the Dead* due to your involvement in *Dawn of the Dead*?

BB: Not at all, not at all. The worst thing George said was "fast zombies suck". He is a sweetheart of a man. Have you ever heard anyone say anything bad about George? There is a reason why he is loved so much. That is something to say, being so out there publicly and no one having anything bad to say about you. I'm sure there are bad things said about me. I didn't see any issues anywhere on set.

BS: You went from playing a human character in *Dawn of the Dead* to playing the Butcher zombie in *Land of the Dead*, did you specifically audition for this role?

BB: I did audition for the Butcher role too. I always thought that it would be a lot fun to play a zombie in a movie. Although I didn't get the role based on playing Tucker. I had to audition for it like everyone else.

BS: Playing a lead zombie for an entire movie must be challenging. Even though the character has no dialogue and shows little emotion, it is still able to communicate and is enjoyable to watch on screen. How did you prepare for the role?

BB: I didn't do a lot of preparation for the actual character, but I did work on some of his mannerisms. I worked on getting my own signature zombie walk. I tried to make the walk look as pained as possible. I think the more painful the walk looks, the better the zombie looks. I wanted it to look like I was having trouble walking and falling forward as I moved. I tried to make it my own.

BS: Did George give you any feedback on the Butcher's history or your motivations?

BB: No, he didn't provide any character background. He saw me do the zombie walk and said it was perfect. He had other shit to worry about. There was a lot going on with the film. I think I did okay though.

BS: I've heard that the shoot for the water scene in *Land of the Dead* when the zombies emerge out of the river was extremely cold. Can you tell us a bit about the experience?

BB: Oh it was cold. Hell, it was absolutely freezing. I spent the entire night soaking wet and shaking, but that was a really fun night though. It was the coldest night of the shoot and we shot that entire scene at night. Naturally it warmed up later the following day, but it was really cold. It's a hard life being a zombie, but it's fun to be one. It's fun to kill them too actually.

BS: Well, you've been lucky enough to be on both sides of that.

BB: Indeed. I have perspective, sir. I have perspective as both the killer and the victim.

BS: What can you tell us about the makeup process for the Butcher?

BB: There was a lot of makeup. Each day I would spend about three hours in the makeup chair putting it on and at the end of the day about forty five minutes to take it off. I think it looked fantastic. The effects guys did an outstanding job. As the shoot went along, they got it down to a fine art and were able to do the process a little faster. I had a lot of fun.

BS: Were you uncomfortable at all?

BB: Not at all. I really enjoyed the process. It was something I'd never done before and would definitely do it again.

BS: How did your cameo in *Diary of the Dead* come about?

BB: I heard that they were casting, so I went in for an audition. I always audition. It was only a very small role, but I thought that it would be fun to be involved. You know, keep my legacy going. *(laughs)*

BS: You keep cropping up in zombie movies. I was wondering if you had a secret that helped you out?

BB: Not that I am aware of. Both George Romero and zombies have been very good to me.

BS: You just starred in *Stripperland*. How was that experience?

BB: *Stripperland* was filmed up in Portland and it was a great time. I had a brief cameo in it as the flamboyant Maestro who meets a really ghastly ending. I swear I am becoming "the zombie guy". I am a bit of a living joke at the moment. I seem to be cropping up everywhere in the genre.

BS: Does dealing with death change your perspectives of your own mortality?

BB: Not at all dude, it's just a movie. It has never bothered me much at all. I can easily separate the two and I really don't think about it. It's a job and I do it to the best of my abilities.

BS: With how realistic the effects are, do you get desensitized to the violence?

BB: You do, you really do. I'm at the stage in my career where nothing shocks me anymore. Sure, the films are really gory, but it doesn't shock me at all. Besides, it's a horror movie, it's supposed to be gory. I think to a certain degree we are all desensitized to movie violence either as an actor or as a film fan.

BS: To further cement the Butcher's longevity, in 2006 SOTA Toys released a Butcher action figure. How did it feel to have an action figure modeled after you?

BB: It's a little surreal. It feels like I actually accomplished something with my life. I'm really proud of it, but it's a little weird to be honest. It's me, but it's not me.

BS: Do you own it?

BB: No I don't. I think plummeted in value though and I think you can buy me for ten dollars now.

BS: Actually, I think I paid five.

BB: Well there you go. Thanks for sharing that. I feel so much better now. *(laughs)*

BS: Were you involved with modeling for the figure?

BB: It all came from the production photos taken during filming, so I wasn't involved in the sculpt at all. They did a fantastic job though. I was really impressed when I finally saw it. I'm rather flattered actually. Not everyone gets to be an action figure.

BS: Are there any zombie films in the future for you?

BB: I just recently completed a 3D zombie movie called *Dead Before Dawn*. I've had a lot of people approach me about cameos. I'm a bit of an in joke in the genre now. As long people continue to hire me, I will be happy.

STEVE BARTON

- Dread Central - Chief Editor
- Survival of the Dead (2010) Featured Zombie

Blood Splatter: Dread Central is one of the premiere horror websites and delves deep into all things horror, not just zombies, how did you get into the genre?

Steve Barton: It's funny, everything in my life is either a comedy of errors or a comedy of triumph. Anyone who knows me, knows that I am just an uber fan at heart. I love movie memorabilia and many years ago, my girlfriend came across a cardboard *Jurassic Park* cage on eBay that roared when you pressed a button. It turned out that the guy she won it from lived down the street from me and rather than ship it, he suggested we meet up. The guy ended up being Tony Timpone, from Fangoria Magazine. From there I got to know him and we became good friends and he gave me a job working at Fangoria. After that I went out on my own and started Dread Central with my two partners, Jon Condit and K.W. Low.

BS: That's an impressive start. What are some of your other career milestones?

SB: There are so many. For my biggest fan boy milestone, there is no greater honor than playing a zombie for George Romero on *Survival of the Dead*, especially a zombie that gets to partake in the feast. When you're feasting, you know you've made it and that's an incredible feeling. As a personal milestone, I really feel that it is the embrace of the fans and the support they have given me individually and collectively for both myself and what I do with Dread Central as a whole. There is nothing cooler in knowing that somebody is genuinely excited to meet you or even just coming up and saying "hey man, I really related to that thing you wrote". It's a really good feeling to be held in at least a somewhat higher esteem from the fan base. All I am is just a glorified fan. I live, breath and shit this stuff.

BS: Obviously you are a zombie fan. What appeals to you about the genre?

SB: The thing about zombies is that for years and years, horror movies portrayed monsters as things with fangs or fur and mummies and space monsters and what have you. Zombie movies were obviously around, but nothing like the way George created them. What he did with the movie and ever so wisely, was to make the monsters us. It opened up a whole different set of rules and groundwork. Can you shoot someone you love once they have turned? There are a lot of social aspects and a lot of really, really intense and more realistic frights. It also brings a bigger set of problems than you would have, by say a vampire who you can kill with a cross. *Night of the Living Dead* holds a really special place in my heart.

BS: How did you get into it?

SB: When I was three or four years old back in the seventies, we had this giant black and white console TV in our living room. When I would hear my parents snoring that would be my cue to run into the living room and turn on the TV and watch movies all night. One night I was embarking on my usual routine and flicking through the channels, when I came across this news broadcast about the dead coming to life and this guy was telling us to get to rescue stations and I was like "oh my god!" I ran into my parent's bedroom and turned on the light and they are telling me I'm having a nightmare. I drag them to the TV and of course, what was on was *Night of the Living Dead* and that famous news cast scene. It seemed incredibly real to me. I got my first spanking that night and it was the first time I had ever been disciplined by my parents. As I laid there in bed with my ass throbbing, I realized that I was one hundred percent terrified out of my mind, but at the same time completely safe and I just thought that was the coolest thing in the world. So that's why I just took to horror movies as I have always been after that controlled chaos. Even growing up, the film stayed a real focal point in my life. I'll never forget when I got my first job growing up in Brooklyn, New York. You grow up there and it's mandatory that you get your first job in a pizzeria. I worked an entire summer to save up enough money for a *Night of the Living Dead* VHS copy as owning that movie would be the greatest thing in the world. However, when VHS first came it out it was like ninety bucks or something like that.

A few years after my first gig with Fangoria, I got my first meeting with George. I just couldn't believe I was going to meet him. I come from the dysfunctional family circus and his movies gave me my values, as strange as that sounds. It taught me what's wrong and what's right and maybe sometimes it's better to listen that to react. These are all lessons I learned from these movies, so to say that he is my idol is a bit of an understatement. I met up with his manager, Chris Roe and he and I had spoken a few times and were very friendly with each other. I saw Chris in passing and he handed me the key to George's hotel room. He told me to just hang out there and George would be there soon. I took the key and went to the room. I was in awe of everything. I started calling every single person I knew and said "guess where I am?" I hugged his pillow on his bed and peed in his bathroom to mark my territory. I sat where I thought he would sit. The door finally opened and there was George. I was just in awe, but it only lasted a few minutes, because there is just something so warm about him. There is something so friendly. He just instantly puts you at ease because he treats you like a real person. He doesn't treat people like "oh here's another guy I have to sign something for", which I see a lot of people do. I got a chance to tell him the story about how he is responsible for my first spanking and tell him the story about how I flipped pizza's for a fucking year to buy *Night of the Living Dead*. We became very close friends and this relationship is something which is probably, next to my girlfriend Debbie, my most valued possession.

BS: What are your thoughts on the genre shift to include the viral/plague films such as *28 Days Later*?

SB: There's a lot of grey area. The thing about George's movies is he laid down the ground work. He said "okay, these things, they want to eat us". He never said why and he never really touched on just what brought them back. The door has always been wide open. It could be an infection, it could be a plague. It could be any number of things. There is no one thing etched in stone. I don't have a problem with how people become a zombie. I have a serious beef with people who are able to run at thirty miles an hour when they are dead. That doesn't make sense to me. When you die, your body starts rotting, your tendons become solidified and stiff. You're not running anywhere. That's the biggest liberty that's been taken with the zombie genre. Don't get me wrong, there have been many really good movies with running zombies in them. A lot of people don't remember that *The Return of the Living Dead* has running zombies in it. That's the only thing that just doesn't make sense to me. I don't like my zombies running. There is a whole dimension of fear that these things can get you quickly and that's why I chalk it up to them to being infected and that makes it okay for me. As long there is some sort of semblance of a nod to the guy who created it, whether it be eating flesh or killing them with a head shot, that's fine.

BS: The genre is obviously known for films of all qualities. What are some of your guilty pleasures?

SB: I love the Blind Dead movies. They are just so fucking sleazy in the most glorious of ways. I also love a movie called Burial Ground which stars a kid who looks like a tiny Dario Argento. I like these movies because I like my dead dry. A lot of the Italian movies like *Gates of Hell, Night of the Zombies* and films like that, had zombies that had a really pasty look to them, like they had macaroni on their face. I like my dead to look a certain way. I like when they are rotting and dried like *Zombie*. I loved the zombies in that movie. If the zombies in a movie look cool, I'm a lot more forgiving of the quality of the movie. Let's face it, zombie movies are easy to make, but they are not easy to make well. I've seen a lot of movies where the film maker decided to throw white powder or splash someone with blood and tell them to walk funny. That's not a zombie. If your movie is a zombie film and I can't tell one zombie from the other and it just looks like a big Goth concert, your movie probably sucks. The dead need to look cool. That's why special effects are so important. It doesn't have to necessarily be a disturbingly violent film, but as long as the zombies themselves look really bitching, I'm cool. Another film hardly anyone has heard of is a really dark comedy from the 80's called *Night Life*. That's a hilarious movie with some great zombie effects in it.

BS: I remember that film. It was promoted in Fangoria pretty heavily when it came out

SB: Yes, they sure did. No one knows *Night Life* and any time I mention it they look at me like I am crazy. Another guilty pleasure is *One Dark Night*. It's a brilliant movie. If you've never seen it, it's directed by Tom McLoughlin and it's one of the most single brilliantly made, cheesy funhouse zombie movies you can ever hope to see. It's a about a hypnotist called Raymar who is into telekinesis and he has the power to transcend death. It then goes into this whole hokey fraternity initiation to stay overnight in a mausoleum. They accidentally awaken Raymar who raises all of the bodies from their coffins. Instead of using real actors, what they did in this movie, which is fucking brilliant, is they have these bitching zombies and rather than having them walk, are rolled on dollies. It sounds ludicrous but you need to see

211

it to experience how fucking cool it is. It's like walking into a spook show of the highest quality. There is a collectors DVD which has the theatrical cut and the original work print called *A Night in the Mausoleum*. I also love *The Chilling*.

BS: You were a zombie extra on *Survival of the Dead*, was this the first time you have been made up?

SB: No, but it was the first official time. If I could be a professional zombie for the rest of my life, there would be no greater gift.

BS: How did the role occur?

SB: It was about ten years into my relationship with George. One day he calls me out the blue and says "hey Steve, I can't possibly cast you as one of the living, but what would do you think about playing a zombie for me"? I offered to launch myself via sling shot to get there. I got up to the set and it was October 13th and I can't even begin to tell you how cold it was up there, but I was the happiest person on the planet. I got to see George and I'm watching him shoot certain parts of the movie and we were having a blast. To me it was akin to an art student watching Picasso paint. All of a sudden, the call came over the walkie talkie to get me into makeup and I was like "holy shit, this is really going to happen". I head over to the trailer and I'm sitting in Sean Sansom's seat and I said "listen dude, here's the deal. I'm a good friend of George's. I don't want to be grey guy or blood splash guy. I'm bald. You can put latex all over me. You can fuck me up bad and don't worry about how uncomfortable I could be". He turned me into a bitching looking zombie. I walked around and looked at the other zombies and for the most part, they were all held in this one area. But I was like "fuck that' and I walked around and watched the setups and the gags being filmed. We got to the part at the end of the film where we are all in the coral and I had been there for hours. Hours of just standing there and I didn't care. It is the greatest feeling in the world to be surrounded by zombies knowing you are in a Romero movie.

The next day, I arrived back on set there and we were getting ready to get me back into makeup. I am sitting in Sean's chair and he says "tonight, we have some background shots. There is a ton of background work that has to be done and I'm sorry but we can only do the basic makeup thing on you. I told him I was cool with that, I got to do the makeup thing once already, but inside I am crushed and heartbroken. He turns around and he comes back with these major appliances and he starts laughing. He puts me in this really elaborate makeup that took over an hour to do. All of a sudden I went from looking like a really cool zombie to a bitching looking zombie. I was in heaven. My wardrobe consisted of a red plaid shirt and you can guess where that nod was from. I'm bald and I got to be the updated version of the plaid zombie from *Dawn of the Dead*. Instead of the rot on the side of my face, they moved it to the side of my head. I loved it. A lot of people don't realize that when you are making a movie there is a lot of standing around waiting for things to happen. I finally got back on set and we're in the coral. It's four in the morning and we've been standing there since ten o'clock the previous night and no one gives a shit. You're looking at George and you see how animated he is and how much fun he is having and all you want to do is do your best for him. No one is complaining. The hot chocolate lady is coming around and she is like Jesus at his point, because it was about fourteen below. We broke for dinner and I went back and Francois Deganois and Damon Bishop were busy stuffing a body and prepping it. It was cool to see as this was the main body that was going to get ripped up. I am in makeup and I took a couple of pictures with it and then I'm back on set and in the coral for another several hours. Now it's about five in the morning and my close friend Michael Felsher are joking around and having a good time. Mike was going to be the one to get to do the main gag with the body that gets torn apart. George comes up and says "okay this is what we're going to do". Mike you are going to fall on the body from this side and Steve, you are going to come from the other side of the fence and put your elbow on the body to keep it on the floor and you are going to tear into the body, pull out the spine and take a bite. I'm looking at him like "what"? I was perfectly happy being the background guy. I am now in the main feast scene. I remember my jaw trembling. George adds that they only had one body and therefore only one take to get it right.

BS: No pressure then?

SB: No, none at all. *(laughs)* Mind you, at this point at night it's close to twenty below. They are prepping the body and Mike is on the floor and there is a mother and daughter zombie and they each had a leg. They were supposed to pull the legs while Mike and I tore into the body and another guy was there if we needed help. What no one had thought about was that while the body was sitting there for several hours, it froze. Everywhere that the body was supposed to tear was completely frozen. The cameras start rolling and we get ready. George called action and I barrel into the scene. I dig my hands in, but we realize this shit isn't coming apart. I'm yanking and pulling and it's not budging. In my head I know I have to get this right. I had to get the body apart. Being that is was so cold, as soon as the body opened and the blood touched our skin it froze. We were in agony but we knew we had to get the shot. I'm no small guy, but I reached in and felt the spine and pulled as hard as I could. I cut my hand open and it took almost two minutes to rip it all apart. You can see all of this on the extra features on the DVD. It was like ripping open a frozen turkey wearing mittens of pain. We finally did it and the spine came loose. George yells "take a bite, Steve" and it was time for my glory. After a few seconds he yells "cut" and we were exhausted. We stood up and everyone on set was applauding. It was such an amazing opportunity. I couldn't stop saying thank you. The assistants were running to get us hot towels to stop frost bite and I admit to tearing up. It was one of the most amazing things I've ever experienced.

BS: What are your thoughts on the lukewarm receptions *Diary of the Dead* and *Survival of the Dead* received?

SB: *Diary of the Dead* is his most critically acclaimed Dead film, but the fan base was really tepid and when *Survival of the Dead* came out, the fan base was super lukewarm. What people fail to realize is that George is always a little ahead of his time. I remember when *Day of the Dead* came out and people hated it. It was dark and depressing and now it's an undiscovered gem. I think in about ten years, people will see these films and really see what he is going for. People complained that there was too much slapstick. Are you kidding me? This is the same guy who added a pie fight into *Dawn of the Dead* for Christ's sake. People seem to forget this.

BS: I felt *Diary of the Dead* played better on the small screen due to the documentary style of how it was filmed. I didn't particularly like it when I saw it as a theatrical presentation, but when I bought the DVD, I loved it and it is actually my favorite of the six films.

SB: I agree. It's a very intimate movie and I love all of the nods to *Night of the Living Dead*. That is the thing about George's movies. They are polarizing. People either like them or they don't. Let's just say you are in love with Led Zeppelin's fourth album. Do you have them just keep making different versions of Stairway to Heaven or do you want them to keep trying something new? Every one of George's movies tried something new and I think that is commendable.

BS: Is it difficult to separate the fan boy and the seasoned professional during an opportunity like this?

SB: It takes a lot of self-restraint. Believe me, no one knows how lucky I am more than I do. I get to work in an industry that I have loved all of my life and there are parts of it where I just can't help but geek out. One of the things I got to learn while doing this is these actors and directors are like anyone else, they just have cooler jobs. Being able to call a lot of them personal friends is a real honor. Unless it's someone of George's caliber, I'm able to keep my fan boy tendencies in check. There are still moments where I can't believe this is happening. When we were doing the commentary for *Survival of the Dead*, we did it in George's living room with a bottle of vodka. If you listen to the commentary, you'll notice we get a little more shit faced as it progresses. The key is to always be thankful and I am incredibly thankful. There is never a better feeling in the world when someone comes up to you and you know they genuinely appreciate your work. It's always humbling.

BS: Do you think zombie movies are becoming more violent because society is becoming more violent?

SB: Not at all. If you look at *Night of the Living Dead*, it's an ultra-violent movie. It's just shot in black and white. So you don't see it that much. Zombie films are supposed to be violent. That's why I marvel at movies like *Shark Night 3D* getting a PG-13 rating. It's a movie about killer sharks that devour and bite people. I'm sorry to say that when you get bitten there is blood. It's going to be gory.

BS: You can definitely get away with more violence than you used to.

SB: I think that thanks to the likes of Quentin Tarantino, violent movies from the MPAA are getting a bit more of a pass, but that never stops them from trying to exploit an indie filmmaker every so often, like Adam Green was with *Hatchet*. They put him through hell saying "you can't do that in a movie" when all he did was make a movie about a swamp monster with a belt sander that apparently didn't need power. It's all done tongue in cheek, but the MPAA will have a heart attack about that, but *Rambo* can go off on an absolute bloody rampage. It really seems like the MPAA pick and choose their battles, but I think that because such acclaimed filmmakers have made such incredibly violent movies, they've at least loosened their belts a bit.

BS: Where do you see the horror and zombie genre heading?

SB: It see it going right back to where it is now. The genre always seems to go in cycles. What's popular now, will be popular again in ten years. What's popular in ten will be popular again in twenty and so on. We go through phases. The ghost movie phase, then slasher's become big and then we go back to zombies. It's like fashion. As long as there are people out there who love being scared and there are a lot of them, there will always be horror movies. Horror has been around since the cavemen, when they would draw pictures of spirits and monsters on cave walls to frighten their children. People are fascinated with death. It's the ultimate fear. When you can come close to death without actually dying, there is nothing cooler than that. I see the genre sticking around and staying strong. In twenty years, I still see people dissecting George's movies. Who in the world will be looking at *Fast Five* in a few years from now? No one will be, as it is forgettable stuff. What George does is hold up a mirror to you and society and shows you humanities darkest side. If you watch the movies, it's not the zombies that are the problem, it's us. It's always us.

BS: That is the formula that made *The Walking Dead* so successful.

SB: Exactly. The real threat is your friends, you family members, your neighbors. A lot of people don't get that when they make zombie films and that is why so many fail.

On the set of "Survival of the Dead" with George A. Romero, Steve Barton, Richard Fitzpatrick courtesy of Steve Barton.

CHRIS BRIDGES

- A Little Bit Zombie (2012) Special Effects Makeup Artist
- Diary of the Dead (2007) Special Effects Makeup Supervisor (Gaslight Studios)
- Dawn of the Dead (2004) Animatronic Designer (Gaslight Studios)

Blood Splatter: You worked on the *Dawn of the Dead* remake and *Diary of the Dead* with fellow Gaslight Studios special effects artists Kyle Glencross and Neil Morrill, how did you get into the genre?

Chris Bridges: The funny thing with zombies is that it is something that seeks you out. As effects guys, we all start out as young kids doing zombie makeup on ourselves and our siblings. Later in life when we're working in the business, inevitably we always find ourselves on a zombie film. In the mid 2000's, there were a ton of zombie films that came to Toronto. It literally found us.

BS: Are you a fan of the genre?

CB: Absolutely. I'm a big fan. I've loved it since I was a child.

BS: Do you have a favorite film?

CB: *Night of the Living Dead* without a doubt. I was five when I first watched it. My dad sat down with me and made me watch it with him one night and it made a huge impression on me.

BS: Are you a fan of horror in general or are you just attracted to some of the subgenres?

CB: I really am a fan of horror in general. I grew up with all of those kind of movies. The 1980's were my teenage years and I think some of the most popular horror movies came out in this era and they definitely steered me to this career.

BS: What have been some of your favorite scenes in zombie films?

CB: I think one of my favorites has to be the Tar Man zombie from *The Return of the Living Dead*. He is just terrifying and really disgusting to look at. It's a great design and a terrific looking zombie.

BS: How about from a film that you have worked on?

CB: Well the one I really like doesn't have zombies in it. I love the scene that we did in *Dawn of the Dead* when Kim Poirier who plays Monica, gets cut with the chainsaw right before the bus roles over. It was such a gruesome and violent way to go.

BS: Can you tell us a little bit more about how did this effect?

CB: My main duty on *Dawn of the Dead* was animatronics, so I supervised and built all of the animatronic puppets used in the film. For this scene, we had a silicone body of the girl, but underneath she was a fully animatronic puppet. So it was able to scream and have the neck flail about. Basically it could do all the things a human could do when getting cut in half with a chainsaw. It took eight people to puppeteer the final version. There was a large amount of setup because there was a real chainsaw being used. It still had all of the teeth and quite literally was going to cut the puppet in half. The puppeteers and R.D. Reid who played Glen were all crammed in the back of the bus to do the final shot. Inside, the puppet had all of these wires and cables running through it and was really intricate. The chainsaw was mounted on an arm that looked like a see saw and R.D. who was doing the cutting, had to pull down on the arm and slice through the puppet. There was no left or right movement, only up and down. It was critical that he hit that mark. If he didn't hit the mark dead on, it would have ripped all the cables out of the body and probably would have killed everyone in the bus. So it was very nerve wracking for everyone. It had to hit the mark perfectly or things would have gotten very messy.

BS: You bring up an interesting point about the actor needing to hit the mark. It is common place for the

215

effects crew to perform some of the dangerous gags simply because they know what is expected both of themselves and of the props used. Was there a reason you used R.D. instead of one of the effects crew?

CB: It was because of the way it was shot. The actor had to be in the scene. There were two, maybe three camera's in the bus and every one of them saw him, so we had no choice. Once you get the rig, the actor and the various crew all crammed in there, you run out of space quickly.

BS: What other animatronics did you set up for the film?

CB: In the Reflex Sports store, there is a zombie that gets a croquet mallet handle rammed through its head. It goes in through the jaw and out of the top of its head. We had cameras on the ground pointing up and the puppet then came into frame. On the count of three, we jammed the mallet in and rammed its brains through the top of its head. The cool thing about this effect is there was no CGI used at all. We also didn't add any animatronics to the eyes, but you could almost swear that the eyes cringe when the mallet goes in. I am really proud how this effect turned out. It is one of the effects that really hit home.

BS: Was there a lot of CGI used in the film?

CB: There was quite a bit of CGI used in certain scenes, but we also used a considerable amount of practical effects. We actually used a lot more than people would think. In many cases, scenes where we used puppets and props, viewers have sworn we used CGI. For example, any time someone is ran over, we used a dummy. The guy getting hit by the ambulance and the box truck reversing over the zombies were all dummies. There was no CGI used in the main setup.

BS: That really surprises me. I would have put money on the scene where the zombies get backed over by the box truck was CGI.

CB: There may have been some minor tweaks in post-production, but as far as what we shot on set, it was all practical effects. We build three or four dummies, tied them up and had the van hit them. It was really effective.

BS: How about as their heads hit the truck? Was the blood added to the dummies heads?

CB: That's where some of the post-production CGI would come in. I'm not offended by that at all. In some ways it makes our lives a little easier. Blood splatter is one of those things that is a complete wild card. You could do an effect one hundred times and you would get a hundred different effects. Blood splatter can be very hard to orchestrate, so using CGI ensures the shot is exactly what the director wants and is right the first time. I'm all for that.

BS: You are definitely in the minority of people I have spoken to about using CGI blood.

CB: Don't get me wrong, I'm not saying it is one hundred percent right all the time, but in certain instances in can make our lives a little easier. When it's done wrong, it looks terrible.

BS: How does your zombie creation process work?

CB: In any zombie movie you have three types of zombie. You have the hero zombie which gets a lot of up close screen time. These zombies are generally sketched out and designed in advance. They are custom made for actors and a lot of time and money goes into them. Then you have your medium range zombies that are put together with generic appliances and paint and behind that are the ones with minimal detail. When we create our hero zombies we use the usual reference materials, medical journals, webpages and that kind of thing.

BS: That seems to be a common source of reference in the industry. Is this a prerequisite?

CB: The fact is we need these materials to make our effects look realistic. There is only so much we can pull from our imagination. Sometimes it is hard for an effects artist to visualize, say for example a crushed limb. We need the visual stimulus to give us that extra edge. As extreme as it is, you just need

216

this to help you with the creation process.

BS: Is it hard to separate yourself from the realism of the effects?

CB: I can't speak for everyone, but personally, I find the source material really disturbing because it is real. I have a really hard time looking at some of the images needed to conduct my research.

BS: Are there any particular areas that are worse than others?

CB: For me, burns are a really hard area to research. I don't know what it is about them, but it's a really hard area for me. However, once they go on the actor, I'm fine with all of it. I can completely separate myself from the reality and source from the makeup.

BS: Did you have any reservations about joining *Dawn of the Dead* due to the fan outrage?

CB: Absolutely not. I was aware of the concerns and that many fans were calling for Tom Savini to be doing the makeup. Fans were obviously upset that George Romero wasn't involved and the movie was being made without the key players. I get that, but on the other hand it was a job and it was a really exciting one too. I have no regrets.

BS: Where there any shots that made it into the final release that surprised you?

CB: There is a great zombie kill that didn't make it into the final film which disappointed me. It was a really cool head shot. I can't really say I'm surprised that shots made it in to the film as it is a zombie movie and it's supposed to be gory. If you're going to be offended by the gore, don't watch a zombie movie. There is a scene that was really disturbing when it was filmed though. It was the one at the end of the film when they are escaping the mall in the buses and they are surrounded by hundreds of zombies. There is a part where a zombie is hanging on the side of the bus and Ty Burrell who played Steve, cuts through his legs with a chainsaw. No big deal right? This is what got to me though. The man who played the zombie was a double amputee and we built fake legs for him. We filled them with blood and tied him to the side of the bus. What really freaked me out was that less than twelve inches below where his body ended, we cut through his legs with a real chainsaw. This affected me for a couple of reasons. The first is I couldn't believe that this guy was okay with a real chainsaw being that close to him. Keep in mind he couldn't really see it, but he could certainly feel it. Once again, an actor is using a real chainsaw and any slip up there would have been dire consequences. The other reason is that this guy is a double amputee. What is he thinking as his prosthetic legs are being cut off? What kind of emotional effect does this have on someone, especially with an amputee? I'm really glad that scene made it into the movie. When you watch the film, you think that it is just a zombie getting its legs cut off but there is so much more to it than that.

BS: Was this the same actor who dropped down from the ceiling and attacked Bart in the parking garage?

CB: Yeah. It was the same guy. He did a really great job.

BS: Have you ever found yourself pushing the envelope to see how far you can go?

CB: The thing about zombie movies, even horror movies as a whole, is we are always trying to push the envelope. We get the script and these new and improved ways of killing people and creatures are presented to us. I wouldn't say that we are pushing the envelope all the time, but someone somewhere definitely is. We obviously have a helping hand as we ultimately build the effects, but I think going to extremes is a team effort. It was that way on *Diary of the Dead*. Working for George is definitely one of my career highlights. The greatest thing about working on a Romero movie is that he gives you the freedom to do what you want. He asks you if there is a kill you would like to try and if so to give it a shot. If it's cool he'll shoot it. That was how we came up with the IV pole gag.

BS: Neil Morrill mentioned the brain storming session you had with George at his apartment and some of the gags like the IV pole and a liposuction gag that ultimately wasn't filmed. Were there any other cool zombie deaths that came out of that meeting that didn't make it on screen?

CB: Not that I can think of, but the zombie nurse getting shocked with the defibrillator did come out of it.

BS: How did you shoot that scene?

CB: Right after she is electrocuted, we stopped the camera, she stepped out of the scene and we attached the eyelids with the eyeballs hanging out and she stepped back into frame. A little post work helped with the effect and I think it turned out great. There was a brief cut, but otherwise the scene is seamless. We also made up Greg Nicotero as the zombie doctor in the same scene.

BS: Have you ever been made up as a zombie?

CB: I haven't. I've been able to dodge that bullet a number of times. I don't know why, but I just feel more comfortable behind the camera. However, there was one day on *Dawn of the Dead* where there were over one hundred extras running in a mob down the street. One of the guys and I decided to join in and run with them. We went over to the blood station and picked up a couple of buckets of blood and dumped them over our heads. We were soaked to the bone, but we blended in. In a few minutes we take off and sprint down the street. They yelled out cut and we filtered out of the crowd and we were laughing about how we were going to be in the movie. Two minutes later, an assistant director walks up to us and tells us that we can't do that and to not do it again. We couldn't figure out how they knew. There were literally hundreds of extras in the scene. It didn't take too long to realize it was because we had logos on our t-shirts. That is a huge no-no on set due to endorsement issues, so we stood out like sore thumbs.

BS: Does working with the dead and dying affect your views on mortality?

CB: Absolutely. You know when you look at these images, especially the reference materials, you really get an appreciation for how fragile and delicate the human body really is. Sometimes I sit down and wonder how we work at all. So much can go wrong and so much can hurt us. It does affect me and while it doesn't keep me up at night, it does make me aware. Some of the reference books I have, I have to close them after a few minutes as they can make me so nauseous. It is so graphic.

BS: Why do you think it is more acceptable to portray violence against zombies than it is against humans, even though they are technically us?

CB: I think that we just think of zombies as mindless and soulless bags of meat. If you have ever been stuck in traffic and experienced road rage, you know that for a brief second, you want to get out of your car, grab your tire iron and take it to a person's windshield. You just can't do that, but to a zombie you can. You can take your frustrations out as it is dead and it is trying to get you. We've managed to disembody the zombie and so there are no morality issues connected to killing it.

BS: Are there any other zombie films in your future?

CB: I just finished up *A Little Bit Zombie* and I possibly have something coming up in the spring.

BS: Can you share any funny stories?

CB: Man, I have a ton. It's been a while since I thought about some of these movies and now it's all coming back. On *Diary of the Dead* when Greg Nicotero was the doctor zombie, he was squirmy in the makeup chair. I don't know if he really likes have the makeup applied, but Kyle Glencross was getting him ready. He just wouldn't quite sit still. He was really fidgety. On *Dawn of the Dead*, when the box truck is reversing over the zombies, one of the zombies is my supervisor, Shaun Smith. Shaun brought a head of himself from Los Angeles and we threw it on one of the dummies. He got a huge kick out of it and I got perhaps a little too much enjoyment out of it.

BS: If you woke up tomorrow and the zombie apocalypse had started, how would you do?

CB: I think I would do very well. I would outlast the outbreak for sure. I know all the mistakes people make and I won't feel sorry for my friends. If they turn into a zombie, you have to kill them. It is every man for himself.

EVERETT BURRELL

- Night of the Living Dead (1990) Special Makeup Effects Supervisor
- The Return of the Living Dead (1985) Uncredited
- Re-animator (1985) Special Makeup Effects Artist
- Hard Rock Zombies (1985) Special Makeup Effects Artist
- Day of the Dead (1985) Special Makeup Effects Artist

Blood Splatter: How did you get into the zombie genre?

Everett Burrell: I saw *Night of the Living Dead* on television when I was really young and was a fan of that type of genre. I love science fiction, fantasy and horror but I really lean towards horror. When *Dawn of the Dead* came out, my dad was living in Maryland at the time and I begged him to take me to go and see it. I had heard so much about it from the horror magazines at the time and I was already a big Tom Savini and George Romero fan anyway. I saw that film and it really changed my life. It was really cool. It was underground, bitching and really subversive. It was gory but it had great story and great character. It wasn't just what you call splatter porn or torture porn nowadays. It had a really great story and had really amazing violence. However, some of it was very cartoony and that kind of violence didn't really appeal to me as it wasn't realistic.

When I was in high school, I started working on making my own short films. I was doing stop motion animation and making my own visual effects and I ordered Tom Savini's book Grand Illusions through the mail. I was supposed to get a signed copy and when I got it delivered and it wasn't signed. I remember how disappointed I was. After reading through the book, I was like "wow someday it would be great to work with Tom Savini".

Cut to years later and I was good friends with John Vulich. John had been corresponding with Tom through the mail, sending him photos of his masks and stuff and John was hired as one of the crew members on *Day of the Dead* to go to Pittsburgh to help Tom out. I guess at some point they realized they needed more help so they called me and Howard Berger of KNB EFX, who was my roommate at the time. We were living in California and we went out to Pittsburgh to work on *Day of the Dead*. I was always a fan of the genre and always wanted to be a part of it and that was how I got into it for real. I ended up in Pittsburgh with Greg Nicotero, Howard Berger, John Vulich, Mike Trcic and David Kindlon and was working for Tom. It was kind of a dream come true.

BS: That's quite a roster.

EB: It was a really fun but hard learning experience for all of us. A lot of great people came out of that movie. You should listen to the commentary on the UK version of the *Day of the Dead* DVD. It was all of us, Nicotero, Michael Deak, myself and Howard. It's a great commentary. If you get the chance to listen to it, I really recommend it. I'm pretty sure it was the British version. It's amazing.

So to answer your question, *Dawn of the Dead* really inspired me to get into the genre. I remember the *Dawn of the Dead* board game board game which I still have somewhere. I was really excited to be a part of it and working on *Day of the Dead* was huge. Ironically before I worked on *Day of the Dead*, Howard and I worked on *The Return of the Living Dead*. I did *Hard Rock Zombies* as one of my first films, but that was kind of cheesy, I'm not overly proud of it. *The Return of the Living Dead* was just a weird experience, but it came out great and it is a really fun film.

BS: I wasn't aware that you had worked on *The Return of the Living Dead.*

EB: Yep. Howard and I were brought in to do some insert effects. Bill Munns got fired from the movie and ended up that Tony Gardner got a chunk of it. Howard and I did some stuff and Kenny Myers did a lot of stuff it. We did a bunch of weird zombie effects like people getting pinned with an axe and that kind of thing. It was fun.

BS: I did notice some difference with the quality and effects of the zombies throughout the film now that you mention it. Which other shots did you work on?

EB: There was a scene, Bill Munns god love him, he tried his best. He did this scene where it was a yellow corpse that gets it head cut off and runs around the room.

BS: Yeah, I believe it's the first zombie they encounter in the film.

EB: That's right. Howard and I did inserts of the pick axe going into its head and sawing off its head. The shots of him actually running around are from Bill. We did an insert body and worked on that sequence.

BS: As far as zombie films go, it wasn't one of the gorier films out there. The shot you just mentioned certainly comes to mind as a shot that should have had way more blood and gore but didn't. Did they make you hold back on the splatter effects?

EB: To be honest, I think they were playing it a little more comedic than serious, whereas, in my opinion *Day of the Dead* has some of the best bites in zombie film history. They were designed by John, Mike Trcic and Tom and they came up with these amazing gags. That was such a fun film. The one thing with Tom is that he is sort of a magician. He loves to come up with really fun gags and he inspired us all to continue that mentality throughout our careers and continue to come up with fun gags. Honestly, John, Trcic and Tom, they are the three creative forces behind that film hands down. We all kind of assisted and helped out. Nicotero, Berger, Deak, Kindlon and myself. Dave did mechanics and Howard and I were sort of like short stops. Greg was helping out a lot with behind the scenes coordinating. I think *Day of the Dead* really raised the bar for both the zombie and horror genre in general.

BS: *Day of the Dead* was one of the first zombie movies I saw as a kid. The scene with the soldier's head being pulled off and the high pitched scream he emits, still send shivers down my spine. It was such an unnatural and terrifying sound. This coupled with the visuals, made for a very disturbing scene. It does highlight the considerable improvement effects in the years between *Dawn of the Dead* and *Day of the Dead*. The first zombie seen in *Day of the Dead* is Dr. Tongue which I think outshines any zombie up to that point.

EB: Dr. Tongue was great. I love Tom, but I think him being stuck in Pittsburgh, he didn't understand a lot of the Los Angeles techniques. The 1980's really were the heyday of makeup effects. From 1980 to 1989 all kinds of cool shit was going down in L.A. Steve Johnson was a great pioneer. Rick Baker and Stan Winston, obviously those guys were doing amazing shit too. I worked nonstop from 1983 to 1989. I never had a day off.

BS: Your movie credits do seem pretty full during that time frame.

EB: Honestly. I worked nonstop. It was right around the actor's strike or something, I don't know what it was, hit in 1989 and I remember I had three months off and I thought it was the end of the world.

BS: From a horror stand point, that era was an amazing time for horror movies. *Day of the Dead* was way ahead of its time from a makeup standpoint.

EB: I agree, but I think *Day of the Dead* has issues as a film. *Dawn of the Dead* is a much better movie. *Day of the Dead* is dark and depressing where as *Dawn of the Dead* has a lot of hope at the end. It sort of reflects how the movie was made. We were stuck in the Wampum Mine up in Beaver Falls, Pennsylvania and that was a very depressing location to be in. The film has a lot of layers and I remember the original script being a lot more complicated.

BS: Were there any significant changes?

EB: Well Bub was involved a whole lot more and there was a subplot involving genetic soldiers.

BS: Bub is another really iconic zombie. It would have been interesting to see what else Romero had planned for him.

EB: I think Bub turned out great and is a really good character. A stand out zombie for sure, but there was a lot more planned for him.

BS: So which was your favorite zombie film to work on?

EB: I think the *Night of the Living Dead* remake. John and I had a lot of fun coming up with cool new zombies. We did tons of research on that and we played with a bunch of new techniques. We did a lot with gelatin and really tried to come up with some interesting new takes on zombies and ideas and back stories for each zombie. I don't think it really came out on the film because Tom Savini was unfortunately going through a bad personal time in his life and I think George stepped in to help direct the movie at a certain point. I think the film could have been way better but the circumstances didn't allow it. I think Tom forgot about why he was so good at effects. He was so worried about making his film he forgot the effects. There are a lot of missed opportunities in that movie. We had a lot of fun working on it and it was really interesting to be a part of that legend and come up with a new look.

BS: It is definitely one of the better horror remakes out there. What inspired you for your zombie makeup in *Night of the Living Dead*? I have read rumors that you and John used images of concentration camp victims for the emaciated look of the zombies, is that true?

EB: There is a store in Los Angeles called the Amok Book Store and it's this eclectic, weird book store that has a lot of strange reference material. They used to sell John Wayne Gacy paintings on the walls. I remember John was really mad as he went back to go and buy one and it was gone. This is talking back in the 1980's before anyone really knew who Gacy was in terms of a cult celebrity. Now they're worth a fucking fortune. That's not to say it's right to give money to a child murderer because it's not, my point is, it was just that type of book store. Anyway, we found this video on concentration camp victims. I'd never seen anything like it before. These days you can see this type of thing on the History Channel all the time. John and I really studied that film. It was horrible to look at, trust me, I don't want to make light of the situation by any means. We thought the closest thing to real zombies and the living dead would be prisoners of war or concentration camp victims because they are not being fed and are starving. The one thing we noticed, that no matter how skinny you get, the things that don't shrink are the cartilage. The ears don't shrink as there is no fat in them. There is no fat in your nose. Your face shrinks as all the fat goes away but your ears look big. We did this thing where we made slush latex ears for the zombies so it made their faces look smaller. We also added a really boney nose and we did things with fake eyeballs. Instead of using contact lenses we actually sculpted the face out and we put eyeballs inside so that the zombies would never blink and always have this weird stare. So there are all kinds of techniques we tried.

BS: So what other types of inspiration do you use to create zombies?

EB: We had loads of medical reference books. We actually went to see an autopsy in Pittsburgh. A bunch of us went to look at dead bodies and we saw the color of the skin. They were very yellow, way more yellow than we thought they would be. I thought that was always a myth.

BS: I have heard that real life dead trauma is very different from the Hollywood versions and that dead bodies don't rot and damage the way you would expect them to.

EB: No it's not the same. It really surprised me. We learned a lot of from that. As the skin is already turning yellow, you then get bloated and start to rot, you tend to go green because the way the flesh deteriorates. The coroner's office would open this drawer and a bloated body would be sitting there and it would be dark, dark green. It was really disgusting, but at the same time it was really interesting. I remember going in there and someone telling me to not breathe through my nose, only through my mouth because I would throw up. The smell will get you as soon as you go in. So I spent the entire time trying to breathe through my mouth and never smelling through my nose once.

BS: That bad?

EB: Awful. Another thing was all the dead corpses had this weird look on their face that is called the Death Grin. They all had this strange smile. The coroner said it's the way the muscles tighten in the face when you die. Almost like a weird "Joker" grin.

BS: Having seen all this up close, does it become difficult to distance yourself from the realism when making the wounds and bodies?

EB: Yeah, there are certain books I have seen that are just awful. There is a great book that we all use called Medicolegal Investigation of Death by Spitz and Fisher. Actually John still has my copy. It is a legendary book that we all use. Everybody has it. There is a famous page, 511. Have you heard this story?

BS: Can't say that I have.

EB: Well, it has different chapters and each one reflects certain ways of death. One chapter has gunshot wounds, there's a chapter on animals eating people. A woman had died in her apartment and her poodles had eaten her face off. That kind of thing. There is a section under weird sexual deaths where people accidentally kill themselves doing strange sexual things and there is this page called page 511 and this old skinny guy is in a bed. He had manufactured these and I swear to God I am not kidding you when I say this, three feet long dildo's that he was shoving up his butt using some weird trapeze device. He had this weird and horrible expression on his face as though he died of a heart attack in the middle of it. It's legendary. Interview Vulich or Nicotero or anyone from that era and they'll know what I'm talking about. Just say page 511 and gauge their reaction. That book was influential in every zombie movie in the 1980's. A lot of zombies came right out of that book. It's a great book. I don't mean great as in awesome, I don't want to be weird about it, it really is a horrible book to look at, but it's in black and white and is astonishingly creepy and really riveting, you can't tear your eyes away from it. It's incredibly powerful.

BS: How do you design zombies?

EB: I think there are two schools of thought on zombies. There is the cartoony zombie and then there is the realistic zombie. I love Bernie Wrightson, the American artist known for his horror illustrations and comic books and I love the way he draws. However, to translate Bernie's stuff into a screen zombie is really hard to make look real and scary. So one of the things John and I tried to do on the remake of *Night of the Living Dead* was base everything on reality like concentration camp victims or prisoners of war. We used medical books to try to base all the zombies off a real deaths and real things and I think that was our design process. My mentality going in to the real world of visual effects is that I have to base everything off of some kind of reality. So a lot of reference is important. I think if you just make it up or base it off of other zombies it becomes a bad VHS copy of a bad VHS copy. You want to be original, but at the same time you want to be real.

BS: Do you look for a specific type of actor when creating zombies?

EB: You want to pick great looking actors. That really important because if you just pick a giant round faced guy, that isn't going to help you. You want people who have a really good look with features you can accentuate. Being skinny really helps as you can always add. It is much harder to cut away.

BS: What are your thoughts on CGI blood?

EB: It's made things easier from a cleanup perspective, but I miss the real squibs. I was watching *Rome* the other day and you can just tell when they use stage blood versus CGI. Sometimes they enhance stage blood with digital highlights, but it just doesn't look right. It floats in the air and doesn't have the right specula highlights. Nothing beats a good head squib. In *The Departed* they used digital squibs when Leonardo DiCaprio got shot. It just makes me miss the real world interaction.

BS: I think this takes the "lived in" feel out of the film. Especially in the zombie genre where the characters get more bloodied and bruised as the film continues.

EB: I agree one hundred percent. Digital has made people lazy.

BS: Zombie films are known for their extravagant zombie kills and character death scenes, which has been your favorite that you created?

EB: I think when Joe Pilato gets ripped in half in *Day of the Dead*. We all worked on that gag. I think it turned out really cool.

BS: It's definitely one of the high points. How did you film that?

EB: Joe was sitting underneath a raised floor. The guy had to sit in that position for hours and hours while he was made up. Nicotero was what we called the "gut boy'. He handled all the pig guts and he brought in a big bucket of pig guts. We had to spoon them in and still Joe had to sit there while the guts started to rot and stunk up the place pretty bad. We had one take to do it in and we did it.

BS: Did you have the same issues with the pig guts as they did in *Dawn of the Dead*?

EB: Not at the time, but I know we came back from Florida after Christmas to do the reshoots in the at Wampum mine, the power had been turned off and Nicotero had to clean out the fridge. It was disgusting.

BS: I could imagine. So how about your favorite death scene from a film you didn't work on?

EB: There are so many great ones. I love the splinter in the eye scene from *Zombie*. *Dawn of the Dead* has a ton of great ones. The helicopter blade gag and the man getting his head blown off with the shot gun are fantastic.

BS: So what other effects did you work on in *Day of the Dead*?

EB: I worked on the scene with Miguel getting his arm cut off. That was fun. I love all of the bites in *Day of the Dead*. They are tremendous. There's a part where Miller gets bitten on the neck, right before when Nicotero gets shot. I love that one.

BS: How about for *Night of the Living Dead*?

EB: There was a really skinny black guy that we worked on. He was in cancer remission and we did this really cool chest makeup on him. It was great as we were able to put the squibs under the appliance as opposed to under the shirt. I shot him in the head with a blow gun to get the entrance. Then we did the entrance wound. *Night of the Living Dead* had some great gags. There should have been more, but that film got in trouble quickly when Tom had some personal issues to deal with. I think they missed the boat on some great zombie deaths. We had some really cool stuff planned but it never got shot.

BS: I know Tom hasn't spoken well of the experience.

EB: His wife filed for divorce like the first day we started shooting so that didn't help. It was a really bad time for Tom and the film didn't work out the way he planned. It's a shame as it had so much potential.

BS: You've worked on some more obscure zombie films such as *Hard Rock Zombies*. How was that experience compared to something like *Day of the Dead*?

EB: God, that was my first movie, so I was just happy to be there. I was just flinging blood around and didn't get to design anything. I was an assistant and was helping put blood on people. I had nothing to do with any of the designs. I just showed up to lug shit around.

BS: Obviously the film had a much lower budget. How do you approach these types of films? Do you strip back the effect and rely on tricks of the camera?

EB: The one cool thing about gore effects is if you splatter blood on someone you get an immediate reaction. Blood is really cheap to make. So from that point of view once you start putting blood on people, you get the results immediately.

BS: So what are your thoughts on the current resurgence in zombie popularity?

EB: I'm loving it. The last ten years have been great. The remake of the *Dawn of the Dead* was amazing.

I loved *28 Days Later* and I thought *Zombieland* was fantastic. I think the crowning achievement has to be *The Walking Dead* though. I think Greg and KNB EFX did a great job. It's a great show and it's really engaging. There are so many great zombie things out and they are taking it to the next level. I think it's really fun. I love that whole mythos and the whole end of the world. *I Am Legend* captured that, but was a little to CGI driven for my tastes. There is so much room out there right now for great zombie films. There are so many great things to look forward to. The zombie thing is getting bigger and bigger.

BS: So no preference on fast versus slow zombies?

EB: Fast zombies, slow zombies, I don't care as long as they are cool zombies.

BS: Were there any effects that made it to the final cut of *Day of the Dead* that surprised you?

EB: I think *Day of the Dead* is very gory throughout. I worked on *Re-animator* and that's got a lot of weird shit in it. Like the severed head eating a woman out. That's pretty intense and was pretty over the top. We read a script one time where a zombie attacks a pregnant lady and rips out her baby and eats it. That was a little crazy.

BS: Which film was that?

EB: It never got made. It's sort of a legendary script. It was this over the top zombie move with non-stop shit like that. I can't remember the name though.

BS: Is it easy to go over the top with the effects as zombie films are so graphic in nature?

EB: The MPAA monitors that stuff pretty tightly, especially on R rated films. You have to be really careful with what you do. However, things have been changing a lot lately. I mean take a look at *The Walking Dead* for example. They have been able to get away with things you could never have done on cable a few years ago. I think you can get away with even more on cable than you can on an R rated movie these days. It's really surprising.

BS: You were a zombie extra in *Day of the Dead*. Where can we find you?

EB: Towards the end of the movie there is a male nurse zombie who gets shot in the head. That was me. We were all zombies at some point during the film. John Vulich was the zombie who gets the shovel in the face and gets his head cut off and I think he played a second one too. Greg Nicotero played Private Johnson.

BS: How about any other films?

EB: No, that was it. I was never really into being on camera. I'm much more comfortable staying behind the camera.

BS: Can you share any funny on set stories?

EB: I'm sure everyone you speak to who was on *Day of the Dead* has stories from that film as we had so many. I remember there was one time when Tom was working on the Dr. Tongue zombie. He had put the foam skin on the face and was drilling a hole near its mouth. The drill bit caught the skin and ripped it completely off the head and twisted around the drill. We all laughed so hard. Tom got pretty upset and walked out of the room.

BS: Was it easy to fix?

EB: Yeah, we fixed it easily enough. So much shit like that happens. It was a really fun shoot.

BS: Are there any other zombie films in your future?

EB: I'd love to do more. I love the genre.

STUART CONRAN

- Shaun of the Dead (2004) Prosthetic Effects Designer
- Braindead/Dead Alive (1992) Creature and Gore Effects: Technician

Blood Splatter: How long have you been in the business?

Stuart Conran: I started work in 1986 on *Hellraiser* as a trainee with Bob Keen's company Image Animation.

BS: How many films have you worked on?

SC: I've lost count to be completely honest. There are obviously stand out films that you really remember for various reasons, such as for the experience or the work, there are the ones you would rather forget and then the others that you may have done a day on here and there. I don't know if that counts though. As an estimate, I would say about sixty films, then there's a lot of television stuff, shorts, promos and ad's.

BS: How did you get into the zombie genre?

SC: It was never a conscious decision. It can be very difficult to drive your career in the direction you want it to go, so I kind of fell into it. Getting onto *Braindead (Dead Alive)* came from contacting the New Zealand Film Commission and production companies prior to a trip I took around New Zealand. Working on *Braindead* led to being recommended and contacted for *Shaun Of The Dead,* so it was a very lucky turn of events.

BS: Are you a fan of the genre?

SC: I'm a big fan of the horror genre in general and I love the zombie genre, especially when it's done particularly well.

BS: What inspired you to work with zombies?

SC: What I love is how different the stories can be, no two are the same. You could set a zombie film practically anytime, anywhere.

BS: Do you have a favorite zombie film?

SC: I think it would be a stand-off between Romero's *Day of the Dead* and Tom Savini's *Night Of The Living Dead* remake. Both have such an amazing atmosphere and give you the feeling that you could find yourself in those situations. As well as being quite dark and a bit more serious than most zombie films. From a makeup effects point of view, they really shine as great examples of 1980's makeup effects at its pinnacle, with great make-ups and gags.

BS: When creating a zombie, how does the design process work?

SC: It will always start with the director's brief and the script. Are the zombies old and dry, fresh and bloody, ultra real or stylized? That kind of thing. There are so many different directions you can go. From a director's brief I will go through books, magazines and comics for reference, picking out ideas and inspirations along the way. After that comes the sculpting.

BS: What do you use as inspiration for the varying degrees of decay and damage? Have you used anything controversial in either makeup or inspiration?

SC: There are always the forensic reference books that come out from time to time. They can help as a springboard for an idea and can be really useful as a reference for the randomness and shapes of injuries and coloring. Sometimes a director would have done their own research and have a particular look in mind that has been sourced from real material. I always feel that the real thing is never quite how you would expect it to look and think it's best to use a bit of creative license.

BS: Knowing that this reference material is real, does it make the job harder at times?

SC: I have worked for makeup designers that send a whole bunch of nasty reference stuff, which I find really difficult to look at. I am quite squeamish really. On *Saving Private Ryan* we had some Ministry Of Defense reference material that was quite graphic, but ultimately not very real looking.

BS: Do you go into it with a predetermined idea for the way the zombies look or do you improvise?

SC: For a hero or a continuity or character zombie it would usually be a designed set look, guided by the script and director's requirements and description. For the generic zombie hoard, it's a case of improvise and make it up as you go, as per the requirements. On *Shaun of the Dead* I got to the point of including bloody handprints on zombies faces as if they had been grabbed before being bitten, in an attempt to add a bit of variety.

BS: Zombie films are known for extravagant zombie kills and character death scenes, which has been your favorite that you have created?

SC: It would have to be David's death from *Shaun of the Dead*. It was a real team effort with lots of elements to it that all came together perfectly. I had used the vinyl material we used for the skin and guts before and always thought it would be a great material for that kind of effect, so it was the perfect chance to use it. We set up a dry run on the stage a few days prior to filming the real thing, for a show and tell of how it would play out. We had a crew member standing in as David with a ropey old dummy and there were a few unsure looking faces around. There was always a feeling of expectation around it, so it was really satisfying when it all came together.

BS: How about your favorite zombie death scene from other movies you have not been involved in?

SC: Probably Rhodes' death from *Day Of The Dead*. It has become a classic, along with the behind the scenes story to go with it. His acting, or maybe it's just him reacting, really adds to it. Whenever I watch it, I can't help but gag a bit.

BS: Have you ever been a zombie extra in one of the films you've worked on?

SC: Yes. I'm in *Braindead* at the very top of the stairs for the zombie "Mexican wave" shot that ends up on Richard Taylor's reanimated, flesh stripped head. I was also in *Shaun of the Dead* in one of the bar scenes near the very end. Again, it was deep background with me doing some arm acting at the back of the crowd.

BS: Okay, onto *Shaun of the Dead*. It's definitely one of the better zombie films in recent history. You did most of the major zombie effects in the movie, which one was your favorite?

SC: There are lots of favorites in there for different reasons. I was pleased with how the hulking zombie character worked out, as he is really the only full on prosthetic zombie character in the film, apart from zombie Ed. It was also one of the first prosthetic effects that went on-set. He got a great response from everyone, especially Edgar Wright, Nira Park, Simon Pegg and Nick Frost so it felt like a great start to the job. He also made it onto the front cover of Fangoria.

BS: The record throwing scene is one of the more memorable moments in the film, how did you create it?

SC: For the hulking zombie getting hit in the face, his prosthetic was designed with the intention of the record going in his eye, so that eye was closed up to avoid any problems down the line and comfort for the actor during shooting that scene. We filmed with the actor Mark Donovan up to and including the action of him being hit with the record. We took him away and applied a small plate with the broken record shard attached and a small prosthetic to cover that. He did the same action with his head jerking back as if being hit by the record and the record breaking in his face was added digitally. Both are great examples of makeup effects and digital work coming together and complimenting each other rather than replacing. When the zombie cashier, Mary played by Nicola Cunningham, is hit by one, I did a cut on her face that was covered by a patch of skin on some monofilament and fishing line. Her hair covered the skin patch and line, so when the line was whipped away her hair flew up with it, to give the impression of the record whipping by. The record was added digitally.

BS: Were all the records CGI?

SC: Some of the records were. Floppy practical ones were thrown for real as well as wax ones that would shatter and others were digital.

BS: David's death was by far the most graphic scene in the movie, how did you design it?

SC: It's one of the oldest tricks in the book and has been done loads of times before, but this time Edgar wanted it to be slightly different in that David is "crowd surfing" over the zombie hoard but not quite making it. It was basically the actor Dylan Moran on a pole arm rig built by the special effects department with a dummy body resting on him which had a gut filled chest and stomach cavity, layered vinyl skin and blood. The people crowding around the dummy body helped obscure his body underneath. Dylan was also wearing a neck prosthetic attached to the false body, which was cut open as the scene progressed give the appearance of his head getting torn off.

BS: Did it play out as you intended?

SC: As it turned out, Dylan needed to be lowered more within the crowd than above it, for people to be able to grab hold of the body and tear it apart. Incidentally, I requested that the zombies tearing into the body should be makeup effects people so they would be familiar with the materials and how the effect worked.

BS: Scenes this graphic, generally end up on the DVD director's cut. Were you surprised it made the final theatrical cut?

SC: Yes, I was surprised. You're expecting it to cut away because it's so graphic, so I was really happy it was there in its entirety.

BS: Were there any scenes you worked on that did get cut or toned down in the final edit?

SC: No, everything we shot was in the final film. In fact for the final pub scenes Edgar and Nira were keen to up the ante. They wanted to make the zombies progressively gorier towards the end, so more and more generic wounds and blood were added courtesy of Jane Walker and her team. There was an additional week of filming sometime after the main shoot for the added scene where Shaun and Liz leave the pub and are saved by the military which arrive and mow down the zombies outside the pub. There were lots of squibs, blood and spurty head shots.

BS: How about the dart sticking in Shaun's head?

SC: That shot was done by Jane. It was originally supposed to be on my build list, then it moved on to the effects shops list, but in the end Jane did it with a lightweight dart loosely fixed to Simon's head. The blood was added digitally.

BS: *Braindead* is considered by many zombie fans to be the pinnacle of zombie splatter, how did you get involved with this project?

SC: Getting onto *Braindead* came from contacting the New Zealand Film Commission and production companies prior to a trip around New Zealand. I basically posted my CV off to New Zealand to every production company on the film commission list. Sometime later I got a phone call at work from Richard Taylor who was heading up the build. He said to get in touch when I arrived in New Zealand. We arranged to meet, I showed my portfolio and started work a week or so later.

BS: Was this the bloodiest film you have worked on?

SC: Most definitely. The house interior was built as a raised set, to allow for puppeteering and operating various effects during the shoot. Towards the end, when it was at its bloodiest a hole was cut into the floor to enable us to sweep all the blood and gore into dust bins underneath the set. It was so sticky that the floor tiles would come off and stick to your feet. The set became quite rancid with the fermenting blood and apple pulp.

BS: How far did you push the envelope?

SC: It was pushed pretty far, as the budget and build time were concerned. Technically the makeup effects were quite inventive but not ground breaking, but where I think it really came alive was in Peter's Jackson's camera work and editing. It was amazingly inventive and it was really cool to watch the camera set-ups for some of those incredible shots.

BS: Were you given boundaries to work in or was it a bit of a free for all?

SC: There were definitely some boundaries. The whole film was storyboarded out in this book we made and each of us was given a copy. It had each effects shot sketched out and broken down into its various components. It really helped, so everyone knew what was needed of the effect they were working on. We also spent an evening round Peter's house watching horror and zombie videos for reference, a gag from here, a shot from there. There were other bits and pieces that were a bit of an organized free for all, limbs, guts, generic heads etc. I actually still have that book. *(Images from this book can be found starting on page 230).*

BS: How did you shoot the scene of the character losing the skin on his legs?

SC: It was a combination of a few things. A pre-cut dummy body was used for the close-ups of it coming apart in the door, with cutaways to his face. It had rope threaded through which were it dressed as guts, so the body could just be pulled apart from either end with the rope guts stretching between the two. The top shot was with Jed Brophy wearing a fake chest with him through a hole in the floor. For the shot after, where he walks toward camera on his hands, Jed was wearing a fake chest hanging down with him on a slant board, wheelbarrow style. Then there was a dummy which had articulated legs for other shots. I think it works so well because the viewer is seeing it from all angles, with the help of all of those different tricks.

BS: In many of the gore scenes there is a lot going on. Are the effects designed for multiple takes or is a single shot opportunity?

SC: Most of the effects were repeatable after a cleanup and costume change, as well as having repeats of effects that can't be reset. I can't remember if there were any one off's, but it was the kind of film where there was always the time to set up an effect.

BS: Can you share any funny on set stories from the zombie films you've worked on?

SC: There is one that springs to mind and it is from *Shaun Of The Dead*. At the end of the film where they are under siege in The Winchester, the older zombie woman who bites Ed completely missed her mark where the blood bladder and perforations were on the prosthetic. I also don't think she realized the amount of blood that was going to come out either. It was blood mixed with compressed air and there was quite a bit of pressure there. After getting a face full of blood she just froze and looked absolutely shocked. It got a big laugh and to make it even funnier, Simon Pegg ran in with a Polaroid and snapped off a picture of her.

BS: Are there any zombie films in the future for you?

SC: Unfortunately there not many zombie films are made in the UK with the budget to feature loads of make-up effects these days, but you never know what's around the corner. I would love to work in the genre again.

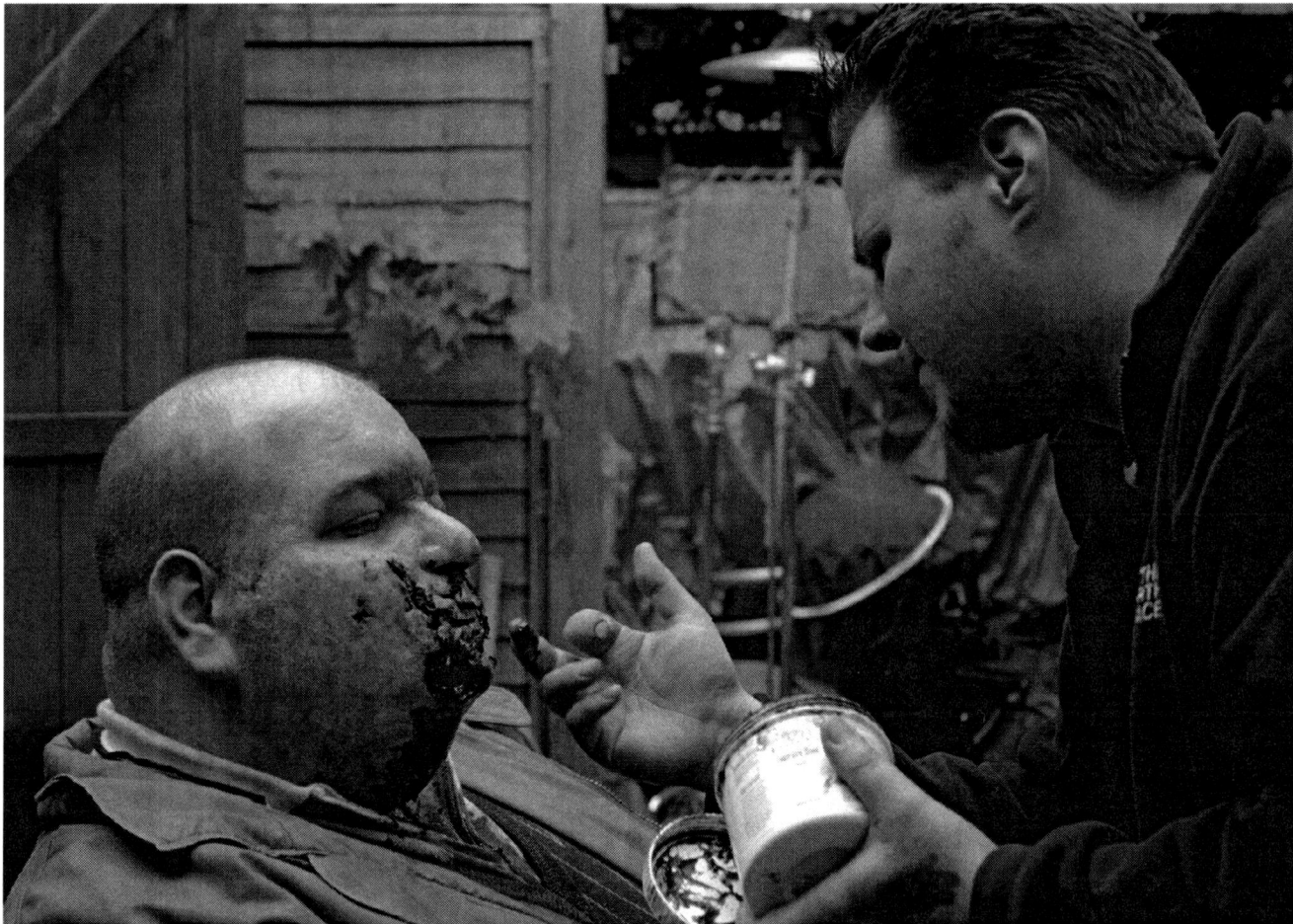

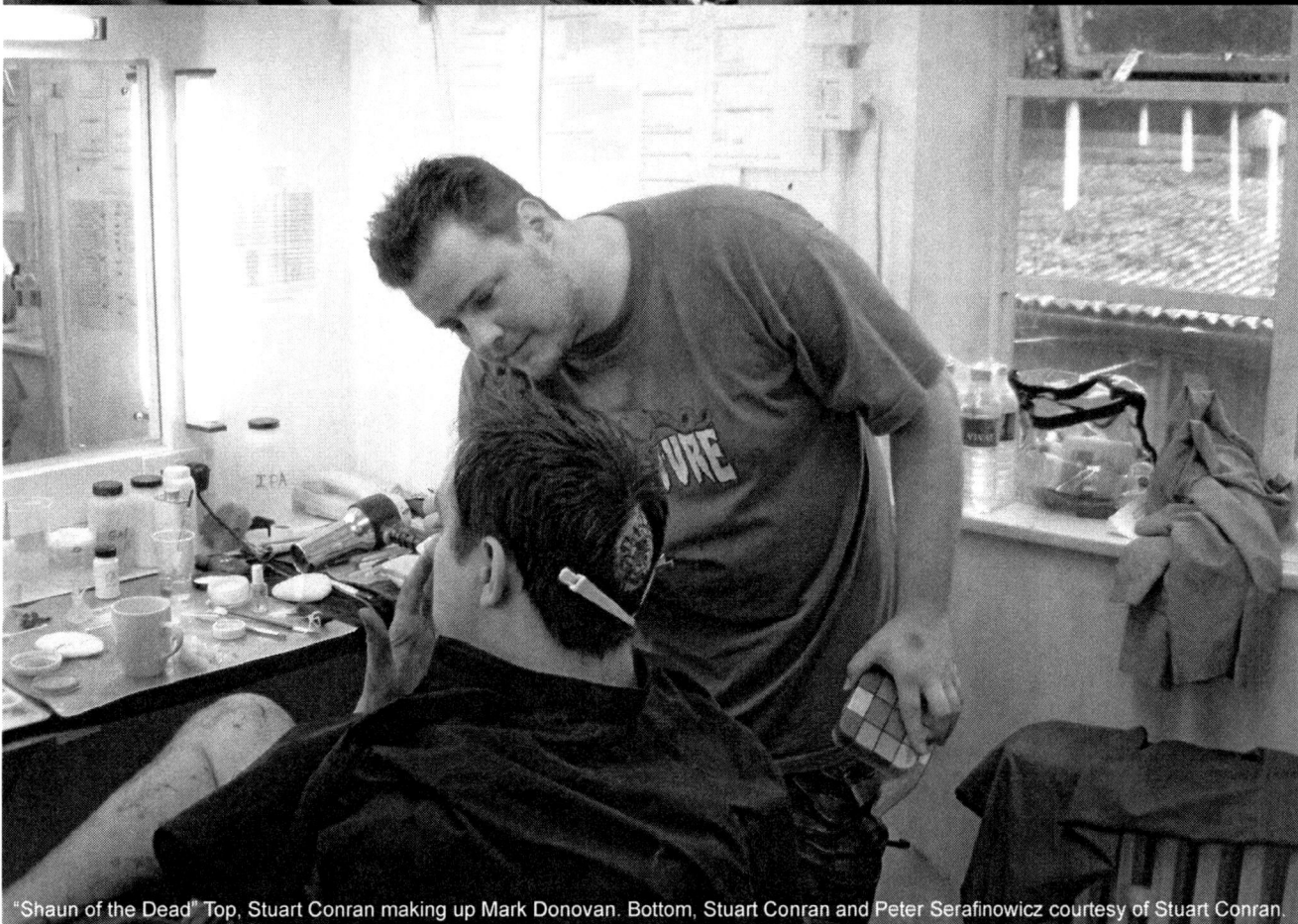

"Shaun of the Dead" Top, Stuart Conran making up Mark Donovan. Bottom, Stuart Conran and Peter Serafinowicz courtesy of Stuart Conran.

229

Sc 109 (5)

SCROAT IS KUNG FU-ED TO PIECES (2)

A FAKE TORSO section, with PULL-OFF LEGS will then be used. The TORSO drops to the ground (shot from behind).

A quick shot of the actor, buried to his waist - his SHOULDER AND THIGH WOUNDS to be dressed.

His head is kicked off - A DUMMY HEAD, pulled off the TORSO SECTION.

The TORSO is kicked into the grave.

NYLONS PULL LEGS OFF DUMMY.

ACTOR BURIED UNDER GROUND TO THIGHS

PUPPETS HEAD PULLED OFF

"Braindead" special effects production sketches courtesy of Stuart Conran.

Sc 150

BARRY'S SKELETAL LEGS

BARRY is pulled through the hole in wall. His legs are chewed away from his HIPS DOWN. Just his SOCKS and SHOES remain, the rest is bone.

The Actor will have his body through a hole in the floor. The FAKE BODY SECTION will start from his arm pits, hooking over his shoulders. The plastic skeleton to be used from the pelvis down.

His FEET will have RODS attached at the back on the HEELS. These rods will provide leg movement.

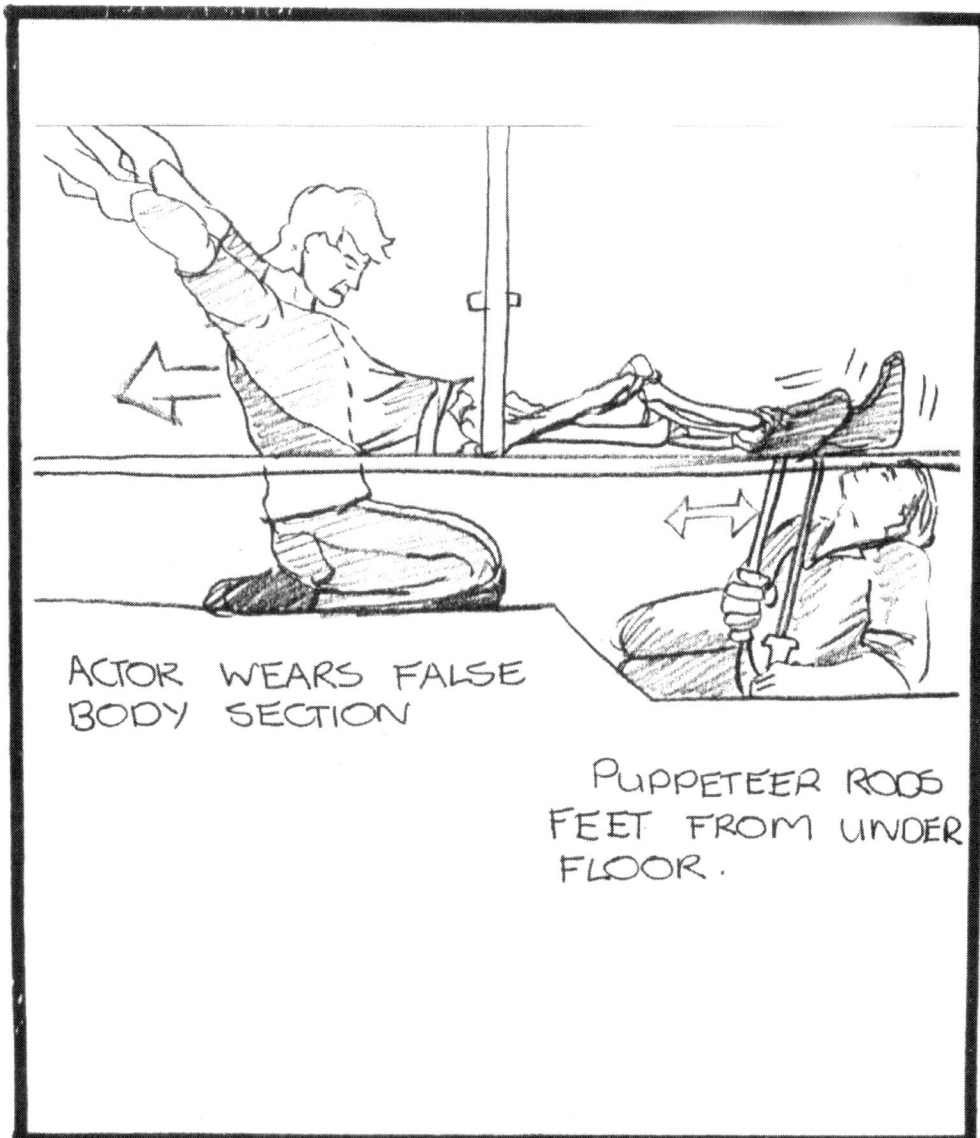

ACTOR WEARS FALSE BODY SECTION

PUPPETEER RODS FEET FROM UNDER FLOOR.

Sc 150 (2)
MANDY'S DEATH

A fist comes punching out of MANDY'S mouth. She has been punched by VOID through the back of her head, from behind. His hand grabs RITA'S face.

DUMMY MANDY head with WIG will be used for initial shot of hand emerging from mouth. Non-articulated head and shoulders.

Back of the head is open. No blood tubes.

FOAM VOID'S HAND to be rigged for the actress to hold in her mouth, under Bob's prosthetic face piece.

MANDY dangles like a puppet from VOID'S hand.

DUMMY BODY with FAKE MANDY HEAD and WIG, to be attached to VOID actor's arm.

PROSTHETIC ARM MOUNTED ON ACTRESS

PUPPET OF MANDY THAT CAN HAVE AN ARM PASSED THROUGH IT.

Sc 162 (3)

LAWRENCE'S HEAD SHEARED IN HALF (3)

3. LAWRENCE'S TOP HALF HEAD.
This is a non-articulated FAKE HEAD. It will be kicked
around, so will have to be quite tough.

4. PARTIAL PROSTHETIC.
This is to simulate LAWRENCE'S HEAD lying on the ground
in close-ups. The real actor's head will be used, with
the top half sticking up through a hole in the set. The
PROSTHETIC PIECE will wrap around his face to provide the
torn flap of skin that rests on the ground.

ROUGH DUMMY VERSION OF LAWRENCES HALF HEAD.

A FACIAL PROSTHETIC IS ADDED TO THE ACTOR, HIS HEAD IS PLACED THROUGH A HOLE IN THE FLOOR.

VOID

For all future VOID EFFECTS, the following will be used:

(All close-ups of the UPPER and LOWER HALVES with use the
REAL ACTOR).

1. REAL ACTOR WITH CHEST RIG.
The Actor will be supported by a skateboard rig on his
feet. He will walk on his hands. A CHEST SECTION will be
built to hang from his shoulders.

This set-up is for low front-on shots only.

ACTOR WALKS ON HIS HANDS
WITH HIS FEET ON A
SKATEBOARD TROLLEY.

FAKE CHEST SECTION
HANGS FROM SHOLDERS

Sc 173

<u>LES DISMEMBERS ZOMBIES</u>

LES chops ZOMBIES up with the meat cleaver in a slightly comical montage.

This effect will be achieved by using MEGA BLOOD TUBES and BODY BITS - ARMS, LEGS and HEADS. SHOULDER RIGS and STUMPS ... all stuff used before.

The last shot will be a wide shot of a PILE OF BODY BITS. Some real, others fake. As many BODY BITS as possible.

Sc 178 (6)
   MOWER MULCHING (1)

   LIONEL chop ZOMBIES with the MOWER.

   These effects will be achieved in several ways:

   1. FAKE MOWER RIGGED WITH BLOOD TUBES.
   For shots from LIONEL'S POV. Seeing the back of the
   mower, with blood flying in all directions.

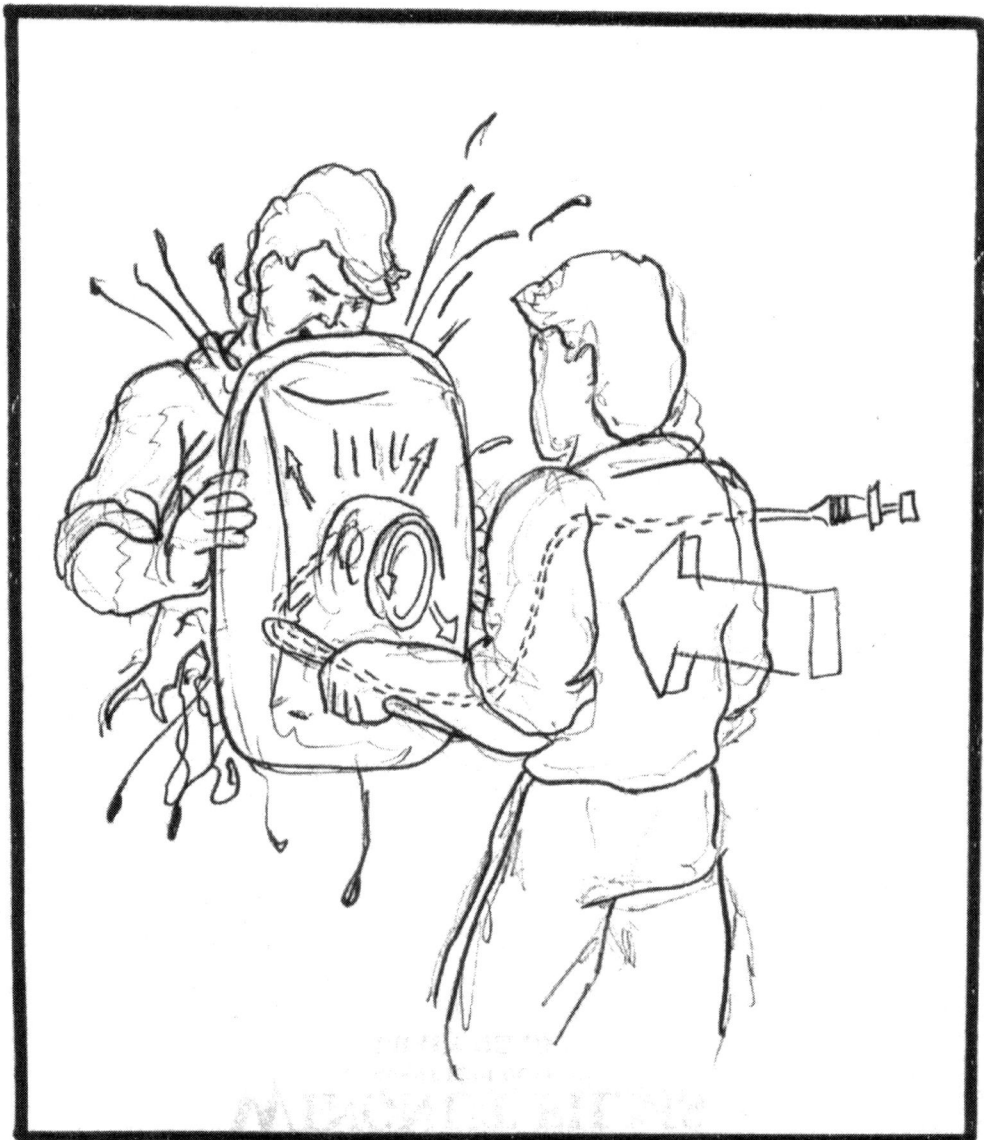

Sc 178 (7)
    MOWER MULCHING (2)

    2. GELATINE BODY BITS.
    For shots of actual contact with the mower blades. These
    body bits rigged with blood and offal to splatter.

Sc 178 (8)
   MOWER MULCHING (3)

    3. FAKE ARMS AND LEGS.
    To be tossed around on cue.

Sc 181

LAWRENCE'S HEAD BLENDED

PAQUITA puts LAWRENCE'S TOP HALF HEAD into the BLENDER
BOWL. We see him staring out through the GLASS. She
flicks the switch. GREEN GOOP splatters the GLASS bowl.
The HEAD vibrates, and sinks into the blades. Bit's fly
out.

The BLENDER BOWL and BODY will have a cut-out hole large
enough for the ACTOR'S HEAD.

TUBES will spurt GOOP against the glass. The ACTOR lowers
his head below the table top, during the shot. CHUNKS of
HEAD are shot out of the BOWL with compressed air during
the shot.

ACTORS HEAD WITH PROSTHETIC FITTED, PLACES HEAD THROUGH HOLE IN BOTTOM OF BLENDER.

ACTOR LOWERS HEAD THROUGH HOLE AS GOO AND BLOOD SQUIRTS AROUND BOWL.

Sc 182

UNCLE LES "SPINE PUPPET"

The ZOMBIE UNCLE LES staggers toward LIONEL. His head
snarls and bobs around on the end of his spine.

PAQUITA uses the CRICKET BAT to knock his head off. It
splatters against the wall like a melon.

ACTOR (possibly an UNCLE LES DOUBLE) has his head tucked
between his arms. The ZOMBIE HEAD PUPPET is ROD and WIRE
and HAND PUPPET controlled. It is non-articulated.

The REAL UNCLE LES will be used for close ups, with a
small neck prosthetic.

MELISSA COWAN

• The Walking Dead (2010) Bicycle Girl

Blood Splatter: How did you get into the zombie genre?

Melissa Cowan: I didn't specifically go looking to be in the zombie genre to be perfectly honest, it was something that just happened. I have always been a big zombie fan and I love watching zombie movies, so when the chance came up, I jumped at it.

BS: How did you get the role of Bicycle Girl? Did you audition for it explicitly or was it offered to you?

MC: One of the casting companies that I had been working with for a while called me out of the blue one day and requested pictures of me in a bikini. I sent in the pictures and didn't hear anything back for two weeks. In the meantime I was searching everything I could find about a zombie show that was in pre-production in Atlanta. I came across an article on *The Walking Dead*, but still didn't know for sure if that was it or not. Two more weeks go by and I heard nothing. Then out of the blue they call me back and said the director likes my look and would like for me to come in for an audition. They stated he was flying in from Los Angeles the next day to meet me. At this point, I still didn't know what show this was for or who was even behind it. So I get to the audition all dolled up and they hand me the script for the first episode. As I sat there reading it, some of the names on the script started standing out to me and I knew it was going to be big. Frank Darabont's name is the obvious one that stood out the most. Much to my surprise, a few minutes later, guess who comes and gets me? I knew that I was going to have to blow this audition out of the water. I had always wanted to work with Frank.

BS: How was the interview?

MC: It went really well and afterwards we sat around and talked for a while. I remember he said two things that completely made my day. The first being that I was too pretty for this role and they had their work cut out for them. The second thing he said within minutes of meeting me was that it was like love at first sight. I knew I had the part before I even left. We were already talking about me traveling to Los Angeles and what would be expected of me. I thought it was funny, because on my way home, I called my casting agent and told them it went really well and that I felt I pretty much got the role and I'll be going to Los Angeles the following week. He told me to calm down and he'd let me know something when knew for sure. Not even a minute after we hung up the phone, my phone rang and it was my agent. He laughed and told me I was right and congratulations. I felt honored and happy to have been chosen for this role out of all of the people that submitted and auditioned for it. In the beginning I had no idea that it would be this big or get this much recognition. I am very happy with the outcome.

BS: Can you tell us about how the makeup process went for bicycle girl?

MC: The makeup process for Bicycle Girl was awesome. It was a very long and insightful process. They flew me out to Los Angeles for a few days, which is where the makeup process started. There I got to work with literally some of best in the business. The first step was to complete a full body cast, which was done of my face, neck, back and torso. The molding process was, in my opinion the most interesting part of it all. They did the molding in stages with the head being the most entertaining. I would compare that experience to being buried alive. It was pretty neat. Also while I was in Los Angeles, I had the mold of my mouth and teeth made up so I could have custom zombie teeth. Which they let keep after shooting had been completed.

I went out to Los Angeles in May 2010 and we started filming in June. KNB EFX did a phenomenal job on every aspect, They totally surpassed every vision that I had in my head of this and when I finally saw the pieces coming together, I couldn't believe it. I remember each makeup fitting or test, I was speechless and even on the day of filming, I was speechless. That was when I knew that this was huge. Once we got on set the day of filming, it was a long process. I arrived on set around four in the morning, ate breakfast and then the real journey began.

The makeup process from start to finish took about four and a half hours. A lot of people ask me if it was hard sitting there for that long, but in all actuality, it really wasn't. At any given moment there would be anywhere from two to six people working on me, which leads to good laughs and good conversations, as you would imagine. There was never a dull or boring moment and the time actually went by pretty fast. It was a great learning experience for me and was very rewarding. I had done other bit parts in horror TV shows and movies before, but this was the most elaborate yet.

Now as far as the makeup applications and the way they felt, that's a whole new chapter. The three pieces were not that heavy, but given the heat and humidity it made it very interesting and unforgettable. I had on the three big pieces, the face, back and torso and smaller prosthetics all over my body and of course all of those pieces were covered in makeup as well, so it was sticky, itchy and hot. Even those things combined there was no reason to complain. I literally had a smile on my face all day. I just went with the flow and let things run their course.

BS: Would you do it again?

MC: I would do it again in a heartbeat, even under the exact same circumstances. Hell, I would do it under worse conditions. We filmed for pretty much the entire day and did all of my scenes. In between takes and in between breaks they were constantly touching up the makeup, prosthetics and making sure everything was perfect. I must say they all did an outstanding job, given the conditions with the heat and humidity. I am sure that a lot of the makeup and stuff was melting as well as rubbing off when I was crawling around on the ground.

BS: Were you wearing contacts or were the eyes CGI?

MC: My eyes were actually contacts and they were very thick. They were custom fitted and covered my entire eye. They looked a lot different from the contacts that the other zombies wear. Wearing the contacts was fun and different and I actually had to have a navigator to guide me around and lead me as they were very cloudy and difficult to see out of. I could only see maybe a hands length in front of me when I had them in. During shooting, they had to keep putting drops on my eyes because the contacts were drying them out.

BS: Other than the legs, was anything else CGI?

MC: No, there wasn't much CGI used at all. Some of the gunshot wound was digitally enhanced though.

BS: How many times did they make you up for it?

MC: I was only made up one complete time as Bicycle Girl. We filmed all of my scenes in one day, which explains the long hours. Could you imagine having to go through a four and half hour process every day or multiple times? That would be really interesting, but I would do it though. However, there were a few make up tests, fittings and other things that we had to do, but that was just to make sure everything fit and looked good for the day of filming.

BS: Bicycle Girl featured heavily on promotional artwork such as posters. Were you involved in any of the photo shoots?

MC: Actually, there was a green screen on set the day we filmed. We completed the photo shoot the same day as filming. The makeup was exactly the same, but there were some minor digital enhancements added afterwards.

BS: You play multiple zombies in *The Walking Dead*, how did the makeup process vary between those characters and Bicycle Girl?

MC: It was completely different each time I was made up. This ranged from the techniques used to apply the makeup to the types of prosthetics used. It was also a lot faster to be made up as a background zombie. All of the other zombies that I played and pretty much all of the other zombies on set, only went through a short makeup process that lasted anywhere from twenty minutes to an hour.

GINO CROGNALE

- The Walking Dead (2011) Special Effects Makeup Artist
- The Rage (2011) Key Makeup Artist
- Planet Terror (2007) On-set Special Makeup Effects Artist
- Land of the Dead (2005) On-set Special Makeup Effects Artist

Blood Splatter: How did you get into the zombie genre?

Gino Crognale: As a special effects artist, the fun part of the job is doing zombie films. It allows us to get creative and a zombie film is something that we all want to do at some point in our career. I've been at KNB EFX since 1990 and Greg Nicotero and myself were working on *Sin City* in 2004. He comes up to me and asked if I wanted to spend the fall in Toronto working on zombies for *Land of the Dead*. It was one of those moments and there really wasn't even an answer needed. First of all it's George Romero and second of all, it's zombies. At some point in your career, you have to do a zombie movie. Right now I am working on *Oz* and creating Munchkins and all the film staples, but I just came off of *The Walking Dead* and I really miss it. The ability to change who ever sits in your chair is just simply amazing. You can use generic appliances and makeup and turn each actor into something unique and terrifying.

BS: Do you have a favorite zombie movie?

GC: My favorite zombie film is the original *Dawn of the Dead*. It has such a memorable place in my life. I was in high school when it came out and I was on the hunt to learn about make up effects. Tom Savini's work on that film was pivotal in my decision to pursue this art as a career. I can't thank Tom enough.

BS: Are you given guidelines to what the dead should look like when you take on a project?

GC: We are given a general idea as to what they should look like. There are some general guidelines in place with *The Walking Dead*. We would exaggerate some features and appliances, but there is definitely a look that *The Walking Dead* has that we are instructed to stick with. They should be skinny and have sunken in features. You are given the framework and you create something to fit in that world.

BS: What do you use as inspiration as varying degrees of decay and damage?

GC: For years we would use forensic books. Tom Savini had a lot of great books for us to use when we were first starting out. A lot of these books show decomposition and trauma to the body. You could see how the wounds would open up and the color they would turn. I think everyone from our generation did the same thing and that allowed us to get a foundation of reference materials and then just go from there. We dramatize the wounds too and add something cool to the look. Then you inspire others who take something from what you have done and they take it a step further. That's how it progresses but it's all kept within the realm of the human condition.

BS: Is it difficult to distance yourself because the effects do resemble real life so closely?

GC: I am in my twenty sixth year of doing this, so I am really past having any issues seeing the effects first hand. I love this job. It's cool and it's a lot of fun. Years ago when I was on *Texas Chainsaw Massacre 2* with Tom Savini, I had to sculpt a character who was completely skinned in the movie. Back then, I had Tom's forensics books and I was physically sculpting right out of the book. I was doing my best to make it anatomically correct. That was rather creepy when all is said and done. Now it's gotten to the point where it doesn't bother me at all. I suppose you could say I'm desensitized, but if I saw something in real life that was that damaged, I would probably completely freak out. We know in the realm of film that making it look real and cool is what we are shooting for. In the film business we can enhance things and trump them up a bit to make them look even better on film. I think that is a really great thing to do. A lot of it is painting and finishing touches that add blood and pus and details like that.

BS: Which is your favorite kill in a movie you worked on?

GC: We had some great kills in *Land of the Dead*. One that I worked on was the priest zombie. It had a flip top head rig, which bit down after it was severed. I think it turned out pretty cool and was very different for the time.

BS: So how about your favorite scene from a film you weren't involved in.

GC: One of my favorite zombie kills would be helicopter zombie in *Dawn of the Dead*. I remember seeing for the first time and I didn't see that coming. Like everyone, I thought the copter noise would lead to David Emgee getting bit. When the top of the head flies off the zombie and he falls to the ground, that was awesome.

I love a lot of the stuff that John Vulich and Everett Burrell did on the remake of *Night of the Living Dead*. They did some really great stuff there. I loved the really skinny zombie they did. As far as the kills, I love all of Savini's stuff in *Dawn of the Dead*. I think those first bites that he did over thirty years ago are still really effective. Tom did some really great stuff there. When we did *Land of the Dead*, Greg wanted to take the bite scene even further. We designed these bite plates that we put on the actors and I felt that they worked really well in the film. There is a scene early in the film when they are in the store and the guy gets bitten on the arm while reaching for some cigars. I played the cop zombie who bites him and the arm is actually Greg's. Greg staged the whole scene and I think it was a really effective gag. We basically took Tom's original idea and updated it with newer materials and techniques that Tom didn't have access to at the time.

BS: Is it common for special effects artists to be involved in close up effects shots like that?

GC: Absolutely. A lot of directors will trust our opinion and in some cases will let us stage it. This allows us to hide the tubes and blood packets. Some director's feel like they are losing control if they can't set up all of their scenes, but it really helps us when we can do it. We know how it is going to work. We've built it and tested it and so we know the gag better than anybody. Greg is really good with staging and I think that is why *The Walking Dead* has been turning out so well.

BS: Are you surprised they have been able to get away with as much as they have on *The Walking Dead*?

GC: I don't know if I am surprised, just because television is where it is now. I'm pleased to see them taking these chances on the screen and I think that's great. Kudos to AMC for allowing the envelope to be pushed. Everyone who appreciates our genre can now have it in their house. It's not something reserved for movies anymore. It is a genuine zombie film in episodic form.

BS: You were the police officer in *Land of the Dead* and the bartender in *Undead or Alive*. Do you enjoy the makeup process?

GC: I love doing it. It's one of those opportunities where we build these effects and appliances and we've been putting it on actors for years, so when we're given the chance to be on screen, it's awesome. I could do it forever. Greg asked me to be on *The Walking Dead* this season, but my schedule wouldn't work, so hopefully next year. It's one of the coolest things to experience.

BS: Why do you think it is more acceptable to portray violence against zombies than it is against humans?

GC: I think it's just because they represent death. If we were in that situation and these dead things were walking around, we'd take some joy in killing them. They belong to no one. The rule is you have to kill the brain, so the death naturally becomes violent.

BS: Have there been any effects shots that made it in the final versions that surprised you?

GC: No. Pretty much everything we create gets shot. What the viewer sees on the film is probably twenty percent of the actual scene. We get to see everything being shot in its most raw form and it happens before the editing takes place. The camera rolls on before and after the scene, so I have seen pretty much everything there is. They cut away for actor reactions and other establishing shots, so what I see is just part of the whole. These films are the cornerstone of our careers. We want the gore in there as much as the fans do. You have to deliver, but you have to do it to a point without the MPAA crucifying your movie. It's a really fine line to walk.

BS: What are your thoughts on the genre including the viral and plague style films of late?

GC: I love them. I think these types of films are fun. They really add to the whole apocalyptic feel that is so important to a zombie film. You are thrown together with a bunch of people you don't know and you have to figure out and survive this thing. As far as the gore goes, it comes hand in hand with this type of film. There are no rules anymore. Anything goes. You have to kill with whatever you can get your hands on. It's how it would be. It's cool that these filmmakers are setting up these scenarios. Even *Shaun of the Dead* which is a comedy is realistic of how people would be.

BS: Do you think the genre is reflection on social fears?

GC: I think it does go hand in hand. Even George's original films pertained to the times. I think filmmakers have to play in that arena. It's what is relevant to the world. I think when films draw on these ideas and fears and dramatize them, it is a good narrative. *Contagion* is a great example of how these things spread. When you're watching a film like *28 Days Later* and there is a chance it could really happen, it makes you think. The familiar makes you think and it's a great tool to have at our disposal.

BS: Do you find yourself gravitating towards CGI to enhance practical shots?

GC: CGI is a great tool. When it works, it really works and it's a great supplement to traditional prosthetics. Merging the two can produce spectacular results. Take a look a Bicycle Girl from the first season of *The Walking Dead*. Without using CGI she is just another decayed zombie. With it, she is missing her legs and I don't think it would have had the same impact without it. In the right context it can be a very helpful tool.

BS: Effects artists are known for using non-conventional methods to achieve new effects on camera. What tricks have you used?

GC: A non-conventional technique I like is using panty hose for skin. When it is stretched you can paint it, add blood to it and it will tear and dangle like torn flesh. To be honest, a lot of the tricks that we use are based on the old school effects. They just work and you don't fix what isn't broken.

BS: Can you tell us about some of the effects you have done for *Planet Terror*?

GC: We did tons of zombie type makeup effects and they were all infected. Robert Rodriguez was very specific about the bubbly skin and giant skin tumors. Every night we were making up stunt guys and each other. In that movie I got to play a zombie eating the brain of a cop lying on a police car. It's a quick shot, but it's there. We also worked on Quentin Tarantino's transformation and when Tom Savini was pulled apart by zombies.

BS: Were these shots all prosthetics?

GC: Absolutely. Everything we did was physical. Both Robert and Quentin are very much into that and prefer the traditional effects over using CGI. They are really old school filmmakers. Every film I have done with them has been the same way. It's cool for us as it puts the ball in our court and we have to deliver.

BS: Do you think you get better performances from actors when they have something tangible to work with on screen?

GC: I really do. I think actors need something physical to respond to as it is part of their craft. I know some actors have made the adjustment because they are put in that situation so much, that they are used to working with nothing. I've seen it first hand with some really good actors struggling to give a strong performance with nothing in front of them. If you have a good monster scare, you are going to get a better reaction from an actor if a monster jumps out of the dark as opposed to expecting them to react to a green screen.

BS: How do you handle conflict if a director insists on an effect or makeup appliance you find artistically or morally offensive?

GC: It can be really tough at times. You always try your best to work with the director, but ultimately they must have the final say. There have been a lot of times where they have asked me for certain things that I don't agree with, but you have to take a step back and realize that this is what they are paying for and the director always has the final say. If you become difficult, you get a reputation and you won't work as much.

BS: Are there any new zombie films for you?

GC: *The Walking Dead* season three.

BS: Can you share a funny story from any of the zombie movies you have worked on?

GC: I actually don't have any I can repeat from the zombie genre, but I have a really good one from *Texas Chainsaw Massacre 2*. We were shooting a scene in a parking garage and the gag was Leatherface was fighting some college students. The scene got cut ultimately, but this guy was in a "roach coach" and sticks his hand out to give Leatherface the middle finger and his hand is cut off. We found a guy who was an amputee and we attached a fake arm. Tom Savini and I were in the "roach coach", I am holding the arm and Tom is pumping the blood. The camera was set up but they could see me and Tom, so we tucked in really tight and they yelled action. The second they start shooting, Tom starts yelling. They cut the arm and we start pumping blood and the whole time Tom is yelling like something is wrong. As soon as we ducked down, Tom hit the lever of the coffee machine and the entire time he is getting scolding hot coffee pouring down his leg. The poor guy had to sit there and take it for the entire scene. He had on a pair of white painters pants and they were stained all the down the side. He had been in agony for the entire scene.

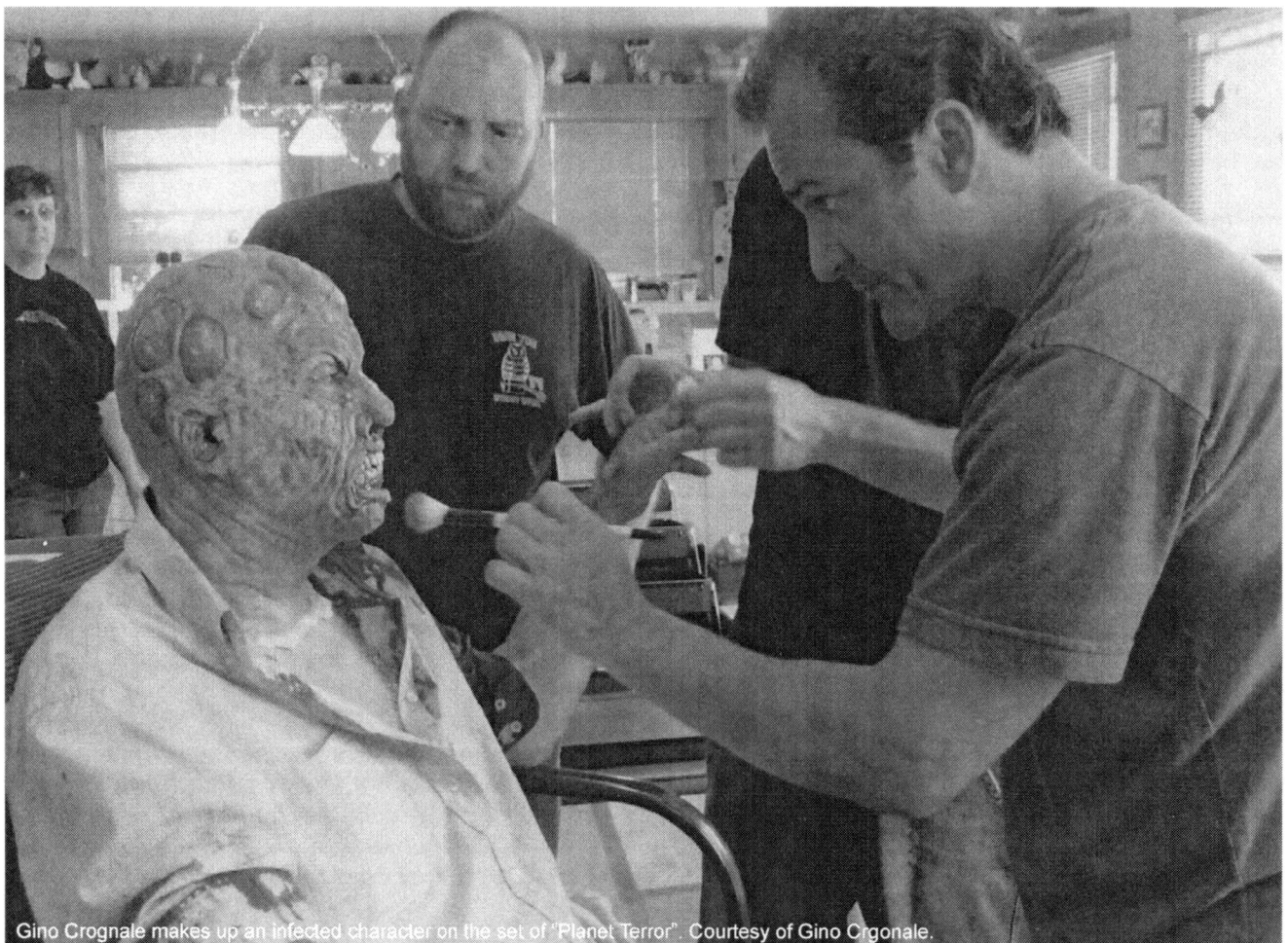

Gino Crognale makes up an infected character on the set of "Planet Terror". Courtesy of Gino Crgonale.

ANDREW CURRIE

• Fido (2006) Director, Writer

Blood Splatter: *Fido* is obviously created by someone who loves zombies, how did you get into the genre?

Andrew Currie: I think it was seeing Romero's original *Night of the Living Dead* at a midnight screening when I was a teenager. It screwed me up so much, but in a good way of course. I couldn't get some of the images out of my head, especially the girl zombie killing her mother in the cellar. I liked how the black guy getting shot in the head at the end by this all-white posse suddenly turned the movie into something political. Later Romero made more directly political films like *Dawn of the Dead* and *Day of the Dead*, which were really inspiring to me. In fact Bub from *Day of the Dead* really inspired the character of *Fido*. I even shot a scene that was an homage to Bub, that ended up cut out of them movie. It was *Fido* in a barn. He sees a razor and picks it up and tries to shave, which Bub did in *Day of the Dead*.

BS: Up until *Fido* you had mostly worked in television and shorts. Was it your intention to work on a zombie movie as your first wide release?

AC: I was always focused more on features than anything. It just takes time to develop them, especially when you're writing them as well. I didn't specifically set out to make a zombie movie. I had made a short film *Night of the Living* through the Canadian Film Centre. It was about a kid who was an avid horror fan, with a vivid imagination. His alcoholic dad goes off the wagon and when the boy sees his dad drunk, he thinks his father's turned into a zombie. He tries to connect with the zombie, feeds him raw meat and that kind of thing. It combined drama and horror and some humor and I really liked how it turned out. It got me excited about the whole idea of cross-genre and how that could work.

BS: Were you expecting *Fido* to have such a loyal following in the zombie community?

AC: The support I've received has been amazing. I really appreciated the fact that even gore lovers embraced it. *Fido* is obviously a different type of zombie movie in the sense that it's not trying to be frightening. The focus was really on the humor and on taking a satirical look at George Bush's reign of fear based politics. I really felt that zombies were a perfect metaphor for that kind of satire. The parallels between the zombies in *Fido* and the issue of illegal immigration were really fun to draw on and hopefully got people thinking and talking a bit. With what's going on in Arizona that issue's probably more relevant now then it was a few years ago.

BS: Do you have a favorite zombie film?

AC: There are so many great ones, but I'd still pick *Night of the Living Dead* because it defined the genre and was made with such direct, visceral power. Even though it was made in the 1960's it still blows me away today, which is pretty amazing.

BS: Were any other titles considered for the movie?

AC: We knocked around a few, but nothing great. In Japan the distributor called it *Zombino*, which I thought was pretty funny. The artwork for the Japanese release was very weird but really great.

BS: How closely did the final film follow the original script?

AC: We went through a lot of drafts of the script, so it changed a lot. Although it's close to the script we went into production with. I did cut out a pretty long subplot that had a really big 'boy and his dog' theme, where Timmy and Fido go on a road trip together. It was a good thing to cut because it made the film way too slow, but I still liked it. After Fido gets into trouble, Timmy and Fido run away. They walk all night, then hide in a barn. In the morning Timmy wakes up and discovers Fido eating a farmer. It makes Timmy realize that he can't keep Fido, so he takes him to a river, which is the border into the wild zone and forces him to leave by throwing rocks at him. Of course Fido won't go and Timmy goes into the river after him and nearly drowns. Fido rescues Timmy and takes him back home. It was classic 'boy and his dog' stuff that I really liked, but there was enough of that in the movie already and it really made the movie lag in the middle so we cut it out. It is in the DVD extras though.

BS: Horror-comedies walk a very fine line trying to balance humor and scares and *Fido* certainly succeeds in this area. Does this make filming a horror-comedy more challenging?

AC: I think horror-comedy is a really tough genre, mainly because there's always a line you need to draw between the two. Do you push more into horror, or more into comedy? Whatever path you choose you're going to alienate some people and have others embrace it even more. I wanted to focus more on the dead pan humor of the world and the characters, so I put the line closer to the comedy than horror.

BS: *Fido* is known for having bright and vibrant colors. Were these deliberately enhanced to contrast the bleakness and desolation of the "Wild Zone"?

AC: Yes. From the very beginning I had this idyllic small town Americana in my head. I loved the idea of having this sweet innocent world, juxtaposed with zombie violence and blood. The colors really helped sell that 1950's innocence and I wanted the wild zone to be harsher and much more real. We shot in the interior of British Columbia and the wild zone was actually a huge area that had been obliterated by wild fires, so it felt like a really appropriate place to shoot those scenes. I was really lucky to color time *Fido* at the Warner Bros. post facility in Los Angeles. They had this amazing facility, but only did their own movies at that time. They decided to open it up to independents as well and I think we were the first. We had Jan Yarbrough and Ray Grabowski as colorists and they had just done a bunch of research on the Technicolor look for *The Aviator* and really knew how to achieve the look I wanted. It made it so much easier and so much better in the end.

BS: How much involvement did you have on the design of the zombies?

AC: I was heavily involved in all the design aspects of the movie. It really was a labor of love type project, so it was great to be that involved. We went through a lot of different issues with the look of the zombies and decided to follow a very specific logic. We rated the zombies depending on what work they were intended for. So household, domestic zombies would be rated a one. They'd be the most attractive zombies, no missing body parts and facial disfigurations. The number two zombies would be rougher, maybe a missing eye, or a few lesions. They would do other work within the community and number three zombies were the factory workers. They could be really rotting with open lesion, but as long as they could still do their jobs it was okay.

BS: What is your favorite scene in the movie?

AC: I tend to be pretty hard on my own work, so it's tough to answer that. I probably like the scene when Timmy finds Fido eating the old lady next door the best, or where he has to kill her with a garden shovel. I also like the sequence when Timmy is tied to a tree and telling Fido to go for help. I really like that idea of a boy and his dog movie for adults and I think those scenes both really captured that.

BS: How do you direct a lead actor who has no lines, especially someone as animated as Billy Connolly?

AC: It's pretty hilarious. Billy is such a talker and so funny. He had us constantly howling between takes. Directing actors is pretty much the same whether they have lines or not, it's so much about motivation. The fun thing about Fido as a character is his motivations were much more than the average zombie, he was protective of Timmy and attracted to Mom, so it was fun to watch Billy pull that off.

BS: Were there any other scenes or graphic shots that didn't make it past the censors?

AC: The MPAA were really hard on us and gave us an R-rating. They kept telling me how much they loved the movie, but that it was just too gory by a few frames. For a month or so we tried to make changes to drop the rating, but they kept asking for more and more, it felt like borrowing money from a loan shark who keeps upping the amount you owe. So eventually we just said fuck it and went with the R-rating.

BS: Many directors and effects artists give themselves cameos as zombies in their films. How about you?

248

AC: I'm one of those guys who usually likes to stay behind the camera. In this case though, I did want to be a zombie getting shot in the head. However, production was so consuming I never had the time to get into makeup and dressed with squibs, so I didn't get the chance in the end.

BS: Are there any other zombie films in the future for you?

AC: I love zombie movies and so many good ones have come on lately that it feels a little flooded, but I'd like to. We've been in development with Lionsgate to do *Fido* as a TV series down the road, so we'll see where that ends up. Right now I'm heading into pre-production on an R-rated comedy called *My Asshole Neighbor*, which I'm really excited about.

BS: Can you share any funny on set stories from *Fido*?

AC: We laughed a lot during the shoot. One incident I remember is when we had Fido tossing one of the kids into the forest. We had this short stunt guy dressed as a little boy and our stunt Fido tossing him. He really launched him a long way and the stunt guy did this little moan that made us all crack up. There's a scene when the Dad played by Dylan Baker is going golfing alone. Timmy asks him if other dad's take their kids golfing. Dylan's line was "no, no they don't", then he leaves. However, instead Dylan said "yes, yes they do" and then leaves. It was so funny in the moment, but unfortunately didn't work in the edit. There was one time when Billy Connolly's manager came out from New York. He was a very classy guy and Billy had blood bags hidden in his mouth. He walked up to his manager to say hi, while biting on them. It was hilarious watching the reaction and how happy it made Billy to get it. He really is such a great clown. Also, after we finished shooting I was doing an additional dialogue recording session for Fido's moans and groans. Billy was in Australia doing his stand up tour, so we had to do it over an audio link only. I was in Vancouver and Billy was in Australia, looking at a monitor with the footage. I started trying to talk him through what I needed and it became really obvious that it was a bad idea to do it this way. Billy openly mocked the process, then we laughed, then he did a bunch of experimental moans and groans and roars.

BS: If you heard on the news that the dead have risen, how would you fair in the zombie apocalypse?

AC: Probably not too well. I'm Canadian so I don't own a gun, or really know how to use one. That and I never plan ahead, so I'd have to go out for food and supplies, which would be risky. On the other hand I am naturally paranoid, which is a good thing in a zombie apocalypse. I run really fast. I'm not sure. Yeah, I think I'd get killed pretty quickly.

Andrew Currie directs Carrie-Anne Moss on the set of "Fido" courtesy of Andrew Currie.

TONY GARDNER

- Zombieland (2009) Special Makeup Effects Supervisor
- The Return of the Living Dead (1985) Uncredited
- Michael Jackson's Thriller (1983) Special Makeup Effects Artist

Blood Splatter: How did you get involved in the zombie genre?

Tony Gardner: I guess you could say I got thrown into it. I was hired by Rick Baker to work on Michael Jackson's *Thriller* music video while I was still in college. I didn't know what the concept of the music video was at the time, I was just excited to have been offered a job in the industry. I was a student at USC and I was offered the job at the end of summer vacation. I was given four weeks of work on *Thriller*, which stretched out into eight weeks once filming was done. Thanks to the fact that I was able to go on set as well as be in the video, I was able gain some great insights on how the industry works in many areas, all within that one project. The entire experience gave me a great perspective and came at a time in my life when I was trying to decide what I wanted to do with my future.   I have always been a fan of the zombie genre, so this was a great opportunity and a wonderful way to start. The greatest part was that the project ended with me continuing to work for Rick Baker for another four years. It was the best "on the job" training anyone could ever ask for.

BS: How was your experience on *Thriller*?

TG: As far as *Thriller* went, it was a lot of long hours working late into the night at the shop, but I loved every minute of it. It was a very enjoyable experience with a lot of great people. Rick had all of these great ideas and designs, but he also gave his crew a lot of artistic freedom as well. We all built zombie characters of ourselves and we were able to be in the music video as those characters. What was nice was that all of the artists on the makeup effects crew brought a different style to their individual zombies, which made for an interesting collection of undead characters. Everyone on the makeup effects crew was as enthusiastic about the project as I was. The best part though, was that I was able to be involved in the entire experience from the designing and creating, to the application and then even the performing on set. It was a really exciting time for me.

While I was working on *Thriller*, I had started building a corpse prop in my free time. I had been helping build makeup appliances and masks for performers to wear in order to create zombie characters. I wanted to try to do something different and take some of my zombie ideas even further. The finished dead body prop that I built was a very emaciated upper body torso of a dead female with long blond hair. I took some pictures of it and a few months later I happened to have those photos with me when I was asked to go to a meeting with Dan O'Bannon at his house to talk to him about a film called *The Return of the Living Dead*. We were meeting to talk about dentures for Brian Peck and Beverly Randolph who played Scuz and Tina respectively. Those those photographs lead to Dan asking me to build the animatronic half corpse character for his film. That actually worked out so well that it eventually lead to other films and makeup effects opportunities in the industry for me. It is weird to think that dead bodies opened the door for me, but that is how it happened. It was an unexpected launch to my career.

BS: Do you have a favorite zombie film?

TG: I wouldn't say I have a favorite film, but I do have a lot of favorite moments. I love Griffin Dunne's character in *An American Werewolf in London* hanging out in the movie theater and having a casual conversation with David Naughton while he's rotting away to nothing. I find that there are certain images or scenes like that one that really stand out and stick with me more than just an entire film most of the time. The first *Friday the 13th* movie was so "in your face" with shocking makeup effects and had some really great visual images. Kevin Bacon on his bunk getting impaled with an arrow, in particular. It was completely unexpected and so well done. I tend to remember those moments more than complete movies more often than not. Those early Tom Savini films seemed to all have at least one of those "What the...?" makeup effects moments in each one of them.

BS: It was a twenty five year gap between filming *The Return of the Living Dead* and *Zombieland*, was this a conscious delay?

TG: Not at all. I love doing zombie movies, but unfortunately there just weren't any zombie movie projects coming my way, so nothing happened.

BS: How did you get involved with *Zombieland*?

TG: Ruben Fleischer who directed the film, had already produced a couple of MTV shows that my company Alterian Inc. had been asked to provide makeup effects for. We had also both worked with the folks from MTV's *Jackass* and Ruben had also seen some of our prosthetics work there. Ruben and I talked a bit, but not in depth regarding any particular future projects. He came across as a very level-headed producer who definitely knew how to shoot things. He was a fan of the zombie genre too, which was great. A year later he was putting together a crew for his directorial debut, *Zombieland* and we sat down then to discuss different zombie concepts and we just clicked. We had both pulled some reference materials of what we were interested in doing for his film and it turned out that we were completely in synch on direction and execution.

BS: On more than one occasion you have been investigated by the F.B.I for the realism of your effects. Has this affected your career in anyway?

TG: *(laughs)* It certainly has not affected it a negative way at all. It is a little nerve-wracking being approached by someone with a gun and a badge and being questioned while you're trying to work, but I actually look at it as a compliment to the realism of my effects. It certainly validates that I am doing a good job, in my opinion at least. It is definitely an extreme reaction, but we do our special effects to get reactions. When *127 Hours* was released, audiences were really shocked with the makeup effects sequences and some people were even passing out. As the person responsible for the makeup effects, my immediate response was to feel really bad that someone had reacted in that way. Half a second later that feeling was overtaken by the relief that we were able to accomplish such a realistic effects sequence. The truth is, what makes a makeup effect succeed isn't necessarily just how great that particular effects is, it really depends on how those effects are presented to the audience that has the most impact and defines their reaction. I have been fortunate to have had some really great responses to my effects work and that is a wonderful feeling. However, it's also necessary to acknowledge the director's presentation of the effect, the actor's ability to make you relate to the effect and sometimes even the sound effect that adds the audio punch to your visual image.

BS: You've been around a lot of blood and gore in your career. Does it become difficult to separate yourself from the realism of the effects?

TG: I personally have to look at reference material from a more artistic or aesthetic perspective, otherwise the case study that I'm referencing and the emotional involvement of the people involved in the case study can get me a little overwhelmed. I'm not one to watch surgery for reference, I think I would probably pass out. In fact I know I would. If I can find a way to distance myself I will. Then I can handle the reality and the content of what I am looking at. I always try to review reference material in the context of the specifics that I need at that moment for that particular effect. I try to focus on muscle color or anatomy or whatever is most relevant for the stage of work we're in at the moment, but it's a hard thing to do. I wouldn't make it in the real world. I've seen some of this carnage in real life and it is completely different from the anatomy books. At a first look, my reaction is that the colors and the textures of the materials in these close up photos I'm looking at are fascinating. Then I'm told that I'm looking at the torso of a person that died from stab wounds received at a kid's birthday party and the experience becomes all too real and a bit overwhelming for me. Suddenly the almost-abstract image in the medical photo becomes a human being and not just a point of reference. That is when it can really get to you.

BS: Have you ever done makeup effects on friends or family members?

TG: That is an interesting thing too. I make up my kids a lot and I've used my daughter in a few shoots. My oldest, Brianna, was in the film *Shallow Hal* when she was seven years old and I had to design and apply a burn makeup on her. The context of the film was sort of a stylized reality, as the movie was a comedy and we were trying to lighten the impact of the burn a bit. To see your child made up like this makes you really appreciate the fact that your kid is alive and healthy and well. There is this switch that flips on and off in your head as a parent. Part of the time you are applying the makeup and watching the edges and making sure the color looks correct in the light. Then the switch flips and you're the parent and you're worried about your child. Watching other people react to her is really interesting. They'll be afraid for her or be scared to even talk to her. It is really powerful watching how a person reacts to an injured child.

I was directing a Daft Punk music video and I had Brianna in a body suit which made it look like she has no skin, but it was also really stylized. I still found it hard to look at her and had to disconnect to be able to finish the job. I'm also working on the effects for a video about drunk driving and my youngest daughter Kyra, who will wear pretty much anything, will be in it. This one is really disturbing for me due to the realism of the effects required, as well as the scenario my daughter will be involved with. I think if you lose yourself in the scenario that is happening on film, the emotional turmoil comes right to the top. As a human being, I really think that as your life situation changes, your perspective on your work will change.

BS: Why do you think it is more acceptable to portray intense violence against zombies than it is against humans?

TG: I think it is acceptable because you are dealing with something that you don't consider to be human. It is almost human so that you can relate to it, but you can also beat the shit out of it and not get in trouble. With a zombie there is a free license to be violent and I think that is part of the appeal of the genre to some people. We touched on this a bit with Woody Harrelson's character in *Zombieland*. He enjoyed the violence and the zombie kills and was always looking for the next way to do it. He wasn't dealing with a person anymore. The audience was able to relate to him because he wasn't looked at as someone going around killing humans. He was killing monsters that were threatening his life and that was acceptable. I also think that having a human being as the threat gives the impression of a more even battle. You are not fighting a giant and unbeatable monster. If anything, the zombie is at a disadvantage. There are a lot of layers to it.

BS: Many zombie films and horror movies in general have scenes that can be extremely violent and in some cases distasteful. How do you handle it if you are asked to create an effect that you morally offensive?

TG: If I got to that point, I would have assumed that I picked the wrong film. There is definitely a disconnect creating violent scenes on zombies. If I didn't want to leave the project, I would have someone else be responsible for that particular piece. It really depends on the context as well. When choosing a project, you read the script ahead of time and talk with the director, so scenes you find offensive should be well addressed up front and never come as a surprise to anyone. If the film changed during production and something came up and sometimes it does, I would have another crew member do it who is more comfortable with it. I would not walk off of a project.

BS: What are your thoughts on the change to CGI?

TG: I feel like that merging the two is the greatest thing. The makeup process is generally an additive process, meaning you can only add material onto what is there. The integration of CGI has allowed for addition and subtraction. You can now have decayed zombies with no legs moving around the camera much easier than before. CGI is the next step in the makeup process that allows us to take makeup effects to the next level. The use of digital allows for you to keep working in correct proportion and scale as well. If you are trying to create a prosthetic head with intense decay on an actor, you have to build up with prosthetics to achieve the look you're after before you can start taking away material. This can really affect the scale and proportion of the person you are working on. By adding digital effects into the mix, you can create something really unique and the end result can be something amazing. I don't gravitate towards one method over the other and a film's budget will certainly help in dictating where you need to apply your efforts.

BS: You're one of the few special effects artists who have worked in costume design. How did this role come around?

TG: My journey into costume designing actually happened while I was working on *Thriller*. It was my first glimpse into the makeup effects profession and I watched the makeup effects crew building their character's body suits and wardrobe to wear in the video. It was a really interesting process as they were building the complete character and not just the head and the hands. This was more than just a simple makeup appliance for a character. *Thriller* was one of my first impressions of the industry and it seemed like a natural progression to continue with that mindset. On other earlier projects we were working with costumes that wouldn't fit over the appliances that the actors were wearing. We therefore ended up making modifications to make the costumes fit. As time went on, I ended up just designing the whole character.

As a designer you find yourself looking at a more complete vision when you can see the entire character design as your starting point. Obviously this vision includes what the character is wearing. When we are sketching out the designs for a character, we are not drawing the actors naked, we are putting clothes on them and creating the entire character. So by default we end up involved in costume design from the very beginning.

BS: Have you ever found yourself pushing the envelope to see how far you can go in one of your zombie films?

TG: The zombie genre definitely encourages you to push the envelope. They are meant to be violent films and push people's buttons. I think that part of the appeal of the genre is the carnage and violence. It is the same as when someone goes to see a scary movie. There is a certain level of expectation that is there that the film should deliver. It's a cathartic experience.

In pushing the envelope regarding realism for the non-genre projects like *127 Hours*, it makes the experience far more believable for all involved. If you are able to get an audience member to pass out in one of your films, you know you've pushed it just right.

Tony Gardner surrounded by zombies on the set of "The Return of the Living Dead" courtesy of Alterian Inc. and Tony Gardner.

253

KYLE GLENCROSS

- Resident Evil: Afterlife (2010) Prosthetic Makeup Artist
- Diary of the Dead (2007) Special Makeup Effects Supervisor) (Gaslight Studios)
- Land of the Dead (2005) Prosthetics Makeup Artist, Special Makeup Effects Artist (Gaslight Studios)
- Dawn of the Dead (2004) Prosthetics Technician, Special Makeup Effects Artist (Gaslight Studios)

Blood Splatter: How did you get into the zombie genre?

Kyle Glencross: I would have to say it's been a bunch of lucky coincidences. I think for those of us who do makeup effects, the film business in Toronto taking off in the field of horror was a big deal. It just happens to be zombies, zombies, zombies. I can't complain as it was a dream of mine as a kid to work with George Romero and work on a zombie movie.

BS: You have some high profile zombie films under your belt, which was your favorite film that you worked on?

KG: My favorite film to have worked on was probably *Dawn of the Dead* remake although some people would probably hate the answer.

BS: Why do you say that?

KG: Due to the politics of zombie films, there were many people bothered by the fact that *Dawn of the Dead* was being remade. However it was one of the best summers I have had. My supervisor on the shoot was the amazing David Anderson. Our work shop was in the abandoned mall in which they shot the film and we had the run of the place. We had a badminton court, basketball court, skateboarding and the entire mall to screw around in. It was awesome. During the day we did actually work though and spent our time creating all the zombie makeups and gags.

BS: Are you a fan of the genre?

KG: I am a huge fan of the genre. I thought I was a zombie when I was a kid. Many, many of the makeup effects I did as a youth revolved around the zombie.

BS: What inspired you to work with it?

KG: One of my main inspirations would have to be anything and everything from Michael Jackson's *Thriller* video and the making of *Thriller*, which I still watch quiet often.

BS: Do you have a favorite zombie film?

KG: That's a tough one. Maybe something Italian.

BS: Which film have you enjoyed working on the most from a creativity standpoint?

KG: The film I enjoyed most would have to be *Diary of the Dead*. We supervised that one for George under the consultation of Greg Nicotero. It was a blast to get to work with both of them for a second time. We had a chance to make some cool stuff, I think.

BS: Zombie films are known for extravagant zombie kills and character death scenes, which has been your favorite that you have created?

KG: My favorite zombie death would have to be a toss-up between the melting acid head zombie death in *Diary of the Dead* and the mallet through the head in *Dawn of the Dead*. I think that both are lovely gags.

BS: How about your favorite zombie death scene from other zombie movies you have not been involved in?

KG: That is an easy one. It's the gag in the original *Dawn of the Dead* where the zombie gets the top of his head taken off by the helicopter. It is hilarious, I love it.

BS: What do you use as inspiration for the varying degrees of decay and damage?

KG: It's funny, but actually I'm a little squeamish, so I don't go through the medical texts as many artists do for reference. I just work it until it looks gross to me. I find that usually works. You have to imagine most viewers have never seen anything that organic or ill like what we create, so they have no reference themselves. Gore is gore as I see it and it is open for interpretation.

BS: When creating a zombie, how does the design process work? Do you go into it with a predetermined idea or do you improvise?

KG: The design process works in a couple of different ways. In some situations we will have predetermined zombie designs created by visual artists which are then approved by production. Films such as the *Dawn of the Dead* remake or *Land of the Dead* work this way. However, even though we have these designs to work with, there always seems to be some flexibility to create your our looks. These are usually similar in design but still have some original zombie flare. Zombies allow us to be open for some different and creepy interpretations.

BS: With the advent of CGI allowing for more decomposing and wounds, do you find yourself still using traditional methods or gravitating more to CGI?

KG: I feel there is a nice combination of CGI and practical effects nowadays. I think everyone has gotten over the smoke and mirrors of CGI and are now realizing that a combination of both are much more realistic. I also have found that many directors are going back to practical effects, simply because it is something that is tangible. It's real and you can visually understand it on a film set. It's not just a tennis ball on a stick. I think an example of a nice combination of CGI and practical was the acid zombie head in *Diary of the Dead*. It's a great gag, but some situations do require complete CGI elements or landscape and sets. There is incredible CGI work being created and developed daily. I'm just a sucker for the old school. I love miniatures and matte paintings. I'm afraid I've dated myself. Next question please.

BS: Have you ever been a zombie extra in one of the films you've worked on?

KG: Yes I played Bubkus the clown in *Diary of the Dead*, the zombie who bites the dad at the kid's birthday party.

BS: That scene was great. I find scenes that involve children are a lot more uncomfortable when they cross that boundary. Have there been any effects shots that made it to the final cut that surprised you?

KG: There was one scene in *Land of the Dead*, in which the zombie pulls the guys guts out by stuffing his arm in through the mouth, down to the stomach, then retrieving the intestines back out. That was pretty cool. It takes a lot to shock me and I'm a little desensitized to things these days. Zombie movies have been over the top since *Dawn of the Dead* and I was messed up by them at an early age.

BS: *Resident Evil: Afterlife* was filmed in 3D, did you approach the prosthetics and make up differently than for a 2D feature?

KG: In dealing with 3D and the final look of a zombie, it is still very open in terms of detail work. I found that the makeups didn't really change all that much. If you were doing a very clean, precise makeup, such as a character makeup or old age you find that you have to be a bit more precise.

BS: How has the integration of high definition affected your work?

KG: High definition, now that's a whole other ball of wax. That can be really troublesome because of the crisp resolution.

BS: When creating background and hero zombies, is there a particular type of actor you look for that determines roles?

KG: I think I can speak for everyone when I say that when picking hero zombies we try to look for tall, thin, folks to create upon. They just leave more room to build on. That thin skeletal frame goes along way when creating the undead. However, considering who casting sometimes send to you, you have to take what you get and go from there. Everyone has that inner zombie no matter their shape or size. It gives variety and it is realistic as people of all shapes and sizes die. That is when you have to be really creative and start using all of your tricks and techniques to find that zombie inside your actor regardless of their body type.

BS: Can you share any funny on set stories from the zombie films

KG: I do have one humorous story, at least one you can print. We were working nights on *Land of the Dead*. Our on-set zombie wrangling assistant director was trying to motivate our background zombie actors, stumbling around set moaning and groaning with his rendition of a zombie. He then started to growl "brains, mooooore braaaains". Then from the background one of the producers yelled "wrong movie bonehead!" Romero started laughing and a small group of us guys were on the ground howling. That's some inside zombie nerd story, barely anybody else got it.

BS: Are there any zombie films in the future for you?

KG: I don't have anything in the works as of now, I may be sculpting a few pieces for *Resident Evil: Retribution* for Paul Jones, who is supervising. However, with the recent addition of my new baby girl, I think I'm going to take it easy and work some normal hours, not the zombie film hours.

Kyle Glencross has banana lips on the set of "Diary of the Dead" courtesy of Gaslight Studios.

DANIEL GOMMÉ

• The Dead (2011) Production Designer

Blood Splatter: How did you get involved with The Dead?

Daniel Gommé: I grew up with Howard and Jon Ford and I've known them since I was six. They were both horror and zombie fans and they were able to get what we call in England "video nasty's" that we'd sit around and watch. These are the banned horror movies that you could only get imported on bootleg VHS from the US and Europe. While they were getting ready to start shooting *The Dead,* they were looking for a military plane to shoot the opening sequence in and I happened to have contacts that could get them one. That's really how I came on board. I wouldn't have touched the movie if I didn't know the capabilities of Howard and Jon. I knew they were going to do something amazing and I think the movie turned out to be quite fantastic. I had always wanted to do a horror film, but the right one had not come along yet. Despite all the problems we had on set, we had a lot of fun.

BS: How did you get into production design?

DG: When I was a kid, I would design and make cardboard movie sets and that was how I got interested in stage and production design. It's always been a passion of mine. I still really enjoy working with miniatures and these days, they are at a level of quality where you can't tell them apart from full size sets. The level of detail now can be absolutely outstanding. It's very easy to trick audience into thinking a miniature set is either full scale or a CGI environment and I take pride in audiences thinking my miniatures are full sized sets. My job as a production designer is to collaborate with the director and director of photography to establish the visual feel and specific aesthetic needs of the project. The production designer guides key staff in other departments such as the costume designer, stylists, the special effects director and the locations manager among others, to establish a unified visual appearance to the film.

BS: Can you tell us about some of the miniature work you did for The Dead?

DG: There was one scene I worked on that ultimately got cut out. I had created a DC-47 miniature for a scene where the plane crashes into the sea and it was a nightmare to shoot. When you are shooting water scenes with miniatures, things can get very complicated due the fact that water droplets can make the effects look disproportionate if you're not careful. As the movie was getting a theatrical release, you have to be really considerate to what you are shooting, because once it is blown up to the big screen, miniatures can look fake if other environmental variables are factored in. We didn't want to take the risk.

A lot of the interiors were actually filmed in the UK and they blend seamlessly into the film. I've done production design on two James Bond movies and the price tag on some of those sets is in the millions. I was definitely working with a much smaller budget with *The Dead.* On the audio commentary the Ford brothers didn't reveal which sets were shot on location and which were created in a studio. If you're good at creating a set, no one will ever realize they are looking at one. If viewers can instantly tell that it is a set, you've screwed up big time. I'm really pleased with how the sets turned out and you can't tell which scenes were shot in Africa and which ones were set on a soundstage back in England. That is when you know you have done your job right.

The horror genre is a very difficult one to get right. If you don't make it scary enough, it almost becomes a comedy and throughout the film, our focus was on getting it right. I also worked on the costumes for the film too. My guide on the James Bond movies was an art director called Alan Tompkins. He's retired now, but he was hired by Steven Spielberg to work on *Saving Private Ryan* and *Band of Brothers* and he is a military wizard at designing. We put a lot of thought into how the soldiers looked. We had toyed with making them Delta Force, but we didn't know how the audience would respond if we killed off a whole bunch of elite soldiers at the beginning of the film. We then talked about making them United Nations soldiers, but the director's didn't like the color of their uniforms. We wanted something that was more of a desert color instead of blue. It's only a small scene, but we wanted everything to be believable and accurate. So we decided to make them mercenaries instead and every detail, even down to the type of guns they were using was accurate for the location. I believe it is really important to keep a close eye on details like that because even if the general audience does catch an inconsistency, someone out there will. I tried really hard to be consistent with these small details.

BS: *The Dead* is known as much for the problems that occurred behind the scenes as it is for the quality of the film. What can you tell us about some of the issues that occurred?

DG: We were shooting in a dangerous part of Africa and we all saw different problems throughout the shoot. I think Rob Freeman who played the lead had it the worst. He caught Malaria and almost died. There have been some reviews that have not been too kind about his acting and that's a bit unfair. A lot of the crew came down with it, but he had the worst of it all. When he's running around and sweating on camera, he is running a fever from a full blown Malaria infection. He was extremely ill, but wouldn't take the prescribed medication. He is one of those people who prefers to use the alternative and homeopathic remedies and he got really sick. We were robbed, held at knife and gun point and had money and equipment stolen. We were constantly stopped for money and held up by so many things you could never plan for on a film set. It was a really challenging shoot. It took almost five weeks just to get our equipment into the country even after the cast and crew had arrived.

Sometimes we would not even make it to the location for the shoot because we would be stopped at gunpoint. Many of these times, our vehicles and equipment were impounded until we could hand over enough cash to appease them and this was just the police. Howard was mugged at knife point on the first day of shooting and he had his money, driver's license and credit cards stolen. Then shortly after that he was pulled over and was nearly put in jail for driving without the license that had been stolen. It was a mess.

BS: With all the issues that you had during production, what kind of atmosphere was there on set?

DG: The atmosphere was actually really good. There were definitely some tempers flaring up at times and there were moments when things got a little tough, but the same can be said for any movie set. It happens all the time. We were working really long hours and a good portion of the crew came down with Malaria, so naturally things got a little heated at times, but there was no animosity or other issues. We all pulled together and made a great film. The one interesting thing about this movie is that there was not an assistant director on the set. Howard and Jon did it all themselves. In contrast to how badly things were going behind the scenes in Africa, the shots we did back in England went really well. It was definitely a shocking contrast to the African portion of the shoot.

BS: With how intense the shooting became, were there any instances of people throwing in the towel and leaving the production?

DG: No, not at all. There were definitely some arguments at various points, but there were no broken friendships or people storming off the set. One of two things will happen in a production like this. Either people close ranks and they band together or they explode and everything goes to pieces. We were lucky that the former happened. We really did fight in the face of adversity and I think it speaks volumes as to the quality of the cast and crew.

BS: Were any of these locations scouted out prior to production? It seems like a lot of these problems could have been alleviated in pre-production.

DG: Howard and Jon had previously made some commercials over there and hadn't experienced any issues at all. They thought they knew the area really well. They went in with an idea of what locations they wanted. Things were completely different with the movie. I think it's because the production size was much bigger and we had a larger crew and it was harder to fly under the radar. With the commercials, they were a smaller production and they drew far less attention.

BS: There are some amazing locales in the movie. Whereabouts in Africa did you shoot?

DG: We were really lucky to be able to shoot on location in some never before seen locales in Burkina Faso, which is a French speaking territory in West Africa. We also shot in Ghana and did some filming in the Sahara Desert. At the time we were shooting, there was actually a lot of green in the desert that

The DC-47 set on "The Dead" courtesy of Danile Gommé.

259

we weren't expecting. We just assumed that all we would see would be sand and dunes. It really was a surprise. It looked beautiful.

BS: How long was the production in Africa?

DG: We were out there for a good four and a half months in total. We had some breaks in between which made the overall shoot about ten months long.

BS: Did the constant interruptions in production change the time frame for shooting?

DG: We actually didn't go over believe it or not. Considering there were times when I couldn't even make it out to the location because it was in the middle of nowhere, we stayed on schedule. We were able to use a lot of the locals as extras and stage hands for the film. We paid them £2 a pay and this was considered a lot of money. We gave the car we used in the film to one of the locals after we were done with it and he was able to use it for deliveries, so we were able to give something back to the community. It was a terrible car, but it was a life saver to the guy. This is the kind of poverty that is out there. It was dreadful. We were filming in villages that had real people suffering from all kinds of illnesses and devastating poverty. It's a very different world out there.

BS: How about the budget? Did the issues with robbery affect how much of the budget was wasted?

DG: Again, it didn't, at least not that I am aware of. Overall, Howard and Jon kept pretty quiet about the fiscal side of things. We did lose a lot of money to thieves and police officers, but the fallout was not felt on set. The production budget was not affected. I don't know if they found additional funds or cut money elsewhere, but we didn't feel it on set at all.

BS: Do you think a lot of the local trouble you encountered was because they thought it was a huge Hollywood production was coming into town with bottomless pockets?

DG: No, I actually don't so. The corruption was rampant and especially centered around the police. Howard and Jon went out to grab lunch one day and they were sitting in a traffic jam and a guy tapped on the window with a machete demanding money. If you looked like a tourist, they would rob you. Being on a film set had nothing to do with the problems we experienced. That's just the kind of environment it is out there.

BS: Can we find you in the film anywhere?

DG: Actually, yes you can. I am one of the soldiers in the plane at the beginning of the movie.

BS: Do you have anything else zombie related on the horizon?

DG: There is a script for *The Dead 2* currently being written, which I am really excited about. There are some great ideas and locations being discussed for the follow up. Hopefully we won't have the problems we had with the first. I'm sure there will be a host of new ones. *(laughs)*

BS: Do you think the negative experiences will make you a little more guarded going into a sequel?

DG: Not at all. We have a location in mind for the next film, but it is a much more stable location. We can't say where it is yet, but we will all have to get our vaccinations before we go. It will be a tough shoot, but the country is nowhere near as corrupt. Although, we can create some great sets so that if we can't shoot where we want, we can always do the sets back home. For *Die Another Day*, we couldn't shoot in North Korea so we did it at Pinewood Studios and got the shot we needed. It isn't always about money or budgets, sometimes you just can't get where you want to go. Sometimes it is just out of your hands. That's when production design becomes so important. It's the details that really set you apart and help with the believability of the set. For the plane scene in *The Dead*, the DC-47 is still being used in Africa. It is a very common military plane that dates back to the Second World War. America hasn't used it since the 1960's. It's small details like this that make the film stand out. I was able to find one in England that was in pieces. We picked it up, repainted it and was perfect for what we needed.

EMILY HAGINS

- Zombie Girl (2009) Herself
- Pathogen (2006) Director, Producer

Blood Splatter: How did you get into the film industry?

Emily Hagins: I started making short films with my home video camera. Since my dad has a background in advertising, he taught me at a very early age that filmmaking was composed of a process consisting of pre-production, production and post-production. When I made my first movie at nine years old, he made sure I had the script, storyboard, shot plan, learned rudimentary camera angles and figured out iMovie before I started editing. He guided me, but didn't do anything for me and since then, the process has become more complex as my projects have become more complex.

BS: Your entrance into the zombie genre is unique not only because of your gender, but also because of your age. What made you decide to shoot a zombie film?

EH: I was scared of almost everything, even Halloween until I saw my first zombie movie. It was an Australian zombedy called *Undead*, which I saw at a twenty-four hour movie marathon called Butt-Numb-A-Thon when I was eleven. It was the first time I realized a horror movie could be both funny and scary and that was the kind of movie I wanted to make for my first feature. At that point, I started watching zombie and horror movies almost obsessively, trying to learn how they were made.

BS: Are you a fan of the zombie genre?

EH: I am, I love the genre.

BS: What are some of your favorite films?

EH: I have loads. Some of my favorites are probably the original *Night of the Living Dead*, *Undead*, *Shaun of the Dead*, *Braindead (Dead Alive)*, *The Evil Dead* trilogy and *Night of the Living Dorks*. Most recently, I very much enjoyed the first season of *The Walking Dead* and I love the comics too.

BS: How familiar were you with the zombie genre prior to shooting *Pathogen*?

EH: Though I hadn't seen any horror movies until *Undead*, I got a sense that there were rules that a zombie movie watching audience wanted a filmmaker to follow. I watched a ton of movies for research on zombie speed, skin tone and texture based on levels of decay, ability to speak and groan. That type of thing. This all helped me take the elements I loved to create my own zombie look.

BS: What do you think the appeal is of zombie movies?

EH: I think Harry Knowles put it best. There's something inherently scary about knowing all the people you care about are now trying to kill you.

BS: Which films inspired you in the creation of *Pathogen*?

EH: *Undead* was the biggest inspiration for tone. I took some of the zombie qualities from George Romero's movies like *Night of the Living Dead*, *Dawn of the Dead* and *Day of the Dead*. I also took some scare techniques from *The Evil Dead*, such as what I dub the "shower curtain effect". This is when a character hears a zombie in the other room and they have to be behind this one door. They open it and then, nothing. Then there's a shower curtain and the zombie just has to be there and then, it's not there. The suspense drops. Then the zombie pops up behind the character.

BS: Who are some of your influences?

EH: As a director, some of my biggest influences are Danny Boyle, Peter Jackson, Edgar Wright, Jon

261

Favreau, Guillermo del Toro and Stanley Kubrick.

BS: Do you think your age or gender has either restricted you or given you an advantage in any way?

EH: I think it affects the way I get certain things for my movies and how I see the world around me at the time. I've been asked if I would ever want to remake one of my movies to fix the mistakes or use better technical resources, but I think each one stands as landmark in where I was in maturity and growth as a filmmaker.

BS: What is your favorite zombie film?

EH: I think overall I'd say *Shaun of the Dead* or *Braindead (Dead Alive)*. They both have the fun quirky tone that I love most in zombie movies.

BS: Do you think coming to the genre with a fresh perspective has benefitted you?

EH: Yeah, I think it definitely has. While I was able to do research on the genre, I knew that I wanted to tell a zombie story through the perspective of awkward middle school kids. This really hasn't been done before.

BS: You've taken a very active role in *Pathogen* with writing, directing, editing and producing. Do you have a preference?

EH: Directing, most definitely. I'm thankful for the experience of wearing many hats on *Pathogen* and I do like those other jobs. I want to learn about the other aspects of filmmaking so I can effectively ask for what I want, but I'd like to mainly focus on developing as a director.

BS: As a child what was the first horror movie to have an impact on you?

EH: I would say the zombie movie *Undead*. I have been really lucky to see a lot of the classic horror movies on the big screen, thanks to the Alamo Drafthouse or the Paramount Theatre located here in Austin. Some of those titles include *The Shining, The Thing, Halloween, The Haunting* and *The Evil Dead*. Getting the whole big screen movie theater experience for those films really scared the bajeezus out of me.

BS: Where did you draw your inspiration from for the effects shots as you were scripting them?

EH: The "shower curtain effect" I described from *The Evil Dead* was a big part of how I developed my scare techniques. Another thing I love about *The Evil Dead* and *Braindead (Dead Alive)* especially is how many crazy oozy liquids come out of the zombies. It's such a fun, specific effects quality of zombie movies and I wanted to take advantage of that in my movie. In addition to the corn syrup blood mixture, we used other mixtures like oatmeal, smoothies, honey and even lettuce to add some texture.

BS: How much of a budget did you need to shoot *Pathogen*?

EH: Since the process took so long, most of our money went to buying a pizza here and there, so it was just little chunks of money instead of a "budget" to work with. My family isn't wealthy at all though, so we could only spend sparingly. Over the course of three years, we estimate spending about $7,000.

BS: How did you raise the funds?

EH: Since then, I have used the crowd funding website IndieGoGo to fund my most recent feature, *My Sucky Teen Romance*, a teen vampire comedy.

BS: Many film productions working with lower budgets invent new ways of creating special effects. What shortcuts did you take for budgetary reasons?

EH: A lot of food products were purchased at the grocery store to pose as organs and made up goopy bodily liquids. My mom has worked as an artist for many years and she was able to help find cheap

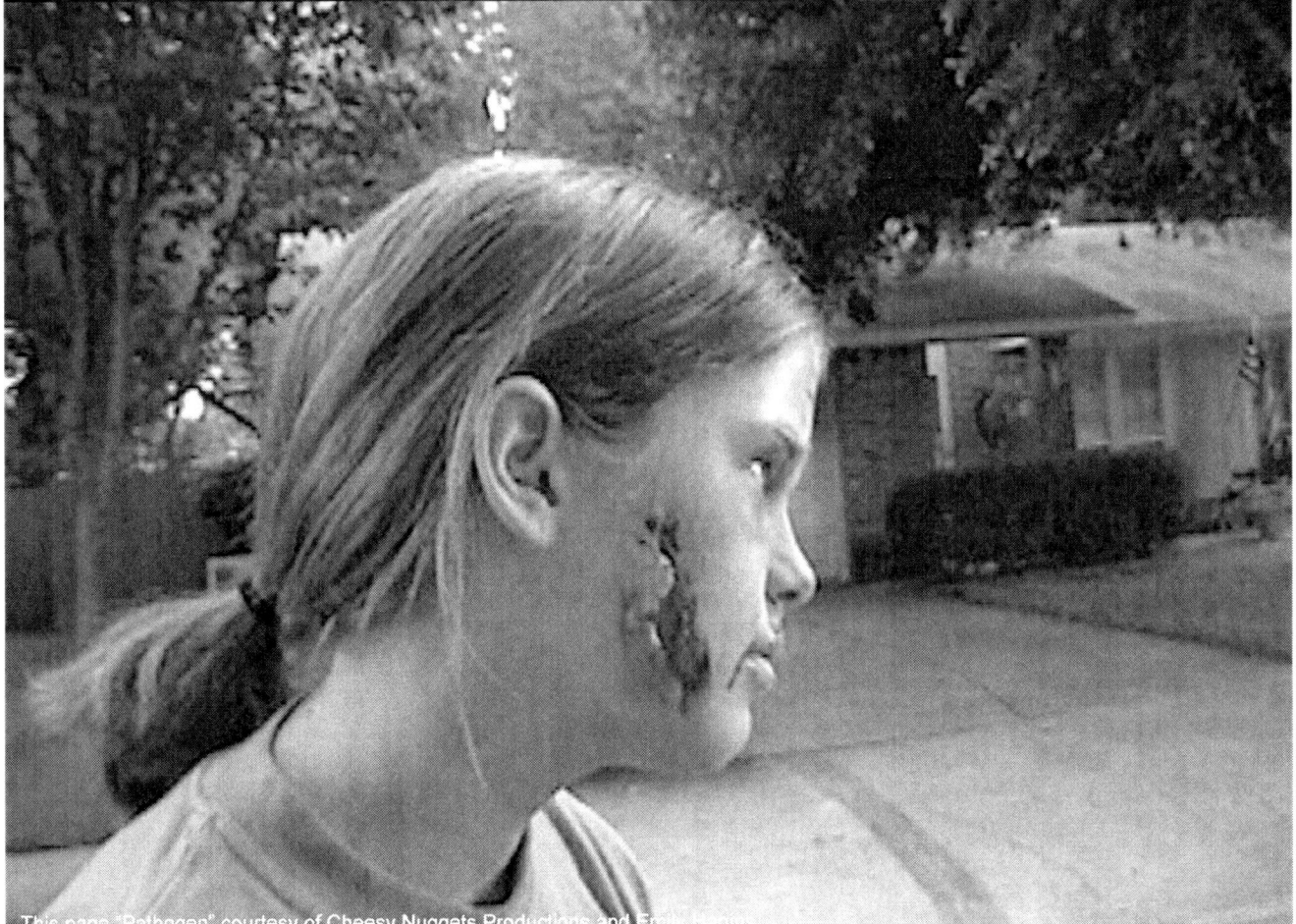

This page "Pathogen" courtesy of Cheesy Nuggets Productions and Emily Hagins

263

ways to create the things we needed effects wise, including a decapitated head. We also bought a lot of Halloween make-up right after alloween when all those kits were on sale. Those came in really handy at times.

BS: Have you been surprised at the positive interest in the movie and your career?

EH: Yes, but I'm very thankful to have made a movie that falls in a genre with such as a supportive audience. As long as they're having a good time with the movie, they don't care what your budget was or how you made it. It seems contradictory, but the horror community is full of some of the nicest people in the world.

BS: *Pathogen* deals with a virus that causes the outbreak. Many recent films like *28 Days Later*, *Quarantine* and *The Crazies* have shifted the zombie genre from having zombies simply rising from graves to becoming infected mutants. What are your thoughts on this recent shift in the genre to include movies like these?

EH: I think there are aspects about the rapidly growing developments in technology that are both scary and fascinating to writers, which can cause a lot of "what if" scenarios in the horror genre. I think it's an interesting premise to be explored and it's always a pleasure to see a well done horror movie like *The Host* for example, come out of that curiosity.

BS: Most twelve year old's are having nightmares about zombies, not making films about them. What scares you?

EH: I actually had a lot of zombie dreams while I was making *Pathogen*.

BS: Did any of your dreams end up in the script?

EH: I did incorporate a few of the elements from my dreams into *Pathogen*. However, there are plenty of things that scare me outside of the zombie genre. Since it's Halloween season haunted houses are one example.

BS: What advice can you give someone breaking into the zombie genre?

EH: Do your research and find out what you like and don't like about other zombie movies. Find your own take on the sub-genre and determine whether it's perspective or cause of outbreak or both. Make sure at the end of the day you're just telling a good story that's important to you,

BS: Are there any zombie films in the future for you?

EH: I hope so, I definitely have a lot of love for the genre, but for the mean time, I'm headed in a more comedy focused direction with *My Sucky Teen Romance*. I guess we'll see where things take me from there.

BS: Can you share any funny on set stories from the zombie films you've worked on?

EH: Since Austin, Texas is a very film-friendly city, there is quite a lot of film production always going on in town. I remember while we were working on *Pathogen,* there was one time we were at the grocery store and we were buying corn syrup, chocolate syrup, red dye and yellow dye in large quantities for some of the effects and the checkout clerk immediately asked why we needed to make so much fake blood. That was really funny.

BS: If you woke up tomorrow morning and the zombie apocalypse had started, how do you think would you fare?

EH: I sure hope I would do well. I at least know that it won't take me twenty minutes of exposition to figure out I'm in zombiegeddon.

LLOYD KAUFMAN

- CEO and founder of Troma Entertainment
- Atom the Amazing Zombie Killer (2011) Actor
- Poultrygeist (2006) Director, Producer, Writer, Actor

Lloyd Kaufman: I have an idea for a new zombie film, although it is probably not original. I want to make a movie where the humans bite the zombies and the zombies turn into nerd's and computer geeks. I think you could get a funny script out that. The entire population is turning into geeks. This is the yang part of the zombie genre. It could be a really good commentary on society.

Blood Splatter: So basically it is zombies turning into zombies?

LK: Exactly. You could have a zombie tearing someone apart and then getting bitten by a nerd and then ten minutes later they are sitting in front of the television playing video games eating popcorn and pizza. I think that this will be my next project.

BS: Is there anything else currently in the works for you?

LK: I am currently writing *The Toxic Avenger Part Five: The Toxic Twins*. It will deal with the zombification of humans as they are being brainwashed by the media and consumerism. One of the twins will turn into a Toxic Avenger and the other will turn into a hot Gyno.

BS: Troma's contributions to the zombie genre have been significant and you've been actively involved in the genre for over thirty five years. What appeals to you so much about it?

LK: I just love zombies. I am in the world of satire and *Poultrygeist: The Night of the Chicken Dead* deals with an American Indian chicken zombie, so it is not likely to scare anyone. It is not your typical scary zombie movie. The reason I chose the zombie format for the film is because of big media. The media is controlled by a number of devil worshipping conglomerates who advertise fast food over and over again and also to kids, none the less. People go to fast food restaurants like zombies and eat this crap and by doing so, they support organizations that have factory farms. These farms treat workers abysmally and create obese teenagers and do nothing good at all for society. So I thought the zombie format worked, because most of my movies have political and social commentaries containing huge amounts of sex and violence and occasional singing and dancing. I also like how every little fan boy who has a video camera these days is making a zombie movie. There are hundreds of them. If you check my credits on IMDB.com you will see I've been in over two hundred movies and over half of them involve zombies. I was in one just recently where a guy was bitten by a mosquito and that was how people turned.

BS: Troma now owns the rights to *White Zombie*. How did you obtain it?

LK: Troma bought a company called Rowan group and *White Zombie* is one of the films in the collection. We now own the best print available of the film and we're really pleased with that.

BS: Was *Night of the Living Dead* an influence on you?

LK: Of course. I do believe that George Romero is the most underrated American director ever. Although too many people forget that zombies were around before Mr. Romero. I wrote a piece on *Night of the Living Dead* a while back for a book about the film. I said that I thought Romero's use of the black protagonist in 1968 was really cool, but I also think that perhaps it was also embracing the underdog of the gay community. There was a big discussion about coming out of the basement in the film and I think he was subtly dealing with the debate of coming out of the closet. It makes sense, as all of his movies are visionary, from *Martin* to *Survival of the Dead*. Most people talk about the color of the characters skin, but I think he was giving a shout out to gay rights.

BS: Are there any other zombie movies you are fond of?

LK: I loved *Colin*. I thought making the movie from the zombies perspective was a really great angle. It was good to see something different. Troma tries to embrace the little guy in the industry. We have lots of new director's and Gyno's in particular.

BS: You've mentioned Gyno's a couple of time. I'm not familiar with the term.

LK: We use that word instead of woman or female because they are both politically incorrect words. Both have variances of the male term, so we embrace the underdog cause. For that reason I really like the film *Stacy*. It has got plenty of gore and violence and is a metaphor for the wave of teenage suicides. One of my recent peeves is the horror genre is supposed to be so underground and hip, but yet it is the most male orientated, good old boy network out there. There are very few Gyno directors in the world of horror. Troma has used plenty of Gyno directors and I think it is an outrage that there aren't more out there. To me, Gyno's know more about horror than any man does and ever could. They menstruate and carry another human inside them. It is amazing and terrifying.

BS: So what exciting news has come from Troma lately?

LK: *Redneck Zombies* has just become available in Walmart and in the forty years of Troma, this is the first time any of our movies have been sold there. This movie is also significant in that it was completely shot on video tape. It was the first movie that broke through that barrier and we were able to distribute it. In those days it was extremely hard to get anything out that wasn't shot on celluloid. *Redneck Zombies* was a seminal movie in that respect. It is the only Troma movie to break through the hymen of Walmart.

BS: What was the first horror movie to have an impact on you as a child?

LK: *Bambi*. My mother took me when I was very young to see it in the movies. I was in the fetal position for weeks afterwards. I was absolutely horrified. It was terrifying.

BS: You have frequently been listed as the inspiration of countless people. Who inspires you?

LK: Definitely the classics. I made the mistake of going to Yale, where I was roomed with a couple of movie nuts just by kismet. They pounded the auteur film theory and as I was fluent in French, I started reading the Cahier de Cinema, the Notebooks of Cinema which the Cinematheque Francaise published and I bought into all of it. In those days they were written by François Truffaut and Claude Chabrol who were critics before they were filmmakers. I really bought into the idea that the director must be the author of the movie. The filmmakers I took inspiration from were Buster Keating, Charlie Chaplin, John Ford, Fritz Lang and of course Roger Corman. Corman proved to me that you can make low budget movies with good scripts and good acting with style and they could be successful. Warhol was a big influence too. Breaking the fourth wall was huge for me. I am also influenced by Stan Brakhage, who is the greatest visual artist of my lifetime. A few us brought him to Yale in my freshman year and showed *The Art of Vision*.

BS: You been involved with all elements of film production, including acting, producing, writing and directing. Where do you prefer to be and why?

LK: I think I enjoy the filmmaking part. It is incredibly stressful, but I love directing. There is a huge amount of stress and you work eighteen hour days. Producing a Troma movie, you learn to sleep on the floor, eat sandwiches three times a day and learn how to defecate in a paper bag. We have produced an amazing documentary about the making of *Terror Firmer*. It is an amazing film and it is finally getting some traction. I made it in 1999 and it is my most personal movie. It's based on my first book "All I need to know about filmmaking, I learned from the Toxic Avenger". It deals with the independent artist versus the mainstream. We did one about *Citizen Toxie* called Apocalypse Soon and the best one we did was for *Poultrygeist*, called Poultry in Motion: The Truth is Stranger than Chicken.

BS: Troma has stood by the zombie genre through its numerous ups and downs over the years. What does Troma look for when either producing or distributing a zombie film?

LK: The movies we look to buy or acquire must be one of a kind. *Redneck Zombies* stands on its own and it is not a copy of anything out there. People keep telling me that they are going to give me the next

266

Poultrygeist or *Toxic Avenger*. I don't need those as I have already made them. What I need is something new and fresh. In terms of my own zombie films, I don't start out wanting to make a zombie film. I have my own social and political themes like fast food which is an abomination. Fast food is what inspired *Poultrygeist*. It is about how the country has been defiled by McDonalds, Burger King and Kentucky Fried Chicken. It is about how they destroy animals and the people who work for them. They destroy the people's health who get addicted to their products and it is addictive, despite what they say. There is absolutely nothing good about what they do. The zombie theme just came from how people go to them either on foot or in their cars and sit there staring vacuously, eating French Fries and chicken that is crammed full of drugs and hormones and you watch them as their eyes are glazed over and half of them are obese. The children are the same and they are like zombies. There are chemicals in there that make people addicted. The giant media conglomerates spew out hours of commercials daily that advertise these places. The movie companies give away toys in the fast food so the kids can go into Burger King and stuff their fat faces. They are all zombies. I don't consider myself an expert on zombies, but I do enjoy the movies.

BS: Do you have a favorite zombie movie either from Troma or elsewhere?

LK: I loved *Shaun of the Dead* when it came out. Certainly my favorite Troma movie for the time being is *Poultrygeist*. I've noticed a lot of horror directors are now doing horror musicals. As far as a favorite movie outside of Troma, I would have to say *Stacy*. I like the fact it has a feminist theme to it and caters to the underdog. Many of my films have Gyno leads in them. Even in *Tromeo and Juliet*, it is Juliet's film for sure. If you look at my movies, it's the Gyno's who are the strong characters.

BS: You wrote some of the songs for *Poultrygeist* and it was your first song writing efforts since *Tromeo and Juliet* in 1996. What made you decide to return to songwriting?

LK: Being a gay married man, I have wept my way through many a Judy Garland or Barbra Streisand musical. I am a major musical comedy fan. Not just a fan, but a musical comedy air conditioner too, occasionally. I felt this would be an opportunity to mix in some songs. Troma is a brand unto itself, because we don't make genre movies. We own about eight hundred films in our library, but we have only produced about a hundred of them. The ones I have done have mixed multiple genres, so you can't really classify them in a particular category. I was very much inspired by *The Happiness of the Katakuris* by Takashi Miike. When he when was younger, he was a major fan of Troma and he wrote a big defense in Japanese about *Citizen Toxie*. Apparently some of the Japanese critics didn't get the film and he gave an explanation about why he thinks the film is a masterpiece. *The Happiness of the Katakuris* gave me the courage to put singing and dancing in my film.

BS: Are you comfortable with distributing a movie you find morally offensive?

LK: No, not at all. We have a movie called *Blood Sucking Freaks* and in 1974 when we got involved, it seemed funny and it still is funny, but I don't think I would have acquired it. It is too misogynistic.

BS: Troma has many zombie films with graphic and violent scenes, what shocks you?

LK: Hypocrisy. People who get Nobel Peace prizes who haven't earned them and people who claim to be public servants who do nothing for the people. I find it shocking that people like Tom Cruise earn twenty five million a movie, while a good portion of the world gets by on a dollar a week. Our society glamorizes it.

BS: What is more important to you, fan acceptance or critical acclaim?

LK: I never read the reviews, I care about the fans. That's why I go to comic book and movie conventions. I'm out there in the trenches. I listen to the fans and to what they want. The critics don't know anything. That's not really fair, some of them used to, but these days, most don't know. They know that they want to get on the junket to see the new Robert De Niro movie. The New York Times knows it has to lick ass to get advertising. I don't have any respect for the media. Vincent Canby, one of the greatest reviewers in the history of cinema, reviewed *The Toxic Avenger* when it was originally released in New York. He had the originality and interest to have it as his lead review that week. These days, only the big blockbusters or current trendy releases get that treatment. I have total respect for the fans. We wouldn't be here without our fans. The fans want our movies and we don't have to brainwash them with millions of dollars in advertising telling them what they should see. We don't have the budget for that and we don't need it.

BS: That is why I have taken a different approach with the reviews in this book as there are so many good, but obscure movies that get panned from critics and reviewers or overlooked or ignored completely.

LK: That's a great angle. It is easy to beat up on the independent. A good example is Variety magazine. It is basically a house organ for the big studios. When one of the critics at Variety has the nerve to give a negative review of a mainstream $100,000,000 piece of crap, they can get fired and they do get fired. History is full of Variety critics who have been fired for being honest.

BS: Why do you think it's more acceptable to portray violence against zombies than it is against humans? Is it thinly masked violent tendencies of human kind?

LK: I don't know if it is more acceptable. Look at *The Toxic Avenger*. I crush the head of a thirteen year old kid. No one gave a shit. We also blew away a Seeing Eye dog and we received tons of letters on it. What is unacceptable is violence to animals and I don't know if it is more acceptable to portray violence on zombies than on humans as no one has complained. I think the only time it is unacceptable is when it is shown to children. *The Toxic Avenger* journey has been an interesting one. It is a very violent movie and it was made into a Saturday morning children's cartoon. It has also been an Off-Broadway musical written by David Bryant of Bon Jovi and is about to go on Broadway.

BS: How does working with the dead affect your view on your mortality?

LK: I am just a sad clown waiting to die. I just don't have the guts to pull the trigger. When you are sixty five, I don't know how much value you can be to humankind. There are a lot of old people who are just pains in the ass. Although, having such an ego, I will try and hold on as long as I can.

BS: There are many violent scenes in your movies. Is it difficult to distance yourself from the realism of the makeup due to the fact that it does resemble real life so closely?

LK: Not at all. While our films are violent, it is cartoon violence. It is Monty Python type violence and there is no reality there. People are not going to go out and emulate this kind of thing. Our fans are smarter than that. There is nothing in a Troma movie that is worse than what is in the real world. The scene in *The Toxic Avenger* where the kids are driving around and hitting old ladies for points actually comes from a story in the New York Times. The Troma movies are amateur compared to what happens in real life. We are basically Tom and Jerry and the Python's really influenced us.

BS: What are your thoughts on the shift to CGI over more traditional prosthetics?

LK: I am going to use CGI in my next movie, but only because it works for the script. *Poultrygeist* only utilizes CGI twice. Once was to digitally remove fishing line from a prop and then we used it to make some small smoking wounds on the chicken. I didn't grow up with video games or CGI, so it is not that important to me. If I do an explosion in a Troma film, we will really blow something up. The same goes for car crashes and location shooting. The only movie with CGI that really worked for me was *District 9*.

BS: Horror is a million miles away from Broadway, where you originally wanted to start you career. Do you ever think about going back and revisiting your first passion?

LK: I am definitely a fan of musical comedy. I did that with *Poultrygeist* and I am peripherally involved with *The Toxic Avenger* musical. I'd love to do *Pal Joey* by Richard Rodgers and Lorenz Hart, because the movie with Sinatra was poorly done. The original play is great. It is really dark and the songs are amazing.

BS: If you woke up tomorrow morning and the zombie apocalypse had started, how would you fare?

LK: I would not go with the military. I would hang out with the specialists. I would search out Max Brooks. He wrote the book on how to survive a zombie outbreak. I use that book all the time as I always run into zombies in the movie industry.

MICHAEL KENWORTHY

• Return of the Living Dead Part II (1987) Actor

Blood Splatter: It's unusual for a child to be so heavily featured in a zombie movie. How did you get your role in *Return of the Living Dead Part II?*

Michael Kenworthy: That's a good question. It is one that I have come to learn over the past year has set me apart from my peers. Many fans have made me aware that I was the first "Zombie killer kid" so to speak. Others have identified with the fact that I was a kid like themselves when they first saw the movie struggling with the one thing kids face the most and that is no one listens to them. I have met many people that actually used to go in their back yards and play Jessie versus the Zombies, which I had no idea about and was truly amazed and humbled to hear. The director had worked with children before, I believe in one of the *Meatballs* movies and knew that children brought veracity to a production, especially when fear was supposed to be involved, however campy the movie may be.

The actual audition process was quite lengthy. At that time there were not as many child actors as there are today, but having started when I was five and having already done forty commercials and dozens of television shows and short films helped. It was narrowed down to a small group of other child actors and I believe I auditioned seven or eight times. I can't say what was going through the producers and directors minds, but in the end I got the part.

BS: Were your parents okay with you being in a horror film?

MK: Believe it or not, they were great with it. They had no problems at all, as long as they didn't have to be on the sets with me. Fortunately my cousin Stacey Salley was my guardian and even made a few cameos. Oddly, my parents were not okay with me being a regular on a television series though. Although, I later came to fully understand why. I was supposed to play Ben Sever, the youngest brother on *Growing Pains*, but my parents declined, deciding it might not be good for my childhood. I'm not sure how the movie was better. As a consolation, they made me the next door neighbor, Kris Kooseman who appeared in the foreground, background and as a special guest in many episodes over the years. In fact, they even gave me a role in one of the spin of shows called *Just the Ten of Us.*

BS: How much exposure did you have to the zombie genre prior to *Return of the Living Dead Part II?*

MK: Actually none. I did not watch the first *Night of the Living Dead* until after getting the role and to this day that black and white film is one of the all time best and eeriest films I have ever seen. Since then, I have become a zombie fan boy of sorts and I love all things horror.

BS: Were you aware of the popularity of *The Return of the Living Dead* prior to accepting the role?

MK: No, I was just a little too young, plus the first film had a bit of nudity in it and perhaps was a bit too hardcore for my parents.

BS: Do you have a favorite zombie movie?

MK: The original *Night of the Living Dead*, hands down.

BS: What appeals to you about the horror and zombie genre?

MK: Zombies were real people too. Seriously, that's a tough question, it's like asking a comic book fan why they love their comics. Aside from growing up with a keen bias towards everything zombie, over the years a counter culture has arisen based on the genre that I gravitated to and found a comfortable place in. Much like a Trekky would at a Star Trek Convention I suppose. On a much more serious note, over the years, studying anthropology, the Next Generation and the Discovery Channel, I have come to learn that every ancient civilization had not only a word or words for zombies, but a great deal to say about them. Even the Bible does for that matter. For many cultures throughout history they are a very real thing and according to the Bible, we will see them come the apocalypse. I'll be ready, crossbow in hand.

BS: How does a child prepare for a role in a horror movie?

MK: You have to remind yourself of the time you got in really big trouble with your Dad and he told you to get the leather belt so he could spank you with it. It wasn't considered abuse back then, he was just being a good dad, I swear.

BS: That would do it for sure. How was your experience on the set?

MK: It could not have been better. I loved every single moment of it, except when they made me leave because of child labor laws. I could have and would have worked all night, every night surrounded by all the amazing zombies created by Kenny Myers and the crew. Most of the zombies worked for low pay and out of passion, so the overall feeling on the set was of a warm community. I have to admit, there were some times when you looked out across the fog filled sets, indoors or outside and I would see dozens of zombies crawling and I would forget for a second it was not real. It was the kind of thing a kid like myself would have done for free, it was so exciting. Especially the times when we went into the small towns, like Sierra Madre and everyone came out to greet us and bring us treats. In fact, it was only a year ago that they took down the mock cemetery in Sierra Madre. It had lasted over twenty years.

BS: As a child on the set of a horror movie, how do you deal with the detailed and graphic makeup?

MK: I was fascinated with the process. It was pre-CGI, so it would take six to eight hours for some actors to go from human to zombie and I was enthralled by the entire process. I would often spend my spare time watching just how the movie magic was created. Doing so also took away from most creepiness I might feel at seeing the zombies in full makeup. As I said before, there were definitely times when fatigue would set in and you would look around and forget was real and what was not and get a chill or two.

BS: Does the director handle you in a special manner to make filming easier?

MK: He knew how to work with us kids very well. There was really only one scene where the written word in the script did not translate to dialogue well for me and I had some difficulty with it. It was the scene when I was on the phone trying to call the Army and National Guard. It was written as a much longer scene with an entire extra page or two of phone time, but for whatever reason, perhaps my own tiredness, I found the dialogue so cumbersome that we never got through it all and had to shorten the scene. I left feeling like I had let the director down that day.

BS: Were there any moments where the filming got too intense for you?

MK: Not at all. I was a kid in a candy story the entire time.

BS: After *Return of the Living Dead Part II* you starred in *The Blob* and then seemed to disappear from the film industry. Was there any particular reason for this decision?

MK: Whilst I did stop making movies, I did not disappear right away. I continued to do dozens of commercials and television shows, a foreign film and a lot of theater. Then I got to that age where I was about sixteen or seventeen and they could cast someone eighteen to play someone my age year without the child labor law restrictions. I thought that was going to slow me down for a couple of years and that is when I delved deep into theater, training and even teaching. The opportunity of a lifetime came along and this time the decision was all mine, not my parents. I was offered a six year contract to play Brian Austin Green's character in *Beverly Hills 90210*. Naturally, I said yes, but with five weeks or so before production started, I had a change of heart. I was in a musical with a friend of mine having the time of my life and work had slowed so I was actually going to school on a more regular basis. I had just sold a couple of scripts I had written and it dawned on me that six years was a very long time. I had grown up with all the other child actors of my generation and many of them had become super famous and complained to me of the pitfalls of fame that they had experienced. I saw their lives getting increasingly darker along with the circle of friends they hung out with. So one day I realized that acting is all I had been doing since I was five years old. I had built some fame, but had not quite crossed the tipping point and that if I ever

Michael and other kids having fun on the set of "Return of the Living Dead Part II" courtesy of Michael Kenworthy

wanted to try to live a normal, namely an anonymous life and perhaps get a college education, this would be my last chance. Wiser than I realized at the time, I decided to back out of 90210. Well, apparently, no one had ever done this to Aaron Spelling before and I was in for a shocker. I first told my agent who was appalled and gave me Aaron's number saying she refused to call on my behalf. Incidentally, she never spoke to me again. She had been my agent since I was five. So, I called Mr. Spelling, told him my decision and he exploded on me with a sailors tongue and threats to this day I still cannot recall, except for that I would never work for him in this town again.

After that phone call I only had a little high school left, so I decided to take it easy, stick to theater and go to college. Little did I know that college would introduce me to technology and I have had several great technology based businesses since then. Coming full circle, with the rise of the zombie culture I have been asked to go on convention tours and been approached to restart my acting career, so that is just what I aim to do.

BS: What advice can you give child actors who are looking to break into the horror genre?

MK: Well, I don't encourage child actors into anything but theater, as I have seen what it has done to far too many of the kids I grew up with. One should not begin until they are at least sixteen if not eighteen in my opinion. A childhood is too precious and innocent of a time to devote to Hollywood, but if you are going to act, I found that the genre picks you.

BS: Do you plan to ever return to the zombie genre?

MK: Yes, stay tuned. I have got some great things lined up, but have learned the hard way to never announce anything before the ink is dry.

BS: Can you share any funny stories from the set of *Return of the Living Dead Part 2*?

MK: The other kids and I were a real handful on set. We were always running around and having fun in the various sets. There were the occasional scrapes and bruises and once I got a piece of glass in my eye. As far as anything funny, a problem that occurred several times is that the other actors and I would be walking across an area that was dark with shallow graves. Many had zombie actors inside and we would often step on them by mistake. Other than that, I had the biggest crush on Marsha Dietlein while we were shooting.

Michael and zombie extras in "Return of the Living Dead Part II" courtesy of Michael Kenworthy.

ROBERT KURTZMAN

- The Rage (2007) Director, Writer, Producer, Special Makeup Effects Producer
- Undead or Alive: A Zombedy (2007) Special Makeup Effects Producer
- Army of Darkness (1992) Special Makeup Effects
- Bride of Re-Animator (1990) Special Makeup Effects Artist
- Evil Dead II (1987) Special Makeup Effects Unit Crew
- Night of the Creeps (1986) Makeup Effects Artist
- Re-Animator (1985) Special Makeup Effects Artist

BS: How did you get started in the special effects industry?

RK: I grew up in a small farm town in Ohio and was always into horror movies. I would frequently stay up and watch the late night horror shows. My mother was an artist so I was always around art of some kind. I started drawing when I was young and I had a thing for horror and fantasy. I figured early on that I wanted to do special effects and had to decide how to do that from Ohio. I found there was a school in Los Angeles run by Joe Blasco and went there for twelve weeks. I went out there when I was nineteen and hit the ground running. I worked on movies like *Re-animator* and *Troll* at MMI and Empire Pictures and started out doing low budget movies and building my resume. I went to art school for a year and dropped out. I didn't want to be a commercial artist in that sense. I was just into monsters and creatures and fascinated how that stuff was made.

BS: What appeals to you about the horror and zombie genre?

RK: It's funny because there are so many zombie things out right now that you would think it would be burned out, but it isn't. There is something about being eaten by a human being that is really disturbing. I love how the disease transfers and causes the zombification and I think that is why zombies are so scary. It's that fear of being eaten alive.

BS: So which was your favorite zombie film you have worked on?

RK: I am partial to *Evil Dead 2* and *Army of Darkness*, even though they aren't technically zombie films.

BS: Why these films in particular?

RK: Well Sam Raimi, of course. He brings a certain energy to his movies when he is filming. It was really cool watching him come up with these cool camera things and ideas with almost no money. Those movies had very little money and so they were packed with energy and everyone was so into making the movie that it was a fun family unit that was formed. On *Evil Dead II*, we were in North Carolina for three months shooting in this old school house with the sets built in the gymnasium and we were young and it was this big fun thing for us. We were on location shooting a monster movie and we were all fans of the first *Evil Dead* so it was a ball. The same thing for *Army of Darkness*. You were a kid fulfilling a fantasy of being on a movie that was like *Jason and the Argonauts*. There were skeleton warriors, guys on horseback and explosions going off everywhere and it was just fun.

BS: Do you have a favorite zombie film?

RK: I usually go back to the original *Dawn of the Dead* or *Day of the Dead*. I liked the remake of *Dawn of the Dead* too. That was pretty cool. There are a few that have been around in recent years that have been interesting, but they are all starting to be the same lately.

BS: You mention the remake of *Dawn of the Dead*. What are your thoughts on zombies running?

RK: I guess that comes from everyone asking why they can't outrun them. I prefer the lumbering drag-your-feet zombies. I think that was the appeal. Yeah, sure you could outrun one or two, but what if you run into a dozen or fifty? Then you've got serious issues. I love the Italian zombie movies like *Zombie* and *City of the Living Dead*. I went through that phase for a while.

BS: What are your thoughts on the genre shift to include viral and plague movies such as *The Rage*?

RK: I think even in the original *Dawn of the Dead* they touch on that it could be viral. They need an explanation and the scientific one is the easiest now. Also, there is the whole contagion thing with the fear of Aids and catching a disease like that. It hits the mark a bit closer to home with what is going on in the world.

BS: Do you think this reflects public fears of bioterrorism?

RK: I think it is part of it and the fact that nature is fighting back. There are these strange infections and skin diseases happening to people and they can't stop it. There is more and more of it lately and I think it has to do with the pollutants and the environment fighting back. It also has to do with us digging up stuff that has been dormant for years. We are in areas of the world unearthing things were we shouldn't be. There are areas of this planet that we don't know a lot about and these things just keep popping up.

BS: Which is your favorite death scene or makeup that you have created?

RK: I loved the full body makeup we did for Kathleen Kinmont in *Bride of Re-animator*. It was a ten piece makeup that took us nine hours to put her in. I loved how we did the muscle structure and exposed flesh. We put KY blood on it so it that it wouldn't be covered in thick blood you couldn't see through. This way we could show more of the detail. That it still one of my favorite effects I have done.

BS: How about your favorite death scene or makeup from a film you haven't worked on?

RK: It's still the exploding head in *Dawn of the Dead*. That is still one of my favorites. There's some really cool stuff out there right now, but it's all digitally augmented. There's some really cool stuff in the new *Dawn of the Dead* where the box truck runs over a group of zombies. My head goes towards scenes like the exploding head in *Scanners*. I loved doing the split body in *Jason Goes to Hell: The Final Friday*, but those aren't really zombies. I suppose Jason is technically a zombie.

BS: You mentioned CGI, what are your thoughts on the heavy reliance on CGI in recent films?

RK: It's good and it's bad. It's obviously a great tool to have in your arsenal, but unfortunately it's a sign of the times. Schedules have gotten so short on prep and on shoot for a lot of films that it is almost required to do things in CGI, because you don't have the time to do it practically any more. Everybody complains about using CGI blood, but when you're only on a set for a few days, you don't have time for cleanup between takes. It comes down to shooting the plate and adding it in later. It's almost to the point where you can't do it on certain sized projects. Everyone thinks that it's more expensive than doing it practically and it's not. If you have to build a mechanical puppet rig, it's going to cost $20,000 to show a guy getting cut in half. Or you can shot it on a plate and cut the actor in half using CGI and it'll cost $5,000. It's just the nature of the beast.

BS: Are you a fan of CGI blood?

RK: It depends. There are some films where I've seen it done really well and I've seen it done really poorly. It's not easy to get it to look right. Then you see a movie like *Rambo* and all of the blood is CGI and it looks really cool.

BS: I think one of the biggest issues is continuity and showing where the blood falls.

RK: Absolutely. If you notice, it's done more in really quick shots now to avoid continuity issues. There is a show on MTV called *Death Valley*. They have a ton of really cool CGI gun shots gags, but they are done really quickly. Back in the early eighties movies like *The Thing* had over a year of research and development work before the film even started shooting. There was a lot of opportunity to push the boundaries and really see what you could do. These days they just don't give you the time to figure out anything new. There is no time to set it up and work out the logistics. It's frustrating. Even on a two hundred million dollar movie, you give them a figure to do something and they tell you it's way out of their range.

BS: So what do you think about the current trend of movies going 3D?

RK: It's obviously adding money to the coffers in the box office. It's not a sure thing though. There are movies that have been released where they slap 3D on top of it and expect it to do well just because it's 3D and it's flopped. As a filmmaker, I am not crazy about 3D. I've been on a couple of sets that have used 3D cameras and it just seems like you are limited. Unless you have the money for five 3D cameras or can convert your 35 mm footage for the non 3D cameras, you are not always going to get the shots you want. On an action scene it's great to have five or six cameras set up. That way you can get multiple angles. On a smaller film, using two cameras you experience limitations with the footage you can gather and 3D gives those same limitations. You're locked into a medium and wide shot and can't get the extra close ups. You're really limited on coverage. It's the same as IMAX cameras. The really big films like *Avatar* or *Transformers* can afford the extra cameras, but if you are on a modest budget around fifteen million, five million of your budget is going on cameras and that just isn't practical. I'd rather shoot it and if they think it's worth doing in post-production, then that's fine. I don't even actively seek out 3D movies just because of the 3D element. I was on *Leatherface 3D* just recently, applying makeup for KNB EFX and they had the 3D cameras and the monitors in the tents. If you put on the 3D glasses, you could see the film in 3D in real time as they were shooting it. It was a really cool process. The thing is, there is a really technical side to this style of filmmaking. It adds another technician to the crew and after every take you ask how it looked and the tech replies that it doesn't look good in 3D so you have to reshoot it. It can definitely slow things down quite a bit.

BS: Is creating more realistic violence on movies like *Hostel* harder to do psychologically than movies that have the fantasy element.

RK: Even when we are doing the more tongue in cheek movies we try to make the violence look real. You try to make it look like it would in reality. You study medical books and see how the wounds are supposed to look. I really try to play down the cartoonish elements. I'm personally not a fan of the slasher movies. I like my horror a little more edgy. Movies like *Hostel* just aren't fun to me because they are too serious and more brutal. I love the Sam Raimi and Peter Jackson style films. Even the *Friday the 13th* movies are a little more tongue in cheek and don't take themselves too seriously. There are movies that I can watch and think they are brilliant, but not watch them again. Movies like *Frontiers* and *Martyrs*, I really enjoyed when I watched them, but I was so affected by them that I couldn't watch them again. They are not the kind of film I could watch over and over again. If a movie affects me so deeply, then I just can't watch it again. I would much rather go out and rent *Fright Night* or *The Return of the Living Dead* again as I have a completely different reaction.

BS: What do you use as reference for creating zombies?

RK: Obviously I use a lot of photos of dead bodies. They are really good when trying to emulate bone structure. The best thing is skinny actors that have the emaciated look but a lot of the time they just give you heavy stunt guys and it's hard to make them look like zombies. You just need to exaggerate the bone structure to make the skin look like it's sunken in. The key is to not to cover it with so much blood that you lose the detail.

BS: How does the zombie creation process work for you?

RK: I always start off with sketches but as soon as I see the actor, it always changes based on their build and facial features. You have to work around the actor. I will take a photo of the actor and then do a life cast. I use Photoshop to design the look then send it out to the director. It can get frustrating as you make dozens of changes until they see what they want. Then it changes again when you get to start sculpting. It's a never ending process until the time you mold it. Then it's locked.

BS: Do you have the freedom to create the zombies how you want them to look or are you limited by the director's vision?

RK: They usually give me the basic idea and then I can run with it and do what I feel is going to be best for the film. For instance on *Undead or Alive*, there is an Indian curse that reanimates the dead. There wasn't a disease or anything, so the zombies didn't have pustules or anything like that. As it was a western we went with all the brown and yellow tones. On a movie like that, where you have fifty or so zombies, you don't get the chance to mold from a life cast. You work with a photo and go from there. The new silicone appliances look so much better and allow for them to mold around the actors face, so it is a bit more forgiving.

BS: In addition to the visual effects, you were also the director on *The Rage*. Did you approach the effects differently?

RK: Yes, but on any film I direct, I am hands on laying out how we are going to do stuff and what we are going to build. With *The Rage* we were on a really tight schedule and shot it in twenty-four days. On that one it was a viral infection and these zombies were more infected with pustules and such. As the director, I had everything planned out, but things always change when you get on set and you have to go with the flow. Once you do your homework, you have the ability to lose shots or change things on the set. I'll storyboard some sequences if I need to. I really enjoyed doing *The Rage* because I had the ability to just have fun with it. I did some things on the fly and was able to see what the actors were going to do. The opening fight scene is one of my favorites in the movie. We had a blast with it. We went in there and knew that we had coverage from three different sides of the room. We set up our masters and started shooting. Once we got into the fight, it was just handheld craziness. We were sitting on doorway dollies and refrigerator boxes and apple crates as guys pushed me around the room in the middle of the action. It was real guerilla style and really fun.

BS: Did you find that directing limited you with the special effects or did you push the envelope even further?

RK: On my own films, I always find myself sticking more things in than I could afford to do. What are you going to do? All you are trying to do is put everything you can into the film and try to go that extra mile. I even try to do it on other people's movies and a lot of time I get pissed off because they don't even use it. They give you a list of things they have to have and when they start shooting they change their minds.

BS: Have there been any shots that you were surprised ended up in the final version of a film you worked on?

RK: It certainly is not as restrictive as it was in the 1980's. Back then they used to crack down a lot more than they do now. In the 1980's and 1990's we always found ourselves building these really cool gags that never made it into the movie because of the ratings issues and that get so disappointing. I'd really love to do another big zombie film again. It would have to be something different though, as it's all been done at this point.

BS: Is it easy to find yourself going over the top with gore?

RK: Honestly, it depends on the director. They usually want you to go overboard so that they have an unrated directors cut that can be used for the DVD. A lot of times you film something and the directors realizes that could cost them their R rating, so you shoot two versions of it, a non-bloody version and the gory version.

BS: Have you ever been a zombie in any of the films you have worked on?

RK: Actually yeah, I was one of the frat guys in *Night of the Creeps*. I walk in front of the bus wearing contacts. We all made heads that split open for everyone on the show. All of the frat guys were played by the effects guys. We didn't have time for them to wait to cast them, so we just did it ourselves. The director was really cool about that.

BS: Can you highlight some of the effects that you created in *The Rage*?

RK: As I said, I loved the opening fight scene. I was really happy with the fight sequence and that actually has some digital changes done to it. Everyone always draws attention to how bad the birds looked, but we didn't even have the budget of a Sci-Fi Channel show. It was really hard. A lot of times the birds are mistaken for stop motion, but they weren't.

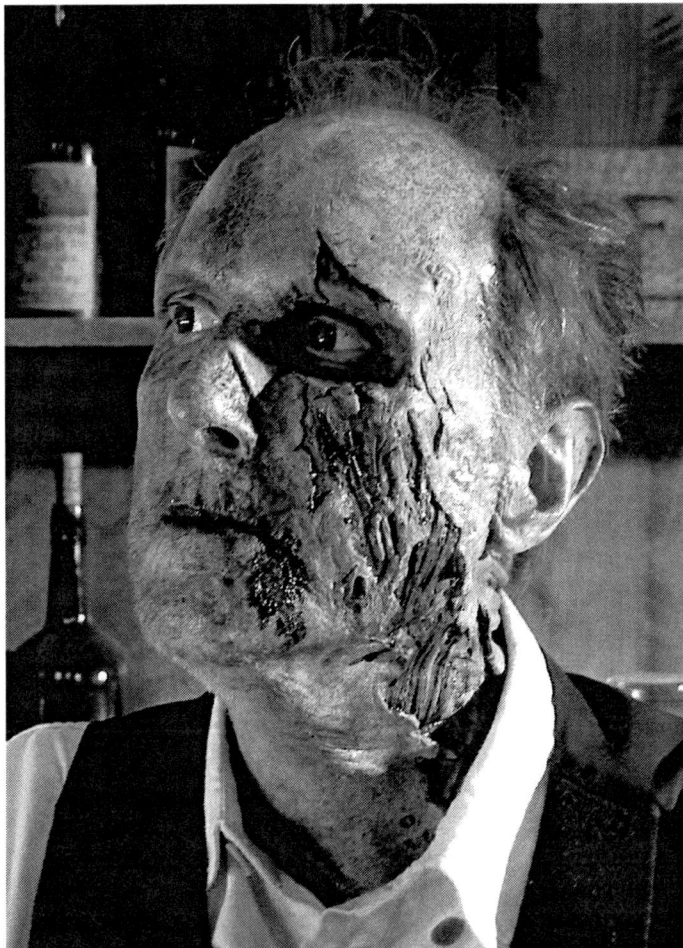

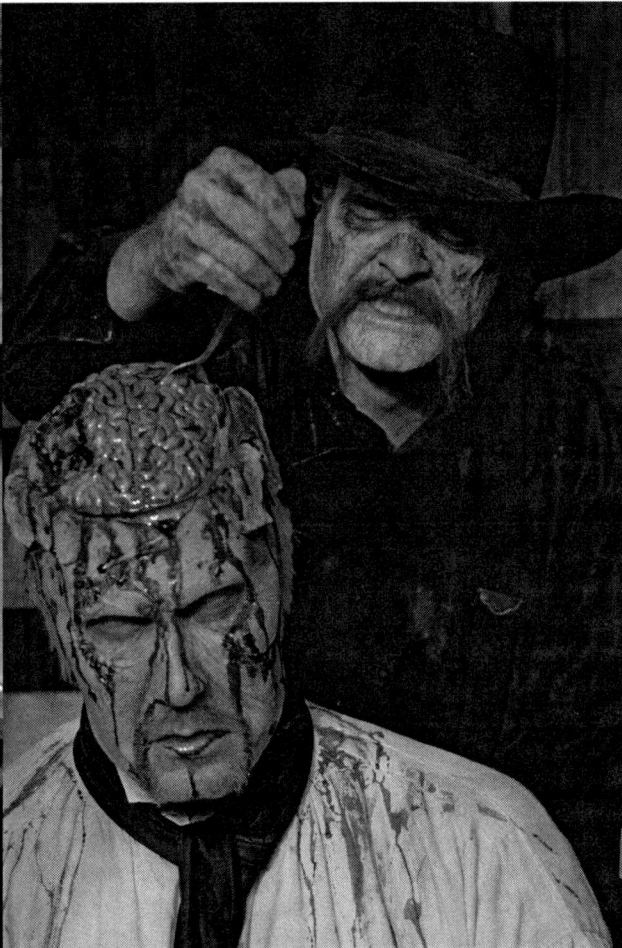

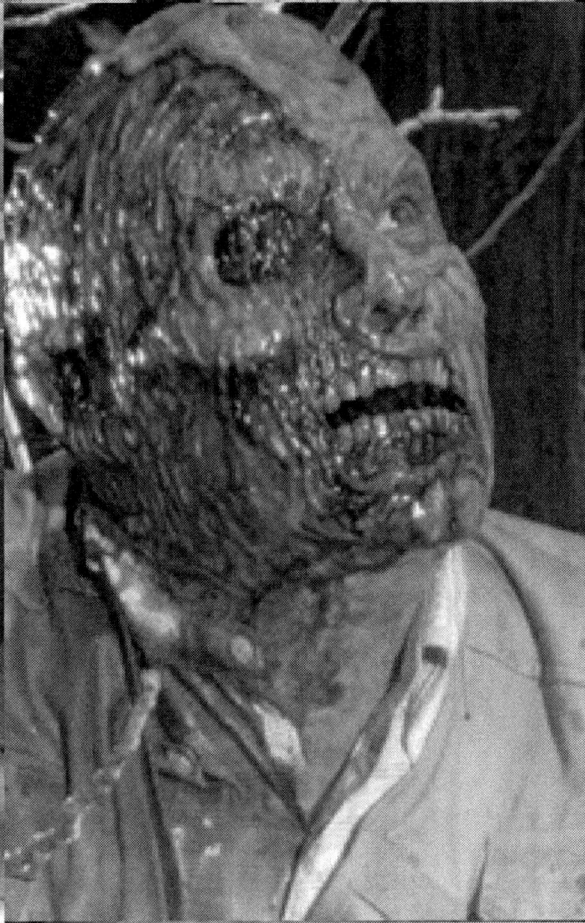

At top, "Undead or Alive". Bottom, "The Rage" courtesy of Robert Kurtzman.

277

JOSHUA LONG

• Axed (2011) Director, Writer, Producer, Editor

Blood Splatter: How did you get into the zombie genre?

Joshua Long: Zombies started with me at an early age. My mum tells me that she is to blame for it as she had the video of Michael Jackson's *Thriller* and when I was four years old I would make her play it over and over again. I would be really scared of it and would watch it while I hid behind the couch. I can't remember that, so I get the feeling my mum is pulling my leg. However, to this day I have to hide behind a couch whenever I watch *Thriller*. I actually grew up having a fascination with Ray Harryhausen films and I loved stop motion monster films. This started a real obsession with horror films. The first zombie flick I remember watching was *The Return of the Living Dead*. It scared the shit out of me, but it also got me really interested in effects makeup. I remember watching it when I was eleven and asking myself why the skeleton had eye lids. After watching that film, I started tracking down all the classics like *The Evil Dead* and *Dawn of the Dead*. It really helped that I hit puberty really early so I was able to go to the video store at the age of fourteen and hire out any rated film I desired. I think mum clued onto me when I brought a copy of *I Spit on your Grave* home when I was fourteen. It wasn't until I saw T*he Evil Dead* and *Dawn of the Dead* that I really wanted to make horror films.

BS: What is your favorite zombie film?

JL: I have a lot of favorites and have collected zombie films for a very long time. Films like *Zombie Flesh Eaters*, *Night of the Living Dead*, *Braindead (Dead Alive)*, *Cemetery Man (Dellemorte Dellemore)* and *Shaun of the Dead* are films that I could watch over and over. My favorite zombie film is *Dawn Of The Dead*. It's the best zombie film hands down. I love the dread of the film. It's so overwhelming, but it also has a sense of hope. I hate the zombie films where the characters have no chance and no hope. What's the point of watching that? The characters always make smart decisions in the film and it treats the audience with respect. There is nothing I hate more than when a character makes the most ridiculous decision. I love the setting of the world. They know how to deal with the zombies, but they need to make the moral decision of if it's right or wrong. The audience also needs to make that decision and it is such a great gore film in its own right. It's one of those films that I watch once a year, so it still stays fresh.

BS: Are there any films that inspired you with the creation of *Axed*?

JL: With *Axed,* I wanted to make a film that brought together the worlds of my two favorite films, *The Evil Dead* meets *Dawn of the Dead*. The film has so many nods to other films. I remember at the time I wanted to make a point of making a film that has the new fast paced running infected versus the old school slow walking dead. So it was kind of an in joke for the hard core fans of the genre. At the time, I watched *28 Days Later* and I thought the film was great, but it always bugged me why the infected never seem to eat the flesh and rather just spit blood all over their victims. I wanted to make the guts fly. I wanted *Axed* to feel modern like *28 Days Later* but have it meet *The Evil Dead, Dawn Of The Dead, Zombie Flesh Eaters* and *The Crazies* but sound like Goblin had done the score. I also wanted it to have that cool low budget, indie fun to it like *Bad Taste* meets *Versus*. The major inspiration for *Axed* was Sam Raimi's film *Within The Woods. Within The Woods* was Raimi's shorter version of *The Evil Dead* that they then used to get the funding for the longer film. That's what we wanted to do. To make a film that doesn't really play like a short film and leave the viewer wanting more and make it for no money. So we can say "hey look what we made off $10, imagine if you gave us $20".

BS: The production values of *Axed* exceed that of many full length features, what formal training do you have?

JL: Thanks mate, that really means a lot to me. I really wanted it to look like we had more money than we actually did. I got a degree majoring in film making and acting and I got out of university thinking I would just walk straight into Hollywood, just like everyone does. I basically got the degree and couldn't get any work at all. To this day I am still a wage slave. Where I live in Brisbane, Australia it is very tough to get any kind of film job and most of my buddies have given up. That's why we made *Axed* to give us something to do. It was either make *Axed* or go get a real degree. I made *Axed.*

BS: How much of a budget did you need to shoot *Axed*?

JL: The thing with *Axed,* is that I really wanted the flick to look a lot more expensive than it really cost. It's all about obstacles and how to rethink your film to get around all the things that get in your way. The story line changed so much due to budget. Myself, along with the two other producers and even my parents put in our own hard earned cash for the budget. The whole film cost around $10,000 Australian, which at the time the Australian dollar was about 46 cents American. So the entire budget for *Axed* was about $5,000 American dollars. I knew the thing that would kill me would be shitty makeup, so we spent about $8,000 on makeup and had to cut a lot of corners. Most of the rest was spent on gas masks, props, food and guts. A lot of guts. We also spent a lot of money on chocolate topping which we mixed with red food color for blood, as we couldn't afford prop blood. So that left about $300 for equipment. My dad built a homemade camera crane for me with a robotic head and I borrowed a Sony Z1 HDV camera that only had a zoom lens. That's the trick right? How to get around obstacles. How do we make a really cheap camera look expensive? Well we wanted to grade the film to look like it was an old Italian cannibal film that had a shitty transfer onto home video and then the home video had been watched a million times. The camera was perfect.

BS: How did you raise the funds?

JL: Nobody would give us any money to make a film that is that fucked up, but that is what I wanted. I wanted a small budget and the power to make the film as brutal and nasty as possible. Mum is so proud.

BS: Obviously with such a tight budget corners have to be cut. Can you elaborate on how you streamlined the process in any way while still maintaining quality control?

JL: We did have to cut corners, but time was something I had for free. I have spent thousands of hours on this film because I refused to pay myself. I remember we didn't have a proper green screen so the director of photographer used a sheet of pool table felt he had. We used that behind the actors when they were in front of the corpse pile. The major corners we had to cut were with makeup. We tried to be smart with it though. One example was the major effect where the lead character Bruce, played by the amazing Kazuya Wright, is dragged out of the corpse pile by an infected. They have a bit of struggle and Bruce kicks him to the ground before swinging the axe into the top of his head, leaving the axe wedged into his face. This was our biggest effect and we had to be clever. We couldn't afford to make a good dummy head if the character had hair. So we made sure we cast a bald actor. We also couldn't afford an armorer so we build all the guns ourselves. Which was kind of cool, because we threw in a tribute to the guns of *Bad Taste.* As we didn't have an armorer we also couldn't afford squibs. I knew we needed a lot of squib hits, but knew we had no money. We designed what we called the Bloodinator. Which was basically an insect sprayer that we attached to a length of garden hose. The idea is to pump the insecticide sprayer about a hundred times and fill the hose with fake blood. Then you hold the bit of hose behind the head of the gunshot victim and time it so they react at the same time as you press the spray button. It worked like a charm. Squibs normally cost you $150 a day to set up, $25 each squib and $600 a day to hire the crazy guy with all the guns to work the squibs. With the Bloodinator I had endless squibs for $15.

BS: Did it always work?

JL: I have worked with squibs before and the Bloodinator worked better. Obviously you have to be creative in hiding the garden hose. I was on the set of a film once where the actor had a squib attached to him and suddenly it went off when no one was ready. It really hurt his hand and was very dangerous. This kind of crap will never happen with the Bloodinator as it uses air pressure, not little bits of dynamite that someone you don't know has put together.

BS: Was this always intended to be a short film?

JL: The film was never meant to be a short. It doesn't play at all like a short. It plays like a feature and the viewer hopefully wants more. We knew we didn't have the cash for a feature so we wanted to use this film to get some funding. It's one thing to be a great short film maker, but to be a half decent feature film maker is a different beast. I wanted *Axed* to prove that if I was given the chance to make a feature, that it would be kick ass. I wanted *Axed* to be that film that would give more in thirty minutes than most feature films would give you in two hours.

BS: How involved were you with the zombie effects?

JL: In the end I got more involved than I would have liked due to money. *Axed* was split into two different shoots two years apart. During the first shoot we did the most extensive zombie stuff with a company called Sharp FX headed by a great artist called Russell Sharp. That's where most of the budget went on the foam latex zombie masks. What we got for the money was amazing. They are great, great artists those guys. I met with Russell originally and got some head casts done for four zombies. I had spoken with him and I wanted the zombies to look more like Gianetto De Rossi had done the makeup rather than Tom Savini. What I mean is, I wanted them to have that brown, clay, mummified look. The Sharp FX guys were really great to work with and I knew based on their work that I would at least have a film where the zombies looked great. That's a great trick with low budget films, make the zombies look great and everyone thinks you had heaps of cash. They ended up doing four major zombie designs and then they cut the pieces up and made more pieces out of them so they could mix and match them. So out of those four molds we got enough foam latex appliances to do thirty zombies.

On the second round of shooting two years later, the Sharp FX guys had moved away to a different part of Australia and I couldn't afford to pay for them to fly back. The artists we had on the second shoot weren't as experienced in prosthetic makeup, so I had to tone it down a bit. I ended up even doing one of the molds myself. The mold I did was in the scene where Bruce is escaping after the executions and a soldier is tackled by a infected and has his finger bitten off. I did the Alginate cast and poured the latex to make the fake arm that squirts blood all over the gas mask of the solider. I didn't know what I was doing but it was something that had to be done. The arm turned out pretty crud, but I just made sure I shook the camera I bit so I would get away with it.

BS: Can you tell us a bit about makeup process?

JL: The makeup process for the major zombies was a long one. They had to get up at about four in the morning and get three hours of makeup done at a house, then driven out to the quarry set which was in the middle of nowhere in rural Sunshine Coast hinterland. It was really tough on the artists also, because we were shooting at the end of the Australian summer and the temperature was really making a mess of the makeup as it was up to 40 degrees Celsius in that quarry. The longest makeup was the zombie played by Georgia Potter, who bites off the nose of a ghoul. She had her whole rib cage exposed. That took at least four hours to apply. Georgia Potter was also the little girl zombie in *Undead*. When I heard that, I really needed her in the flick. I love little tributes like that.

BS: What is your favorite effect in *Axed*?

JL: My favorite effect is probably the leg of the hanging woman being cut off at the shin with the hand saw. It's not the best executed effect but let's face it, that shit's fucked up and you won't see any Hollywood film going that ape shit.

BS: Did you utilize any CGI for the film?

JL: The film has extensive CGI in it. That is why the film took so long, because I didn't know how the hell to do it and had to rely on others to get that stuff done. Most of the cool CGI shots that I like are the front head bullet hits. When you match them up with the Bloodinator's back of the head bullet hit, it works like a charm. The hardest CGI effects in the film are the corpse pile and the nuke. That was the major flaw with *Axed* and why it took so long. We had Hollywood ideas with a $10 budget. So this CGI stuff takes a very long time. The best thing people can do with CGI is use it in places that you don't expect. I hate it when you can tell it's CGI and I am always looking for it. My favorite CGI shot is one that you wouldn't even know was CGI. We shot the overhead view of Bruce's whole family in the grave and I got into post and realized that we totally forgot to add an exit wound on the lead actress's fore head. So they added a bullet wound in post. That took ages. I wish I had more crew at the time so someone was doing continuity. I will never make that mistake again.

BS: Did you find yourself intentionally pushing the envelope to see how far you could go?

JL: Yes. There is no point in making a film that doesn't take risks. I wanted to make a film that I will like. Ultimately, I want it to be good and punch above its weight. I knew since I was putting up all the money that I could call the shots. I also knew if it was only for it's brutality, then *Axed* would be remembered for that. I then tried to put beauty into the film as much as I could. I want that mix of opposites. Doom, gloom, dread and hope. I also wanted my film to stand out as far as Australian cinema goes. This kind of film has not been made in Australia. I wanted to respect the great films that came before like *Undead*. I wanted to do what they did, but do it in thirty minutes.

BS: Can we find you in *Axed* anywhere?

JL: I play a soldier who gets his hand chopped off. The hand then falls to the ground and the gun in the hand goes off and shoots the other soldier in the head. That was a fun, but scary experience. We split the shot up into the shot where the lady swung the machete down into the prop hand cutting it off and the blood squirts everywhere. We also shot a version where she swings down into my real hand stopping just before she hit my hand. I knew just before we were set to shoot that something was up when the lady who was playing the machete swinging ghoul was complaining about not having her contacts in. I knew I had to take this one for the team. I said action and when she swung the machete down she missed timed the stop point and nearly broke my wrist. I was so very glad I got my dad to blunt the machete the night before.

BS: Are there any more zombie films in your future?

JL: I hope so. I want to make the feature version of *Axed*. I want it to find its core audience, which is the people reading this book. I really hope everyone reading this book gets to see *Axed*. I am a huge zombie film fan and I made the film for zombie fans. To all those filmmakers out there that want to make a zombie film, I say don't give up. You can do it. Don't listen to the nay sayers that put shit on zombie films.

BS: Can you share any funny stories from the set?

JL: The set was a fun place to be. When you use a lot of blood on set it's always a bit more fun. Most of the time because what you're using to create these awful looking effects is kind of innocent stuff. Like we have a brutal death scene where the victim smells like chocolate and to this day I still can't eat any chocolate topping on my ice cream. I remember one time we were shooting in the quarry. It was very hot and we had about fifty extras there who were working their bums off. The whole time I had promised that if they work hard then we would blow up a head at the end of the day. So we were set to blow the head and everyone was crowded around to check it out. To give you a bit of background on the head, because we didn't have much money we cut corners a lot and the head was one of those corners. We had the actors head cast and instead of making a foam latex head filled with blood and guts and getting an explosives expert to blow it up, which is what you would do if you had cash, but remember we are working with a $5,000 budget here. The effects crew, instead of using foam latex made a cast of hollowed out plasticine head which looked identical to the person. Because we didn't have the money to hire an explosives expert, the makeup team made up an air compression rig which worked similar to the Bloodinator. It was basically a long tube on a stand that you would fill with blood and it would be linked to an air compressor and when the trigger was pulled it would shoot blood everywhere. Anyway we rigged that under the head and shoved a cork down the tube so it would shoot out through the head and blow it up. The makeup crew assured me they had tested a different head and it worked awesome. So we were set to go and we got the whole crowd to count it down and when the trigger was pressed, the cork shot out of the top of the fake head through the top, but it didn't explode how to was meant to and we didn't see any blood. It was a complete fizzer and everyone was there to see us fail, it was really embarrassing. I still have the head at home.

One of the great experiences with *Axed* was working with Kazuya Wright. He was an absolute godsend. He had a great love for Bruce Campbell so it was a perfect mix. On set he asked me if he could roll down a cliff. An actor like that is hard to find. One who can cry and then roll down a cliff while dodging pretend bullets.

ED MARTINEZ

- Cowboys and Zombies (2011) Special Effects Makeup
- Retardead (2008) Director of Special Effects
- The Dead Pit (1989) Special Makeup Effects Artist

Blood Splatter: How did you get into the zombie genre?

Ed Martinez: I got into science fiction and horror at a really young age and I enjoyed the creature feature type television shows. Every city has their own horror host and they would show all the classics like Dracula, Frankenstein, the Wolfman and the Ray Harryhausen stop motion films. That got me into everything after that. Comic books were also a big influence on me. I would spend hours reading them and that got me got into drawing. Soon I was creating zombies and monsters from my own designs. The main turning point, as I assume was with everyone else in the genre, was watching *Night of the Living Dead* for the first time. It had a major impact on me and I remember watching it late at night in the dark with my younger sister. It definitely gave me nightmares for a long time after that.

BS: Do you have a favorite zombie film?

EM: Of course, I love the original Romero trilogy. They are the pinnacle of zombie cinema for me, but in recent years there have been some really good films released like *Shaun of the Dead* and *Zombieland*. I am also a huge fan of the Italian genre too.

BS: Is the zombie genre something you seek out to work on?

EM: Oh, for sure. I do anything I can with the genre. So far I have worked on shorts, music videos and feature length productions. For guys like me, Halloween is a really big time for zombies. For the past few years, Google have hired me to do the makeup for their annual Halloween party called the Googleween Zombie Machine. We have about eight makeup artists on hand and we make a cemetery and props. They love it. All the employees dress up as zombies and for hours we make up the employees as zombies.

BS: What is your favorite zombie kill?

EM: I have soft spot for *The Dead Pit* as that was my first film. The main character in the film, Dr. Ramzi has a huge death scene at the end. To this day, this sequence is still one of the most elaborate death scenes I have ever worked on. I would actually like to work on a sequel to the film if that ever came about. I also really like the scene in *Retardead* where we had a body torn apart. This was a definite homage to Rhodes dying in *Day of the Dead*. I always felt that scene had such a huge impact on the audience and I wanted to pay my respects.

BS: You mentioned *The Dead Pit* was your first zombie movie. What can you tell us about the experience?

EM: I did get my zombie start working on *The Dead Pit* and it was a really intense shoot. It was the first film I'd done where I had to have a crew and figure out the look of the film. We only had a certain amount of hours to shoot as it was mostly filmed at night. We would have to start getting the actors made up before the sun went down and we had to make up 150 zombies in one setting. It was really hectic at times. Like most special effects artists, I am a student of the masters, Dick Smith, Rick Baker and Tom Savini. Whenever they would reference an anatomy book or medical reference guide in an interview, I would do my best track it down and use it. I found some great medical books that way. One of the first books I bought was the "Color Atlas of Human Anatomy" by Johannes Wilhelm Rohen. *The Dead Pit* called for certain medical procedures and in particular, a lobotomy and so I spent a lot of time researching how lobotomies are done and one of the books had ViewMaster reels in the back. They had pictures of brain operations and I was able to use these in my workshop while I was sculpting. Some of the procedures they did in the sixties were barbaric and I wanted to convey that with the effects. I even recreated some of the tools used back then to do the lobotomies. Believe it or not, it was a modified ice pick. They would hammer this into the side of the eye socket and do a scooping motion to sever the ganglia. It's really horrifying if you look at it what it is. We added blood tubing and made the tool retract and it turned out really well.

The hospital where we shot *The Dead Pit* was a mental hospital and it had a pretty sordid history. A lot of the elements of the film actually came from the history of the hospital. Doctors there had performed a lot of these types of procedures in the past. It was actually an active hospital when we were shooting and it was huge. It sat on acres upon acres of land. Certain wings had been closed down years before and were boarded up, but we were able to shoot there. There is so much history behind the building. In the 1906 San Francisco earthquake, the building was heavily damaged and portions of it collapsed. There are pictures at the facility and it was very similar to the Overlook Hotel in *The Shining*. The administration building was lined with pictures of patients tied to trees with bed sheets after being made homeless from the earthquake. Almost sixty patients were killed in total. On the grounds, there was a mass grave for the patients who died and was quite literally a dead pit. The director and writer of the film knew all about the history and the various cold spots and where the patients had been lobotomized or killed.

When they let us go into the buildings to shoot, it was really creepy. It was like a million dollars of art direction for free. They were huge buildings that still had all of the medical equipment left inside. There were old dentist chairs complete with instruments and tools. In the movie there is one scene where a man's eye is drilled out with a dental drill and we were able to use the original props. So the film has a great level of authenticity that many viewers may not even realize. The filmmakers were actually shooting a different movie on the set and liked it so much, they turned *The Dead Pit* around really quickly. The setting is perfect for the overall atmosphere of the film. There were a lot of effects in the script that I had never done before, such as the meltdowns, so there was a bit of a learning curve for me. I also did a lot of studying to determine how a corpse looks after it has been stored in formaldehyde. The skin starts to wrinkle the same way your fingers do when they have been in water for too long. The flesh goes translucent and you can see bones beneath it. This doesn't make for your typical looking zombie. I made up buckets of Methylcellulose, which is more commonly used to make slime and I added a thinner to it to make it look less congealed. We had two baby pools on set and one was filled with blood and the other with slime. The standard routine was we would make up the zombie, then have them stand in the pool and they were covered in slime. This made them look like they had just crawled out of a vat of formaldehyde. That coupled with the blood made for a really gooey and sticky mess. It gave them really wet look that you don't see very often. The actors were pretty miserable though. All they had on were hospital gowns and most didn't even have underwear on. These poor actors were just wearing a thin gown and they were sprayed down with this mess. It was a night shoot, so they were they were all standing outside shivering. I'm really glad I wasn't one of them to be honest.

BS: Did you notice anything strange occurring at the hospital because of its history?

ED: Oh, I have a ton of stories about things like that. There were strange things happening all of the time. Some were related to the supernatural history of the building, while others were tied to the existing residents. We were given cart blanche on the entire shut down wing of the hospital, so we could go anywhere we wanted. However, there was still an active part of the hospital in use and had patients living there. We were eating breakfast one morning on set and a couple of the patients had escaped from their rooms and were having sex in the bushes outside of the window. On more than one occasion we'd be shooting or eating and there would be patients in the window behind us jacking off. We saw some really crazy shit during the shoot. It's scary to think of people being in a place like that. The problem was that our extras who were playing the patients wore the same color outfits as the real life patients. There were times when we were shooting and you'd see the zombie patients and from a distance you couldn't tell which were actors and which ones belonged there.

BS: How about some of the more unexplainable occurrences?

ED: While we were doing research for the film and the hospital, we found out about the lobotomies and the patients they were doing them to. Some of them were just simply bored housewives who didn't need this kind of treatment at all. That was scary in itself. You know how certain haunted locations have cold spots, which are basically areas in the building that experience an unexplained drop in temperature? There were loads of cold spots all over the place. I would be in the building that housed my workshop and at night when the crew was filming on the other side of the campus, I would be there alone and I would hear footsteps in the building. I knew no one else was supposed to be there, so I'd call in on the radio and ask if anyone had been sent over and they'd tell me no. I'd stop what I was doing and go take a walk to see what I could find. I never found anyone, but I did find cold spots throughout the hospital. There was one room that I went in to that had been used as a punishment room. There was a chair that had been bolted to the floor facing the corner of the room and had leather restraint straps on the arms. It was a small room about the size of a bathroom and when the patients were bad, they would be tied into the chair and forced to stare at the wall. If this room had a voice, I'm sure it would be screaming. All of the walls were undamaged except the corner of the room which was the area the patients were forced to stare at. It was like an intense heat beam had been focused on the wall and all the paint was bubbled and peeling. The room had a really disturbing feel to it and it was not a room you wanted to be locked in on your own. Anytime I needed to go in there, I would always prop the door open. There were other rooms that had cold spots too. The operating room where they performed the lobotomies had a really dark vibe to it. There were nights where we were shooting at four in the morning and there were only a handful of us on set and we would hear noises and footsteps and the room would suddenly go cold. There was a real sense of despair on the set. We thought that some of it was other crew members playing games, because we all knew about the history of the hospital, but the crew was always accounted for and we could not find the source. I really believe that buildings can hold onto bad feelings and suffering. A lot of really bad and tragic things happened behind those walls.

BS: You mentioned a possible sequel. Is this something anyone has seriously looked into?

EM: The director of photography had written a script on spec a while back about Sister Clair, the crazy nun. I think I would have a different take on it, but it does look like there is fan interest in a sequel.

BS: What can you tell us about the scene where Dr. Ramzi melts?

EM: That scene actually got a reshoot at the end of filming and ended up being something quite different from what was originally scripted. We had a set amount of money and we used that up before we got to the end of the film. We reached the end of the shooting schedule and there were some effects that we weren't happy with. They closed down the production and went off to do some editing and at the time there was a film festival in Milan, Italy. They took eighteen minutes and went to the festival and they sold the foreign rights outright for more than the films budget up to that point. We had spent $200,000 up to that point and they came back from the festival with an additional $300,000 in their pockets. We did a reshoot and were able to regroup and finish up the effects. We were able to revisit the death of Dr. Ramzi and give him a very elaborate death scene that involves a multi layered puppet that could melt.

BS: Have you been a zombie extra in any of the films you've worked on?

EM: No, unfortunately I haven't. The zombie films I have done have been lower budget films, so I am usually one of the only effects guy on hand and there is no one to put me in makeup. It is incredibly difficult to do a makeup job on yourself, so I don't. I have had zombie makeup done on myself, but never in a movie. I'm like Tom Savini in that respect, in that I don't really like being covered in glue and make up. The removal process is not fun for me at all. We do have the makeup put on ourselves so we can see what the actor is experiencing. I think it is essential for any makeup artist to be aware of what the person sitting in your chair is going through. Their comfort is an important factor of the makeup process. I teach classes on life casting and I find that some artists are more concerned about the cost of materials rather than the comfort of the model or actor. If your subject is claustrophobic, you can do the cast in multiple sessions, so there are always ways to work around things. I've had someone in my chair freak out during the life cast and I take the mold off and help them to calm down. It's critical for them to know that they are more important than the makeup.

BS: So what else have you done in the genre?

EM: I was involved in the huge marketing event for season one of *The Walking Dead*. Right before the season premiere, AMC did this worldwide marketing event. AMC shipped makeup out to me directly from Greg Nicotero and the guys at KNB EFX. We got a bunch of Prosaide transfers and went to a hotel and we spent a day making up dozens of zombies. A bus then showed up and took them to all of the popular landmarks in San Francisco to take pictures for AMC's website. I guess they did the same thing in New York, Mexico, London, Japan and a bunch of other cities. It was really cool to be a part of it.

ROB MCCALLUM

- Resident Evil: Afterlife (2010) Concept Artist, Storyboard Artist
- Survival of the Dead (2009) Storyboard Artist
- Land of the Dead (2005) Storyboard Artist
- Resident Evil: Apocalypse (2004) Concept Designer: Nemesis, Storyboard Artist

Blood Splatter: How did you become a storyboard artist?

Rob McCallum: It kind of came from me drawing comics and my love of films. I had seen the storyboards that Mike Ploog had drawn for *The Thing* in a magazine as a kid and had always thought it was a great crossover between comics and films. When I came to direct my own shorts while I was at Glasgow School of Art, I did my own boards. I had been drawing a comic for the doomed Stan Lee's Excelsior Line. I worked on it for almost two years then found out it had been put on hold indefinitely. I was pretty sickened that my work wouldn't be seen and by comics in general after that. The next day I received a call from a Hallmark film looking for a board artist and my name had been given to them by a comic's editor. I got the job, so everything ended up working out.

Then, when I moved to Canada, I dropped some samples off at a studio and they saw I could draw and asked me to do some prop designs. Not long after, I was boarding for them and word spread about me in town and that was that. One nice thing that closed the circle was last year when I got to work on *The Thing* remake. I loved that because Ploog's amazing boards for the John Carpenter film were what made me aware that there was even a thing called storyboards.

BS: How did you get into the zombie genre?

RM: I've always loved horror films and drawing monsters. In my portfolio I have some samples of zombie boards from a television pilot, plus all my zombies and things from over the years which helped me get the storyboarding job on *Resident Evil: Apocalypse*. There were loads of undead in there.

BS: Are you a fan?

RM: I am, yes. A picky fan, but a fan none the less. Zombie stories have flooded the horror genre and there are a lot of really bad films out there. As with all genres, there are some gems though.

BS: Do you have a favorite zombie movie?

RM: I wouldn't say I have one ultimate favorite. *Night of the Living Dead, Shaun of the Dead, Day of the Dead* are all on the list. I also love Charlie Brooker's *Dead Set*, a UK television show.

BS: How does the storyboard process work in relation to the overall film process?

RM: The storyboards are used as a blueprint, often replacing the script when describing the action to the departments. Sometimes they are followed exactly, other times they are a guide. It really depends on the film and what is possible on the day.

BS: Do you generally complete the storyboards before the film shoots or is it more of an organic process with the storyboards changing as the film evolves?

RM: There are times where I do both. As always, it depends on the film. Some films, I come in to board a sequence, it's locked and I move onto the next sequence. Other times, the boards are always changing. I had a job last year where I was revising the boards right up until they filmed the sequence. Hours before in fact.

BS: How much of the script do you receive prior to starting to draw?

RM: I usually get the whole script prior to starting to draw. I usually know it very well by the time I'm done.

BS: Where can we see some of your particular designs in the George Romero or *Resident Evil* movies?

RM: There are some of my sequences in all the films I've worked on. That's nice when that happens but you never expect that. Things can always change. Small ideas make it in there, but it all melts in with the other ideas. As for actual design, I designed Nemesis on *Resident Evil: Apocalypse* and it was built very close to my design by Paul Jones. I also did a lot of storyboarding for the film. On the *Resident Evil: Afterlife* movie, I wasn't doing the storyboards, I was a concept artist. A lot of the look of the burnt out and destroyed Los Angeles came from paintings I did under the guidance of the production designer and director. Film work is such a collaborative effort, that it's often so tricky to be able to claim any design as your own.

BS: Your storyboards for the scene in *Land of the Dead* where Big Daddy leads the zombies out of the river, features a striking resemblance to the Eugene Clarke who played Big Daddy in the film. Were your drawing based on photographs of Eugene or was Eugene hired based on your images?

RM: I was given photographs of Eugene prior to shooting and I was able to base all of my designs from those.

BS: How closely did you work with George Romero on the designs for *Land of the Dead* and *Survival of the Dead*?

RM: I worked very closely with George. We had a really nice back and forth going on.

BS: Your storyboards feel more like a comic book narrative telling a story as opposed to images simply giving camera and stage direction. Is this intentional and is it common in the community?

RM: I always try to make my boards "a good read". I try to get the feel of the whole thing and give an idea of how the sequence will look when finished. I can't say for others though.

BS: How do you handle drawing a storyboard that you find morally offensive?

RM: It hasn't happened to me yet.

BS: Zombie films are known for extravagant zombie kills and character death scenes, which has been your favorite that you have drawn?

RM: I liked drawing the zombie getting the arrow in the face in *Land of the Dead*. I had a few weeks of gore and fun kill boards. I spent ages just drawing the most awfully horrible ways to die. There are some on my site. I had a guy getting his groin pulled off and his guts landing on the zombie under him. There was a guy getting his head and spine pulled out. I had all sort of expensive ideas, but some made it into the film in creative ways. The head and spine one was done in silhouette.

BS: Were there any scenes cut from either the Romero or *Resident Evil* movies you storyboarded that you were attached to?

RM: I find it's easier not to get attached to scenes, so that way it doesn't really bother me when it happens.

BS: Can you tell us about some of the concept drawings you have done for the Romero zombie movies?

RM: All of the stuff I've done for George has been storyboards. I boarded most of *Land of the Dead* and I did the heads on poles bit of *Survival of the Dead.*

BS: Why do you think it's more acceptable to portray violence against zombies than it is against humans? Is it thinly masked violent tendencies of human kind?

RM: It seems to be the case, doesn't it? I think it's probably because zombies are sort of removed from

Scene 108 Shot 6

WIDE - BIG DADDY SPLASHES IN.

CUT TO

Scene 112 Shot 4

CW BIG DADDY - ZOMBIES
BEHIND HIM.

"Land of the Dead" storyboards courtesy of Rob McCallum.

287

normal humans. Plus, they are softer and come apart more easily, which makes for a lot of comedy potential.

BS: Many special effects artists use pictures from medical journals and morgues as reference points for wounds and damage on humans. Where do you draw your inspirations from?

RM: I don't use references when I create my zombies. I have an idea how humans work physically and then draw how they look like with bits of that showing. I have to think of what the zombie is going to be doing and then work from there. If its biting someone, then it needs a jaw and an arm to grab them with.

You really don't have to for the boards, but since I'm drawing them anyway, I mix up the injuries. The main injuries on a zombie are always going to be how they died and what happened during that process. It gives them a story. It keeps them interesting to look at.

BS: Have you ever drawn yourself or people you know into a storyboard?

RM: I don't draw myself into my boards.

BS: Is there any particular reason why?

RM: I try not to draw things that might distract from the sequence. I used to though from time to time. On *Land of the Dead*, that waterfront sequence has Shaun and Ed in there. I had just seen *Shaun of the Dead* and drew them in, then heard that Edgar Wright and Simon Pegg were coming over to do cameos. Some people assumed that was the scene they would be in from my little drawn for myself background pictures. They shambled into my office, unrecognizable under blood and makeup. I gave them copies of the boards. They were very nice guys.

BS: Are there any zombie films in the future for you?

RM: Who knows? I was recently offered a job on the new *Resident Evil* movie *Resident Evil: Retribution* but unfortunately I wasn't available.

Shaun and Ed from "Shaun of the Dead" have cameos in this storyboard from "Land of the Dead" courtesy of Rob McCallum.

NEIL MORRILL

• Diary of the Dead (2007) Special Makeup Effects Supervisor (Gaslight Studios)
• Land of the Dead(2005) Special Makeup Effects Artist (Gaslight Studios)

BS: How did you get into the zombie genre?

NM: A friend of mine, Stuart Conran asked me to do some dailies with him on *Shaun of the Dead*, but unfortunately I wasn't available at the time. He told me to give his friend Paul Jones a call when I got to Canada and from there I started working on *Silent Hill*. I soon heard that Greg Nicotero was coming up to Toronto to start working on *Land of the Dead*. The way the movie industry works is that you get jobs based on recommendations from other jobs and I was able to get on board with *Land of the Dead* and the ball started rolling from there.

BS: Are you a fan of the zombie genre?

NM: Oh yeah, I am a fan. The weird thing is that being a special effects guy, you don't get the same buzz when you watch the movies play back as you used to. When I was younger, before I got into effects, the films were more exciting. It's a bit of a downer as movies were more fun then. Now, don't get me wrong, I really love what I do, I just get to see the magic happening from the other side of the camera now. So it's a trade off.

BS: Many people I have spoken to have said that the hours on a zombie movie are worse than other films. Is that something you've experienced too?

NM: Very much so. There is so much makeup to do and it takes hours to put on and then take off at the end of the day. The rest of the crew is usually long gone before we finish. Sometimes we've even had the electricity turned off as the electricians want to go home. The night shoots can be really tough at times.

BS: Were you a fan of George Romero before you signed on to *Land of the Dead*?

NM: Yeah I was a big, big fan of *Dawn of the Dead*. In the U.K it was one of the banned films and even when it was officially released, it was edited. Fortunately I was able to get hold of a European bootleg copy. I was also a fan of Tom Savini's and had his Grand Illusions special effects book.

BS: A lot of people in the industry have sworn by that book. It's been mentioned time and time again in interviews.

NM: It's a really great book.

BS: Do you have a favorite zombie film?

NM: The original *Dawn of the Dead* without a doubt. More recently I have really enjoyed *28 Days Later*. I love the intensity of the film and it's definitely tapping into people's fears a bit more.

BS: What has been your favorite death scene that you worked on?

NM: It has to be from *Diary of the Dead*. While we were in pre-production, Kyle Glencross, Chris Bridges and I went to George Romero's apartment to talk about the effects in the film. Greg Nicotero was there and we were sitting around and George told us that he had written a bunch of stuff but he wanted to know how we wanted to kill zombies. He basically gave us cart blanche on new ways to kill zombies. I had a massive panic attack as it is not often you get an opportunity like that, but it was an amazing experience.

There is a scene in the hospital where a zombie is stabbed with an IV pole. That was originally supposed to be a liposuction machine. We just couldn't find a way of writing it in to the scene and making it cohesive. The sequence we did with the IV pole is a great scene though. There are a few CGI elements, but we used a retractable pole and a fiber glass chest on the actor. He had blood packs on his chest that burst when the pole hit them. For the kill, we created a silicone puppet head and jammed the pole through it, pushing brain out the back. It came out really good and we only had one take to do it in. Joe Dinicol who played Eliot was under a lot of pressure to get it right.

BS: *Diary of the Dead* is shot in a very interesting manner with the handheld camera style of shooting giving it a more realistic feel to it. Did you have to approach the effects differently because of this?

NM: The makeup was essentially the same as what we would do on a normal film. The problem that George presented for us was that he wanted everything to happen live on camera with no cuts. That was a huge challenge. With normal blood gags you will have people off camera with tubes and compressed air, but we couldn't do anything like that. Everything we built had to be self-contained. So we came up with different ways of doing things. For example, if someone was bitten on the neck, we had appliances with bladders underneath and then the tubes would run down to squeeze balls hidden underneath their arms and then they could squeeze on demand. Essentially when you see these things happening on the film, they are really happening at that time.

BS: How about the scene at the beginning of the movie with the man climbing off the stretcher and being shot in the chest?

NM: We created a fake chest for him and put squibs on it. We covered the squibs with wax to hide them. I'm really proud of that scene, because it is not often you see someone getting shot in the chest with no shirt on. It came out really well. It was really challenging to do, but I think it turned out to be a really great scene and really set the theme for the film.

BS: Is it hard to distance yourself from the reality of the effects, especially with a film like *Diary of the Dead* where the shooting is done on a real time basis with less of the regular behind the scenes pieces showing?

NM: It definitely was for some of the set pieces. A lot of people assume that because we work with gore and violence, that we are really into it, but in all honesty I am really squeamish. I can't stand the sight of my own blood. I'm certainly not desensitized at all, but it is a job and you know that you are not seeing reality.

BS: What is your favorite zombie death?

NM: I really liked Rhodes getting torn apart in *Day of the Dead*.

BS: Which effect are the most proud of?

NM: I really liked the Ridley makeup that we did in *Diary of the Dead*. It worked because Philip Riccio who played him did such a good job. He had the walk down and everything. That is the thing with special effects. Even if the makeup is amazing, if the actor isn't into it, it loses it's impact and can spoil the makeup effect significantly.

BS: What can you tell us about the acid attack?

NM: Kyle applied the makeup and I did the head. There were some CGI elements to this particular shot. We did a series of makeups that gave him the various looks of the face melting. We created a head that could melt that was added in by CGI. We put Alka Seltza and such in the head to give the impression that the skin and bone were melting. As the budget was tighter on this film, I think the CGI crew was less flamboyant and that really helped.

BS: What are your thoughts on CGI?

NM: To be honest, I kind of like it, but the problem with it is if you put too much money into CGI, it can get overdone and detracts from the movie. Many of the people using CGI have a technical background over an artistic one and it definitely shows on some movies. I've tried some of the high end applications and I can still sculpt a head faster than I can do it on a computer. However, I like the look of CGI when it's done well.

BS: Were there any shots that made it to the final cut of *Land of the Dead* or *Diary of the Dead* that surprised you?

NM: There was one scene that I was really surprised they kept in *Diary of the Dead*. It was the scene that featured the kid getting shot in the head with the arrow For some reason, I didn't think that shot would ever be seen. It looked really cool, but you have to be careful with what you do to children and I felt this really pushed it.

BS: Have you ever pushed the envelope to see what you could get away with?

NM: Many of the ideas we presented to George during our meeting seemed completely over the top but he just sat there telling us how awesome these ideas were. Things that we thought we pretty shocking we was just eating it up. The news reporter who gets bitten on the mouth at the beginning of *Diary of the Dead* also came from that session. You always see people getting bitten on the arm or on the neck, rarely on the lip. I don't even know where we could go after some of the scenes we did.

BS: Have you ever been a zombie extra?

NM: No, actually I haven't. I was almost in *Diary of the Dead*, but they had too many extras so it didn't pan out. My only screen time was working the blue screen suit when Ridley gets his head sliced in half with a sword and even then I was digitally erased. In *Land of the Dead*, a few of the effects guys were able to get cameos. They had to stand around for hours in makeup and it was assumed they could put up with it. I wouldn't mind doing it if it came up though.

BS: So no fears of being in makeup at all?

NM: Oh no, not at all.

BS: Are there any more zombie movies in your future?

NM: I am actually in the process of doing some work for *Resident Evil: Retribution* but it's all hush-hush right now as we are still in production. It's all top secret, but some of the designs look really cool and hopefully be something no one has seen before.   I did a few days on *Resident Evil: Afterlife* as well. That was a lot of fun. You know the zombies that have the weird flower looking things that come out of their mouths?

BS: I sure do. What did you call those?

NM: They're called weird flower things. *(laughs)* I worked on those, although I don't know what the technical phrase was for them. I did all of the sculpting.   A lot of people thought they were completely CGI, but there was actually a practical prop involved to begin with. The actor would hold it in his mouth and reference pictures were taken. It was then created in CGI to enable it to be animated and make it a little easier on the actor.

BS: Can you share any funny on set stories?

NM: We tried out some new effects in *Diary of the Dead*. We were making some vacuuform dentures that would fit over the actor's lips to give the impression that the lips had been torn away during an attack. All of the teeth were exposed. However George took it upon himself to start referring to everyone who wore them as "banana lips" and that seemed to stick throughout the shoot.

BS: How would you survive in the zombie apocalypse?

NM: I always wanted to build a bunker in the bottom of my house. I would probably get really technical and have air and water filtration systems. I would keep it fully stocked and be able to survive down there. Yeah, I would be that guy.

MICHAEL MOSHER

- Day of the Dead (2008) Special Makeup Effects Artist
- Resident Evil: Extinction (2007) On-set Makeup Effects Technician: Tatopoulos Studios
- Dead & Breakfast (2004) Special Makeup Effects Supervisor

Blood Splatter: How long have you been doing special effects?

Michael Mosher: I've been doing makeup on friends and family since I was about nine years old. I poured my first foam latex appliance when I was sixteen. This was back in the days of the old R and D foam latex, before gelatin was back in vogue and years before silicone was used as an appliance material.

BS: How did you get into the zombie genre?

MM: I love makeup in general, not just horror, so I do whatever makeup I am hired for. Zombie movies are just more fun. One can only do foundation and powder for so long before he wants to get back up to his elbows in rubber.

BS: Are you a fan of the zombie genre?

MM: I hope I don't make enemies here, but I'm not specifically a fan of any genre and so many horror films are just bad. There are great and bad films in every genre, of course. I'm a fan of movies that try hard to be exactly what they strive for. A good story is always a must. Film is all about the story.

BS: You have quite the range of zombie films under your belt. From high profile blockbuster movies like *Resident Evil: Extinction* to the quirky and obscure like *Dead and Breakfast*. Which one was your favorite to work on?

MM: By far *Dead and Breakfast* was the most fun.

BS: I loved that film. Why was that?

MM: We got to be so incredibly creative. I've been in the biz for over twenty years and have over seventy film and television projects under my belt and by far *Dead and Breakfast* was the most creative. We had over thirty six major effects for a ridiculously small budget, all shot in nineteen days. I had a small but super talented crew, Ralis Kahn, Rocky Faulkner and Richard Redlefsen. All great makeup artists who work all the time.

BS: The zombie genre is known for extravagant zombie kills and character death scenes. All three of the zombie films you have worked on have had some great examples of this. Which has been your favorite that you created?

MM: There have been some good ones, but the one that was the most challenging and came out exactly the way I'd imagined was the big chainsaw decapitation on Eric Palidino who played David in *Dead and Breakfast*. When I explained how I wanted to do it, the guys in my shop didn't think it would work, but it did. It was a huge pain in the ass and probably the most expensive single effect in the film, but it was totally worth it.

BS: You say that it came out exactly how you imagined. Are there times where that doesn't happen?

MM: No, never. Of course. I've had connections break and much less blood come out where it's supposed to and cover me and the crew instead. I've had exploding heads that didn't quite explode and I did what should have been a beautiful scalping for a film. Alas, it was shot badly and looked more like someone getting a hat taken off, rather than someone was being scalped.

BS: Are there any other zombie movies you are a fan of?

292

MM: I loved *28 Days Later.* It was original. It was just gory enough without being cliché and I love that the zombies ran.

BS: That was certainly a big change to the zombie genre that divided fans. Any particular reason you liked the running zombies?

MM: If zombies are mobile, they should have some reasoning left. If all they are just mindless blobs, I don't find it all that scary. They should be able to chase after their food.

BS: What do you use as inspiration for the varying degrees of decay and damage?

MM: I try to at least start with something forensic.

BS: Have you used anything controversial?

MM: No, nothing controversial. I stick with rubber and fake blood. I've never used real guts or real blood and I have a reputation of being very kind to my actors when I can.

BS: So no sheep intestines then?

MM: No, I don't like anyone uncomfortable for long periods of time and actors appreciate it. So does the crew when my supplies don't smell.

BS: When creating a zombie, how does the design process work? Do you go into it with a predetermined idea or do you improvise?

MM: Define improvise. Every film is a bit different. For *Dead and Breakfast*, the zombie makeup is makeup I didn't even do. That was white face with dark circles. My crew and I did the blood effects and most of the specialty props. For *Day of the Dead*, we had a huge supply of appliances, stock and custom and we mixed and matched and made a lot of it up as we went along. *Resident Evil: Extinction* was incredibly well planned. We had makeup tests, we had paint schemes on maquette's in the trailer that we followed, but the actual appliances were stock and pretty small. So every stunt man got a different set of lumps and bumps most every day, to make them look like there were more super undead than there really were.

BS: With the advent of CGI allowing for more decomposing and wounds, do you find yourself still using traditional methods or gravitating more to CGI?

MM: If I go CGI at all, I prefer eighty percent real effects and twenty CGI. I hate CGI Blood. It looks like crap and it never lands on anything. I think that CGI has its place in makeup effects and occasionally you see something that's really impressive. Most of the time though, CGI is used because they think it's going to save money by not doing it on set. In the long run, it may save time on set, but it almost never saves money. CGI is expensive. We did a head shot on the female zombie for *Resident Evil: Extinction* that was an entrance and exit with no squibs. I thought the director was going to have to change his pants he was so happy. Originally, production wanted to do it CGI. My friend Ralis Kahn was able to talk them into giving us the opportunity to do it live and that same rig was used over and over and over in the Vegas stuff to do bullet hits that would have been done CGI or by the pyro guys who took a long time to reset. We took three minutes.

BS: I'm surprised you didn't use squibs. Can you share with us how you achieved this?

MM: It was a fairly simple, but very reliable high pressure air rig. There was one tube with a T-split, one under the makeup on her forehead and one in the back. It shoots about 3oz of blood at well over 150 pounds of pressure and it looks great in the film.

BS: Zombie films continue to push the boundaries, have there been any effects shots that made it to the final cut that surprised you?

MM: I don't get shocked by gore. The MPAA never ceases to amaze me in that you can show some dude getting his arms and legs ripped off, but you can't show a full frontal penis or sex. Sex is dirty, but violence is okay. They're horrible human beings. The simple fact that you can't use precedence baffles me. If it's good enough for one movie, it should be good enough for every film, but they can just make up rules as they go along.

BS: Have you found yourself intentionally pushing the envelope to see how far you can go?

MM: Sadly, I'm often constrained by the script and the story. I will suggest more creative ways for actors to go sometimes. However, re-writing someone else's script is incredibly rude. Unless I'm involved in the creative process from early on, I just make what they want, just hopefully better than they imagined it.

BS: Recently we have had *Resident Evil: Afterlife* in 3D and there is rumor that the *Zombieland* sequel could be a 3D film. How do you think 3D technology benefits these types of films?

MM: It doesn't and as the box office has been showing it. 3D is not a way to add money onto your returns. I think it's great for some stuff, but does *Remains of the Day* need to be re-released in 3D? Nope, it sure doesn't.

BS: When creating background and hero zombies, is there a particular type of actor you look for that determines roles?

MM: That depends on what the script calls for. Ideally, an older zombie would want to be super skinny, like the cigarette zombie from *Resident Evil: Extinction*, but I've seen some fat zombies be very effective.

BS: Have you ever been a zombie extra in one of the films you've worked on?

MM: Nope. I love getting my makeup done, but I've simply never had the time.

BS: How does working with images of the dead affect your views on mortality?

MM: I've been an atheist since I was about twelve, so my view of the dead is different than those who are religious. I also never want to grow old. Living in Los Angeles makes you very aware of the ageism that goes on in our little world. Every day after I turned forty I've woken up feeling a bit older and I hate it. So it's not the pictures of the dead that affect my views of mortality, it's actually getting old. Pictures are just research to me, although seeing it live and in person would actually affect me more. It would no longer be photography or art at that point and I think the smell would affect me more than anything. I have a vivid sense of smell.

BS: Have you ever done an effect you feel went too far?

MM: Not yet, but I certainly hope to one day. Some of the stuff we did for *Train* was very graphic, but it was all the in the script and I didn't design it.

BS: How do you react to seeing a loved one in bloody makeup?

MM: I used to make up friends more than I do now. I love it when they really get into character and make the makeup come alive. My own reaction is rather boring. All I see is someone I know under a lot of rubber and the dread that I probably have to clean it off in an hour.

BS: Effects artists are known for using non-conventional methods of creating special effects. What tricks have you used that some may consider unusual?

MM: I used to be a magician for a living, so I've done a number of effects that were based off of magic illusions. I designed a microphone stand to impale through a zombie for *Dead and Breakfast*, but we ran out of time to shoot it. It went in the back and out the front, all in one shot on a live actor. One of these days I'll get to use it. It's vaguely based on a stage illusion called Impaled.

BS: Your effects are in the nightmares of countless fans. What scares you?

MM: Being unsuccessful, being poor, becoming old. The normal stuff. I don't care for spiderwebs. Yuck.

BS: If tomorrow you heard on the news that the dead have risen, how would you fair in the apocalypse?

MM: I think I'd do well. I mean the most it would last would be two weeks right? How long does it take a corpse to rot into a pile of useless goo? I can last that long, as long as I have milk and cereal.

BS: Are there any zombie films in your future?

MM: Sadly no. As I get older, I have less and less energy for huge effects films. It's a genre for artists who can work the hours that indie movies work. The higher up the ladder I go and the older I get, the less I like working more than fourteen hour days. I think in general the crew stops doing their best work around then. I've been on films where we did twenty hour days. Once I shot a twenty seven hour day.

BS: Can you share any funny on set stories from the zombie films you've worked on?

MM: There are so many. Some I can tell. Some I'd probably get killed for.

BS: Well, in the interest of not signing your death warrant, how about one you can share?

MM: When we were doing the chainsaw decapitation with Eric Paladino in *Dead and Breakfast*, we mostly used Methocel blood, because it doesn't collect bugs and it doesn't thicken in cold weather and it was a freezing February in San Francisco. However, we ran out and had to use regular corn syrup blood. We ultimately pumped over four and half gallons of blood through that tubing. By the end of the day, poor Eric was drenched in blood and the corn syrup blood was starting to dry and stick his armpit hairs to his body and thicken up because of the cold. It was all very uncomfortable for him. To make things worse, he got back to the hotel at the end of the night to shower only to find out that his wallet was soaked through and his money, credit cards and driver's license were all died pink. His license was pink for two years until it expired.

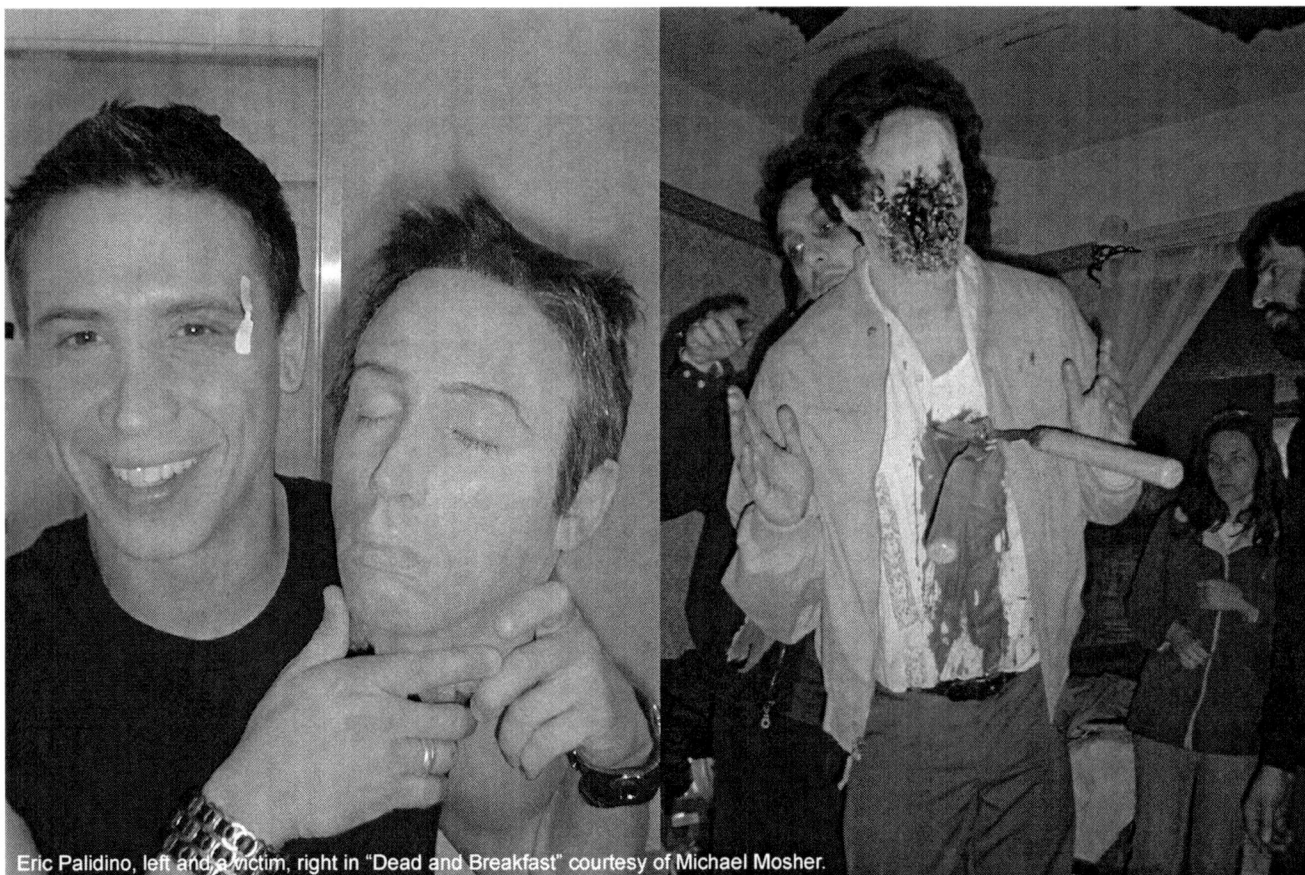

Eric Palidino, left and a victim, right in "Dead and Breakfast" courtesy of Michael Mosher.

GREG NICOTERO

- The Walking Dead (2011) Special Makeup Effects Supervisor
- Survival of the Dead (2009) Special Effects Makeup Consultant
- Diary of the Dead (2007 Special Makeup Effects Producer
- Planet Terror (2007) Special Makeup Effects Designer
- Land of the Dead (2005) Special Makeup Effects Supervisor
- Army of Darkness (1992) Special Makeup Effects
- Bride of Re-Animator (1990) Special Makeup Effects and Bride Effects Creator
- Evil Dead II (1987) Special Makeup Effects Unit Crew
- Day of the Dead (1985) Special Makeup Effects Artist

Blood Splatter: How did you get involved with *Day of the Dead*?

Greg Nicotero: I grew up in Pittsburgh and my uncle had worked with George Romero on *The Crazies*. I was fourteen at the time and I became good friends with George and Chris. When they were shooting *Creepshow*, they had invited me to come out from Monroeville to visit the set. They had actually offered me a job as a personal assistant on the film, but I was about to go away to college, so I had to turn them down. I went to visit the set and that is where I first met Tom Savini. I had previously visited the set of *Dawn of the Dead* at Monroeville Mall, but I didn't really know anybody at the time. I was there for just one or two nights just watching what was going on. When I went out to visit *Creepshow*, I went in and looked for George and found my way into Savini's workshop. It was in the corner of this big gymnasium where the whole interior of the basement of the college for the film was built. It was a movie set and offices combined. Tom and I hit it off and became really good friends. So, not only did I expand my friendship with George by visiting the set a lot, but I became friends with Tom. I was this inquisitive and excitable kid who loved movies and wanted to learn. Initially I was going out there to see George, but then my friendship with Tom grew and I went to visit him. I would see him building creatures like Fluffy and all that stuff. By the time *Creepshow* had wrapped, I was well ensconced in the Romero/Savini family.

Three years later in 1984, I called George and told him I was coming to visit for lunch. When I got there, he told me they had just been green lighted for *Day of the Dead* and asked me if I wanted a job. I was determined not to make the same mistake twice after turning them down on *Creepshow*, so I instantly said yes. I called Tom and told him that I had just been hired on for *Day of the Dead* and that I wanted to be his assistant. That job didn't even exist and what George and production loved about it was that it allowed Tom to be free to be creative and come up with the gags. He didn't have to worry about the day to day tasks like ordering materials and keeping supplies together. It was a win-win situation for everybody. I was able to gain experience and Tom was able to work on new zombies and gags. I remember reading the first draft of the script and it was a really big film. It had bits of *Survival of the Dead* in it and it had lots of ideas that ended up in *Land of the Dead*. When I read the first draft, I loved it. It was epic and I would joke that it was *The Ten Commandments* of zombie movies. It was budgeted at eight million dollars. What happened was, they couldn't get an R rating for the film and United Film Distribution had issues with putting up that kind of money and not be able to play it in a lot of theaters. So the options were an eight million dollar R rated movie or a three million dollar unrated movie. So before we even started shooting, the budget was cut by five million. We kept the bones of the movie, but it was a lot more contained than George's original vision. It is still a great movie and I can remember virtually every detail about it, because it was so ingrained in my brain. However, it certainly wasn't the film it started out as.

Another thing that made a big impression on me at a young age was that Tom was a big gadget guy. A lot of his early career he spent time documenting his effects on set so he would have a record of it. My dad was also very interested in the audio visual stuff and loved VCR's and cameras, so I ended up being the documentarian on *Day of the Dead*. If I wasn't involved in the execution of the effect, I was videotaping it and recording it for posterity. Being behind the lens was a whole new experience for me and I certainly took that into my future career. Every other film I did after that, I documented everything. Many of the bonus features on DVD's like *Evil Dead II* comes from footage that I shot, because I learned with Tom to document everything. We spent six months working on *Day of the Dead*. We started July 23rd 1984 and we started shooting in October and went until Christmas. We came back for a couple of weeks in

January 1985 for some pickups. On that movie I met Everett Burrell, Howard Berger, John Vulich, Mike Trcic and David Kindlon. Guys I would continue to work with throughout my career and in Howard's case, become his partner for twenty five years. After that movie wrapped, I went to New York and worked with Richard Rubenstein and Laurel Entertainment for a while and from there I went to Los Angeles.

BS: Has your career taken the path you expected?

GN: I had no idea where it was going to go. I was pre-med and I was going to be a doctor. I was about to take my medical school entrance exams, so the idea was that I was going to take a semester off school, go and work on *Day of the Dead* just to say that I did and then go back to school. So the fact that I went from Pittsburgh to New York to Los Angeles within a year was just crazy. I was working in Stan Winston's studio, then I went on to *Evil Dead II* and three years later I had started my own company. I had no idea that would happen. The beauty of being twenty years old and having that freedom is I just went wherever life took me. When I went to New York to work for Richard on *Tales from the Darkside*, I had no idea what it was like to live in New York City. I was just a kid and it was nothing I planned. It just all happened. At that time I had the freedom to go where the job took me. I went to North Carolina to work on *Evil Dead II* and then I went back to New York to work on *Creepshow 2* and I bounced around. If you had asked me in 1984 when I first started working on *Day of the Dead*, if I had aspirations to own my own effects shop and to be one of the prominent makeup effects artists in the industry, I would never have imagined that. I was just happy to be working on a zombie movie.

BS: Do you have a favorite zombie film?

GN: I love *Dawn of the Dead*. I think *Dawn of the Dead* and *Jaws* are the greatest movies of all time.

BS: Despite having so many major blockbusters under your belt, you keep returning to the zombie genre. What is the appeal to you with zombies?

GN: I grew up in Pittsburgh and I lived twenty minutes from Evans City where the cemetery from *Night of the Living Dead* is located. I used to drive to the Monroeville Mall to go Christmas shopping. You have certain towns that are defined by specific things. Pittsburgh is defined by two things, sports teams and zombies. *Night of the Living Dead* put Pittsburgh on the map and in the late sixties when the steel industry was crashing and the city was really in a big financial hardship, to see a little Hollywood East starting to develop in Pittsburgh was a big deal. There was a television show called Chiller's Theater that I would watch every Saturday night and the host was Bill Cardille, who was Lori Cardille's dad. So I spent a lot of my formative years watching this show and following George Romero's movies. I love zombie stuff and I have had the opportunity to be a zombie in five of George's movies. I have the world record for most zombie performances in a George Romero movie. I love that I have been able to be a zombie so many times for him. It is something I grew up loving and am fortunate enough to be able to work on a lot of great zombie projects. I have always been involved in some capacity. I went from the early Romero stuff to *Land of the Dead* and then consulting on both *Diary of the Dead* and *Survival of the Dead*. Even though I was off shooting *Inglorious Basterds*, George always wanted to know that I was around if he needed me.

BS: How does your family feel about seeing you in made up on screen and then subsequently killed?

GN: My mom doesn't really like it too much. I showed her a picture of one of my makeups from season one of *The Walking Dead* and she didn't even recognize me. She didn't believe it was me. I had a cameo on *From Dusk Til' Dawn* and my hair was really long and I get into a little altercation with Tom Savini's character. I showed that to my kids and they didn't believe it was me either. It is a fun rush to be able to be a zombie and look at the makeup to see how it all comes together. It is thrilling. My kids are now old enough to know it is all make believe, so they love it. My son is actually going as a zombie for Halloween this year and I gave him one of the masks from *The Walking Dead* that we used last year. There is an action figure of me from the first season coming out soon and I am really excited to be a part of that.

BS: That's right, the deer eating zombie. This was your first action figure of you correct?

GN: It is. There have been other action figures from characters I have created, but this is the first one of me. It was really fun to have Todd McFarlane make a toy of me.

BS: Which film did you enjoy working on the most?

GN: I would have to say *Day of the Dead*. Everett and Howard were eighteen. I was twenty and we were all under twenty one years old working for Tom. The irony was that we weren't even old enough to drink at the bar in the hotel in Pittsburgh. We were all young kids with this enormous enthusiasm to be working on a George Romero movie. It was so much fun and it was an amazing experience. We went to work every day in the Wampum Mines in Beaver Falls and it was freezing. I think it was fifty degrees in there. We didn't see the sun for three months, as we went to work early in the morning before sunrise and left long after sunset. We were in this limestone mine and it was a really amazing time. There is no way I can beat that experience. Having the chance to become friends with Howard and Everett and everyone, it really changed the perspective of my career. If we didn't have a good time, I would have gone back to college and I would have finished up med school and that would have been it. To be a part of that history is just awesome. I remember on set we were talking about *The Evil Dead* and how cool it would be if they did a sequel. I've had the opportunity to work on sequels to the George Romero movies and then with sequels with Sam Raimi. I couldn't even have imagined being a fan and going to see every movie and then being a part of it. All of a sudden I had a group of people I could share my love of movies with. This was something I'd never had before. Tom and George were the closest I had ever gotten to that, but they were a bit older than I was. So to have an opportunity to hang out with guys my age and nerd out about horror movies was great. I remember us going to see *The Terminator* and *A Nightmare on Elm Street* while we were shooting *Day of the Dead* and it just fueled my interest and enthusiasm for the effects industry.

BS: Do you think the genre shift to include viral and plague movies is a reaction to public fear of bioterrorism and pandemics like H1N1?

GN: I think it absolutely does. *28 Days Later* did a lot for the modern zombie movie, even though we all know they are not zombies and are called infected. I think between *28 Days Later* and *Shaun of the Dead*, they redefined the genre. *Resident Evil* came out around the same time and I remember there being a shift where all of sudden zombie movies were being made again. In my opinion, those three films changed the perception of zombie movies and *28 Days Later* added the adrenalized fast moving zombies which heightened the terror of getting caught and torn apart. *Shaun of the Dead* took the genre seriously again, even though it was a comedy. It went back to the traditional zombie stuff. I loved the Spanish film *[REC]* as well, although I'm not a fan of the American remakes of foreign films. I would much rather watch the original source material. I thought *[REC]* was great and patient zero in the attic was so creepy looking. You couldn't tell if it was a man or a woman. It was soiled and really skinny and just really eerie. All of those movies opened the doors for George to do *Land of the Dead*.

BS: Should zombies be able to run?

GN: No. No way man. I just never imagined that with the atrophy of muscles and the decomposition of tissue, that there is no way that their muscles would allow them to. That is why *28 Days Later* didn't bother me because it was an infection. They weren't dead and there was no decomposition of muscle or flesh, whereas the *Dawn of the Dead* remake had zombies running at fifty miles an hour. I have nothing against the movie, it is just not my cup of tea.

BS: Is it easier to do effects on zombies than it is to do violent effects against humans?

GN: Very much so. It is much easier psychologically to maim or mutilate something that is a monster than it is to a human. There is a completely different human response. If you watch a movie like *Last House on the Left* or *The Hills Have Eyes* where horrible things are happening to human beings, it is just hard to watch as it makes you uncomfortable. You cannot psychologically help but put yourself or your loved ones into those positions and think about what you would do. If it is a monster, it is a little easier for you to digest and comprehend when that you know it is something that would probably never happen. Zombie gags can be really outrageous though. Take Peter Jackson's *Braindead (Dead Alive)* for example. It is a really entertaining film and the gags are just crazy and over the top. You don't get an emotional response from that movie, but you have a blast watching it. It is a different experience because it is happening to zombies. If it was happening to real people, you would react differently.

BS: Is it thinly masked violent tendencies of human nature than allows zombie violence to be acceptable?

GN: I think not looking at them as humans makes a huge difference. That is also where you get into big issues with the ratings board. On *The Walking Dead*, what we are able to do to zombies versus humans is a huge difference. I remember on *Evil Dead II*, we did everything to change the color of the demonic possessions. There was black blood, there was green blood and we threw some brown in there too. This was all intentional, as red blood has a very different visual and psychological effect than other colored blood does. The reason it is more acceptable in society to see a zombie get its head blown off, is that its blood is brown. If the blood was red you would have a different visceral reaction to it.

BS: So how does working with images of the dead affect your views on mortality?

GN: As the son of a doctor, I have a very realistic view on mortality. I used to listen to him talk about patients and in my pre-med years I interned at a couple of hospitals. I was the guy that went around to the patients rooms with the EKG charts. I would do cardiograms on incoming patients and go to the intensive care unit. I remember walking into the ICU and there was an old man who had been there for a couple of weeks and one time I went in and he was gone. I asked what had happened to the guy and they matter of fact told me he had passed away. It was really strange for me in that it was because I was that a point in my life where I was being trained to treat sick people and I processed it differently. You can't get emotionally attached to people. If you do and they die, then you have that sense of loss every time it happens. For me it was a very different reaction to human mortality, because of my upbringing and my understanding of the medical field. At a young age I would see patients of my dads who he would cure and those that wouldn't make it. When I was twelve, I heard about a person who over dosed and drank a gallon of antifreeze. I remember asking why someone would do such a thing and being told that they were on drugs. It affects at how you look at things. So when you see that kind of thing in the theatres, it is always scary. I will always look at that scene in *Zombie*, where the woman has her eye impaled on a splinter of wood, as one of those seminal moments in movie history. I remember I tried to claw my way out of the theater. I was mortified that they never cut away from that scene.

BS: While we are on the subject of medical images, Everett and John told me to say page 511 to you.

GN: *(laughs)* There was a book that we had called the Mediological Investigation of Death. It was a coroner's text book for autopsy and medical school review. Every single chapter was a different death. One chapter was plane crashes and another was blunt force trauma. There was one chapter on auto erotic asphyxiation and on page 511 there was this old man who had built this horrible contraption of dildo's and had actually died in the middle of pleasuring himself. I was working on *Day of the Dead* and this became our code word. 511 was just something we would start saying to each other, meaning that something was really fucked up.

BS: Do you still have the t-shirt?

GN: You know what, I don't. I do still have my crew shirt from *Day of the Dead* though.

BS: How do you rectify personal morals with getting a pay check when you are hired to complete an effect with questionable subject matter or something you don't agree with?

GN: It is a movie. There has never been a time where I've said absolutely not. No matter if someone finds it offensive or immoral, there will be someone who finds it entertaining. If you look back to the sixties and seventies to movies like *The Exorcist* and the public outcry as to how objectionable they found the film was, it is crazy. It is just fantasy. You have to have the ability and understanding to differentiate the fantasy and the reality. There have been a couple of times when I was in a movie thinking about how disturbing certain scenes were. I remember the original *Mother's Day* and I was really turned off by the brutalization of women. I also remember watching *Maniac* and back then I went to the movies just to see the effects. I didn't care what the movie was about. If Tom Savini's name was there, I would watch it. I thought *Maniac* was just sick and couldn't figure out who would like such a film. Yet, there was an audience for it and the effects that Tom did were so visceral, they had a major impact. Some people may not agree, but it is an art form. What I like about it is that our society allows us to express ourselves in that way. Without that ability, the film industry would not be where it is today.

BS: Have there been any scripts you have read and shied away from?

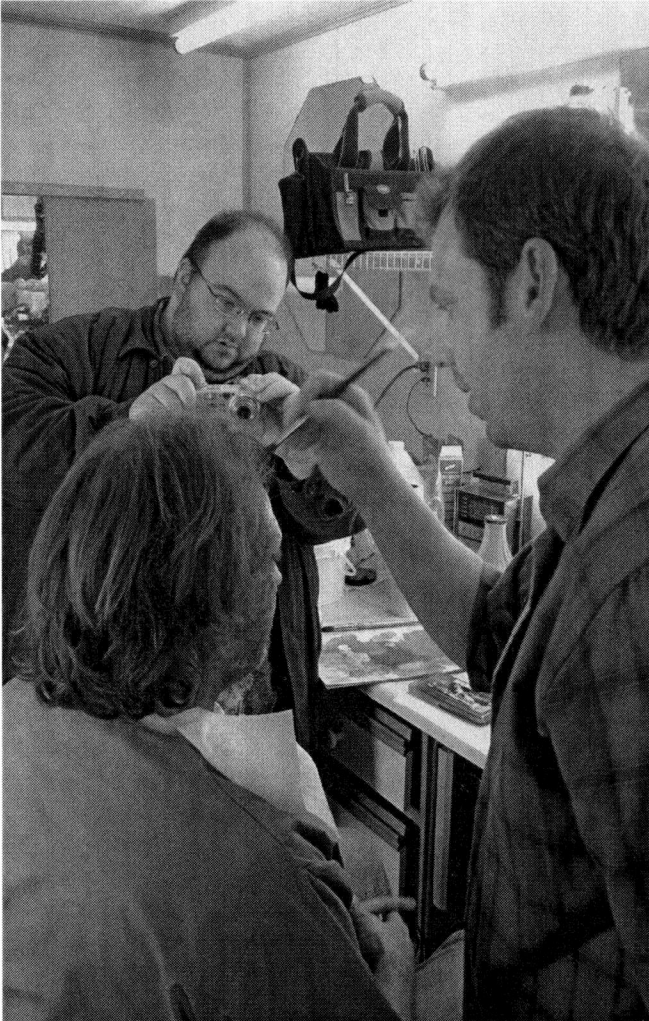
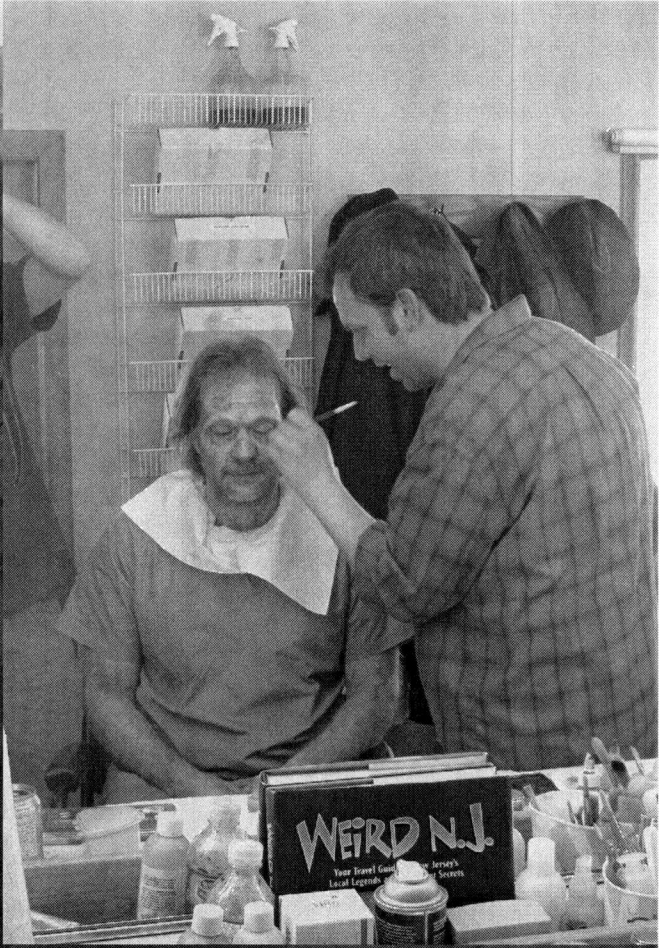
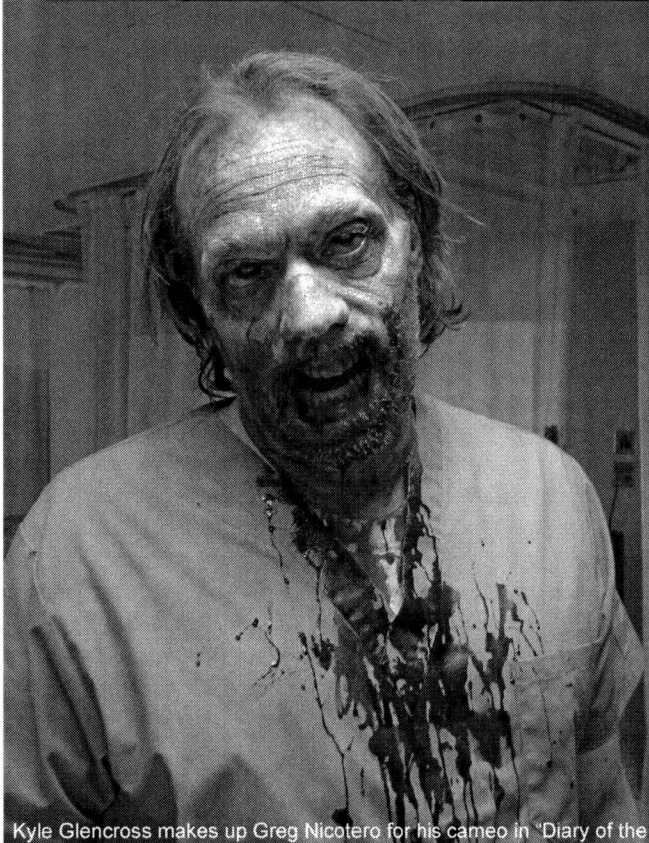
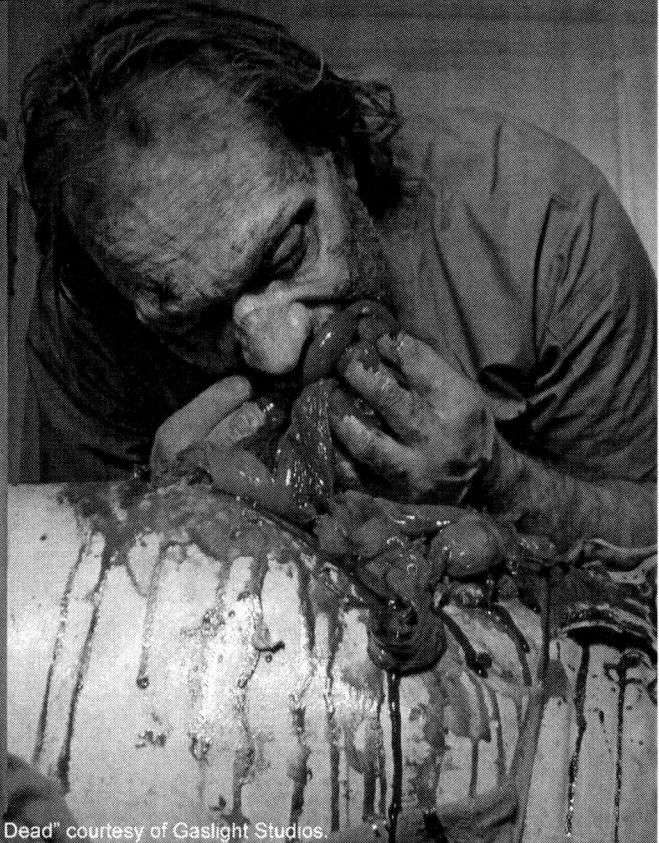

Kyle Glencross makes up Greg Nicotero for his cameo in "Diary of the Dead" courtesy of Gaslight Studios.

GN: There have been a handful I have read and wondered what they were thinking. It was less about the effects themselves and more about the tone of the movie. There was one script I read a while back where a man cuts open a woman's stomach and rips a baby out and I just didn't get it.

BS: Have you ever done an effect you feel went too far?

GN: I don't know if I'd say anything has gone too far, but there have been scenes I have seen played back where I wonder what the fuck were we doing. There was a scene in *Dr. Giggles* where a young boy is hiding in his dead mother's stomach and when he is found by the police, he cuts his way out with a scalpel. It was really disturbing.

BS: Do you have any effects trademarks such as a bite mark or wound?

GN: Not specifically. There is a certain aesthetic that I like to use for blood gags that we use over and over. I think that is because everytime I do a blood gag, I want to improve on it and do it better. The great thing about *The Walking Dead* is the cast and crew is so enthusiastic every time we come out of the trailer with new zombies. The one big thing Tom taught me was nothing is more real than real. On *Day of the Dead,* we used real pig entrails for Rhode's death scene. We did a gag on *The Walking Dead* recently and we called a local slaughter house and got real entrails and looking at it through the camera and seeing it, it looks so real and adds a lot to it. It is one thing to see a silicone or foam latex prosthetic torn open to see more latex underneath, but it is another to rip skin open and see real meat in it. It plants a whole new impression in your head. It really is powerful.

BS: I heard you had to clean out the fridge on *Day of the Dead.*

GN: I did and I will never forget that. What happened was we were shooting in Florida in December 1984 and we shot two weeks. We shut down for Christmas and came back in early January. What we didn't realize was that they had shut the power off in the facility where we were working. When we came back after the holiday, we were walking down the hallway and were about a hundred yards away from Saviniland, as we called his workshop and we could smell the rotting guts. We could have called the slaughterhouse and gotten more guts, but we were shooting the scene with Joe Pilato the next day. Instead I dumped them in a bucket with Clorox and cleaned them. I didn't even think about being unable to reverse the decomposition or the rotting smell. We loaded the torso up with both fake guts and real guts. Some of the zombie extras actually put ear plugs up their nose to avoid having to smell the guts.

BS: Which has been your favorite zombie or character death scene that you have created?

GN: I would have to say the death of Amy, played by Emma Bell, in *The Walking Dead* on season one. We spent a lot of time choreographing that sequence, having her stepping out of the RV in a particular way. I blocked the whole scene with her and I ended up getting into makeup and doing the biting. I had rehearsed with her a bunch of times and on the final take, I grabbed her wrist and she froze. She had never seen the bite or skin rip before, so when it happened she saw the wound and she went stiff for a second. Then she freaked out and started screaming. I told her before the scene that I was going to grab her arm and try to bite her more than once, so it was her job to get away from me. Right after I bit her there was this weird moment where she froze and looked wide eyed at the wound, then I tried to bite her again and it became this struggle. When we cut, she told me she didn't know what to do and it looked so real. One second I was there, my teeth were sinking to her arm and blood was everywhere. I told her that it was real and she had done a great job. The result was so unexpected that it stopped her dead in her tracks. Emma is a great actress and the scene turned out fantastic.

BS: How about your favorite zombie death scene from a film you have not been involved with?

GN: The first bite in the original *Dawn of the Dead* or when Taso Stavrakis has his stomach torn open in the mall are still so ground breaking. It was so unexpected, but these days, zombie fans want this kind of thing in every movie and it has become a staple of the genre. That is what fans put their money down for. I think the best bite is the one on Miller's neck in *Day of the Dead.*

BS: You just directed your first episode of *The Walking Dead.* Do you plan to direct more in the future?

GN: I think so. I directed a short film last year and I directed *The Walking Dead* shorts that aired on the AMC website. It had about four and a half million hits I believe. I certainly feel like moving in that direction. It is really rewarding and you get to direct an amazing cast and work with Andrew Lincoln, Sarah Wayne Callis and Jon Bernthal.

BS: Were you familiar with the comic book before coming on board?

GN: I was actually. I bought the first issue when it came out. I was working in Austin with Robert Rodriguez and went to Austin Comics, saw it and bought two. I gave the other to Robert and was all excited that there was a comic book about zombies available. I loved the art style.

BS: Do you think they will take Rick down the same path he takes in the comic book? The story turns really dark in later issues. In fact all of the characters suffer tremendously in situations never shown on television before.

GN: I have no idea. I know things gets really, really dark, but it is really hard to say. The show has already deviated significantly from the comic, so it is really hard to see where they will take Rick.

BS: Effects artists are known for using non-conventional methods of creating special effects. What tricks have you used that some may consider unusual?

GN: We use oatmeal to make brains. A lot of the times when we do head exit wounds and brain hits, we mix oatmeal into the blood. When we were shooting *Pulp Fiction*, we added it to Samuel Jackson and John Travolta's hair when they shoot Marvin in the head in the back seat of the car. It adds some really cool looking chunks to the blood. A lot of the skins and bites that we do, we use gelatin skins and sometimes we will put chicken skin underneath it to give it a little extra weight and meat to it.

BS: One of my favorite bites is the one that yourself and Gino Crognale did on *Land of the Dead* in the convenience store.

GN: You know what is good about that bite is the way we built it. We had a vaccuuformed piece that went on my arm then there was a bladder beneath it. We drilled some holes in the bladder and put strips of latex flesh and gelatin over the top of it. It was designed so that the zombie could take a bite in more than one spot and would bleed from under the plate. You get this really great meaty rip. It is a little harder for me to be objective on these effects because I worked on them, so I will always refer to stuff that I didn't do as my favorite effects.

BS: What are your thoughts on the increased use of CGI?

GN: Watching *I Am Legend*, I wanted to jump off of a building. They spent so much time creating these characters that I just didn't believe were real or in the same room. Both makeup effects and visual effects are great tools and they are the most successful when they are both used to complement each other. When Rick Grimes is running down the street in Atlanta shooting zombies in the head, is it practical on a television shooting schedule to put squibs in the head of every zombie? No fucking way. It makes more sense to put the blood in with CGI afterwards. The zombies drop and we put the CGI in later. There are obviously instances where CGI just doesn't cut it. Take the scene in the *Dawn of the Dead* remake where Ving Rhames' character shoots Andy in the head. The CGI effects used are a very different visual than say the exploding head in *Scanners* or the head shot in *Dawn of the Dead*. Although, even the exploding head in *Scanners* we can't do anymore because of using the shotgun. The problem we have these days, is if you create a prosthetic head and you use explosives to blow it up you get smoke in the effect and that can ruin the shot.

BS: Your effects are in the nightmares of countless fans. What scares you?

GN: Spiders. I hate spiders. I fucking hate them. In season two of *The Walking Dead,* we were shooting this scene where we had a fake well in the ground and a bloated zombie was down there. We went over to the well to figure out how we were going to film it and there was a big spider over there. I told them that I wanted nothing to do with it and left.

JIM OJALA

- Deadgirl (2008) Special Makeup Effects Artist and Designer
- Poultrygeist: Night of the Chicken Dead (2006) Creature Effects: Baby Zombie Chick Puppet
- House of the Dead 2 (2005) Special Makeup Effects Lab Technician: Almost Human

Blood Splatter: In addition to some of the bigger Hollywood films such as *Hellboy II: The Golden Army* and *X-Men: The Last Stand* you've worked on a few obscure zombie movies, are you a fan of the genre?

Jim Ojala: Absolutely yes. My career actually started in the genre with a cable access show that I did back in Minnesota. It was an over the top horror-comedy called *My Three Scums* about a family of monsters and zombies and how they got by. Based on the success there, Troma Entertainment invited me to come out to New York to work for them.

BS: Troma has made a huge impact on the zombie genre, which film did you start out on there?

JO: My first film at Troma was *The Toxic Avenger IV: Citizen Toxie* where I was in the makeup effects department. I had an amazing time there.

BS: Do you have a favorite zombie film?

JO: It's still the original *Dawn of the Dead*.

BS: You have a lot of different style horror films under your belt. Do you approach the effects on a zombie differently than you would a standard horror?

JO: It's tough because it's all been done so many times and so many times really well. You can't keep reinventing the wheel. On *Deadgirl*, we had several meetings with the directors ahead of time. They made it very clear that the look of the dead girl was really important to them. It was imperative to see how she evolved during the film with the various stages of decomposition. We wanted to move away from the standard look and bring in some other worldly colors. We applied some tones that we weren't used to using in zombie films.

BS: What did you use as a reference points?

JO: My main reference was photos of decomposed bodies and there was one particular picture that was deeply disturbing of this woman who had been drowned. She was a murder victim who had been thrown in water and it was weeks until she was found. Her skin was really well preserved, but it took on this strange grayish blue tone with a subtle hint of purples and greens. It was something you really weren't used to seeing. It was a really strange mix. I brought some of that into the dead girl and it was one of the things I tried to bring to the table to change it up a bit.

BS: *Deadgirl* definitely had a much darker story than many other zombie films and had some really disturbing images. Can you highlight some of the effects from the film?

JO: There were several shots that were really intense. The biggest one that was exciting to do and came off really well was her bullet wounds that festered over the course of the film. We created a full fake torso for Jenny Spain who played the dead girl and we pumped a really nasty greenish mucus-like pus out of the wounds when Noah Segan, who played J.T. squeezed them. That was a great effect and it looks really gross on film. One of the cool things about the movie was that it didn't go for a lot of shock value. There was just a really disturbing atmosphere over the whole thing because of the films extreme subject matter. I think that's one of the reasons why the movie is so strong and it's become this modern cult classic. If you read the synopsis of *Deadgirl*, it could be this nasty and trashy film. But because they did it artfully and tastefully, touching the subject matter of raping a dead woman found in a basement that doesn't die, it really had some strength to it. That was the big thing that attracted me to the subject matter. I spoke to the director's many times before coming on board and knew they were taking it very seriously and it wasn't going to be a cheesy type of film. I knew the screenwriter, Trent Haaga from way back in the Troma days. So I trusted how they were going to handle it. If it was going to be some trashy exploitation flick, I probably would not have gotten involved because it wasn't a lot of money. I knew that in talking to them and reading the script that it was a good film to get involved with and it was going to be done right.

BS: Is it harder to create special effects for a movie where the subject matter is darker and more grounded in reality?

JO: There is a real fine line that you walk with this type of film. There are so many factors that can cause things to go sour. I was so incredibly lucky that Jenny was so cool and we were able to break the ice really early on. We had the same sense of humor and got on really well. I had to do five hours of makeup on her every day with her butt naked throughout. I had to put fake pubic hair on her and if we weren't totally cool with each other it would have been incredibly uncomfortable and would have affected the movie. The main thing is having the right feeling on set among people.

BS: If this had been a human instead of a zombie, it would have bordered on a rape or snuff film. Why is it acceptable to portray such graphic violence on a zombie, especially as it was once human?

JO: I have a few different viewpoints on that. I've hung out with degenerates and weirdo's and creeps when I was a teenager. Those kids in *Deadgirl*, I know those kids exist. I thought it was important that the film showed this darker side of people and that some kids on film aren't always the Spielberg type kids. There are horrible people out there, but I think it's important to tell those people's stories as well. It's a really tough line though and my original makeup girl quit on me on the very first day of shooting. She had read the entire script at that point and was appalled. She thought I was a disgusting pig and that everybody associated with the film was as well. I knew the film was going to be done tastefully, but I just couldn't convey it to her.

BS: I think people read scripts differently too. Maybe she had issues with the subject matter stemming from personal experiences?

JO: That's exactly it. She poured out to me that she had been abused, so the way she read the script, it struck a nerve with her personally and I can't fault her for that.

BS: Had the film been based on a woman instead of a zombie, do you think it would have been released?

JO: It's hard to say. It would probably have been released unrated and I would not have gotten involved with the film. That is something I would not have been interested in participating in. It would have been a pretty tough sell for anyone. You need to have the fantasy element to be able to ride that line. Without it, it's just this really harsh and mean spirited film that probably would not have found an audience. The character that Shiloh Fernandez plays is the moral compass and counters the evil kids. If they had both indulged completely with having fornicated with the body, I also would not have gotten involved. There was the moral dilemma and someone trying to do the right thing. That is always important and is what ultimately attracted me to the film.

BS: How do you handle conflict if a director wants an effect that you find morally offensive?

JO: It depends if it was immoral, but still artistic. Usually if I bump heads, I can help the director come to terms with a possible alternative. We both get what we want with the effect, but it's something we can both live with.

BS: So how do you separate human mortality and death from the fantasy of death in zombie films? Is it something that starts getting to you psychologically dealing with it so much?

JO: Actually yes it does. I have to look at a lot of dead bodies and I've seen a lot of bad stuff over the years. I have a lot of books that have a lot of really graphic images in them. It can really get to you after a while. There's nothing cool about death. It sucks. That is one of the interesting things about death. When you look at book about it and see it up close, nothing looks cool. Death is sloppy and messy and gross and it's nothing to be glorified. I really get bummed out with it at times, so I only look at the reference materials when absolutely necessary. I have been able to get desensitized to some degree.

BS: Is that a defense mechanism?

JO: Absolutely. It's the same as any other job that deals with that kind of subject matter. A doctor dealing with sick and dying children has to become desensitized else they could not perform the job. It becomes a necessity. You will crack up and fall apart if you don't put the wall up. It's what protects your morals and your sanity.

BS: Were you able to add in any effects ideas that weren't in the script?

JO: A few yes. Most of the effects ideas were already scripted, but there was one big effect at the end that I was able to bring it. When the dead girl escapes and she attacks Noah Segan's character, it wasn't really written what she was going to do to him, just that she was going to do something. I looked in my stock to see what I had available and I had a great split lip effect. I made dentures for Noah with gums that went really high and we put a cleft lip type appliance over the dentures and over his top lip. We then have Jenny bite his face and tear away the lip. I think the effect came out really well.

BS: You also worked on *House of the Dead 2*. Did you have any reservations approaching the film knowing how badly the first *House of the Dead* movie was blasted by fans and critics alike?

JO: Yeah, I definitely did. It's also one of those things where there is no way it could be any worse. I was on Rob Hall's Almost Human team for that one. He'd already taken the job and I came in and helped build everything and worked on set. We spent some time with Sid Haig and everyone and had a good time. I think that there are some really cool makeup effects on that film.

BS: Which was your favorite effects shot in *House of the Dead 2*?

JO: I liked the scene where Sticky Fingaz gets his head blown off. That was a really good one. It's always fun to come on set and do a gag like that where we can add one hundred pounds of pressure and blow a head off its shoulders.

BS: With a destructive gag like that, I would imagine it's very cost prohibitive to build multiple props. Do you only have one chance to get it right?

JO: Actually, we are able to do more than one take if needed. We structure the head like a puzzle and we cut it into six or seven pieces. We then strategically place the pieces back together and put an air mortar in the neck. The head is filled up with blood and brains and the top part is placed back and on you hit the switch and blow it apart. Within an hour you are able to do it again. It's a great looking effect.

BS: What is your favorite effects shot from a zombie movie you haven't worked on?

JO: I still think the scene in the original *Dawn of the Dead* when the zombie bites his wife on the arm and neck is amazing. It still holds up so well. I love a lot of the head explosions too. You never see a head explosion these days that is as good as in *Dawn of the Dead* or *Scanners*.

BS: Because of the shotgun?

JO: Exactly. You won't be on a set these days that will allow that for insurance and obvious safety reasons, but it looks better than any other way you can do it.

BS: Many of these shots are getting replaced with CGI these days, what are your thoughts on the change from more traditional effects to CGI?

JO: It's definitely getting better as years go by, but for me it's on a case by case basis. There are some films that I see effects that are done really well and others that just look like video games. I think where you start to get in trouble is when you start doing too much character stuff. Take the new *Fright Night* for example. At the end, the Jerry Dandrige character has CGI over all of his makeup. As an audience member I am not scared anymore and it takes me out of the realm of fantasy because I can't relate to it. The original *Fright Night* holds up so well with its effects. They are doing the same thing done back then now with CGI and it just doesn't look right.

BS: Do you think CGI has made it harder on actors as they have nothing tangible to work with?

JO: I definitely think it's easier for actors who have a theater background, as they are generally used to working with less on stage. Much is left to the imagination and they seem to do better. Actors who don't have that seem to be left hanging a lot and some of their performances are stilted as they have nothing to react to.

BS: You also did some work on the Troma movie *Poultrygeist* and Troma is known for over the top gore and splatter. Did you approach the effects differently knowing this?

JO: Absolutely. I love the movies that Troma Entertainment puts out. They approached me about doing the effects for the film, but unfortunately I was booked at the time and I couldn't commit. Instead I asked if I could do one effects shot to help out. I picked the zombie chicken and worked on that. The story line was over the top so it allowed me to go over the top with the effects. As the chicken is possessed by dead Indians, I really went crazy with the colors and features. I made one that could have the head bitten off and spray green goo everywhere. As I had already done some work with those guys, I knew exactly what to expect.

BS: What are your thoughts on the genre shift to include plague and viral movies?

JO: It's a great time to scare the public. These fears of terrorism and political corruption are lying just under the surface. These themes are very relevant in today's society. It's a good time to be making horror movies, especially those that touch on a nerve.

BS: If you woke up tomorrow morning and the zombie apocalypse had begun, how would you fair?

JO: I don't have any guns. All I have is a knife and baseball bat. I wouldn't have much more going for me than that.

Behind the scenes of "Deadgirl" courtesy of Jim Ojala.

CHRISTINE PARKER

- A Few Brains More (2011) Director, Producer, Writer, Cinematographer
- Fistful of Brains (2008) Director, Producer, Writer, Cinematographer, Editor
- The Forever Dead (2007) Director, Producer, Writer, Cinematographer, Editor, Composer

Blood Splatter: How did you get in the film industry?

Christine Parker: I had been laid off from my job and so I decided to go back to school to study video production. I had always been interested in movies and how they came together. I was taking a class in broadcast technology and the teacher wanted to show the fun side of putting a film together. He asked if we would write a zombie movie and he would direct it. I wrote and produced a movie short called *Second Death*. We had so much fun on the film that we decided to form our own production company and we filmed *The Forever Dead*. That is how I found the core group that I work with.

BS: Your career is unique in that it's rare to find women heavily involved in the zombie genre. Were you aware of this void in the genre prior to directing *The Forever Dead*?

CP: No I wasn't. It never really occurred to me. While I was working on *The Forever Dead*, I came into contact with Heidi Honeycutt. Heidi runs Planetfury.com and she really supports women in the horror industry and she has helped me a lot. She showed me what to look out for and how to get my movie out there and there and promote it.

BS: Do you think your gender has either restricted you or given you an advantage in any way?

CP: I don't think it's made it that hard in all honesty. In fact, I have gotten into some festivals because I was female and I haven't had any issues as far as people discriminating because of my gender. It's actually really helped me.

BS: The genre as a whole is one dominated by males, what appealed to you about zombies?

CP: I think it's interesting in that it puts a magnifying glass on humanity. How would you face someone you love who wants to eat you? You have to dig deep inside and find the strength to kill them. It's a really hard choice and not everyone could do that.

BS: Do you have a favorite zombie film?

CP: I love both *The Evil Dead* and *Evil Dead II* movies but they are not technically zombie movies. *Braindead (Dead Alive)* has to be my favorite zombie film.

BS: It's also a lot rarer to find graphically violent films directed by women, why do you think this is?

CP: I am trying to make up for the fact that I don't show boobs in my movies. I am compensating by pumping up the gore.

BS: Do you think coming to the genre with a fresh perspective has benefitted you?

CP: I think so. I don't think I'm as jaded as some of the people who have been doing it for a while. No one has told me what I'm not supposed to do. I wasn't told that you're not supposed to do a period piece for your second film. They are some of the most difficult films to do without a budget and I've now done two of them.

BS: You've taken a very active role in your films with writing, directing, editing and producing, do you have a preference?

CP: I love editing. The editing process is my favorite part. I really enjoy taking all of the shots that don't make much sense and putting them together to form a story.

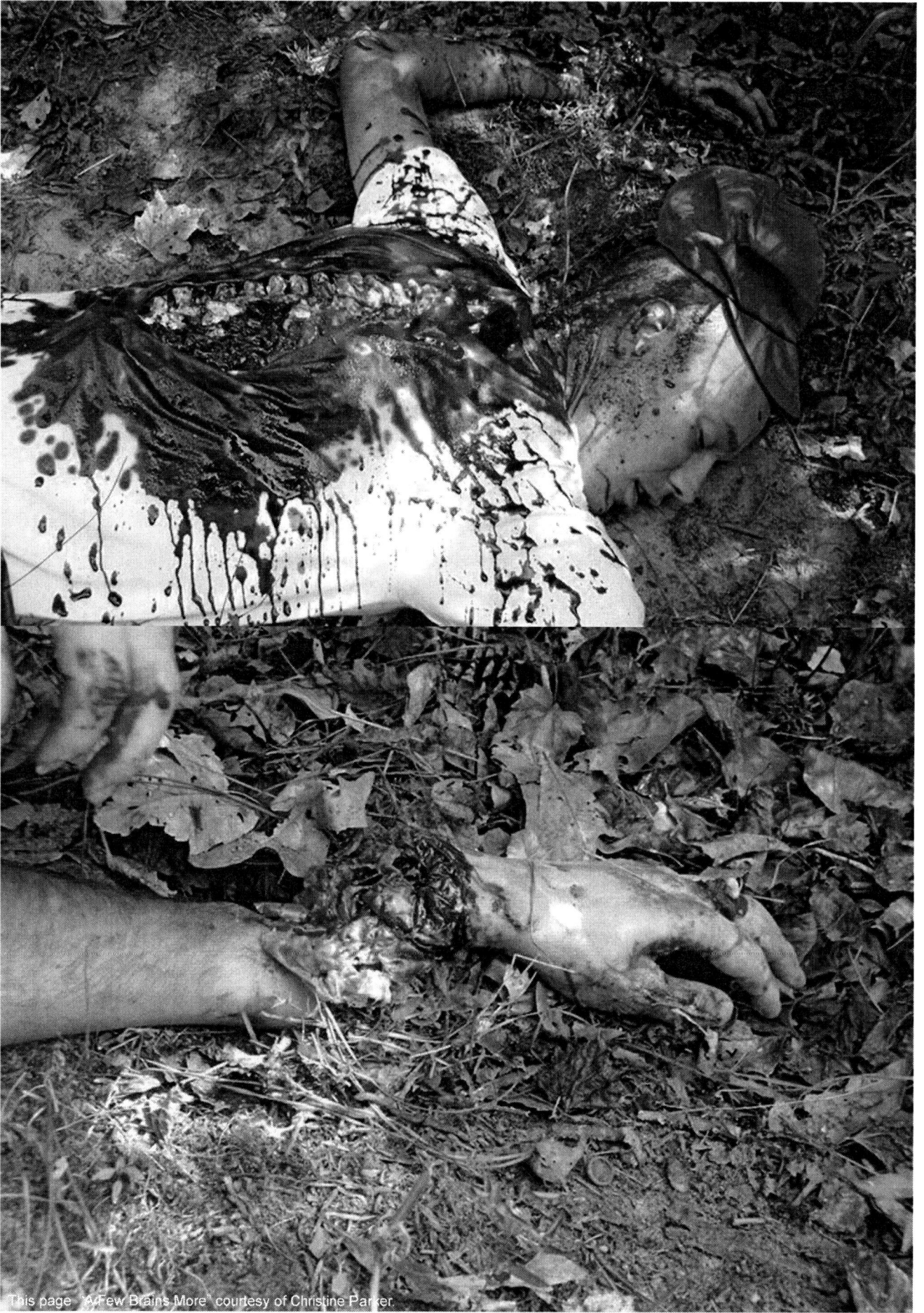

308

BS: Were there any particular movies that inspired you in the making of these films?

CP: None specifically. Obviously a couple were named after the Clint Eastwood movies. I watched a lot of cowboy movies growing up and they were homage to the old westerns. It wasn't any particular zombie film I had in mind, I just tried to do something completely different.

BS: As a child what was the first horror movie to have an impact on you?

CP: *House of Wax* with Vincent Price. I didn't actually watch a lot of zombie films as a kid. It wasn't until I was older when I started watching the likes of *The Evil Dead, Braindead (Dead Alive)* and obviously George Romero's films.

BS: There are many violent scenes in your movies, how involved are you with the special effects*?

CP: I wrote everything in the script that I wanted to see and left it up to my poor special effects guy to pull it off. Bill Mulligan, the special effects artist and I worked closely together, so I was always right there telling him we need more of this or that.

BS: Where did you draw your inspiration from for the effects shots as you were scripting them?

CP: Honestly, I just made it up as I went along. I thought about what would be the most devastating thing that could happen. I tried to come up with shots that people could connect with.

BS: Many films productions working with lower budgets invent new ways of creating special effects. What shortcuts did you take for budgetary reasons?

CP: In *The Forever Dead,* I had decided that I wanted a zombie rabbit for the film. At first we thought we could create some kind of animatronic rabbit, but our special effects guy quickly told us it was not possible to make it look good with the budget we had. So we ended up getting a dead rabbit from a rabbit farm and put it on a string.

BS: How much of a budget did you need to shoot a film like *Fistful of Brains*?

CP: We worked with less than $10,000 for each feature.

BS: How did you raise the funds?

CP: When I first started this, there wasn't Kickstarter or IndieGoGo type stuff around. So I came up with the idea of selling credits to my movie on eBay. I got a huge following by selling them for a dollar a piece and then if you paid $20 you would get a DVD. That is how I funded *The Forever Dead*. When people saw I had actually made a movie, they wanted to contribute more to *Fistful of Brains*. We had one guy in particular who contributed most of the funding for that film because he believed in what we were doing.

BS: What are your thoughts on the shift to CGI and the over dependence on using digital shots over more traditional prosthetics?

CP: I think CGI is way over done, especially on some of the sci-fi movies. Since it's not always done really well. I think it can get really distracting if it's not done right. People should use the two together to enhance practical effects. I think it's used as a crutch far too often.

BS: Did you implement much CGI on your films?

CP: We used a little, but it's mostly hands on practical effects.

BS: Do you think the genre shift to include viral/plague films such as *28 Days Later* and *Planet Terror* is a natural social reaction to increasing threats of viral pandemics and bioterrorism?

CP: I think that is part of it. It is the end of the world fear that many people have. I think in times of war, horror films become more prevalent, because it's a form of escapism. Seeing something terrifying on screen, like a zombie, makes reality a little easier to deal with.

BS: Zombie films definitely have a unique style of violence to them. Why do you think it's more acceptable to portray violence against zombies than it is against humans?

CP: I think because really the person they were is not there anymore. They can't reason and they don't have any more emotion. They become eating machines. That is something I have been trying to change in my movies by marrying zombies and humans together to make it harder against the people who are fighting against them, because they are more human.

BS: Do you think it is thinly masked violent tendencies of human kind?

CP: Absolutely. I've had a few people who have come on as extras after having a bad week at work and they just love to tear somebody apart. It makes them feel good.

BS: How does working with the dead affect your view on your mortality?

CP: I am completely desensitized to it. I see how it's made and I'll be filming it wondering if a shot isn't gory enough and then I'll watch it with an audience who will say it's disgusting. I see it so much, I don't realize how over the top it is.

BS: Does the desensitization become a prerequisite to being able to finish the job?

CP: Yes. If I was getting violently ill any time I see something like that, I wouldn't be able to do anything.

BS: How do you feel about zombie movies using children either as zombies or victims?

CP: I'm not a big fan of cinematic implied violence against children. I don't really like violence against women either. However, you have to realize that you can't just have adult male zombies walking around. So you have to cover everything and it's a difficult thing of course. I don't want to do it in a way that manipulates people. If I do stuff like that, I usually try to make it funny in a B-movie slapstick kind of way.

BS: Your films have creatures in them that give people nightmares, what scares you?

CP: Bills. Bills give me nightmares. Seriously though, I think supernatural movies scare me the most.

BS: What advice can you give someone breaking into the zombie genre?

CP: Have a good time with it and don't stress over money. You can do a lot with a little, sometimes you just have to be really creative. You may not get the budget you want for your first film, but if you get out there and make your film and people see you are serious, it's easier to get funding for the next movie.

BS: Are there any zombie films in the future for you?

CP: We may try and do a sequel to *A Few Brains More* but we'd like to try something different as well that departs from the zombie genre.

BS: Can you share any funny on set stories from the zombie films you've worked on?

CP: While we were shooting my last film, they were taking a wax cast of my daughter's head and they didn't put enough Vaseline on her face. Unfortunately, when the wax was pulled off it ripped all of her eye lashes out. The poor girl was seventeen at the time and was very embarrassed.

BS: If you woke up tomorrow morning and the zombie apocalypse had started, how would you fare?

CP: I think I'd do pretty well. I am resourceful and can adapt to change.

BRIAN PAULIN

- BloodPigs(1990) Special Makeup Effects Supervisor
- Bone Sickness (1985) Uncredited

Blood Splatter: How did you get into film making?

Brian Paulin: I started making movies as an outlet for my special makeup effects. As I was learning effects I quickly became tired of spending hours and hours on creating an effect with the end result being just a few pictures. It wasn't satisfying enough. I always had an interest in trying to film short stories and creating effects for them was the push I needed to get started. Once I did, I really enjoyed being able to tell stories visually and movie making became my main interest.

BS: What are some of your inspirations?

BP: The horror genre is my main inspiration, of course. I still study other films and try to figure out what it was that made them so great. The works of George Romero, Tom Savini, Lucio Fulci and John Carpenter have a major influence over what I do. I am also fascinated by the writing of H.P. Lovecraft. No one has ever topped the bizarre imagination of that man. Asian cinema inspires me to go further with concepts for horror. Nature itself has a strong influence over me. A simple walk through the woods can ignite so many ideas in my mind. I love filming in the woods.

BS: What appeals to you about the zombie genre?

BP: A good zombie movie contains some of the best horror visuals. To me the ultimate horror visual is a fogged out, overgrown graveyard at night. Once you have a decayed skeletal corpse crawling its way out of its grave, that is pure atmospheric horror. Zombies, when done right, are the creepiest movie monsters there are, in my opinion. Skeletons are already an iconic symbol of horror and Halloween. Now have them walking and ripping the living to pieces and you have the making of a classic.

BS: Do you have a favorite zombie film?

BP: *The Return of the Living Dead* is my favorite zombie movie. That film has so much energy, atmosphere and the Tar Man zombie. The creepiest looking zombie ever created. My second favorite would be Lucio Fulci's *Zombie*. That movie is pure atmosphere.

BS: Are you surprised that *Bone Sickness* has garnered such a cult following?

BP: I am. When you are working at the level I am, you never know if anyone is going to enjoy your movie. It wasn't our intention. The reason we make any of our movies is to have fun. It's our way of celebrating the horror genre. Simply watching horror films was no longer enough. We had to participate somehow.

BS: *Bone Sickness* has also gathered quite the reputation among gore and zombie fans. How did the film come about?

BP: We decided to make *Bone Sickness* because I had received so many emails from people saying that they would love to see what we would do with a zombie movie. We started filming in the spring of 2002 and at that time, the zombie genre had been dead for almost ten years. We decided to make a zombie movie that would contain all fully rotted zombies in the style of the great Italian zombie films and to make it as gory as possible. We wanted to go as far as we could with the gore and make sure the movie delivered. Half way through filming something simply clicked and the gore flowed out of us more than it ever had before.

BS: Were there any scenes that didn't make it to the final film?

BP: Since we had a second chance to go back and fix some things for the Unearthed Films edition, everything that I wanted to put into the original version made it into their DVD release.

BS: How much did you have to pay Rich George to eat worms?

BP: I didn't have to pay him anything. I told him my idea and he went for it knowing it was going to be a stand out scene in the movie and it was. That scene is always the first thing people mention and Rich loves the attention he received from it.

BS: Was it his idea or yours to film that scene?

BP: I came up with the idea. It seemed like a natural progression for the character to go through and I knew that if we filmed it without any cutaways as the worms came out of his mouth, it would have a huge impact on the viewers. Luckily Rich was all for it. I also made sure to include behind the scenes footage on the dvd where you see Rich putting the worms in his mouth just in case anyone still doubted it.

BS: How many takes were needed?

BP: I am pretty sure what you see in the movie is what we shot. I didn't want to make him do more than he had to. The filming went really smoothly. However, what didn't go as smoothly was when we decided to add more worms to end of the Unearthed Films version. It is the scene when Rich vomits them on my face, possessing me and then I vomit them as well. I had bought the worms, but we had to cancel filming that night and we didn't get to film until the following weekend. So we are all set to start filming, I grab the worms and find that they have all died. It was too late to go and buy more so we said "the hell with it, let's get it done". So we took turns stuffing our mouths with these nasty dead, hardening worms. The worst part was this weird secretion that was seeping from their bodies. We were worried that it was going to make us sick.

BS: Did you intentionally keep pushing the envelope to see how far you could go?

BP: When it came to the gore, yes,, but I did hold back with some ideas I had because I still wanted the movie to have a traditional zombie feel to it. I had tossed around some more bizarre ideas for Rich's character as he became a "Necro Junkie". I had thought of some mutation ideas where things were growing from his body, but dropped those thinking that they strayed too far away from being a traditional zombie movie.

BS: Your zombies have a "Blind Dead" feel about them. Where did you draw your inspiration from?

BP: The dusty, rotted Italian zombies. Lucio Fulci's style zombies for the most part. I like my zombies slow, plodding along without looking at anything. I do not like having zombies looking around because there is so much life in people's eyes. I think when filmmakers have zombies looking at things, that gives them life that they shouldn't have.

BS: Many find the content of *Bone Sickness* shocking. What shocks you?

BP: The only thing in movies that truly shocks me is pointless and inexcusable cruelty towards animals. There is no excuse for it and it is stupid.

BS: Why do you think it's more acceptable to portray violence against zombies than it is against humans? Is it thinly masked violent tendencies of human kind?

BP: I guess because zombies are not real, so the violence towards them doesn't feel real when watching it. If there are any masked violent tendencies, it may come from the natural instinct to protect your family and yourself from something that has proven it will destroy them and you without mercy.

BS: What kind of budget did you need for *Bone Sickness*?

BP: I needed a hell of a lot more than what I had, that's for sure. I would have loved to have had even $10,000 to shoot it. To shoot the movie properly, we would have needed at least $50,000. Yet we still managed to get the movie into major retail chains and foreign distribution with the tiny $3,000 budget.

BS: How did you raise the funds?

BP: Everything was paid out of our own pockets. My wife Stacey, Rich George and myself were all working full time jobs and we paid for what we could when we could do it. We even had to borrow money to get our original DVD's manufactured.

BS: How involved were you with the special effects?

BP: I did all of the special makeup effects in *Bone Sickness* and all of my other movies. I realized long ago that I did not want to move to California to become a professional effects artist. So I am content being the makeup artist for Morbid Vision Films.

BS: Can you give us any insights on how some the effects were created?

BP: Most of the effects were made with foam latex from the traditional way of sculpting and molding to create appliances. The nude girl who was cut in half was sitting on the floor with a false floor built around her waist. A fake stomach was applied to her body that was made in a way so my character could reach inside and pull out organs. The fully skinned corpse that attacks Darya Zabinski towards the end was created by making appliances and gluing them to tight clothing so the actor could simply put these skinned clothes on to avoid hours of application to his body. The corpses head was a full head pullover appliance that only needed to be glued around the mouth and neck. For the attack scene we built a fake bed around Darya and a torn torso was hidden under her shirt. The goblins were all facial appliances.

BS: *BloodPigs* raised the bar for more graphic violence. Did you set out to up the ante on this one?

BP: Yes. We wanted to make the goriest and bloodiest movie we had ever done. I wanted to display more gore and bodily horror and Rich came up with an air pressure blood sprayer that can explode three gallons of blood within five seconds. So now when it's called for, we have geysers of grue at our fingertips.

BS: What lessons did you learn while making the films?

BP: The main thing I learned while shooting *Bone Sickness*, *Fetus* and *BloodPigs* was not to bother spending months writing the perfect script because everything changes once you are on set anyway. What sounded great on paper has a habit of not working visually on set. As a movie moves along during filming, many new ideas surface that you didn't think of while sitting behind a computer typing. If a production has the freedom to expand during its creation, it has the freedom to evolve into something much greater than the original idea. Unfortunately in the studio system, this is hardly ever allowed.

BS: What tips can you offer new filmmakers looking to get into the zombie genre?

BP: Be creative. There are hundreds of zombie films out there now that are all doing the same thing and it has become boring. Put in the effort to make your zombies look good. So many of these films just have normal looking people with a bit of blood around their mouths and some black around the eyes. That does not make a monster. Oh and please do not waste horror fans time with another zombie comedy.

BS: Where do you go from here? Are there any more zombie films in your future?

BP: The next movie I want to make will be about flying witch heads. There are going to be a lot of creature effects in that one and there may be some zombie type creatures in it. I want to explore other concepts and storylines for a while. I may go back to zombies someday, but it won't be in the near future.

BS: Can you share any funny stories from the set of any of your zombie films?

BP: At the very end of *Bone Sickness* after the end credits, is the shot of the goblin perched on top of the chimney of a house. I was filming from the back yard so from the street all you could see was Rich in costume up there. A car slowed down and asked Rich if he was okay as if they were worried he might jump. I don't know if they even noticed the goblin makeup. Rich just waved and told them "yeah, I'm fine". Then he laughed his ass off.

MIKE PEEL

- The Zombie King (2012) Head of Special Effects Makeup
- Zombie Diaries 2: World of the Dead (2011) Special Effects Coordinator
- Zombie Diaries (2006) Special Makeup Effects Artist

Blood Splatter: How did you get involved with *Zombie Diaries*?

Mike Peel: My involvement with the first *Zombie Diaries* came about as a result of working on Kevin Gates' first film, *The Unseen*. I was working alongside two other effects artists, Marcus Murray and Scott Orr and as a result of getting on well with Scott, we became friends. We stayed in touch and when he was approached to head up the effects for *Zombie Diaries,* he invited me to create some of the effects for the film.

BS: Are you a fan of the zombie genre?

MP: I'm a huge fan of the zombie genre. The first zombie film I remember watching was Hammer's *Plague of the Zombies*, when BBC2 used to show late night horror films on a Friday night. My Dad would record them for me and I'd be up at the crack of dawn watching them before anyone was awake. From then on in, I was hooked.

BS: Do you have a favorite zombie film?

MP: By far my favorite zombie film is still *Dawn of the Dead.* I saw this when I was thirteen and it was at a time when I was just getting into the blood and gore films and it just amazed me. To sit there and watch a helicopter blade take a zombie's head off filled me with awe and fascination. I'll still sit and watch it now and just be mesmerized by the effects. Obviously as I've grown, the importance of the film has shifted from just the effects to the narrative, the storytelling, the characters journeys and the truly biting social commentary that Romero was aiming for.

BS: When creating a zombie, how does the design process work? Do you go into it with a predetermined idea of how the zombie will look or do you improvise as you go?

MP: When I'm designing zombies I'll have a rough idea of the look that I want to create. This is usually determined by the script and the director. If it's a fresh just bitten zombie, then the design will need to reflect that they haven't started to decompose yet. A lot of the time, most directors that I have worked with have been happy for me to just create zombies from scratch, so I do tend to improvise as I go. During the sculpting process, I'll sometimes find a feel or even a character for the zombie. If there is bone or skull showing through, then I'll highlight this area, while on others I might add a more diseased look. With a lot of scripts the detail for the zombies is literally 'a zombie approaches'. Every now and then the script will call for a more detailed and defined look, so I'll then work with the director to create that image.

BS: Zombie films are known for extravagant zombie kills and character death scenes, which has been your favorite that you have created?

MP: I think one of my favorite kills was on a short film from a few years back. The scene was shot as a POV and the director, James Bushe had rigged up the HD camera to sit on a helmet on his head. We see the zombie bite into a neck, with blood and gore aplenty and as he attacks the next character he's swiftly dispatched with a corkscrew in the eye. This stands out as it was all a continuous shot, so we had to prep both the victim and the zombie and let it run in real time.

BS: How about your favorite zombie death scene from other zombie movies you have not been involved in?

MP: I'd have to say that one of my favorite death scenes committed to screen is the lawnmower carnage in *Braindead (Dead Alive)*. It's a complete gorefest.

BS: Which zombie are you the most proud of?

MP: The zombie that I'm most proud of is a fairly recent creation. I got involved with a chat group looking for zombies to take part in Alice Cooper's Halloween Night of Fear at the Alexandra Palace, London. Originally I'd signed on to be a zombie as it looked fun and I'd get a free ticket for the gig. This got me thinking to create a zombie version of Alice himself and not looking anything like him and not being willing to shave my beard I drafted in David Sellicks who is a great zombie performer. Everything on this project worked well, even though I had three days to life caste, sculpt, mold and cast. It was worth it as the undead Alice went down well and we even had a guy from Devon theorizing about the prosthetic and loving how we had captured the essence of Alice Cooper himself.

BS: Which effect are you the most proud of?

MP: One of the stand out effects that I've created was simple, but very effective. It's the scene in *Zombie Diaries 2: World of the Dead* when the young boy, having just stabbed Cane is confronted and then shot in the head whilst trying to escape from the soldiers. We knew that we wanted a blood splatter on the wall but there wasn't any room to have an effects artist operate the gag, especially as he was to be running. So trying to follow him with tubing and a blood rig and stay out of shot was nigh on impossible. So I came up with the idea for the rig to be hidden under the actors coat and he basically operated it himself. With a few rehearsals and good timing we managed to pull off the effect.

BS: Can you tell us a bit about some of the specific effects that you created for *Zombie Diaries*?

MP: Some of the effects that I created for the first *Zombie Diaries* included several pullover face masks, a few zombie dummies that we then set fire to and a burnt and a crispy zombie. This was actually played by one of the main characters, doubling up as an extra. I was drafted in along with Cesar Alonso as an effects artist for this project by Scott Orr. We all had a hand in most things from the life casting, sculpting, applying and blood and gore on the shoot.

BS: Effects artists are known for using non-conventional methods of creating special effects. What tricks have you used that some may consider unusual?

MP: I know that every effects artist has their own methods of creating effects and more than likely their own recipes for certain things like blood, brain matter, guts and gore. A few years back, I needed a lot of guts and gore for a body being ripped open. I only had a miniscule budget, so I opted for almost the real thing and went mad at the supermarket basically buying all types of livers, kidneys, hearts and chicken giblets. At the time it was a cheaper option than making fake ones. I know that Tom Savini did the same for *Day of the Dead* and that looked fantastic. As much as you plan and design an effect, sometimes you are still scratching your head and even up to the last minute you're thinking about how the hell to do it. On one occasion a few years back I was approached to create an exploding head. So already in my mind I knew that it would need to be a fairly light and breakable head and I could maybe connect up an industrial air compressor and blow up the head that way. I ended up creating the head in wax and even though I'd pre-scored the inside it just wasn't working. So with the idea of the head blast in *Scanners* in my mind, we decided to shoot it for real with a local farmer and his shotgun to help us out. The head was filled with blood, gore and brain matter and was blown to bits perfectly. It wasn't conventional, but we created the desired effect.

BS: Is it difficult to distance yourself from the realism of the makeup due to the fact that it does resemble real life so closely? Is it necessary to desensitize yourself?

MP: There aren't many jobs that require you to look at dead bodies for a living, let alone recreate them. When researching the look of certain zombies, it is essential to know what you are going to be creating and to make it as realistic as possible. There are a lot of websites, books and reference materials to seek out and in this day and age, a decomposing body or burn victim is only a click away. I'll admit that over the years I have become slightly desensitized to real life injuries and view them not as dead bodies of people who had a life, but as research material. Although I still feel squeamish when anything involves children.

BS: Why do you think it's more acceptable to portray violence against zombies than it is against humans?

MP: I think that as a whole, society has accepted what a zombie is, what they do and how the best way is to kill them. As a result, they are part of popular culture and the zombie lore is so ingrained in people's minds, that any kind of violence against the undead is widely accepted. It's because they aren't people anymore, although while they are more human than certain horror monsters and creatures, they are still fictional creations.

BS: What kind of budget were you working with on *Zombie Diaries*?

MP: I think in total the overall budget for the first *Zombie Diaries* was around the £10,000 mark, so we were all working purely for expenses and because we all loved zombie films. We had no idea at the time that it would do as well as it did.

BS: How does a lower budget affect how you create effects? Do you cut back or find alternate ways to step around these restrictions?

MP: Working on a lower budget production is always going to be a challenge, as I can't always get the artist that I'd like and be able to pay them for their work. In some ways though, it is artistically liberating as most directors and productions understand that they are asking a hell of a lot for very little and accept that as long as you can create the effect they require, then you are free to make it from whatever you can. I've re-used so many different moulds and props especially for zombie films. My work ethic doesn't change regardless of the project and budget. If it's a good story and I'm interested enough to be involved, then I'll always put my best work into it.

BS: After the success of the first *Zombie Diaries* movie, were you given a larger budget for the sequel?

MP: There was an effects budget for *Zombie Diaries 2: World of the Dead*, which was nice and I had the luxury to hire people for the prep and shoot.

BS: Does the handheld style method of shooting make it harder to perform the needed effects shots?

MP: The handheld style used on both the *Zombie Diaries* films was a little restricting sometimes with regards to performing some of the effects. With most shoots, you'll a have a locked-off shot or scenes where the camera is static and ready to capture the effects needed. The camera style on the two films was part of the story and a way to put the audience in the movie. So as an effects artist, I wanted everything that we'd created to be seen so that you could get the full effect. In keeping with the story, the zombies weren't the main focus of the film, so even if I'd set up a specific zombie or effect it might only have been glimpsed briefly in the films. We also lost a lot of the prosthetics and effects with the night vision camera mode in the second film, as the hours of applications and really cool zombies just didn't register on screen.

BS: With the advent of CGI allowing for more decomposing and wounds, do you find yourself still using traditional methods or gravitating more to CGI?

MP: I'm very much old school and love to create in the real world. Most of the directors and productions I've worked alongside with have all wanted practical effects. I've seen this especially on a low budget films as they want to see, touch and feel what they are paying for. There have been a few occasions when CGI has been added afterwards, usually to bulk up a gunshot blast or spraying blood. The mix of practical and CGI effects has become intrinsic in a lot of today's films and I'm certainly not averse to seeing it used with my creations if the script requires it.

BS: Have you found yourself intentionally pushing the envelope to see how far you can go?

MP: There are always new materials and new methods of working, so I'm always trying to push the envelope of what I can achieve. Trying different methods and materials is part of the job and if you stick with the same things, your work can sometimes feel very stale. I am always looking for ways to challenge myself and my work.

BS: How do you handle conflict if a director insists on an effect or makeup appliance that you don't agree with or it conflicts with your morals?

MP: I'll have to say that so far I've not been in a position that has brought me into conflict with a director insisting on an effect that would test my morals. We got a bit close to the bone on the first *Zombie Diaries* when we shot the young girl in the head. That had a few interesting reactions afterwards, but never at the time did we think it was too much or too violent. The script required the effect, so it was filmed. There was one scene that was eventually written out of the original *Zombie Diaries* script which was a full on zombie rape scene. A zombie was imprisoned in a shed and had been abused many times. When I first read that scene, I was in two minds as to whether I wanted to be involved in it, but it got cut in the end.

BS: Have you ever been a zombie extra in one of the films you've worked on?

MP: I did actually play a zombie in the first *Zombie Diaries* and I think I get about two seconds of screen time. If you watch closely, it's the scene when the journalists are leaving the farmhouse and running past the zombies. Unbeknownst to the cast, I hid in one of the old farm buildings so when they had run past the zombies they did know about, I stumble out and literally scared them shitless. The scream you hear on screen was completely real and very satisfying. Most of the crew from the first film crop up somewhere in the film, as some days there weren't as many zombies. We all appear as extras along the way.

BS: What advice can you give someone looking to get into the effects industry?

MP: My advice for anyone wanting to get into the effects industry is just go for it. Take time to develop your skills and your portfolio and if you've never tried something, experiment with different materials and find what you are comfortable using. The down side is that a lot of the materials aren't cheap, so you really have to be dedicated and willing to get started. When I first started I had a few books and Grand Illusions was my bible. I knew the theory of creating things, but it wasn't until I started making things myself that I really started to learn. There are plenty of courses on offer which are pricey, but you'll get the help and advice of industry professionals. I did toy with this idea for a while, but I liked being on set and learning as I go.

BS: Are there any zombie films in the future for you?

MP: I had a rest from zombies for a while. 2010 was a bumper year and I worked on four different zombie related projects. After the zombie Alice Cooper, I worked on a music video for a Russian rapper and I am currently prepping for a film called *The Zombie King* which stars Corey Feldman and Edward Furlong in their first UK horror film.

BS: Can you share any funny on set stories from the zombie films you've worked on?

MP: A lot of weird things happen on film sets and they usually involve me for some reason. We had one instance during the shoot on *Zombie Diaries 2: World of the Dead* where not only did it start to snow mid shoot, but as we were leaving the location late on evening, the whole convoy slowed and then stopped. I was in the back of the producer's car with one of the directors and was quite surprised when a policeman approached the car and wanted to know from the driver what was going on. It was the producer's father's house that we were shooting in. As we looked out there was quite a large police presence and I'm sure that one of the other drivers had a tazer pointed at this head. What had happened was that one of the neighbors had seen a car leaving the grounds at high speed and the driver was covered in blood. Add to this that we had been firing blanks on the premises and the neighbors knew that the owner was away. They'd called the police saying that they thought there had been a robbery involving firearms. We had a lot of fun scrambling to find where we had put our call sheet to prove we weren't actually armed robbers, but a film crew.

Staying with the police theme, I got pulled over a few years back after a night shoot, as one of my tail lights was out. The fact that I was almost home and the roads were deserted got me off with a caution. At some point during my talk with the officer, I suddenly remembered that I still had a fake dismembered bloody body in my trunk and tried to look as innocent as possible from there on in. I'm so glad he didn't want to look in the trunk. That would have been interesting to explain.

NICK PLANTICO

- Humans Versus Zombies (2011) Pyrotechnician, Special Effects Supervisor
- Bite Me (2010) Safety Consultant
- The Dead Undead (2010) Special Effects
- Trailer Park of Terror (2008) Stunt Coordinator
- Flight of the Living Dead (2007) Special Effects Supervisor, Stunt Coordinator

Blood Splatter: How did you get into the special effects industry?

Nick Plantico: I started in stunts, but a couple of years after I started I was working on a war movie and the effects guy blew me up twice. The second time knocked me down and burned off a lot of my hair and I figured that I had better learn that side of it too. I learned what I could and after a few years I hooked up with a couple of top effects guys that took me under their wings and taught me a lot. I still work with them to this day. I got better and learned more and eventually starting coordinating special effects as well as coordinating stunts. The first film that I helped to produce, *Curse of the 49'er*, has a ton of action in it and I won Best Special Effects with it at ScreamFest.

BS: How about the zombie genre?

NP: I have worked in all genres in the past thirty years, but I have a lot of fun doing horror, especially zombie films. Within the zombie genre you have a lot of freedom to get creative with the effects and stunts. We often get a script and it will say "the zombie hoard attack". That's when it gets fun, coming up with unique and fun ways to kill zombies.

BS: Are you a fan of the genre?

NP: I am a huge fan of horror in general, everything from the classic Universal horror films to the latest and greatest work of today's artists and filmmakers, but zombie films have a special place in my heart and I am slowly getting known for them. On my website, there are three demo reels of my work. There is my stunt coordinating reel, my special effects coordinating reel and of course my zombie kill reel.

BS: Do you have a favorite zombie film?

NP: That is a tough question, there are so many out there and several are really entertaining. It's not really mainstream, but I really enjoyed *Fido*. I was already a huge Billy Connolly fan and I just love the entire look and feel of that one. Lately I caught a French film called *The Horde* which was a different take on the genre. I also liked *Dead Snow* from Norway and of course, the works of George Romero. I love how he makes a very entertaining exploitation film, but throws in social commentary to make you think.

BS: Which was your favorite zombie film to work on and why?

NP: I'd say that *Flight of the Living Dead* would have to be my favorite, although all of them were fun. On *Flight of the Living Dead*, I got to work with the amazing make-up effects artist Brian Wade. We had worked together on another film called *Sabretooth* and we meshed really well. I am currently working on a script that he is designing the makeup for.

BS: Which zombie film have you enjoyed working on the most from a creativity standpoint?

NP: Again, *Flight of the Living Dead*, working with Brian Wade is always a good time and we had a lot of freedom to create kills and action sequences together. We had a limited budget and a short time to do everything, but the creative juices flow better under pressure for me and on a zombie film, that means the blood flows and splatters.

BS: Zombie films are known for extravagant zombie kills and character death scenes, which has been your favorite that you have worked on?

NP: In *Flight of the Living Dead* I had a character spray flaming hairspray at a zombie and light it on fire from the chest up, on an airplane set. That one was fun and the stuntwoman, Dorenda Moore, ended up winning an award for the stunt. On the same film, Brian and I worked out a scripted gag that had an umbrella shoved into a zombie's mouth, coming out the back of her head. That was cool enough, but the payoff was that we rigged the umbrella to pop open after going through.

BS: How about your favorite zombie death scene from other movies you have not been involved in?

NP: I have to give that one to the master, Tom Savini. In *Day of the Dead* when they tore Rhodes in half while he was still alive, Joe Pilato yells at the zombies that are eating him, "choke on them!" That has to be one of the greatest death scenes ever done. *Shaun of the Dead* and others have paid tribute to that scene and rightfully so. It still makes me smile when I see it to this day.

BS: Have you ever been a zombie extra in any other of the films you've worked on?

NP: I'm actually in most of them. In *Flight of the Living Dead*, when the zombies break through the floor of the plane and drag the first person down, it's my arm wrapped in cables that punches through and grabs him. As a joke, on *Humans vs. Zombies* when the zombies break into the church, it's my arm that punches through the window. I also am the zombie that gets lit on fire by a Molotov cocktail.

BS: Can you tell us a bit about some of the effects that you created for *Flight of the Living Dead*?

NP: Wow, that one was non-stop. I did tons of effects on that one. I built all the blood hits for when the zombies are shot. I rigged the exploding heads that Brian Wade and his crew had made for me. We rigged the planes overhead compartments to open and close during turbulence. We blew a breakaway wall section up and then pulled it off with cables to simulate the plane getting hit by a missile while in flight. I worked on rigging the miniature plane crash into the mountain and we did the explosion in the hold at the end that included four dummy zombies filled with explosives. There was also a propane fireball that rolled through the real plane set and a ton of small spark and bullet effects.

BS: You bring a lot of different skills to the table that haven't been discussed so far, in particular stunts. Stunt work and effects work are two very different skills sets. How did you get into stunt work?

NP: I actually started out in stunt work, I studied to be a marine biologist, but the summer before I was going to join the Navy a friend of mine took me on a set. I saw guys blowing up things and wrecking cars. My reaction was to ask where I signed up. I got very lucky in that I was mentored by Yakima Canutt, the grandfather of stuntmen. He came up with camera techniques and safety standards that we still use today. It was an honor to have him teach me what he did and I actually owe my career starting out to his support. As for effects and stunts, while they are different, they overlap a lot, especially on horror projects. While I don't do digital effects, I do shoot the live action plates and elements that the digital effects artists use and as a friend once said, I speak geek. I had to learn the new wave of effects, at least in theory, so I can communicate with the digital artists and be able to understand what they need from me.

BS: Can you tell us about some of the stunts you have worked on in zombie films?

NP: Almost every zombie film has to have at least one flaming zombie, so body burns are a staple of the genre. We also do a lot of wirework and ratchets to fly the zombies and their victims. On *Flight of the Living Dead*, one of the characters, played by the great actor, Erick Avari, is crawling through the air ducts of the plane when turbulence hits. He falls through the ceiling of the plane, bounces off the overhead compartments and the seats and falls into the hold of the plane through the hole in the floor that the zombies tore through, with wires wrapped around his neck. He ends up hanging like a piñata as the zombies move in for a meal. The stunt was done by Erick's double on the film, Roger Stoneburner.

BS: Have any of the stunts gone wrong? If so, how do you handle that?

NP: Luckily very few stunts go wrong, we plan them out and rehearse as much as possible and during the planning and rehearsal the coordinators job is to try to figure out what can go wrong and eliminate it. There always will be accidents and we have trained medics that are on set, just in case of a mishap.

Stunt performers will get scrapes and bruises, that is part of the job, but the plan is for everyone to go home and be able to come back the next day, ready to work again.

BS: For *Flight of the Living Dead* you were both the special effects supervisor and the stunt coordinator. How do these work hand in hand?

NP: They overlap so much sometimes that the lines blur. One example was that I had to know what materials to make the burn mask out of so that it wouldn't melt during the zombie burning sequence. I also designed and ordered the breakaway walls for the shot when the missile hits the plane. I had to know what to make them out of, how much explosive to use and how to rig the cable pulls that yanked the pieces away after the explosion. We also had two stuntmen on cables that flew out after the wall blew up and another stuntman strapped into a plane seat on a track that flew him and the seat out of the set. It all has to work together to get the shot and keep the performers and crew safe. As a stunt coordinator, I find it very helpful to be able to communicate with other effects coordinators when I am just doing the stunts and someone else is coordinating the effects.

BS: Do you approach zombie effects and makeup differently if you are performing stunt work with an actor who is in makeup?

NP: Definitely. Often the makeup will hinder movement and vision, so we have to adjust that when it involves an actor doing action or a stunt performer.

BS: Does the type of makeup differ? For example, do you need special fire retardant makeup?

NP: Sometimes it will. If I am doing a burn in makeup, the flame retardant gel that I use to protect myself will often cause the makeup to run off an appliance. It's important that the makeup effects artists know what we are going to be doing with their work, so they can adjust their materials accordingly.

BS: You worked on *Bite Me*, the webs series for *Dead Rising 2*. How does working on a web show differ from a DVD or theatrical release?

NP: The biggest difference is usually the budget and that translates into time. Most web series have very short shooting schedules and *Bite Me* was one of them. The crew stepped up and we made a project that everyone could be proud of. The first episode got three million hits in the first month and the series has over ten million views so far.

BS: You were the safety consultant for this series. Is this just for stunts or other aspects of film making?

NP: It was for everything. I kept the insurance company happy and helped where I could. With a tight schedule and a heavy workload, people get tired and that is when accidents can happen. Luckily, there were no issues with *Bite Me*. It was a great cast and crew and they pulled it off.

BS: Are there any zombie films in the future for you?

NP: Actually, in addition to coordinating the stunts and special effects, I have been asked to help produce season two of *Bite Me*. We are in pre-production right now and are about to shoot a feature-length continuation of the storyline. It will be broken up into episodes for the web and then released onto DVD. There is a much bigger budget and the scope and scale of the story and action have increased greatly.

BS: Can you share any funny on set stories from the zombie films you've worked on?

NP: There have been several, but one stands out. While in Pittsburg, Texas filming *Humans vs. Zombies*, we had a lot of locals playing zombies for the big scenes. While filming a scene where about a hundred zombies are running in to attack the heroes, one of the actors throws a Molotov cocktail at me and I light on fire. As soon as I started burning, the entire running horde of zombies stopped in their tracks, staring at me as I walked up the street, burning. The assistant director yelled at them to keep coming and they resumed running in. I guess it's not every day in a small east Texas town that you see someone walking calmly down the street. On fire.

MARC PRICE

• Colin (1990) Director, Writer

BS: *Colin* is an interesting addition to the zombie genre not only because of its incredibly low budget but also from its original narrative. How did the story come about?

MP: I was with a bunch of friends watching the European cut of *Dawn of the Dead*. We hadn't seen that version before as the one released here in England had some scenes cut out of it. There had been a shooting at a school in Scotland and the scene where Peter shoots the children was cut out of the movie. The next morning I woke up thinking how much I'd love to make a zombie movie and making it from the zombie's perspective. From there, the idea grew. It was originally going to be a short instead of a feature. I played with it and tried to come up with an idea that could carry it to feature length.

BS: Are you a fan of the zombie genre? If so, what inspired you to work with it?

MP: I'm certainly a fan of the Romero movies. Those are the films that I saw that introduced me to the genre, particularly *Dawn of the Dead*. I really responded to *Day of the Dead* and the idea of Bub completely blew me away. I always wanted to make a zombie film, but I couldn't think of an idea that felt unique, so the concept of making a film from the zombie's point of view definitely tied into what I loved about *Day of the Dead*.

BS: Do you have a favorite zombie film?

MP: So that's a tricky one for me. I love *Dawn of the Dead*, but I also really love *Day of the Dead*. Then you get into the not-quite-zombies like *28 Days Later* which I also really like. It's always tempting to say something really obscure to earn some cool points among zombie fans, but I'll be perfectly honest, these are the films that rocked my world when I saw them.

BS: Why did you decide to make the film on such a tight budget?

MP: It wasn't really a decision, to be fair. I looked at what the movie was. I resent the notion of having to fill in a heap of forms before people will tell you your movie isn't worth making. I haven't really experienced it first hand in all honesty but the notion of it bothers me. This is a system that is put in place always by organizations meant to encourage young filmmakers, but I find it very off putting especially when you are a young filmmaker. You are enthusiastic and you have a lot to learn, there is just not much of a system in place for filmmakers to make those mistakes on those early films, which they are very much entitled to do and need to do to grow as filmmakers. I got my first camcorder at twenty one and that was the camera I ended up using to shoot *Colin*. I just thought, "hey, we've got what we need here, so let's make the movie using this". I knew that this was a difficult sell anyway. It's a movie with hardly any dialogue and a narrative that is deliberately scattered and designed to not make a great deal of sense, but ultimately will reward the audience for making it to the last scene. I then hopefully present a movie that is worth revisiting. That was the intent for me. We take a lot of risks making a movie like this. So there wasn't any money and I was living on overdrafts at the time.

BS: How do you direct an actor whose screen time mainly consists of actions and no dialogue?

MP: I made it clear to Alastair Kirton who played Colin, about how he was never really on his own when it came to playing the character. The big challenge was he couldn't emote. He couldn't talk and we didn't want to use flashbacks scattered throughout to tell the story. We took all of these tools away from him. We explained that the actor he was performing with was the camera, if that makes sense. The idea is whatever he would do, he camera would be there to help communicate what he needs to communicate as a character to the audience. He was brave to take this role. Alastair was working on a previous film that I had shot and I realized the story was there and the performances were okay, but it was a dull and flat film. I was struggling to make the film interesting as we were editing and the idea for Colin came along. I wanted to ditch the film, which I ultimately did. Alastair was involved with that and I felt bad about it. I really liked him as an actor, but what we had done so far had hardly any dialogue and we had this joke where he would finally get to speak in something and I told him I'd like him to play the lead character in a film I am working on and he said "yeah, wicked, I'll finally get to talk" and I said "yeah, the thing about that is, you're a zombie and you don't get any dialogue in the movie". He loved the challenge and we really enjoyed working together. We had a really good rapport. At the beginning of the movie when we started shooting, I remember the first night Alastair stayed over as he was shooting the next morning. We had known each other at arm's length for a while, but we weren't really close and I remember looking back at that awkwardness of not knowing someone very well and having to entertain them and be a good host and now he's one of my best friends. That definitely came through making *Colin*.

BS: *Colin* achieved effects that movies with budgets a thousand times larger are unable to do, how much of the budget was assigned to special effects?

MP: To be fair, in terms of a budget we didn't say that we had money put aside for effects. We spent about £50 give or take and we just looked to see what we had available to us. The makeup effects guys would bring their own equipment that they had either acquired on other sets or had in their supply. They would use that to create the zombies. Michelle Webb who directed the effects team would show us how to do the zombie makeup and leave her equipment with us and go to do fashion makeup, which is more her thing. She would come back to see what we've done and "say great, now try this" and she would show us something else. So that is how we got through that. It just came with Michelle. I would work on little projects as well, such as teaching film to young filmmakers and they saw what we were doing and they wanted to work on a zombie movie. So what we ended up doing is making a zombie film and utilized those resources. There were little sneaky ways around it.

BS: What did you use as a foundation for the effects?

MP: Liquid latex came in quite handy. We all became familiar enough with it to create wounds of varying degrees. Some looked great, some didn't. Luckily a lot of the injuries were freshly bitten with fresh blood so we could bruise them up and cover the injures with blood which we made using golden syrup, I think it's corn syrup in the US. We added black and red food coloring to get the texture right and we used flour a lot.

BS: For the makeup?

MP: Actually for whenever I wanted an impact shot. There is a scene during the house siege where the door gets kicked off, when Kate Alderman is hiding upstairs. We had taken the door of the hinges and I'd countdown from three, we'd push the door, the camera would shake and someone off camera would blow a handful of flour to simulate dust. In post production we added a loud cracking sound and the shot comes alive. That is how we did little tricks like that.

BS: How much of the makeup was custom made?

MP: In the house siege scene we didn't have enough makeup people to cover the amount of people who showed up. We had gotten to the time where I needed to start shooting and I asked how many zombies we had and three people put their hands up. I told those three to face the camera slightly and everyone face away and act like zombies. What we would do is then take two people into makeup, they could then come on screen and face the camera and we'd then take two more and we got through the day like that. I knew that the scenes would be intercut during editing, so that the scene wouldn't have an obvious progression of zombies facing the camera as the scene went on. I knew we'd be able to cut it and logistically it worked out really well.

BS: The effects quality was very good. How much experience have you had in the industry?

MP: I don't even know if I am in the industry now. I am doing the same thing as I've always done. I am a fan of film and the magic of filmmaking has always intrigued me. I've always been interested in how a fan sees a film. *Jurassic Park* has just been released again and I remember seeing it when it first came out and I would always look around at the audience during key moments to see how they reacted. It's really cool to see how people react to a film. A friend of mine hadn't seen *Alien* and I got to watch it with her for the first time. She knew something was going to come because I would turn and stare at her waiting to see her reaction. She'd tense up knowing that something cool was about to happen. Of course I threw in a few fake stares to fuck with her and not ruin all of the surprises. I just love seeing that. It's not really that I have a lot of experience in the industry, but I have a lot of experience in the audience and what I would like to see. That is what I tried to do with *Colin*.

BS: Did you have to come up with any new ways of creating effects to fit in the budget?

MP: The whole ethos behind the film and any film for that matter is that you have to work with what you've got. In our case, we didn't have anything, so we had to get creative in a lot of aspects. Which I kind of enjoy and if I ever get to make more movies, it's something I want to hang on to. I know guys who worked on the *Harry Potter* movies and even they say that they didn't get enough money to get what they need. Not that I refer to my films as art, but there is that art from adversity thing and I like the idea of that. Ultimately you are trying to achieve an emotional response from an audience. You have to look at the best way to achieve it with what you've got. I like finding that out. I don't like to prepare too much and I want to find it as I go. I have the movie in my head and I've seen it and it's exciting and that is the film we find as we are shooting it. I really enjoy that part of the process which is why I try to encourage a lot of improvisation from the actors. Anyone can throw in ideas as that is what makes an interesting film.

BS: Which was your favorite effects shot in the film?

MP: That's an interesting one. There is a visual effect I am really fond off. Leigh Crocombe played the first zombie in the film and he gets stabbed in the head about a hundred times. He was playing about with a visual effects program and there was a shot I had of slingshot guy taking a shot at a zombie and then the zombie falls. I thought it looked like the zombie was hit with a shoe lace. I asked if he could add a digital splat and a mist of blood splatter. He had a go at it and I think it turned out great. It's a subtle effect that many don't notice. That is my favorite visual shot in the film. As a practical effect, I liked the shot of the guy who gets his throat bitten in the house siege. Blood pours out of his neck wound and it was really simple. One of the zombies had a mouthful of blood and wrapped his mouth around the victim's neck and let a load of blood out. I cracked pasta shells to enhance the audio of the throat getting torn. It's little things like that I enjoyed.

BS: Did the effects meet your expectations?

MP: I think most of the time they did. It's how you cut them together in post production. I think most of the effects shots if we had let them play out in long continuous shots, you would have seen the cracks very quickly. It's about getting the perfect moments and then cutting then something. That's what happens when you shoot. You see these perfect moments and take them and put them with more perfect moments. I was working on a film recently with a friend of mine and he asked me to direct a zombie film he had written. I asked him why he didn't want to direct it himself and he told me he'd never directed before. I told him that he should direct and I would come and hang out and if he got stuck, I could help him out. We were shooting a scene with someone's neck getting bitten and something went wrong with the effect. They were talking about trying to reset up the effect which would have taken a couple of hours, so I took the footage they had shot up to that point and worked on editing it. It's about taking a failed shot, finding a shot that works and putting it all together with post production. I think that is how you work with special effects. So yes, everything did meet my expectations.

BS: Which was the most challenging effect to create?

MP: There was one we didn't use in the end actually. I wanted this low angle of a building with two people standing on the edge holding their hands like they were going to jump. Below that I wanted a load of zombie hands reaching up and clawing at them. The guy is pulling her towards the edge but she is resisting. She pulls away and falls off the building. He's looking around at her screaming and a zombie grabs him and he steps over the edge. I wanted the camera to follow him down and land with a crunch. You don't see the impact as the camera closes in behind Colin's shoulders as he watches everything happen. The fall doesn't kill the guy, but he can't get away from Colin. Who bites him on the face and kills him. The ironic thing is the guys who needed to do the shot, couldn't do it then, but have since learned how. The shot in the final film is not continuous. The main error I made in the shot was, as the guy lands, I pan to Colin, then pan back and everything thinks we switched a dummy for the actor which we didn't do. The actor was there the whole time. We added a digital blur to simulate him hitting the car.

BS: Which was your favorite zombie or character death scene?

MP: That is a really hard questions because there are bits in most of the film that I liked. I really liked Leigh's zombie at the beginning of the film. He wasn't gentle with Al at all. He was shoving his ass against the cabinets and really trying to bite him. Leigh is normally a really shy guy, so seeing him be a wicked zombie was cool. There were finer details that most don't notice, like the grass stains on his shirt that show where he was attacked coming home and dragged along the grass. I also like his death, getting stabbed in the head that many times. Justin Hayles, who did a lot of the effects, is the guy who gets snapped in half and pulled through the window. That was a really great shot. I ripped it off, or rather I should say, borrowed it from *The Blob* remake.

BS: How about your favorite zombie death scene from other zombie movies you have not been involved in?

MP: I really like Rhodes' death in *Day of the Dead*.

BS: Were you a zombie extra in the film?

MP: I was actually in the film a couple of times. You can hear me in the street battle scene shouting orders. I was actually shouting directions off camera to the cast members, but they sounded so vague we kept them in. It really worked well for the scene. I pop up as one of the zombies when Colin first comes out. You see some legs running past the camera and a zombie lurching towards it and that was me. You also see a dude with a shopping trolley and that was me as well.

BS: Are there any zombie films in the future for you?

MP: I have an idea for a television series. It's nothing to do with *Colin* but follow that same idea of the apocalypse. In this story, the apocalypse has passed and it details how England starts getting on its feet again. Zombies have been trained and returned back to their family members. It isn't successful and what you have is a system where people are getting their loved ones back, but it's like they have Alzheimer's and don't remember their previous lives.

BS: Can you share any funny on set stories from the making of *Colin*?

MP: Man, we have so many. We had a blast shooting the film. I think one of my favorite ones is when we were shooting the street fight scene. All of the neighbors on the street were fine with what we were doing and they knew what we were working on. However, I think someone with a sense of humor thought it would be funny to call the police, as it looked like there was a real riot taking place. There were no real explosions, just practical effects. We were shooting the scene and there was lots of screaming and blood and body parts everywhere and someone went and called the police on us. So we are in the middle of shooting and this one single policeman shows up. I can only assume it was because he didn't believe that there was a riot happening in our quiet neighborhood. When he showed up he had this look of horror on his face as he saw bloody people walking around. I switched out the camera just in case he tried to confiscate it. I didn't want to lose the footage we'd shot and took an empty one with me and went over to see him. I told him we were students shooting a film and he was so relieved he didn't have to face a riot on his own. He laughed and took some photos on set with us and we asked him to be in the movie, but he had to continue walking his beat so he wasn't able to. That was such a funny situation. I swear you can't make things like this up.

BS: What has been the one of your favorite moments after the release of *Colin*?

MP: There was recently a German dub released and it's always really interesting to see how you sound in another language. We all forgot at the time, but there is a scene in the film where Alastair says "shit" and the German voice over said "scheiße". When we watched it back we couldn't stop laughing. It made me wish we'd put in more cool swear words to see how they translated into other languages.

This page "Colin" courtesy of Nowhere Fast Film Productions and Marc Price.

325

JOHN RUSSO

- Escape of the Living Dead (2012) Director, Screenwriter, Key Special Effects Artist
- Children of the Living Dead (2001) Executive Producer
- Night of the Living Dead 30th Anniversary Edition (1998) Director: New Scenes
- Night of the Living Dead (1990) Producer
- Night of the Living Dead (1968) Screenwriter

BS: *Night of the Living Dead* was and continues to be a landmark film in the zombie genre. With its release, all of the rules were rewritten. Up until *Night of the Living Dead*, zombies had never eaten humans before, this was a massive change for the genre, what made you decide to make them cannibals?

JR: In the early stages of the film, George Romero and I were working on script ideas and doing some writing on a collaboration basis. My original story had to do with aliens who came to earth in search of human flesh.

BS: That's quite a distance away from how the final ended up. How did the aliens become zombies?

JR: George wrote about forty pages of a story that eventually became the first part of *Night of the Living Dead*. The lead female, Barbara, was being attacked but he didn't say or seem to know who the attackers were or what they were after. To make a long story short, I suggested that they should be dead people in search of human flesh.

BS: That was definitely a turning point for the genre. How closely did the final release follow your original vision once the core features were in place?

JR: We stuck to our vision throughout the shooting of the film. The movie follows the script in every meaningful aspect.

BS: So any other changes were minimal?

JR: We only changed or added some things without destroying the overall vision.

BS: Some of the visual effects are absolutely terrifying and years ahead of its time. Did the graphic effects on screen mirror your vision?

JR: We scrupulously stuck to our original vision in every way that we possibly could. We carefully considered every move and every decision, including decisions affecting the graphic portrayal of violence and flesh-eating in the movie.

BS: Reviews from when the movie came out ranged from disgust to outright hysteria. Was this the impact you were expecting?

JR: We knew we had made a good movie and we were therefore hoping for good reviews, of which we got many, especially in the long run.

BS: Were you a fan of the zombie genre prior to *Night of the Living Dead* ?

JR: I never really thought that there was much of a zombie genre prior to *Night of the Living Dead*. I think we changed all that and really made the genre its own.

BS: That is a very good observation. Up until then, I think the zombie was little more than a Saturday matinee monster.

JR: Absolutely. I just felt that the zombies I had seen in movies up to that time were not very frightening at all. They really didn't do very much.

326

BS: I agree completely. In fact, the start of this book is the turning point that *Night of the Living Dead* brought about.

JR: When we turned zombies into flesh-eaters, that changed everything in the genre.

BS: Were there any scenes you were surprised that made it to the final cut?

JR: I was not surprised by anything concerning what ended up in the final cut mainly because I was intimately involved with the entire process. I worked very closely with George and producer Russ Streiner, among many others.

BS: What is your favorite special effects shot from any zombie film you have been associated with and why?

JR: I don't know that I have a favorite special effects shot because I am always more concerned with the story and character development. I'd have to say that the stabbing of Helen Cooper by her daughter Karen in *Night of the Living Dead* has to rank among the best. As far as a non zombie film goes, I also think the death of Janet Leigh in the opening scene shower in *Psycho* is as well.

BS: *Psycho* is a great example of a genre defining moment. Killing off a lead actress so early on in the film was unheard of at the time, as much as *Night of the Living Dead* killing off the entire cast was. This certainly set a trend for future zombie films. You are currently slated to direct the film adaptation of your 2005 comic book miniseries *Escape of the Living Dead*, can you tell us a bit about it?

JR: The comic books and graphic novel tell as much about the story as anyone would need to know. Although the story is a sequel to *Night of the Living Dead*, it is not set in the continuity of George's universe or the *Return of the Living Dead* saga.

(Author's note: Escape of the Living Dead and its multiple sequels are currently available through Avatar Press)

BS: How effects driven is the film?

JR: To my way of thinking, almost no good movie or story should be "effects driven." Good movies and stories depend mainly on plot, theme and character development. The effects are secondary.

BS: Do you prefer traditional prosthetics or CGI?

JR: I think CGI is really overdone nowadays. It is to the point where plot, theme and character development are quite often short-changed, which is a mistake and often a recipe for disaster for many films.

BS: Who are you considering for the cast in *Escape of the Living Dead?*

JR: I want very much to keep Kristina Klebe, Tony Todd and Kane Hodder in the cast and I hope I can prevail on this.

BS: Those are some great actors with roots firmly in the horror genre, especially Tony Todd who was in the 1990 *Night of the Living Dead* remake. You are noted for a cameo role as a zombie in the original *Night of the Living Dead*, do you plan to appear as a zombie in *Escape of the Living Dead?*

JR: No, I don't. These days I prefer to concentrate on my role behind the camera and to give it my full attention, in lieu of trying to do cameos or acting just for kicks.

BS: What can the fans of the zombie genre expect from you in the future?

JR: What can zombie fans expect of me in the future? Well, you already know about *Escape of the Living Dead*, but I have a couple more books and movies either under contract or in development and fans will hear all about them when the publishers or distributors are ready.

SEAN SANSOM

- Resident Evil: Afterlife (2010) Key Prosthetic Makeup Artist, Creature Effects Artist
- Survival of the Dead (2009) Special Makeup Effects Artist
- Land of the Dead (2005) Special Makeup Effects Artist, Prosthetics Makeup Artist
- Resident Evil: Apocalypse (2004) Special Makeup Effects Artist
- Dawn of the Dead (2004) Prosthetics Technician, Special Makeup Effects Artist

Blood Splatter: You have some very high profile zombie films under your belt. How did you get into the zombie genre?

Sean Sansom: Working on horror films in Toronto wasn't uncommon at the time, but there had never been a zombie film. It seemed like the sub-genre had long been abandoned for serial killer and torture films. For many years, a script called *Pontypool* had been floating around. We could hardly wait for that film to happen as anything with a zombie was good news, but it quietly went away. A year or so later, we all found ourselves working on the *Dawn of the Dead* remake like a bunch of giddy school girls, not knowing that we would be doing a zombie film almost every year for the next six years. Funny enough, when *Pontypool* finally did get off the ground, none of us were available to work on it because of the other zombie flicks. Go figure.

BS: Are you a fan of the genre?

SS: Of course. Having grown up watching every zombie film I could get my hands on, I was more than happy to contribute to the genre that had always put a smile on face.

BS: Do you have a favorite zombie film?

SS: That's a tough one. I really like George's first two "Dead" films, but the one I watch the most is *Zombie.* They're all very good, but the latter really stands out. Maybe it's because of the ridiculously drawn out eye splinter scene, or the crazy zombie vs. shark?

BS: Which was your favorite zombie film to work on and why?

SS: I'll have to say from a creative standpoint, it would be the *Dawn of the Dead* remake. The build was done here in Toronto headed by David Anderson of AFX Studios and we had an amazing crew and a lot of fun. Building, testing and coming up with the various effects, is always the most rewarding when it looks great on screen. Plus, it was the first zombie film that all of the local crew got to work on. Our shop was in the mall itself, so we were able to duck in and out during filming to finish something that inevitably shot in the following week. We had a regulation sized badminton court thanks to Zack Snyder, as well as an area for basketball in the shop. We worked long hours, but hardly noticed because we had so much fun. It was like summer camp with zombies. From a nostalgic standpoint, it would be *Land of the Dead.* Working on a George Romero zombie film and also working again for Greg Nicotero and the KNB crew, I couldn't have asked for a better combination. We got to be involved with some cool gags and make-ups. I am very grateful to have had the chance to work on both of these films.

BS: There was a lot of controversy with the remake of *Dawn of the Dead* from a purist's perspective. Did you have any reservations approaching the project?

SS: None at all, I was just happy that finally there was a zombie movie being made. I thought it was a good update and retelling of the story and we got to create a different zombie "look".

BS: Which zombie are you the most proud of?

SS: I really liked the "Number 9" character from *Land of the Dead.* KNB designed and created all the pieces, I just applied it, but Jennifer Baxter was such a great actress to work with, she really sold the look she was given.

BS: Zombie films are known for extravagant zombie kills and character death scenes, which has been your favorite that you have created?

SS: I like them all. We've done so many, it's hard to remember who did what and in which film, so I couldn't give you a favorite. Usually with a scene like that, it's such a collaborative effort that there's at least three or four of us involved. We get to put our heads together and come up with something as gory as possible. It was good times.

BS: How about your favorite zombie death scene from a zombie movie you have not been involved in?

SS: Well, there's that eye-splinter scene from *Zombie*.

BS: What sources of inspiration did you use to create the zombies, both recently dead and more decayed?

SS: We usually use forensic and medical reference books for realistic injuries or trauma, but for zombies you have to take it a few steps further. We try to make them look different from other zombie films, but you can't help but pay homage to your favorites. I'm still a big fan of the zombies in the *Night of the Living Dead* remake and now with *The Walking Dead*, they're going to be tough to surpass.

BS: Is it difficult to distance yourself from the realism of the zombie and wound makeup due to the fact that it does resemble real life so closely?

SS: Not at all. The makeups are usually so over the top to start with, or at least at a level that isn't a common occurrence in the real world. It's usually the subtle stuff that has a more lasting impression, an injury or accident that has happened to yourself or someone you know.

BS: When creating a zombie, how does your design process work? Do you go into it with a predetermined idea of how the zombie will look or do you improvise as you go?

SS: It all depends on the script, really. We'll get an overall idea of how fresh or rotten the zombies are and then we'll get input from the director on what they're looking for. From that, we present designs which usually consist of various stages and we'll do some make-up tests. That gives us our overall guideline in which to follow for all the zombies, as a whole. We then design specific zombies that are featured, so that they stand out and become their own character.

BS: Can you tell us a bit about some of the specific effects that you created for *Dawn of the Dead*?

SS: We had so much work to pull off during a short period of time that we usually teamed up on specific effects and characters during the prep. I was directly involved with the little zombie girl attack, the pregnant zombie, the chainsaw accident, zombie Andy's head shot and on set for a lot of the other effects, but not alone. Some of us did however, get to create one character from start to finish and apply it on set. They were mainly one-scene only, but featured nonetheless. I made a zombie that has half of his face stripped down to the bone and he's pushing against the glass outside the mall when they first arrive.

BS: How about for the *Land of the Dead*?

SS: None of us local crew had anything to do with the build, as it was all done by KNB. We were the support crew for the KNB guys, there to handle all the set work. My main task was to apply the makeup to Number 9 and as many hero, stunt and background zombies as possible. There was a lot of body wrangling, blood gags and it was usually all hands on deck.

BS: How about for the *Survival of the Dead*?

SS: For that one, Greg Nicotero was our consultant and KNB supplied us with some very juicy wound appliances, as well as a full-sized horse lying on its side. Everything else we made with our small five man crew and four weeks of prep. We had to have almost everything built before we went to camera, as it was all shot on location with all of us present to apply zombie make-ups. Whatever you see on film, the five of us all had a hand in creating.

BS: Zombie films continue to push the boundaries, were there any effects shots that made it to the final cuts of your films that surprised you?

SS: Not really, because we've usually seen these shots before. There's always the editing that saves a scene from being removed completely. For the really gory scenes, they usually shoot the hell out of it with multiple cameras and sometimes if it allows, multiple takes. Luckily they cut it down and trim it to fit, otherwise, we'd lose the scene all together.

BS: Is it easy to find yourself pushing the envelope to see how far you can go?

SS: Like I said, we've seen all the gore, the only difference now, is we're seeing the use of CGI to help cleanup and accentuate what we do. I think the only thing to push now is the way the zombies look, which KNB is doing a fine job with *The Walking Dead*.

BS: Have you ever been a zombie extra in one of the films?

SS: Never. I've been close many times, but maybe one day.

BS: Are there any zombie films in the future for you?

SS: Not at the moment, but you never know. I haven't had withdrawals yet and with all the other zombie projects coming out, I think I'll be okay for now.

BS: Can you share any funny on set stories from the zombie films you've worked on?

SS: Along with everyone else you've talked to, that could be a whole other book. None are as good as the "unplugged fridge full of guts" story, so I won't even try to compare.

BS: Can you offer a zombie makeup tip for aspiring special effects artists who may be reading the book?

SS: Try adding instant coffee to your blood. It gives it an old and dried-out look. It looks great and it keeps you awake.

Sean Sansom, left, applying makeup to Steve Barton "Survival of the Dead" courtesy of Steve Barton.

TOM SAVINI

- The 4th Reich (2013) Actor
- Planet Terror (2007) Actor
- Land of the Dead (2005) Actor
- Dawn of the Dead (2004) Actor
- Zombiegeddon (2003) Actor
- Children of the Living Dead (2001) Actor
- Night of the Living Dead (1990) Director
- Day of the Dead (1985) Special Makeup Effect
- Dawn of the Dead (1978) Makeup and Cosmetic Special Effects, Actor

Blood Splatter: You've been actively involved in the zombie genre for over thirty years. What appeals to you so much about it?

Tom Savini: Appeals to me? Is that the way to say it? Do I like it? Yes, I do. I have done ever since seeing George Romero's original *Night of the Living Dead* for the first time. I think it's because the possibilities are really exciting. I love the idea that what was once human is now walking around using primal animal instincts. The idea that a dead body is being moved around by something that perhaps never moved a body around, in other words, never had arms or feet or eyes to use to motivate itself. I think it's just an interesting idea.

BS: What are some of your favorite zombie films?

TS: I really liked *Shaun of the Dead*, because it is just brilliant. I also really liked *Zombieland* as well.

BS: You've been involved with all elements of film production including acting, stunts, special effects and directing. Where do you prefer to be and why?

TS: These days I prefer acting and directing over anything else. Acting is the hardest thing to do and directing is the top of the wire as far as the creation process goes.

BS: If you hadn't entered the film industry, what other career would you have taken?

TS: I would have chosen choreography for the stage.

BS: You are frequently identified as the inspiration for many effects artists both amateur and professional. Who inspires you?

TS: My inspirations come from the classics, Jack Pierce, Dick Smith, Rob Bottin and Rick Baker.

BS: Which effect or technique that you have created are you the most proud of?

TS: I like the magic trick aspect behind my mind set as an effects artist.

BS: *Dawn of the Dead* was one of the first movies you worked on. How did you get involved with the production?

TS: *Dawn of the Dead* was actually the fourth film I did make up makeup effects on. George sent me a telegram while I was doing a play down south that said "start thinking of ways to kill people. We have another gig". That was the beginning.

BS: Were you aware at the time that your effects were to have such a strong impact on the effects industry and in particular the zombie genre?

TS: Nope. I had no idea at all.

BS: Effects artists are known for using non-conventional methods of designing and executing effects such as coffee grounds and Karo syrup for blood, what non-conventional methods have you used the gore fans would be surprised to read?

TS: One of the things I have used before is Rice Krispies and latex to create the look of dirt and rot on Nate's corpse from *Creepshow*.

BS: *Dawn of the Dead* is considered ground zero for zombie gore. While *Night of the Living Dead* was violent, much was implied. Few effects like this had been seen before, did your time in Vietnam as a combat photographer influence this?

TS: I think I am the only special effects makeup artist who has seen real gore and violence first hand and had to photograph it during my tour of duty in Vietnam. It was a brutal and shocking lesson in anatomy and that is why my special effects have the reputation of realism that they have.

BS: Is it necessary to desensitize yourself from the realism of the makeup due to the fact that it does resemble real life violence that you have seen so closely?

TS: It's for too late for me now. I became extremely desensitized during Vietnam. It was a survival mechanism and it was one I needed to have to retain my sanity.

BS: Zombie films are known for extravagant zombie kills and character death scenes, which has been your favorite that you have created?

TS: There have been many, but I think that the helicopter zombie scalping in *Dawn of the Dead* is a really good one and the disemboweling of the soldiers in *Day of the Dead*. Joe Pilato being torn to shreds and the zombies yanking off Taso Stavrakis's head in *Day of the Dead* are also up there.

BS: How about your favorite zombie death scene from other zombie movies you have not been involved in?

TS: Definitely the eye being gouged on the large splinter in Fulci's *Zombie*.

BS: On *Dawn of the Dead* and *Day of the Dead*, were you given parameters to work with in regardless to zombie look or were you given free reign?

TS: Yep, I was given free rein to do what I wanted.

BS: You recently returned to special effects in *Redd Inc.* after an almost decade long absence. What prompted your decision to return?

TS: There were a couple of reasons that made me decide to return. I had the chance of working with the great make up effects guys at MEG and the opportunity to go to Australia and shoot.

BS: I assume the industry has changed a bit. Were you able to keep abreast of the new materials and techniques?

TS: Of course. I have my makeup effects school located in Pittsburgh. I keep up on all of the latest techniques and materials there.

BS: Do you approach the effects on a zombie film differently than a standard horror film?

TS: Nope, they are all just special effects.

BS: Why do you think it's more acceptable to portray violence against zombies than it is against humans? Is it thinly masked violent tendencies of human kind?

TS: Yeah, I really think it's a thin excuse to beat the shit out of other humans.

BS: How does working with the dead and staring at death affect your view on mortality, considering the things you have seen in real life?

TS: It really doesn't. I personally don't see it as staring at death at all. What I am staring at is just latex, Karo syrup and prosthetics. It's easy, but this also goes back to the desensitization thing.

BS: Is it harder to create special effects when the subject matter is darker and more grounded in reality?

TS: Absolutely it is. I really don't like the real maniacs and perverts that exist in real life.

BS: Having seen death in real life and how it differs from a lot of Hollywood style death, do you prefer to see the realism or the glamorized over the top style gore?

TS: I prefer the realism of death, but I see it so rarely in the shit that Hollywood keeps putting out.

BS: Despite your close connections with George Romero, there was a lot of controversy with the remake of *Night of the Living Dead* from a purist's perspective. Did you have any reservations approaching the project?

TS: Nope, not at all. I was just doing the best I can as usual.

BS: Your negative experiences during the production of *Night of the Living Dead* are well documented, did this influence your decision to step away from the Directorial role?

TS: No, neither my personal issues that were happening off set or the numerous production issues I went through on the set had any effect on my decision to no longer direct at all. What did factor in for me though, was the fact that it wasn't a hit. That entirely affected that part of my fate. It has since gained popularity in the community. *Citizen Kane* wasn't a hit when it came out either and so many classics that exist today.

BS: Was it difficult to turn over the special effects reins to John Vulich and Everett Burrell having been so involved with George's previous movies?

TS: Not at all, I completely trusted them.

BS: It has been noted that the film did not live up to your expectations. What scenes could we have seen that did not make it to the final cut?

TS: There are plenty of scenes cut throughout the film. If you can find it, it's all in the twenty five minute documentary that's part of the supplemental material on the DVD. We discuss some of things in that feature.

BS: You had a cameo on the *Dawn of the Dead* remake, how were you approached for this role?

TS: Actually I wasn't approached at all. I called them and told them I wanted to be in it.

BS: James Gunn the original screenwriter had received death threats about his involvement with it. Did you have any reservations about it considering the outrage from fans of the original?

TS: I personally didn't know anything about it and I really wouldn't care if I did. I'd still have done it.

BS: Were you approached for the *Day of the Dead* remake that came out in 2008?

TS: No and I didn't bother to see it.

BS: How do you feel seeing such beloved movies as *Dawn of the Dead* and *Day of the Dead* receiving remakes and unofficial sequels of such varying quality?

TS: I really don't care.

BS: Zombie films continue to push the boundaries, were there any effects shots that made it to the final cuts of *Dawn of the Dead* or *Day of the Dead* that surprised you?

TS: I was surprised that any of it made it on the screen to be perfectly honest with you. We pushed the envelope pretty hard on both of those films and got some really gory stuff in there.

BS: How do you handle conflict if a director insists on an effect or makeup appliance that you don't agree with or it conflicts with your morals? Have you ever walked off of a project?

TS: Nope, that sort of thing has never happened to me before.

BS: Have you ever done special effects on people you know and care about?

TS: Yes, of course I have. I think every makeup effects artist has at some point.

BS: Is it harder to see someone you care about bloodied and torn as opposed to a stranger?

TS: No, not at all. Actually I find that it's much more fun when it's someone you know.

BS: How does your family feel about seeing you in makeup and dying on screen?

TS: Honestly, it's a big goof to everyone. That is because I am there I am sitting with them it's really no big deal to them or me.

BS: Your ground breaking special effects and horrific creations have given millions of viewer's nightmares, what scares you?

TS: Spiders and razor blades scare me.

BS: How do you feel about the shift to CGI and the over dependence of using digital shots over more traditional prosthetics and makeup effects?

TS: I actually love CGI. I really wish we had it earlier when I was creating the stuff.

BS: What are your thoughts on the genre shift to include viral and plague films such as *28 Days Later* and *Planet Terror*? Do you think this genre change is a natural social reaction to increasing threats of viral pandemics and bioterrorism?

TS: No, I don't really try to think about such stuff at all.

BS: Are there any zombie films in the future for you?

TS: Yep, but I'm not allowed to talk about it right now. There's confidentiality agreements and all that. You know how it is.

BS: Can you share any funny on set stories from the zombie films you've worked on?

TS: Yeah, maybe someday when I write my biography. *(laughs)* That's really an essay question though. There have been loads over the years. The guts turning to rot and stink in the refrigerator that was unplugged for two weeks before we used them on Joe Pilato in *Day of the Dead* is a good one. I'm sure Greg Nicotero has told you the story about how he got stuck cleaning it out when we got back to the mine.

BS: If you woke up tomorrow morning and the zombie apocalypse had started, how would you fare?

TS: I'd fare great. I am a crack shot, but that would be too easy. I would hunt them with a bow and arrow, or wait till they were real close and practice martial arts on them.

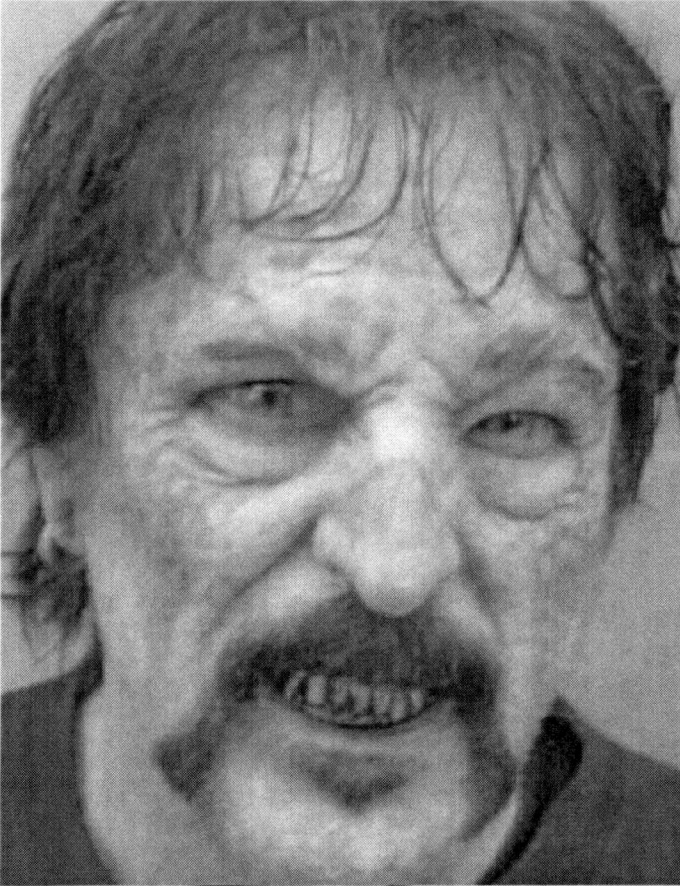

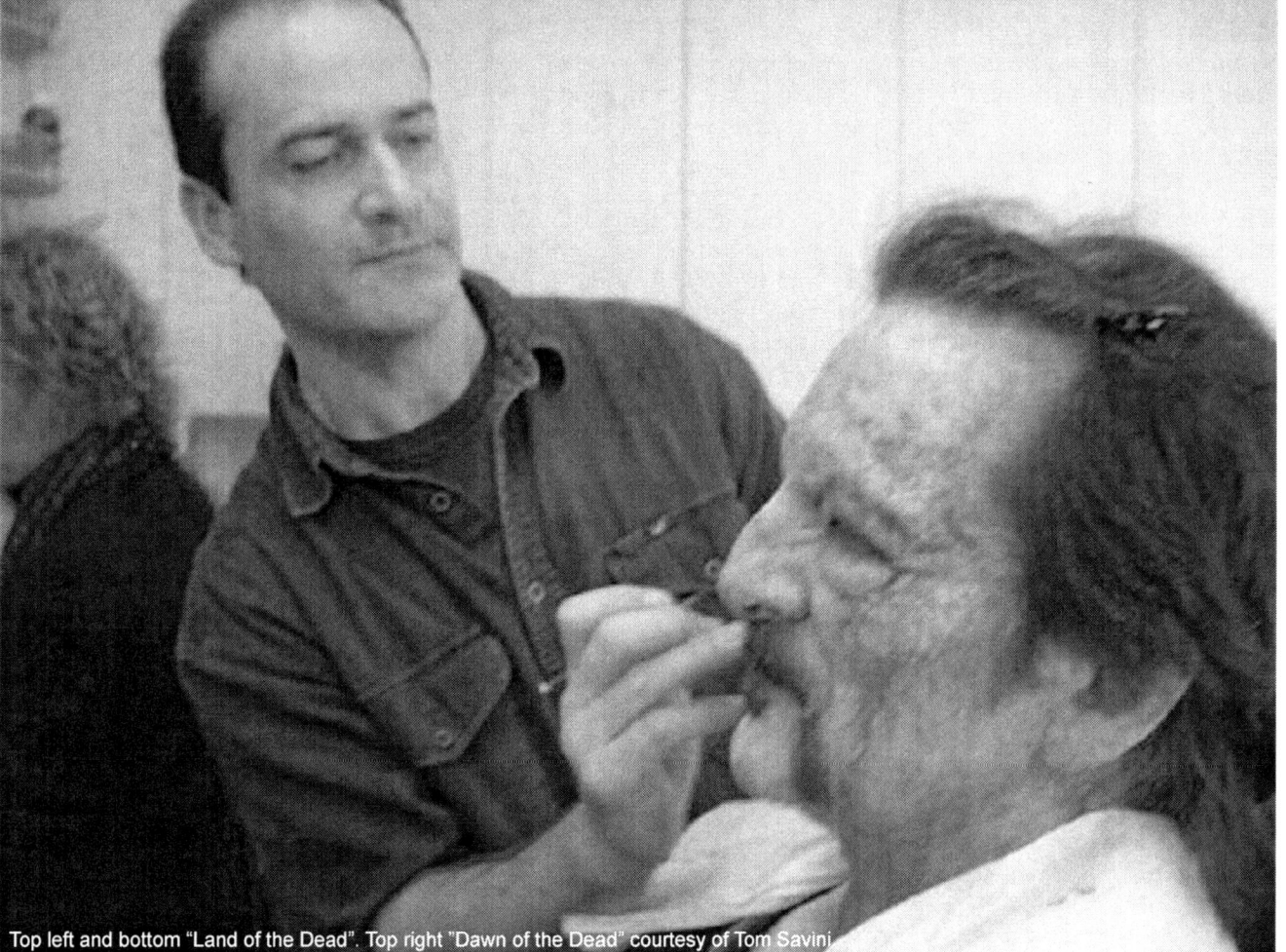

Top left and bottom "Land of the Dead". Top right "Dawn of the Dead" courtesy of Tom Savini.

TOBY SELLS

•Quarantine 2: Terminal (2011) Key Special Effects Makeup Artist
•The Walking Dead (2010) Special Effects Makeup Artist
•The Crazies (2010) Special Makeup Effects Artist
•Collapse (2010) Special Makeup Effects Artist, Special Makeup Effects Designer
•Zombieland (2011) Special Makeup Effects Artist
•Dance of the Dead (2008) Makeup Department Head, Special Makeup Effects Artist, Special Makeup Effects Designer

Blood Splatter: How did you get into the effects industry?

Toby Sells: Zombies were just one of many creatures and characters that have fueled my love for makeup effects. As far as how I got into the zombie genre, I think that I just got slowly sucked into the zombie craze. Of course as a kid I saw the original *Night of the Living Dead* and in the 1980's I saw *Day of the Dead* and *The Return of the Living Dead*. I thought they were very cool and scary and they all helped gravitate me towards doing makeup. I was interested all types of effects, but mostly I did characters like werewolves, old age makeups and *The Planet of the Apes*. Really, just anything that was strange, scary or intriguing.

BS: How did you get involved with *The Walking Dead*?

TS: *The Walking Dead*, is a KNB show, Greg Nicotero is the makeup effects designer. All I can say is that I am so very lucky to be one of his hired guns on it.

BS: Which other zombie films have you worked on?

TS: I was the designer on an indie zombie film that was picked up by Sam Raimi's Ghosthouse Underground called *Dance of the Dead,* we had a ridiculously low make up effects budget and not a lot of time, but we pulled it off and I thought the movie turned out really good.

BS: How was it working on *Zombieland*?

TS: I worked on *Zombieland*, for Tony Gardener's Alterian Studios. It was a super talented makeup effects team to work with. Steve Prouty and Jamie Kelman ran the show for Tony and it was just tons of fun. Some nights we would have up to 185 Zombies and another ten or twenty hero zombies. It was a physically hard shoot. The theme park segment of the movie was supposed to take place in Los Angeles, but we actually shot it at 'Wild Adventures' in Valdosta Georgia, on the Georgia and Florida border in February. The average temperature was around 27 degrees on most days. I have to laugh every time I watch it as the theme park looks so warm on film.

My shop did an independent film in Iowa called *Collapse*, which I absolutely loved, it has a great twist. The entire production team was one of the kindest groups of people I have worked with. The zombies that my company did were more "infected" type zombies. We only had four weeks to prep for it and what has just become the norm in the indie world, not on a big budget. However, for what it was, my crew rocked. The movie has not been released at this time, but I am excited to see it.

I worked on the remake of *The Crazies* for Robert Hall's Almost Human. I actually had one of my make ups from that show make the cover of Fangoria magazine. It was a makeup of one of the hunters Brett Wagner from The Speed Channels show *Pass Time*. Robert and I did that makeup together. During *The Crazies* we were told not to say "zombie", they were "infected", but it seems like a lot of fans of the genre have seemed to except the film as a 'quasi-zombie film'.

BS: You also worked on *Quarantine 2: Terminal* which is another entry in the zombie/not zombie infected hybrid genre. How was that?

TS: I also keyed *Quarantine 2: Terminal* for Robert Hall and yet again, we were told to call them 'Infected',

336

which I think in this show they were as there was nothing supernatural about them, but they sure did resemble rabid zombies. I always love working with Rob, he is such a fun and talented guy. He is such a fan of what we do and as a fan of the whole genre you have no choice but to just be a geek around him. It's always a great working atmosphere with Rob.

BS: Which was your first zombie movie?

TS: The first zombie film I worked on was a low budget indie that I won't mention. It is pretty rough. I won't even put it up on IMDB.com.

BS: How about your favorite?

TS: The favorite is a hard call. They all have their place in my heart for various reasons. *The Walking Dead* is probably the tops though. I love the story, the graphic novels. I think what AMC has done with it awesome. The fact that is on TV is also just a milestone. Working for Greg Nicotero and with all the talented guys from KNB is such great honor and experience. I have known Greg since 1988. He turned me onto the garage kit model fad and action figures. He calls me a big geek and a nerd, but that is actually big compliment coming from Nicotero, I love the guy, he is one the best people I know in the industry. He and Bob Kurtzman took me under their wing and treated me like a little brother. I didn't have a car, so I would sometimes stay at their apartment on weekends. We would watch tons of monster movies and go different hobby shops and Toy Stores. Those are still some of the most memorable times in my life.

BS: So you're obviously a fan of the genre. What inspired you to work with it?

TS: I am a fan of the genre. I was really into monsters, creatures and alien make ups and masks early on and then I discovered zombies in a slow progression, I remember lots of cartoons in the old horror magazines of the early 1970's and seeing *Night of the Living Dead* when I was eleven or twelve of course sparked my interest in zombies, so I just added another character to my list of cool makeups to practice.

BS: Do you have a favorite zombie film?

TS: I have tons of favorite zombie films, it's hard for me to pin point just one and there are so many good ones out there now. I will say that I love the original *Dawn of the Dead*, right along with the remake. I know there are some folks out there that want to shoot me for saying that, but I did like the remake. I absolutely loved the makeup effects that Dave Anderson and his crew did. Dave is another super cool make up effects dude.

BS: Which film have you enjoyed working on the most from a creativity standpoint?

TS: Wow, each project seems to have its great points. I had a blast on *Zombieland*, We were given certain guide lines and parameters to fallow, but each zombie was our own creation. We had hundreds of generic silicone gel filled prosthetics, so we were just mixing and matching. I find *The Walking Dead* to be just as creative and fun to be involved in.

BS: Zombie films are known for extravagant zombie kills and character death scenes. Which has been your favorite that you have created?

TS: That one I can't answer, as every kill has had its place in my heart. I do like the good old bleeding neck bite gag though. There have been some really cool ones that I have come up with that we have not gotten to do yet for one reason or another, so I will keep those on the down low for future use.

BS: How about your favorite from other zombie movies you have not been involved in?

TS: I really enjoyed *Shaun of the Dead* because of the comedy and the parodies of more serious zombie movies. *Day of the Dead*, *Dawn of the Dead*, Tom Savini's work still holds up today. Actually Tom gave me Dick Smiths phone number, so I have to credit him for getting me started in the business. I seem to like those that were made in the late 1970's and early 1980's because that was such a great time in my life, I had already made up my mind that I was going to do makeup effects for a living. I remember going to see *Dawn of the Dead* at the theater with two of my class mates from dental lab school and telling them that was what I wanted to do, not those damn teeth. The ironic part is that I am making teeth, but for *The Vampire Diaries* and other shows.

BS: The 1990 *Night of the Living Dead* remake found itself with a slight controversy when it was mentioned that some of the zombie effect were based on concentration camp victims. What do you use as inspiration for the varying degrees of decay and damage on your zombies? Have you used anything controversial?

TS: I personally think that the holocaust and concentration camps in World War II are horrific examples of how evil that the human race can be. I actually have a friend whose father escaped one of the camps at the age of ten tell me the story and I balled like a baby. That being said, I have to just shake my head at anyone that would try to make a makeup effects artist out to be a bad person by basing a character off of that. It happened. It is one of the most tragic things that has happened in our history as humans. I have asked producers for the skinniest actors for zombies before and I think I have used the words concentration camp victim to describe just how thin we would like them. If my memory serves me right, I think he was Jewish. He agreed and sure didn't make a big issue out it. I love all people, all races, religions and sexual orientations. Does it make me a bad person if I say that the zombie should have hair that looks like it's falling out from chemotherapy? Hell no it doesn't. My father was taken from me by cancer and that is still a hard thing for me after fourteen years. Will I say cancer patient to describe a certain look, or holocaust, or retarded, yes I will. I have designed a retarded type character before. They are just words used to for comparison and description not slurs or insults. I will now get off of my soap box. *(laughs)*

BS: When creating a zombie, how does the design process work? Do you go into it with a predetermined idea or do you improvise?

TS: Here is a good example. When I am working on a zombie project, we have certain predetermined perimeters that we follow. We literally have a "name of the movie"' zombie look that we try to keep. However, each individual actor or stunt person has his or her own personal look and distinguishing features that we try to use to accentuate that predetermined look. Referring back to your previous question, if I see a super thin actor or actress, I try my best to get them in my chair. I made up *Zombieland* zombies for four weeks solid. It took a conscious effort on the next zombie project to not make them look like *Zombieland* zombies. They were a bit bloodier and fresher. If you notice the zombies that we did for *Zombieland* did not have prosthetics around there brows and cheek bones that give them the sunken eye look. Ironically, when my company did *Collapse*, the zombies were more like *Zombieland's*. It all goes back to the original concept of the project and what they are looking for. I do a lot of research, if the FBI should confiscate my computer they would think I am some kind of serial killer or mentally deranged person. I have files of real photos of dead people, accident and suicide victims. They really are sad. It's tragic that these were real people with friends, families and dreams, but they do help me when designing a character or a gag. I sometimes feel as if I am invading their privacy, but ultimately it helps me with my job. I am sure some of these departed souls were horror movie fans, so maybe they look at me from the other side and say "cool, glad I could help in some strange way". I think the photos that have really bothered me were photos of children. It does remind me of how precious life is though.

BS: I know what you mean. Seeing children in zombie films never really bothered me, but since becoming a parent I have a much harder time with it. I don't think I could stand seeing my daughter being shot or attacked on screen. I think that parental defense mechanism would kick in. No one wants to think of their child getting hurt.

TS: I think subconsciously that maybe that is what the horror and suspense movies do for us. It has a way of reminding us that we are alive and that it's a sweet thing.

BS: With the advent of CGI allowing for more decomposing and wounds, do you find yourself still using traditional methods or gravitating more to CGI?

TS: Here is the part where some dork will say "he's just saying that because he is losing work". CGI has its place in the story telling process. As much as we would like to think that the masses cultivate toward the theaters to see our makeup effects work, the majority don't. It's all about the total package that ends up on the screen, namely the story. CGI has been a great tool for us and I personally have suggested and used the incorporation of practical makeup effects and CGI. Ultimately it makes the end product more believable. Now, the thing that just irks me is when a whole movie is done with motion capture and everyone is like "how awesome, makeup effects are no longer needed". Bull shit I say, bull shiteth. It stills looks like a cartoon, true, a well done cartoon, but never the less a cartoon. This should sum it up for the people that proclaim that CGI will replace make up effects. CGI hit its pinnacle in little old movie back in 1993 called *Jurassic Park*, nothing has topped it.

BS: Yeah, I agree. There really hasn't been a whole lot of CGI centered films that have had the heart of *Jurassic Park*.

TS: I rest my case your honor.

BS: Have you ever been a zombie extra in one of the films you've worked?

TS: No, I honestly can't stand to wear prosthetics. The glue and the removal process gives me the willies. Tom Savini actually has the same phobia. I will put it on someone else all day, but don't get a drop of glue on me. With that being said, I am very attentive to the actor or extra I am working on. A lot of extras don't know what they are getting in to. Many of them have worked in haunted houses, so they usually have had a non-prosthetic makeup done or painted on makeups. The real thing is very different and it can be a long and grueling process.

BS: Have you been in any of your films at all?

TS: I did play an Israeli store clerk in *Dance of the Dead* and I had a whole four or five words. I get killed off screen, so I was makeup and blood free.

BS: Have you found yourself intentionally pushing the envelope to see how far you can go?

TS: I will not say which project, but of course. I was the makeup effects designer on a show and the folks above the line wanted to keep the makeup effects at a PG-13 level. Keep in mind that these were all gore effects and they just did not look or feel right. It was kind of like Captain Kangaroo and Mr. Rogers pole dancing on stage with Lady GaGa and as they say in here in the south, "it needed to be put down". So every take, I pumped triple the blood, made the puppets wounds much bigger at the last minute, anything that I could do make it better. Without that spurt of blood it just didn't feel real and had no shock value at all. In the end they never said a negative word, they were very happy and I think it helped sell the movie.

BS: Recently we have had *Resident Evil: Afterlife* in 3D and there is a rumor that *Zombieland 2* could be a 3D film if it gets green lighted. How do you think 3D technology benefits these types of films?

TS: As far as 3D goes, I personally do not enjoy them because of some eye issues that I have. A lot of people find them fun, so I am certain if they can make the second *Zombieland* as fun as the first, the 3D aspect may just be cool. I think the benefit for the makeup effects department is that with 3D the effects can be right up in your face.

BS: Are there any zombie films in the future for you?

TS: It seems as if the zombie craze is still hot. I think now that more of the general public has been exposed to zombies thanks to shows like *The Walking Dead* and *Zombieland*, we will see more quality zombie movies, so I guess I better keep brushing up on my zombie skills.

BS: When creating background and hero zombies, is there a particular type of actor you look for that determines roles?

TS: Yes, we love people with high cheek bones, thin, almost sickly looking. That kind of goes back to the controversial question thing. It also depends on the look that we are going for. With the zombies that we did for *Collapse*, I went with the thought of everyone dies. Tall, short, fat, skinny and so it was much easier to pick and choose our zombies. We also had zombies of all ages. I think some shows have been a bit shy about having a five year old child corpse walking around. Many times we will put some of our mid-range and deep background zombies in masks. Keep in mind that they are far better than any mask that the public can usually buy, but they are still masks. The only problem I have experienced with the masks is that many of the extras are always wanting to get up in the camera and get their screen time and that will always ruin the illusion. We can sometimes use an actor that may not have the perfect face for a make up, put him in a mask and boom, you have one very cool zombie.

BS: Many special effects artists have gone into directing. Is that something you have considered?

TS: Yes, I have considered it. I really like the whole process that goes on. The vast majority of the world will never get to see or be a part of such a wonderful, creative machine. I consider myself very blessed to get to do what I do, to be a small part in such a large well-oiled machine. Would I like to play quarterback and direct? Sure I would. I am still learning every aspect of film making that I can and I have only skimmed the surface, but hopefully I will get the opportunity to test those waters someday. It would of course have to be an effects driven show, that's what I know and it's what I feel more comfortable with doing.

BS: Can you share any funny on set stories from the zombie films you've worked on?

TS: Wow, believe it or not that is a really hard one. There have been a few things that occurred on set with zombies and actors, but being the class clown all my life, most of the funny stuff is usually something that I have done. I love pranks and practical jokes. I don't really have any stories that won't incriminate me on this one. I have great memories from *Zombieland* though. The makeup effects team we had for the month that we did the "Pacific Play Land" makeups with, were not only talented as hell but all we did was laugh. Lee Grimes, Jonah Levy, Leigh Ann Yandle, Jamie Kelman, Steve Prouty, Gabe DeCunto, Corey Castellano, Bill McCoy and I just had a blast. Although, I have to say that Lee Grimes kept me in stitches. There was a day or two that I had the flu and we were doing eighteen hour days in Valdosta Georgia. It got as cold as twenty seven degrees and needless to say I felt like death on a cheese cracker. Lee kept me laughing throughout and that meant a lot to me. It all has been fun, more laughter than tears, but there have been a few of those over the years.

BS: You were on an episode of The Discovery Channel's *Dirty Jobs* correct?

TS: I was. I was a featured guess on *Dirty Jobs* a few years back.

BS: How was that experience?

TS: It was a lot of fun and although the segment is pretty funny, there was a lot of great stuff that couldn't be aired on TV. Mike Rowe was a lot of fun to hang out with. We actually turned him into a zombie for the episode.

BS: So where do you see yourself heading?

TS: Who knows? I have been blessed to get to do what I do for a living. I was ten years old when I made my first latex mask. I remember telling people in my home town that when I grew up, I was going to make monsters for movies. That was a long shot for a kid from east Tennessee. I did it though, with a lot of help and support from my family and friends and my surrogate grandfather, a sweet old guy by the name of Dick Smith. I am a lucky man.

BS: If you woke up tomorrow and the zombie apocalypse had started, how would you fair?

TS: I like that question. I bet you haven't had this answer before. I would actually use Isopropyl Myristate. It's deadly to zombies. It's a makeup remover we use on prosthetic make ups. I would just freaking drench them in it. Eventually they would all be clean and just be actors, stunt people and extras. Game over man.

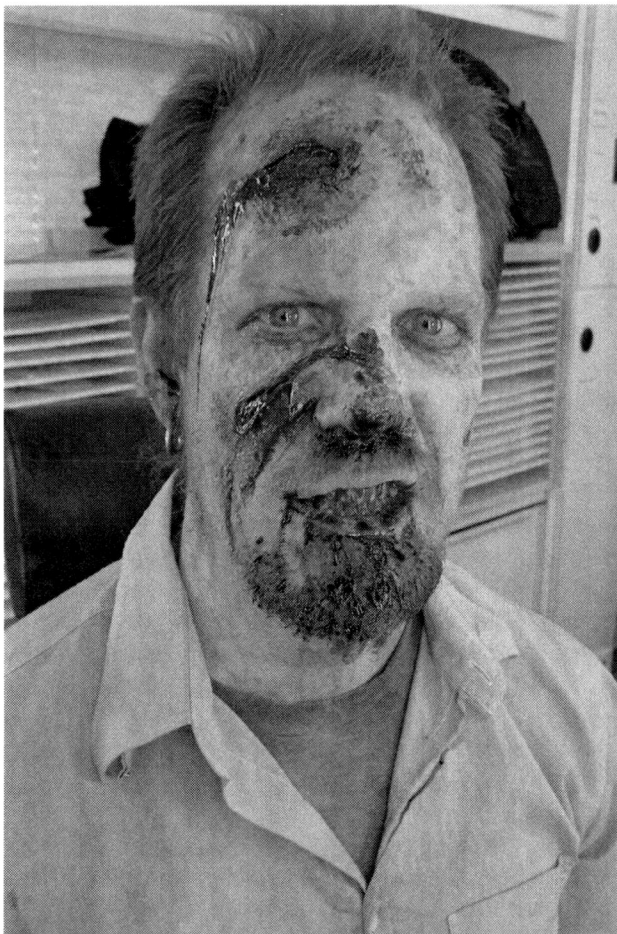

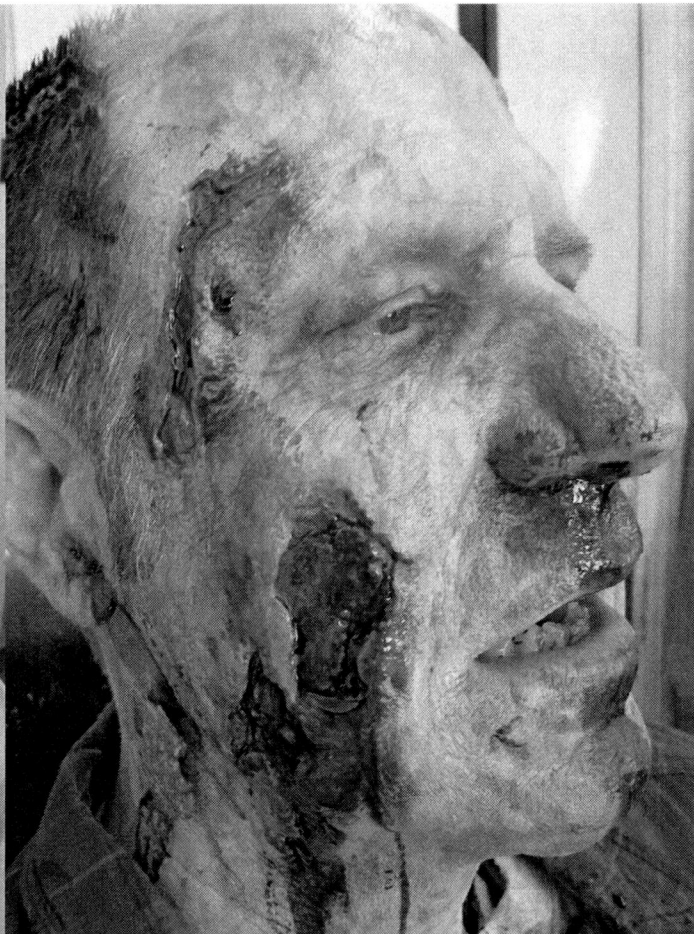

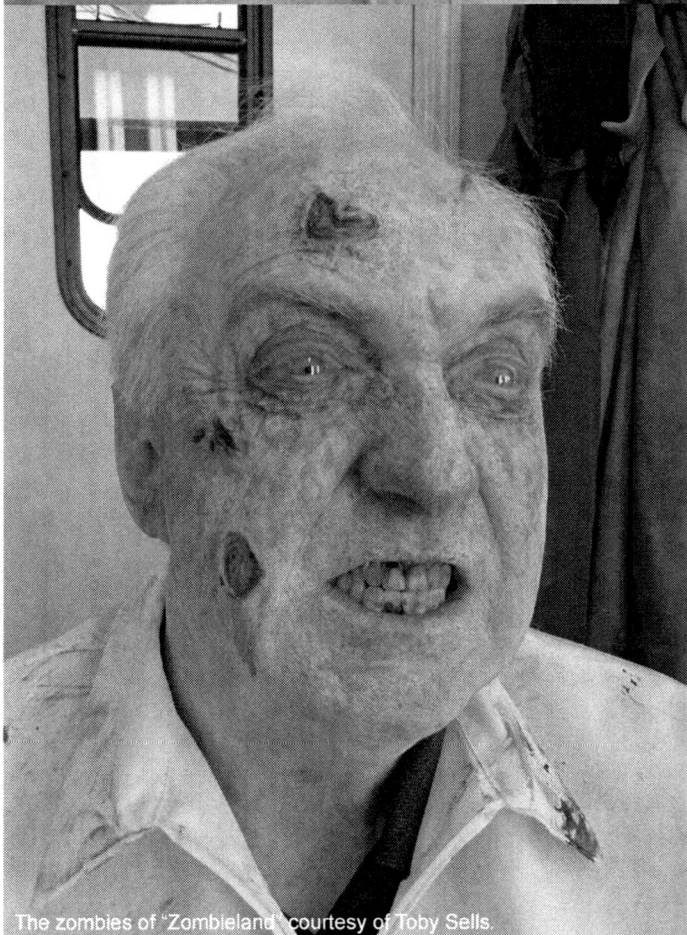

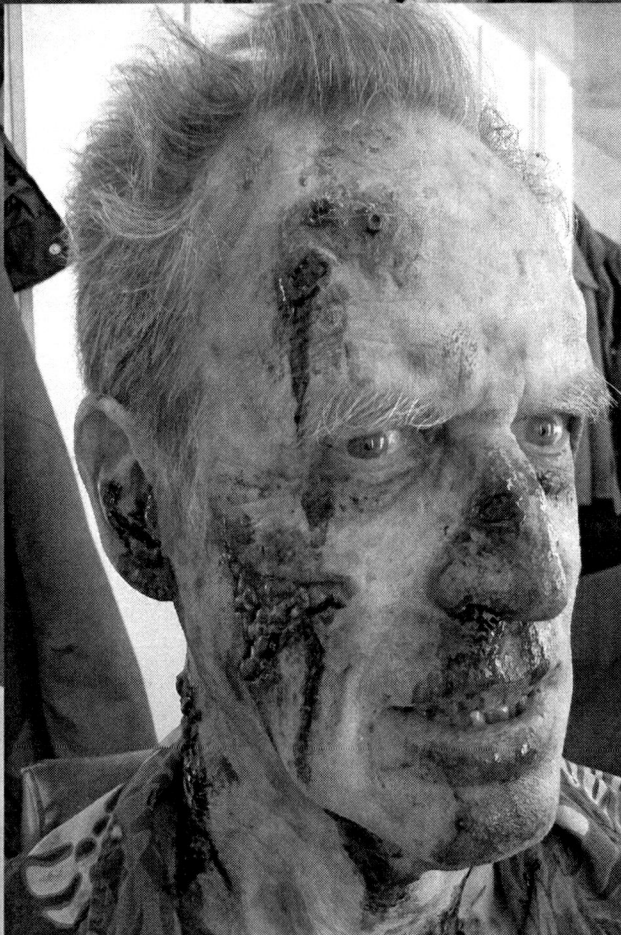

The zombies of "Zombieland" courtesy of Toby Sells.

TODD SHEETS

- Zombie Bloodbath 3: Zombie Armageddon (2000) Director
- Zombie Bloodbath 2: Rage of the Undead (1995) Director, Writer
- Zombie Bloodbath (1993) Director, Writer, Producer
- Zombie Rampage (1989) Director, Writer

Blood Splatter: While loved in the zombie fan community, the *Zombie Bloodbath* saga hasn't received many kind words from critics. What are your thoughts on how the critics have treated you?

Todd Sheets: You have to realize that when we started making the series, no one was making zombie movies at all. I only made these movies as I wanted to give something back as a young filmmaker. I was way too ambitious and I didn't have the means to make the movie as large as I took on. We were shooting *Zombie Bloodbath* during the Mississippi and Missouri rivers flood of 1993. We literally had to boat out to our locations at times because our buildings were underwater to the point where only tops were showing. It was a huge flood and I think it rained for almost three quarters of the year. So of course, there are parts of the movie that don't make sense, because I literally had to cut stuff to get through the shooting schedule. We couldn't film what we needed. Then to have people tearing me apart when all I was trying to do was make a tribute to the genre I loved so much was hard. It was me putting everything I loved about the zombie genre growing up into a film. I wasn't trying to be a huge star, I was just doing what I love.

BS: You have a name for yourself as the king of the shot on video phase. How did you get into film making?

TS: One of my first memories as a child is of a drive-in triple bill for *Night of the Living Dead*, *Sssssss* and *The Boy Who Cried Werewolf*. It was a really cool time as these movies really stuck with me and I became a creature buff. My dad had a Super 8 camera and every holiday he would get a bunch of film to record us. One summer he had some extra film just sitting there doing nothing and it really bothered me. I decided to use the film and make my own Frankenstein movie with my friends. There was an old stone house up in the woods that looked like a ruined castle. I grabbed the camera and started filming. I had a blast doing it and being involved with the whole creation process. After I paid my dad back for the film I took, I would buy more film at any chance I could get. I made some science fiction films, especially after *Star Wars* came out. *Night of the Living Dead* and *Star Wars* both had a huge impact on me. People can be as jaded as they want about George Lucas, but most people in the industry today would not be there if it wasn't for him. Both he and George Romero changed the face of filmmaking forever.

BS: So what appeals to you about the Zombie genre?

TS: I just loved how scary it is and because *Night of the Living Dead* was in black and white, you couldn't tell them apart from humans. They didn't have green skin and they were just normal people. It dawned on me that this could be your neighbor or your best friend or someone from your family. Zombies have this insane creep factor about them. A year after I saw *Night of the Living Dead*, I saw a preview for *Let Sleeping Corpses Lie*. That took it even further in that it was in color. I just went nuts over this film. I saw *Dawn of the Dead* when it first came out and fell in love with that too. I really got into the Italian phase after Fulci's *Zombie* came out.

BS: It's been 11 years since your last film, where did you go?

TS: It actually hasn't been that long. I have had a lot of trouble trying to get IMDB.com to update my page. It's been a nightmare trying to get them to list them. I have made four movies since then and they are getting ready to be released on DVD soon. I have actually been going back and remastering some of the older films I have done. I was working on the *Zombie Bloodbath* trilogy and there were some encoding issues with some of the discs I was not happy with. Part three has some weird shake on some of the discs that was not on the master. I have been working with the distributor to make sure this does not happen again. It is something to do with the encoding on a batch of DVD's which sucked, as I got a ton of hate mail attacking me on the release, but it wasn't my fault.

BS: How is the remastering process going?

TS: It's really hard. Trying to remaster these films has been tough, as a lot of them were shot on older video formats and these deteriorate over time. I have had to clean up the images and match them with the original sound tracks. Doing this frame by frame is very tedious and I've been doing it for almost four years now. I also have some scripts that I am looking at including a remake of the original *Zombie Bloodbath*. I have a German distributor looking to help and if I can get just a little more money, I'll get it done.

BS: Will this be closer to your original vision?

TS: Exactly. I'm going to do it how I wanted to initially. I have updated some of the original ideas and plan to make it one of the goriest zombie films out there. The other three films aren't in the zombie genre. I've focused on quantity, now I want to focus on quality. I love making films and want to do it right. I was a young filmmaker when I started and to be honest, I have disowned most of my films before *Zombie Bloodbath*. I really did try to make *Zombie Bloodbath* a good film, but I had so many internal and external factors working against me. I had over seven hundred zombies to deal with and a really limited budget. Add in the flood and it was a really hard time. You can definitely see an improvement between the three films. Most directors never let their earlier movies get seen by the public. They just bury them. The difference is, I released mine to the world and took my baby steps in public. I'm still judged on movies I made over twenty years ago and I have grown a lot since then.

BS: M. Night Shyamalan has released some of childhood movies as supplemental material on his DVD releases and they are terrible. However fans and critics gushed over them, saying how cute they were. Other filmmakers get slammed for putting out films like this. It certainly had its charm, but had a non-famous director released this, they would have been crucified. It is an interesting double standard.

TS: Exactly. I've actually read reviews that say the next time I pick up a camera, someone needs to shoot me. Who wants to read stuff like that? All horror directors have their highs and lows. Take Wes Craven for example. I think he has made three great movies and the rest is junk. I think *Scream* really hurt the genre as it made horror a parody of itself. Do I send him hate mail? Of course I don't. I just choose to not watch the films again. Then you look at *Nightmare on Elm Street* and you can overlook the bad ones. I know I'm not a great filmmaker, but I'm doing my best and I enjoy it. I make these movies because I want to give something back. You know makes this all worth it? It's when I get an email from a kid or someone in another country who tells me they had a horrible day and they came home and *Zombie Bloodbath* was in the mail. They tell me they watched it with their friends and had a laugh and enjoyed it. That is what it's all about and that pushes me to make more movies. But when I have people who threaten to kill my mom if I make another movie, it gets really hard. It's just a movie. Some people take it on such a personal level to the point where it's insane. I didn't set out to ruin their day. We had all kinds of production issues throughout the film. We had an investor who pulled out and that left us short on cash. We had a crew of forty people working day and night for no money trying to get the film made. Considering the struggles we were up against, it's a miracle we were able to finish the first film at all. A lot of people who own the VHS versions of the original *Zombie Bloodbath* aren't aware that they own unfinished versions. These are not the same versions that came out on DVD. Some of those early tapes have temporary soundtracks. I put all of these great shots into the first edit and then I was going to start editing the film and cut it down until I was happy with it. What happened was I had these unscrupulous producers who took the unfinished film to a local distributor and put the film out without my knowledge. I needed an extra week to trim the film down and this was in the day when the editing suite was two decks next to each other. It was a completely manual process. They took my film and released it without my permission.

BS: How did the shooting go for *Zombie Bloodbath 2: Rage of the Undead*?

TS: When part two of the saga came around, I had already learned a lot, but there are still things that I don't like about it and parts that don't make sense. I shot the film on various formats and some of it was shot in 16mm. When it got processed, we used a light meter and did everything to retrieve it, but the footage was shot at night and it was too dark. We couldn't salvage any of it. We had already used up our budget and we couldn't do any reshoots, so we lost three crucial scenes from the film. The scenes with the scarecrow don't make sense at times, but I lost some major footage. Many thought I had ripped off

Natural Born Killers by shooting in multiple formats, but the funny thing is, I had finished my film long before that movie came out, but as I am an independent, it takes much longer to find distribution. What actually inspired me was a music video by Iron Maiden called Wasting Love. They shot it in three different formats. One was a grungy looking 16mm stock, one was black and white and then they did one 35mm color one and it looked really cool.

BS: What kind of budget were you looking at for *Zombie Bloodbath 2: Rage of the Undead* and *Zombie Bloodbath 3: Zombie Amrageddon*?

TS: I think we spent about $1,200 on the second film and about $1,500 on the third. We had to buy some digital effects. We were at the cutting edge at the time, but I look at the effects now, especially the space shuttle scene and I think if that isn't cheese, I don't know what is. At the time, no one had the 3D digital workstations. Were the effects perfect? Hell no they weren't, but they really were ahead of their time.

BS: Were you surprised that the films have gained a cult following?

TS: I was very surprised. I went to Chiller Theater and I remember sitting at the table and I looked up at a line of people wanting me to sign stuff. I couldn't believe it. I was signing and getting writer's cramp. I had young guys coming up to me saying that I had inspired them to make their own movies. It was a great feeling and that is why I have slowed down and started to take this much more seriously than I used to. This happened again recently at Cinema Wasteland and it really is the most amazing feeling. I am still humbled by it.

BS: A lot of the zombie films you have worked on have been panned by critics and fans alike, but I find there is a certain charm about low budget zombie films. Indeed it is a genre filled with low budget films made by fans for fans. How do you react to these reviews that just don't seem to get it?

TS: When people review my older movies, I have to agree with them. I was just a kid when I was making them. I had a ton of fun doing it, but I was just a kid. However, when someone starts attacking my later films and me as a person, that is when things get really tough. I think what hurt me more was when I would visit review websites and reply to some of the negative comments. I'd say that there is no need to be this harsh and then I was called a reviewer bully. I was never rude, but I got attacked for standing up for myself. I couldn't win. It's really hard to get your skin thick enough to withstand that much abuse. I don't see how anyone can.

BS: Zombie films are known for extravagant zombie kills and character death scenes, which has been your favorite from a film that you have worked on?

TS: One of the standouts for me is a scene in *Zombie Bloodbath* involving Jerry Angell on the bridge when his guts are ripped out by a group of zombies. They don't just simply pull them out through his stomach like they would do in other zombie films, they pull them out of his butt. We built this elaborate rig filled with gooey stuff and chunks of flesh and pieces from the local butcher. It was the grossest thing, but it got a really good reaction.

In *Zombie Bloodbath 2: Rage of the Undead*, there is a scene where a bad guy gets taken down and in a tribute to the Italian films, we pop his eyeballs out. The zombies then reach into the eye sockets and pull the guy's brains out. It was really gross. We were like kids in a candy store figuring out how to make scenes like this come together.

BS: As a director, do you have an idea of how the special effects will play out throughout the film or do let the effects crew take the lead.

TS: I was really hands on with the effects. I helped create the makeup and effects and in some cases, was helping apply it to the actors. While I enjoyed it, it wasn't always possible as there were always tasks I needed to start or finish. In the first film I was really hands on and we were training and learning as we filmed. I had a couple of guys who had a little effects experience. For *Zombie Bloodbath 2: Rage of the Undead,* I was able to get some guys who had a bit more experience with makeup. As I was growing they were too. It was fun watching the process evolve. For a film like that with next to no budget, you have to take on multiple roles, else the film will never get finished. I have worked multiple roles on my films throughout my career.

BS: Have you been a zombie extra in any of your films?

TS: I was a zombie in the first *Zombie Bloodbath*. I was the zombie that comes out of the basement and is hit in the chest with a claw hammer. The guy who was supposed to do it originally did the first take and got nailed in the chest and was done. I went ahead and put on the fake chest and took a beating. I had claw hammer scars on my chest for weeks.

BS: Your films are filled with graphic and violent scenes, what shocks you?

TS: I don't want to see this kind of thing in real life. I don't like seeing people hurt. That is part of the thrill of the horror genre. One of the producers on the film wanted us to put a social message at the end of the film. I was really against it, but the producers are who fund the film, so you have to take what they want into consideration. It was a really preachy message about society that will definitely get cut when I re-release it.

BS: Can you share any funny on set stories from the zombie films you've worked on?

TS: There was one time when I had finished shooting and was leaving the set with one of the prop corpses in the back of my car. My windows were all bloodied from shooting and I get pulled over by the police. Trying to explain that was fun.

While we were filming *Zombie Bloodbath* during the flood, after we were done shooting, about fifty of us, all in zombie makeup and attire would go down to the river and help the National Guard sandbag the banks. That effort earned us a lot of local and national news. In fact, Fox sent a reporter down to do a story on the zombies who were helping to save the town. As she was wrapping up, I had one of the zombies jump out of a car she was walking by. She screamed bloody murder and they ended up running it on Fox national news.

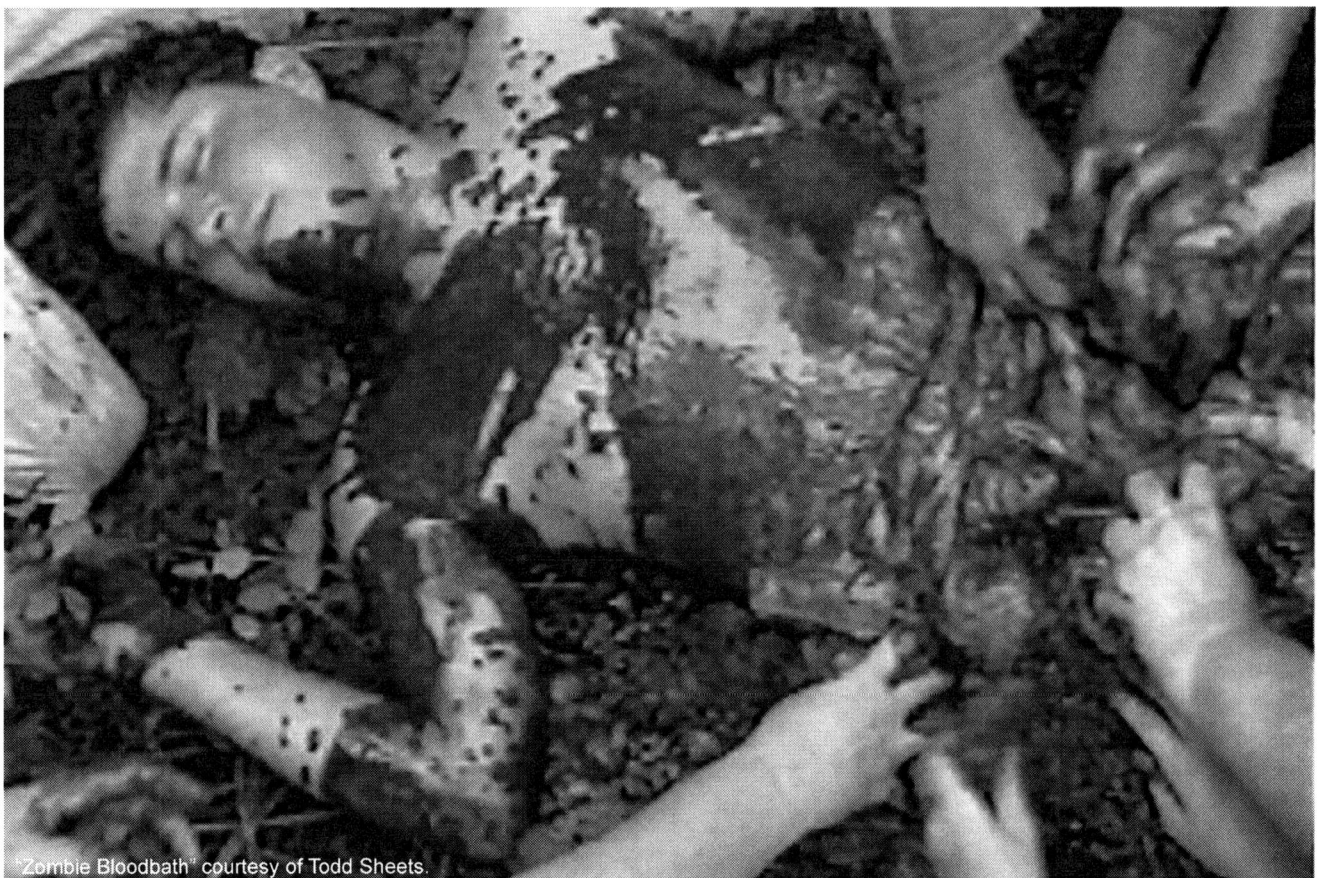

"Zombie Bloodbath" courtesy of Todd Sheets.

WARREN SPEED

• Zombie Women of Satan (2009) Director, Producer, Writer, Actor

Blood Splatter: How did you get into the zombie genre?

Warren Speed: I think zombies are just really cool. It's just the way it is. Like many people, I started watching zombie films in my early teens.

BS: What is your favorite zombie film?

WS: To be honest it's probably the remake of *Dawn of the Dead* starring Sarah Polley and Ving Rhames and directed by Zack Snyder.

BS: How did the story for *Zombie Women of Satan* come about?

WS: It all stemmed from the title that popped into my head one day and I just thought I've got to make a movie where all the zombies are sexy girls without many clothes on.

BS: Was this always going to be a role for your alter ego, Pervo the Clown?

WS: I've had a fascination with clowns for a very long time and the Pervo character had been floating about in my head for quite a while before I got the movie idea. The movie was the perfect opportunity to debut the character.

BS: How much of a budget did you need to shoot it?

WS: We had a budget of about £70,000 for the entire film.

BS: How did you raise the funds?

WS: I was able to pull most of it from my life savings, but I also had some help from other people for reduced rates.

BS: The production values on *Zombie Women of Satan* exceed that of many higher budget features, what formal training do you have?

WS: Personally, I'd just previously made a couple of short films, but I've been performing on stage for years as a stand-up comedian, burlesque performer and actor. I had lots of help from a professional film crew put together by my co-producer Steve O'Brien.

BS: Are there any plans to make a sequel?

WS: I would love to and I do have a script already written. Unfortunately it all depends purely on me finding outside investment to get it off the ground. This time I cannot invest my life savings into a movie again.

BS: How involved were you with the zombie effects?

WS: Actually, not very much at all. They were all down to Jez Hunt and Mark Danbury with some help from a few other talented individuals. Jez and Mark truly did an amazing job with the meagre effects budget they had.

BS: How different was the final version from earlier drafts?

WS: Hardly any different to be honest, although we had to change the story line slightly during filming as one significant cast member had to leave the set for personal reasons for a few days which led to us

On the set of "Zombie Women of Satan" courtesy of Warren Speed.

347

actually enhancing the secondary story lines.

BS: The dialogue in the film feels very free flowing. How much of it was ad libbed?

WS: Seymour Mace, who played Johnny Dee Hellfire, ad libbed the most and in the process came up with most of the movie's funniest and most memorable lines.

BS: Although you weren't heavily involved with the effects, what can you tell us about the makeup and effects process from a director's standpoint?

WS: Jez and Mark improvised to a large extent. All of the zombie girls were sprayed a shade of pale white which was quite harsh on them really as they had to stand about in their underwear for an hour or so when the weather wasn't really that great.

BS: What is your favorite effect in *Zombie Women of Satan*?

WS: It think it is definitely the effect when Pervo chainsaws the zombies head in half. If we'd had the budget for a second camera it would have been even more spectacular as the blood spurted about fifteen meters in to the air.

BS: Did you utilize any CGI for the film?

WS: *(laughs)* Yeah, I wish.

BS: Did you find yourself intentionally pushing the envelope on effects to see how far you could go?

WS: We had a very tight shooting schedule and hardly any money, so it was really more of a case of what's the best we can achieve within our limits. I know Jez and Mark could've done much, much more if they'd simply had more time and money.

BS: Are there any more zombie films in your future?

WS: *Zombie Women of Satan 2* is the only other zombie film that's part of my future plans. I do have three other movie scripts in development though, although none feature zombies.

BS: Will Pervo the Clown appear in any more zombie films?

WS: He'll definitely be in *Zombie Women of Satan 2* of course, if that happens. There's a slightly similar character in one of my other movie scripts. Similar in that he's a kind of freaky clown but different enough that it's certainly not Pervo.

BS: If zombies came back from the dead tomorrow, who would you kill first and why?

WS: I'd sensibly kill the ones nearest to me first of course, but it would be really fun to hunt down kill the likes of Elvis Presley and Michael Jackson.

BS: What demands can we see on Pervo's rider for his trailer?

WS: *(laughs)* Lots of chocolate, red wine and condoms.

BS: Can you share any funny stories from the set?

WS: The first time we shot the bit where Johnny rips off the gaffer's tape over Pervo's nipples, the tape was pretty sticky and it really bloody hurt. I made sure it wasn't so sticky for future takes. Also, one of the topless zombie girls took a dive onto a crash mat during her death scene and rather hurt her boobs as they splattered on the mat, which was really funny for everyone else watching.

JOHN VULICH

- Return of the Living Dead: Rave to the Grave (2005) Makeup Effects Supervisor
- Return of the Living Dead: Necropolis (2005) Makeup Effects Supervisor
- Night of the Living Dead (1990) Special Makeup Effects Supervisor
- Day of the Dead (1985) Special Makeup Effects Artist

BS: How did you get into special effects?

JV: I did special makeup effects as a hobby when I was a teen. I used to make 8mm movies with a group of friends and I would always do my own makeup effects for it. My parents set up a lab in my garage for me so I could hone my skills and have somewhere to work. Through the course of trying to learn, I found that there wasn't much material out there back in the seventies. I think there was Michael Westmore's book The Art of Theatrical Makeup for Stage and Screen and that was about it. We obviously didn't have the internet where you can browse hundreds of sites to get makeup tips. There just wasn't that much material widely available back then, so you were somewhat on your own. Part of supplementing my knowledge was trying to contact whatever makeup people I knew were in the business and bug them for information. I got in touch with Tom Savini and Tim Burman and they were kind enough to share information with me when I needed it. Tom Savini and I developed a friendship via telephone and mail and he was giving me advice and mentoring me on how to do effects. Through that relationship he told me that if he ever got out to Los Angeles he would bring me on as part of the crew. True to his word, he brought me on board when he was working on Friday the 13th Part IV. I subsequently found out years later that their main interest in hiring me was to get a series of masks that I had made. I used to make various creature masks and would take them to the local costume store to sell them to further subsidize the hobby. I had about a dozen masks that hadn't been widely distributed and the director wanted to use them to decorate Corey Feldman's bedroom in the film. After that I started making the rounds and getting my name out there.

BS: How did you get into the zombie genre?

JV: A good friend of mine, Mike Deak and I were out drinking one night and we had read there was going to be a sequel to Dawn of the Dead. As a huge fan of the previous two movies, I told him I was determined to get involved with the film. When I worked with Tom on Friday the 13th Part IV, I told him that was my aspiration. I wanted to be doing this for the rest of my life. Tom went back to Pittsburgh and I had heard through the grapevine that they had started filming, so I just figured I'd lost the chance. A few months into the film, Tom finally called me and wanted me to gather some of my work to showcase my makeup. I put together a bunch of new makeup's and tested them on Howard Berger, who was living at the same apartment complex at the time and sent them over to Tom. He was really happy with what I had put together and he made arrangements to have me flown out and be a part of the crew.

BS: Are you a fan of the genre?

JV: For sure. There is something so enduring about the zombie genre. It went dormant for quite a while in the late eighties and nineties, but now it is in full swing. I am shocked with the quality these days. It's better than it has ever been. There is certainly some kind of sociological reason why it's made such a comeback. I would imagine it has to do with the whole sociopolitical climate we find ourselves in these days. The idea of the dead rising just resonates with people in a way it hasn't in the past. It reflects a fear of people losing their identity and becoming mindless drones.

BS: What is your favorite zombie film?

JV: Off the top of my head, I would have to say Dawn of the Dead. The original one of course. I think the remake was technically interesting as they did some great gags and effects, but none of the characters were engaging. They didn't spend enough time with the characters and you don't feel vested in their plight. Whereas the original spends more time on character development and you really care about them. You genuinely care when one of them dies. It's far more emotionally engaging from that standpoint. As an effects guy, I am cognizant that our effects are meaningless unless they are staged properly and have some emotional context to drive them. I get so disappointed when our effects are there simply for window dressing and this happens all too often in the industry. Take *The Walking Dead* for example. I think Robert Kirkman is very aware of the need for character development and it is an important aspect of any story. So often people are attracted to the superficial aspects of filmmaking and don't give the attention to characters that they should.

BS: Which film have you enjoyed working on the most from a creativity standpoint?

JV: That's a hard question as I like them all for different reasons. On *Day of the Dead* I was still very young and new to the industry. I was absorbing everything and working closely with Tom Savini. Tom approaches effects from more of a theatrical stage magician point of view, which was alien to my experience. There is certainly a different mind set that accompanies that style of work. It was little things like hiding parts of people's bodies under panels and disguising the effects and rigging that don't necessarily fall under the repertoire of makeup effects. He would come up with these effects that I didn't think could possibly work. We'd stage them and try out a prototype that would work perfectly. It was a great lesson to learn at such an early stage in my career. It taught me to not limit myself. He really is one of the masters of blood tubing and splatter. It is a lot harder than it looks.

I really enjoyed working on the *Night of the Living Dead* remake as we were trying to find a different angle to make things look fresh. Our big focus was to find details that weren't apparent. We studied prisoner of war footage and tried to find imagery that would look like the living dead. We didn't want to do the typical rotten corpse that had just crawled out of the grave, as that would not have fit with the timeline of the story. I think we did some really great things with the zombies that hadn't been done before. On *Return of the Living Dead: Necropolis* and *Return of the Living Dead: Rave to the Grave*, we were shooting from the hip a little bit and they were more of a free for all. We had boxes of appliances left over from other productions and we built up wounds with silicone. *Night of the Living Dead* was a lot more rigid and with this we just wanted to have fun with it and get back to our roots. It was more chaotic aesthetically and we didn't want to repeat ourselves. Each film I've done has offered something different for me that I have really enjoyed. *Day of the Dead* was my initiation, *Night of the Dead* was more thought out and more methodical and *Return of the Living Dead* was just fun. I've pulled something from each of them.

BS: Everett told me to mention page 511 to you.

JV: *(laughs)* That comes from a forensic pathology book we used. One of the requirements of our profession is that if you want your effects to look realistic, you have to look at pictures of crime scenes and autopsy images. None of these books are pleasant at all to look it. It just comes with the territory. The dildo's this guy was using were the size of your leg. They were huge. As a kid in my twenties, I had never seen anything like this before. It was such an extreme way to die. There was one time when we posed Tom on the floor surrounded by cardboard tubes in homage to the picture. I have the Polaroid somewhere. I think Greg Nicotero made up t-shirts of it at some point.

BS: Does it become difficult to distance yourself from the realism of the makeup?

JV: Definitely earlier in my career when I first saw it. It would really disturb me. The more I saw it, the less it bothered me. I think the whole page 511 thing is a defense mechanism to prevent that kind of thing from affecting me. If you deal with people who work with death on a frequent basis like doctors or soldiers, they trivialize it. I was doing some research for *The Dark Half* and was talking to a pediatric surgeon and they were really callous about it. At face value it seems really harsh, but you realize it is a coping mechanism. It is not meant to be disrespectful, it is how you can get through it without going crazy. Looking at these pictures it is easy to add the human element. These people had lives and loved ones and if you dwell on that, you would go insane. When we were doing *Night of the Living Dead*, we studied concentration camp photos for our zombies. I was interviewed by the L.A Times and the interviewer completely lambasted us, saying we were sadists and took a sadistic delight from look at horrific imagery. This couldn't have been any further from the truth. I think he had his own agenda and wanted us to look bad. There is definitely a touchy aspect of doing this. It may look distasteful, but it's purely for research and to make us effective at what we do.

BS: Which has been your favorite death scene that you have worked on?

JV: Many times in a script, the deaths are not detailed and it is left up to the effects crew to design them. For *Day of the Dead*, we did a round table at Tom's house and brainstormed some new deaths to add into the film. One of the ones I threw out was based on George's rule that a zombie can only die if the brain is destroyed. So I thought about what would happen if the top part of head was severed and the brain was left intact? It couldn't move as it didn't have a jaw or anything to help. That was how the scene where the zombies head is cut off with a shovel came about. Tom liked the idea and I asked if I could play the part in the film, so that was how I got my cameo in *Day of the Dead*. I also play another zombie in the cave scene as well. I'm in a pastel suite with a goatee. I was rigged up with a load of squibs and had a blast doing the scene. They took a mold of my head and did some head squibs. On the *Night of the Living Dead* remake we did this great shotgun head blast that was unfortunately cut out of the film. I found out years later that a lot of the scenes that were cut out, the MPAA was going to allow the editor to put back in, they just wanted to trim the scene, but I think he misunderstood and took out the entire scene.

BS: So what made the head shot so cool?

JV: We used live fire arms to pull it off. We waited until the end of the day and shot a prop head with a real shotgun. You just can't do that these days. It's the best look for that type of effect, but the risk factor of an accident is too high. There are strict regulations for the use of firearms on a set.

BS: Were you aware of the controversy with the remake of *Night of the Living Dead*?

JV: I wasn't really familiar with any controversy. Was there?

BS: There was a level of anger from a select area of the fan base in reaction to the film being remade. Although it was not quite as severe as the backlash received on the *Dawn of the Dead* remake.

JV: I wasn't aware of that either.

BS: It was very harsh. James Gunn who wrote the film, received death threats due to his involvement. They had to jump on the PR train very quickly and announced that there was no reason to remake *Dawn of the Dead* and that it was a re-envisioning.

JV: Maybe I just wasn't that immersed in the fan community at the time because I wasn't aware of anything. We were huge fans of the original movie, so we were just chomping at the bit to be involved in remaking such a great film. There certainly was no disrespect involved at all. It was being made by most of the same people who did the original too, so I think there was some added validity to that, that may be missing from other remakes. It is not like it was just someone else hacking at it. I'm not one hundred percent happy with how it turned out, but I really like it. I think that with a remake or a sequel for that matter, there is a lot of premeditation that goes into it and expectations are generally a lot higher because the product is so well established with the fan base. There is something about going with the gut instinct and when you are doing something first, you don't have quite as much pressure.

BS: What are your thoughts on the shift to CGI?

JV: I've seen instances where I really liked it. I liked the CGI blood splatter that they used in *Hot Fuzz*. I'm really not opposed to it at all. I know a lot of my contemporaries have issue with the migration because they feel threatened by it. There is a lot of crappy CGI out there unfortunately, but there is a lot that is really good. The same can be said for traditional effects though. Both the technology and artistry have increased considerably in recent years. I know that many times with practical effects you can't get the blood to go where you want it to go and sometimes it can require a few takes to get it right. You are dealing with liquid and tubing and a slight variation in room temperature can affect the viscosity. It can get really frustrating to get blood to do what you want it to do. CGI does remove the variables. I think working the two hand in hand creates some amazing results. In Christopher Nolan's *Inception*, I thought most of it was CGI but when you watch the behind the scenes footage, you realize that a considerable amount of the effects are practical. The scene with the train driving in downtown Los Angeles was a practical effect. They took a semi-truck and dressed it up to look like a train and then they added CGI effects for the asphalt being torn up. It is this marriage of the two which has brought some truly amazing results. Everett and I were playing with this kind of back in the eighties and I think we were some of the first in the industry to be doing that.

BS: Are there any more zombie films in your future?

JV: I am not sure. One of my business partners co-owns the rights to *The Return of the Living Dead* franchise. We talk every now and then about making another movie. My idea is to do a prequel that is based on the mythology established in the movie and John Russo's book.

BS: Can you share any on set stories from any of the zombie films you have worked on?

JV: With Tom Savini, there is always a ton of things gone on behind the scenes. He loves using dangerous things, like crossbows and darts and we had these metal sticks with cotton swabs on the end. We were grinding them down to make blow darts out of them and someone got shot in the ass by Tom. As retribution, Tom had to bend over and get shot. It went two or three inches into his butt. About an hour later they all panicked and went to the hospital to get tetanus shots. This kind of thing went on all the time. Tom is a huge practical joker. There was one time he cracked me in the face with a bull whip.

BS: I've heard there were a lot of jokes played on the set of *Day of the Dead*.

JV: Oh very much so. When we were on set, we ended up getting into an ongoing war with the accountant. One day, Tom had set up an explosive charge the size of a baseball on a piece of wood with igniters. He knew the accountant was stopping by at a specific time and when the accountant came through the door, Tom set the charge off. The explosion was much bigger than we had expected and was deafening. The accountant went into a standing fetal position and went into shock. They felt the vibrations all the way over to the set and we could hear the radio buzzing asking what the hell had happened.

BS: So is the real reason the budget was reduced so heavily nothing to do with ratings and everything to do with Tom torturing the accountant?

JV: *(laughs)* I hope not. The accountant certainly got us back though. We had an old beat up station wagon that we used to get around the set. One day we were leaving the mine and before we exited the big cave doors, smoke starts seeping in from under the dashboard. Within seconds the car is full of smoke and Tom's freaking out that the car is on fire. We throw the doors open and dive out of the car. I'm still in the back of the car trying to get out and we see the accountant with the munitions physical effects guy driving by pointing and laughing at us. They had rigged a smoke device that was tied to the headlights.

The cemetery zombie from the updated "Night of the Living Dead" courtesy of Columbia Pictures.

CLIFF WALLACE

- World War Z (2012) Animatronic Workshop Supervisor
- 28 Weeks Later (2007) Special Effects Makeup Designer
- 28 Days Later (2002) Prosthetics Makeup Effects

Blood Splatter: How did you get into the special effects industry?

Cliff Wallace: I saw *The Howling* and that's what did it for me. I hadn't really considered makeup effects as a career until that time, although I'd always been interested in the fantastique. In fact, at the time, I was doing a media studies course and thought I would probably move into promo production or advertising. At least, that was the fall back position if rock and roll star didn't work out. From the moment I saw Rob Bottin's werewolf effects, I resolved to finding out everything I could about makeup effects. It wasn't as easy as it is now as there was no internet and so information was pretty scarce. I read all the articles and books I could find and wrote to the effects artists chiefing any movies that were shooting in the UK at the time. I got to meet Rick Baker and Christopher Tucker that way and just spent a couple of years in my bedroom building up a portfolio. My first job was on Clive Barker's *Rawhead Rex* and whilst I was on that I heard about *Hellraiser* and managed to talk my way into a job on the film.

BS: Are you a fan of the zombie genre?

CW: I'm probably more of a creature nut as I find I can let my imagination go a lot more. I've always found the human body and facial structure to be quite restrictive as a canvas, I always want to stretch it and rearrange it. There's been some great zombie movies though and some really awesome designs.

BS: Do you have a favorite zombie film?

CW: My favorites are probably the ones I watched as a kid. In the UK there used to be a television program called *Appointment with Fear* that showed double bills of old Hammer and Amicus movies and I have a fondness for those. *Plague of the Zombies* I like a lot and the makeup in *Tales from the Crypt*. Both projects are the work of Roy Ashton. I haven't seen *Shock Waves* for years, but I always liked the idea of Nazi Zombies. I saw *Dawn of the Dead* on a double bill with *Scanners*, which was a pretty cool night out and I think Tom Savini's stuff on *Day of the Dead* was hugely imaginative.

BS: How did you become involved with the *28 Days Later* and *28 Weeks Later* franchise?

CW: If I remember rightly, I think we were recommended by a special effects guy we'd just done a war film with. Embarrassingly, he didn't get the job but I met up with Danny Boyle and Andrew MacDonald and we just sort of clicked. I'd established a reputation for doing good gore stuff and being able to come up with stuff on the fly and that seemed to be the way the movie was going to be shot. It was done very quickly with lightweight DV cameras, minimal lighting and mostly on locations around London. It really was guerilla film making.

BS: While not technically zombie films in their truest sense, the *28 Days Later* and *28 Weeks Later* films have been embraced by fans of the genre. What are your thoughts on the genre shift to include infected and viral creatures? Do you think this is a sign of the times with fears of bioterrorism?

CW: Yeah I think it single handedly jump started the new wave of zombie movies, although while we were making it, use of the "z" word was strictly forbidden. It uses the vernacular of a zombie movie, but I think anyone who is a fan of the genre can see that. The writer, Alex Garland certainly knew that, although it mixes in elements of British science fiction literature too, John Wyndham is a big influence as was J.G. Ballard. Also a UK TV series from the late 70's called *Survivors* played a huge part in the creation. I think the viral aspect of it was more interesting to Danny and the whole notion of sudden uncontrollable rage was something that was being mentioned in the media a lot at the time. We had air rage and road rage. It was everywhere. There had also been the Kenneth Noye case in the UK which had certainly been a major influence. The book, The Hot Zone about the spread of the Ebola virus was something we talked about too in that initial meeting. So if horror movies are made to reflect the concerns of the times, those elements all played a part. Of course a few days after we started shooting on *28 Days Later* September 11th happened and that event changed the nature of the film to a certain extent. It certainly changed peoples attitude towards its themes. It became more about the fragility of human life and how it can just be obliterated in an instant. It shows how unsafe our cities are and all those elements colored not only the shooting of the film, but how it was ultimately received. It is in much the same way *28 Weeks Later* became about the aftermath of the Iraq conflict. Consciously or subconsciously those things tend to surface, rightly or wrongly and horror, more than any other genre, always attains a cultural subtext.

BS: What do you use for inspiration with the makeup on an infected character?

CW: The nature of the virus was that it was hugely virulent and you could be infected by just one drop of blood. It was also a psychological virus, so the makeup had to reflect that. With Rage, the blood is literally boiling over and this is why we made the veins more prominent. It's also why we went for the red contact lenses. The blood leaking from every orifice was an Ebola virus reference, as that infection liquefies the internal organs, so the results are similar. We knew from the start that there wasn't going to be a traditional "zombie goggle" makeups. After all, these weren't reanimated dead people. We also knew that the look of the infected was going to be very much determined by the way the movie was going to be shot and there simply wasn't going to be the time for heavy prosthetics on the infected characters.

BS: Where do you draw inspiration for the wounds on the victims of zombie and viral attacks?

CW: We used a lot of pathology books as reference together with the descriptions from the Hot Zone book. We wanted the violence to seem as raw and graphic as possible. Danny is a great one for reference material and all the news footage that the chimps are being subjected too at the start of the film was all stuff that we had recreated from footage he'd shown us. The violence in *28 Days Later* is shocking because it's so sudden. I think, Naomie Harris just hacking Noah Huntley's arms off is one people always flag up. In fact his arm was never supposed to come off like that. Naomie just totally got into it and Danny just kept the cameras rolling.

BS: What are your thoughts on the effects shift to CGI?

CW: I think CGI can be a great tool, I'm not a fan of completely CGI created effects, but certainly as an effects artist CGI opens a number of possibilities for combinations of effects. That is how it seems to work best for me. Effects are after all, magic tricks and I think that you should use any means possible to sell the effect. The problem I have with CGI used on its own is that there is no element of magic there. The audience knows it's created on a computer, end of story. I would certainly question the use of CGI to create something that is basically human anatomically. So CGI zombies are always going to be something of a non starter for me. CGI enhanced zombies taking away elements of anatomy however, is another kettle of fish.

BS: Can you highlight some of the specific shots you worked on in *28 Days Later*?

CW: A lot of the stuff we did for the movie hopefully isn't recognized as such. The news reel footage I've mentioned and the various chimp puppets we made, I am very proud of. There's a lot of dummy work, particularly in the church and in the grounds of the army base. There is the fake head of the soldier that gets his eyes squished out and the Chris Ecclestone dummy that gets pulled from the car. The most noticeable ones and probably the things we spent longest on were the dummies of Jim's parents. One thing we talked about an early stage was that at the height of a rage attack we should catch a glimpse of, to use a 'Cronenbergism' the 'shape of rage'. This was going to be some physical manifestation of the psychological virus that you'd catch sight of for a fleeting second. Danny was and is, very taken with the works of Francis Bacon and he wanted these glimpses to be 'Baconesque'. I wanted to do something like the subliminal glimpses of demons in *Jacob's Ladder* and to that end we set about creating some images that could be created very simply, using minimal prosthetics, teeth etc, then distorting the features by stretching tights over people's faces or taping them down or wrapping elastics bands round them, then doing multiple exposures and Photoshopping over the top. Dom Hailstone, who is a great artist and video director, worked on these and put together a series of quite nightmarish imagery that we were all very excited about. At the end of the day, the CGI company didn't think they could replicate the sort of imagery we'd come up with, or not for the budget they had anyway. It was a bit of a body blow, but it would have taken the movie in a different direction and made it probably more arthouse than it ended up being. Commercially it probably would have damaged the project, but the photos still weird me out a little even after all this time.

BS: How about *28 Weeks Later*?

CW: After the success of *28 Days Later* we'd always hoped there would be a sequel but it took over five years to come along. It's a very different beast from *28 Days Later* and I think the work we did reflects that to a degree. I think we were all disappointed that Danny wasn't going to be back at the helm, although he did direct the pre credit sequence, which I think is one of the best bits of the film. We built a great dummy for that first sequence that gets ripped apart by the motorboat that Robert Carlyle escapes in. It was graphic stuff, obviously too graphic, One of the problems I had with the script was that it was too much like a zombie movie. There was a little too much biting in it. By the time *28 Weeks Later* was made, the zombie resurgence that *28 Days Later* had started was well underway and the script kind of reflected that, I think we managed to get it back to the original a bit.

BS: Were there any scenes in particular that were changed to be less zombie-like?

CW: We changed Roberts Carlyle's attack on his wife, so that it became more about the rage and just using everything at his disposal, rather than just biting her as it was in the original script. Luckily we'd built a nice dummy of Catherine McCormack, which Robert just systematically destroyed in his attack. It was in a pretty rough state by the end of it. We also made loads of dummies for the tube station and dummies of the main characters for various stunts. There were a couple of exploding head gags, one of the medical officer who becomes infected near the start of the film, which worked out pretty well. Most of the work we did was involved with the now infamous helicopter scene.

BS: That is definitely one of the highlights from the film. How was that scene was done?

CW: We were filming the medical officer scene when this scene was first talked about. The making of documentary filmed me staggering around with the remains of that puppet strapped to me. We showed that to the director and I said to him that if he gave give us a couple of weeks we could come up with a bunch of stuff like this that he could use in the sequence. I'm not sure of the time line, but there's a similar sequence in *Planet Terror* and of course in the *World War Z* book. They might have influenced the sequence or it might have been a *Dawn of the Dead* reference but it certainly wasn't in the script we started with and it was a sequence that just got bigger as the weeks went on. We filmed a lot of aftermath stuff on location and there were a lot of nods to Savini's *Day of the Dead* stuff in there. Plus we put in a few puppets and exploding heads, together with a few of the kind of things the making of guys had shown the director. There's a soldier staggering around whose been almost cut in two by the rotor blade and I think that one worked well. The rest of the stuff was shot in the studio a couple of months later. The effects supervisor made a running rig and we made a series of bodies that could by pulled apart then reassembled that were mounted on the rigs legs and its these that you see the helicopter tearing into. There was also a rotor blade set up that we'd just line dummies up in front of a guillotine and cut them to pieces. So there's a lot of practical stuff mixed in there with the CG in that sequence. I think there is a lot more than most people imagine. Regardless of the realism of the event, the helicopter would surely crash after striking the first couple of zombies, I think it's a neat scene and it was great fun to be involved with. I'm especially happy that the producers and director just let us run with it and come up with stuff. That doesn't happen too often.

BS: Can you share a funny story from the set of *28 Days Later* or *28 Weeks Later*?

CW: I do have a story from *28 Days Later*, however it wasn't funny at the time it happened. A couple of days after the September 11th attacks, we were filming the petrol station scene. As I've said before, the film was made very much on the hoof and I don't think the sort of security measures in regards to filming and the need to obtain permits were quite as strict as they are today. The special effects department knew it was pretty much going to be a one take wonder, so they ramped up the explosion to make sure. Unfortunately, it was a little larger than anyone had imagined and the garage happened to be on the flight path to London City Airport. Within ten minutes of the explosion, virtually every fire engine in London arrived. Suffice it to say we had to finish shooting early that night.

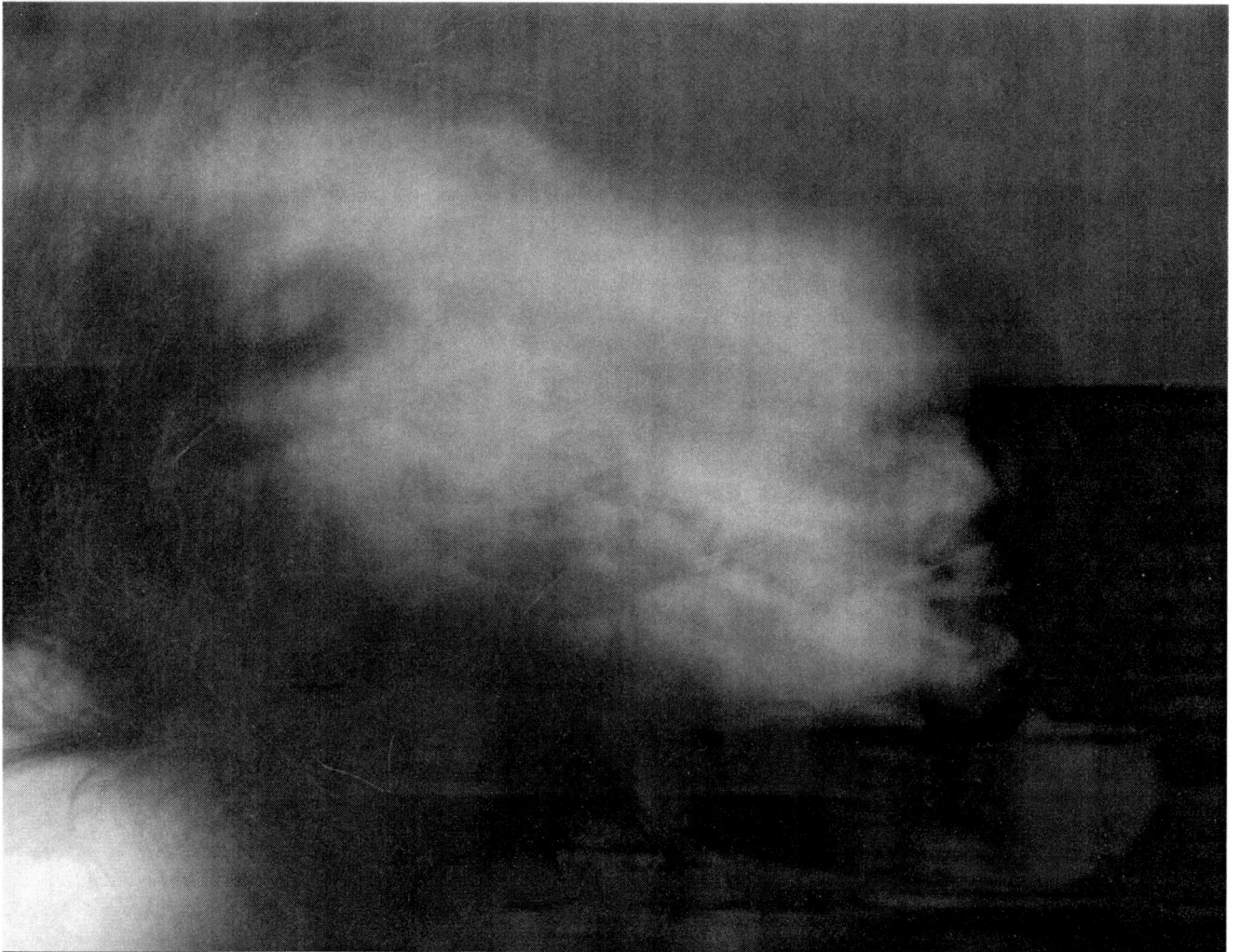

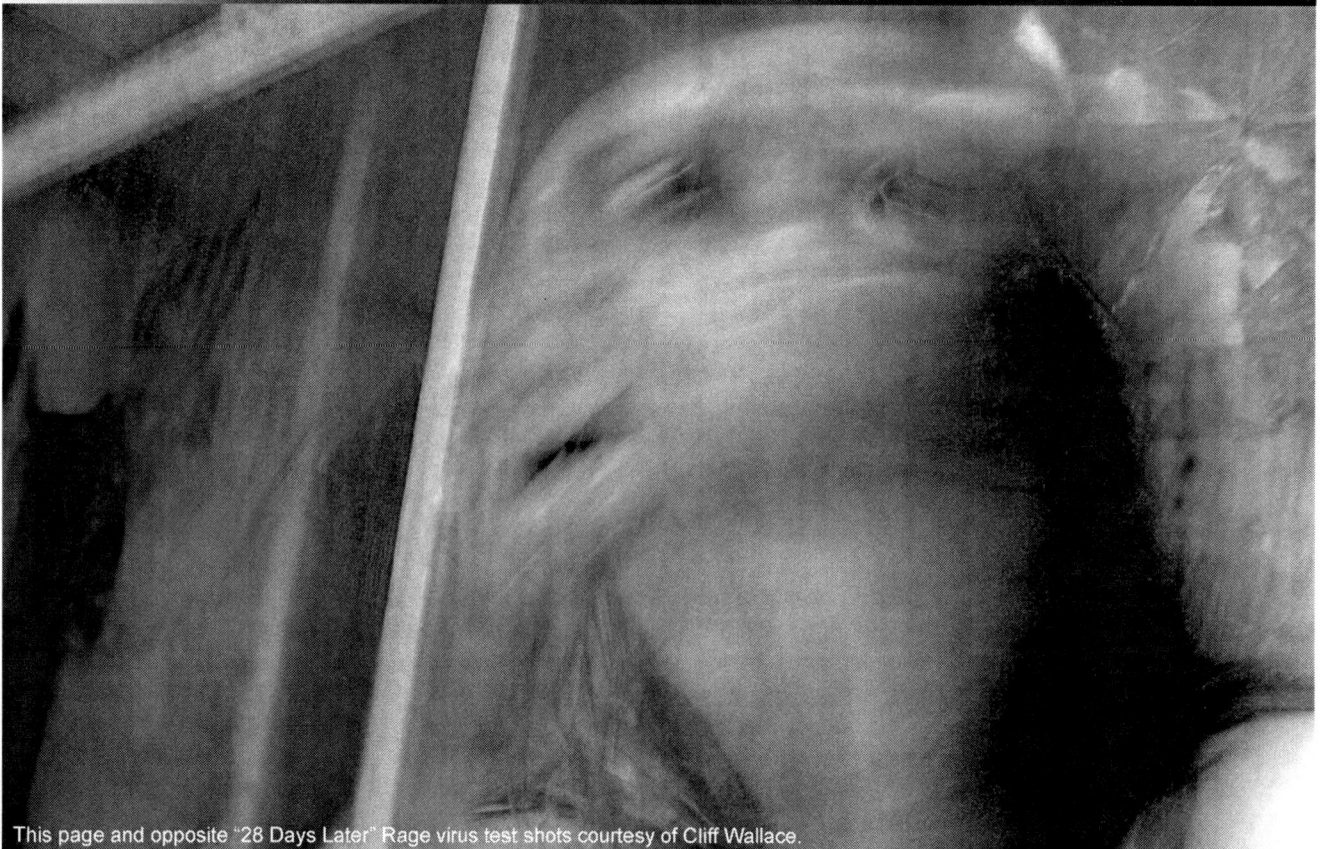

This page and opposite "28 Days Later" Rage virus test shots courtesy of Cliff Wallace.

5 JOURNAL OF THE DEAD

Over the past year, I have been fortunate enough to speak with some truly amazing and extremely talented people. I have gained great insights into the making of the zombie genre and the special effects industry as a whole. However, as the interviews started to wrap up, I realized something was missing. During the conversations, it didn't take long for common themes to emerge. Small things such as a favorite film, or a favorite effect, an anecdote about another interviewee or a shared method of research, began to stand out and connect with each other. Almost every interview tied into another somehow, but at the center of it all there was a hole. I have chatted with the people who design and create the makeup, the storyboard artists and the directors who bring it all together, but ultimately, what was missing was what happens underneath the makeup from the life cast to the final application. While I have been able to speak to a few people who have gone under the brush, I have not discussed the entire process in depth. Part of this has to do with actors signing non-disclosure agreements and in another case the length of time since they were made up. I needed to report on the final steps of the creation process. I needed to become a zombie.

This was not going to be a project that I could easily do at home. While I've had a lot of experience sculpting latex and bite wounds, to compliment the level of professionalism presented so far in this book, it would be necessary to look beyond the scope of my abilities. I needed to have someone at the top of their game perform this transformation if it was to seamlessly fit with the rest of the content. My first choice was to reach out to someone who had been a strong supporter of the project since day one. Toby Sells has been involved with Blood Splatter since we first spoke in November 2010. Indeed our first phone interview had to be scrapped as we spent ninety minutes talking about makeup and our love of films. We barely touched on the topic of zombies. Toby has made his mark on the genre with some of the biggest zombie productions in the market. Currently he is working on AMC's *The Walking Dead* and previously on *Zombieland* and *The Crazies*. While this idea sounded great on paper, I had this nagging voice at the back of my head telling me that hiring a Hollywood professional was going to be next to impossible. To my surprise, Toby responded quickly with an overwhelming yes and within a few days my flights were booked and the contracts were signed. The entire process was to be completed over two trips to allow for Toby to create my life cast and then I was to return for the final makeup application.

In August 2011, I traveled to Toby's Creature FX Workshop in Atlanta, Georgia to meet with him and start the first stage of the makeup. Assisting with this phase was Mark Ross who has worked with Toby on numerous features, including *The Walking Dead*. As one of the few allowed into Toby's workshop with a camera, I was immediately a kid again and my fan boy side poured out. I was surrounded by zombies, dead bodies, bloody torsos and everything in between. I had only been approved to take photos of the makeup session but I wanted to snap pictures and trying to take everything in. Fortunately I was able to keep my cool and celebrated the moment with a big grin. Toby's enthusiasm is infectious and soon we were chatting away like old friends. Although I arrived at a little before nine, we didn't get started until almost noon. That's what happens when you put two movie geeks in the same room. As it turned out, Toby was just as, if not more excited than I was for this opportunity. He expressed his excitement at being able to work on me with no established boundaries for the age of the zombie or cause of death which can come with other productions. Naturally, I had come in to the session with a few ideas, but after hearing how excited Toby was, I decided he should take the lead. He quickly laid out his ideas and I must admit they far exceeded any that I had.

Before the process began, Toby covered every detail of what we were about to undertake. He wanted to ensure that there would be no surprises or discomfort. The first step would involve taking an impression of my teeth. I've never had braces or retainers, so I haven't had any negative experiences getting impressions done. Toby mentioned that some people are nervous about the molds due to previously choking in the dentist's office while inclined. This is simply alleviated by sitting upright. Toby tried a couple of different plates before we found two that fit comfortably.

To make the molding material, a powder called Dental Alginate is mixed with distilled water. Distilled water is preferred, as tap water contains chlorine which causes the Alginate to clot. After a minute of mixing, the powder turns into the gel and it is placed in the dental plate. The plate is then placed on my lower teeth and I bite down for the next five minutes. The plate is removed and Toby checks to make sure the imprint is acceptable.

While Toby headed to the back part of the workshop to pour the plaster for the bottom cast, Mark prepared the second batch of Alginate for the top tray and took the mold of my upper teeth. Five minutes later Mark approved the second mold. We met up with Toby who was finishing up plastering the lower teeth. He was pleased with how the molds came out and was already starting to prepare the plaster for the second set. A few minutes later the casts were finished and we headed back to the main room.

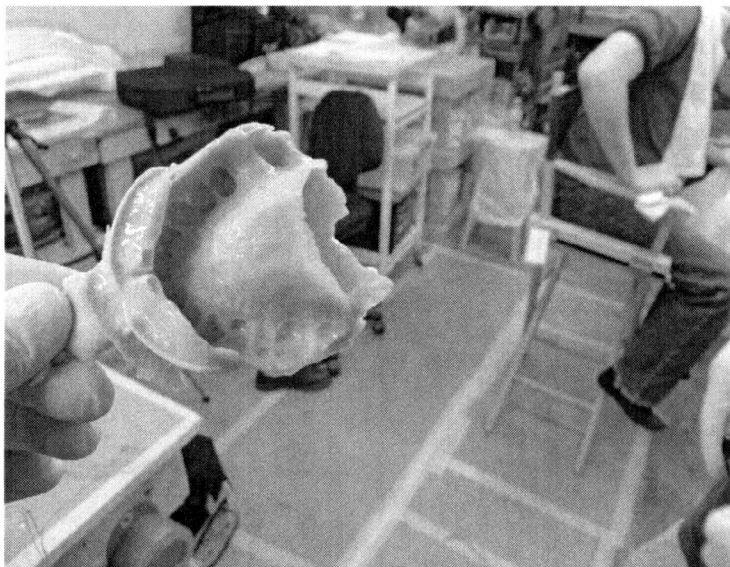

So far so good. I wasn't expecting a set of teeth to be made, so I was already quite pleased. Toby has some outstanding examples of his dental work on display and informed me he does all of the teeth for *The Vampire Diaries*. The second stage of the day was the life cast of my head. If I were to be completely honest, it was the one part I was dreading. I am a little claustrophobic and the thought of my head being completely covered didn't fill me with warm fuzzy feelings. As one of my friends so eloquently put it "why the fuck would you do this if you are claustrophobic?" Why? Because to the best of my knowledge, no one else has ever written about it.

As before, Toby talked over what was about to happen and asked if I had any concerns. I mentioned the claustrophobia and he told me to relax, breathe deeply and that he hadn't killed anyone yet. I certainly didn't intend to break new ground there. The first step involved fitting me for a bald cap. My hair needed to be slicked back with gel and the cap was trimmed around my ears and the back of my neck. Toby traced around my hairline with a marker and I was ready to go. The next step involved the first application of Alginate. Once again, distilled water was used to prevent clotting, but the difference this time was that the water needed to be cool. The Alginate sets very quickly and if the water is warm, it sets while the coat is being applied. I closed my eyes and Toby and Mark applied the Alginate.

Within a few minutes my ears, eyes and mouth were covered with only my nostrils exposed. The water was so cold that when the Alginate was applied it would take my breath away, causing me to promptly inhale through my nose. On more than one occasion Toby or Mark had to clean Alginate out of my nostrils. It's a very weird feeling. The closest I can come to describing is that it is like being underwater. I wouldn't say it was terrifying by any means, but it certainly makes you aware of the limitations of your senses. You can't see and you can't speak. All sound is deadened and I really did need to focus on breathing. Toby was well aware of my uneasiness and was professional and considerate. He constantly checked in to see how I was doing. My enthusiastic thumbs up a bit of a contrast to the discomfort I was actually going through. Maybe discomfort is a bad choice of word, as that makes it sound like the procedure is uncomfortable. It wasn't. Any issues are purely psychological. After a few minutes with my breathing steady and the alginate starting to warm up, I started to get very relaxed.

Before we started, Toby had mentioned that some people fall asleep during the process and I can certainly understand why. With dulled senses, a feeling of meditation washes over you. I'm glad I didn't though. I can only imagine how freaked out I would be to wake up and not be able to see or talk. After five minutes, Toby and Mark started to apply the plaster bandages which took another four or five minutes. During this stage, the mask started to gain a little weight and continued to get warmer. By this point any feeling of claustrophobia was long gone and I sat there peacefully in the dark as the mask hardened. Toby tapped a pencil on the mask a few times. As it dries it emits a different echo. After five minutes, the mask was hard and ready to be removed. The entire process was over in fifteen minutes but it felt longer. Would I do it again? Absolutely.

I leaned forward as Toby and Mark started to pry the back of the negative impression off of my face. Meanwhile I am furrowing my brow, rolling my eyes and lightly puffing my cheeks to loosen the mold.

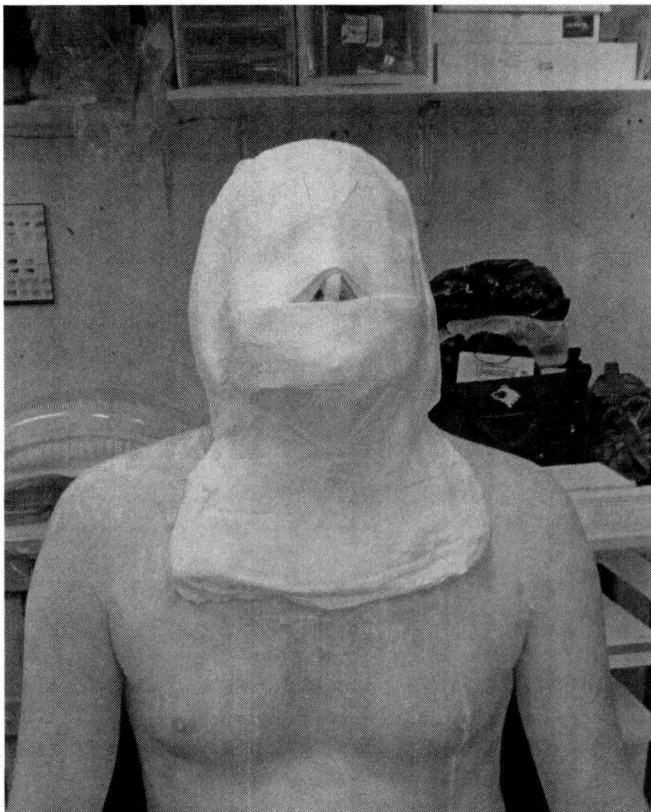

After a minute or two of gentle manipulation, the cast slid forward into my hands. Wasting no time, Toby heads back to the other room while Mark cleans me up. Normally I would have worn a shirt for this, but the shirt I brought was an original *Ghostbusters* one and Toby couldn't bring himself to get plaster on it. It was certainly poor planning on my part.

In the back area, Toby has started pouring Ultacal 30, a gypsum product that is much harder than plaster, into the mold. For the next fifteen minutes he continues to brush plaster onto the sides of the impression. This concluded the first part of the makeup session and I needed to come back in five weeks to see the finished product and go under the brush for the final makeup application.

The five week wait between the life casting and final application was agonizing. While I was back in Phoenix finishing up research for the rest of the book, Toby and his crew were hard at work preparing the next stage of my makeup. He would send me periodic photo's detailing his progress and the days slowed to a crawl. From the life cast, Toby created an epoxy resin reproduction of my face. On the copy of my face, Toby then sculpted what would eventually become my zombie prosthetic. He then made an epoxy resin mold of the sculpture, from this he fabricated a silicone gel filled prosthetic which would be applied to my face. Toby also started work on the acrylic teeth.

Having planned the second trip a little better than the first, I allowed myself time to check into a hotel the day before and I spent the evening in my hotel room looking at the latest teaser pictures Toby had sent me while web chatting with my wife and daughter. All the while I was chomping at the bit to get back over to his studio. At the crack of dawn, I was up and a couple of hours later I was sitting in Toby's chair ready to go.

Mark Ross was on hand to help out again along with Scott Fensterer, one of the sculptors for *Robot Chicken*. Both would be assisting Toby throughout the session. As before, Toby's chief concern was my comfort level and at all times he kept me informed of what he was doing and it how could affect me. At no time during the entire process was I uncomfortable. I thoroughly enjoy the makeup procedure and any complaints I would have would be more to do with not being able to it every day as opposed to any discomfort. After some chit-chat, Toby gathered his supplies and we got started.

The first order of business was to fit me with a bald cap. This was similar to the fitting I had when Toby took the life cast, but this time that my hair was coated in Gafquat to make it lay completely flat. My zombie was going to have very thin hair, almost to the point of being bald, so it was important that my scalp was completely smooth. To put it in perspective, traditional hair gel or spray is one percent of the strength. After the skull cap was fitted, Toby applied a special antiperspirant to my face and chest to prevent sweat from causing the paint to run and the appliances to lift off. After ten minutes, the skull cap was secured and we were ready to go.

The makeup came together quickly as Toby applied the facial prosthetic. It was glued down with Telesis silicone adhesive and instantly blended into my face. I was surprised how pliable it was, the Prosthetic

moved with any facial expressions I made. 99% alcohol was applied to the edges to ensure a seamless blend between silicone and flesh. While Toby worked on attaching the mask, Mark and Scott started to apply the various wounds that would be covering my torso, shoulders and arms. Instead of standard latex, the prosthetic wounds were Prosaide transfers. Prosaide transfers are a relatively new method of creating detailed wounds. They are a flexible prosthetic appliance that is made from Prosaid Adhesive. They are attached to tattoo transfer paper and applied to the skin allowing full movement. Multiple transfers were applied showing gaping wounds, decay and pustules. Even before the paint was applied the work looked striking. The pustules were a particularly nice touch as I have always felt that zombie skin would have infections and open sores. On my stomach, Toby created a custom third degree silicone wound. He used a red based mix for the interior to help the coloring and the edges were built up with a flesh tone silicone.

The majority of the time was spent painting and detailing. Toby used an airbrush and Skin Illustrator liquids to give my skin a dried and rotten look. He used a mix of browns, greens and purples which he applied over multiple layers. He drew thin snake lines of dark brown across my skin to simulate veins full of stagnant blood and the purples and greens created subtle bruising under the skin. The skin had a very uneven patchiness that replicated having had more sun exposure on certain parts. Toby applied numerous subtle techniques that only a zombie fanatic who really knows his undead would think to do. As my zombie had been dead a while, adding fresh blood would not have been consistent with the rest of the makeup. Scott used instant coffee to create a thick congealed substance and applied it to the wounds. It was nice touch and added volumes to the overall design. It really provided an aged affect to the blood and allowed it to have an oozing effect, while still showing the discolorations that would naturally occur. Such details and continuity are the marks of a real professional. Although now, I will always associate the smell of coffee with being a zombie.

For the final touch, Toby added wisps of hair to the back and sides of my head. It was a slightly lighter color than my natural hair and staring at myself in the mirror really set me back a bit. There is a psychological aspect to special effects that isn't discussed very often and one that became apparent to me on more than one occasion throughout the process. During my interviews I asked the effects artists about how working with makeup affects their views on mortality, but I didn't consider the impact it could have on the actor being made up. Watching the process in the mirror is really interesting as you see the transformation from healthy to dead slowly happening. This it isn't just a mask that is pulled over your head, it really gives you a glimpse into an older and frailer version of yourself. My cheeks started to sink in and my brow became more pronounced. In addition to adjusting to the physical changes, as Toby and Scott started painting and detailing the various wounds, especially the gaping wound on my stomach, I found myself flinching. Due to the realism of the effects, I had to reprogram my brain that the wounds were not real. While this may seem ridiculous, as the logical part of your brain knows it is make believe, there is a part of you that naturally recoils in defense. In the interviews I conducted, I spoke with many of the effects artists about the desensitization of seeing the effects so many times. I would assume the same psychological walls would need to be put up by an actor who goes under the brush on multiple occasions. While there are zombie makeup effects that completely disguise the actor beneath, I think those where the actor is still somewhat recognizable beneath it all can take its toll. Stepping up to a mirror and seeing myself as a rotten corpse, really set me back a bit. It happened on more than one occasion throughout the day. It's a very weird experience to describe.

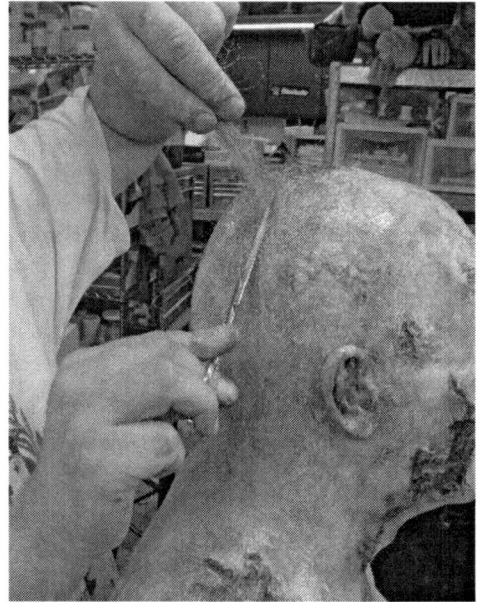

With the makeup finished, we went out into the woods to take some photos. After posing with and chewing on severed limbs and clawing my way between trees, we heard a faint bell ringing in the distance signaling the ice cream man was pushing his cart down the street. Toby and I glanced at each and didn't even need to communicate what should happen next. Toby steps out to buy an ice cream and few seconds later I shuffle out into the street, groaning and reaching for the poor elderly ice cream man. His eyes go wide and he starts to back away from the cart. Toby tries to calm the poor guy down but we realize he doesn't speak English. After some charades and me stepping out of character, the poor fellow settled down a bit, gave Toby his ice cream and posed for a few pictures. He seemed to be a bit more comfortable around me, although he continued to throw a few wary glances my way. With no one left in the neighborhood to terrorize, I reluctantly went back into Toby's studio and we started the removal process.

Removing the makeup took just over an hour. Scott used Isopropyl Myristate to remove the paint and appliances quickly and painlessly. My hair was still caked to my head and it felt like I was wearing a crash helmet. Before long I slowly transformed into a living human again and my adventures as a zombie were over. I didn't get the chance to shower before heading out for sushi with Toby. I was getting some really strange looks from our waitress, who was no doubt wondering why my hair was flaking and why I was wearing eyeliner. Once Toby explained it was makeup and I was not some Goth with a major dandruff issue, she relaxed a bit.

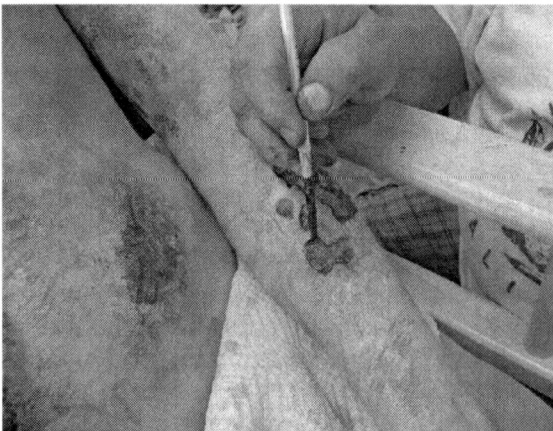

I am extremely happy with the final design and I think Toby did an outstanding job. I feel this design definitely has a Fulci's *Zombie* feel to it. I love the old decayed style of zombie. Of course, being made up like this has done nothing to quench my desire to perform as a zombie in a feature length production and hopefully that will be the next step in my zombie career. My gratitude and thanks go out to Toby for this once in a lifetime opportunity. His generosity, professionalism and talent are outstanding and I hope that our paths cross again in the future.

Full color pictures of the makeup session with Toby are available at www.zombiebloodsplatter.com. Click on the "Book Owners" link and enter "makeup" for the password.

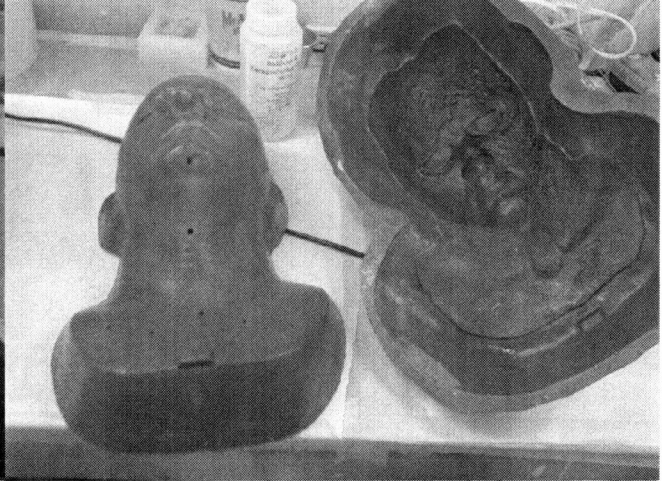
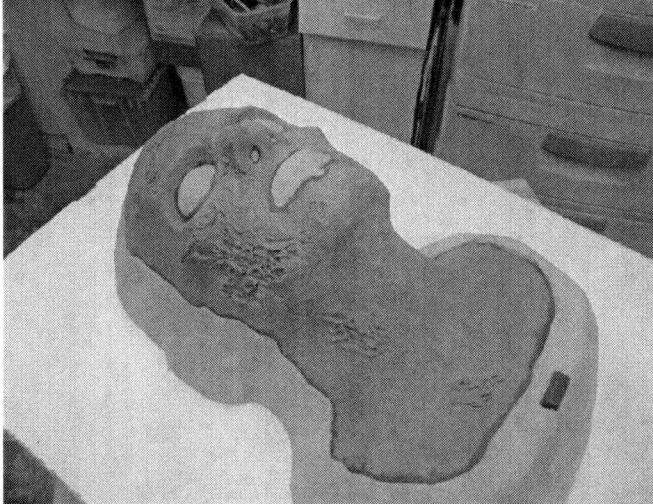
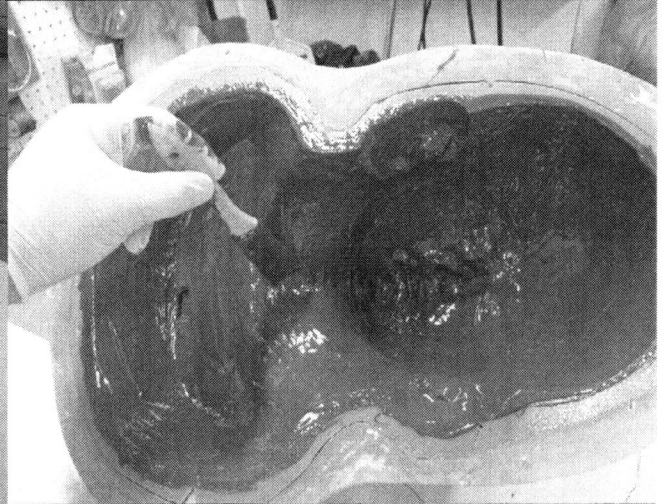

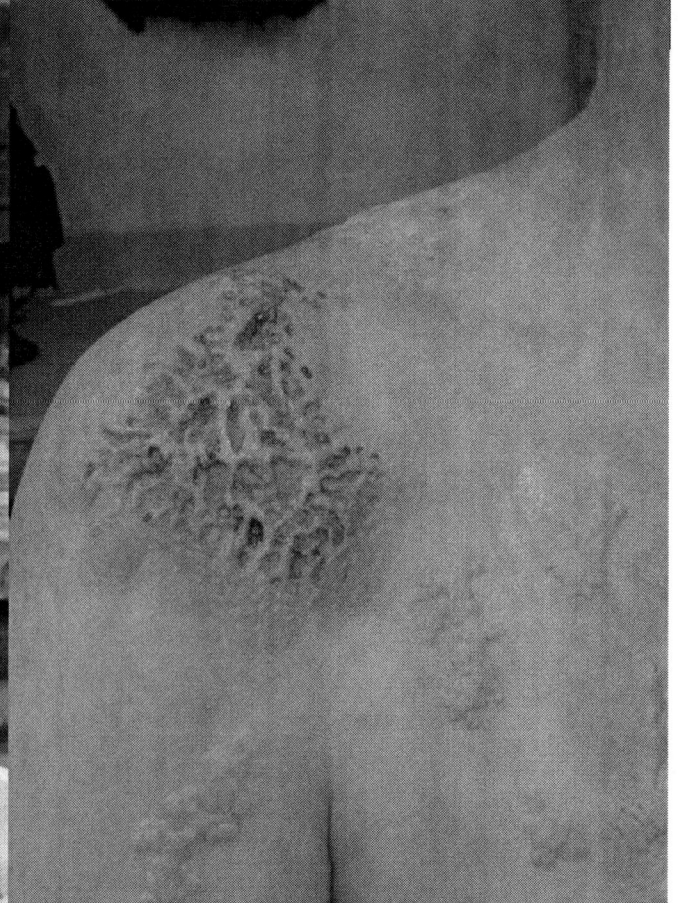

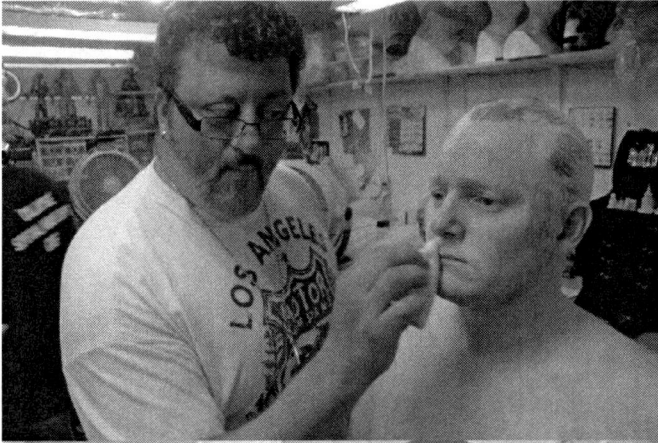
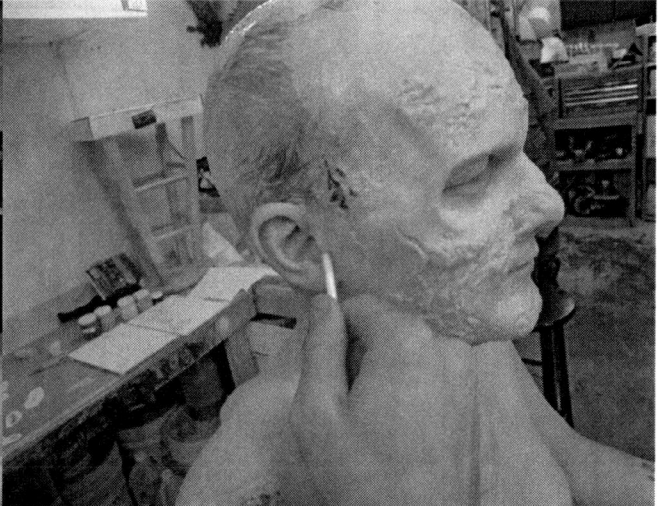
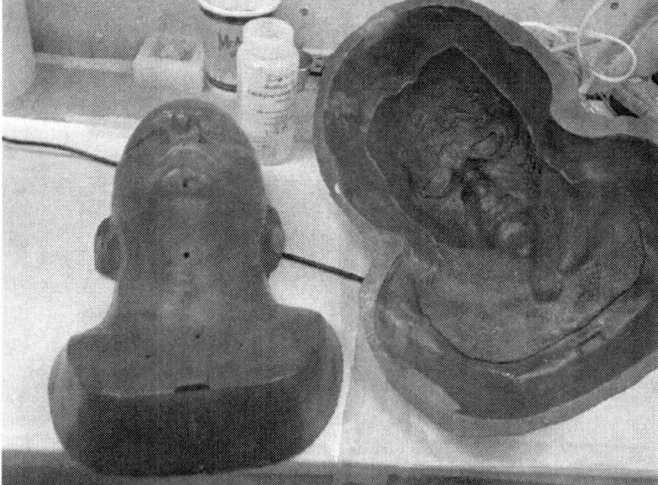

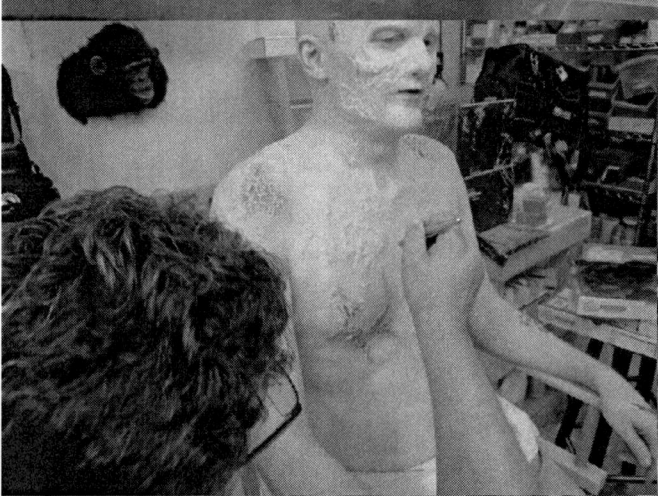

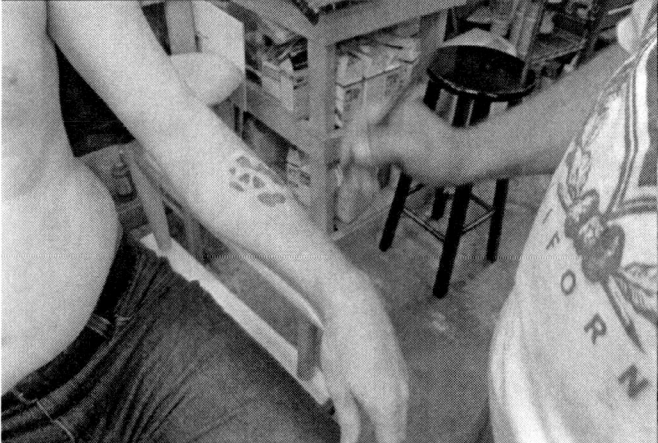
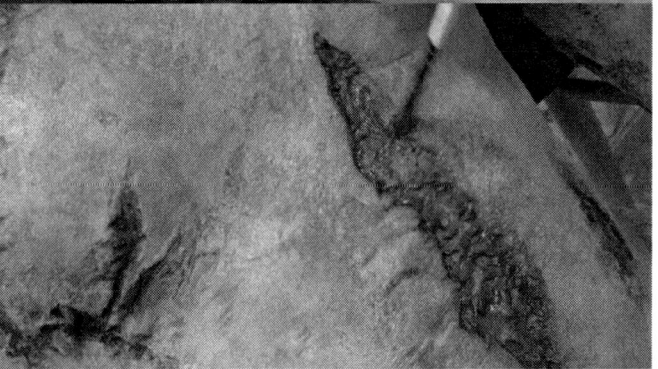

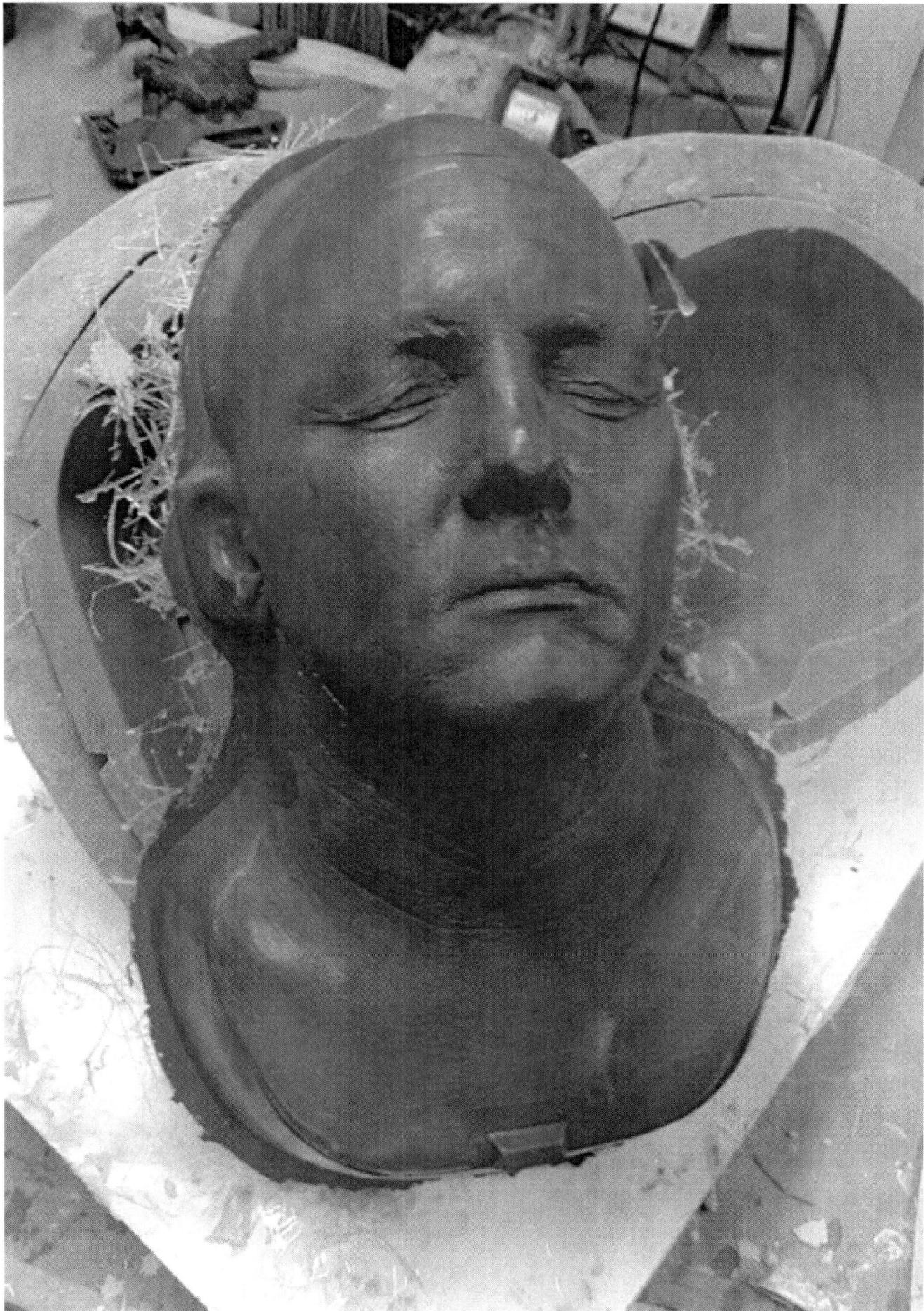

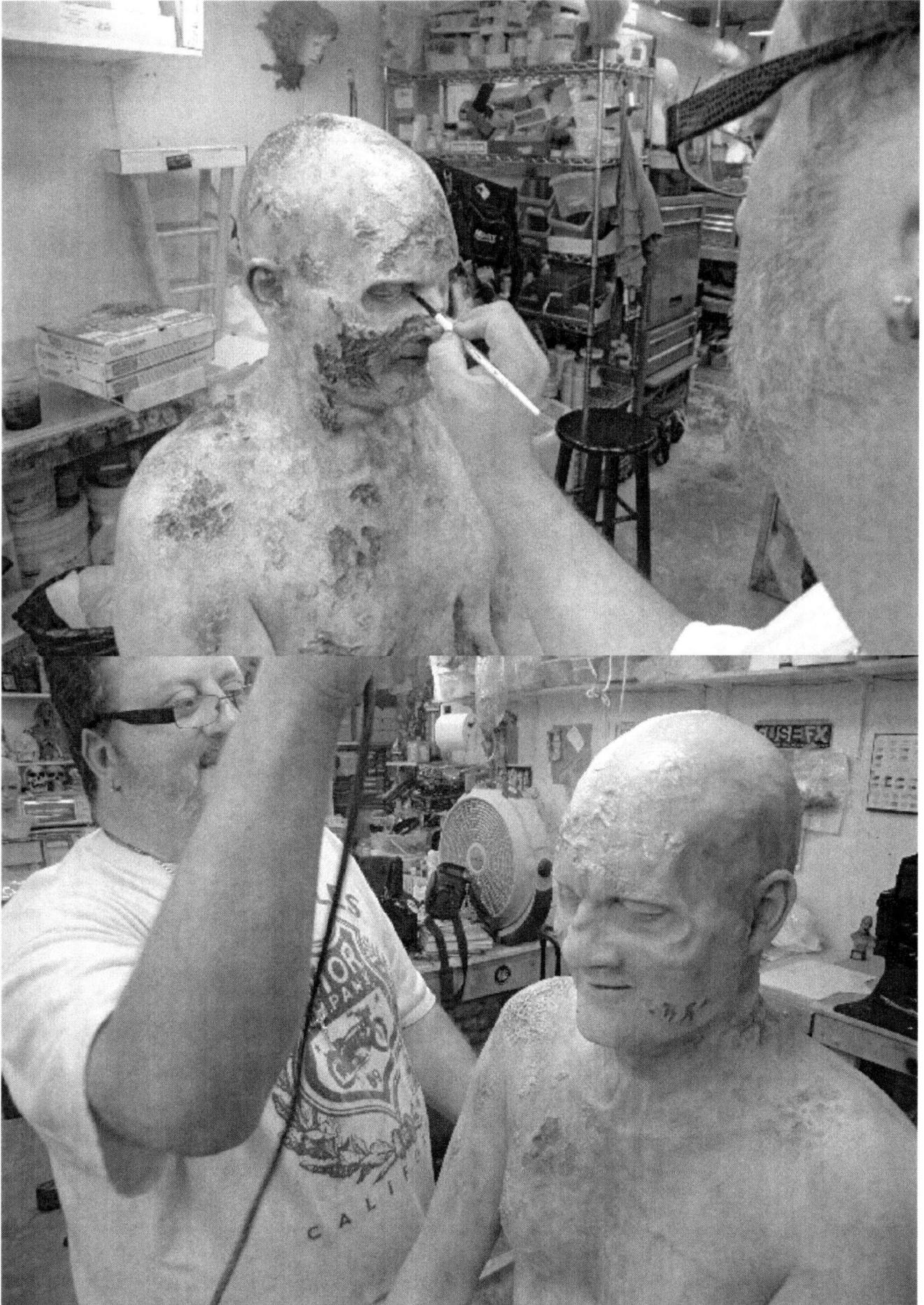

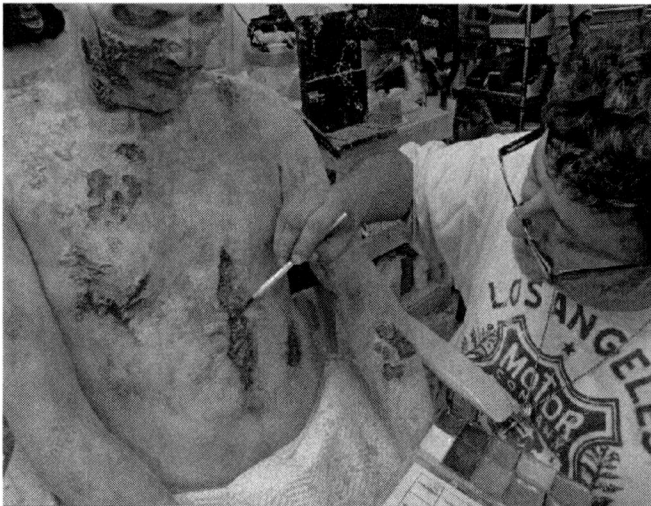
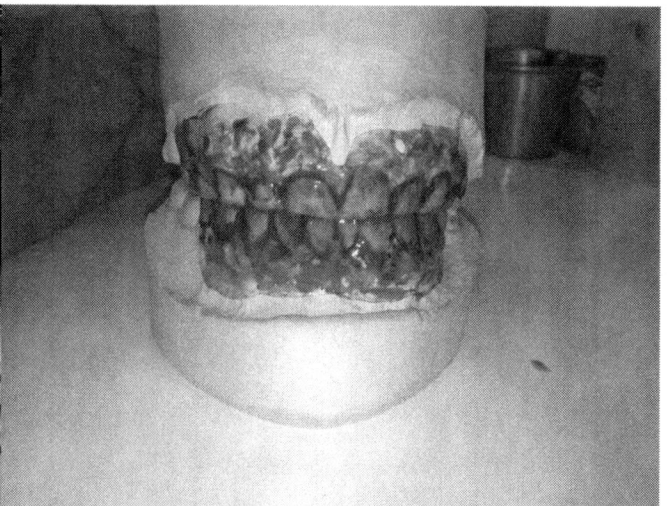
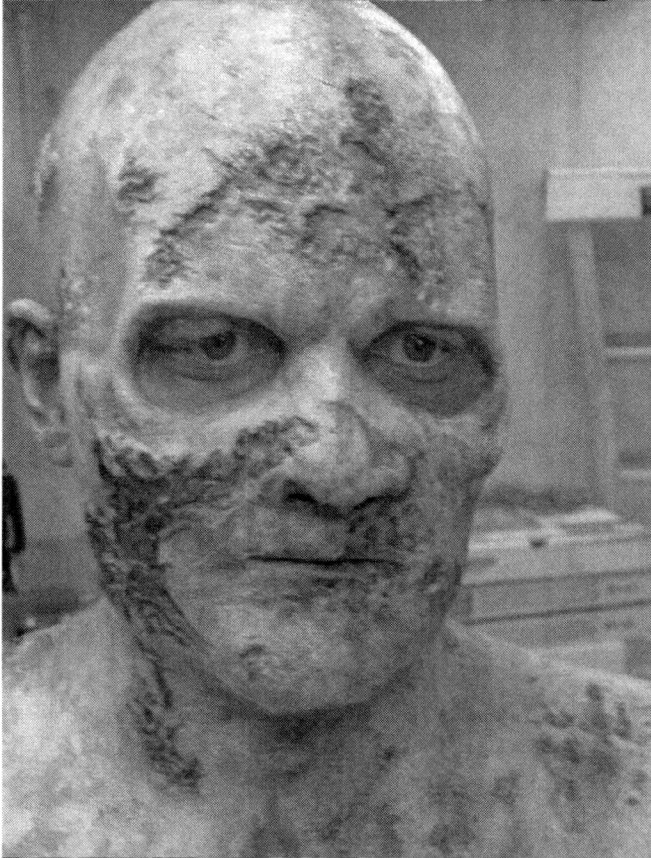
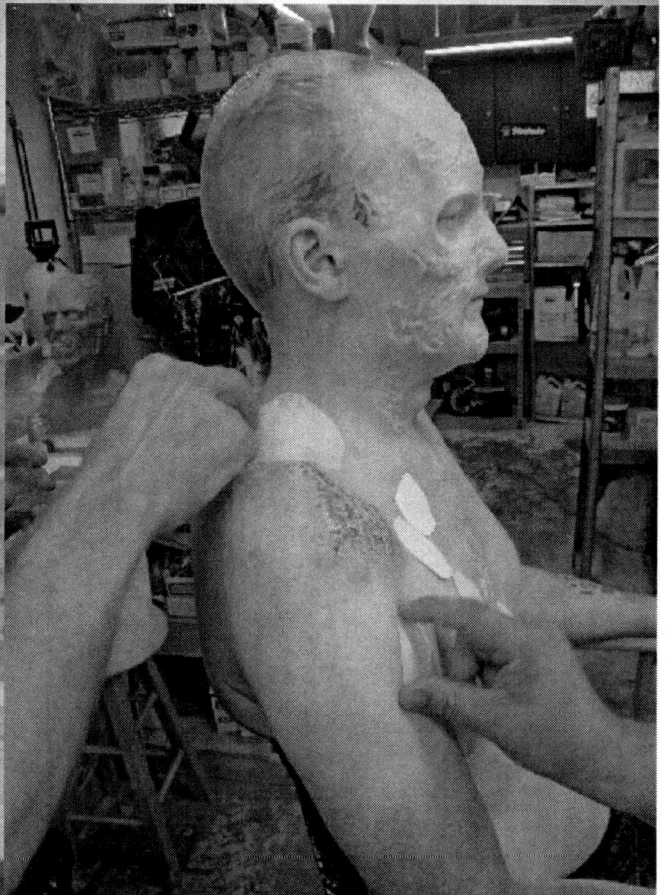
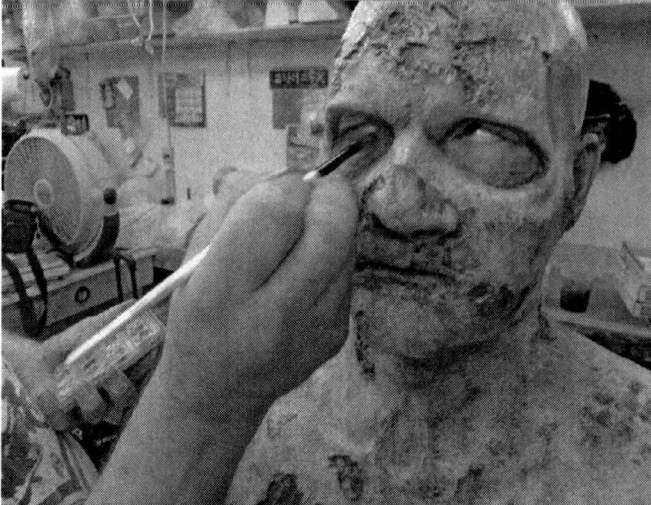
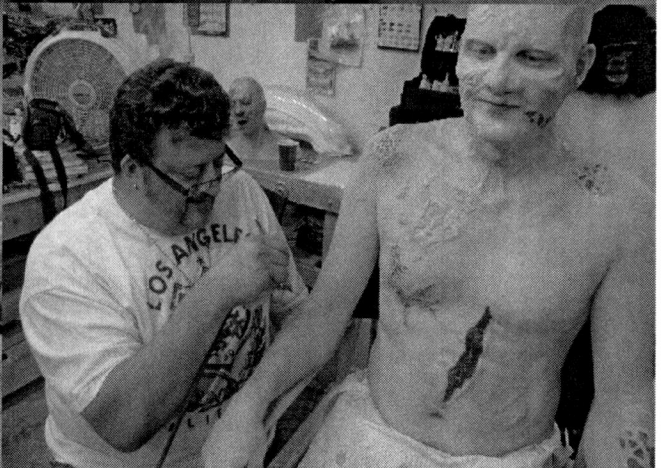

INDEX

#

127 Hours 251, 253
28 Days Later 3, 6, *202, 203, 204*, 211, 223, 245, 264, 278, 289, 298, 309, 321, 324, 353, 354, 355
28 Weeks Later 6, 7, 201, *202, 203, 205*, 295, 353, 355
4th Reich, The 331

A

A Few Brains More 307, 308, 310
A Grave for the Corpses 8, *203, 204*
A Little Bit Zombie 215, 218
A Nightmare on Elm Street 298, 343
A Virgin Among the Living Dead 8
Aaah! Zombies!!! 8, 9, 10, *203*
Abram, Christopher 11
Acomba, David 122
Ada: Zombilerin Dugunu 11, *203*
After Sundown 11, *203, 204, 205*
Against The Dark 11, *202, 203, 204*
Alberti, Marc 117
Alçina, Jaume 117
Alderman, Kate 322
Alien 322
Alien Dead 12
All Souls Day 12, *202, 203*
Allen, Caleb 164
Alonso, Cesar 315
American Zombie 12, *203*
An American Werewolf in London 250
Anderson, David 254, 328, 337
Anderson, Matthew R. 67
Anderson, Paul W.S. 142, 143
Angell, Jerry 344
Aragão, Rodrigo 119
Argento, Dario 211
Army of Darkness 13, 14, *203, 205*, 273, 296
Art of Vision, The 266
Ashton, Roy 353
Aso, Masahiro 102
Astro Zombies 14, *205*
Atom the Amazing Zombie Killer 265
Attack Girl's Swim Team Vs. Undead 14, *202*
Automaton Transfusion 14, *202, 203*
Autumn 15, *203*
Avari, Erick 319
Aviator, The 248
Awaken the Dead 15, *203, 205*
Axed 16, 17, *201, 202, 205, 203*, 278, 279, 280, 281

B

Bacchus, John 200
Bacon, Kevin 250
Bacon, Francis 354
Bad Taste 278, 279
Baker, Dylan 249
Baker, Rick 220, 250, 282, 331, 353
Balagueró, Jaume 141
Ballard, J.G. 353
Bambi 266
Band of Brothers 257
Banks, Boyd 206, 207
Barker, Clive 353
Barker, Steve 129
Bartlett, Michael 183, 185
Barton, David P. 61
Barton, Steve 170, 171, 206, 210, 330
Battle Girl 18
Battlefield Baseball 18, *203, 205*
Bava, Lamberto 103
Baxter, Jennifer 328
Beast Within 18
Bell, Emma 301
Beneath Still Waters 18, *202, 203*
Beneath The Surface 19
Benevich, Eddie 67
Berger, Howard 32, 219, 220, 297, 298, 349
Bernsen, Corbin 58
Bernthal, Jon 302
Bessai, Carl 157
Beverly Hills 90210 279
Beyond Re-animator 19
Bianchi, Andrea 33
Big Tits Zombie 20, *203*
Bio Cops 20, *203*
Bio Zombie 21, *203*
Biophage 21, *203*
Birman, Matt 80
Bishop, Damon 212

Bishop, Gregg 43
Bite Me 318, 320
Black Magic 21
Black, James 173
Blasco, Joe 273
Blob, The 270, 324
Blood Creek 22, *202*
Blood Moon Rising 22, *203, 205*
Blood of the Beast 22
Blood Sucking Freaks 267
Bloodlust Zombies 23, *202*
Bloodpigs 23, 24, *201, 203, 311, 313*
Bloodsuckers from Outerspace 24, *203*
Boll, Uwe 107
Bone Sickness 24, 25, *201,203, 205, 311, 312, 313*
Boneyard, The 26
Bong of the Dead 26, *201, 202, 203, 205*
Boni, Luca 84
Book of Zombie 27, *203*
Bookwalter, J.R. 66, 129
Bottin, Rob 331, 353
Bowker, John 134
Boy Eats Girl 27, *202, 203*
Boy Who Cried Werewolf, The 42
Boyle, Danny 6, 261, 353, 354, 355
Bradley, Stephen 27
Brain Dead 27, *202*
Braindead 28, 29, 30, *201, 202, 203, 205*, 225, 226, 227, 261, 262, 278, 298, 307, 309, 314
Brakhage, Stan 266
Bride of Re-animator 32, 33, 273, 274, 296
Bridges, Chris 206, 215, 293
Broadstreet, Jeff 125
Brooker, Charlie 285
Brookshire, Jeff 15
Brophy, Jed 228
Brothers, Deagol 117
Bruiser 208
Bryant, David 268
Bubba's Chili Parlor 33, *203, 205*
Burial Ground 33, *201, 202, 203*, 299
Burman, Tim 349
Burrell, Everett 206, 219, 244, 297, 298, 333, 350, 351
Burrell, Ty 217
Bushe, James 314
Buttcrack 34
The Beyond 19

C

Cade, Blaine 85
Callis, Sarah Wayne 302
Canby, Vincent 267
Cannibal apocalypse 34, *205*
Canutt, Yakima 319
Cardille, Bill 297
Cardille, Lori 297
Carlyle, Robert 355
Carnage, Art 173
Carpenter, John 285, 311
Carruthers, Bob 185
Carter, John N. 187
Castellano, Corey 340
Cavalline, Ryan 76
Cemetery Man 34, *202, 203*, 278
Chabrol, Claude 266
Channell, Justin 77
Chaplin, Charlie 266
Cheng, Wai-Man 20
Children of the Living Dead 35, *203, 205*, 326, 331
Children Shouldn't Play With Dead Things 35, *203*
Chilling, The 212
Choking Hazard 35
Chown, Greg 113
C.H.U.D - Bud the C.H.U.D 35
Citizen Kane 333
City of the Living Dead 36, *202, 203*
Clark, Bob 35
Clarke, Eugene 115, 286
Clavell, Ana 56
Clement, Brian 87, 118,
Coburn, Glen 24
Colin 36, 37, *201, 203*, 266, 321, 322, 323, 324, 325
Collapse 336, 340
Condit, Jon 210
Conna, Edward 67
Connolly, Billy 248, 249, 318
Conran, Stuart 29, 30, 159, 160, 161, 206, 225, 229, 289
Contagiun, 245
Cook, Bob 165
Cook, Todd Jason 75
Cooper, Alice 315, 317

Corman, Roger 266
Corpses 39
Cousins, Brent 155
Cowan, Melissa 206, 241, 242,
Cowboys and Zombies 39, 40, *201, 203, 205*, 282
Cranefield, Paul 27
Craven, Wes 343
Crazies, The (1973) 296
Crazies, The (2010) 264 , 336, 358
Creatures From The Pink Lagoon 42, 43
Creepersin, Creep 128
Creepshow 296, 332
Crocombe, Leigh 323, 324
Crognale, Gino 114, 115, 206, 243, 246, 302
Crudo, Richard 11
Cullen, Charles E. 122
Cummins, James 26
Cunningham, Nicola 227
Currie, Andrew 88, 93, 94, 206, 247, 249
Curse of the 49'er 318
Curse of the Cannibal Confederates 43, 44, *203*
Curse of the Screaming Dead see Curse of the Cannibal Confederates
The Chilling 212

D

D'Amato, Joe 85, 135, 179
D'Amato, Vince 173
Dahan, Yannick 106
Danbury, Mark 346, 348
Dance of the Dead 43, *202, 203*, 336, 339
Darabont's, Frank 241
Dark Half, The 350
Darling, Shawn 102
Davies, Rhys 191
Dawn of the Dead (1978) 3, 46, 47, 48, 49, *201, 203, 205*, 212, 213, 219, 200, 223, 243, 244, 247, 261, 273, 274, 278, 289, 296, 297, 298, 302, 303, 305, 314, 321, 331, 332, 334, 337, 338, 349, 353, 355
Dawn of the Dead (2004) 3, 50, 51, *201 , 202, 203, 205, 207*, 208, 209, 215, 217, 218, 223, 254, 255, 274, 302, 328, 329, 331, 333, 335, 346, 351
Dawn of the Living Dead 50
Day of the Dead (1985) 3, 54, 55, 52, 53, *201, 202, 203, 205*, 213, 219, 220, 222, 223, 224, 225, 226, 247, 261, 273, 285, 290, 296, 297, 298, 299, 301, 315, 319, 321, 331, 332, 334, 336, 337, 349, 350, 351, 352, 353, 355
Day of the Dead (2008) 55, 56, *201, 202, 203, 205*, 282, 295, 293, 333
Day of the Dead 2: Contagium 56, *201, 202, 203, 205*
Day X 57, *203*
Days of Darkness 57, *201, 202, 203*
De Niro, Robert 267
De Ossorio, Amando 100, 125, 148, 169
De Rossi, Gianetto 280
Dead, The 58, 59, *201, 202, 203, 205*, 257, 258, 259, 260
Dead 2, The 260
Dead Air 58, *203*
Dead Alive see Braindead
Dead and Breakfast 60, *201, 202*, 295, 293, 294, 295
Dead and Buried 61
Dead and Deader 61, *201, 202, 203*
Dead and Rotting 61
Dead and the Damned, The see Cowboys and Zombies
Dead Before Dawn 209
Dead Clowns 62
Dead Country 62
Dead Creatures 62
Dead Hate The Living, The 63, *202*
Dead Heat 63, *205*
Dead Heist 63, *202, 203, 205*
Dead Hunter 64, *203, 205*
Dead Life 64, *203*
Dead Meat 64, *203*
Dead Men Walking 65, *203*
Dead Moon Rising 65, *201, 202, 203*
Dead Next Door 66, *203*
Dead Outside, The 66
Dead Pit, The 66, 68, 60, 72, *202, 203*, 282, 283
Dead Rising 2 320
Dead Set 285
Dead Snow 67, *201, 202, 203*, 318
Dead Summer 67
Dead Undead, The 67, *201, 202, 203, 205*, 318
Deadgirl 74, *202, 303, 304*, 306
Deadlands 2: Trapped 7 4, *204*
Deadlands 7 4, *204*
Deak, Michael 219, 220, 349
Death Metal Zombies 75, *204*
Death Valley 274

Death Valley: The Revenge of Bloody Bill 75, 202, 204
DeCunto, Gabe 340
Deganois, Francois 212
Dekker, Fred 123
Dellamorte Dellamore see *Cemetery Man*
Demon Slaughter 76
Departed, The 222
Devil's Playground 76, 202, 204
Diani, Chris 42, 43
Diary of the Dead 77, 78, 80, 201, 202, 203, 204, 207, 209, 213, 215, 217, 254, 255, 289, 290, 291, 296, 297, 300
DiCaprio, Leonardo 222
Dickens, Jordy 162
Die and Let Live 77, 204
Die Another Day 260
Die You Zombie Bastards! 82
Die Zombielager 82, 201, 204, 205
DieNer 82
Dietlein, Marsha 151, 272
Dinhut, Patrick 61
Dinicol, Joe 290
Dinter, Mathias 125
Dirty Jobs 340
Dobes, Marek 35
Doghouse 83, 202, 203, 204
Donovan, Mark 226, 229
Doomed 83, 204
Dorm of the Dead 84
Dowdle, John Erick 138
Dr. Giggles 301
Dread Central 210
Dudelson, Glenn 56
Dunne, Griffin 250
Durán, Juanjo 117

E

Eastwood, Clint 309
Eaters: Rise of the Dead 84, 201, 202, 203, 204
Eberhardt, Thom 123
Ecclestone, Christopher 354
Edges of Darkness 85, 202, 204
Electric Zombies 85
Elkayem, Ellory 153
Emerson, Caleb 82
Eren, Murat Emir 11
Erotic Nights of the Living Dead 85, 204
Ertürk, Talip 11
Escape of the Living Dead 326, 327
Evans, Joey 33
Evil 86, 201, 202
Evil 2 86, 201, 204, 205
Evil Dead, The 87, 261, 262, 278, 307, 309
Evil Dead 2: Dead By Dawn 87, 88, 273, 296, 297, 299, 307
Evollove, Darcy 166
Exhumed 87, 296
Exorcist, The 299

F

Fangoria 210, 226
Farmer, Donald 84
Fast Five 214
Faulkner, Rocky 295
Favreau, Jon 261
Feeding the Masses 88, 89, 204
Feldman, Corey 317, 349
Felsher, Michael 212
Fensterer, Scott 361, 362
Fernandez, Juan 117
Fernandez, Shiloh 304
Ferrin, Chad 101
Fido 88, 91, 92, 93, 94, 201, 202, 204, 241, 247, 248, 249, 318
Fingaz, Sticky 305
Fistful of Brains 95, 96, 201, 204, 307, 309
Fitzpatrick, Richard 214
Fleischer, Ruben 194, 251
Flesh Freaks 95, 202
Flesheater 98, 205
Flight of the Living Dead 98, 202, 203, 204, 205, 318, 319, 320
Ford, Howard 58, 59, 257, 258, 260
Ford, John 266
Ford, Jonathan 58, 59, 257, 258, 260
Forest of the Dead 99
Forever Dead, The 99, 201, 204, 307, 309
Fragasso, Claudio 179
Francis, David J. 187
Franco, Jesus 8, 118, 127
Fratto, Marc 195
Freeman, Rob 258
Fresnadillo, Juan Carlos 6
Friday the 13th 250, 275
Friday the 13th Part IV 349

Fright Night (1985) 275, 305
Fright Night (2011) 305
Frontiers 275
Frost, Nick 160, 226
Fujiwara, Ken'ichi 186
Fukuda, Yôhei 128
Fulci, Lucio 19, 36, 107, 178, 311, 312, 332, 342, 362
Furlong, Edward 317
Furst, Griff 110

G

Gangs of the Dead 100, 202, 204
Garden of the Dead 100
Gardner, Tony 13, 149, 195, 196, 197, 206, 250, 253, 336
Garland, Alex 353
Garland, Judy 267
Gaslight Studios 78, 80, 81, 256, 302
Gates of Hell 211
Gates, Kevin 183, 185, 314
Gebroe, David 186
George, Rich 25, 312
Ghost Galleon 100
Ghost Lake 100
Ghostbusters 360
Ghoul School 101
Ghouls, The 101, 201, 202
Girls Zombie 102, 204, 205
Girolami, Marino 186
Glencross, Kyle 81, 206, 213, 218, 254, 256, 289, 290, 300
Goldblatt, Mark 62
Gommé, Daniel 257, 259
Gordon, Stuart 141
Grabowski, Ray 248
Graham, Ryan 117
Grapes of Death, The 102, 204
Grau, Jorge 112
Grave Mistake 102, 203, 204
Graveyard Alive 103
Graveyard Disturbance 103
Gray, Charles F. 90, 91, 92
Green, Adam 214
Green, Brian Austin 270
Griffin, Richard 88
Grimes, Lee 340
Growing Pains 269
Gunn, James 333, 351
Gut Pile 103

H

Haaga, Trent 303
Hack, Jason 57
Hagins, Emily 130, 131, 206, 261, 263
Haig, Sid 126, 305
Hailstone, Dom 354
Hall Jr., Dale 175, 176
Hall, Kenneth J. 116
Hall, Robert 305, 336, 337
Halloween 262
Hamedani, Kevin 198
Happiness of the Katakuris, The 267
Hard Rock Zombies 103, 219, 223
Harel, Gadi 74
Harrelson, Woody 196, 252
Harris, Naomie 354
Harryhausen, Ray 278, 282
Harsone,Peter B. 154
Hart, Lorenz 268
Hatchet 214
Hartsell, Chuck 105
Haunting, The 262
Hayes, John 100
Hayles, Justin 324
Heavener, David 50
Hell of the Living Dead 104, 201, 204
Hellboy II: The Golden Army 303
Hellraiser 225, 353
Hells Ground 104, 202
Hendricks, Chad 110
Hide and Creep 105, 204
High School Girl Zombie 105, 204
Hills Have Eyes, The 298
Hinzman, S. William 98
Ho, Meng Hua 21
Hodder, Kane 327
Honeycutt, Heidi 307
Host, The 264
Hostel 275
Hot Fuzz 351
Howling, The 353
Huntley, Noah 354

I

I Am Legend 224, 302
I Am Omega 110, 203, 204
I Sell the Dead 110
I Spit on your Grave 278
Inception 351
Inglorious Basterds 297
Insane in the Brain 110
Irving, David 35
Islas, Ricardo 185

J

Jackass 251
Jackson, Michael 250, 254, 278, 348,
Jackson, Peter 28, 261, 275, 298
Jackson, Samuel 302
Jacob's Ladder 354
Jaissle, Matt 121
Jason and the Argonauts 273
Jason Goes to Hell: The Final Friday 274
Jaws 297
Johnny Sunshine 110
Johnson, Steve 220
Jones, Paul 293
Junk 111, 201, 204, 205
Jurassic Park 210, 322, 339
Just the Ten of Us 269

K

Kahn, Ralis 295
Kalangis, John 117
Kanefsky, Rolfe 39
Kasten , Jeremy 12
Kaufman, Lloyd 135, 206, 265
Kawano, Kôji 14
Keates, Roland 7, 48
Keating, Buster 266
Keen, Bob 225
Kellisch, Oliver 109
Kelly, Brett 121
Kelman, Jamie 336, 340
Kennedy, Jake 57
Kenworthy, Michael 151, 206, 269, 271, 272
Kephart, Elza 103
Khan, Omar 104
Kindlon, David 219, 220, 297
Kinmont, Kathleen 32, 274
Kirkman, Robert 350
Kirton, Alastair 38, 321, 324
Kitamura, Ryûhei 174
Klebem Kristina 327
Klimovsky, León 174
KNB EFX 78, 80, 219, 241, 275, 284, 328, 330, 336
Knowles, Harry 261
Kohnen, Matthew 8, 9, 10
Komizu, Kazuo 'Gaira' 18
Koszulinski, Georg 22
Kragelund, Scott 27
Kren, Marvin 163
Kubrick, Stanley 262
Kurtzman, Robert 32, 87, 139, 140, 206, 273, 277, 337

L

Lamelin, Don 89
Land of the Dead 3, 111, 113, 114, 201, 202, 203, 204, 205, 207, 208, 243, 244, 254, 255, 256, 285, 286, 287, 288, 289, 291, 296, 297, 298, 302, 328, 329, 331, 335
Landis, John 169
Lantz, Dan 23
Lara, Julián 64
Lasen, Jim 34
Last House on the Left 298
Lattanzi, Claudiov 179
Leatherface 3D 275
Lee, Grace 12
Lee, Jay 189
Lee, Stan 285
Leigh, Janet 327
Lenzi, Umberto 122
Leonard, Brett 66
Let Sleeping Corpses Lie 112, 342
Leutwyler, Matthew 60
Levin, Thunder 120
Levy, Jonah 340
Lewnes, Pericles 142
Lincoln, Andrew 302
Lindbergh, Carl 158
Linnea Quigley's Horror Workout 112
Livelihood 117, 201
Living Dead Girl, The 116
Living in a Zombie Dream 116, 201
Long, Joshua 16, 17, 206, 278
Lovecraft, H.P. 311

Low, K.W. 210
Lucas, George 342

M

MacDonald, Andrew 353
Mace, Seymour 348
Mad, The 117, 202
Magariños, Germán 180
Make Out with Violence 117
Malanowski , Tony 43, 44
Mallorca Zombie 117, 204
Maniac 299
Mansion of the Living Dead 118
Margheriti, Antonio 34
Martin 265
Martinez, Ed 40, 68, 70,72, 147, 206, 282
Martyrs 275
Maslansky, Paul 199
Masonberg, Hal 132
Mattei, Bruno 104, 178, 199
McCallum, Rob 206, 285, 287, 288
McCormack, Catherine 355
McCoy, Bill 340
McCrae, Scooter 158
McDonald, Bruce 135
McFarlane, Todd 297
McKinney, Brockton 162
McLoughlin, Tom 128, 211
McMahon, Conor 64
McQuaid, Glenn 110
McQueen, Mark 76
Meat Market 118, 204, 205
Meat Market 2 118, 201, 204
Meatballs 269
Merkelbach, Andrew 62
Mervis, Peter 65
Miike, Takashi 267
Mikels, Ted V. 14
Miller, Steven C. 15
Minami, Masashi 105
Minarovich, Adam 177
Miner, Steve 55
Monty Python 268
Moore, Dorenda 319
Moran, Dylan 227
Morin, Grégory 130
Morrill, Neil 81, 206, 213, 289
Mortuary 119
Mosher, Michael 60, 144, 206, 295, 295
Moss, Carrie-Anne 249
Mother's Day 299
Motor Cross Zombies From Hell 119
Mud Zombies 119, 201, 202, 203, 204, 205
Mulcahy, Russell 145
Mullaney, Kerry Anne 66
Mulligan, Bill 309
Mulva Zombie Ass Kicker 120
Munns, Bill 219, 220
Muroga, Atsushi 111
Murphy, Jason 199
Murray, Bill 196
Murray, Marcus 314
Mutant Vampire Zombies From the 'Hood 120, 202, 204, 205
My Asshole Neighbor 249
My Dead Girlfriend 121
My Sucky Teen Romance 262, 264
My Three Scums 303
Myers, Kenny 219, 270

N

Nakano, Takao 20
Natural Born Killers 344
Naughton, David 250
Necro Files, The 121
Neighbor Zombie, The 121, 202
Newman, Thomas 26
Nicolaou, Ted 173
Nicotero, Greg 2, 115, 206, 218, 219, 200, 223, 224, 243, 244, 254, 269, 284, 289, 296, 300, 328, 329, 334, 336, 337
Night Life 122, 211
Night of the Bums 122, 201
Night of the Comet 123
Night of the Creeps 123, 273, 276
Night of the Living Dead (1968) 1, 124, 204, 210, 213, 215, 219, 221, 222, 223, 225, 247, 261, 265, 278, 285, 297, 326, 331, 332, 336, 337, 342
Night of the Living Dead (1990) 124, 202, 203, 204, 219, 221, 222, 223, 244, 326, 329, 331, 333, 338, 349, 350, 351, 352
Night of the Living Dead 30th Anniversary (1998) 204, 205, 244, 326
Night of the Living Dead 3D 125, 126, 202, 203, 204
Night of the Living Dorks 125, 261

Night of the Seagulls 125
Night of the Zombies 211
Nightmare City 122, 201, 204, 205
Nighy, Bill 161
Ninja's Vs Zombies 127, 204
Nolan, Christopher 351
Nott, Gerald 139
Noussias, Yorgos 86
Noye, Philip 353
Nudist Colony of the Dead 127

O

O'Bannon, Dan 148, 250
O'Brien, Steve 193, 346
O'Rawe, Timothy 101
O'Sullivan, Jerry 103
Oasis of the Zombies 127, 205
OC Babes and the Slasher 128
Oh, Young-doo 121
Ojala, Jim 75, 136, 206, 303, 306
One Dark Night 128, 211
Onechanara 128, 201, 204, 205
Orr, Scott 314, 315
Ortega, Juan 117
Outpost 129, 202
Oz 243
Ozone 129

P

Pal Joey 268
Palidino, Eric 60, 295, 295
Parés, Pablo 130, 132
Paris by Night of the Living Dead 130, 201, 202, 204, 205
Park, Nira 226, 227
Parker, Christine 95, 96, 99, 206, 307, 308
Parker, David 63
Parkinson, Andrew 62
Pass Time 336
Pathogen 130, 131, 204, 261, 262, 263, 264
Paulin, Brian 23, 24, 25, 206, 311
Paulin, Stacey 313
Peck, Brian 250
Peel, Mike 184, 206, 314
Pegg, Simon 226, 227, 228, 288
Pendergast, Conall 95
Perez, Rene 39
Phillips Thomas L. 163
Phillips, Glasgow 172
Phillips, Scott 164
Pierce, Jack 331
Pilato, Joe 222, 223, 301, 319, 332, 334
Piper, Brett 141
Pirro, Mark 127
Plaga Zombie 130, 204
Plaga Zombie 2 132, 201, 204
Plague of the Zombies 314, 353
Plague, The 132, 202
Plaguers 133
Planet of the Apes, The 336
Planet Terror 3, 133, 201, 202, 204, 205, 243, 245, 246, 296, 309, 324, 355
Plantico, Nick 206, 318
Platoon of the Dead 134
Plaza, Paco 141
Ploog, Mike 285
Pogue, John 139, 339
Poirier, Kim 215
Polley, Sarah 346
Pontypool 135, 202, 203, 207, 328
Poole, Mark E. 65
Popko, Rick 146
Porno Holocaust 135
Potter, Georgia 280
Potter, Harry 323
Poultrygeist 135, 135, 201, 204, 205, 265, 266, 267, 268, 303, 305
Premutos Lord of the Living Dead 136, 201, 202, 203, 205
Presley, Elvis 348
Price, Marc 36, 37, 206, 321, 325
Price, Vincent 309
Prior, David A. 191
Prouty, Steve 336, 340
Psycho 327
Psychomania 138
Pulp Fiction 302

Q

Quarantine 3, 138, 202, 264
Quarantine 2: Terminal 139, 202, 204, 336, 337
Querut, Pierre 8
Quick and the Undead 139, 202, 204
Quiro, Jose 105

Quiroz, Eduardo 105

R

Rage, The 139, 140, 201, 202, 203, 243, 273, 274, 276, 277
Raiders of the Living Dead 141, 205
Raimi, Sam 14, 87, 88, 273, 275, 278, 298, 336
Rambo 214, 274
Ramsey, Tor 35
Randolph, Beverly 250
Rapp, Mark 21
Rawhead Rex 353
Ray, Fred Olen 12
Re-animator 141, 202, 224, 273
[Rec] 141, 219, 298
[Rec 2] 141, 202, 204
Redd Inc. 332
Redlefsen, Richard 295
Redneck Zombies 142, 201, 204, 266
Reid, R.D. 215, 216
Reigle, Blake 19
Remains of the Day 294
Resident Evil 142, 202, 203, 204, 205, 286, 298
Resident Evil: Afterlife 143, 201, 202, 203, 204, 205, 285, 286, 291, 328, 339
Resident Evil: Apocalypse 145, 202, 203, 204, 205, 285, 286, 328
Resident Evil: Extinction 144, 145, 201, 202, 203, 204, 205, 295, 293
Resident Evil: Retribution 256, 288, 291
Retardead 146, 147, 201, 203, 205, 254, 282
Return in Red 148
Return of the Blind Dead 148, 204, 205
Return of the Living Dead, The 148, 149, 204, 211, 215, 219, 250, 253, 275, 278, 311, 336, 352
Return of the Living Dead Part II 150, 151, 202, 203, 204, 205, 269, 270, 271, 272
Return of the Living Dead 3 150, 153, 201, 202, 203
Return of the Living Dead: Necropolis 152, 201, 202, 203, 204, 205, 349, 350
Return of the Living Dead: Rave to the Grave 152, 201, 202, 203, 204, 205, 349, 350
Revenge of the Living Dead Girls 154
Revolting Dead, The 155
Reynolds, Todd 116
Rhames, Ving 302, 346
Rising Dead, The 155, 204, 205
Ristori, Marco 84
Robert, Gary 119, 198
Robinosn, Luke 161
Robot Chicken 361
Rocher, Benjamin 106
Rodgers, Richard 268
Rodriguez, Robert 133, 245
Roe, Chris 211
Rohen, Johannes Wilhelm 282
Rollin, Jean 8, 102, 116, 187
Rome 222
Romero, Chris 296
Romero, George 1, 46, 47, 49, 55, 77, 111, 124, 167, 207, 208, 209, 210, 211, 212, 213, 214, 219, 220, 221, 225, 243, 245, 247, 256, 261, 265, 286, 289, 291, 296, 297, 298, 309, 311, 321, 326, 327, 328, 331, 333
Roost, The 155
Ross, Mark 359, 360, 361
Ross, Peter John 106
Roush, Michael 107
Route 666 155
Rowe, Mike 340
Rubenstein, Richard 297
Rumbelow, Steven 15
Russo, John 124, 206, 326, 352
Ryoo, Hoon 121

S

Sabbath 156, 204
Sabretooth 318
Sáez, Hernán 130, 132
Salley, Stacey 269
Sansom, Sean 206, 212, 328, 330
Sarmiento, Marcel 74
Sars Wars 156, 202, 203, 204
Sato, Sakichi 169
Saving Private Ryan 226, 257
Savini, Tom 2, 54, 124, 206, 217, 219, 220, 221, 224, 225, 243, 244, 245, 246, 280, 282, 284, 289, 296, 298, 299, 311, 315, 319, 331, 334, 335, 337, 339, 349, 350, 351, 352, 353, 355
Saxon, John 183
Scanners 302, 305, 315, 353
Schnaas, Andreas 179

Schotten, William Victor 64, 156
Schumacher, Joel 22
Scott, Robert 174
Scream 343
Seaver, Chris 120
Segan, Noah 303, 305
Sellicks, David 315
Sells, Toby 206, 336, 341, 358, 359, 360, 361, 362, 374
Serafinowicz, Peter 229
Serpent and the Rainbow, The 156
Sessions, Steve 62
Severed: Forest of the Dead 157
Shadow: Dead Riot 157, 201, 202, 203, 204, 205
Shadows of the Dead 158
Shah, Krishna 103
Shallow Hal 251
Shark Night 3D 213
Sharp, Don 138
Sharp, Russell 280
Shatter Dead 158
Shaun of the Dead 3, 158, 159, 160, 161, 201, 202, 203, 204, 225, 226, 228, 245, 261, 262, 267, 278, 282, 285, 288, 293, 298, 319, 331, 337
Sheets, Todd 181, 182, 188, 206, 342, 345
Sherman, Gary 61
Sherman, Samuel M. 141
Shining, The 262
Shirley, Chance 105
Shock Waves 162, 353
Shyamalan, M. Night 343
Sibley, S.N. 8
Sick and the Dead 162, 201, 204, 205
Siege of the Dead 163, 204, 205
Silent Hill 289
Simmons, Sean 163
Sin City 243
Singleton, Brian 99
Skelding, Sean 165
Skiba, Brian 22
Skin Crawl 163
Smith, Dick 282, 331, 338, 340
Smith, Joshua D. 182
Smith, Shaun 218
Snyder, Zack 49, 207, 328, 346
Soavi, Michele 34
Spain, Jenny 75, 303, 304
Specht, John 85
Special Dead 163
Speed, Warren 192,193, 206, 346, 347
Spelling, Aaron 272
Spielberg, Steven 257, 304
Spierig, Michael 172
Spierig, Peter 172
Sssssss 342
Stacy 163, 202, 204, 266, 267
Star Wars 342
Stavrakis, Taso 301, 332
Stiff Odds 164
Stink of Flesh, The 164, 201, 204
Stinnett, Duane 100
Stone, Emma 196
Stoneburner, Roger 319
Storm of the Dead 165
Streiner, Russ 327
Streisand, Barbra 266
Stripperland 165, 166, 202, 204, 205, 207, 209
Su, Michael 83, 155
Survival of the Dead 3, 168, 171, 202, 203, 204, 205, 210, 212, 213, 265, 285, 286, 296, 297, 328, 329, 330
Survivors 353
Sykes, Brad 133
Symmes, Daniel 126

T

Takeuchi, Tetsuro 177
Tales from the Crypt 353
Tales from the Darkside 297
Tarantino, Quentin 213, 245
Taylor, A.J 51
Taylor, Richard 226, 227
Ten Commandments, The 296
Tenney, Kevin 28
Terminator, The 298
Terror Firmer 266
Texas Chainsaw Massacre 2 243, 246
Tharpe, Tyler 148
Thing, The (1982) 262 274, 285
Thing, The (2011) 285
Thomas, Scott 98
Thriller 169, 250, 253, 254, 278
Timpane, Justin 127
Timpone, Tony 210
Todd, Tony 327
Tokyo Zombie 169, 204
Tombs of the Blind Dead 169
Tomomatsu, Naoyuki 163, 189Tompkins, Alan 257

Tomplins, Alan 257
Tonibadoiro, Pakito Bien 188
Toro, Guillermo del 262
Tort, Frederic 117
Toth, Wayne 153
Toxic Avenger, The 267, 268
Toxic Avenger IV, The Citizen Toxie 266, 267, 303
Toxic Avenger Part Five: The Toxic Twins 265
Trailer Park of Terror 318
Train 294
Travolta, John 302
Trcic, Mike 219, 220, 297
Troll 273
Troma 265, 266, 267, 268, 303, 305
Tromeo and Juliet 267
Truffaut, François 266
Tucker, Christopher 353

U

Ugarek, Gary 75
Undead 172, 202, 204, 205, 261, 280
Undead or Alive 172, 202, 203, 204, 244, 273, 275, 277
Urban Evil 173

V

Vampire Diaries, The 338, 359
Vampires Vs. Zombies 173
Vargas, Alex 117
Vengeance of the Dead 173
Versus 174, 202, 204, 205, 278
Video Dead, The 174, 175
Vulich, John 206, 219, 220, 221, 224, 244, 297, 299, 333, 349

W

Wade, Brian 318
Wagner, Brett 336
Walker, Jane 227
Walking Dead, The 3, 214, 223, 241, 243, 244, 245, 246, 261, 284, 296, 297, 299, 301, 302, 329, 330, 336, 337, 339, 350, 358, 359
Wallace, Cliff 206, 253, 356
Wan, Derek 157
Wantha, Taweewat 156
Wasting Away see Aaah! Zombies!!!
Watson, Chris 193
Webb, Bo 63
Webb, Michelle 37, 322
Werner, Byron 75
Wesley, William 155
West, Jake 83
West, Ti 155
Westmore, Michael 349
White Zombie 265
Whitney, John 106
Wiederhorn, Ken 150, 162
Wild Zero 177, 202, 204, 205
Wiseguys vs. Zombies 177, 202
Wingenfeld, Justin 163
Winston, Stan 220
Wirkola, Tommy 67
Within The Woods 278
Witt, Alexander 145
Woelfel, Jay 100
Wolcher, Jonas 82
Wolff, Wolf 18
World War Z 353, 355
Wright, Edgar 158, 226, 227, 261, 288
Wright, Kazuya 279, 281
Wrightson, Bernie 222
Wyndham, John 353

X

X-Men: The Last Stand 303

Y

Yamaguchi, Yūdai 18
Yandle, Leigh Ann 340
Yarbrough Jan 248
Yeager, Matt 110
Yip, Wilson 21
Yuzna, Brian 18, 19, 29, 33, 150

Z

Zabinski, Darya 313
Zombie 178, 202, 204, 205, 211, 328, 329, 332, 342
Zombie 3 178, 204, 205
Zombie 4: After Death 179, 204, 205

Zombie 5: Killing Birds 179
Zombie 90: Extreme Pestilence 179, 202, 204
Zombie Apocalypse Now 180, 202, 204
Zombie Bloodbath 181, 204, 205, 342, 343, 344, 345
Zombie Bloodbath 2: Rage of the Undead 181, 202, 204, 342, 343, 344
Zombie Bloodbath 3: Zombie Armageddon 182, 204, 342, 344
Zombie Campout 182, 202, 204
Zombie Death House 183
Zombie Diaries 183, 184, 202, 204, 314, 316, 317
Zombie Diaries 2: World of the Dead 183, 185, 202, 204, 205, 314, 315, 316, 317
Zombie Driftwood 185, 204
Zombie Farm 185, 204
Zombie Flesh Eaters 278
Zombie Girl 261
Zombie Holocaust 186, 202
Zombie Honeymoon 186, 202, 203
Zombie Hunter Rika 186, 202, 205
Zombie Island Massacre 187, 205
Zombie King, The 314, 317
Zombie Lake 187, 205
Zombie Night 187, 204
Zombie Penetrator 188
Zombie Rampage 188, 204, 342
Zombie Self Defense Force 188, 202, 204, 205
Zombie Strippers 189, 190, 202, 203, 204, 205
Zombie Undead 191, 202, 204
Zombie Wars 191, 202, 204, 205
Zombie Women of Satan 192, 193, 202, 204, 205, 346, 347, 348
Zombie Women of Satan 2 346
Zombiegeddon 193, 331
Zombieland 3, 194, 195, 196, 197, 202, 203, 204, 205, 223, 250, 251, 252, 282, 294, 331, 336, 337, 338, 339, 358, 362, 374
Zombieland 2 339, 340, 341
Zombies Anonymous 195, 202, 203
Zombies Gone Wild 198
Zombies of Mass Destruction 198, 202, 203, 204
Zombies of Sugar Hill 198
Zombies the Beginning 199, 202, 204, 205
Zombies Zombies Zombies 199, 202, 204, 205
Zombiez 200

373

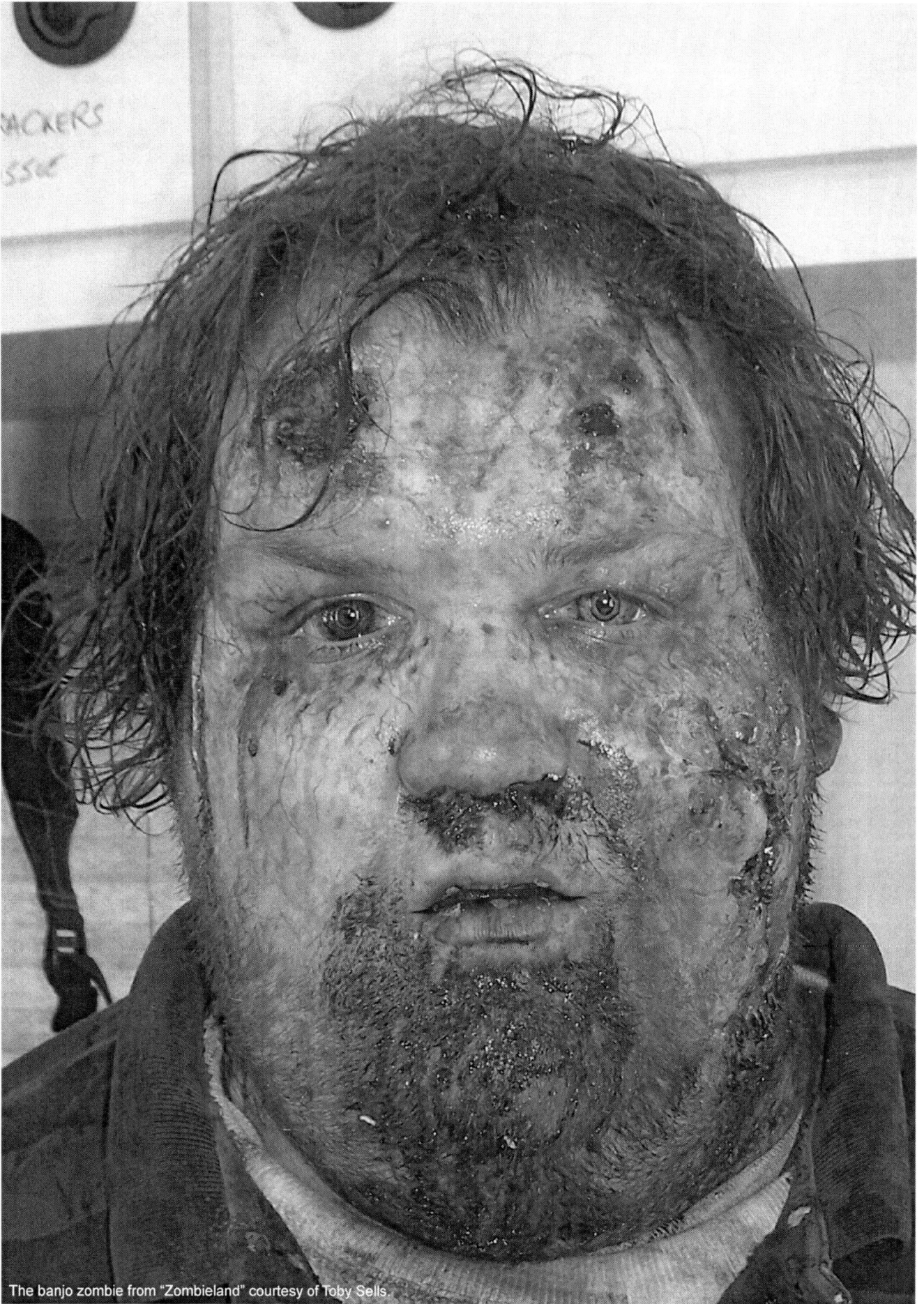

The banjo zombie from "Zombieland" courtesy of Toby Sells.

CPSIA information can be obtained at www.ICGtesting.com
Printed in the USA
BVOW050009270312

286137BV00010B/3/P